BRITISH WRITERS

BRITISH WRITERS

JAY PARINI

Editor

SUPPLEMENT VI

Charles Scribner's Sons
an imprint of the Gale Group
New York • Detroit • San Francisco • London • Boston • Woodbridge, CT

Charles Scribner's Sons
an imprint of The Gale Group
27500 Drake Rd.
Farmington Hills, MI 48331-3535

Library of Congress Cataloging-in-Publication Data

British Writers. Supplement VI / Jay Parini, editor in chief.
    p. cm.
    Includes bibliographical references and index.
    ISBN 0-684-80641-X
    1. English literature—Bio-bibliography. 2. English literature—History and criticism. 3. Authors, English—Biography. I. Parini, Jay.

PR85 .B688 Suppl. 6
820.9—dc21
[B]   00-063504

The paper used in this publication meets the requirements of ANSI/NISO Z39.48-1992 (Permanence of Paper).

Acknowledgments

Acknowledgment is gratefully made to those publishers and
individuals who permitted the use of the following materials in copyright:

PETER ACKROYD Excerpts from "Only connect . . . ,"
and "the diversions of Purley" from *The Diversions of
Purley and Other Poems* (London: Hamish Hamilton,
1987). Copyright © 1987 by Peter Ackroyd. Reprinted
with the permission of the author.

ANDRÉ BRINK Excerpt from "Andre Brink: In Tune
with His Times" by John F. Baker reprinted from *Publisher's Weekly* 243: 48 (November 15, 1996). Reprinted
with the permission of *Publisher's Weekly*.

GEORGE MACKAY BROWN Excerpts from "Under
Brinkie's Brae: Wheel of the Year, December" from
Northern Lights: A Poet's Sources. Excerpts from *For the
Islands I Sing*. Excerpt from *Magnus, Beside the Ocean of
Time*, excerpts from "Ikey," and "The Paraffin Lamp"
from *Winter Tales*, excerpts from "The Storm," "The Old
Woman," and "The Hawk" from *Selected Poems 1954-
1992*, excerpts from "The Jars," "The House," and
"Orkney: The Whale Islands" from *The Wreck of the
Archangel*, excerpts from "Lux Perpetua" from *Following
a Lark*. All reprinted with the permission of John Mur-
ray (Publishers), Ltd. Excerpt from "The Way of Litera-
ture: An Apologia" from *The Tablet* (June 12, 1982).
Reprinted by permission.

BASIL BUNTING Excerpts from "Briggflatts," "Aus
Dem Zweiten Reich," "Chomei at Toyama," "The
Spoils," and Odes I.1, I.3, I.5, I.29, and II.1 from *Complete
Poems*. Copyright © 2000 by the Estate of Basil Bunting.
Reprinted with the permission of Bloodaxe Books Ltd.

J. M. COETZEE Excerpts from "The Vietnam Project"
from *Dusklands*. Copyright © 1974 by J. M. Coetzee.
Excerpts from *Waiting for the Barbarians*. Copyright ©
1980 by J. M. Coetzee. Excerpts from *The Life and Times
of Michael K*. Copyright © 1984 by J. M. Coetzee.
Excerpts from *Foe*. Copyright © 1987 by J. M. Coetzee.
All reprinted with the permission of Viking Penguin, a
division of Penguin Putnam Inc. and The Random
House Archive & Library. Excerpts from *Boyhood: Scenes
from a Provincial Life*. Copyright © 1997 by J. M. Coetzee.
Reprinted with the permission of Viking Penguin, a
division of Penguin Putnam Inc. and the Peter Lampack
Agency, Inc.

DONALD DAVIE Excerpts [3 lines] from "The Poet-
Scholar" from *Essays in Criticism* V: 1 (January 1955).

Copyright © 1955 by Donald Davie. Reprinted with
permission. Excerpts from "Among Artisans' Houses,"
"Belfast on a Sunday Afternoon," "The Garden Party,"
"Time Passing, Beloved," "The Fountain," "A Gathered
Church," "A Winter Talent," "Heigh-ho on a Winter
Afternoon," "With the Grain," "A Letter to Curtis Brad-
ford," "Barnsley Cricket Club," "In California," "The
Hardness of Light," "The North Sea," "Sunburst,"
"Turnstall Forest," "A Winter Landscape near Ely,"
"Orford," "July, 1964," "Or, Solitude," "Revulsion,"
"England" "Six Epistles to Eva Hesse," "Bedfordshire,"
"Cheshire," "Sussex," "In the Stopping Train," "Morn-
ing," "Thom Gunn in Los Altos, California," "Winter's
Talents," "Summer Lightning," "Brilliance," and
"Though dry, not dry" from *Collected Poems*. Copyright
© 1990 by Donald Davie. Reprinted with the permission
of Carcanet Press, Ltd.

T.E. HULME Excerpt from Canto XVI by Ezra Pound.
From *The Cantos*. Copyright 1934, 1948 by Ezra Pound.
Reprinted with the permission of New Directions Pub-
lishing Corporation and Faber & Faber, Ltd.

NORMAN MACCAIG "In Deserts" and excerpts "Hid-
den Law" from *Riding Lights*. Copyright © 1955 by Nor-
man MacCaig. "Summer Farm," "Byre," "Sound of the
sea on a still evening," "Connoisseur" and excerpts from
"July Evening," "Failed Mystic," and "Mutual Life,"
"Country House," "Wet Snow," "The Rosyfingered,"
"Double Life," "The Wreck," "Clachtroll," "Roses and
Thorns," "Celtic Twilight," "November Night, Edin-
burgh," "Country Bedroom," "Nude in a Fountain,"
"Feeding Ducks," "Two Ways of It," "Spate in Winter
Midnight," "Edinburgh Courtyard in July," "Midnight,
Lochinver," "Moonrings," "Loch Sionascaig," "Bull,"
"Fetching Cows," "Aspects," "Icy Road," "Neglected
Graveyard, Luskentyre," "Numismatist," "Transforma-
tions," "Structures," "It's Hopeless," "Sure Proof,"
"Inarticulates," "A Man in My Position," "A Man in
Assynt," "Basking Shark," "Sparrow," "Country
Dance," "Inward Bound,""Invasion of bees," "Where
we are," "Interruption to a Journey," "Sounds of the
Day," "Responsibility," "Assisi," "Writer's Conference,
Long Island University," "Circle Line," "Hotel Room,
12th Floor," "Fog at Dusk," "Leaving the Metropolitan
Museum," "Camera Man," "Neighbor," "Highland bar-
becue," and "Blackbird in a Sunset Bush," "Birthdays,"

v

ACKNOWLEDGMENTS

"Between Two Nowheres," "Highland Funeral," "Toad," and "Variations of Ten Summer Minutes" from *Collected Poems*. Copyright © 1990 by Norman MacCaig. Excerpts from "After Eden" from *The Sinai Sort*. Copyright © 1957 by Norman MacCaig. Excerpts from "Blue Chair in a Sunny Day" from *A Common Grace*. Copyright © 1960 by Norman MacCaig. Excerpts from "King of Beasts" from *Surroundings*. Copyright © 1966 by Norman MacCaig. Excerpts from "On a Croft by the Kirkcaig," and "Small Boy" from *Voice Over*. Copyright © 1988 by Norman MacCaig. All reprinted with the permission of The Random House Archive & Library. Excerpt from an untitled poem ["The closer fist clamped my ell-head in / ... man of sea"] from *The New Apocalypse*. Reprinted with the permission of Routledge. Excerpt from "rhetoric in winter" by G. S. Fraser. From *The White Horseman*, edited by J. F. Hendry and Henry Treece. Reprinted with the permission of Routledge. Excerpt from "Over the apparatus of the spring is drawn" by W. S. Graham. From *Cage Without Grievance* (Glasgow, 1942). Reprinted with the permission of Nessie Graham. Excerpt from "The Four Seasons of War" by J. F. Hendry. From *The Bombed Happiness*. Reprinted with the permission of Routledge.

DEREK MAHON Excerpts from "In Carrowdore Churchyard," "A Portrait of the Artist," "As It Should Be," "Afterlives," "Last of the Fire Kings," "The Snow Party," "An Image from Beckett," "The Apotheosis of Tins," "The Mute Phenomena," "The Disused Shed in Co. Wexford," "The Hunt by Night," "Courtyards in Delft," "Alien Nation," "Ovid on West 4th," "A Swim in Co. Wicklow," and "Shapes and Shadows" from *Collected Poems*. Copyright © 1999 by Derek Mahon. Reprinted with the permission of The Gallery Press, Loughcrew, Oldcastle, Co Meath, Ireland. Excerpts from "The Art of Poetry LXXXII: Derek Mahon" by Eamon Grennan from *The Paris Review* (Spring 2000). Copyright © 2000. Reprinted with permission. Excerpts from "Four Walks in the Country Near Saint Brieuc," "Homecoming," "Lives," "What Will Remain," "An Image from Beckett," "Rage for Order," "Beyond Howth Head," "Thammuz," "The Banished Gods," "The Sea in Winter," and "Girls on the Bridge" from *Collected Poems*. Copyright © 1999 by Derek Mahon. Reprinted with the permission of The Gallery Press, Loughcrew, Oldcastle, Co Meath, Ireland. Excerpts from "Pythagorean Lines" by Gerard de Nerval from *The Chimeras*, translated by Derek Mahon. Copyright © 1982 by Derek Mahon. Reprinted with the permission of The Gallery Press, Loughcrew, Oldcastle, Co Meath, Ireland. Excerpts from "Beauty and the Beast" from *The Hudson Letter*. Copyright © 1995 by Derek Mahon. Excerpt from "Smoke," "Death in Bangor" from *The Yellow Book*. Copyright © 1997 by Derek Mahon. Reprinted with the permission of The Gallery Press, Loughcrew, Oldcastle, Co Meath, Ireland. Excerpt from the introduction to *The Complete Short Stories of Saki* by Christopher Morley. Copyright 1930, © 1957 by The Viking Press, Inc. Reprinted with the permission of Viking Penguin, a division of Penguin Putnam Inc.

EDWIN MUIR Excerpts from *An Autobiography*. Copyright 1954 by Edwin Muir. Reprinted with the permission of The Hogarth Press/The Random House Archive & Library. Excerpts from "Childhood," "Horses," "Variations on a Time Theme," "Troy," "The Sufficient Place," "The River," "The Good Town," "Adam's Dream," "One Foot in Eden," "The Horses," "The Song," "I Have Been Taught," "To J.F.H. (1897-1934)," "The Grove," "Suburban Dream," "Too Much," "The Journey Back," "The Transfiguration," from *Collected Poems*. Copyright © 1960 by Willa Muir. Reprinted with the permission of Oxford University Press, Inc. and Faber & Faber, Ltd. Excerpt from "Little Gidding" by T. S. Eliot from *Four Quartets* in *Collected Poems 1909-1962*. Copyright 1922, 1925, 1927 1941 by T. S. Eliot. Copyright 1936 by Harcourt, Inc., renewed © 1964 by T. S. Eliot. Reprinted with the permission of Harcourt, Inc. and Faber and Faber Limited. Excerpts from "The Annunciation," "The Incarnate One," "The Difficult Land," and "Dream and Thing" from *One Foot in Eden*. Copyright © 1956 by Edwin Muir. Reprinted with the permission of Faber and Faber, Ltd.

NORMAN NICHOLSON Excerpt from "Now in the Time of This Mortal Life." Excerpts from "The Holy Mountain," and from "The Bow in the Clouds" from *Five Rivers* (London: Faber & Faber, 1944). Copyright 1944 by Norman Nicholson. Excerpts from "Old Main Street, Holborn Hill, Millom," "The Pot Geranium," and "The Seven Rocks" from *The Pot Geranium* (London: Faber & Faber, 1954). Copyright 1954 by Norman Nicholson. Excerpts from "On the Dismantling of Millom Ironworks," "Weeds," "The New Cemetery," "At the Musical Festival," and "Sea to the West" from *Sea to the West* (London: Faber & Faber, 1981). Copyright © 1981 by Norman Nicholson. Excerpts from *Prophesy to the Wind* (London: Faber & Faber, 1950). Copyright 1950 by Norman Nicholson. Excerpts from *A Match for the Devil* (London: Faber & Faber, 1955). Copyright © 1955 by Norman Nicholson. All reprinted with the permission of David Higham Associates, Ltd. Excerpt from "Letter to Lord Byron" by W. H. Auden. From *W. H. Auden: Collected Poems*, edited by Edward Mendelson. Copyright 1940, renewed © 1968 by W. H. Auden. Reprinted with the permission of Random House, Inc.

PETER REDGROVE Excerpts from "Lazarus and the Sea," and "Bedtime Story for My Son" from *The Collector*. Copyright © 1960 by Peter Redgrove. Excerpts from "At the Edge of the Wood," "The Ghostly Father," and "Mr. Waterman" from *The Nature of Cold Weather*. Copyright © 1961 by Peter Redgrove. Excerpt from "At the White Monument" from *At the White Monument*. Copy-

ACKNOWLEDGMENTS

right © 1963 by Peter Redgrove. Excerpt from "The Force" from *The Force.* Copyright © 1966 by Peter Redgrove. Excerpts from "Young Woman with the Hair of Witches and No Modesty, " "The Idea of Entropy at Maenporth Beach," "Water-Witch, Wood-Witch, Wine-Witch" from *Dr. Faust's Sea-Spiral Spirit.* Copyright © 1972 by Peter Redgrove. Excerpt from "The Famous Ghost of St. Ives" from *The Weddings at Nether Powers.* Copyright © 1979 by Peter Redgrove. Excerpt from "Streets of the Spirits" from *The Apple Broadcast.* Copyright © 1981 by Peter Redgrove. Excerpts from "The Funeral," "The Quiet Woman of Chancery Lane," "The College in the Reservoir," "The Man Named East," and "The Harmony" from *The Man Named East.* Copyright © 1985 by Peter Redgrove. Excerpts from "Three Aquarium Portraits" from *From Every Chink of the Ark.* Copyright © 1977 by Peter Redgrove. All reprinted with the permission of Routledge. Excerpt from "The Flying Ace" from *The Times Literary Supplement* (July 14, 2000). Copyright © 2000 by Peter Redgrove. Reprinted with the permission of the author. Excerpt from "Aube," by Arthur Rimbaud, translated by Helen Rootham. From *Prose Poems from the Illuminations of Arthur Rimbaud.* Reprinted with the permission of Faber & Faber, Ltd. Excerpt from "poem" by Tom Scott. From *The White Horseman,* edited by J. F. Hendry and Henry Treece. Reprinted with the permission of Routledge.

ANNE STEVENSON Excerpts from "To My Daughter in a Red Coat," "Sierra Nevada," "Siskin," "Travelling Behind Glass," "Generations," "North Sea off Carnoustie," "The Price," "With My Sons at Boarhills," "If I Could Paint Essences," "Transparencies," and "Sonnets for Five Seasons," "Making Poetry," "Re-Reading Jane," "The Fiction-Makers," "From an Unfinished Poem," "An April Epithalamium," "Signs," "Letter to Sylvia Plath," "From My Study" and "Trinity at Low Tide" from After You Left" from *Collected Poems 1955-1995.* Copyright © 1965 by Anne Stevenson.

Excerpts from "Green Mountain, Black Mountain" from *Minute by Glass Minute.* Copyright © 1982 by Anne Stevenson. Excerpts from "Forgotten of the Foot" and "Taking Down the Christmas Tree" from *The Fiction-Makers.* Copyright © 1985 by Anne Stevenson. Excerpts from *Correspondences.* Copyright © 1974 by Anne Stevenson. Excerpts from "After you left" from *Four and a Half Dancing Men.* Copyright © 1993 by Anne Stevenson. All reprinted with the permission of Oxford University Press, Ltd. Excerpts from "England," "Reversals," and "The Spirit Is Too Blunt an Instrument" from *Reversals.* Copyright © 1969 by Anne Stevenson. Reprinted with the permission of University Press of New England and Oxford University Press, Ltd. Excerpts from "Granny Scarecrow," and "Going Back" from *Granny Scarecrow.* Copyright © 2000 by Anne Stevenson. Reprinted with the permission of Bloodaxe Books Ltd. Excerpts from "A Dialogue of Self and Soul," "Among School Children," "Two Songs From a Play," and "The Circus Animals" "Desertion" by William Butler Yeats. From *The Collected Poems of W. B. Yeats, Revised Second Edition,* edited by Richard J. Finneran. Copyright 1928, 1933 by Macmillan Publishing Company, renewed © 1956, 1961 by Bertha Georgie Yeats. Copyright 1940 by Georgie Yeats, renewed © 1968 by Bertha Georgie Yeats. Reprinted with the permission of Simon & Schuster, Inc. and A. P. Watt, Ltd. on behalf of Michael Yeats. Excerpt from "Lapis Lazuli" from *The Collected Poems of W. B. Yeats, Revised Second Edition,* edited by Richard J. Finneran (New York: Simon & Schuster, 1989). Reprinted with the permission of A. P. Watt, Ltd. on behalf of Michael Yeats.

A.N. WILSON Excerpt from "Thoughts about the Person from Porlock" by Stevie Smith. From *The Collected Poems of Stevie Smith.* Copyright © 1972 by Stevie Smith. Reprinted with the permission of New Directions Publishing Corporation.

Editorial and Production Staff

Project Editors

ANNA SHEETS NESBITT
PAMELA PARKINSON

Contributing Editor

ALJA COLLAR

Copyeditors

JANET BYRNE
ANNE JEANETTE JOHNSON
GINA MISIROGLU
GREG TEAGUE

Indexer

REBECCA VALENTINE

Permission Researcher

FRED COURTWRIGHT

Production Manager

EVI SEOUD

Buyer

STACY MELSON

Publisher

KAREN DAY

Contents

Chronology

Late 7th century Earliest predictions claim that *Beowulf* may have already been written and completed

731 An Anglo-Saxon monk, Bede, writes *Ecclesiastical History of the English People*

732 The Battle of Tours halts the Moorish conquest of Europe

735 Egbert serves as the first archbishop in England's second archbishopric, located in York

793 The first recorded appearance of the Vikings comes from the island of Lindisfarne, Scotland.

800 Charlemagne is crowned Emperor of the western Roman Empire

896 England's Alfred the Great ends the threat of the Danes

899 Death of Alfred the Great

959–975 **Reign of Edgar (great-grandson of Alfred the Great and first king of a united England)**

975–978 **Reign of Edward (the Martyr)**

978–1016 **Reign of Aethelred (the Unready)**

999 Eastern and western Europeans fear the end of the world

1016 **Reign of Edmund**

1016–1035 **Reign of Canute, by conquest**

1037–1040 **Reign of Harold I**

1040 Duncan I, King of Scotland, is murdered, and Macbeth assumes his thrown until 1057, when Macbeth is murdered by Duncan's son

1040–1042 **Reign of Harthacanute**

1065 Westminster Abbey is consecrated.

1042–1066 **Reign of Edward (the Confessor)**

1066 **Reign of Harold II**

1066 At the Battle of Stamford Bridge, Harold II's army defeats Harald III, king of Norway, and his men, who have invaded England

1066 The Normans, led by William the Bastard (to become William the Conqueror), defeat Harold II at the Battle of Hastings and conquer England

1066–1087 **Reign of Norman William I (William the Conqueror)**

1085–1086 The Doomsday Book, a census of England, is ordered by King William the Conqueror

1087–1100 **Reign of William II (Rufus)**

1095 At the Council of Clermont, Pope Urban Ii called Christians to war; the first crusade lasts until 1099, and other crusades follow until the fall of the last Christian stronghold in 1291

1100–1135 **Reign of Henry I**

12th century Oxford University is founded

1120 Anglo-Saxon scientist Welcher of Malvern pioneers the measurement of the earth in degrees, minutes, and seconds of latitude and longitude

French philosopher Peter Abelard's *Sic et non*

1121 Concordat of Worms

1128 Scotland's David I founds the Abbey of Holyrood

1135–1154 **Reign of Stephen**

1136 Abelard's *Historia Calamitatum*

1139 Matilda, daughter of Henry I and cousin of King Stephen, challenges for the throne of England, but withdraws her claim in 1148

1140 Matilda is elected "Lady of the English"

1141 King Stephen is captured during the seige of Lincoln Castle, and Matilda rules for 6 months

1154–1189 **Reign of Henry II**

CHRONOLOGY

1159 John of Salisbury writes his *Policraticus*, a work of political philosophy

1164 At the Council of Clarendon, King Henry II issues the Constitutions of Clarendon, extending jurisdictions of civil over church courts

1170 Thomas Becket, long-time foe of King Henry II, is murdered by King Henry's men in Canterbury Cathedral

1189–1199 Reign of Richard the Lionhear (Coeur de Lion)

1199–1116 Reign of John

1215 The Magna Carta, a charter limiting the power of the monarchy, is reluctantly signed by King John

1216–1272 Reign of Henry III

1217 Cambridge University is founded

1247 Death of Robin Hood, identified as Robert, Earl of Huntington

1266–1273 St. Thomas Aquinas' *Summa theologiae*

1272–1307 Reign of Edward I

1276 The prince of North Wales, Llewelyn II, refuses to pay homage to England's Edward I, who invades North Wales and forces Llewelyn to surrender

1282 Llewelyn II leads a second attack against Edward and fails; Wales falls to English rule

1297 William Wallace (Bravehart) leads attacks against British troops in an attempt for Scottish sovereignty

1305 William Wallace is captured, tried, and hanged

1307–1327 Reign of Edward II

ca. 1325 John Wycliffe born
John Gower born

1327–1377 Reign of Edward III

ca. 1332 William Langland born

1337 Beginning of the Hundred Years' War

ca. 1340 Geoffrey Chaucer born

1346 The Battle of Crécy

1348 The Black Death (further outbreaks in 1361 and 1369)

ca. 1350 Boccaccio's *Decameron*
Langland's *Piers Plowman*

1351 The Statute of Laborers pegs laborers' wages at rates in effect preceding the plague

1356 The Battle of Poitiers

1360 The Treaty of Brétigny: end of the first phase of the Hundred Years' War

1362 Pleadings in the law courts conducted in English
Parliaments opened by speeches in English

1369 Chaucer's *The Book of the Duchess*, an elegy to Blanche of Lancaster, wife of John of Gaunt

1369–1377 Victorious French campaigns under du Guesclin

ca. 1370 John Lydgate born

1371 Sir John Mandeville's *Travels*

1372 Chaucer travels to Italy

1372–1382 Wycliffe active in Oxford

1373–1393 William of Wykeham founds Winchester College and New College, Oxford

ca. 1375–1400 *Sir Gawain and the Green Knight*

1376 Death of Edward the Black Prince

1377–1399 Reign of Richard II

ca. 1379 Gower's *Vox clamantis*

ca. 1380 Chaucer's *Troilus and Criseyde*

1381 The Peasants' Revolt

1386 Chaucer's *Canterbury Tales* begun
Chaucer sits in Parliament
Gower's *Confessio amantis*

1399–1413 Reign of Henry IV

ca. 1400 Death of William Langland

1400 Death of Geoffrey Chaucer

1408 Death of John Gower

1412–1420 Lydgate's *Troy Book*

1413–1422 Reign of Henry V

1415 The Battle of Agincourt

1420–1422 Lydgate's *Siege of Thebes*

1422–1461 Reign of Henry VI

1431 François Villon born
Joan of Arc burned at Rouen

1440–1441 Henry VI founds Eton College and King's College, Cambridge

1444 Truce of Tours

1450 Jack Cade's rebellion

ca. 1451 Death of John Lydgate

1453 End of the Hundred Years' War
The fall of Constantinople

1455–1485 The Wars of the Roses

CHRONOLOGY

CHRONOLOGY

CHRONOLOGY

CHRONOLOGY

CHRONOLOGY

Cromwell defeats the Scots at Preston

The Thirty Years' War ended by the treaty of Westphalia

Parliament purged by the army

1649–1660 Commonwealth

1649 King Charles I tried and executed

The monarchy and the House of Lords abolished

The Commonwealth proclaimed

Cromwell invades Ireland and defeats the royalist Catholic forces

Death of Richard Crashaw

1650 Cromwell defeats the Scots at Dunbar

1651 Charles II crowned king of the Scots, at Scone

Charles II invades England, is defeated at Worcester, escapes to France

Thomas Hobbes's *Leviathan*

1652 War with Holland

1653 The Rump Parliament dissolved by the army

A new Parliament and council of state nominated; Cromwell becomes Lord Protector

Walton's *The Compleat Angler*

1654 Peace concluded with Holland

War against Spain

1655 Parliament attempts to reduce the army and is dissolved

Rule of the major-generals

1656 Sir William Davenant produces *The Siege of Rhodes*, one of the first English operas

1657 Second Parliament of the Protectorate

Cromwell is offered and declines the throne

Death of Richard Lovelace

1658 Death of Oliver Cromwell

Richard Cromwell succeeds as Protector

1659 Conflict between Parliament and the army

1660 General Monck negotiates with Charles II

Charles II offers the conciliatory Declaration of Breda and accepts Parliament's invitation to return

Will's Coffee House established

Sir William Davenant and Thomas Killigrew licensed to set up two companies of players, the Duke of York's and the King's Servants, including actors and actresses

Pepys's *Diary* begun

1660–1685 Reign of Charles II

1661 Parliament passes the Act of Uniformity, enjoining the use of the Book of Common Prayer; many Puritan and dissenting clergy leave their livings

1662 Peace Treaty with Spain

King Charles II marries Catherine of Braganza

The Royal Society incorporated (founded in 1660)

1664 War against Holland

New Amsterdam captured and becomes New York

John Vanbrugh born

1665 The Great Plague

Newton discovers the binomial theorem and invents the integral and differential calculus, at Cambridge

1666 The Great Fire of London

Bunyan's *Grace Abounding*

London Gazette founded

1667 The Dutch fleet sails up the Medway and burns English ships

The war with Holland ended by the Treaty of Breda

Milton's *Paradise Lost*

Thomas Sprat's *History of the Royal Society*

Death of Abraham Cowley

1668 Sir Christopher Wren begins to rebuild St. Paul's Cathedral

Triple Alliance formed with Holland and Sweden against France

Dryden's *Essay of Dramatick Poesy*

1670 Alliance formed with France through the secret Treaty of Dover

Pascal's *Pensées*

The Hudson's Bay Company founded

William Congreve born

1671 Milton's *Samson Agonistes* and *Paradise Regained*

1672 War against Holland

CHRONOLOGY

CHRONOLOGY

Death of Sir Charles Sedley

1702–1714 Reign of Queen Anne

1702 Clarendon's *History of the Rebellion* (1702–1704)

Defoe's *The Shortest Way with the Dissenters*

1703 Defoe is arrested, fined, and pilloried for writing *The Shortest Way*

Death of Samuel Pepys

1704 John Churchill, duke of Marlborough, and Prince Eugene of Savoy defeat the French at Blenheim

Capture of Gibraltar

Swift's *A Tale of a Tub* and *The Battle of the Books*

The Review founded (1704–1713)

1706 Farquhar's *The Recruiting Officer*

Deaths of John Evelyn and Charles Sackville, earl of Dorset

1707 Farquhar's *The Beaux' Stratagem*

Act of Union joining England and Scotland

Death of George Farquhar

Henry Fielding born

1709 The *Tatler* founded (1709–1711)

Nicholas Rowe's edition of Shakespeare

Samuel Johnson born

Marlborough defeats the French at Malplaquet

Charles XII of Sweden defeated at Poltava

1710 South Sea Company founded

First copyright act

1711 Swift's *The Conduct of the Allies*

The *Spectator* founded (1711–1712; 1714)

Marlborough dismissed

David Hume born

1712 Pope's *The Rape of the Lock* (Cantos 1–2)

Jean Jacques Rousseau born

1713 War with France ended by the Treaty of Utrecht

The *Guardian* founded

Swift becomes dean of St. Patrick's, Dublin

Addison's *Cato*

Laurence Sterne born

1714–1727 Reign of George I

1714 Pope's expended version of *The Rape of the Lock* (Cantos 1–5)

1715 The Jacobite rebellion in Scotland

Pope's translation of Homer's *Iliad* (1715–1720)

Death of Louis XIV

1716 Death of William Wycherley

Thomas Gray born

1717 Pope's *Eloisa to Abelard*

David Garrick born

Horace Walpole born

1718 Quadruple Alliance (Britain, France, the Netherlands, the German Empire) in war against Spain

1719 Defoe's *Robinson Crusoe*

Death of Joseph Addison

1720 Inoculation against smallpox introduced in Boston

War against Spain

The South Sea Bubble

Gilbert White born

Defoe's *Captain Singleton* and *Memoirs of a Cavalier*

1721 Tobias Smollett born

William Collins born

1722 Defoe's *Moll Flanders, Journal of the Plague Year*, and *Colonel Jack*

1724 Defoe's *Roxana*

Swift's *The Drapier's Letters*

1725 Pope's translation of Homer's *Odyssey* (1725–1726)

1726 Swift's *Gulliver's Travels*

Voltaire in England (1726–1729)

Death of Sir John Vanbrugh

1727–1760 Reign of George II

1728 Gay's *The Beggar's Opera*

Pope's *The Dunciad* (Books 1–2)

Oliver Goldsmith born

1729 Swift's *A Modest Proposal*

Edmund Burke born

Deaths of William Congreve and Sir Richard Steele

1731 Navigation improved by introduction of the quadrant

Pope's *Moral Essays* (1731–1735)

Death of Daniel Defoe

William Cowper born

1732 Death of John Gay

1733 Pope's *Essay on Man* (1733–1734)

CHRONOLOGY

Lewis Theobald's edition of Shakespeare

1734 Voltaire's *Lettres philosophiques*

1737 Edward Gibbon born

1738 Johnson's *London*

1740 War of the Austrian Succession, 1740–1748 (King George's War in America, 1744–1748)

George Anson begins his circumnavigation of the world (1740–1744)

Frederick the Great becomes king of Prussia (1740–1786)

Richardson's *Pamela* (1740–1741)

James Boswell born

1742 Fielding's *Joseph Andrews*

Edward Young's *Night Thoughts* (1742–1745)

Pope's *The New Dunciad* (Book 4)

1744 Johnson's *Life of Mr. Richard Savage*

Death of Alexander Pope

1745 Second Jacobite rebellion, led by Charles Edward, the Young Pretender

Death of Jonathan Swift

1746 The Young Pretender defeated at Culloden

Collins' *Odes on Several Descriptive and Allegorical Subjects*

1747 Richardson's *Clarissa Harlowe* (1747–1748)

Franklin's experiments with electricity announced

Voltaire's *Essai sur les moeurs*

1748 War of the Austrian Succession ended by the Peace of Aix-la-Chapelle

Smollett's *Adventures of Roderick Random*

David Hume's *Enquiry Concerning Human Understanding*

Montesquieu's *L'Esprit des lois*

1749 Fielding's *Tom Jones*

Johnson's *The Vanity of Human Wishes*

Bolingbroke's *Idea of a Patriot King*

1750 The *Rambler* founded (1750–1752)

1751 Gray's *Elegy Written in a Country Churchyard*

Fielding's *Amelia*

Smollett's *Adventures of Peregrine Pickle*

Denis Diderot and Jean le Rond d'Alembert begin to publish the *Encyclopédie* (1751–1765)

Richard Brinsley Sheridan born

1752 Frances Burney and Thomas Chatterton born

1753 Richardson's *History of Sir Charles Grandison* (1753–1754)

Smollett's *The Adventures of Ferdinand Count Fathom*

1754 Hume's *History of England* (1754–1762)

Death of Henry Fielding

George Crabbe born

1755 Lisbon destroyed by earthquake

Fielding's *Journal of a Voyage to Lisbon* published posthumously

Johnson's *Dictionary of the English Language*

1756 The Seven Years' War against France, 1756–1763 (the French and Indian War in America, 1755–1760)

William Pitt the elder becomes prime minister

Johnson's proposal for an edition of Shakespeare

1757 Robert Clive wins the battle of Plassey, in India

Gray's "The Progress of Poesy" and "The Bard"

Burke's *Philosophical Enquiry into the Origin of Our Ideas of the Sublime and Beautiful*

Hume's *Natural History of Religion*

William Blake born

1758 The *Idler* founded (1758–1760)

1759 Capture of Quebec by General James Wolfe

Johnson's *History of Rasselas, Prince of Abyssinia*

Voltaire's *Candide*

The British Museum opens

Sterne's *The Life and Opinions of Tristram Shandy* (1759–1767)

Death of William Collins

Mary Wollstonecraft born

Robert Burns born

1760–1820 **Reign of George III**

1760 James Macpherson's *Fragments of Ancient Poetry Collected in the Highlands of Scotland*

CHRONOLOGY

William Beckford born

1761 Jean-Jacques Rousseau's *Julie, ou la nouvelle Héloïse*

Death of Samuel Richardson

1762 Rousseau's *Du Contrat social* and *Émile*

Catherine the Great becomes czarina of Russia (1762–1796)

1763 The Seven Years' War ended by the Peace of Paris

Smart's *A Song to David*

1764 James Hargreaves invents the spinning jenny

1765 Parliament passes the Stamp Act to tax the American colonies

Johnson's edition of Shakespeare

Walpole's *The Castle of Otranto*

Thomas Percy's *Reliques of Ancient English Poetry*

Blackstone's *Commentaries on the Laws of England* (1765–1769)

1766 The Stamp Act repealed

Swift's *Journal to Stella* first published in a collection of his letters

Goldsmith's *The Vicar of Wakefield*

Smollett's *Travels Through France and Italy*

Lessing's *Laokoon*

Rousseau in England (1766–1767)

1768 Sterne's *A Sentimental Journey Through France and Italy*

The Royal Academy founded by George III

First edition of the *Encyclopaedia Britannica*

Maria Edgeworth born

Death of Laurence Sterne

1769 David Garrick organizes the Shakespeare Jubilee at Stratford-upon-Avon

Sir Joshua Reynolds' *Discourses* (1769–1790)

Richard Arkwright invents the spinning water frame

1770 Boston Massacre

Burke's *Thoughts on the Cause of the Present Discontents*

Oliver Goldsmith's *The Deserted Village*

Death of Thomas Chatterton

William Wordsworth born

1771 Arkwright's first spinning mill founded

Deaths of Thomas Gray and Tobias Smollett

Walter Scott born

1772 Samuel Taylor Coleridge born

1773 Boston Tea Party

Goldsmith's *She Stoops to Conquer*

Johann Wolfgang von Goethe's *Götz von Berlichingen*

1774 The first Continental Congress meets in Philadelphia

Goethe's *Sorrows of Young Werther*

Death of Oliver Goldsmith

Robert Southey born

1775 Burke's speech on American taxation

American War of Independence begins with the battles of Lexington and Concord

Samuel Johnson's *Journey to the Western Islands of Scotland*

Richard Brinsley Sheridan's *The Rivals* and *The Duenna*

Beaumarchais's *Le Barbier de Séville*

James Watt and Matthew Boulton begin building steam engines in England

Births of Jane Austen, Charles Lamb, Walter Savage Landor, and Matthew Lewis

1776 American Declaration of Independence

Edward Gibbon's *Decline and Fall of the Roman Empire* (1776–1788)

Adam Smith's *Inquiry into the Nature & Causes of the Wealth of Nations*

Thomas Paine's *Common Sense*

Death of David Hume

1777 Maurice Morgann's *Essay on the Dramatic Character of Sir John Falstaff*

Sheridan's *The School for Scandal* first performed (published 1780)

General Burgoyne surrenders at Saratoga

1778 The American colonies allied with France

Britain and France at war

Captain James Cook discovers Hawaii

Death of William Pitt, first earl of Chatham

Deaths of Jean Jacques Rousseau and Voltaire

William Hazlitt born

1779 Johnson's *Prefaces to the Works of the English Poets* (1779–1781); reissued in 1781 as *The Lives of the Most Eminent English Poets*

Sheridan's *The Critic*

Samuel Crompton invents the spinning mule

Death of David Garrick

1780 The Gordon Riots in London

1781 Charles Cornwallis surrenders at Yorktown

Immanuel Kant's *Critique of Pure Reason*

Friedrich von Schiller's *Die Räuber*

1782 William Cowper's "The Journey of John Gilpin" published in the *Public Advertiser*

Choderlos de Laclos's *Les Liaisons dangereuses*

Rousseau's *Confessions* published posthumously

1783 American War of Independence ended by the Definitive Treaty of Peace, signed at Paris

William Blake's *Poetical Sketches*

George Crabbe's *The Village*

William Pitt the younger becomes prime minister

Henri Beyle (Stendhal) born

1784 Beaumarchais's *Le Mariage de Figaro* first performed (published 1785)

Death of Samuel Johnson

1785 Warren Hastings returns to England from India

James Boswell's *The Journey of a Tour of the Hebrides, with Samuel Johnson, LL.D.*

Cowper's *The Task*

Edmund Cartwright invents the power loom

Thomas De Quincey born

Thomas Love Peacock born

1786 William Beckford's *Vathek* published in English (originally written in French in 1782)

Robert Burns's *Poems Chiefly in the Scottish Dialect*

Wolfgang Amadeus Mozart's *The Marriage of Figaro*

Death of Frederick the Great

1787 The Committee for the Abolition of the Slave Trade founded in England

The Constitutional Convention meets at Philadelphia; the Constitution is signed

1788 The trial of Hastings begins on charges of corruption of the government in India

The Estates-General of France summoned

U.S. Constitution is ratified

George Washington elected president of the United States

Giovanni Casanova's *Histoire de ma fuite* (first manuscript of his memoirs)

The *Daily Universal Register* becomes the *Times* (London)

George Gordon, Lord Byron born

1789 The Estates-General meets at Versailles

The National Assembly (Assemblée Nationale) convened

The fall of the Bastille marks the beginning of the French Revolution

The National Assembly draws up the Declaration of Rights of Man and of the Citizen

First U.S. Congress meets in New York

Blake's *Songs of Innocence*

Jeremy Bentham's *Introduction to the Principles of Morals and Legislation* introduces the theory of utilitarianism

Gilbert White's *Natural History of Selborne*

1790 Congress sets permanent capital city site on the Potomac River

First U.S. Census

Burke's *Reflections on the Revolution in France*

Blake's *The Marriage of Heaven and Hell*

CHRONOLOGY

Edmund Malone's edition of Shakespeare

Wollstonecraft's *A Vindication of the Rights of Man*

Death of Benjamin Franklin

1791 French royal family's flight from Paris and capture at Varennes; imprisonment in the Tuileries

Bill of Rights is ratified

Paine's *The Rights of Man* (1791–1792)

Boswell's *The Life of Johnson*

Burns's *Tam o'Shanter*

The *Observer* founded

1792 The Prussians invade France and are repulsed at Valmy September massacres

The National Convention declares royalty abolished in France

Washington reelected president of the United States

New York Stock Exchange opens

Mary Wollstonecraft's *Vindication of the Rights of Woman*

William Bligh's voyage to the South Sea in H.M.S. *Bounty*

Percy Bysshe Shelley born

1793 Trial and execution of Louis XVI and Marie-Antoinette

France declares war against England

The Committee of Public Safety (Comité de Salut Public) established

Eli Whitney devises the cotton gin

William Godwin's *An Enquiry Concerning Political Justice*

Blake's *Visions of the Daughters of Albion and America*

Wordsworth's *An Evening Walk* and *Descriptive Sketches*

1794 Execution of Georges Danton and Maximilien de Robespierre

Paine's *The Age of Reason* (1794–1796)

Blake's *Songs of Experience*

Ann Radcliffe's *The Mysteries of Udolpho*

Death of Edward Gibbon

1795 The government of the Directory established (1795–1799)

Hastings acquitted

Landor's *Poems*

Death of James Boswell

John Keats born

Thomas Carlyle born

1796 Napoleon Bonaparte takes command in Italy

Matthew Lewis' *The Monk*

John Adams elected president of the United States

Death of Robert Burns

1797 The peace of Campo Formio: extinction of the Venetian Republic XYZ Affair

Mutinies in the Royal Navy at Spithead and the Nore

Blake's *Vala, Or the Four Zoas* (first version)

Mary Shelley born

Deaths of Edmund Burke, Mary Wollstonecraft, and Horace Walpole

1798 Napoleon invades Egypt

Horatio Nelson wins the battle of the Nile

Wordsworth's and Coleridge's *Lyrical Ballads*

Landor's *Gebir*

Thomas Malthus' *Essay on the Principle of Population*

1799 Napoleon becomes first consul

Pitt introduces first income tax in Great Britain

Sheridan's *Pizarro*

Honoré de Balzac born

Thomas Hood born

Alexander Pushkin born

1800 Thomas Jefferson elected president of the United States

Alessandro Volta produces electricity from a cell

Library of Congress established

Death of William Cowper

Thomas Babington Macaulay born

1801 First census taken in England

1802 The Treaty of Amiens marks the end of the French Revolutionary War

The *Edinburgh Review* founded

1803 England's war with France renewed

The Louisiana Purchase

Robert Fulton propels a boat by steam power on the Seine

CHRONOLOGY

CHRONOLOGY

Wordsworth's *The White Doe of Ryl-stone*

Anthony Trollope born

1816 Byron leaves England permanently

The Elgin Marbles exhibited in the British Museum

James Monroe elected president of the United States

Jane Austen's *Emma*

Byron's *Childe Harold* (Canto 3)

Coleridge's *Christabel, Kubla Khan: A Vision, The Pains of Sleep*

Benjamin Constant's *Adolphe*

Goethe's *Italienische Reise*

Peacock's *Headlong Hall*

Scott's *The Antiquary*

Shelley's *Alastor*

Rossini's *Il Barbiere di Siviglia*

Death of Richard Brinsley Sheridan

Charlotte Brontë born

1817 *Blackwood's Edinburgh* magazine founded

Jane Austen's *Northanger Abbey* and *Persuasion*

Byron's *Manfred*

Coleridge's *Biographia Literaria*

Hazlitt's *The Characters of Shakespeare's Plays* and *The Round Table*

Keats's *Poems*

Peacock's *Melincourt*

David Ricardo's *Principles of Political Economy and Taxation*

Death of Jane Austen

Death of Mme de Staël

Branwell Brontë born

Henry David Thoreau born

1818 Byron's *Childe Harold* (Canto 4), and *Beppo*

Hazlitt's *Lectures on the English Poets*

Keats's *Endymion*

Peacock's *Nightmare Abbey*

Scott's *Rob Roy* and *The Heart of Mid-Lothian*

Mary Shelley's *Frankenstein*

Percy Shelley's *The Revolt of Islam*

Emily Brontë born

Karl Marx born

Ivan Sergeyevich Turgenev born

1819 The *Savannah* becomes the first steamship to cross the Atlantic (in 26 days)

Peterloo massacre in Manchester

Byron's *Don Juan* (1819–1824) and *Mazeppa*

Crabbe's *Tales of the Hall*

Géricault's *Raft of the Medusa*

Hazlitt's *Lectures on the English Comic Writers*

Arthur Schopenhauer's *Die Welt als Wille und Vorstellung (The World as Will and Idea)*

Scott's *The Bride of Lammermoor* and *A Legend of Montrose*

Shelley's *The Cenci,* "The Masque of Anarchy," and "Ode to the West Wind"

Wordsworth's *Peter Bell*

Queen Victoria born

George Eliot born

1820–1830 Reign of George IV

1820 Trial of Queen Caroline

Cato Street Conspiracy suppressed; Arthur Thistlewood hanged

Monroe reelected president of the United States

Missouri Compromise

The *London* magazine founded

Keats's *Lamia, Isabella, The Eve of St. Agnes, and Other Poems*

Hazlitt's *Lectures Chiefly on the Dramatic Literature of the Age of Elizabeth*

Charles Maturin's *Melmoth the Wanderer*

Scott's *Ivanhoe* and *The Monastery*

Shelley's *Prometheus Unbound*

Anne Brontë born

1821 Greek War of Independence begins

Liberia founded as a colony for freed slaves

Byron's *Cain, Marino Faliero, The Two Foscari,* and *Sardanapalus*

Hazlitt's *Table Talk* (1821–1822)

Scott's *Kenilworth*

Shelley's *Adonais* and *Epipsychidion*

Death of John Keats

Death of Napoleon

Charles Baudelaire born

Feodor Dostoyevsky born

Gustave Flaubert born

1822 The Massacres of Chios (Greeks rebel against Turkish rule)

CHRONOLOGY

Byron's *The Vision of Judgment*
De Quincey's *Confessions of an English Opium-Eater*
Peacock's *Maid Marian*
Scott's *Peveril of the Peak*
Shelley's *Hellas*
Death of Percy Bysshe Shelley
Matthew Arnold born

1823 Monroe Doctrine proclaimed
Byron's *The Age of Bronze* and *The Island*
Lamb's *Essays of Elia*
Scott's *Quentin Durward*

1824 The National Gallery opened in London
John Quincy Adams elected president of the United States
The *Westminster Review* founded
Beethoven's Ninth Symphony first performed
William (Wilkie) Collins born
James Hogg's *The Private Memoirs and Confessions of a Justified Sinner*
Landor's *Imaginary Conversations* (1824–1829)
Scott's *Redgauntlet*
Death of George Gordon, Lord Byron

1825 Inauguration of steam-powered passenger and freight service on the Stockton and Darlington railway
Bolivia and Brazil become independent Alessandro Manzoni's *I Promessi Sposi* (1825–1826)

1826 André-Marie AmpΣre's *Mémoire sur la théorie mathématique des phénomΣnes électrodynamiques*
James Fenimore Cooper's *The Last of the Mohicans*
Disraeli's *Vivian Grey* (1826–1827)
Scott's *Woodstock*

1827 The battle of Navarino ensures the independence of Greece
Josef Ressel obtains patent for the screw propeller for steamships
Heinrich Heine's *Buch der Lieder*
Death of William Blake

1828 Andrew Jackson elected president of the United States
Henrik Ibsen born
George Meredith born

Dante Gabriel Rossetti born
Leo Tolstoy born

1829 The Catholic Emancipation Act
Robert Peel establishes the metropolitan police force
Greek independence recognized by Turkey
Balzac begins *La Comédie humaine* (1829–1848)
Peacock's *The Misfortunes of Elphin*
J. M. W. Turner's *Ulysses Deriding Polyphemus*

1830–1837 **Reign of William IV**

1830 Charles X of France abdicates and is succeeded by Louis-Philippe
The Liverpool-Manchester railway opened
Tennyson's *Poems, Chiefly Lyrical*
Death of William Hazlitt
Christina Rossetti born

1831 Michael Faraday discovers electromagnetic induction
Charles Darwin's voyage on H.M.S. *Beagle* begins (1831–1836)
The Barbizon school of artists' first exhibition
Nat Turner slave revolt crushed in Virginia
Peacock's *Crotchet Castle*
Stendhal's *Le Rouge et le noir*
Edward Trelawny's *The Adventures of a Younger Son*

1832 The first Reform Bill
Samuel Morse invents the telegraph
Jackson reelected president of the United States
Disraeli's *Contarini Fleming*
Goethe's *Faust* (Part 2)
Tennyson's *Poems, Chiefly Lyrical*, including "The Lotus-Eaters" and "The Lady of Shalott"
Death of Johann Wolfgang von Goethe
Death of Sir Walter Scott
Lewis Carroll born

1833 Robert Browning's *Pauline*
John Keble launches the Oxford Movement
American Anti-Slavery Society founded
Lamb's *Last Essays of Elia*

CHRONOLOGY

Carlyle's *Sartor Resartus* (1833–1834)
Pushkin's *Eugene Onegin*
Mendelssohn's *Italian Symphony* first
performed

1834   Abolition of slavery in the British
Empire
Louis Braille's alphabet for the blind
Balzac's *Le Père Goriot*
Nikolai Gogol's *Dead Souls* (Part 1,
1834–1842)
Death of Samuel Taylor Coleridge
Death of Charles Lamb
William Morris born

1835   Hans Christian Andersen's *Fairy
Tales* (1st ser.)
Robert Browning's *Paracelsus*
Samuel Butler born
Alexis de Tocqueville's *De la Democratie en Amerique* (1835–1840)

1836   Martin Van Buren elected president
of the United States
Dickens' *Sketches by Boz* (1836–1837)
Landor's *Pericles and Aspasia*

1837–1901   Reign of Queen Victoria

1837   Carlyle's *The French Revolution*
Dickens' *Oliver Twist* (1837–1838)
and *Pickwick Papers*
Disraeli's *Venetia* and *Henrietta Temple*

1838   Chartist movement in England
National Gallery in London opened
Elizabeth Barrett Browning's *The
Seraphim and Other Poems*
Dickens' *Nicholas Nickleby*
(1838–1839)

1839   Louis Daguerre perfects process for
producing an image on a silvercoated copper plate Faraday's
Experimental Researches in Electricity
(1839–1855)
First Chartist riots
Opium War between Great Britain
and China
Carlyle's *Chartism*

1840   Canadian Act of Union
Queen Victoria marries Prince Albert
Charles Barry begins construction of
the Houses of Parliament
(1840–1852)
William Henry Harrison elected
president of the United States

Robert Browning's *Sordello*
Thomas Hardy born

1841   New Zealand proclaimed a British
colony
James Clark Ross discovers the
Antarctic continent
Punch founded
John Tyler succeeds to the presidency after the death of Harrison
Carlyle's *Heroes and Hero-Worship*
Dickens' *The Old Curiosity Shop*

1842   Chartist riots
Income tax revived in Great Britain
The Mines Act, forbidding work
underground by women or by children under the age of ten
Charles Edward Mudie's Lending
Library founded in London
Dickens visits America
Robert Browning's *Dramatic Lyrics*
Macaulay's *Lays of Ancient Rome*
Tennyson's *Poems*, including "Morte
d'Arthur," "St. Simeon Stylites,"
and "Ulysses"
Wordsworth's *Poems*

1843   Marc Isambard Brunel's Thames
tunnel opened
The Economist founded
Carlyle's *Past and Present*
Dickens' *A Christmas Carol*
John Stuart Mill's *Logic*
Macaulay's *Critical and Historical
Essays*
John Ruskin's *Modern Painters*
(1843–1860)

1844   Rochdale Society of Equitable Pioneers, one of the first consumers'
cooperatives, founded by twentyeight Lancashire weavers
James K. Polk elected president of
the United States
Elizabeth Barrett Browning's *Poems*,
including "The Cry of the Children"
Dickens' *Martin Chuzzlewit*
Disraeli's *Coningsby*
Turner's *Rain, Steam and Speed*
Gerard Manley Hopkins born

1845   The great potato famine in Ireland
begins (1845–1849)
Disraeli's *Sybil*

CHRONOLOGY

CHRONOLOGY

Olive Schreiner born
Tennyson's *Maud*
Thackeray's *The Newcomes*
Trollope's *The Warden*
Death of Charlotte Brontë

1856 The Treaty of Paris ends the Crimean War
Henry Bessemer's steel process invented
James Buchanan elected president of the United States
H. Rider Haggard born

1857 The Indian Mutiny begins; crushed in 1858
The Matrimonial Causes Act
Charlotte Brontë's *The Professor*
Elizabeth Barrett Browning's *Aurora Leigh*
Dickens' *Little Dorritt*
Elizabeth Gaskell's *The Life of Charlotte Brontë*
Thomas Hughes's *Tom Brown's School Days*
Trollope's *Barchester Towers*

1858 Carlyle's *History of Frederick the Great* (1858–1865)
George Eliot's *Scenes of Clerical Life*
Morris' *The Defense of Guinevere*
Trollope's *Dr. Thorne*

1859 Charles Darwin's *The Origin of Species*
Dickens' *A Tale of Two Cities*
Arthur Conan Doyle born
George Eliot's *Adam Bede*
Fitzgerald's *The Rubaiyat of Omar Khayy‡m*
Meredith's *The Ordeal of Richard Feverel*
Mill's *On Liberty*
Samuel Smiles's *Self-Help*
Tennyson's *Idylls of the King*

1860 Abraham Lincoln elected president of the United States
The *Cornhill* magazine founded with Thackeray as editor
James M. Barrie born
William Wilkie Collins' *The Woman in White*
George Eliot's *The Mill on the Floss*

1861 American Civil War begins

Louis Pasteur presents the germ theory of disease
Arnold's *Lectures on Translating Homer*
Dickens' *Great Expectations*
George Eliot's *Silas Marner*
Meredith's *Evan Harrington*
Francis Turner Palgrave's *The Golden Treasury*
Trollope's *Framley Parsonage*
Peacock's *Gryll Grange*
Death of Prince Albert

1862 George Eliot's *Romola*
Meredith's *Modern Love*
Christina Rossetti's *Goblin Market*
Ruskin's *Unto This Last*
Trollope's *Orley Farm*

1863 Thomas Huxley's *Man's Place in Nature*

1864 The Geneva Red Cross Convention signed by twelve nations
Lincoln reelected president of the United States
Robert Browning's *Dramatis Personae*
John Henry Newman's *Apologia pro vita sua*
Tennyson's *Enoch Arden*
Trollope's *The Small House at Allington*

1865 Assassination of Lincoln; Andrew Johnson succeeds to the presidency
Arnold's *Essays in Criticism* (1st ser.)
Carroll's *Alice's Adventures in Wonderland*
Dickens' *Our Mutual Friend*
Meredith's *Rhoda Fleming*
A. C. Swinburne's *Atalanta in Calydon*

1866 First successful transatlantic telegraph cable laid
George Eliot's *Felix Holt, the Radical*
Elizabeth Gaskell's *Wives and Daughters*
Beatrix Potter born
Swinburne's *Poems and Ballads*

1867 The second Reform Bill
Arnold's *New Poems*
Bagehot's *The English Constitution*
Carlyle's *Shooting Niagara*
Marx's *Das Kapital* (vol. 1)
Trollope's *The Last Chronicle of Barset*

CHRONOLOGY

1868   Gladstone becomes prime minister (1868–1874)

Johnson impeached by House of Representatives; acquitted by Senate

Ulysses S. Grant elected president of the United States

Robert Browning's *The Ring and the Book* (1868–1869)

Collins' *The Moonstone*

1869   The Suez Canal opened

Girton College, Cambridge, founded

Arnold's *Culture and Anarchy*

Mill's *The Subjection of Women*

Trollope's *Phineas Finn*

1870   The Elementary Education Act establishes schools under the aegis of local boards

Dickens' *Edwin Drood*

Disraeli's *Lothair*

Morris' *The Earthly Paradise*

Dante Gabriel Rossetti's *Poems*

Saki (Hector Hugh Munro) born

1871   Trade unions legalized

Newnham College, Cambridge, founded for women students

Carroll's *Through the Looking Glass*

Darwin's *The Descent of Man*

Meredith's *The Adventures of Harry Richmond*

Swinburne's *Songs Before Sunrise*

1872   Max Beerbohm born

Samuel Butler's *Erewhon*

George Eliot's *Middlemarch*

Grant reelected president of the United States

Hardy's *Under the Greenwood Tree*

1873   Arnold's *Literature and Dogma*

Mill's *Autobiography*

Pater's *Studies in the History of the Renaissance*

Trollope's *The Eustace Diamonds*

1874   Disraeli becomes prime minister

Hardy's *Far from the Madding Crowd*

James Thomson's *The City of Dreadful Night*

1875   Britain buys Suez Canal shares

Trollope's *The Way We Live Now*

1876   F. H. Bradley's *Ethical Studies*

George Eliot's *Daniel Deronda*

Henry James's *Roderick Hudson*

Meredith's *Beauchamp's Career*

Morris' *Sigurd the Volsung*

Trollope's *The Prime Minister*

1877   Rutherford B. Hayes elected president of the United States after Electoral Commission awards him disputed votes

Henry James's *The American*

1878   Electric street lighting introduced in London

Hardy's *The Return of the Native*

Swinburne's *Poems and Ballads* (2d ser.)

Edward Thomas born

1879   Somerville College and Lady Margaret Hall opened at Oxford for women

The London telephone exchange built

Gladstone's Midlothian campaign (1879–1880)

Browning's *Dramatic Idyls*

Meredith's *The Egoist*

1880   Gladstone's second term as prime minister (1880–1885)

James A. Garfield elected president of the United States

Browning's *Dramatic Idyls Second Series*

Disraeli's *Endymion*

Radclyffe Hall born

Hardy's *The Trumpet-Major*

Lytton Strachey born

1881   Garfield assassinated; Chester A. Arthur succeeds to the presidency

Henry James's *The Portrait of a Lady* and *Washington Square*

D. G. Rossetti's *Ballads and Sonnets*

P. G. Wodehouse born

1882   Triple Alliance formed between German empire, Austrian empire, and Italy

Leslie Stephen begins to edit the *Dictionary of National Biography*

Married Women's Property Act passed in Britain

Britain occupies Egypt and the Sudan

1883   Uprising of the Mahdi: Britain evacuates the Sudan

Royal College of Music opens

CHRONOLOGY

T. H. Green's *Ethics*

T. E. Hulme born

Stevenson's *Treasure Island*

1884 The Mahdi captures Omdurman: General Gordon appointed to command the garrison of Khartoum

Grover Cleveland elected president of the United States

The *Oxford English Dictionary* begins publishing

The Fabian Society founded

Hiram Maxim's recoil-operated machine gun invented

1885 The Mahdi captures Khartoum: General Gordon killed

Haggard's *King Solomon's Mines*

Marx's *Das Kapital* (vol. 2)

Meredith's *Diana of the Crossways*

Pater's *Marius the Epicurean*

1886 The Canadian Pacific Railway completed

Gold discovered in the Transvaal

Ronald Firbank born

Henry James's *The Bostonians* and *The Princess Casamassima*

Stevenson's *The Strange Case of Dr. Jekyll and Mr. Hyde*

1887 Queen Victoria's Golden Jubilee

Rupert Brooke born

Haggard's *Allan Quatermain* and *She*

Hardy's *The Woodlanders*

Edwin Muir born

1888 Benjamin Harrison elected president of the United States

Henry James's *The Aspern Papers*

Kipling's *Plain Tales from the Hills*

T. E. Lawrence born

1889 Yeats's *The Wanderings of Oisin*

Death of Robert Browning

1890 Morris founds the Kelmscott Press

Agatha Christie born

Frazer's *The Golden Bough* (1st ed.)

Henry James's *The Tragic Muse*

Morris' *News From Nowhere*

Jean Rhys born

1891 Gissing's *New Grub Street*

Hardy's *Tess of the d'Urbervilles*

Wilde's *The Picture of Dorian Gray*

1892 Grover Cleveland elected president of the United States

Conan Doyle's *The Adventures of Sherlock Holmes*

Shaw's *Widower's Houses*

J. R. R. Tolkien born

Rebecca West born

Wilde's *Lady Windermere's Fan*

1893 Wilde's *A Woman of No Importance* and *Salomé*

1894 Kipling's *The Jungle Book*

Moore's *Esther Waters*

Marx's *Das Kapital* (vol. 3)

Audrey Beardsley's *The Yellow Book* begins to appear quarterly

Shaw's *Arms and the Man*

1895 Trial and imprisonment of Oscar Wilde

William Ramsay announces discovery of helium

The National Trust founded

Conrad's *Almayer's Folly*

Hardy's *Jude the Obscure*

Wells's *The Time Machine*

Wilde's *The Importance of Being Earnest*

Yeats's *Poems*

1896 William McKinley elected president of the United States

Failure of the Jameson Raid on the Transvaal

Housman's *A Shropshire Lad*

1897 Queen Victoria's Diamond Jubilee

Conrad's *The Nigger of the Narcissus*

Havelock Ellis' *Studies in the Psychology of Sex* begins publication

Henry James's *The Spoils of Poynton* and *What Maisie Knew*

Kipling's *Captains Courageous*

Shaw's *Candida*

Stoker's *Dracula*

Wells's *The Invisible Man*

1898 Kitchener defeats the Mahdist forces at Omdurman: the Sudan reoccupied

Hardy's *Wessex Poems*

Henry James's *The Turn of the Screw*

C. S. Lewis born

Shaw's *Caesar and Cleopatra* and *You Never Can Tell*

Alec Waugh born

Wells's *The War of the Worlds*

Wilde's *The Ballad of Reading Gaol*

CHRONOLOGY

1899   The Boer War begins
Elizabeth Bowen born
Noël Coward born
Elgar's *Enigma Variations*
Kipling's *Stalky and Co.*

1900   McKinley reelected president of the United States
British Labour party founded
Boxer Rebellion in China
Reginald A. Fessenden transmits speech by wireless
First Zeppelin trial flight
Max Planck presents his first paper on the quantum theory
Conrad's *Lord Jim*
Elgar's *The Dream of Gerontius*
Sigmund Freud's *The Interpretation of Dreams*
V. S. Pritchett born
William Butler Yeats's *The Shadowy Waters*

1901–1910   **Reign of King Edward VII**

1901   William McKinley assassinated; Theodore Roosevelt succeeds to the presidency
First transatlantic wireless telegraph signal transmitted
Chekhov's *Three Sisters*
Freud's *Psychopathology of Everyday Life*
Rudyard Kipling's *Kim*
Thomas Mann's *Buddenbrooks*
Potter's *The Tale of Peter Rabbit*
Shaw's *Captain Brassbound's Conversion*
August Strindberg's *The Dance of Death*

1902   Barrie's *The Admirable Crichton*
Arnold Bennett's *Anna of the Five Towns*
Cézanne's *Le Lac D'Annecy*
Conrad's *Heart of Darkness*
Henry James's *The Wings of the Dove*
William James's *The Varieties of Religious Experience*
Kipling's *Just So Stories*
Maugham's *Mrs. Cradock*
Stevie Smith born
Times Literary Supplement begins publishing

1903   At its London congress the Russian Social Democratic Party divides into Mensheviks, led by Plekhanov, and Bolsheviks, led by Lenin
The treaty of Panama places the Canal Zone in U.S. hands for a nominal rent
Motor cars regulated in Britain to a 20-mile-per-hour limit
The Wright brothers make a successful flight in the United States
Burlington magazine founded
Samuel Butler's *The Way of All Flesh* published posthumously
Cyril Connolly born
George Gissing's *The Private Papers of Henry Ryecroft*
Thomas Hardy's *The Dynasts*
Henry James's *The Ambassadors*
Alan Paton born
Shaw's *Man and Superman*
Synge's *Riders to the Sea* produced in Dublin
Yeats's *In the Seven Woods* and *On Baile's Strand*

1904   Roosevelt elected president of the United States
Russo-Japanese war (1904–1905)
Construction of the Panama Canal begins
The ultraviolet lamp invented
The engineering firm of Rolls Royce founded
Barrie's *Peter Pan* first performed
Cecil Day Lewis born
Chekhov's *The Cherry Orchard*
Conrad's *Nostromo*
Henry James's *The Golden Bowl*
Kipling's *Traffics and Discoveries*
Georges Rouault's *Head of a Tragic Clown*
G. M. Trevelyan's *England Under the Stuarts*
Puccini's *Madame Butterfly*
First Shaw-Granville Barker season at the Royal Court Theatre
The Abbey Theatre founded in Dublin

1905   Russian sailors on the battleship Potemkin mutiny

CHRONOLOGY

After riots and a general strike the czar concedes demands by the Duma for legislative powers, a wider franchise, and civil liberties

Albert Einstein publishes his first theory of relativity

The Austin Motor Company founded

Bennett's *Tales of the Five Towns*

Claude Debussy's *La Mer*

E. M. Forster's *Where Angels Fear to Tread*

Henry Green born

Richard Strauss's *Salome*

H. G. Wells's *Kipps*

Oscar Wilde's *De Profundis*

1906   Liberals win a landslide victory in the British general election

The Trades Disputes Act legitimizes peaceful picketing in Britain

Captain Dreyfus rehabilitated in France

J. J. Thomson begins research on gamma rays

The U.S. Pure Food and Drug Act passed

Churchill's *Lord Randolph Churchill*

William Empson born

Galsworthy's *The Man of Property*

Kipling's *Puck of Pook's Hill*

Shaw's *The Doctor's Dilemma*

Yeats's *Poems 1899–1905*

1907   Exhibition of cubist paintings in Paris

Henry Adams' *The Education of Henry Adams*

Henri Bergson's *Creative Evolution*

Conrad's *The Secret Agent*

Daphne du Maurier born

Forster's *The Longest Journey*

Christopher Fry born

André Gide's *La Porte étroite*

Shaw's *John Bull's Other Island* and *Major Barbara*

Synge's *The Playboy of the Western World*

Trevelyan's *Garibaldi's Defence of the Roman Republic*

1908   Herbert Asquith becomes prime minister

David Lloyd George becomes chancellor of the exchequer

William Howard Taft elected president of the United States

The Young Turks seize power in Istanbul

Henry Ford's Model T car produced

Bennett's *The Old Wives' Tale*

Pierre Bonnard's *Nude Against the Light*

Georges Braque's *House at L'Estaque*

Chesterton's *The Man Who Was Thursday*

Jacob Epstein's *Figures* erected in London

Forster's *A Room with a View*

Anatole France's *L'Ile des Pingouins*

Henri Matisse's *Bonheur de Vivre*

Elgar's First Symphony

Ford Madox Ford founds the *English Review*

1909   The Young Turks depose Sultan Abdul Hamid

The Anglo-Persian Oil Company formed

Louis Bleriot crosses the English Channel from France by monoplane

Admiral Robert Peary reaches the North Pole

Freud lectures at Clark University (Worcester, Mass.) on psychoanalysis

Serge Diaghilev's Ballets Russes opens in Paris

Galsworthy's *Strife*

Hardy's *Time's Laughingstocks*

Malcolm Lowry born

Claude Monet's *Water Lilies*

Stephen Spender born

Trevelyan's *Garibaldi and the Thousand*

Wells's *Tono-Bungay* first published (book form, 1909)

1910–1936   **Reign of King George V**

1910   The Liberals win the British general election

Marie Curie's *Treatise on Radiography*

Arthur Evans excavates Knossos

Edouard Manet and the first post-impressionist exhibition in London

CHRONOLOGY

Filippo Marinetti publishes "Manifesto of the Futurist Painters"
Norman Angell's *The Great Illusion*
Bennett's *Clayhanger*
Forster's *Howards End*
Galsworthy's *Justice* and *The Silver Box*
Kipling's *Rewards and Fairies*
Norman MacCaig born
Rimsky-Korsakov's *Le Coq d'or*
Stravinsky's *The Firebird*
Vaughan Williams' *A Sea Symphony*
Wells's *The History of Mr. Polly*
Wells's *The New Machiavelli* first published (in book form, 1911)

1911 Lloyd George introduces National Health Insurance Bill
Suffragette riots in Whitehall
Roald Amundsen reaches the South Pole
Bennett's *The Card*
Chagall's *Self Portrait with Seven Fingers*
Conrad's *Under Western Eyes*
D. H. Lawrence's *The White Peacock*
Katherine Mansfield's *In a German Pension*
Edward Marsh edits *Georgian Poetry*
Moore's *Hail and Farewell* (1911–1914)
Flann O'Brien born
Strauss's *Der Rosenkavalier*
Stravinsky's *Petrouchka*
Trevelyan's *Garibaldi and the Making of Italy*
Wells's *The New Machiavelli*
Mahler's *Das Lied von der Erde*

1912 Woodrow Wilson elected president of the United States
SS *Titanic* sinks on its maiden voyage
Five million Americans go to the movies daily; London has four hundred movie theaters
Second post-impressionist exhibition in London
Bennett's and Edward Knoblock's *Milestones*
Constantin Brancusi's *Maiastra*
Wassily Kandinsky's *Black Lines*
D. H. Lawrence's *The Trespasser*

1913 Second Balkan War begins

Henry Ford pioneers factory assembly technique through conveyor belts
Epstein's *Tomb of Oscar Wilde*
New York Armory Show introduces modern art to the world
Alain Fournier's *Le Grand Meaulnes*
Freud's *Totem and Tabu*
D. H. Lawrence's *Sons and Lovers*
Mann's *Death in Venice*
Proust's *Du Côté de chez Swann* (first volume of *À la recherche du temps perdu*, 1913–1922)
Barbara Pym born
Ravel's *Daphnis and Chloé*

1914 The Panama Canal opens (formal dedication on 12 July 1920)
Irish Home Rule Bill passed in the House of Commons
Archduke Franz Ferdinand assassinated at Sarajevo
World War I begins
Battles of the Marne, Masurian Lakes, and Falkland Islands
Joyce's *Dubliners*
Norman Nicholson born
Shaw's *Pygmalion* and *Androcles and the Lion*
Yeats's *Responsibilities*
Wyndham Lewis publishes *Blast* magazine and *The Vorticist Manifesto*

1915 The Dardanelles campaign begins
Britain and Germany begin naval and submarine blockades
The *Lusitania* is sunk
Hugo Junkers manufactures the first fighter aircraft
Poison gas used for the first time
First Zeppelin raid in London
Brooke's *1914: Five Sonnets*
Norman Douglas' *Old Calabria*
D. W. Griffith's *The Birth of a Nation*
Gustav Holst's *The Planets*
D. H. Lawrence's *The Rainbow*
Wyndham Lewis's *The Crowd*
Maugham's *Of Human Bondage*
Pablo Picasso's *Harlequin*
Sibelius' Fifth Symphony

1916 Evacuation of Gallipoli and the Dardanelles

CHRONOLOGY

Battles of the Somme, Jutland, and Verdun
Britain introduces conscription
The Easter Rebellion in Dublin
Asquith resigns and David Lloyd George becomes prime minister
The Sykes-Picot agreement on the partition of Turkey
First military tanks used
Wilson reelected president president of the United States
Henri Barbusse's *Le Feu*
Griffith's *Intolerance*
Joyce's *Portrait of the Artist as a Young Man*
Jung's *Psychology of the Unconscious*
Moore's *The Brook Kerith*
Edith Sitwell edits *Wheels* (1916–1921)
Wells's *Mr. Britling Sees It Through*

1917 United States enters World War I
Czar Nicholas II abdicates
The Balfour Declaration on a Jewish national home in Palestine
The Bolshevik Revolution
Georges Clemenceau elected prime minister of France
Lenin appointed chief commissar; Trotsky appointed minister of foreign affairs
Conrad's *The Shadow-Line*
Douglas' *South Wind*
Eliot's *Prufrock and Other Observations*
Modigliani's *Nude with Necklace*
Sassoon's *The Old Huntsman*
Prokofiev's *Classical Symphony*
Yeats's *The Wild Swans at Coole*

1918 Wilson puts forward Fourteen Points for World Peace
Central Powers and Russia sign the Treaty of Brest-Litovsk
Execution of Czar Nicholas II and his family
Kaiser Wilhelm II abdicates
The Armistice signed
Women granted the vote at age thirty in Britain
Rupert Brooke's *Collected Poems*
Gerard Manley Hopkins' *Poems*
Joyce's *Exiles*
Lewis's *Tarr*

Sassoon's *Counter-Attack*
Oswald Spengler's *The Decline of the West*
Strachey's *Eminent Victorians*
Béla Bartók's *Bluebeard's Castle*
Charlie Chaplin's *Shoulder Arms*

1919 The Versailles Peace Treaty signed
J. W. Alcock and A. W. Brown make first transatlantic flight
Ross Smith flies from London to Australia
National Socialist party founded in Germany
Benito Mussolini founds the Fascist party in Italy
Sinn Fein Congress adopts declaration of independence in Dublin
Eamon De Valera elected president of Sinn Fein party
Communist Third International founded
Lady Astor elected first woman Member of Parliament
Prohibition in the United States
John Maynard Keynes's *The Economic Consequences of the Peace*
Eliot's *Poems*
Maugham's *The Moon and Sixpence*
Shaw's *Heartbreak House*
The Bauhaus school of design, building, and crafts founded by Walter Gropius
Amedeo Modigliani's *Self-Portrait*

1920 The League of Nations established
Warren G. Harding elected president of the United States
Senate votes against joining the League and rejects the Treaty of Versailles
The Nineteenth Amendment gives women the right to vote
White Russian forces of Denikin and Kolchak defeated by the Bolsheviks
Karel Čapek's *R.U.R.*
Galsworthy's *In Chancery* and *The Skin Game*
Sinclair Lewis' *Main Street*
Katherine Mansfield's *Bliss*
Matisse's *Odalisques* (1920–1925)
Ezra Pound's *Hugh Selwyn Mauberly*

CHRONOLOGY

Paul Valéry's *Le Cimetière Marin*
Yeats's *Michael Robartes and the Dancer*

1921 Britain signs peace with Ireland
First medium-wave radio broadcast in the United States
The British Broadcasting Corporation founded
Braque's *Still Life with Guitar*
Chaplin's *The Kid*
Aldous Huxley's *Crome Yellow*
Paul Klee's *The Fish*
D. H. Lawrence's *Women in Love*
John McTaggart's *The Nature of Existence* (vol. 1)
Moore's *Héloïse and Abélard*
Eugene O'Neill's *The Emperor Jones*
Luigi Pirandello's *Six Characters in Search of an Author*
Shaw's *Back to Methuselah*
Strachey's *Queen Victoria*
George Mackay Brown born

1922 Lloyd George's Coalition government succeeded by Bonar Law's Conservative government
Benito Mussolini marches on Rome and forms a government
William Cosgrave elected president of the Irish Free State
The BBC begins broadcasting in London
Lord Carnarvon and Howard Carter discover Tutankhamen's tomb
The PEN club founded in London
The *Criterion* founded with T. S. Eliot as editor
Kingsley Amis born
Eliot's *The Waste Land*
A. E. Housman's *Last Poems*
Joyce's *Ulysses*
D. H. Lawrence's *Aaron's Rod* and *England, My England*
Sinclair Lewis's *Babbitt*
O'Neill's *Anna Christie*
Pirandello's *Henry IV*
Edith Sitwell's *Façade*
Virginia Woolf's *Jacob's Room*
Yeats's *The Trembling of the Veil*
Donald Davie born

1923 The Union of Soviet Socialist Republics established

French and Belgian troops occupy the Ruhr in consequence of Germany's failure to pay reparations
Mustafa Kemal (Ataturk) proclaims Turkey a republic and is elected president
Warren G. Harding dies; Calvin Coolidge becomes president
Stanley Baldwin succeeds Bonar Law as prime minister
Adolf Hitler's attempted coup in Munich fails
Time magazine begins publishing
E. N. da C. Andrade's *The Structure of the Atom*
Brendan Behan born
Bennett's *Riceyman Steps*
Churchill's *The World Crisis* (1923–1927)
J. E. Flecker's *Hassan* produced
Nadine Gordimer born
Paul Klee's *Magic Theatre*
Lawrence's *Kangaroo*
Rainer Maria Rilke's *Duino Elegies* and *Sonnets to Orpheus*
Sibelius' *Sixth Symphony*
Picasso's *Seated Woman*
William Walton's *Façade*

1924 Ramsay MacDonald forms first Labour government, loses general election, and is succeeded by Stanley Baldwin
Calvin Coolidge elected president of the United States
Noël Coward's *The Vortex*
Forster's *A Passage to India*
Mann's *The Magic Mountain*
Shaw's *St. Joan*

1925 Reza Khan becomes shah of Iran
First surrealist exhibition held in Paris
Alban Berg's *Wozzeck*
Chaplin's *The Gold Rush*
John Dos Passos' *Manhattan Transfer*
Theodore Dreiser's *An American Tragedy*
Sergei Eisenstein's *Battleship Potemkin*
F. Scott Fitzgerald's *The Great Gatsby*
André Gide's *Les Faux Monnayeurs*

xl

CHRONOLOGY

Hardy's *Human Shows and Far Phantasies*
Huxley's *Those Barren Leaves*
Kafka's *The Trial*
O'Casey's *Juno and the Paycock*
Virginia Woolf's *Mrs. Dalloway* and *The Common Reader*
Brancusi's *Bird in Space*
Shostakovich's *First Symphony*
Sibelius' *Tapiola*

1926 Ford's *A Man Could Stand Up*
Gide's *Si le grain ne meurt*
Hemingway's *The Sun also Rises*
Kafka's *The Castle*
D. H. Lawrence's *The Plumed Serpent*
T. E. Lawrence's *Seven Pillars of Wisdom* privately circulated
Maugham's *The Casuarina Tree*
O'Casey's *The Plough and the Stars*
Puccini's *Turandot*

1927 General Chiang Kai-shek becomes prime minister in China
Trotsky expelled by the Communist party as a deviationist; Stalin becomes leader of the party and dictator of the Soviet Union
Charles Lindbergh flies from New York to Paris
J. W. Dunne's *An Experiment with Time*
Freud's *Autobiography* translated into English
Albert Giacometti's *Observing Head*
Ernest Hemingway's *Men Without Women*
Fritz Lang's *Metropolis*
Wyndham Lewis' *Time and Western Man*
F. W. Murnau's *Sunrise*
Proust's *Le Temps retrouvé* posthumously published
Stravinsky's *Oedipus Rex*
Virginia Woolf's *To the Lighthouse*

1928 The Kellogg-Briand Pact, outlawing war and providing for peaceful settlement of disputes, signed in Paris by sixty-two nations, including the Soviet Union
Herbert Hoover elected president of the United States

Women's suffrage granted at age twenty-one in Britain
Alexander Fleming discovers penicillin
Bertolt Brecht and Kurt Weill's *The Three-Penny Opera*
Eisenstein's *October*
Huxley's *Point Counter Point*
Christopher Isherwood's *All the Conspirators*
D. H. Lawrence's *Lady Chatterley's Lover*
Wyndham Lewis' *The Childermass*
Matisse's *Seated Odalisque*
Munch's *Girl on a Sofa*
Shaw's *Intelligent Woman's Guide to Socialism*
Virginia Woolf's *Orlando*
Yeats's *The Tower*

1929 The Labour party wins British general election
Trotsky expelled from the Soviet Union
Museum of Modern Art opens in New York
Collapse of U.S. stock exchange begins world economic crisis
Robert Bridges's *The Testament of Beauty*
William Faulkner's *The Sound and the Fury*
Robert Graves's *Goodbye to All That*
Hemingway's *A Farewell to Arms*
Ernst Junger's *The Storm of Steel*
Hugo von Hoffmansthal's *Poems*
Henry Moore's *Reclining Figure*
J. B. Priestley's *The Good Companions*
Erich Maria Remarque's *All Quiet on the Western Front*
Shaw's *The Applecart*
R. C. Sheriff's *Journey's End*
Edith Sitwell's *Gold Coast Customs*
Thomas Wolfe's *Look Homeward, Angel*
Virginia Woolf's *A Room of One's Own*
Yeats's *The Winding Stair*
Second surrealist manifesto; Salvador Dali joins the surrealists
Epstein's *Night and Day*

Mondrian's *Composition with Yellow Blue*

1930 Allied occupation of the Rhineland ends

Mohandas Gandhi opens civil disobedience campaign in India

The *Daily Worker*, journal of the British Communist party, begins publishing

J. W. Reppe makes artificial fabrics from an acetylene base

John Arden born

Auden's *Poems*

Coward's *Private Lives*

Eliot's *Ash Wednesday*

Wyndham Lewis's *The Apes of God*

Maugham's *Cakes and Ale*

Ezra Pound's *XXX Cantos*

Evelyn Waugh's *Vile Bodies*

1931 The failure of the Credit Anstalt in Austria starts a financial collapse in Central Europe

Britain abandons the gold standard; the pound falls by twenty-five percent

Mutiny in the Royal Navy at Invergordon over pay cuts

Ramsay MacDonald resigns, splits the Cabinet, and is expelled by the Labour party; in the general election the National Government wins by a majority of five hundred seats

The Statute of Westminster defines dominion status

Ninette de Valois founds the Vic-Wells Ballet (eventually the Royal Ballet)

Coward's *Cavalcade*

Dali's The *Persistence of Memory*

John le Carré born

O'Neill's *Mourning Becomes Electra*

Anthony Powell's *Afternoon Men*

Antoine de Saint-Exupéry's *Vol de nuit*

Walton's *Belshazzar's Feast*

Virginia Woolf's *The Waves*

1932 Franklin D. Roosevelt elected president of the United States

Paul von Hindenburg elected president of Germany; Franz von Papen elected chancellor

Sir Oswald Mosley founds British Union of Fascists

The BBC takes over development of television from J. L. Baird's company

Basic English of 850 words designed as a prospective international language

The Folger Library opens in Washington, D.C.

The Shakespeare Memorial Theatre opens in Stratford-upon-Avon

Faulkner's *Light in August*

Huxley's *Brave New World*

F. R. Leavis' *New Bearings in English Poetry*

Boris Pasternak's *Second Birth*

Ravel's *Concerto for Left Hand*

Peter Redgrove born

Rouault's *Christ Mocked by Soldiers*

Waugh's *Black Mischief*

Yeats's *Words for Music Perhaps*

1933 Roosevelt inaugurates the New Deal

Hitler becomes chancellor of Germany

The Reichstag set on fire

Hitler suspends civil liberties and freedom of the press; German trade unions suppressed

George Balanchine and Lincoln Kirstein found the School of American Ballet

Beryl Bainbridge born

Lowry's *Ultramarine*

André Malraux's *La Condition humaine*

Orwell's *Down and Out in Paris and London*

Gertrude Stein's *The Autobiography of Alice B. Toklas*

Anne Stevenson born

1934 The League Disarmament Conference ends in failure

The Soviet Union admitted to the League

Hitler becomes Führer

Civil war in Austria; Engelbert Dollfuss assassinated in attempted Nazi coup

Frédéric Joliot and Irene Joliot-Curie discover artificial (induced) radioactivity

Einstein's *My Philosophy*

Fitzgerald's *Tender Is the Night*

Graves's *I, Claudius* and *Claudius the God*

Toynbee's *A Study of History* begins publication (1934–1954)

Waugh's *A Handful of Dust*

1935   Grigori Zinoviev and other Soviet leaders convicted of treason

Stanley Baldwin becomes prime minister in National Government; National Government wins general election in Britain

Italy invades Abyssinia

Germany repudiates disarmament clauses of Treaty of Versailles

Germany reintroduces compulsory military service and outlaws the Jews

Robert Watson-Watt builds first practical radar equipment

Karl Jaspers' *Suffering and Existence*

André Brink born

Ivy Compton-Burnett's *A House and Its Head*

Eliot's *Murder in the Cathedral*

Barbara Hepworth's *Three Forms*

George Gershwin's *Porgy and Bess*

Greene's *England Made Me*

Isherwood's *Mr. Norris Changes Trains*

Malraux's *Le Temps du mépris*

Yeats's *Dramatis Personae*

Klee's *Child Consecrated to Suffering*

Benedict Nicholson's *White Relief*

1936   Edward VII accedes to the throne in January; abdicates in December

1936–1952   Reign of George VI

1936   German troops occupy the Rhineland

Ninety-nine percent of German electorate vote for Nazi candidates

The Popular Front wins general election in France; Léon Blum becomes prime minister

Roosevelt reelected president of the United States

The Popular Front wins general election in Spain

Spanish Civil War begins

Italian troops occupy Addis Ababa; Abyssinia annexed by Italy

BBC begins television service from Alexandra Palace

Auden's *Look, Stranger!*

Auden and Isherwood's *The Ascent of F-6*

A. J. Ayer's *Language, Truth and Logic*

Chaplin's *Modern Times*

Greene's *A Gun for Sale*

Huxley's *Eyeless in Gaza*

Keynes's *General Theory of Employment*

F. R. Leavis' *Revaluation*

Mondrian's *Composition in Red and Blue*

Dylan Thomas' *Twenty-five Poems*

Wells's *The Shape of Things to Come* filmed

1937   Trial of Karl Radek and other Soviet leaders

Neville Chamberlain succeeds Stanley Baldwin as prime minister

China and Japan at war

Frank Whittle designs jet engine

Picasso's *Guernica*

Shostakovich's Fifth Symphony

Magritte's *La Reproduction interdite*

Hemingway's *To Have and Have Not*

Malraux's *L'Espoir*

Orwell's *The Road to Wigan Pier*

Priestley's *Time and the Conways*

Virginia Woolf's *The Years*

1938   Trial of Nikolai Bukharin and other Soviet political leaders

Austria occupied by German troops and declared part of the Reich

Hitler states his determination to annex Sudetenland from Czechoslovakia

Britain, France, Germany, and Italy sign the Munich agreement

German troops occupy Sudetenland

Edward Hulton founds *Picture Post*

Cyril Connolly's *Enemies of Promise*

du Maurier's *Rebecca*

Faulkner's *The Unvanquished*

Graham Greene's *Brighton Rock*

CHRONOLOGY

Hindemith's *Mathis der Maler*

Jean Renoir's *La Grande Illusion*

Jean-Paul Sartre's *La Nausée*

Yeats's *New Poems*

Anthony Asquith's *Pygmalion* and Walt Disney's *Snow White*

1939 German troops occupy Bohemia and Moravia; Czechoslovakia incorporated into Third Reich

Madrid surrenders to General Franco; the Spanish Civil War ends

Italy invades Albania

Spain joins Germany, Italy, and Japan in anti-Comintern Pact

Britain and France pledge support to Poland, Romania, and Greece

The Soviet Union proposes defensive alliance with Britain; British military mission visits Moscow

The Soviet Union and Germany sign nonaggression treaty, secretly providing for partition of Poland between them

Germany invades Poland; Britain, France, and Germany at war

The Soviet Union invades Finland

New York World's Fair opens

Eliot's *The Family Reunion*

Seamus Heaney born

Isherwood's *Good-bye to Berlin*

Joyce's *Finnegans Wake* (1922–1939)

MacNeice's *Autumn Journal*

Powell's *What's Become of Waring?*

1940 Churchill becomes prime minister

Italy declares war on France, Britain, and Greece

General de Gaulle founds Free French Movement

The Battle of Britain and the bombing of London

Roosevelt reelected president of the United States for third term

Betjeman's *Old Lights for New Chancels*

Angela Carter born

Chaplin's *The Great Dictator*

J. M. Coetzee born

Disney's *Fantasia*

Greene's *The Power and the Glory*

Hemingway's *For Whom the Bell Tolls*

C. P. Snow's *Strangers and Brothers* (retitled *George Passant* in 1970, when entire sequence of ten novels, published 1940–1970, was entitled *Strangers and Brothers*)

1941 German forces occupy Yugoslavia, Greece, and Crete, and invade the Soviet Union

Lend-Lease agreement between the United States and Britain

President Roosevelt and Winston Churchill sign the Atlantic Charter

Japanese forces attack Pearl Harbor; United States declares war on Japan, Germany, Italy; Britain on Japan

Auden's *New Year Letter*

James Burnham's *The Managerial Revolution*

F. Scott Fitzgerald's *The Last Tycoon*

Huxley's *Grey Eminence*

Derek Mahon born

Shostakovich's *Seventh Symphony*

Tippett's *A Child of Our Time*

Orson Welles's *Citizen Kane*

Virginia Woolf's *Between the Acts*

1942 Japanese forces capture Singapore, Hong Kong, Bataan, Manila

German forces capture Tobruk

U.S. fleet defeats the Japanese in the Coral Sea, captures Guadalcanal

Battle of El Alamein

Allied forces land in French North Africa

Atom first split at University of Chicago

William Beveridge's *Social Insurance and Allied Services*

Albert Camus's *L'Étranger*

Joyce Cary's *To Be a Pilgrim*

Edith Sitwell's *Street Songs*

Waugh's *Put Out More Flags*

1943 German forces surrender at Stalingrad

German and Italian forces surrender in North Africa

Italy surrenders to Allies and declares war on Germany

Cairo conference between Roosevelt, Churchill, Chiang Kai-shek

Teheran conference between Roosevelt, Churchill, Stalin

CHRONOLOGY

Eliot's *Four Quartets*
Henry Moore's *Madonna and Child*
Sartre's *Les Mouches*
Vaughan Williams' *Fifth Symphony*

1944   Allied forces land in Normandy and southern France
Allied forces enter Rome
Attempted assassination of Hitler fails
Liberation of Paris
U.S. forces land in Philippines
German offensive in the Ardennes halted
Roosevelt reelected president of the United States for fourth term
Education Act passed in Britain
Pay-as-You-Earn income tax introduced
Beveridge's *Full Employment in a Free Society*
Cary's *The Horse's Mouth*
Huxley's *Time Must Have a Stop*
Maugham's *The Razor's Edge*
Sartre's *Huis Clos*
Edith Sitwell's *Green Song and Other Poems*
Graham Sutherland's *Christ on the Cross*
Trevelyan's *English Social History*

1945   British and Indian forces open offensive in Burma
Yalta conference between Roosevelt, Churchill, Stalin
Mussolini executed by Italian partisans
Roosevelt dies; Harry S. Truman becomes president
Hitler commits suicide; German forces surrender
The Potsdam Peace Conference
The United Nations Charter ratified in San Francisco
The Labour Party wins British General Election
Atomic bombs dropped on Hiroshima and Nagasaki
Surrender of Japanese forces ends World War II
Trial of Nazi war criminals opens at Nuremberg

All-India Congress demands British withdrawal from India
De Gaulle elected president of French Provisional Government; resigns the next year
Betjeman's *New Bats in Old Belfries*
Britten's *Peter Grimes*
Orwell's *Animal Farm*
Russell's *History of Western Philosophy*
Sartre's *The Age of Reason*
Edith Sitwell's *The Song of the Cold*
Waugh's *Brideshead Revisited*

1946   Bills to nationalize railways, coal mines, and the Bank of England passed in Britain
Nuremberg Trials concluded
United Nations General Assembly meets in New York as its permanent headquarters
The Arab Council inaugurated in Britain
Frederick Ashton's *Symphonic Variations*
Britten's *The Rape of Lucretia*
David Lean's *Great Expectations*
O'Neill's *The Iceman Cometh*
Roberto Rosselini's *Paisà*
Dylan Thomas' *Deaths and Entrances*

1947   President Truman announces program of aid to Greece and Turkey and outlines the "Truman Doctrine"
Independence of India proclaimed; partition between India and Pakistan, and communal strife between Hindus and Moslems follows
General Marshall calls for a European recovery program
First supersonic air flight
Britain's first atomic pile at Harwell comes into operation
Edinburgh festival established
Discovery of the Dead Sea Scrolls in Palestine
Princess Elizabeth marries Philip Mountbatten, duke of Edinburgh
Auden's *Age of Anxiety*
Camus's *La Peste*
Chaplin's *Monsieur Verdoux*
Lowry's *Under the Volcano*

Priestley's *An Inspector Calls*
Edith Sitwell's *The Shadow of Cain*
Waugh's *Scott-King's Modern Europe*

1948 Gandhi assassinated
Czech Communist Party seizes power
Pan-European movement (1948–1958) begins with the formation of the permanent Organization for European Economic Cooperation (OEEC)
Berlin airlift begins as the Soviet Union halts road and rail traffic to the city
British mandate in Palestine ends; Israeli provisional government formed
Yugoslavia expelled from Soviet bloc
Columbia Records introduces the long-playing record
Truman elected of the United States for second term
Greene's *The Heart of the Matter*
Huxley's *Ape and Essence*
Leavis' *The Great Tradition*
Pound's *Cantos*
Priestley's *The Linden Tree*
Waugh's *The Loved One*

1949 North Atlantic Treaty Organization established with headquarters in Brussels
Berlin blockade lifted
German Federal Republic recognized; capital established at Bonn
Konrad Adenauer becomes German chancellor
Mao Tse-tung becomes chairman of the People's Republic of China following Communist victory over the Nationalists
Peter Ackroyd born
Simone de Beauvoir's *The Second Sex*
Cary's *A Fearful Joy*
Arthur Miller's *Death of a Salesman*
Orwell's *Nineteen Eighty-four*

1950 Korean War breaks out
Nobel Prize for literature awarded to Bertrand Russell
R. H. S. Crossman's *The God That Failed*
T. S. Eliot's *The Cocktail Party*
Fry's *Venus Observed*

Doris Lessing's *The Grass Is Singing*
C. S. Lewis' *The Chronicles of Narnia* (1950–1956)
Wyndham Lewis' *Rude Assignment*
George Orwell's *Shooting an Elephant*
Carol Reed's *The Third Man*
Dylan Thomas' *Twenty-six Poems*
A. N. Wilson born

1951 Guy Burgess and Donald Maclean defect from Britain to the Soviet Union
The Conservative party under Winston Churchill wins British general election
The Festival of Britain celebrates both the centenary of the Crystal Palace Exhibition and British postwar recovery
Electric power is produced by atomic energy at Arcon, Idaho
W. H. Auden's *Nones*
Samuel Beckett's *Molloy* and *Malone Dies*
Benjamin Britten's *Billy Budd*
Greene's *The End of the Affair*
Akira Kurosawa's *Rashomon*
Wyndham Lewis' *Rotting Hill*
Anthony Powell's *A Question of Upbringing* (first volume of *A Dance to the Music of Time*, 1951–1975)
J. D. Salinger's *The Catcher in the Rye*
C. P. Snow's *The Masters*
Igor Stravinsky's *The Rake's Progress*

1952– **Reign of Elizabeth II**
At Eniwetok Atoll the United States detonates the first hydrogen bomb
The European Coal and Steel Community comes into being
Radiocarbon dating introduced to archaeology
Michael Ventris deciphers Linear B script
Dwight D. Eisenhower elected president of the United States
Beckett's *Waiting for Godot*
Charles Chaplin's *Limelight*
Ernest Hemingway's *The Old Man and the Sea*
Arthur Koestler's *Arrow in the Blue*
F. R. Leavis' *The Common Pursuit*

Lessing's *Martha Quest* (first volume of *The Children of Violence*, 1952–1965)

C. S. Lewis' *Mere Christianity*

Thomas' *Collected Poems*

Evelyn Waugh's *Men at Arms* (first volume of *Sword of Honour*, 1952–1961)

Angus Wilson's *Hemlock and After*

1953 Constitution for a European political community drafted

Julius and Ethel Rosenberg executed for passing U.S. secrets to the Soviet Union

Cease-fire declared in Korea

Edmund Hillary and his Sherpa guide, Tenzing Norkay, scale Mt. Everest

Nobel Prize for literature awarded to Winston Churchill

General Mohammed Naguib proclaims Egypt a republic

Beckett's *Watt*

Joyce Cary's *Except the Lord*

Robert Graves's *Poems 1953*

1954 First atomic submarine, *Nautilus,* is launched by the United States

Dien Bien Phu captured by the Vietminh

Geneva Conference ends French dominion over Indochina

U.S. Supreme Court declares racial segregation in schools unconstitutional

Nasser becomes president of Egypt

Nobel Prize for literature awarded to Ernest Hemingway

Kingsley Amis' *Lucky Jim*

John Betjeman's *A Few Late Chrysanthemums*

William Golding's *Lord of the Flies*

Christopher Isherwood's *The World in the Evening*

Koestler's *The Invisible Writing*

Iris Murdoch's *Under the Net*

C. P. Snow's *The New Men*

Thomas' *Under Milk Wood* published posthumously

1955 Warsaw Pact signed

West Germany enters NATO as Allied occupation ends

The Conservative party under Anthony Eden wins British general election

Cary's *Not Honour More*

Greene's *The Quiet American*

Philip Larkin's *The Less Deceived*

F. R. Leavis' *D. H. Lawrence, Novelist*

Vladimir Nabokov's *Lolita*

Patrick White's *The Tree of Man*

1956 Nasser's nationalization of the Suez Canal leads to Israeli, British, and French armed intervention

Uprising in Hungary suppressed by Soviet troops

Khrushchev denounces Stalin at Twentieth Communist Party Congress

Eisenhower reelected president of the United States

Anthony Burgess' *Time for a Tiger*

Golding's *Pincher Martin*

Murdoch's *Flight from the Enchanter*

John Osborne's *Look Back in Anger*

Snow's *Homecomings*

Edmund Wilson's *Anglo-Saxon Attitudes*

1957 The Soviet Union launches the first artificial earth satellite, *Sputnik I*

Eden succeeded by Harold Macmillan

Suez Canal reopened

Eisenhower Doctrine formulated

Parliament receives the Wolfenden Report on Homosexuality and Prostitution

Nobel Prize for literature awarded to Albert Camus

Beckett's *Endgame* and *All That Fall*

Lawrence Durrell's *Justine* (first volume of *The Alexandria Quartet,* 1957–1960)

Ted Hughes's *The Hawk in the Rain*

Murdoch's *The Sandcastle*

V. S. Naipaul's *The Mystic Masseur*

Eugene O'Neill's *Long Day's Journey into Night*

Osborne's *The Entertainer*

Muriel Spark's *The Comforters*

White's *Voss*

1958 European Economic Community established

CHRONOLOGY

Khrushchev succeeds Bulganin as Soviet premier

Charles de Gaulle becomes head of France's newly constituted Fifth Republic

The United Arab Republic formed by Egypt and Syria

The United States sends troops into Lebanon

First U.S. satellite, *Explorer 1*, launched

Nobel Prize for literature awarded to Boris Pasternak

Beckett's *Krapp's Last Tape*

John Kenneth Galbraith's *The Affluent Society*

Greene's *Our Man in Havana*

Murdoch's *The Bell*

Pasternak's *Dr. Zhivago*

Snow's *The Conscience of the Rich*

1959 Fidel Castro assumes power in Cuba

St. Lawrence Seaway opens

The European Free Trade Association founded

Alaska and Hawaii become the forty-ninth and fiftieth states

The Conservative party under Harold Macmillan wins British general election

Brendan Behan's *The Hostage*

Golding's *Free Fall*

Graves's *Collected Poems*

Koestler's *The Sleepwalkers*

Harold Pinter's *The Birthday Party*

Snow's *The Two Cultures and the Scientific Revolution*

Spark's *Memento Mori*

1960 South Africa bans the African National Congress and Pan-African Congress

The Congo achieves independence

John F. Kennedy elected president of the United States

The U.S. bathyscaphe *Trieste* descends to 35,800 feet

Publication of the unexpurgated *Lady Chatterley's Lover* permitted by court

Auden's *Hommage to Clio*

Betjeman's *Summoned by Bells*

Pinter's *The Caretaker*

Snow's *The Affair*

David Storey's *This Sporting Life*

1961 South Africa leaves the British Commonwealth

Sierra Leone and Tanganyika achieve independence

The Berlin Wall erected

The New English Bible published

Beckett's *How It Is*

Greene's *A Burnt-Out Case*

Koestler's *The Lotus and the Robot*

Murdoch's *A Severed Head*

Naipaul's *A House for Mr Biswas*

Osborne's *Luther*

Spark's *The Prime of Miss Jean Brodie*

White's *Riders in the Chariot*

1962 John Glenn becomes first U.S. astronaut to orbit earth

The United States launches the spacecraft *Mariner* to explore Venus

Algeria achieves independence

Cuban missile crisis ends in withdrawal of Soviet missiles from Cuba

Adolf Eichmann executed in Israel for Nazi war crimes

Second Vatican Council convened by Pope John XXIII

Nobel Prize for literature awarded to John Steinbeck

Edward Albee's *Who's Afraid of Virginia Woolf?*

Beckett's *Happy Days*

Anthony Burgess' *A Clockwork Orange* and *The Wanting Seed*

Aldous Huxley's *Island*

Isherwood's *Down There on a Visit*

Lessing's *The Golden Notebook*

Nabokov's *Pale Fire*

Aleksandr Solzhenitsyn's *One Day in the Life of Ivan Denisovich*

1963 Britain, the United States, and the Soviet Union sign a test-ban treaty

Britain refused entry to the European Economic Community

The Soviet Union puts into orbit the first woman astronaut, Valentina Tereshkova

Paul VI becomes pope

President Kennedy assassinated; Lyndon B. Johnson assumes office

CHRONOLOGY

Nobel Prize for literature awarded to
George Seferis
Britten's *War Requiem*
John Fowles's *The Collector*
Murdoch's *The Unicorn*
Spark's *The Girls of Slender Means*
Storey's *Radcliffe*
John Updike's *The Centaur*

1964   Tonkin Gulf incident leads to retaliatory strikes by U.S. aircraft against North Vietnam
Greece and Turkey contend for control of Cyprus
Britain grants licenses to drill for oil in the North Sea
The Shakespeare Quatercentenary celebrated
Lyndon Johnson elected president of the United States
The Labour party under Harold Wilson wins British general election
Nobel Prize for literature awarded to Jean-Paul Sartre
Saul Bellow's *Herzog*
Burgess' *Nothing Like the Sun*
Golding's *The Spire*
Isherwood's *A Single Man*
Stanley Kubrick's *Dr. Strangelove*
Larkin's *The Whitsun Weddings*
Naipaul's *An Area of Darkness*
Peter Shaffer's *The Royal Hunt of the Sun*
Snow's *Corridors of Power*

1965   The first U.S. combat forces land in Vietnam
The U.S. spacecraft Mariner transmits photographs of Mars
British Petroleum Company finds oil in the North Sea
War breaks out between India and Pakistan
Rhodesia declares its independence
Ontario power failure blacks out the Canadian and U.S. east coasts
Nobel Prize for literature awarded to Mikhail Sholokhov
Robert Lowell's *For the Union Dead*
Norman Mailer's *An American Dream*
Osborne's *Inadmissible Evidence*
Pinter's *The Homecoming*

Spark's *The Mandelbaum Gate*

1966   The Labour party under Harold Wilson wins British general election
The Archbishop of Canterbury visits Pope Paul VI
Florence, Italy, severely damaged by floods
Paris exhibition celebrates Picasso's eighty-fifth birthday
Fowles's *The Magus*
Greene's *The Comedians*
Osborne's *A Patriot for Me*
Paul Scott's *The Jewel in the Crown* (first volume of *The Raj Quartet*, 1966–1975)
White's *The Solid Mandala*

1967   Thurgood Marshall becomes first black U.S. Supreme Court justice
Six-Day War pits Israel against Egypt and Syria
Biafra's secession from Nigeria leads to civil war
Francis Chichester completes solo circumnavigation of the globe
Dr. Christiaan Barnard performs first heart transplant operation, in South Africa
China explodes its first hydrogen bomb
Golding's *The Pyramid*
Hughes's *Wodwo*
Isherwood's *A Meeting by the River*
Naipaul's *The Mimic Men*
Tom Stoppard's *Rosencrantz and Guildenstern Are Dead*
Orson Welles's *Chimes at Midnight*
Angus Wilson's *No Laughing Matter*

1968   Violent student protests erupt in France and West Germany
Warsaw Pact troops occupy Czechoslovakia
Violence in Northern Ireland causes Britain to send in troops
Tet offensive by Communist forces launched against South Vietnam's cities
Theater censorship ended in Britain
Robert Kennedy and Martin Luther King Jr. assassinated
Richard M. Nixon elected president of the United States

CHRONOLOGY

Booker Prize for fiction established
Durrell's *Tunc*
Graves's *Poems 1965–1968*
Osborne's *The Hotel in Amsterdam*
Snow's *The Sleep of Reason*
Solzhenitsyn's *The First Circle* and *Cancer Ward*
Spark's *The Public Image*

1969 Humans set foot on the moon for the first time when astronauts descend to its surface in a landing vehicle from the U.S. spacecraft *Apollo 11*
The Soviet unmanned spacecraft *Venus V* lands on Venus
Capital punishment abolished in Britain
Colonel Muammar Qaddafi seizes power in Libya
Solzhenitsyn expelled from the Soviet Union
Nobel Prize for literature awarded to Samuel Beckett
Carter's *The Magic Toyshop*
Fowles's *The French Lieutenant's Woman*
Storey's *The Contractor*

1970 Civil war in Nigeria ends with Biafra's surrender
U.S. planes bomb Cambodia
The Conservative party under Edward Heath wins British general election
Nobel Prize for literature awarded to Aleksandr Solzhenitsyn
Durrell's *Nunquam*
Hughes's *Crow*
F. R. Leavis and Q. D. Leavis' *Dickens the Novelist*
Snow's *Last Things*
Spark's *The Driver's Seat*

1971 Communist China given Nationalist China's UN seat
Decimal currency introduced to Britain
Indira Gandhi becomes India's prime minister
Nobel Prize for literature awarded to Heinrich Böll
Bond's *The Pope's Wedding*
Naipaul's *In a Free State*
Pinter's *Old Times*

Spark's *Not to Disturb*

1972 The civil strife of "Bloody Sunday" causes Northern Ireland to come under the direct rule of Westminster
Nixon becomes the first U.S. president to visit Moscow and Beijing
The Watergate break-in precipitates scandal in the United States
Eleven Israeli athletes killed by terrorists at Munich Olympics
Nixon reelected president of the United States
Bond's *Lear*
Snow's *The Malcontents*
Stoppard's *Jumpers*

1973 Britain, Ireland, and Denmark enter European Economic Community
Egypt and Syria attack Israel in the Yom Kippur War
Energy crisis in Britain reduces production to a three-day week
Nobel Prize for literature awarded to Patrick White
Bond's *The Sea*
Greene's *The Honorary Consul*
Lessing's *The Summer Before the Dark*
Murdoch's *The Black Prince*
Shaffer's *Equus*
White's *The Eye of the Storm*

1974 Miners strike in Britain
Greece's military junta overthrown
Emperor Haile Selassie of Ethiopia deposed
President Makarios of Cyprus replaced by military coup
Nixon resigns as U.S. president and is succeeded by Gerald R. Ford
Betjeman's *A Nip in the Air*
Bond's *Bingo*
Durrell's *Monsieur* (first volume of *The Avignon Quintet*, 1974–1985)
Larkin's *The High Windows*
Solzhenitsyn's *The Gulag Archipelago*
Spark's *The Abbess of Crewe*

1975 The U.S. *Apollo* and Soviet *Soyuz* spacecrafts rendezvous in space
The Helsinki Accords on human rights signed
U.S. forces leave Vietnam

CHRONOLOGY

King Juan Carlos succeeds Franco as Spain's head of state

Nobel Prize for literature awarded to Eugenio Montale

1976 New U.S. copyright law goes into effect

Israeli commandos free hostages from hijacked plane at Entebbe, Uganda

British and French SST Concordes make first regularly scheduled commercial flights

The United States celebrates its bicentennial

Jimmy Carter elected president of the United States

Byron and Shelley manuscripts discovered in Barclay's Bank, Pall Mall

Hughes's *Seasons' Songs*

Koestler's *The Thirteenth Tribe*

Scott's *Staying On*

Spark's *The Take-over*

White's *A Fringe of Leaves*

1977 Silver jubilee of Queen Elizabeth II celebrated

Egyptian president Anwar el-Sadat visits Israel

"Gang of Four" expelled from Chinese Communist party

First woman ordained in the U.S. Episcopal church

After twenty-nine years in power, Israel's Labour party is defeated by the Likud party

Fowles's *Daniel Martin*

Hughes's *Gaudete*

1978 Treaty between Israel and Egypt negotiated at Camp David

Pope John Paul I dies a month after his coronation and is succeeded by Karol Cardinal Wojtyla, who takes the name John Paul II

Former Italian premier Aldo Moro murdered by left-wing terrorists

Nobel Prize for literature awarded to Isaac Bashevis Singer

Greene's *The Human Factor*

Hughes's *Cave Birds*

Murdoch's *The Sea, The Sea*

1979 The United States and China establish diplomatic relations

Ayatollah Khomeini takes power in Iran and his supporters hold U.S. embassy staff hostage in Teheran

Rhodesia becomes Zimbabwe

Earl Mountbatten assassinated

The Soviet Union invades Afghanistan

The Conservative party under Margaret Thatcher wins British general election

Nobel Prize for literature awarded to Odysseus Elytis

Golding's *Darkness Visible*

Hughes's *Moortown*

Lessing's *Shikasta* (first volume of *Canopus in Argos, Archives*)

Naipaul's *A Bend in the River*

Spark's *Territorial Rights*

White's *The Twyborn Affair*

1980 Iran-Iraq war begins

Strikes in Gdansk give rise to the Solidarity movement

Mt. St. Helen's erupts in Washington State

British steelworkers strike for the first time since 1926

More than fifty nations boycott Moscow Olympics

Ronald Reagan elected president of the United States

Burgess's *Earthly Powers*

Golding's *Rites of Passage*

Shaffer's *Amadeus*

Storey's *A Prodigal Child*

Angus Wilson's *Setting the World on Fire*

1981 Greece admitted to the European Economic Community

Iran hostage crisis ends with release of U.S. embassy staff

Twelve Labour MPs and nine peers found British Social Democratic party

Socialist party under François Mitterand wins French general election

Rupert Murdoch buys *The Times* of London

Turkish gunman wounds Pope John Paul II in assassination attempt

U.S. gunman wounds President Reagan in assassination attempt

President Sadat of Egypt assassinated

Nobel Prize for literature awarded to Elias Canetti

Spark's *Loitering with Intent*

1982 Britain drives Argentina's invasion force out of the Falkland Islands

U.S. space shuttle makes first successful trip

Yuri Andropov becomes general secretary of the Central Committee of the Soviet Communist party

Israel invades Lebanon

First artificial heart implanted at Salt Lake City hospital

Bellow's *The Dean's December*

Greene's *Monsignor Quixote*

1983 South Korean airliner with 269 aboard shot down after straying into Soviet airspace

U.S. forces invade Grenada following left-wing coup

Widespread protests erupt over placement of nuclear missiles in Europe

The £1 coin comes into circulation in Britain

Australia wins the America's Cup

Nobel Prize for literature awarded to William Golding

Hughes's *River*

Murdoch's *The Philosopher's Pupil*

1984 Konstantin Chernenko becomes general secretary of the Central Committee of the Soviet Communist party

Prime Minister Indira Gandhi of India assassinated by Sikh bodyguards

Reagan reelected president of the United States

Toxic gas leak at Bhopal, India, plant kills 2,000

British miners go on strike

Irish Republican Army attempts to kill Prime Minister Thatcher with bomb detonated at a Brighton hotel

World Court holds against U.S. mining of Nicaraguan harbors

Golding's *The Paper Men*

Lessing's *The Diary of Jane Somers*

Spark's *The Only Problem*

1985 United States deploys cruise missiles in Europe

Mikhail Gorbachev becomes general secretary of the Soviet Communist party following death of Konstantin Chernenko

Riots break out in Handsworth district (Birmingham) and Brixton

Republic of Ireland gains consultative role in Northern Ireland

State of emergency is declared in South Africa

Nobel Prize for literature awarded to Claude Simon

A. N. Wilson's *Gentlemen in England*

Lessing's *The Good Terrorist*

Murdoch's *The Good Apprentice*

Fowles's *A Maggot*

1986 U.S. space shuttle *Challenger* explodes

United States attacks Libya

Atomic power plant at Chernobyl destroyed in accident

Corazon Aquino becomes president of the Philippines

Giotto spacecraft encounters Comet Halley

Nobel Prize for literature awarded to Wole Soyinka

Final volume of *Oxford English Dictionary* supplement published

Amis's *The Old Devils*

Ishiguro's *An Artist of the Floating World*

A. N. Wilson's *Love Unknown*

Powell's *The Fisher King*

1987 Gorbachev begins reform of Communist party of the Soviet Union

Stock market collapses

Iran-contra affair reveals that Reagan administration used money from arms sales to Iran to fund Nicaraguan rebels

Palestinian uprising begins in Israeli-occupied territories

Nobel Prize for literature awarded to Joseph Brodsky

Golding's *Close Quarters*

Burgess's *Little Wilson and Big God*

Drabble's *The Radiant Way*

1988　Soviet Union begins withdrawing troops from Afghanistan

Iranian airliner shot down by U.S. Navy over Persian Gulf

War between Iran and Iraq ends

George Bush elected president of the United States

Pan American flight 103 destroyed over Lockerbie, Scotland

Nobel Prize for literature awarded to Naguib Mafouz

Greene's *The Captain and the Enemy*

Amis's *Difficulties with Girls*

Rushdie's *Satanic Verses*

1989　Ayatollah Khomeini pronounces death sentence on Salman Rushdie; Great Britain and Iran sever diplomatic relations

F. W. de Klerk becomes president of South Africa

Chinese government crushes student demonstration in Tiananmen Square

Communist regimes are weakened or abolished in Poland, Czechoslovakia, Hungary, East Germany, and Romania

Lithuania nullifies its inclusion in Soviet Union

Nobel Prize for literature awarded to José Cela

Second edition of *Oxford English Dictionary* published

Drabble's *A Natural Curiosity*

Murdoch's *The Message to the Planet*

Amis's *London Fields*

Ishiguro's *The Remains of the Day*

1990　Communist monopoly ends in Bulgaria

Riots break out against community charge in England

First women ordained priests in Church of England

Civil war breaks out in Yugoslavia; Croatia and Slovenia declare independence

Bush and Gorbachev sign START agreement to reduce nuclear-weapons arsenals

President Jean-Baptiste Aristide overthrown by military in Haiti

Boris Yeltsin elected president of Russia

Dissolution of the Soviet Union

Nobel Prize for literature awarded to Nadine Gordimer

1992　U.N. Conference on Environment and Development (the "Earth Summit") meets in Rio de Janeiro

Prince and Princess of Wales separate

War in Bosnia-Herzegovina intensifies

Bill Clinton elected president of the United States in three-way race with Bush and independent candidate H. Ross Perot

Nobel Prize for literature awarded to Derek Walcott

1993　Czechoslovakia divides into the Czech Republic and Slovakia; playwright Vaclav Havel elected president of the Czech Republic

Britain ratifies Treaty on European Union (the "Maastricht Treaty")

U.S. troops provide humanitarian aid amid famine in Somalia

United States, Canada, and Mexico sign North American Free Trade Agreement

Nobel Prize for literature awarded to Toni Morrison

1994　Nelson Mandela elected president in South Africa's first post-apartheid election

Jean-Baptiste Aristide restored to presidency of Haiti

Clinton health care reforms rejected by Congress

Civil war in Rwanda

Republicans win control of both houses of Congress for first time in forty years

Prime Minister Albert Reynolds of Ireland meets with Gerry Adams, president of Sinn Fein

Nobel Prize for literature awarded to Kenzaburo Íe

Amis's *You Can't Do Both*

Naipaul's *A Way in the World*

1995 Britain and Irish Republican Army engage in diplomatic talks

Barings Bank forced into bankruptcy as a result of a maverick bond trader's losses

United States restores full diplomatic relations with Vietnam

NATO initiates air strikes in Bosnia

Death of Stephen Spender

Israeli Prime Minister Yitzhak Rabin assassinated

Nobel Prize for literature awarded to Seamus Heaney

1996 IRA breaks cease-fire; Sein Fein representatives barred from

Northern Ireland peace talks

Prince and Princess of Wales divorce

Cease-fire agreement in Chechnia; Russian forces begin to withdraw

Boris Yeltsin reelected president of Russia

Bill Clinton reelected president of the United States

Nobel Prize for literature awarded to Wislawa Szymborska

1996 British government destroys around 100,000 cows suspected of infection with Creutzfeldt-Jakob, or "mad cow" disease

1997 Diana, Princess of Wales, dies in an automobile accident

Unveiling of first fully-cloned adult animal, a sheep named Dolly

Booker McConnell Prize for fiction awarded to Arundhati Roy

1998 United States renews bombing of Bagdad, Iraq

Independent legislature and Parliaments return to Scotland and Wales

Ted Hughes, Symbolist poet and husband of Sylvia Plath, dies

Booker McConnell Prize for fiction awarded to Ian McEwan

Nobel Prize for literature awarded to Jose Saramago

1999 King Hussein of Jordan dies

United Nations responds militarily to Serbian President Slobodan Milosevic's escalation of crisis in Kosovo

Booker McConnell Prize for fiction awarded to J. M. Coetzee

Nobel Prize for literature awarded to Günter Grass

2000 Penelope Fitzgerald dies

J. K. Rowling's *Harry Potter and the Goblet of Fire* sells more than 300,000 copies in its first day

Oil blockades by fuel haulers protesting high oil taxes bring much of Britain to a standstill

Slobodan Milosevic loses Serbian general election to Vojislav Kostunica

Death of Scotland's First Minister, Donald Dewar

Nobel Prize for literature awarded to Gao Xingjian

List of Contributors

STEPHEN AMIDON. Novelist whose books include *Splitting the Atom, Thirst, The Primitive*, and *The New City*. His criticism has appeared in numerous journals, including the *Times Literary Supplement, The New York Times Book Review, The London Sunday Times*, and *The Atlantic Monthly*. **Wilkie Collins**

PAUL BIBIRE. Formerly a lecturer in the School of English, University of St. Andrews, and of the Department of Anglo-Saxon, Norse, and Celtic, University of Cambridge. Since retirement, he has been an honorary lecturer in the Department of Medieval History, School of History, University of St Andrews, Scotland. Research includes Old English and Old Norse language and literature; West and North Germanic philology; the historical development of the phonological and morphological systems of Old English and Old Norse from their Indo-European and Germanic origins; Old English dialects; the development of Germanic legend and its representation in early English and Scandinavian poetry; Norse paganism and pagan mythology (sources for its knowledge and modes of its understanding); Icelandic sagas and other prose (in particular formal analysis); Norse court (*skaldic*) poetry. **Beowulf**

SANDIE BYRNE. Fellow in English at Balliol College, Oxford. Her publications include works on eighteenth and nineteenth-century fiction and twentieth-century poetry. **George Mackay Brown** and **Saki**

PATRICIA CRAIG Freelance critic. She is a regular contributor to *The Times Literary Supplement, The London Independent*, and *The New York Review of Books*. She has also edited many anthologies including *The Oxford Book of Ireland* and *The Oxford Book of Modern Women's Stories*. She is working on a biography of novelist Brian Moore. **Beryl Bainbridge**

JULIE HEARN. Writer. Julie Hearn is a former journalist who, in 1999, received an M.St. in women's studies from Oxford University. It is a continuing source of amusement to her that she went from writing a weekly mother and baby column for the national *Daily Star* to researching witch-hunting and maternal power in early modern England. She lives with her daughter in a market town near Oxford, where she is writing a novel and recording the memories of elderly women for a local heritage project. **Radclyffe Hall**

DIANA HENDERSON. Author of *Passion Made Public: Elizabethan Lyric, Gender, and Performance* (University of Illinois Press, 1995). Recent articles on early modern domestic culture, women lyricists of the Renaissance, Shakespeare, Sir Philip Sidney, and Virginia Woolf. Current book manuscript: *Uneasy Collaborations: Transforming Shakespeare across Time and Media*. **Henry King**

PHILIP HOBSBAUM. Emeritus Professor of English Literature at the University of Glasgow and Doctor of Letters of that university. Pupil of F.R. Leavis at Downing College, Cambridge; research student with William Empson at the University of Sheffield. Author of seven critical books, including *Metre, Rhythm and Verse Form* (1996); four collections of poems; sixty contributions to reference works; seventy-seven articles, mostly concerned with modern poetry, in academic and literary journals. **Norman McCaig** and **Peter Redgrove**

LABAN CARRICK HILL. Professor of literature at several institutions including Columbia University and St. Michaels College. He has published more than twenty books and is currently working on a cultural history of the Harlem Renaissance for Little, Brown & Company. **J. M. Coetzee**

DILLON JOHNSTON. Professor of English at Wake Forest University, Dillon Johnston founded the Irish Poetry Series and the Wake Forest University Press, which he directs. He is the author of *Irish Poetry After Joyce* (1985, revised in 1997) and *Poetic Economies Of England and Ireland*, 1912-2000. **Derek Mahon**

PATRICK McGUINNESS. Lecturer in French at the University of Oxford, and Fellow of St Anne's College, Oxford. He is the editor of *T. E. Hulme. Selected Writings* (1998), *Symbolism, Decadence and the fin de siècle: French and European Perspectives* (2000), and the author of *Maurice Maeterlinck and the Making of Modern Theatre* (2000). He is the author of a number of essays and articles on English and American Poetry, and received an Eric Gregory Award for Poetry from the Society of Authors in 1998. **T. E. Hulme**

ROBERT NIEMI. Associate Professor of English at St. Michael's College, Colchester, Vermont. He specializes in the study and teaching of American literature, film, and critical theory. Has published books on Russell Banks and Weldon Kees. **André Brink**

SAM PICKERING. Professor of English at the University of Connecticut. He has written fifteen books, twelve of them collections of personal essays, the most recent being *A Little Fling* and *Deprived of Unhappiness*. He has also written *John Locke and Children's Literature In Eighteenth-Century England* and *The Moral Tradition of English Fiction*. **Gilbert White**

NEIL POWELL. Poet, biographer, editor, and lecturer. His books include five collections of poetry—*At the Edge* (1977), *A Season of Calm Weather* (1982), *True Colours* (1991), *The Stones on Thorpeness Beach* (1994), and *Selected Poems* (1998)—as well as *Carpenters of Light* (1979), *Roy Fuller: Writer and Society* (1995), and *The Language of Jazz* (1977). He lives in Suffolk, England and is working on a biography of George Crabbe. **Donald Davie**

WILLIAM H. PRITCHARD. Henry Clay Folger Professor of English at Amherst College. His numerous publications include *Lives of the Modern Poets* (1980); *Frost: A Literary Life Reconsidered* (1984); *Randall Jarrell* (1990); *Talking Back to Emily Dickinson* (1998); and *Updike: America's Man of Letters* (2000). He is an advisory editor for *The Hudson Review* where his essays and reviews appear. He also contributes essays and reviews to *The New York Times Book Review* and *The Boston Globe*. **A. N. Wilson**

PETER SCUPHAM. Poet. Has published ten collections, mostly with Oxford University Press. *Night Watch*, his most recent collection, was published by Anvil Press in 1999. His Collected Poems is due for publication in 2003. He is a Fellow of the Royal Society of Literature and has received a Cholmondeley award for poetry. **Edwin Muir**

D. J. TAYLOR. Freelance writer. His publications include a biography of William Makepeace Thackeray (1999), the novel *Moral Trespass* (1998), and a collection of short stories entitled *After Bathing at Baxter's*. Taylor won a Grinzane Cavor award for Italian translations for *English Settlements* in 1999. **Alec Waugh**

N. S. THOMPSON. Lecturer in English at Christ Church, Oxford. He writes on both modern and medieval poetry, with recent publications on Chaucer and Tony Harrison. In America his poetry and prose have appeared in *The Hudson Review* and *The Southern Review*, and other journals. **Norman Nicholson**

NICOLAS TREDELL. Tutor in Literature, Film and Cultural Studies at Sussex University. He has contributed widely to literary journals in England and America and his eleven books include *The Critical Decade: Culture in Crisis, Conversations with Critics: Interviews with Leading Figures in Literary Criticism*; and *Fighting Fictions: The Novels of B. S. Johnson*. He is Consultant Editor of the Icon Readers' Guides series and has edited Guides to the works of Conrad, Dickens, Fitzgerald, Faulkner, and Martin Amis. He is currently editing *The Icon Critical History of Film Theory* and writing a book called *Notes Towards a Definition of Digital Culture*. **Anne Stevenson**

THOMAS WRIGHT. Editor of the recently published *Table Talk. Oscar Wilde*, the first ever anthology of Wilde's spoken stories. He has written a number of articles on Wilde and related topics in publications such as the *Times Literary Supplement*. He has published an interview with Peter Ackroyd in *The Sunday Telegraph Magazine*. **Peter Ackroyd**

PETER ACKROYD

(1949–)

Thomas Wright

PETER ACKROYD IS one of the most prolific and idiosyncratic English writers of his generation. His works are characterized by their energy and heterogeneity. Within them he blends fact and fiction, the past and the present, high and low culture, tragedy and comedy, and a variety of styles and genres. Critics have typically described Ackroyd's writings as intellectually playful; his books have been compared to intertextual and metafictional games that readers must try to play as best they can. They have also emphasized the intensely artificial and theatrical nature of Ackroyd's work: his novels and biographies have been likened to intellectual pantomimes and to virtuoso linguistic performances. The most astute commentators have understood that, like any performance, Ackroyd's writings resist simple closure. It is not possible, in other words, to find a residual meaning or a content that is behind, or outside, of them; nor is it easy to analyze them in the context of their relationship to the real world.

It is the playful, artificial, and theatrical nature of Ackroyd's work that has occasionally exasperated reviewers. Usually, hostile critics complain that Ackroyd's writings are pointless games and that they do not really "mean" anything. A review of the novel *First Light* (1989), in the *Guardian* (14 April 1989), for instance, was entitled: "But What Does It All Mean, Mr Ackroyd?" Ackroyd never supplies the answer to the reviewer's overwhelming question, either in interviews or in the works themselves, in which he employs a number of strategies to keep meaning unstable and indeterminate. Indeed, although Ackroyd's books frequently hint at the possibility of mystical or transcendental meanings (magical connections across time and archetypal forms of the imagination that manifest themselves throughout English literature), he invariably reminds the reader that these meanings can only exist within the fictional world that he has created. Ackroyd the author can be compared to a conjurer who, having performed a marvelous trick, explains to his captivated audience exactly how it is done. And it is, in the end, this curious mixture of mysticism and skepticism that distinguishes his writing. He has been described as a religious postmodernist and as a writer who "affirms the constructedness of writing while simultaneously attempting to recover its mythopoeic and transcendental function" (Onega, 1999, p. 10). The transcendental element is ever present in Ackroyd's work: an eternal city is always about to be glimpsed, and the secrets of the universe are always on the verge of being revealed. But the city never quite materializes and the secrets remain hidden.

BIOGRAPHY

PETER Ackroyd was born in London on 5 October 1949, the only child of Graham Ackroyd and Audrey Whiteside. His parents separated soon after his birth and he was raised by his mother and grandmother on a council estate in government-subsidized housing near Wormwood Scrubs prison in West London. He had no contact with his father during or after his childhood. In his early years he was exposed to two great influences on his vision of the world: Catholicism, the faith in which he was brought up by his mother, and the city of London, the streets of which he would explore with his grandmother. According to his mother, he was a precocious and ambitious child. He read newspapers at the age of five, wrote a play about Guy Fawkes at nine, and dreamed of becoming a famous tap dancer or a great magician. At ten he was awarded a scholarship to Saint Benedict's, a Catholic public school in Ealing. This offered him escape from the working-class world of his childhood.

In 1968 he entered Clare College, Cambridge. By this time he had discovered his homosexuality. Through hours spent reading alone, he had also realized that he was essentially an autodidact.

Along with fellow undergraduates, such as Kevin Stratford and Ian Patterson, he discovered the works of the New York poets John Ashbery and Frank O'Hara and the Cambridge poet J. H. Prynne. At Cambridge he decided to be a poet; in 1971 *Ouch*, his first volume of poetry, was published. He left the university in 1971 having achieved a double first, the highest possible examination mark. From 1971 to 1973 Ackroyd was a Mellon Fellow at Yale University. In America he met Ashbery and other New York poets, wrote a play (now lost) entitled *No*, which was entirely made up of quotations, and finished the polemical prose work *Notes for a New Culture* (1976). On returning to England in 1973 he entered the world of London literary journalism, becoming first literary editor and then, in 1978, joint managing editor of the English magazine the *Spectator*. Throughout the 1970s Ackroyd wrote book reviews and political articles for the *Spectator*. Through his journalism, which was characterized by an incisive style and a mordant wit, he soon became well known in literary circles. He wrote two further volumes of poetry in this period and two prose works. In 1982, after the publication of his first novel, he left the *Spectator* to become a full-time writer. Since that date to the time of this writing he has written fifteen books (nine novels and six biographies). In addition, he has published several short stories, countless articles, and numerous introductions to a wide variety of books. Since 1986 he has been the chief book reviewer for the *Times*.

A flamboyant London figure, Ackroyd is renowned for his humor, his energy, and his capacity for consuming vast amounts of alcohol. He writes novels in the mornings, researches biographies in the afternoons, and goes to parties in the evenings. His public persona is a combination of Wilde and Dickens, with a dash of Blake. He has been called a modern lord of misrule.

1971–1979

ACKROYD'S first major prose work, *Notes for a New Culture: An Essay on Modernism* (1976), is a history of modernism and a polemic concerning the state of postwar English literature. Ackroyd identifies two antithetical cultural forces, humanism and modernism, that represent different conceptions of language and man. For the humanist, language is a transparent tool through which reality, and the experience of a moral subject, can be accurately represented. Humanist literature is concerned with a transcendental human nature and with universal values; it originates from a monolithic authorial "I." In contrast, modernists view language as an autonomous sign system. Within modernist literature, to paraphrase Ackroyd, language divests itself of signifying force, ceases to identify with truth and meaning, and returns to a state of play. The focus thus shifts away from the world of experience to language itself. Modernists do not regard human nature in transcendental or universal terms; instead, they view the subject as a finite and historical product of language. The modernist writer is not a controlling authorial presence but rather an instrument through which language speaks. Ackroyd argues that, since the 1930s, the humanists, represented by critics such as F. R. Leavis and poets of subjective experience such as Philip Larkin, have dominated English literary culture. This explains its impoverished and dispirited state. Only when England embraces modernism, he argues, and accepts the "death of man" as he finds himself in humanism and subjectivity, will Albion rise again.

Notes is an intensely personal book. It represents Ackroyd's attempt to discover connections and patterns within his vast and miscellaneous reading (in the space of a few paragraphs he refers to Edmund Burke, Rod Stewart, Jacques Derrida, Harold Robbins, and Jacques Lacan). It is also a justification of the kind of modernist poetry he was writing at the time, and an ambitious Poundian bid to create among his contemporaries the critical temper by which that poetry would be judged. It could even be compared to one of Ackroyd's poems, as it evinces the obscurity and the unexpected shifts of perspective found in his verse, or to an extended oration in which he performs a particular kind of polemical language derived from writers such as Sir Philip Sidney, Percy Bysshe Shelley, and T. S. Eliot.

Notes is, in other words, a fittingly modernist production, in which the form complements the theme, rather than a systematic academic study (indeed, at times Ackroyd appears to parody the scholarly tone). Certain reviewers of the book, who pointed out its occasional inaccuracies and bemoaned the absence of footnotes, evidently failed to grasp this fact.

In a preface to the revised edition (1993), Ackroyd states that the preoccupations of *Notes* can be found throughout his mature writings. In an obvious sense this is true; Ackroyd's biographies of Pound and Eliot attest to his continued interest in modernism. He has also maintained a broadly modernist stance. His novels and his biographies confirm his belief in the autonomy of art and language: they are artificial worlds in which words are allowed to play. The concerns of *Notes* certainly inform, and are to some extent dramatized in, Ackroyd's poetry.

It was always Ackroyd's ambition to be a poet. He claims that he never read a work of fiction until the age of twenty-four, when he began reviewing novels for the *Spectator*. After *Ouch* (1971) two further volumes of verse, *London Lickpenny* (1973) and *Country Life* (1978), were published in beautifully produced limited editions by the Ferry Press. These were praised by critics as interesting examples of avant-garde verse. Later Ackroyd revised a selection of the poems contained in these three volumes for publication in *The Diversions of Purley and Other Poems* (1987), a collection to which he also added a few previously unpublished poems. By this time, he had becomes a famous novelist and biographer and it was within the context of his work in these genres that many reviewers read his verse.

Like the poetry of Ashbery, O'Hara, and J. H. Prynne, which he praises in *Notes*, Ackroyd's poetry is without a central perspective or a single style or tone. Fragmentary images (a child pretending to be a plane, a poet with semen on his chin) accumulate in the poems in an apparently random order, and cliché, excerpts from pop songs, and demotic speech are combined with quotations from canonical poetry. In the space of a few lines, the mood changes from melancholy to exultation, and Ackroyd's tone alternates between ironic playfulness and plangent lyricism. In "the hermaphrodite . . ." he mocks the authorial "I" of humanism ("the poet wears violet shades . . . Alas his art is dead," in *Diversions*, p. 60) and replaces it with the "I" of modernist literature, using a number of authorial personae and becoming an instrument through which literary tradition and language speak. Ackroyd's poetry is full of parodies and half-quotations from writers such as Gerard Manley Hopkins, William Butler Yeats, Sidney, and John Keats.

Ackroyd allows himself to be carried away by language. Typically, a poem will begin with a chance word or phrase, such as "Only connect," from which the remainder of the poem appears to follow in an arbitrary but inevitable sequence: "Only connect / sounds of love / come from the head / in a fixed handwriting / name following name" ("Only connect," in *Diversions*, p. 21). In Ackroyd's verse, language, to quote Roland Barthes, is a hurdy-gurdy that is never still. Ackroyd listens to some of its melodies and riffs, and reproduces them in a polyphonic style:

> Your writing is peaceful now, and so starve
> Your dream which looked at itself and drowns
> When Mr Harding reached the parsonage he
> Found that the arch-deacon had been called away
> And a natural hush falls over us, all in your
> Arms.
> ("The Diversions of Purley," in *Diversions*, p. 10)

As readers, we cannot stop the flow of Ackroyd's epiphanic word-music in order to discover a meaning. We can only slide on the surface of these patterns and watch as the words, cut away from their referents, play endlessly with themselves.

Ackroyd maintains that, although he ceased to write verse after the publication of his first novel in 1982, his poetry simply migrated to his prose. On a superficial level this is undoubtedly the case; phrases, and even characters, from his poems appear throughout his novels and biographies. There are also more general connections. The later prose works display the same gift for parody that we find in the poems; and they are equally diverse in form and style. In addition, the characters in Ackroyd's novels and the subjects of his biographies can be compared to the various authorial personae of the poems.

In 1979 Ackroyd published *Dressing Up—Transvestism and Drag: The History of an Obsession*. This short prose work examines transvestism as a historical phenomenon and as an aspect of contemporary culture. Ackroyd argues that modern transvestites are the victims of bourgeois society, in which sexual identities are too rigidly defined. As Peter Conrad noted (*New Statesman and Society*, 30 November 1979), the book is informed by the assumption that an identity is not given but can be created. Ackroyd thus presents the transvestite as a heroic Wildean dandy who denies all that is considered normal and natural and uses clothes and makeup to invent an artificial persona. In this respect, the transvestites in the book prefigure some of the self-created characters that appear throughout Ackroyd's novels, many of which, like

Daniel Moore in *The House of Doctor Dee* (1993), are cross-dressers. In *Dressing Up*, Ackroyd describes a Dionysian culture of theatrical excess and anarchic inversion that represents the "world turned upside down" (this phrase resounds throughout his writing). It is exactly the kind of alternative and carnivalesque world that he will celebrate in many of his later works.

David Sexton, writing in the *Spectator* (10 September 1994), has suggested that this relatively neglected book is important for an understanding of Ackroyd. "Dressing up" is, he argues, the ideal metaphor for Ackroyd's habit of parodying, or borrowing the clothes, of other writers. Viewed in this light, *Dressing Up* is, he suggests, the key to all of Ackroyd's work.

1980–1985

ACKROYD has always described the distinction between biography and the novel as artificial and meaningless; this is certainly true within the context of his own oeuvre. In his work in both genres, he blends historical fact with imaginative fiction and attempts to shape his material into a coherent narrative. In both, he also performs the language of figures from the past. There are numerous connections between themes of his novels and the subjects of biographies. The utopian novel *The Plato Papers* (1999), for instance, followed Ackroyd's 1998 biography of Thomas More, author of *Utopia*.

Ackroyd's first biography, *Ezra Pound and His World* (1980), is a long essay written in the style of Johnson's *Lives of Poets* that contains an outline of Pound's life and a general criticism of his works. Ackroyd presents Pound as an inveterate actor who was incapable of introspection. He emphasizes the poet's gifts as a mimic and his delight in role-play: it is, he remarks, "unclear where the mask ends and the man begins" (p. 98). In this respect Pound is the archetypal hero of Ackroyd biography, as every one of Ackroyd's subjects are described as actors and protean beings. His biographies are catalogues of masks, moods, and contradictions rather than attempts to uncover monolithic personalities. *Ezra Pound* took a notoriously difficult writer and made his life and work accessible to general readers. Ackroyd achieved this with a combination lucid criticism and a prose style that is urbane and witty: "Hemingway taught [Pound] how to box," reads one line, "and [Pound] tried to teach Hemingway how to write" (p. 61).

In the early 1980s the ostentatiously obscure poet of *Ouch* decided to write novels. As has been suggested, this did not mean that he suddenly abandoned modernism but rather that he began to explore conventional literary forms from the perspective of a modernist poet. Certain critics have considered this shift in Ackroyd's career within the context of a general postmodern cultural trend (for instance, Linda Hutcheon in *A Poetics of Postmodernism,* 1988, places Ackroyd's novels alongside those of Umberto Eco and John Fowles in the postmodern genre of "Historiographic Metafiction"). Other commentators (and Ackroyd himself), however, have argued that he belongs to older literary traditions, and that he is simply too unique to be usefully classified as a postmodernist.

His first novel, *The Great Fire of London* (1982), is a highly artificial and self-conscious book that lacks the strong plot and the psychologically convincing characters that are usually associated with realistic fiction. The narrative, which focuses on the director Spenser Spender's attempt to film a version of Dickens' *Little Dorrit* in modern-day London, is slow and desultory. Its main purpose is to link a series of scenes that feature Ackroyd's collection of Dickensian characters. Among them we find a killer dwarf called Little Arthur, a gay Canadian Dickens scholar, and a working-class telephone operator who believes that she is possessed by the spirit of Amy, the heroine of *Little Dorrit*. The novel also contains a number of archetypal London figures, such as tramps and madmen, who appear to be the guardians of specific London locations.

While writing the novel, Ackroyd discovered his great subject: London. In *The Great Fire*, as in many of Ackroyd's later novels and biographies, the city itself is the central character. Ackroyd takes his characters on walking tours of various parts of the city and shows us prisons, hospitals, and gay pubs. He also evokes the particular atmosphere of areas such as Borough and Archway. Ackroyd's London is a diverse and multiple metropolis. As each of his characters inhabits a different London, the book is an anthology of their separate cities. Ackroyd evokes these cities by reproducing the distinct and contrasting languages of his characters in the dialogue and in the passages in which he describes them. Thus, while Spenser is so inspired by flute music that he sees a vision of people walking over a bridge as "a line of energy . . . of irresistible momentum and sweetness" (p. 37), another character only hears in the music a tune that brightens "everything up a bit" (p. 38). Characteristically, Ackroyd does not allow a single character or language to dominate the book.

In the novel and throughout Ackroyd's writings, the noise, energy, and enormity of London seem to diminish the characters, all of whom find it impossible to assert their individual identities or to discover a meaning or a discernible purpose in the city itself. In later works certain figures are liberated and inspired by this loss of self-consciousness and by London's vastness, indeterminacy, and unknowability. In *The Great Fire*, however, the characters are filled with desolation and fear; they are the first "lonely Londoners" of Ackroyd's fiction.

Ackroyd's next novel, *The Last Testament of Oscar Wilde* (1983), is a fictional autobiography. It purports to be the journal Wilde wrote during the final months of his life in Paris in 1900. In it he surveys the splendors and the miseries of the life he described as a "long and lovely suicide." The novel is, as many reviewers noted, a masterful parody of Wilde's style. The following lines, Wilde's comment on the play *Vera,* are typical: "There was poetry in it, but unfortunately none of it was my own. One can forgive Shakespeare anything, except one's own bad lines" (p. 46). *The Last Testament* is the first book in which Ackroyd performs the language of a historical figure. It is, Ackroyd's works suggest, only through parody and through an act of the imagination that we can hope to evoke something of the past. Ackroyd is not concerned, however, with the authentic or objective past that the conventional historian attempts to recover. Throughout his writings he suggests, in fact, that the past can never be entirely or faithfully resurrected because we can only see it from the perspective of our own time. The past of Ackroyd's work is therefore the author's thoroughly self-conscious and partial invention: it is a concoction of fact and fiction that emerges out of a dialogue between a historical period and the present.

Thus, in the novel, Ackroyd does not attempt to recover the authentic Wilde, or the real late nineteenth century. He offers us instead his own particular versions of them. Countless "inaccuracies" are scattered throughout the book (for instance, the historical Wilde was not, as far as we know, illegitimate); Wilde's language is also a conflation of nineteenth- and twentieth-century English. On several occasions, Wilde quotes T. S. Eliot; at other times he appears to allude to poems by a certain Peter Ackroyd.

The Last Testament is an appropriately paradoxical book. By offering us a character that both is and is not the historical Oscar Wilde it makes a pastime out of past time; and although it is written in the form of a confession, the confessor never actually reveals himself. Wilde's language, which is a collection of quotations, embodies his artificiality. The journal, a miscellaneous anthology of prose poems, fairy tales, dreams, letters, and extracts from newspaper advertisements, captures his multiplicity. The novel, which can be compared to a dialogue between Wilde and Ackroyd, was very important for the latter. He found himself as a writer by borrowing another voice: his career as ventriloquist-author began. The novel was awarded the Somerset Maugham Award.

In writing *T. S. Eliot* (1984), his first full-length biography, Ackroyd faced a serious problem. The Eliot estate would not allow him to quote from Eliot's unpublished writings and only permitted him to quote from Eliot's published works in a critical context. In the book, Ackroyd overcomes these difficulties in a number of ingenious ways. First, he wove the style of Eliot's writing into the texture of his own prose. He uses the authoritative tone of Eliot's criticism, for instance, beginning sentences with phrases such as "It is perhaps not inappropriate to note." He also continually employs Eliotic images, such as the river and the sea, and even appears, at times, to parody Eliot's poetry. Ackroyd thus performs Eliot's language in the same way that he had performed the language of Wilde. As he regards individuals as living lexicons or collections of words, for Ackroyd there can be no better way of evoking a biographical subject.

Ackroyd also surmounted the problem by quoting extensively from people who knew Eliot. In consequence, the biography reads like an anthology of diverse and contradictory descriptions of the poet. This is, in fact, the ideal way for Ackroyd to present Eliot; he regards the poet as a paradoxical and protean figure behind whose poses and moods there was no fixed personality. Eliot is thus described as an actor, a mimic, a clown, and a dandy, and as a lover of fancy dress, makeup and the music hall. Ackroyd discovers the attributes of the actor in Eliot's authorship as well. He praises the poet's gift for imitation, pastiche, and parody and his ability to ventriloquize the different voices of English literature. He also describes Eliot's critical works as performances or "dramatic monologues no less rigorously 'worked up' than his poetry" (p. 106).

Ackroyd is at pains to avoid reductive biographical readings of Eliot's verse. Because of Eliot's dramatic virtuosity it is, he suggests, impossible to locate the "true" voice of the poet. Characteristically, he also denies that Eliot's writing has a paraphrasable meaning, and focuses on its formal aspects. He does argue, however, that Eliot's works manifest an idiosyncratic quality: the ability to combine a profound idealism with an equally profound skepticism. As has been suggested, this is also a characteristic of Ackroyd's own writings. It is a characteristic that is exhibited in *T. S. Eliot* itself. While Ackroyd attempts to magically summon up the poet by parodying his language, he is also conscious of the fact that the real Eliot, and the historical period he inhabited, is ultimately beyond his grasp. It is in this context that Ackroyd describes biography as a "convenient fiction" (p. 239). In an interview he amplified this by commenting that, as the real Eliot is irrecoverable, all that the biographer can do is offer readers his or her particular version of the poet (see McGrath's interview). *T. S. Eliot* was awarded the Whitbread prize for the best biography of 1984. It was also the joint winner of the Royal Society of Literature's William Heinemann award.

Ackroyd's third work of fiction, *Hawksmoor* (1985), combines the genre of the doppelgänger tale with that of the metaphysical detective story. The novel contains two narratives set in two different centuries that echo and animate each other. The first, which unfolds in early eighteenth-century London, concerns the diabolic architect Nicholas Dyer, a character very loosely based on the English baroque architect Nicholas Hawksmoor. Like Hawksmoor, Dyer constructs several churches as part of Parliament's plan to rebuild London after the Great Fire. Unlike the historical architect, however, Dyer is an occultist and a murderer who, at the site of his churches, sacrifices his victims. The second narrative is set in present-day London. In it, a detective, who is called Nicholas Hawksmoor, attempts to solve the mystery of a series of murders that have taken place at the sites of Dyer's churches.

The eighteenth-century chapters are presented as extracts from Dyer's journal. In them Ackroyd brilliantly parodies the style of the period: "as I felt the City under my Feet," Dyer writes, "I had a habit of rowling Phrases around my Head, such as *Prophesie Now, Devouring Fire, Violent Hands*" (p. 13). Dyer's language is a patchwork of quotations from early eighteenth-century writers such as Defoe and Christopher Wren (during his research, Ackroyd read almost every book from the period in order to absorb its language). Like Ackroyd's Wilde, however, Dyer echoes writers from later historical periods. It is therefore apparent that he is the artificial creation of a late-twentieth-century novelist.

Artifice pervades the novel. Hawksmoor is little more than a cardboard character from the detective story genre, and there are a number of metafictional scenes. However, Ackroyd's evocation of the period and his descriptions of the murders are so vivid that the reader experiences the uneasy sensation that the book may contain events that are somehow real. James Fenton, writing in the *Times* (26 September 1985), found the novel's mixture of the real and artificial disturbing and compared it to a horrifying literary game that had got out of hand. This ambiguity is one of the great sources of power of Ackroyd's writing: with their blend of history and fiction and evocative realism and artifice, his works constitute twilight worlds that are at once real and unreal. They also suggest that the relationship between art and the world is complex and paradoxical: while works of art comprise autonomous universes they nevertheless influence the way people perceive the world; they can also enter and contaminate reality.

The plot of *Hawksmoor* is elaborate and inexorable. Phrases, characters, and incidents contained in the odd-numbered eighteenth-century chapters are echoed in the even-numbered chapters in which the twentieth-century story develops. Dyer and his "double" Hawksmoor work in the same area of London, for instance, and have assistants and housekeepers with almost identical names. The novel ends with a mystical resolution in which Dyer and Hawksmoor appear to merge into a single being: "And his [Hawksmoor's] own image was sitting beside him . . . They were face to face. . . . And when they spoke they spoke with one voice" (pp. 216–217).

Many of Ackroyd's novels contain narratives that unfold over wide periods of time and involve intricate patterns of recurrence. Events are repeated across different centuries, often in exactly the same area of London. Ackroyd's London is thus an echoic city in which people of the same mental and physical type recur in each generation, inhabit the same areas, and even perform the same tasks. This is why Ackroyd is frequently associated with the idea of reincarnation or eternal return. However, as the critic Brian Finney has pointed out, rather than being a question of a belief in any mystical concept, it is, in the end, a question of language. Echoes can occur across two centuries in *Hawksmoor* for the simple reason that traces of eighteenth-century English survive and reverberate in modern English (the novel demonstrates this by repeating, in the twentieth-century chapters, phrases used in the eighteenth-century sections). It is thus through language that the past continues to animate and influence the present. Ackroyd's books can, in this context, be compared to machines that generate linguistic patterns and resonances across time. *Hawksmoor* was an enormously successful novel. It won both the Whitbread and the *Guardian* prizes for fiction.

1986–1990

LIKE all of Ackroyd's fiction, *Chatterton* (1987) cannot be classed as a conventional realistic novel. It can be read as a philosophical drama, as a short story of literary detection whose momentum is sustained over two hundred pages, or as an essay on authorship and plagiarism. In *Hawksmoor*, Ackroyd offered the reader two interconnecting narratives that take place in two different centuries. In *Chatterton*, like a performer who gradually increases the difficulty of his act in the course of the show, he attempted to link three stories set in three different times. In the part one, which is set modern-day London, a modernist Cambridge poet, Charles Wychwood, discovers a portrait of the eighteenth-century poet Thomas Chatterton (1752–1770). Chatterton, who gained notoriety for forging the verses of a fifteenth-century monk, committed suicide at the age of seventeen. He was later memorialized in the verse of the Romantic poets and in Henry Wallis' Victorian painting *The Death of Chatterton*. In Charles's portrait, however, Chatterton is not depicted as the "marvellous boy" of Romantic legend but as an old man. Charles also finds the manuscript of a confession that appears to have been written by Chatterton, which confirms that the poet did not die in 1770 but instead faked his own suicide and lived on into the nineteenth century. The manuscript, which is reproduced at the beginning of part two,

is a parody of late-eighteenth-century English. In this section Ackroyd also imitates the language and style of the nineteenth-century novel in an account of the painting of Henry Wallis' picture, for which the novelist George Meredith was the model for Chatterton. In part three, Charles's picture and the manuscript are exposed as forgeries. In the transcendental denouement Chatterton appears to meet Charles and Meredith: "I will live forever, he tells them. They link hands, and bow towards the sun" (p. 234).

Part three has been described by Finney as a celebration of the dissolution of the distinction between originality and imitation, and between reality and its representation in art. Like the rest of the novel, it is also a celebration of Ackroyd's idea of authorship. Chatterton, for instance, is presented as a premodern or modernist author rather than as a unique genius of Romantic mythology. Instead of striving to express his particular vision of the world he understands that originality "consists in forming new and happy combinations" (p. 58) and that "the truest Plagiarism is the truest Poetry" (p. 87). Ackroyd is of course commenting on, and justifying, his own intertextual approach to writing. His works are palimpsests that bear the traces of previous writings, or atemporal libraries in which authors from different periods coexist. *Chatterton* itself is a chamber of echoes from writers such as Dickens and Wordsworth. Almost every line of dialogue contains an allusion: if you pricked the characters they would bleed quotations.

Ackroyd is renowned as the ingenious artificer of intertextual labyrinths. But, as critics such as Jeremy Gibson and Julian Wolfreys have noted, there appears to be no center to the mazes he constructs. As has been suggested, it is impossible to discover a meaning behind Ackroyd's writings, as they form autonomous linguistic worlds. In *Chatterton* a character has a vision in the stacks of a library that might serve as a metaphor for Ackroyd's oeuvre and for his conception of literature. "[The books created] some dark world where there was no beginning and no end, no story, no meaning. And, if you crossed the threshold into that world, you would be surrounded by words . . . but if you tried to grasp them they would melt away" (p. 71).

Chatterton is perhaps Ackroyd's most exhilarating and bravura intellectual performance. Events seem to spontaneously crystallize around each other; its style might be compared to an overwhelming polyphonic music made up of the voices of English literature. The novel was short-listed for the Booker Prize.

In their reviews of *Chatterton* critics wondered what kind of book Ackroyd would write next. None of them could have predicted that it would be a relaxed and loosely plotted pastoral novel set in Hardyesque English countryside, in which all of the action takes place in the late twentieth century. The plot of *First Light* (1989) is utterly absurd from a realistic point of view. One strand of the narrative concerns the archaeological excavation of a Neolithic tomb, another, the examination of the stars by a group of modern astrologers. Ackroyd combines these narratives with a number of bizarre subplots. In one a retired music hall impresario searches for his parents; another concerns a farming family that worships the body of their oldest ancestor.

Ackroyd peoples his fantastic novel with a cast of grotesque caricatures. There is a theatrical antiques dealer who utters remarks such as "Put me near a stage and I yearn for tights" (p. 70), a modern-day version of Mrs. Malaprop, and a pair of aging lesbians whose camp conversations border on the surreal: "Is this some lovely new game, Baby Doll? . . . you had better tell me the rules" (p. 311). Along with these comic figures there are characters whose lives are touched by tragedy: an astrologer who goes insane, and a lame woman who commits suicide.

First Light is a promiscuous medley of mirth and sorrow and a pantomime of endless variety. It contains songs, solemn interior monologues, jokes, philosophical debates in which science's claims to objective knowledge are mocked, and several aria-like set pieces in which individual characters tell fairy tales and stories. Within the book Ackroyd employs a dazzling number of styles and tones. There are passages of lofty metaphysical speculation (a character remarks: "I suppose that we could only see the pattern [of time] if we were outside of it. And in that case we would have ceased to exist. So all we can do is make up our stories," p. 264), but these are punctuated by lyrical epiphanies that border on self-parody, and pages of droll music hall dialogue. Dickens referred to this mixture of the solemn and the playful and the tragic and the comic as the "streaky bacon" effect. It is an effect that all of Ackroyd's writings aim to produce. During *First Light* the characters attend a play that is a microcosm of the novel itself. The drama in question is a

performance of Eliot's *The Family Reunion*, which is played by an amateur group as a Gothic melodrama. "The World," we are told, "had been transformed into a pantomimic creation, but this did not mean that it was any the less effective . . . everything had . . . [a] consistency which was not revealed to those who insisted on some distinction between the real and the unreal" (p. 152).

In *Dickens* (1990) Ackroyd had to present the life and work of a well-known literary figure in an innovative way. He attempted to do this by effectively writing a new kind of biography: a hybrid form that, like his novels, is a mixture of historical fact and imaginative fiction. To some extent, he had already experimented with the biographical form in *T. S. Eliot*, by parodying Eliot's style. In *Dickens* he went much further. Not only does his prose frequently recall that of Dickens (one chapter begins: "London. The Great Oven. The Fever Patch. Babylon. The Great Wen," p. 56), but the entire biography reads like a pastiche of a Dickens novel. It opens with a prologue in which Ackroyd imitates the omniscient narrator of nineteenth-century fiction: "Charles Dickens was dead. He lay on a narrow green sofa" (p. xi). It also contains six fictional interludes. In one interlude, several Dickens characters visit Greenwich Fair; another is an imaginary conversation between Wilde, Eliot, Chatterton, and Dickens. In its size (the first edition is 1,200 pages long) and its energy and its variety of moods and tones, the book could also be described as "Dickensian." Ackroyd treats Dickens as a character in a Dickens novel: at times he seems to be possessed by his subject in the same way that Dickens was possessed by his characters.

Dickens, and to a lesser extent Ackroyd's other biographies, appear to be informed by the principle that the style and form of a biography should somehow embody its subject. Thus the life of a man as artificial as Dickens—a man who found it impossible to distinguish between fact and fiction, who thought of his own life as a marvelous story, and who, Ackroyd claims, was "created" by his books as much as he created them—can be written in the style of a novel. Ackroyd's biography is an ambitious project that is, at the same time, conscious of its own limitations. One of the book's epigraphs is taken from Vladimir Nabokov's *The Real Life of Sebastian Knight*, a novel that is similar to *Dickens* in its dramatization of the difficulty of writing literary biography. In the last imaginative interlude, Ackroyd enters the book and asks himself questions about *Dickens*. In the interview he admits that he has "cheated" in one or two places; in addition, he remarks that, as every biographer is a prisoner of his time, his book cannot be the definitive Dickens. Ackroyd also attempts to introduce the "uncertainty principle" into his biography by repeatedly emphasizing Dickens' strangeness and by arguing that, as he did not understand himself, it would be absurd of us to think that we could pluck out the heart of his mystery.

Certain reviewers thought *Dickens* unscholarly (it contains no footnotes); others described its fictional sections as self-indulgent, and some felt that it simply weighed too much. Other critics, however, found Ackroyd's novel approach to the subject and the biographical form refreshing. Ackroyd went on to write a short book about Dickens' work, entitled *Introduction to Dickens* (1991). The influence of the great English novelist is evident throughout his writing; Alberto Manguel, writing in the *Village Voice* (29 March 1988), described Ackroyd as a well-read and intellectual Dickens.

1991–1995

ENGLISH Music (1992), Ackroyd's longest work of fiction to date, offers the reader two narratives. The first is the autobiography of the ventriloquist Timothy Harcombe. In it he describes his working-class upbringing and his relationship with his father, who is a medium and a magician. The other narrative is comprised of a series of visionary (or "virtual reality") chapters in which Timothy enters the fictional worlds of a number of canonical works of English literature. The structure of the novel recalls Ackroyd's biography of Dickens, in which imaginative interludes are scattered throughout the narrative of the hero's life. Ackroyd parodies the styles of the books Timothy enters. One chapter is a pastiche of a Sherlock Holmes story, and another a parody of *Great Expectations*. Ackroyd thus becomes a ventriloquist for the voices of English literature or, as Verlyn Klinkenborg puts it, he turns the whole of the English canon into a parlor game (*New Yorker*, 23 November 1992).

English Music can be read as Ackroyd's essay on Englishness. A quintessentially English quality can, the novel suggests, be discovered throughout English art: it is manifested in English verse from Chaucer to Ernest Dowson, in the "line of beauty" of William Hogarth's engravings, and in the harmonies of William Byrd and Henry Purcell. "The instruments may alter," as one character remarks, "and the form may vary, but the spirit seems always to remain the same" (p. 128).

The vision of English literature that the novel presents can be compared to Ackroyd's vision of London. Like London, the English literary canon is a place in which echoes and patterns of resonance can be traced across the centuries. These patterns are created by language, the substance of literature, which, according to Ackroyd, generates its own lines of force and elaborate repetitions as it moves through time.

Many reviewers criticized the novel's vision of English literature and English culture. The book, which was read as a clear statement of Ackroyd's personal beliefs, was described by some as nationalistic and reactionary. Other critics have interpreted it as an ironic parody of the idea of Englishness and of a homogeneous English literary canon. They have also emphasized the fact that the novel is not necessarily an expression of Ackroyd's private opinions. The concerns of *English Music*, however, are important for Ackroyd. In a number of lectures, such as "The Englishness of English Literature" (1996), and in several interviews, he has expressed his belief in the idea of a Platonic form of Englishness and in a specifically English tradition of writing. However, his conception of English literature is, he claims, far from being elitist or conservative: he has attempted to unearth an unorthodox and hidden English tradition. It is a tradition of English literature and art that is energetic and heterogeneous. Its representative artists and writers focus on the external aspects of the world and delight in the scenic and the theatrical. They are not concerned with interior meaning, realistic characterization, the world of individual consciousness, or ethical judgments. Instead, they celebrate difference and variety and view life as an intensely artificial drama, as a carnivalesque spectacle, or as an elaborate game. Nor are they interested in the idea of an individual originating literary genius: their eclectic work is based on imitation, parody, and pastiche.

Ackroyd associates this tradition with a Catholic culture that has been forced underground since the Reformation and with a sensibility that is particular to London. It thus informs the work of London artists and writers such as Dickens, Blake, Hogarth, and Turner. It is also embodied in multifarious works, such as Sidney's *Arcadia*, and in art forms, such as the Gothic melodrama, which mix comedy and tragedy and laughter and tears. It is a tradition that Ackroyd attempts to exemplify in many of his writings and in *English Music* itself, a heterogeneous novel that the reader is encouraged to enter in the same way that Timothy enters his favorite books.

Ackroyd's seventh work of fiction, *The House of Doctor Dee* (1993), is a ghost story set in a house in Clerkenwell, London, which, in the fictional world of the novel, once belonged to the Renaissance magus Doctor Dee. Matthew Palmer, a twentieth-century historical researcher, inherits the house. On discovering that it is haunted by Dee and by the past, he decides to research its history and the details of Dee's life. The structure of the novel recalls *Hawksmoor;* it is divided into alternating modern-day and historical chapters. The modern chapters, written in contemporary English, outline Palmer's experiences in the house. The sixteenth-century chapters, which are presented in the form of Dee's journal (a cento made up of quotations from Renaissance texts), relate his quest to locate the mystical city of London. The novel thus offers the reader two distinct languages and historical worlds. These worlds also appear strangely similar, however, as incidents and phrases are repeated across the chapters and centuries. At the denouement the two periods (and the two languages) are blended together.

Doctor Dee is a novel full of echoes from other books by Ackroyd. The bridge of light Matthew Palmer sees across the Thames recalls Spenser Spender's vision in *The Great Fire*, and the novel's concern with sexual magic prefigures *Blake*. There are characteristic discussions of the intertextual nature of writing (Matthew suggests that books are "forever engaged in an act of silent communion which, if we are fortunate, we can over hear," p. 129). There are also the familiar passages that call into question the possibility of recovering past time. At the conclusion Ackroyd, in a characteristic Hitchcockian cameo, enters the book and asks: "Does [the past] have some substantial reality? Am I discovering it, or inventing it?" (p. 275).

Like Wilde before him, Ackroyd has turned repetition into an art. It is, however, more than just a question of playful self-plagiarism. Within his oeuvre there are so many echoes and intricate connections that he appears to have deliberately created an inter- or intratextual maze, or an autonomous literature within literature. Entire scenes are repeated in different novels while metaphors, such as the comparison of time to a lava flow, and phrases, such as "I know you. I know you very well," recur throughout his writings. In Ackroyd's oeuvre everything seems to be touching everything else: like his vision of London and the canon of English literature, his body of work is full of patterns of resonance.

Dan Leno and the Limehouse Golem (1994; published in the United States as *The Trial of Elizabeth Cree: A Novel of the Limehouse Murders*) is perhaps Ackroyd's most characteristic production. It is a London novel in the Dickensian tradition that contains a motley troop of characters, numerous coincidences, and a fast-moving plot. Within it, artifice and reality are effortlessly combined and tragedy is mixed with comedy. At the denouement, a young actress dies during the performance of a play that is based on the events narrated in *Dan Leno* itself. The audience, unaware that she is dead, imagines that is just part of the dramatic fun. *Dan Leno* is a detective story set in nineteenth-century London. In it, the police attempt to catch an elusive murderer who, in Ripperesque fashion, kills and mutilates female prostitutes in an area of London's East End called Limehouse. It also contains an account of the trial and execution of a woman convicted of poisoning her husband. Along with these gruesome gothic elements, the novel contains a vivid evocation of the hilarious world of the music hall and an account of the great comic genius and monopolylinguist (a performer who impersonates the voices of a number of people) Dan Leno. "They talk of Tennyson and Browning," as one of the characters puts it, "but believe me, girls, Mr Leno is *it*" (p. 90).

The novel, which can be read as a parody of the late nineteenth-century form of pulp fiction known as the "shilling shocker," is Ackroyd's portrait of late Victorian London, a city vast and capacious enough to contain a number of miscellaneous characters, languages, and contrasting visions of the world. We encounter Karl Marx, who sees reality in terms of dialectical materialism, George Gissing, the author of works of realistic fiction, and the cross-dressing Elizabeth Cree, who enjoys "a bit of a game *en travesti*" (p. 228). The variety and energy of nineteenth-century London animate the style or, rather, the styles, of the book. It contains a forged journal, extracts from court transcripts, newspaper reports and excerpts of stage dialogue. The plot of the novel is imbued with an energy that is at once intoxicating and frightening. Like the plot of *Hawksmoor*, that of *Dan Leno* appears to emerge spontaneously out of London itself. The murderer, for example, believes that he is playing a part in a drama that has been written by the city. "I felt proud," he writes, "to be entrusted with [London's] powers of expression" (pp. 70–71).

The idea that London somehow determines the events that take place within it can be found throughout Ackroyd's oeuvre. As Plato remarks in *The Plato Papers* (1999), Londoners "lived within fantasies and ambitions which the city itself had created, and they felt obliged to act according to the roles allotted to them" (p. 94). Ackroyd's characters thus become trapped within London's vast and mysterious narratives; they are guided by its invisible lines of energy. Some find the experience terrifying and enervating, others are exhilarated and feel a sensation of blissful release. To put it in the terms of Ackroyd's fiction, they hear London's music, join the Dionysian dance, and go on dancing till they drop.

Ackroyd's next work, *Blake* (1995), was a biography of the English Romantic poet. Ackroyd's Blake is a representative English genius. After comparing Blake's gift of seeing visions to that of Caedmon, the first English poet, Ackroyd echoes the Blakean poem he included as one of the visionary chapters in *English Music*: "So are the lives of the poets connected," he writes, "and our English music is sustained by visions" (p. 111). Blake is also described as a characteristic London or "Cockney" visionary. He was, according to Ackroyd, a poet who had the ability to see what he called "infinite London" or "Spiritual four fold London eternal" within the streets of the earthly city. Blake thus joins the other Cockney visionaries of Ackroyd's writing, including George Gissing, Doctor Dee, Matthew Palmer, and Spenser Spender, all of whom glimpse a heavenly city within the fabric of London. Ackroyd's biography is one of the most accessible introductions to a poetic and artistic oeuvre that is generally regarded as eccentric and arcane. In lucid prose Ackroyd explains Blake's personal mythology and identifies the sources of the greatness of his work in its visionary attributes, in its indeterminacy, and in the "extraordinary sensation of power, of violence and of exultation" (p. 289) it affords.

Blake's work is also placed within the tradition of London writing Ackroyd delineated in his lecture "London Luminaries and Cockney Visionaries" (1993). This tradition is similar to the English tradition he outlined in his lecture on Englishness in the sense that its exemplary artists and writers delight in spectacle, variety, artifice, and play. According to Ackroyd, Blake's early work *An Island in the Moon* epitomizes this tradition; it is made up of a mixture high and low literary forms such as dialogues, street cries, songs, and nursery rhymes. It is, we are told, typical of London writing: serious and ironic, idealistic and skeptical, plangent and harsh at the same time. With Blake, as with every London genius, "you cannot have one aspect without all of the others" (p. 282).

Blake can be read as a chapter of the vast book that Ackroyd has been writing for the last twenty years: an imaginative history of London. Once again, the English capital is the informing presence of the book. Ackroyd conjurers up the whole panoply of urban existence through evocations of Blake's walks in the late eighteenth-century city. Blake's London, we are told, is like the London of every period in its violent energy and in its contradictiveness. It exhibits two permanent conditions of the city: a passion for change and an ultimate unknowability. Like the work of other Cockney visionaries, such as Dickens, Defoe, and Ackroyd himself, Blake's art and poetry embody these attributes of the city. This is why Blake is, for Ackroyd, the archetypal London poet and visionary.

1996–2000

ACKROYD'S ninth work of fiction, *Milton in America* (1996), belongs to the genres of the counterfactual novel and the Utopia. In it the English poet and Republican John Milton flees London in 1660 after the fall of Cromwell and crosses the sea to New England, where he attempts to construct an ideal Puritan society. Milton travels to America with a Cockney boy called Goosequill, who comes from a long line of sausage makers. "Goose" is a cross between Sancho Panza and a Shakespearean fool. "I left my mother's womb," he tells Milton, "like a piece of Andover pork" (p. 22). In New England Milton agrees to preside over a community of excessively earnest Puritans. At first all goes well, but when a group of Catholics settle on nearby land, hostilities break out between the two communities.

The Protestant and the Catholic visions of the world are diametrically opposed. While the Puritans emphasize the importance of individual conscience and ethics, the faith of the Catholics is communal and amoral; where the Puritans attempt to convert the native Indians, the Catholics encourage them to combine elements of their own heathenism with Christianity. It is also a question of language. The Puritans believe in the force of simple English and plain scripture while the language of the Catholics is ornate and metaphorical. The Catholic community is described in carnivalesque terms. The Catholics dress in brightly colored clothes, sleep with the native Indians, dance around maypoles and statues of the Virgin Mary, drink continually, and perform marvelous spectacles. Theirs is a world without fixed limits in which identities are fluid and multiple; it is an entirely artificial universe of beautiful surfaces that has no interior meaning. It is, therefore, similar to the carnivalesque worlds inhabited by the music hall artists in *Dan Leno*, the circus performers in *English Music*, and the transvestites in *Dressing Up*.

The idea of the carnivalesque informs much of Ackroyd's work. It can be discerned in the vision of modernist literature as an amoral and autonomous universe contained in *Notes*, and in the conception of the hidden English tradition of spectacle adumbrated in *The Englishness of English Literature*. Ackroyd's writings are suffused with the spirit of the carnival. *Milton in America* can certainly be described as carnivalesque. It offers the reader a variety of forms and styles and the bizarre spectacle of the "double act" of Milton and his sidekick Goosequill.

The subject of Ackroyd's most recent biography was the English Saint, courtier, and writer Thomas More. Unlike many other modern biographies of More, *The Life of Thomas More* (1998) avoids the anachronism of presenting its subject as a post-Reformation individual. Ackroyd regards More as a product of the social and political forces at work within late medieval society and of institutions such as the Church, Oxford University, the family, the legal system, and the court. More is described as a node within a vast network of duties and affiliations: as part of a closed social system in which everyone had a proscribed role, and as a member of a social body rather than a separate individual. As a result, Ackroyd's book reads like a hybrid form of biography and imaginative social history.

Ackroyd's More moves through the legal and political hierarchies of Tudor England with the ease of an actor who can master a variety of roles, or of a player who is adept at a number of difficult games. Ackroyd describes More as a chameleon courtier who effortlessly adapts his character to the situation in which he finds himself. More's authorship is also described in terms of acting. "He was," we are told, "a resourceful actor [who] became an equally skillful rhetorician . . . He had been thoroughly trained in the art of disputation, where it was necessary to take up either side of a question" (p. 52). His works delight in ambiguity, disguise, and impersonation. To understand them it is necessary to expel the post-Romantic notion of self-expression or the idea of a single residual meaning. Ackroyd therefore reads them as meaningless dramas and as word games. *Utopia* is described as an elaborate game of rhetoric in which "the counter-argument . . . is internalized within the narrative" (p. 170): it constitutes, in American professor and literary theorist Stanley Fish's phrase, a "self-consuming" artifact.

Ackroyd suggests that More's writings evince his particular genius and his vision of the world. In this respect he is similar to the other subjects of Ackroyd's biographies. Although More's personality is never directly present in his works in the sense that they express his private opinions, they embody his ironic doubleness of mind and his sense of life as a transient game and as a passing spectacle. For More, the world seemed insignificant because he viewed it within the context of eternity; it had a divine meaning and purpose but these could not be understood in human terms or expressed in language. This is why More's works do not attempt to reach toward an ultimate meaning or to disclose answers and why they simply unfold and then fold back into themselves.

In *The Life of Thomas More* Ackroyd celebrates English Catholic culture. For Ackroyd, Catholic England was an energetic and carnivalesque world in which the sacred and the secular were part of the same reality and in which "opposing forces were held together by bringing them both within the rituals of display and seasonal ceremony" (p. 58). In the biography, More, like Pound, Eliot, Dickens, and Blake before him, is described as a man in whom the forces of his age became incarnate. His death on the scaffold (an episode that Ackroyd typically compares a scene from a mystery play) is viewed as an emblem of that age's passing. The book was awarded the James Tate Black Memorial Prize.

The Plato Papers: A Novel (1999; published in the United States as *The Plato Papers: A Prophesy*) is a utopian novel set in London in the year A.D. 3700. The society of the future can be read as a parody of the Catholic society Ackroyd describes in *The Life of Thomas More*. Its inhabitants participate in elaborate rituals, have a sense of the sacredness of place, and are content to exist without a definite purpose or meaning in their lives. Plato of Pie Corner wears the robe and mask of the orator and gives lectures to his fellow Londoners concerning the past. He describes the "Age of Mouldwarp" (A.D. 1500–2300), a period of misery and ignorance, which ended when the stars dimmed and the sun went black. From fragments of archaeological evidence, Plato reconstructs an amusingly inaccurate picture of Mouldwarpian culture. He describes Freud as a stage comedian, for instance, and Edgar Allan Poe as the social historian of nineteenth-century America ("The Americans," he deduces, "had pale countenances, with thin lips and large eyes . . . they were all of distant aristocratic lineage . . . [and] were a highly nervous people, who suffered from a morbid acuteness of their faculties," p. 31). Plato also misreads *The Origin of Species* as an ironic novel by Charles Dickens, and compiles a glossary of Mouldwarp terms that contains entries such as the following: "*literature*: a word of unknown provenance, generally attributed to 'litter' or waste" (p. 19). In these sections, Ackroyd is as polemical as he had been in his first prose work, *Notes for a New Culture*. He satirizes the materialism, arrogance and rampant individualism of twentieth-century Western society. He also ridicules our pretensions to historical knowledge and pours scorn on the notion of scientific objectivity. In an interesting variant on the traditional utopian novel, the hero, who inhabits an apparently ideal society, becomes fascinated by the dystopian world of Mouldwarp. In what is either a dream vision or an actual journey, he travels to Mouldwarpian London. On his return, he describes late-twentieth-century London as a city that delights in contrast and discontinuity and that exists in a delirious state of perpetual change. Plato, the Luther or the Socrates of his age, is then placed on trial for corrupting the young with his lies regarding his experience.

The novel is a collection of fragmentary papers, some of which are written in the form of the Platonic or Lucianic dialogue. Many of Ackroyd's books contain dialogues. It is a form that appeals to Ackroyd, just as it appealed to More, Blake, and Wilde before him, perhaps because in the dialogue it is possible to present different and even contradictory perspectives at the same time. In *Plato*, as in *Notes* and in *Milton in America*, Ackroyd offers us two opposing perspectives: that of Plato and that of his society. Characteristically, he does not offer the reader a resolution of the dialectic within the novel. Plato may be a charlatan, a madman, a genuine visionary, or indeed all of these things.

CONCLUSION

LIKE his individual writings, Ackroyd's oeuvre cannot be closed: we cannot attribute to it an ultimate meaning or give it a summary definition. This is, as we have seen, because his works deny precisely this kind of reading. It is also due to the fact that he is still alive and continues to be as prolific as ever. Indeed, like his own characters, he appears to be caught up in one of London's inexorable narratives and to have become imbued with the city's indomitable energy. His enormous historical study of London (*London: The Biography*) was published in 2000, to be followed by a nonfictional work, *The Origins of the English Imagination*. Other projected future books include a biography of Shakespeare. Having achieved success with his first play *The Mystery of Charles Dickens*, which was playing in London's West End at the time of this writing, Ackroyd may also write further dramas. It is impossible to predict the nature of these and other future works; nor can we foresee the way in which they will alter our understanding of Ackroyd's oeuvre. To judge by his writing to date they will be artificial, varied, playful, flamboyant, and, above all, elusive performances. Ambiguity and indeterminacy are, in conclusion, the quintessential qualities of Ackroyd's work. He appears to have taken the words of one of the characters in *Dan Leno* as the motto of his authorship: "That's the game, you see. Keep them guessing" (p. 130).

SELECTED BIBLIOGRAPHY

I. BOOKS. *Notes for a New Culture: An Essay on Modernism* (London, 1976; New York, 1976; rev. with a new preface, London, 1993); *Dressing Up—Transvestism and Drag: The History of an Obsession* (London, 1979; New York, 1979); *Ezra Pound and His World* (London, 1980; New York, 1980); *The Great Fire of London* (London, 1982; Chicago, 1988); *The Last Testament of Oscar Wilde* (London, 1983; New York, 1983); *T. S. Eliot* (London, 1984; repub. as *T. S. Eliot: A Life*, New York, 1984); *Hawksmoor* (London, 1985; New York, 1985); *Chatterton* (London, 1987; New York, 1988); *First Light* (London, 1989; New York, 1989); *Dickens* (London, 1990; repub. as *Dickens: Life and Times*, New York, 1990); *Introduction to Dickens* (London, 1991; New York, 1991); *English Music* (London, 1992; New York, 1992); *The House of Doctor Dee* (London, 1993; London and New York, 1994); *Dan Leno and the Limehouse Golem* (London, 1994; repub. as *The Trial of Elizabeth Cree: A Novel of the Limehouse Murders*, New York, 1995); *Blake* (London, 1995; repub. as *Blake: A Biography*, New York, 1996); *Milton in America* (London, 1996; New York, 1997); *The Life of Thomas More* (London, 1998; New York, 1998); *The Plato Papers: A Novel* (London, 1999; repub. as *The Plato Papers: A Prophesy*, New York, 2000); *London: The Biography* (London, 2000).

II. POETRY. *Ouch* (London, 1971); *London Lickpenny* (London, 1973); *Country Life* (London, 1978); *The Diversions of Purley and Other Poems* (London, 1987).

III. MISCELLANEOUS PROSE. "The Inheritance" (short story), in *London Tales*, ed. Julian Evans (London, 1983); Introduction to *PEN New Fiction I*, ed. Peter Ackroyd (London, 1984); Introduction to *Oscar Wilde: The Picture of Dorian Gray*, ed. Peter Ackroyd (London, 1985); Introduction to *Dickens' London: An Imaginative Vision* (London, 1987); "The Plantation House" (short story), in *New Statesman and Society Christmas Supplement* (December 1991); "London Luminaries and Cockney Visionaries," in *LWT London Lecture* (London, 1993; rev. and repub. as "Cockney Visionaries," in *Independent*, 18 December 1993); Foreword and Afterword to *Catalogue of Rare Books offered for sale from the collection of Giles Gordon* (London, 1994); Introduction to *Stephen Harwood: East End Paintings* (London, 1994); Introduction to *Frank Auerbach: Recent Works* (New York; 1994); *Blake and London Radicalism: Times Literary Supplement Talk* (London, 1995); Introduction to *Poems of William Blake* (London, 1995); "A Tale of the Expected" (short story), in *The Guardian* (22 December 1995); "The Englishness of English Literature" (lecture), Proceedings of the XIXth International Conference of Aedean, ed. Javier Pérez Guerra (Vigo, 1996); Foreword to *Enoch Soames, Man of Letters: The Critical Heritage* (London, 1997); Introduction to *The Book of Isaiah* (Edinburgh, 1999); Foreword to *Table Talk: Oscar Wilde*, ed. Thomas Wright (London, 2000).

IV. INTERVIEWS. In sections IV–VI, I have listed a small selection of the interviews, book reviews, and critical studies that are of particular interest. For a more comprehensive list refer to the bibliography in J. Gibson and J. Wolfreys, *Peter Ackroyd: The Ludic and Labyrinthine Text* (New York, 1999; London, 2000).

Patrick McGrath, "Peter Ackroyd," in *Bomb* 26 (winter 1988–1989); Brian Appleyard, "Aspects of Ackroyd," in *Sunday Times Magazine* (9 April 1989); John Walsh, "Confessions of a Monopolylinguist," in *Sunday Times*

(17 May 1992); Mark Lawson, "Nothing Personal," in *The Guardian* (31 August 1995); Susana Onega, "An Interview with Peter Ackroyd," in *Twentieth Century Literature* 42, no. 2 (summer 1996); Thomas Wright, "A bit of a talking to," in *Sunday Telegraph Magazine* (9 February 1997); Tim Adams, "A Life Sentence: London's Biographer," in *Observer* (1 March 1998).

V. REVIEWS. Jeremy H. Prynne, "*London Lickpenny*," in *Spectator* (19 January 1974); Peter Conrad, "Notes For a New Culture," in *Times Literary Supplement* (3 December 1976); David Lodge, "Mine, Of Course," in *New Statesman and Society* (19 March 1976); Christopher Ricks, "The Craft of Criticism," in *Sunday Times* (7 March 1976); Peter Conrad, "The Third Sex," in *New Statesman and Society* (30 November 1979); Lincoln Kirkstein, "Ezra Pound and His World," in *New York Review of Books* (30 April 1981); Galen Strawson, "Failing to Connect," in *The Times Literary Supplement* (29 January 1982); Tom Paulin, "Oscar and Constance," in *London Review of Books* (17–30 November 1983); Christopher Ricks, "The Braver Thing," in *London Review of Books* (1–14 November 1984); James Fenton, "Time Present and Time Past Horrors," in *The Times* (26 September 1985); Alan Hollinghurst, "In Hieroglyph and Shadow," in *Times Literary Supplement* (27 September 1985); Joyce Carol Oates, "The Highest Passion is Terror," in *New York Times* (19 January 1986); Martin Dodsworth, "Existing in Order to Exist," in *Times Literary Supplement* (11–17 September 1987); Robert Nye, "His Mind on His Sleeve," in *The Times* (19 February 1987); Lawrence Danson, "To Catch a Thief," in *New Republic* (22 February 1988); Debis Donoghue, "One Life Was Not Enough," in *New York Times* (17 January 1988); Alberto Manguel, "Untrue Confessions: Many Moods of Thomas Chatterton," in *Village Voice* 33, no. 15 (29 March 1988); Stephen Games, "But What Does It All Mean, Mr Ackroyd?" in *The Guardian* (14 April 1989); Grevel Lindop, "The Empty Telephone Boys," in *PN Review* 15, no. 6 (1989); Craig Raine, "Odds and Ends of a Great Life," in *Observer* (2 September 1990); John Sutherland, "A Terrible Bad Cold," in *London Review of Books* (27 September 1990); James R. Kincaid, "The Sum of His Oddities," in *New York Times* (13 January 1991); Verlyn Klinkenborg, "Peter Ackroyd's Music," in *New Yorker* (23 November 1992); D. J. Taylor, "Fogey Heaven," in *New Statesman and Society* (5 June 1992); Eric Korn, "Evil in EC1," in *Times Literary Supplement* (10 September 1993); David Sexton, "Thereby Hangs a Tale," in *Spectator* (10 September 1994); Iain Sinclair, "The Cadaver Club," in *London Review of Books* (22 December 1994); Jay Parini, "A Thriller—But about Thinkers," in *Boston Globe* (4 June 1995); James Wood, "Little Guignol," in *New York Review of Books* (21 September 1995); Iain Sinclair, "Customising Biography," in *London Review of Books* (22 February 1996); Tony Tanner, "Milton Agonistes," in *New York Times* (6 April 1997); Patrick Collinson, "Defined by His Death," in *Times Literary Supplement* (13 March 1998).

VI. CRITICAL STUDIES. Linda Hutcheon, *A Poetics of Postmodernism. History. Theory. Fiction.* (London, 1988; New York, 1988); Karl Miller, "Long Live Pastiche," in *Authors* (Oxford, 1989); Brian Finney, "Peter Ackroyd: Postmodernist Play and *Chatterton*," in *Twentieth Century Literature* 38, no. 2 (summer 1992); Susana Onega, "British Historiographic Metafiction in the 1980s," in *British Postmodern Fiction, Postmodern Studies 7*, ed. T. D'haen and H. Bertens (Amsterdam and Atlanta, Ga., 1993); Roy Kaveney, "Turn and Turn Again: Sinclair, Ackroyd and the London Novel," in *New Statesman and Society* (9 September 1994); John Peck, "The Novels of Peter Ackroyd," in *English Studies: A Journal of English Language and Literature* 75, no. 5 (1994); Laura Giovannelli, *Le vite in Gioco: Le prospettiva ontologica e autoreferenziale nelle narrative di Peter Ackroyd* (Pisa, 1996); Susana Onega, *Peter Ackroyd* (Plymouth, Eng., 1998); Jeremy Gibson and Julian Wolfreys, *Peter Ackroyd: The Ludic and Labyrinthine Text* (New York, 1999; London, 2000); Susana Onega, *Metafiction and Myth in the Novels of Peter Ackroyd* (Columbia, S.C., 1999).

BERYL BAINBRIDGE

(1933–   )

Patricia Craig

THE LAST THIRTY years of the twentieth century saw the rise to prominence, in varying degrees, of a number of exceptionally stylish, sharp, and idiosyncratic English women novelists, among them the resonant Penelope Fitzgerald, the lucid Jane Gardam, and the fantastical Alice Thomas Ellis. Beryl Bainbridge belongs in this vivid company, whose literary ancestry can be traced back through early Muriel Spark to Stevie Smith's prescription for pointed deviousness, issued in her *Novel on Yellow Paper* (1936), which she called "a foot-off-the-ground novel that came by the left hand." All these writers display an imaginative audacity, aiming for an unexpected angle on things. The first novel written by Bainbridge was so at odds with conventional expectations that it failed to find a publisher until after she had brought out a couple of books, *A Weekend with Claude* (1967) and *Another Part of the Wood* (1968), composed in a style she considered more acceptable to the reading public. Since this style accommodates expressions like "grape-intoxicated Mountaineer," and "three pairs of orbs," it was fortunate that she did not continue to use it. That she did not, was due in part to her friendship with Anna Haycraft (the novelist Alice Thomas Ellis), who, with her husband, Colin Haycraft, ran the Duckworth Press. In 1970 Haycraft read the two published Bainbridge novels and pronounced them "rotten" but asked to see anything else the author might have. Thus *Harriet Said . . .* , the novel written in 1960 and shelved after a publisher had turned it down on the grounds of general indecency and unpleasantness, finally made it into print.

Though the central incident in the plot was derived, albeit obliquely, from reports of a real-life murder that occurred in New Zealand during the 1950s, the mood and atmosphere of *Harriet Said . . .* hark back to the author's Lancashire childhood just after the Second World War. "I am not very good at fiction. . . . It is always me and the experiences I have had," Beryl Bainbridge has reiterated, denying any expertise when it comes to unadulterated invention. She likes to keep things authentic, and the "invented," or borrowed, element in her books, which often consists of some macabre or sensationalist item filched from a newspaper ("life plus a newspaper plot" is her own sardonic summing-up of her early narrative formula), is blended so skillfully with the agitations and contretemps of everyday life—her quintessential subject matter—that it never strikes a jarring note.

BIOGRAPHY

IF writing from her own experience contributes clarity, it is fortunate that Bainbridge's life has been sufficiently varied and eventful to make the exercise auspicious. "There she sat, after twenty-two years of terrors and triumphs that he knew nothing about" (p. 6), thinks the brother of Madge in *A Quiet Life* (1976), the most directly autobiographical of the Bainbridge novels. Like Madge, Bainbridge had a brother some years her senior, a wayward disposition, and a pair of egregiously ill suited parents. She was born in Liverpool on 21 November 1933, the second child and only daughter of a failed businessman turned commercial traveler, full of tall tales, and a mother preoccupied with the niceties of genteel behavior. Both parents were clever and, in their own way, devoted to their children, but the explosive temper of one and the unrealized expectations of the other led to constant bickering and upheavals in the home and created what their daughter called "a climate of strain and anxiety."

By the time she was five or six, at the start of the Second World War, the family had moved to windswept Formby on the Lancashire coast. Like the fictional Madge in her school raincoat and ankle socks, the teenage Bainbridge would spend a lot of her free time out among the sand dunes of the Mersey Estuary, or with friends in the nearby pine woods. She was sent to the Merchant Taylors' School at Crosby on the outskirts of Liverpool, but her schooling does not appear to have had a profound effect on her. It was in the home, discordant or not, that she was encouraged to cultivate her talents: tap dancing, acting, and writing stories. It was plain from the start that the whole-hogging child was destined to make a name for herself in one of these areas—as Uncle Vernon said of Stella, in *An Awfully Big Adventure* (1989), "from the moment she could toddle, he had watched her lurching towards the limelight" (p. 13). However, it was acting that claimed Beryl Bainbridge's first allegiance, from the age of ten, when she began to appear on the Children's Hour Program on the radio. For a time she attended a ballet school in Tring, and then at fifteen she joined the Liverpool Repertory Theatre Company, as an assistant stage manager and "character juvenile" (a young girl not considered pretty enough to merit a starring role). In fact, her acting career continued sporadically until 1972, and included performances in London and provincial theaters, as well as work for radio and television. By sixteen she had met her future husband, the artist Austin Davies, then an art student and temporary scene painter at the Liverpool Rep. Despite her justified misgivings about the course this always volatile relationship was likely to take, she married him in 1954, when she was twenty. The couple settled in what became the Toxteth area of Liverpool, an address that so embarrassed Bainbridge's parents that they kept it from their neighbors. "Liverpool 8 was considered Bohemian and run-down, not to say sordid," Bainbridge recalled in 1981 (*Sunday Times*, 19 July), the summer in which the district became notorious as the scene of furious race riots. In the friendlier 1950s, however, Lascar seamen, Asians, blacks, and mixed-race families mingled happily enough with university and art students and local prostitutes.

Two of Bainbridge's three children were born in Toxteth, the second shortly before her divorce in 1959 (Austin Davies had left Beryl Bainbridge in 1958), and she has drawn on her recollections of the place in several of her novels—for example, *Young Adolf* (1978). She stayed on in Liverpool for another five years and then moved to London at the behest of her ex-husband, who wanted to be within reach of his children. In the 1960s Bainbridge gave birth to a third child, a daughter, whose father is the writer Alan Sharp, the model for the hero of the 1975 *Sweet William*.

After the deprivations of the war and postwar years, the 1960s were an astonishing decade, even if its precepts and certitudes proved as ephemeral or chimerical as anything that had come before. A new buoyancy of spirit was in the air, stimulating for anyone at all susceptible to the change of atmosphere and, for a writer and social observer like Beryl Bainbridge, of the utmost importance to a literary development. A legacy from Bainbridge's early London days is her refusal to make moral judgments about her characters, be they murderers, philanderers, or whatever. This is perhaps her most striking characteristic, after the ability to turn every kind of horror and misery into a comedy of social alignments.

Bainbridge's metropolitan life began in the north London, nineteenth-century-terraced house in which she has lived ever since, aside from a year on a farm in the north of England. According to photographs, the interior of this Camden Town house is as dark, decorative, eccentrically appointed, and full of treasures as the novels of its owner. John Morrish has described it as "a Victorian parlor on steroids" (*Daily Telegraph*, 10 September 1996), crammed with bygone pub advertisements, wind-up gramophones, stuffed animals, and other evocative odds and ends that make it a perfect extension of its owner's personality. During her earliest years here, with three young children, Bainbridge led a precarious existence. Employment in a local winebottling factory resulted in *The Bottle Factory Outing* (1974). By the time the book came out, the author and her ideal publisher had found one another. Duckworth had employed her in their office for a year and thereafter put her on a monthly salary to enable her to write. During the highly productive 1970s, she turned out virtually a novel a year, in a sequence displaying increasing confidence and expertise.

She got off to something of a false start with the two novels published in the 1960s, but her association with Duckworth resulted in the chance to bring out revised versions. "It is seldom," she said, "that an author gets the opportunity of rewriting a published book. Once in print, there's an end on't" (*Times*, August 1981). The new versions of *Another Part of the Wood* and *A Weekend with Claude*, shorter and sharper, came out in 1979 and 1981, respectively. Effectively amended, they lack the gusto and succinctness of their successors. According to Bainbridge, *Weekend* was written partly to impress her estranged husband. It is based on a narrative device, the discovery of a photograph in the drawer of a desk in an antique shop: not a photograph of any historical interest, merely a snapshot dating from 1960, when four oddly assorted friends had come to spend a weekend with the shop's recently divorced proprietor, Claude Perkins. The friends are Lily—the first of the Bainbridge look-alikes—with her chaotic life and romantic expectations; her lodger, "Victorian" Norman; her current stolid boyfriend, Edward; and an old, self-regarding, and obsessive woman with a litany of persecutions, Shebah, who provides the only moment of drama in the novel by getting herself shot in the ankle. One critic (the poet Anthony Thwaite) described Beryl Bainbridge's earliest set of characters as a "mob of solipsists, emotional cripples and bores." The author's deadpan approach to the grotesqueries of normal life is just discernible behind the somewhat mannered overlay. The narrative consists of three monologues, by Lily, Norman, and Shebah. *A Weekend with Claude* (the first version) was fairly well received, went into paperback, and earned its author £25. *Another Part of the Wood* assembles a group of misfits and oddballs in flimsy holiday huts in a wet Welsh wood. The selfishness, spite, and misjudgment of these dreadful people eventually (and inadvertently) cause the death of the youngest among them, a boy of seven or eight, Child Roland; the Byronic resonance is intentional, as in "Childe Rolande to the dark tower came." It cannot be called an attractive theme. A degree of personal anger and bitterness got into both versions of the book, with (as Bainbridge admits) consequent loss of detachment and erosion of the black comic element that spiced up the terrors and traumas of the next group of novels. Child Roland is an innocent and pathetic victim of adult disagreeableness and deficiencies. With subsequent Bainbridge victims, the crucial death, whether accident or accidental homicide, is either almost peripheral to the main story line and therefore doesn't engage the reader's deepest sympathies or is presented as part of a comic scenario, whose effect is thoroughly invigorating (*The Bottle Factory Outing* is a case in point).

Harriet Said . . . (1972) is a much more accomplished novel than *Claude* or *Another Part of the Wood*, but it is more a tale of pervasive corruption than a comedy. A couple of teenage girls, the unnamed narrator and her friend Harriet, the manipulator, egg one another on to more and more shady behavior. Bainbridge takes the usual, over-the-top adolescent emotions and points them in a sinister direction. Everything in this short novel is charged with a kind of desolate lyricism. It is a bleak postwar summer on the Lancashire coast: "Everything seemed damp and sallow, the horizon was flushed green, so that there was no longer a division between earth and sky. The whole world looked sickly and weak; tombstones, slate church and pebbled path tinged with a green unearthly light" (p. 105). Out of boredom, perhaps, or through some essential destructiveness in their natures, the girls engage in a dicey flirtation with an elegant elderly neighbor named Mr. Biggs, whom they dub the Tsar. Harriet's plan (it appears) is to have her friend seduce the Tsar among the sand hills, so that the event may be written up in a secret diary in which the friends record their (magnified) doings. The copulation does in fact take place, but the climax of the action occurs when the narrator, at the instigation of Harriet, smashes in the skull of the Tsar's large wife, who is about to discover them in a compromising situation. The two then run off, leaving old Mr. Biggs to take the rap.

Although some critics have discerned a lesbian undercurrent in the friendship between the two desperately precocious heroines of this novel, it is unlikely that Beryl Bainbridge had this in mind when she wrote it. What she evokes is a half-competitive alliance with a lurid component. The book might be read as a warning about the dangers of leaving imaginative, clever young girls alone, as an enshrinement of amorality, or as a piece of beautifully judged storytelling. Bainbridge has signaled, as clearly as possible, that we are not to attribute out-and-out badness to her central characters: a photograph of herself and a friend, at the appropriate age, are on the dustjacket of the first edition. *Harriet Said . . .* was followed by *The Dressmaker* (1973), which tells the story of Rita, a girl of seventeen in lower-middle-class Liverpool, brought up sedately by a couple of aunts. It is 1944, with the devastation of wartime everywhere around:

When the roof split open, the prams and bedding spilled from the top floor to the next, mingling with Aunt Nellie's rolls of dress material, snaking out wantonly into the burning night. . . . tumbling down through the air to be buried under the bricks and the iron girders—covered now by the grass and the great clumps of weed that sprouted flowers, rusty red and purple, their heads swinging like fox-gloves as the tram lurched round the corner and began the steep ascent to Everton Brow.

(p. 26)

Rita's lackluster life is evoked concisely:

so put down, so without passion, living all her life with the old women down the road. As a child she had never played out in the street, never put her dolls to sleep on the step, never hung around the chip shop on Priory Road. In the air-raid shelter she wore a hat belonging to Aunt Nellie as if she was in church.

(p. 10)

The eruption into this dejected existence of an unsettling force, an illiterate young American soldier, Ira, opens the way for another of Bainbridge's macabre denouements. Rita is infatuated, though the soldier finds her "joyless"; she lacks a capacity for amusement. The poor girl displays all the messy hopelessness peculiar to her age group: the tears, the exaggerations. "Oh, Auntie, I wish I was dead." Soon not Rita but Ira is dead, dead and sewn into a makeshift shroud in the form of an old chenille curtain, by the capable hands of Aunt Nellie, the dressmaker.

What has happened? Ira the dunce, a boy with a sure instinct only in relation to his own erotic needs, had found brassy Aunt Margo more to his taste than docile Rita; Nellie, catching them at it in the storage room, stabs the soldier in the neck with a pair of scissors, causing him to meet his death in a fall downstairs. Aunt Nellie then rises superbly to the occasion. "We haven't had much of a life," she pronounces, stitching grimly away. "I don't see why we should pay for him." Astringent social realism, a sense of murk, a devastating particularity, and a streak of farce all meet head-on in this strong novel (derived in part from Bainbridge's recollections of her father's sisters in their cramped Liverpool home), which gained its author her first nomination for the Booker Prize, as well as an increasing readership in both England and America (where it was retitled The Secret Glass).

Verisimilitude, which is always a feature of Beryl Bainbridge's writing, gains an extra dimension when it is given a comic slant. The bleak, black comedy of The Dressmaker is still quite muted, but its successor, The Bottle Factory Outing (1974), is marked by an upsurge of the impulse toward the blackest revelry. There is something irresistibly Ortonesque about this novel (Joe Orton, 1933–1967, is, of course, the playwright of anarchic and entertaining imbroglios such as Loot, 1966), with its sixteen-stone corpse carried around by agitated Italians, on an outing at an English

stately home. The corpse is crammed into a car and arranged to look drunk and asleep while the cart's other occupants admire the animals in a safari park. Bundled into an elevator and deposited upstairs back at the factory, the corpse is eventually pickled in a wine barrel and set adrift. The corpse is of Freda, organizer of the outing, who has met a mysterious, and probably accidental, death at the hands of a co-worker; either Rossi, the manager, Vittorio, the trainee manager, or Irish Patrick, the van driver (it is never established whom). The blend of low-toned mimesis and grotesque high jinks is striking. The novel begins and ends with a funeral, the second a parody of the first, which brings it full circle.

Instructed by her editor, Anna Haycraft, to use her own experiences as a starting-point for her singular excursions into fiction, Bainbridge acted on the advice to remarkable effect in The Bottle Factory Outing. The Bainbridge stand-in in this novel (her fifth) is Brenda, a thirty-two-year-old divorcee, by no means as abject as she sometimes seems, whom overbearing Freda has taken in hand. Brenda spends her days fending off the advances of Mr. Rossi in the cellar at work, and trying to stand up to flamboyant Freda, whose own energies are concentrated on the ill-omened outing, at which she hopes to effect the seduction of Vittorio. From the opening page on, various events, including the appearance in Brenda and Freda's flat of a mad mother-in-law armed with a pistol, go exorbitantly and wonderfully off the rails. Though critical complaints continued to be voiced concerning Bainbridge's constant resorting to a sensationalist motif, this novel, like its predecessor, was shortlisted for the Booker Prize and won the Guardian Fiction Prize.

The follow-up to Outing is less outrageous, more gently funny. Sweet William (1975) is a slice of irregular, not too desperate life, framed with tenderness and humor. William is an incorrigible womanizer whose characteristic image is on a bicycle, cycling away from one enthralled female or another. Ann, the novel's protagonist, has ditched her sensible fiancé to cater to William's whims, allowing every stable element in her life—friends, job, lodgings, future prospects to drift away from her. The effect of William is overwhelming. "In ten days," thinks Ann, "she had encouraged adultery, committed a breach of promise, given up her job, abetted an abortion. She had not been aware, throughout these happenings, of any unease or distress" (p. 67). If the book has a theme, aside from its re-creation of free-ranging, besotted London days, it's to do with the power of self-deception of various kinds, the willing suspension of the faculty for astuteness.

FAMILY THEMES

BERYL Bainbridge's laconic, ironic eloquence gets full expression in *A Quiet Life* (1976), a tour de force of dynamic edginess and transfigured family history. Freed by her mother's death (her father had died some years earlier, when she was twenty-three) to take a sharp look at the shortcomings and frictions of her Lancashire upbringing, Bainbridge produced a comedy of anxiety-ridden home life. Continuing her practice of presenting herself at various ages and stages—but stylized, objectified—she gives us fifteen-year-old Madge, whose dominant characteristic is a tendency to act up. "She leapt aboard the tram . . . and parked herself on the long bench with lips parted like a movie queen, glancing about theatrically, her shoes swinging clear of the floor and her laces trailing in the dust. She was desperate for attention" (p. 93).

Madge is effectively distanced from the reader by being seen at all times through the apprehensive eyes of her well-meaning older brother Alan, who has taken on the impossible task of trying to keep the peace. Impossible, with Father flying off the handle and venting his fury on a kitchen chair, Mother lamenting the absence of an outlet for her finishing-school accomplishments, and tactless grandparents putting their oar in. Not to mention Madge running wild among the sand dunes, cavorting with German prisoners-of-war, and getting herself talked about in the neighborhood. All this, and more, is held in consummate equilibrium. Out of her unexceptional material, Beryl Bainbridge has fashioned a small miracle of compassion and compression, summing up a whole threadbare but vigorous mode of existence.

In *Injury Time* (1977), a bunch of inexpert bank robbers escaping from the police interrupt a dinner-party. Being held hostage doesn't seem to cause the characters any more upset or terror than the ordinary vexations of day-to-day living. One of the central characters, Binny, is clearly Madge of the previous novel advanced to the age of forty, bereft of husband but abundant in offspring, and no better equipped than her predecessor to tailor her proceedings to a conventional code of conduct. Binny lives in an area of London where old women come out to wail on the balcony in the evening, and illicit copulation takes place behind the garbage cans. (Beryl Bainbridge, playfully, has a photo of her own front door on the cover of this book.) She's the kind of woman who, giving a dinner party with gritted teeth, having demanded of her lover, Edward, that he acknowledge her socially, will unaccountably mislay the second course. The ramshackle social occasion at Binny's is attended by placatory Edward, the first of the author's nervous adulterers (who reappears in Bainbridge's 1980 novel *Winter Garden*); one of Edward's business acquaintances and his woman-of-the-world wife; and—uninvited—Alma, a drunken friend of Binny's. The assembly is about to get more than it bargained for. Edward, in particular, consulting his watch with increasing agitation—he's supposed to be home by eleven o'clock—is never going to make it home at all.

Injury Time is funny, diverting, and composed with all the resources of an adept storyteller, with its portents of disaster, its streets filled with vagrants and "meths-drinkers" (drinkers of cheap alcohol), its unpredictable outrages ("the world was menacing and full of alarms," p. 21), its failures of decorum and order, and its heroine whose querulousness is robust and endearing. Some of the novel's derangement and dishevelment can be put down to the provocations of modern living, the problems of trying to make sense of things in a fearfully shaky universe. However, as the next Bainbridge novel, *Young Adolf*, indicates, pre–World War I Liverpool is no better endowed with shapeliness or repose. This book is based on the premise that Adolf Hitler, as an exceptionally benighted youth, passed the winter months of 1912–1913 with his half-brother Alois and Irish sister-in-law Bridget at their home on seedy Stanhope Street (coincidentally in the area inhabited, some decades later, by Beryl Bainbridge and her husband Austin Davies). Taking her cue from the Chaplin of *The Great Dictator* (1940), adding her own recollections of mid-century Liverpool (such details as the family of nineteen residing next door, and the floorboards torn up in winter for use as firewood, are appropriated from life), and parceling these details up in an atmospheric re-creation of the city of her father's early days (he was born in 1889, the same year as Hitler), Bainbridge pulls off another triumph of comedy and contretemps.

"Hatless, his only luggage a book on Shatterhand of the Wild West, young Adolf had arrived in Liverpool" (p. 11). So we read at the end of chapter 1, and from then on it's downhill all the way, as bleak young Adolf gets punched and knocked over on the alien platform, incessantly falls under tables and trips over Christmas trees, loses his boot on an excursion into the country and has to limp home covered in mud, imagines himself to be the object of pursuit by a sinister official seeking his impoundment as a draft dodger, and eventually finds himself mixed up in a conspiracy to keep bug-infested children of the poor out of the clutches of the City Corporation. Life is a threat and a torment. At the same time, the text allows itself some small mocking pointers to features of the Third Reich. For instance, Bridget Hitler, taking pity on Adolf when he loses some of his clothes, runs up a garment for him out of a piece of mildewed brown linen. Adolf's brief employment at the sumptuous Adelphi Hotel gives him a taste for uniforms and grandeur. A Jewish landlord, Dr. Meyer, befriends him but doesn't sufficiently appreciate his uniqueness. Desperately prone to take umbrage, a bit pompous and priggish Adolf suffers his comic mishaps like a ruffled bantam. It's an extraordinary portrayal, daring and droll. Lesser characters in the novel—hairy Mary O'Leary, the maid of all work; the more innocuous Hitlers; and their infant darling Pat, the mildly licentious Meyer—are expertly delineated too. The city of Liverpool, mettlesome, pungent, forever on the go, and enshrined in a desperate past, strikingly overshadows all the souped-up proceedings.

Around this time, the late 1970s, Beryl Bainbridge was engaged in revising the two unassimilated early novels, as well as taking on some work for British television, including a script for *A Quiet Life* and—an offshoot of *Young Adolf*—a two-part dramatization (with Philip Seville) of *The Journal of Bridget Hitler. Sweet William*, for which she also produced a script, had just been filmed with Jenny Agutter. At the same time, the main body of her work was being extended in several directions. *Winter Garden* (1980) shifts the scene to Russia, and *Watson's Apology* (1984) moves back in time to the mid-nineteenth century. A work of nonfiction (also connected to a television series) took shape as Bainbridge, following in the footsteps of J. B. Priestley, who traveled through England in 1933 and recorded his impressions in the classic *English Journey*, made her own survey of the same ground, half a century later. Her *English Journey* (1984) is more disarmingly personal, more capricious, than Priestley's, but it shows her to be no less inspired as a social commentator, even if she spends a lot of time opting out of modern life by heading for graveyards. She's at ease among yews and tombstones, which appease her yen for the bygone, the macabre, She dons a helmet and goes down a coal mine when she has to, and fulfills her brief by attending a council meeting in Bradford. She admits to being a nostalgist, and laments the obliteration of narrow cobbled streets and back-to-back insanitary housing, deplored by Priestley in his day. At the same time, she is overtaken by sleepiness as she sits in your quintessential English village with the whole weight of half-timbering, the tourist industry, and overpriced antique shops bearing down on her. Still in nostalgic vein, she includes in the book a tribute to her own Formby, with its Norman church, its schoolhouse complete with bell on the roof, its manor house in a wood of pines: a version of the place that never gets a showing in the novels.

With the tenth Bainbridge novel, *Winter Garden*, the Russian location adds an exotic element to the comic bewilderment, absurdity, and frustration of decent, unimaginative Douglas Ashburner (the leading character), whose plans for blissful adultery abroad fall to pieces around him. Having told his wife he is off to Scotland for a fishing trip, Ashburner hastens instead to Heathrow Airport, bearing his redundant fishing tackle, to meet up with his imperious and histrionic mistress, Nina, and a couple of Nina's fellow artists, uncouth Bernard and sardonic Enid, who are bound for Moscow as guests of the Soviet Artists' Union. But something is amiss with Nina, who slumps instead of striding, has gone on the wagon, wrapped herself in a moth-eaten old fur, and come equipped with a mysterious supply of pills, some of which she foists on Ashburner. Once the striking little party reaches its destination, Nina vanishes altogether, to remain tantalizingly just beyond the reach of Ashburner (or so it seems) throughout the rest of the trip. Some of Ashburner's belongings have also gone astray at Sheremetyev Airport, for he is that quintessential Bainbridge character, the person beset by a mischievous and malevolent fate.

Bare-headed in the snow, bereft of his suitcase and his mistress, stupefied by vodka, and harassed by the constant obligation to visit the

People's Institute, attend the Kirov Theatre, and generally absorb the culture of the country, Ashburner remains in ignorance for some time of the fact that, like others in the party, he has caught a mild dose of clap. Things become increasingly hallucinatory as he is whisked off to a Soviet hospital to witness an operation (mistaken for Nina's brain-surgeon husband). An icon-smuggling racket and other intrigues come into the picture. At the same time, the tone remains wonderfully down-to-earth and sportive, as the author keeps control of all her unruly ingredients, and even, by the end, strikes a note at once enigmatic and elegiac. Suitably elegiac, you might say, for *Winter Garden* marks the end of a run of high-spirited undertakings, full of horrors and hilarity, by means of which Beryl Bainbridge's literary impulse was activated throughout the 1970s. It's true that *An Awfully Big Adventure* (1989) returned her, partially, to this mode, but without the sheer gusto and jubilation that characterize it. In place of these qualities come others, equally alluring, a more measured approach, an increase in density and ambitiousness. Clearly, at some stage, she decided it was time for a change.

HISTORY

IT was also time to slow down and take stock. *Watson's Apology* (1984) was three or four years in the making (after the novel-a-year of the previous decade). Bainbridge has said, a bit tongue-in-cheek, that, having run out of incidents from her own life to dramatize, she was forced to turn to history. History, to begin with, gave her a Victorian murder case, on which she then imposed her own fancies and flourishes. The bare facts were these: in 1871, in Stockwell, South London, an elderly clergyman and retired headmaster named John Watson, in his own front drawing-room, grasped hold of a horse pistol and used it to bash in the head of his wife. Starting from this point, Bainbridge moves backwards to construct a tedious, bitter marriage for the pair, he a schoolmaster and dry-as-dust scholar of limited means, she (when they join forces) an aging spinster plucked from dilapidated circumstances in a Dublin lodging house, sharing rooms with an older sister. Anne Armstrong is her name. A low-key, long-drawn-out episode of domestic angst ensues. This is the bleakest of Beryl Bainbridge's works, and the most claustrophobic. It is written with a new formality, though the old briskness still surfaces from time to time: "Taunton, at fourteen, had climbed on to the roof and hurled stones at the drill sergeant. He had offered no excuse for his behaviour beyond claiming that the hot weather had affected him" (p. 122). The book leaves an unusual aftertaste for a Bainbridge novel (and for all its authority and ironic undertone): a weariness and dreariness of the spirit.

The next "Victorian" novel, by contrast, is a piece of juvenilia, "written June to August 1946," disinterred from a trunk or cupboard, titled *Filthy Lucre*, and published by Duckworth in 1986. It's a charming, full-flavored tale—somewhat in the *Young Visitors* mold, crossed with Robert Louis Stevenson—a tale of love, duplicity, suffering, and ruin, written with a precocious understanding of the conventions of melodrama. The previous year, Duckworth had also brought out a selection of Bainbridge short stories, *Mum and Mr. Armitage*, which are mostly entertaining trifles, siphoned off from the main sources of inspiration. And in 1987 came a follow-up to *English Journey*, called *Forever England*, which deals with the contemporary north/south divide in England.

An Awfully Big Adventure (1989), Bainbridge's twelfth novel, once again mines the author's past, deriving its theme and setting from her stint with the Liverpool Rep. The year is 1950. Stella, the central character, is a Bainbridge ingenue but stranger, spikier than her predecessors, with a gift for posturing and disruption. The title is, of course, borrowed from J. M. Barrie's best-known play—"To die," says Peter Pan, "will be an awfully big adventure"—with the fictional theater company about to mount a new production of this "terrible masterpece" (as one of Barrie's original "lost boys" styled it). Indeed, a suspect strand gets into *Peter Pan*, with its dressed-up death mongering and exploitation of children's faith in fairies, and this makes it a fitting backdrop to the Bainbridge brand of home-brewed disquiet.

Sixteen-year-old Stella has been propelled into the theater by her Uncle Vernon, in acknowledgement of her tendency to act, or overact: "She had a boldness of manner, not to be confused with brashness, and an ability to express herself that was amusing, if at times disconcerting" (p. 82). Stella is reaching maturity by fits and starts, not at all smoothly; an infelicitous infancy has not helped the process. There are things in Stella's past, before her life with Uncle Vernon and Aunt

Lily, that will not bear much examination; and this area of the novel shows an intriguing affinity with some of Barrie's motifs: lost mothers, barred windows, the night light in the nursery. This novel, as well as *Sweet William, The Dressmaker*, and *The Bottle Factory Outing*, has been adapted for film, starring Hugh Grant and Alan Rickman.

The story concerns the unrequited affections prevailing among the cast and producers of *Peter Pan* (Stella's included), and also considers the catalytic side of innocence, without a steady disposition to temper it. Odd things start to happen around Stella—half-hearted suicide attempts, a death in the street, an outbreak of temper on the part of her young colleague Geoffrey, a leg fractured in two places, a drowning. She, in the meantime, savors the agitated state of her feelings on account of Meredith Potter, *Peter Pan's* director, and fails to fathom the sudden constraint on the part of two older actresses when she refers to Meredith's absent consort Hilary as "she." Meredith, who sports a monocle, first pays some attention to Stella and then ignores her, so that she is driven into the arms of a middle-aged actor named O'Hara, who is standing in for Captain Hook after an accident with a spear. Disaster follows. The narrative is both tense and funny, and saturated in the atmosphere of mid-century Liverpool, a seedy milieu full of bomb sites, wild old women hawking firewood from prams, murky alleyways, and flea-bitten urchins up to no good. While atmosphere and background are conjured swiftly and surely in Bainbridge's earliest novels, they assume increasing importance from *Young Adolf* on and come to function as extra plot ingredients in the three most recent Bainbridge works, which form a distinctive "historical" group. She came to write these, she says, almost by accident: her publisher offered her a three-book deal and asked what she'd like to write about. "Off the top of my head I trotted out Scott of the Antarctic, the *Titanic* and the Crimea" (interview in *The Times* with Noreen Taylor, 10 May 1998). However, such accidents are often less a product of chance than they seem.

Winter Garden has some pointed allusions to Cherry-Garrard's account of the polar expedition of 1912, *The Worst Journey in the World*. It seems that this journey, with its unimaginable adversities, had been swirling around in Beryl Bainbridge's head for some years before it took reconstructed shape in her 1991 novel *The Birthday Boys*.

The Birthday Boys covers the period between June 1910 and March 1912, when Captain "Titus" Oates left his tent in a blizzard, announcing that he was going outside and might be some time. The Bainbridge narrative consists of five monologues delivered by doomed members of the expedition, starting with Welshman Petty Officer Evans and ending with Oates, each of which advances the journey a bit further, deeper into the frozen nightmare. This gives the book a formal structure and shows how far the author herself has come since she first adopted a similar framework, back in her apprentice work *A Weekend with Claude*. As Petty Officer Evans puts it, "there's a trick to holding attention, to keeping interest at full pitch" (p. 8); Beryl Bainbridge has quickly mastered it. This engrossing novel isn't short on suspense, even though the outcome of the Scott expedition is pretty well known—how the Norwegian Amundsen stole a march on the English party by beating it to the pole, and how, on the return journey, hellish conditions proved lethal to one after another of the English explorers. What was it all for? "I felt there was something splendid, sublime even, in pitting oneself against the odds" (p. 144), said Lieutenant "Birdie" Bowers, who died with Captain Scott and the scientific observer Dr. Edward near One Ton Camp, where help was waiting. His is the conventionally "masculine" expression of a certain mentality—reckless and grandiose—drawn to the most tremendous feats of endurance; one of Bainbridge's achievements, with this novel, is to accord due respect to this high-flown (and quintessentially Edwardian) notion of "man's gallant battle with the elements," while at the same time humanizing and demystifying her characters, getting them out of their Arctic gear and into everyday clothing. Her adept enactment of each distinctive role in turn takes account of nuances of class, personality, and outlook; the overall impression remains of a company petrified in its collective, ice-bound isolation. An austere, lyrical element surfaces now and again in *The Birthday Boys*, along with a compelling ruefulness: "It's hard to behave like a Boy Scout boiling a billycan on the village green when the cold has paralysed one's mind and swollen one's fingers to the size of bananas" (p. 71). And, though she can't help casting a sardonic eye on commonplaces of the day, including public-school assumptions ("They really must learn that the more beastly the conditions, the harder the slog, the better prepared we shall be for the journey next year," p. 105), she never allows a present-day perspective to distort the perceptions of the past. Like all good historical novelists, she thinks herself back into the ethos of the era.

In the wake of Captain Scott's expedition ship, the *Terra Nova*, comes the *Titanic*. Just a month after Scott and his companions died at the pole, one of the key catastrophes of the twentieth century occurred. The ship feted as the original "floating palace," the last word in luxury and invulnerability, went down on its maiden voyage in the north Atlantic after colliding with an iceberg and was immediately subsumed into a common cultural and mythological store. As an infinitely adaptable symbol, the lost *Titanic*, as well as fueling class antagonism when the numbers of steerage passengers who drowned were compared with those of the dead who had traveled in greater comfort, came to stand as a metaphor for absolutely everything from Ulster Protestant supremacy (the ship was, of course, built in Belfast) and materialism in the modern world to the glamorous era before the cataclysm of the First World War.

None of these aspects of the disaster is crucial to the plot of the fourteenth Bainbridge novel, *Every Man For Himself* (1996), though we may be sure that the author is keeping them all in mind, along with certain more personally symbolic insets and reiterations that link a few of her recent works. Bainbridge's *Titanic* novel suggests more than one interpretation for its title phrase—not just the selfishness of everyone concerned to save his or her own skin, or a bracing directive uttered in the moment of extremity, but the essential mystery of other people. The most extreme instance of this, in the novel, is connected to the person of a middle-aged lawyer, Scurra, who comes wrapped in inscrutability, down to the scar on his lip, for which he proffers a variety of explanations. Bitten by a parrot, gored by a bull, wounded in a duel: you can take your pick.

Scurra is one of the characters, real and imaginary, assembled by Bainbridge at the top end of the magnificent ship. The focus of interest in the novel is a young man, Morgan, an invented character, nephew of the real-life J. Pierpont Morgan of the White Star Line, but endowed with shady beginnings like other Bainbridge protagonists. Who was his mother? Who was his father? There are no straight answers to these and other ques-

tions. But it doesn't matter. Morgan's position in society is assured; he wants to be a naval architect, and to this end his uncle has had him placed in the office of Thomas Andrews at Harland & Wolf's Shipyard in Belfast. In the meantime, on board ship, he's enjoying cavorting and flirting with young bloods such as Lord Melchett, a Van Hopper, and a Ginsberg, and a self-willed young American beauty named Wallis Ellery. Believing he's been summoned to Wallis's stateroom, and hurrying there in an excess of jubilation, Morgan finds he has been preceded by Scurra. Unable to leave for fear of discovery, Morgan is forced to eavesdrop on the subsequent bout of lovemaking. This personal drama, which precedes the ready-made drama of the shipwreck, forms a kind of subsidiary climax. Nothing much happens otherwise, though the narrative does contain a few subplots involving chance and coincidence. For example, on the opening page, a man suffers a heart attack and dies in Morgan's arms in a London square. Later, on the *Titanic*, a statuesque singer is on the verge of throwing herself overboard—unaware that she might save herself the trouble since she's destined to go overboard in any case. The attempted suicide is due to the failure of her lover to join her at Cherbourg, as he'd promised. The two incidents, the lover's absence and the death in the street, turn out to be connected. (A further subplot brings in a high couture creation, a wondrous dress, the gown of ice, that functions in the end as nothing more complicated than a symbol of lost, breathtaking beauty and workmanship.)

There were other things caught upon the water—chairs and tables, crates, an empty gin bottle, a set of bagpipes, a cup without a handle, a creased square of canvas with a girl's face painted on it; and two bodies, she in a gown of ice with a mermaid's tail, he in shirt sleeves, the curls stiff as wood shavings on his head, his two hands frozen to the curve of a metal rail. Beyond, where the sun was beginning to show its burning rim, smoke blew from a funnel.

(p. 224)

Every Man for Himself is narrated by Morgan, who survives. He recounts the four days leading up to the chance encounter with the iceberg; and before it plunges us into darkness and death, we've been plunged, with Morgan, into a social whirl, a kind of compressed F. Scott Fitzgerald scenario, involving exuberant young people, older aristocrats with names such as Astor and Vanderbilt, tours of the ship, a fear of class cross-purposes to add an astringent touch. As with *The Birthday Boys* knowing what's in store doesn't diminish the interest of the foregoing urbanities and japes. And, when the crunch comes, a kind of orderly fatalism and paternalistic instinct take over. The mysterious Scurra is still uttering his cryptic pronouncements as he stands braced against a tilting rail: "Remember, Morgan, not the height, only the drop, is terrible" (p. 7). Bainbridge assumes male and female narrative voices with equal facility. Getting under the skin of another person, of whatever gender, is a resource she found available to her from *A Quiet Life* on. With that novel, she made the decision to impersonate someone close to her—her brother—to achieve certain narrative effects. Thereafter, she gained the confidence and aplomb to move into more and more remote and unknown areas, both spatially and psychologically. *Master Georgie* (1998), the third in the historical sequence, takes us from 1840s Liverpool to the Black Sea area during the Crimean War. Like other Bainbridge books, it uses the device of the posed photograph (an art form at the time in its infancy) to define each section and suggest its flavor; it also has three first-person narrators, each of whom comes center stage to take up the story at an appropriate point. And what a story it is—of obsession, class mobility, surrogate motherhood, foreign travel, field hospitals, carnage, and more, and more: all compressed, with the utmost vividness, into 190 pages.

It begins in 1846 with the collapse of a Punch and Judy van—and consequent exposure of the showman's illusion—witnessed by Myrtle, a girl, probably twelve years old, taken as a foundling into the Hardy family of Liverpool, and possessed of an innate inner soundness and shrewdness, despite her extreme and unending attachment to a son of the family, George Hardy ("Master Georgie"). Myrtle's opening narrative gives an account of the death, in a brothel, of her benefactor Mr. Hardy, and of her involvement, by Master Georgie, in a hurried operation to get the dissolute corpse home to its own bed and thereby avoid a scandal. Another person is roped in to lend a hand with these fraught proceedings, a street boy named Pompey Jones, known as "the duckboy," whose fortunes, like Myrtle's, will take an upward turn from this catalytic incident onward. The dead lecher is trundled safely home in a van, coincidentally the overturned Punch and Judy van, which will reappear

years later on the battlefield of Inkerman: thus are certain emblems and fixed points of reference distributed to anchor various elements of the story.

Myrtle, like a good many heroines of Victorian literature, is sent away to boarding school to be "made into a lady"; henceforth she's supposed by many people to be Master Georgie's sister, and has to remind herself to call him George. Pompey Jones—the second narrator—becomes a photographer's assistant; his function in the novel is to act as a kind of minor lord of misrule, a mischief maker, though he's as complex a character as most of the other players in the drama. He is also bisexual, unlike George, who prefers boys, though George is married by 1854 and is the father (clandestinely) of a couple of children by Myrtle, with his wife's, Annie's, connivance, and as a consequence of her miscarriages and eventual infertility. George becomes a surgeon and travels to Constantinople, taking his entourage—wife, children, sister, brother-in-law, and others—with him. When the Crimean War is declared, he sends them back home to England, though both Myrtle, because she refuses to let George out of her sight, and George's brother-in-law Dr. Potter, who is a geologist and an observer (and the third narrator), remain. Along with some 64,000 British, French, and Turkish troops, the remains of the Hardy party sail from Varna to the western shore of the Crimea, where an army camp is set up at Kalamita Bay, before the order comes to march on to Sebastopol. There follow extraordinary scenes of suffering, hallucination, and carnage.

Our progress was slow and lurching. The planks of wood laid down by the picquets had mostly been torn up to be used for firewood, and those that remained had long since sunk into the mud. In places the oak bushes grew thickly, impeding the wooden wheels of the cart. At intervals the mist cleared and the grey columns of marching men could be seen slipping and sliding through the grey daylight. . . . Once, when the fog shifted to reveal a fountain of flame spurting upon the horizon, I conjured up the sunset spreading across the sky beyond the humpbacked bridge, and in the puffs of gory smoke belching along the rise imagined I glimpsed the eucalyptus leaves quivering above the stream.

(p. 181)

Pompey Jones—on a stomach-churning assignment for the Royal College of Surgeons (to photograph wounds)—turns up on the way to Inkerman. The novel ends as it began, with a corpse propped up to look as if it were alive, to be photographed for posterity. Bainbridge seems to be implying here that the photographer's art, like the novelist's, will preserve the moment but may also distort it. *Master Georgie* is written with a staggering conviction and a sure feeling for the strangeness and intensity of the past. Bainbridge was short-listed for the Booker Prize for the fourth time; *Every Man for Himself* was also nominated, as well as winning the Whitbread Novel of the Year award.

CONCLUSION

REGARDLESS of what she says to the contrary, Bainbridge has a strong inventive faculty. As she herself acknowledges, she disappears into whatever aspect of her personality she has chosen to stress, whether it is the hesitant assertiveness of Brenda in *The Bottle Factory Outing* or the teenage rebelliousness of Madge in *A Quiet Life*.

She is not a novelist who has greatly concerned herself with that most English of leitmotivs, distinctions of class. This is partly through having begun her career in the radical, egalitarian 1960s and partly because the subject simply doesn't interest her. When she has to acknowledge its existence, as she does with her historical re-creations, it is treated less as an issue than as a fact of life. For this reason and others, it is hard to classify Beryl Bainbridge, to assign her to any single category of writing—if you try, she immediately ducks out of it. She jettisoned her "newspaper plots" when she'd had enough of them, and went from being a sharp-tongued chronicler of women's discontents to someone riveted, along with her character Morgan, by "the sublime thermodynamics of the *Titanic*'s marine engineering" (p. 36). She takes the technical requirements of an Antarctic expedition in stride.

The little-known English novelist Barbara Comyns (1909–1992) has been cited as a possible influence, though in fact Comyns' faux-naivete and fairy-tale poignancy are as alien to Beryl Bainbridge as the carnival exuberance of Angela Carter or the A. S. Byatt's blend of naturalism, scholarship, and discursiveness. She does not create caustic feminist fables in the manner of Fay Weldon, or even—though this is closer—aspire to a Sparkian obliquity. She is unique and incomparable, a vibrant truth teller, an outstanding entertainer, the laureate of Liverpool, a master of the colorful exigency, a subversive humorist, and possessor of one of the most distinctive voices in contemporary fiction.

SELECTED BIBLIOGRAPHY

I. NOVELS. *A Weekend with Claude* (London, 1967 and 1981); *Another Part of the Wood* (London, 1968 and 1979); *Harriet Said . . .* (London, 1972); *The Dressmaker* (London, 1973); *The Bottle Factory Outing* (London, 1974); *Sweet William* (London, 1975); *A Quiet Life* (London, 1976); *Injury Time* (London, 1977); *Young Adolf* (London, 1978); *Winter Garden* (London, 1980); *Watson's Apology* (London, 1984); *An Awfully Big Adventure* (London, 1989); *The Birthday Boys* (London, 1991); *Every Man for Himself* (London, 1996); *Master Georgie* (London, 1998).

II. STORIES AND JUVENILIA. *Mum and Mr. Armitage* (London, 1985); *Filthy Lucre* (London, 1986).

III. NONFICTION. *English Journey* (London, 1984); *Forever England* (London, 1987).

IV. INTERVIEWS AND REVIEWS. Julia O'Faolain, "Getting Away with Murder," in *New York Times Book Review* (20 March 1977); Lorna Sage, "Comedy of Horrors," in *Observer* (5 November 1978); Diane Johnson, "Young Adolf," in *Times Literary Supplement* (1 December 1978); Beryl Bainbridge, "The Lullaby Sound of Houses Falling Down," in *Sunday Times* (19 July 1981); John Morrish, Interview with Beryl Bainbridge, in *Daily Telegraph* (10 September 1996); Gabrielle Annan, "Only the Drop," in *London Review of Books* (17 October 1996); Noreen Taylor, Interview with Beryl Bainbridge, in *The Times* (10 May 1998); Sarah Rigby, "Mind's Eye," in *London Review of Books* (4 June 1998).

BEOWULF

Paul Bibire

BEOWULF IS UNCONTROVERSIALLY the finest surviving Old English poem and one of the finest from the so-called Dark Ages of western Europe. At 3,182 verse lines it is the longest known Old English poem, and the second longest in any ancient Germanic language after the Old Saxon *Heliand* of 5,983 lines. In range it is of epic scale, and although far shorter than the classical epics, it can in quality of poetry and seriousness of purpose reasonably be compared with the Homeric poems and Virgil's *Aeneid*. It tells the story of a hero, Beowulf, who during a long life fought and slew two troll-like monsters and a dragon. This tale is set against a background of sixth-century Scandinavian heroic legend, war, and rumors of war. It is to this extent a window into the world of Germanic legend. In its central figure, however, it examines heroic endeavor in absolute terms.

PRESERVATION AND PRESENTATION OF THE POEM

THE unnamed poem now known as *Beowulf* is written in Old English, that is, English earlier than about 1120 A.D. It is of unknown authorship. It survives on folios (leaves) 132–201v (129–198v according to the numbering used by Julius Zupitza and Friedrich Klaeber) of a single manuscript, MS BL Cotton Vitellius A. XV, sometimes known as the *Beowulf* or Nowell codex. The manuscript was written around the year 1000 or very soon thereafter. Its medieval origin and history are unknown, though it may have been written in the south of England. There is no record of it before it belonged to Laurence Nowell, dean of Lichfield (d. 1576); his name and the date 1563 are written at the top of its first page. It then entered the collection of Sir Robert Cotton (1571–1631), which is now part of the British Library. Facsimiles of the manuscript, with valuable additional material, have been edited by Zupitza, Kemp Malone, and Kevin Kiernan. Preceding items in the manuscript are three Old English prose texts: an incomplete homily on Saint Christopher, *Wonders of the East*, and *Alexander's Letter to Aristotle*. Following *Beowulf* in the manuscript as now bound is the fragmentary Old English poem *Judith*.

The manuscript was written by two scribes, with the change of scribes taking place in midsentence (within line 1939 of *Beowulf*) at the end of the third written line of folio 175v (172v in Zupitza and Klaeber). There is a pattern of wormholes on folios 192–201, which does not continue into folios 202–209. This shows that *Beowulf* was once at the end of the manuscript, indicating that, although *Judith* was written by the second scribe of *Beowulf*, it was not originally bound as the final text. The composition of the manuscript, and any thematic unity of its texts, have been much discussed.

The manuscript was damaged in a fire in the Cottonian library in 1731. This damage mostly affected the upper outside edges of leaves, which due to scorching have continued to deteriorate. Early transcripts and facsimiles of the manuscript are therefore important in recovering some readings. There is also some damage to the last leaf of the poem, which is torn and rubbed, and substantial water damage to folio 182r (179r in Zupitza and Klaeber), and some of the text on that page is not continuously readable; some visible readings have probably been subsequently touched up. The end of the poem is probably complete, and again indicates that *Beowulf* must have been positioned at the end of the manuscript, since the final words are crammed in below the last ruled line of folio 201v, as if the scribe was trying to fit them all in. The text of the poem therefore seems to be substantially complete.

The poem in the manuscript is divided into "fits": an unnumbered initial section and forty-three numbered sections. These usually vary in length between 43 and 112 lines. The functions of this division are unknown, though sometimes fit breaks seem to appear at structural points in the poem.

The existing manuscript was fairly carefully copied, and the scribes seem to have checked and corrected their own work. Nonetheless, the text of the poem is frequently corrupt, in that it often makes neither sense nor meter. In most instances this corruption can be explained by copying errors, and clearly the scribes did not always understand what they were writing. Sometimes they or previous scribes seem to have mistaken an unfamiliar letter-form from an earlier script; sometimes they mistook an unfamiliar word or earlier form of a word; in both cases this can sometimes make it possible to suggest a date for the earlier exemplar being copied. In some instances the text is so corrupt that it remains unintelligible. The degree and complexity of textual corruption in *Beowulf* indicates multiple layers of copying error, and therefore that the poem had been copied many times before it was copied into the present manuscript. Modern editors can often suggest plausible emendations to restore the text; frequently, however, editorial emendation is no more than guesswork, and alternative guesses are equally plausible.

Punctuation and word division in medieval manuscripts were marked on largely different principles from present practice. Punctuation here is sparse and seems mostly to be structural; compound words are usually divided, but prepositions are usually written continuously with the following word. There is virtually nothing corresponding to the modern use of capital letters at the beginnings of sentences or names, though larger letters are written at the beginning of sections. No metrical line division is indicated. Virtually all punctuation, word division, line division, and capitalization in modern editions are therefore due to editors.

Present-day printed editions always incorporate emendation, and modern word division, line division, punctuation, and capitalization, because they are intended for use by modern readers. They are modern editorial constructs, which depend upon the perception and judgment of their editors. They are therefore necessarily subjective products of their editors' understanding of the poem. The editors make the poem say what they think it says. Happily, the poem has been blessed with scrupulous, sensitive, and thoughtful editors, notably Klaeber and George Jack.

Beowulf is very difficult to translate into modern English. Even where the text is sound and modern understanding of it is secure, translators cannot reproduce the range of implication created within it. The thought-world of the poem is largely alien to that imposed by modern English. Translations that try to re-create the heroic aspects of the poem usually seem bombastic; those that try to reproduce its sense sound stilted. No modern translation into English can be unconditionally recommended. Editions with parallel glosses into modern English give some access to the original poem: of these, Michael Alexander's is most suitable for the beginner, Jack's for the more advanced student.

COMPOSITION OF THE POEM

THE date of composition of *Beowulf* is unknown. Composition has been proposed in any period from the late seventh to the early eleventh century A.D. Dates significantly earlier are improbable on linguistic grounds and because of the Christian presentation of the content of the poem; and the poem obviously cannot be later than the date of its manuscript. The collapse of English cultural activity during much of the ninth century, under the impact of Viking invasions, has caused most scholars to consider that period unlikely. The eighth century, the time of Bede and Alcuin, was the traditionally favored period for composition of the poem, and is supported by some linguistic and metrical evidence. In reaction to this many scholars now favor the tenth century, subsequent to the educational reforms of the Anglo-Saxon king Alfred the Great and the Benedictine Revival. Whether or not the poem was composed late, it seems to record details of earlier periods: for example, boar-helmets (lines 303–306) are only found in the archaeological record of the pre-Viking period.

The place of composition is likewise unknown; an assumed association with the Northumbria of Bede and Alcuin has been supplemented by suggested links with Wessex, and the pre-Viking Anglo-Saxon kingdoms of Mercia and East Anglia, on the basis of supposed dynastic references within the poem. On such grounds it would also be possible to link the poem with the one remaining Anglo-Saxon kingdom, Kent. In short, cases can be made for the composition of the poem everywhere in Anglo-Saxon England.

Circumstances of composition can only be deduced from the poem. Its courtly and aristocratic tone, as well as its obsessive concern with the ethics of kingship, strongly suggest an intended noble or royal audience. But it gives virtually no reference to most of the practical aspects of aristocratic or royal activity, and in particular makes no mention of the legal functions of the king as law-giver and judge, which seem to have been central to Anglo-Saxon kingship. It is also a learned poem; it may contain verbal echoes of Virgil and seems to use philosophical ideas derived from or through the Roman philosopher Boethius. It gives a wide range of allusive and often indirect reference to material from the early parts of the Bible as well as to native legend. It also seems to have been composed in writing, since it appears to contain many internal cross-references of content forward and backward within the poem, sometimes spanning many hundreds of lines. This implies the ability to flip forward and backward in a book. Literacy, however, was largely limited to churchmen for most of the Old English period, and writing materials were usually only available in monastic scriptoria. For these reasons many scholars have assumed a monastic context for the composition and intended performance of the poem. These possibilities are easily reconciled, since many monasteries were founded by kings or noblemen and received subsequent aristocratic endowment. Younger members of noble or royal families often entered the Church and became abbots, and kings not infrequently retired to their monasteries in old age. This removed possible contenders for succession and made provision for an elderly king's incapacity, ensuring that a suitable and vigorous heir could peacefully succeed to the realm. Such monasteries were therefore not only institutions of Christian learning but also effectively aristocratic or royal courts within the Church.

Since the authorship of *Beowulf* is unknown, the method of its composition is also unknown. It has been strongly argued that the poem was composed in oral improvisation, since like all other Old English poetry it uses verbal formulae, that is, semi-stable phrasing echoed widely within the poem and often elsewhere. This view has been much disputed, and is not held by the present writer. Oral techniques may be used in written composition because the work was intended for oral performance or because it was composed in a tradition which had once been oral: both of these are probable for most Old English poetry. *Beowulf* may also have been intended to create the illusion of orality, since it self-consciously recounts ancient tales, some of which must have been received from oral tradition. This is supported by formulaic phrases

such as "I heard," "we have found out by asking," and the absence of references to written sources as such. In any case, formulaic wording and construction are an unreliable test for orality, since they are used in many traditions which are certainly not primarily oral (for instance, in English eighteenth-century pastoral poetry).

Most of those who have tried to study *Beowulf* as a poem believe that it was composed by a single poet, but that belief is based simply upon apparent unity of tone, style, and compositional technique, and upon an internally consistent approach to its content. This does not exclude the use of earlier poetry, perhaps underlying the so-called Finnesburh episode (lines 1068–1159), suggested by Alistair Campbell on the basis of an unusual concentration of rare and archaic vocabulary. Interpolation—insertion of extra material—was suggested on stylistic grounds by J. R. R. Tolkien for lines 175–188, though stylistic peculiarities in this passage are adequately explained by the subject matter, and the passage uses vocabulary and imagery entirely integrated into the poem: for instance, the imagery of hellfire here is arguably required for understanding passages elsewhere, such as the description of the funeral pyre in the Finnesburh episode.

Beowulf is composed in the meter and diction common to all ancient Germanic verse: the surviving poetry of Old English, Old Saxon, and Old High German, and more remotely that of Old Norse, the Scandinavian language of the Vikings. This meter survived into the Middle English period and was revived in poems such as *Sir Gawain and the Green Knight* and William Langland's *Piers Ploughman* in the fourteenth century. The metrical unit is the half line, which is a single rhythmic phrase containing a minimum of four syllables, two of which are usually stressed. Pairs of half lines are linked into lines by alliteration on at least the first stressed syllables in each half line. There is no metrically functional rhyme nor is the number of syllables in the half line significant beyond a minimum of four. There is a specialized poetic vocabulary, almost entirely restricted to nouns which only appear in poetry throughout the ancient Germanic languages. This provides a large body of near synonyms for concepts important to heroic poetry, such as "warrior," "sword," and "renown." The diction also permits large-scale creation of compound nouns, using elements both from ordinary and poetic vocabulary. *Beowulf* appears to exploit this with unusual freedom, and many of its compounds are unique to the poem. The meter and diction appear to have been independently inherited from their common past by all the poetic traditions which used them; they must therefore be old and originally oral.

Old English poetic syntax also differs from that of prose; in poetry, the technique of "parallelism and variation" is frequently used where a sentence is not linear but revolves around repetition of its central concepts, each time expressed in different terms, showing these concepts in different aspects and contexts. *Beowulf* differs in meter, syntax, and diction from most other Old English poems in ways which are likely to be more archaic.

THE STORY OF THE POEM

AGAINST a background of Germanic heroic and Scandinavian dynastic legend, the story of the hero Beowulf is presented. The accounts of Beowulf's three monster fights are the only parts of the poem directly narrated in full, linear, and logical order, and each of the first two is also told continuously, uninterrupted by subordinate narrative. The hero does nothing else directly recounted at firsthand in the poem.

Beowulf is a Geat, that is, from the kingdom of the Geatas (Norse "Gautar"), a historical people who lived in what is now southern Sweden; their name is preserved in Swedish "Väster-" and "Östergötland" (West- and East-Gautland), and in the name of the city of Göteborg (Norse "Gautaborg," fortress of the Gautar; English "Gothenburg"). He is the son of the sister of Hygelac, the king of the Geatas.

For twelve years a troll-like monster, Grendel, has afflicted the court of the aged Danish king, Hrothgar,[1] at Heorot, rampaging around at nighttime eating Danes. The young Beowulf hears of this and sails to Denmark with some companions. Hrothgar eagerly welcomes him when he offers to stay up overnight in Heorot and tackle the monster. The Danes retire to a safe distance. Grendel

comes, and Beowulf wrestles with him; the companions' weapons will not bite on Grendel. Beowulf tears Grendel's arm off and the monster flees, mortally wounded.

The following night Grendel's mother visits the hall to avenge her son and kills another Dane. Beowulf and the others follow the bloodstained track to a strange mere, beneath which the monsters live. He dives into the mere, while the Danes and his followers sit beside it. Grendel's mother grabs him on the way down and takes him into her underwater hall, where they wrestle; his sword will not bite on her head. Beowulf is thrown by Grendel's mother, who sits upon him. But he then sees a second, giantish sword hanging on the wall; he grabs it and beheads her. He then finds Grendel's lifeless corpse and beheads that too. The sword blade is destroyed by the "poison" of Grendel's blood. Meanwhile the Danes have seen the monster's blood in the water and think that Beowulf is dead; they leave. Beowulf swims up through the mere, carrying Grendel's head and the hilt of the sword. His own men meet him and, rejoicing, they return to Heorot with Grendel's head and the sword hilt. After much feasting and gift giving Beowulf goes home and reports the events to Hygelac.

Time passes. Hygelac is long dead, fallen in Frisia, and his son has fallen in dynastic wars against the Swedes. Beowulf has taken the throne and ruled for fifty years. But a runaway slave finds a burial mound full of treasure and steals a cup from it. The dragon which guards the hoard is aroused and burns a royal hall in revenge. The aged Beowulf takes up weapons to deal with the dragon, and with a group of companions challenges it. Only one of the companions, Wiglaf, does not flee in cowardice. Beowulf's sword does not bite upon the dragon's head, and he is wounded in the fight. But Wiglaf stabs the dragon lower down, and Beowulf is able to decapitate it with a second sword. Dying from the poison of the dragon's bite, Beowulf bequeaths the kingship to Wiglaf. The poem ends with Beowulf's funeral pyre and barrow burial; the dragon's treasure is placed in Beowulf's own barrow "as useless as it was before." He is lamented by his men, who ride around the barrow.

This is the main narrative of the poem and the only one told in logical sequence. The synopsis has been deliberately told here in folktale style because the story, and particularly its central

---

[1] Old English used three extra letters, æ (probably pronounced like the *a* of *cat*), þ (mostly pronounced like the *th* of *bath*) and ð (mostly pronounced like the *th* of *bathe*). In this essay, Old English æ is used throughout, but þ and ð are transcribed as *th* in the main discussion, as an aid to the reader. They are only retained in explicit citation or quotation. So Old English *Hroþgar* is transcribed here as *Hrothgar*.

episode, is known from a very large number of other retellings, or "analogues," recorded widely across the world mostly in folktale form. Friedrich Panzer called the basic narrative the "Bear's Son" tale, and Antti Aarne and Stith Thompson refer to it as "The Three Stolen Princesses," but it is also known from many medieval Icelandic sagas (for example, *Grettis saga, Samsons saga fagra, Gull-Þóris saga*) in forms which seem particularly close to *Beowulf*. It may remotely and ultimately be related to myths of a heroic or divine fight against a demonic dragon figure, such as that of Herakles (Hercules) against the Hydra and Apollo against the Python in Greek legend and myth, Indra against Vritra in Hindu mythology, or even that of Thor against the World Serpent in Norse mythology. The story, therefore, was not invented for this poem, and almost all its details appear in many other analogues. It is of immeasurable antiquity and may carry mythic implications.

The poem, however, tells its ancient tale of monster slaying in Christian heroic mode, just as the *Odyssey* tells tales of trickery and magic in epic mode. The poem states that Grendel is a descendant of Cain, the first fratricide, whose offspring were wicked men, monsters, and giants exiled in perpetual feud against God. A feud within a family, the endless cycle of vengeance, can never be brought to an end, for revenge must be taken on those who should take it; compensation paid by those who should receive it. All human beings are members of Adam's family, and all inherit Cain's feud. All human hatred and war follow from this. This interpretation of biblical narrative in terms of Germanic social and legal practice gives the entire poem a strong metaphysical basis.

Grendel attacks the hall because in his exiled misery he cannot bear the sounds of innocent joy coming from it, and above all the bright song of the minstrel telling how God created the unfallen world, just as Hrothgar the king had built the hall as a joyful human microcosm of God's creation. Beowulf's fight with Grendel continues the first feud, which began with Cain and Abel, and which involves all humanity in unending conflict.

And so it proves here: Grendel's mother comes to take vengeance. The description of Grendel's mere (lines 1357–1376) is of a monstrous otherworld, and is closely related to a description of hell in the Old English *Vision of St. Paul*. Unlike in the first fight, Beowulf is nearly defeated in the encounter with Grendel's mother and is only apparently saved by divine intervention. After slaying Grendel's mother with an apparently supernatural sword, the waters of the mere are cleansed. The sword hilt bears an appropriate depiction of the biblical destruction of the Cain-descended giants in the Flood. On Beowulf's return to Heorot, the aged Hrothgar, gazing at the hilt, is moved to a long "sermon" (lines 1700–1784), in which he recounts the downfall of named and exemplary unnamed kings through pride and warns Beowulf against pride.

The narrative of the dragon fight is given a much grimmer tone: on hearing of the dragon, Beowulf fears that he has enraged God, and his preparations for the fight are without any real hope of his own survival. He reminisces at great length on the wars and fratricide in his own dynasty that brought him to his present position. His only claim for himself is that he did not murder his own companions. The dragon is not presented as a metaphysical emblem of diabolical malice, but almost sympathetically, as a creature wronged and seeking vengeance. At Beowulf's death, Wiglaf and the other Geatas expect nothing other than the long-delayed vengeance of Swedes and Merovingians upon their lordless people. Their lamentation for his fall seems also a lament for the passing of all human glory, all human achievement, which vanishes like the smoke of the funeral pyre upon the wind.

Christian heroic mode, loosely termed, was available throughout Old English poetry, and usefully enabled Old English poets to use native heroic diction and literary models for Christian purposes. It is based on the ancient metaphor of the warfare of the Christian soul, presented by Saint Paul (Ephesians 6), and Paul's account of the spiritual armor of the soul given there (vv. 13–17) is certainly echoed almost explicitly in Hrothgar's sermon (lines 1743–1746). This metaphor enables Christian ethics to be mapped upon the pre-Christian heroic values of honor and loyalty. It is used, for instance, when the poet of the Old English poem *The Dream of the Rood* describes Christ as a young warrior as he advances toward Crucifixion, a lord to be slain by his own anguished retainer, the Cross. In *Beowulf*, however, this poetic mode is developed differently and far further, to provide an entire wordview, where heroic glory can stand for all human achievement. But that achievement is wholly subverted by the horrific reality of feud and fratricide, murder and war, the damnable means of death which underlie and end all heroic endeavor. And above heroism, the Christian perspective gives an overarching and timeless metaphysical framework, as it were the view from the other side of death. Within that perspective even the noblest and most beautiful of all human endeavor and achievement is transient and therefore ultimately tragic.

This interpretation of the poem's central narrative is based largely on that given by Tolkien, in *The Monsters and the Critics*, in 1936. It has substantially withstood subsequent shifts in critical fashion, despite obvious dependence upon Tolkien's own melancholic Catholicism; this he may share with those who originally composed and read, performed, or heard the poem.

CHRISTIAN CONTENT IN THE POEM

BEOWULF is very much a Christian poem and was composed for a Christian audience. It makes frequent moral comment upon its content, both directly and in the speeches of some of its characters, particularly Hrothgar. It is particularly concerned with the ethics of kingship: what constitutes a good or a bad ruler. These opposed ideas are constantly elaborated and deepened through the course of the poem. In the first lines of the poem, the "good king" is defined simply as successful in the achievement of honor, with Scyld Scefing, the founder of the legendary Danish dynasty. This gradually develops into a very complex understanding, full of internal ethical tensions, by the time of the memorial lay for Beowulf, who by the end of the poem has himself become the archetypal good king.

Biblical citation in the poem is not infrequent, but overt reference is restricted to the earliest parts of Genesis only: in particular the narratives of Cain and the Flood. This sets the content of the poem firmly in an Old Testament, prepatriarchal context, before revelatory prophecy, before revelation of divinely ordained moral law, let alone before revelation of redemption. The characters of the poem occupy a fallen world, stained by Cain's fratricide, but as yet without revealed knowledge. Any religious understanding they may possess must be acquired through "natural religion," perception of God through observation of the created world, such as described by Paul in Romans 1:19–20. Therefore they know of God, but only as creator and ruler of the world which they inhabit.

He is usually named only in the terms of power and kingship appropriate to Genesis, only rarely as Father, and then usually in Christian comments on the content of the narrative. Christ and the Holy Spirit are not explicitly named.

The poem contains only one explicit reference to paganism (lines 175–188), there described as devil worship; otherwise its characters are presented as pre-Christian, not heathen. However, there may be one instance of inexplicit but probably intentional use of Germanic pagan myth in the poem: the account of a fratricide within the royal house of the Geatas, in which Hæthcyn killed his elder brother Herebeald (lines 2434–2449). This is almost certainly the same story as the Norse pagan myth in which the god Höthr killed his brother Baldr. Quite apart from the names and the central action, the account contains several superficially self-contradictory or nonfunctional "blind" details, which only make sense when interpreted in terms of the myth. The apparent contradictions and discontinuities are emphasized in the wording of the passage, which probably indicates that they are intended to draw attention to the underlying narrative. The myth is recast in terms of heroic legend; it is thereby set within the human world, and so can function in the poem in much the same way as the biblical narrative of Cain and Abel. This pagan myth may also have been used in *The Dream of the Rood*, there applied to the Crucifixion of Christ. Perhaps this shows the attitude that paganism was not merely diabolical delusion or error, but rather a partial and flawed reflection of Christian truth: a useful means for Christians to avoid damning their own pagan ancestors.

There may be considerable inexplicit biblical reference in the poem. The clearest examples are the extended and developed use of David imagery just before Hrothgar's sermon, and the use of imagery derived apparently directly from Ephesians 6 in the sermon (lines 1743–1746).

There is no explicit Christian allegory in the poem, though many scholars have suggested possible allegorical interpretations. Figures such as Grendel and his mother are not presented as allegorical, and are given religious significance by other means. The dragon is given very little overt significance in the poem; it is presented very much as a physical animal, living its own life with its own purposes until unhappily disturbed. But within both Germanic legend and myth, and within Christian imagery, the dragon is not elsewhere a natural animal; at best it is someone, a human or superhuman being, who has taken the form of a dragon. It is a potent religious symbol: the monstrous final opponent of the gods or of God, whether it is the World Serpent, enemy of Thor, or the satanic dragon of the Apocalypse. Neither interpretation is overtly present in *Beowulf*; neither can be excluded.

The use of Christian modes of expression and understanding sets up a great divide within *Beowulf*, between its implied audience and the characters within it. The poem self-consciously looks back to another time, when things were different: those in possession of revealed Christian truth gaze back on a world before prophecy, before law, before revelation, before hope.

LEGENDARY MATERIAL IN THE POEM

BEOWULF contains or refers to many narratives other than its central story. Most of these are presented as if historical, but except in one instance they cannot be historically verified; they are at best regarded as "legendary history," and in many cases simply as legend. The poem seems to show an encyclopedic attitude to legend and to include as many references as it reasonably can. The effect is to re-create the world of Germanic heroic legend around its own central story. This extends the horizons of the poem across the Germanic world and gives a frame of reference for evaluation. One other Old English poem *Deor*, preserved in a late-tenth-century manuscript, also gives brief fragments of a range of legends thematically organized within an overall narrative frame. A similar encyclopedic attitude appears in the Old English poem *Widsith*, which refers to many of the same legends. *Widsith*, preserved in the same manuscript as *Deor* and perhaps containing ancient material, gives catalogs of legendary persons and peoples, Germanic, biblical, and classical, known to the Anglo-Saxons, occasionally with extremely brief fragments of narrative attached to individual figures. These poems show a sense of the unity of bodies of legend, which later produced the large cyclic compilations of the High Middle Ages such as the Norse *þiðreks saga* and *Karlamagnus saga*, and which also affected Arthurian romance and saints' lives.

The story of *Beowulf* is set entirely in legendary Scandinavia of approximately the sixth century A.D. The poem four times refers to one historically verifiable and datable event: Hygelac's raid on Frisia, which ended with his defeat and death at the hands of the Hetware and Merovingians (that is, Franks), for example at lines 2914–2921. Gregory of Tours's *Historia Francorum* (written before 594) and the *Liber Historiae Francorum* (written around 727) record a Scandinavian raid on the lands of the Attuarii, led by one Ch(l)ochilaicus, identified as a Danish king, who was defeated and killed by the Merovingian prince Theudebert in around 521 A.D. Of the name forms as recorded in *Liber Historiae Francorum*, "Chochilaicus" is certainly an attempt to represent an early form of the name which after undergoing regular Old English phonological changes appears in *Beowulf* as "Hygelac." Similarly, "Attuarii" safely corresponds to Old English "Hetware." The identification of the persons and event is therefore secure. Further, the names could not have been borrowed by *Beowulf* from the extant written Frankish sources without an improbably exact knowledge of the phonological development of prehistoric Old English to transform them into the correct English forms. They must therefore have been inherited through an English tradition of Hygelac's Frisian raid, possibly also attested by a reference in the *Liber Monstrorum*. Other events recounted within the poem are also told in Scandinavian dynastic legend, and are there attributed to roughly the same period. *Beowulf* and the Scandinavian legendary texts therefore both report a common body of legend dealing with prehistoric Scandinavia, and some of this legend may have a basis in historical fact.

It cannot be unquestioningly accepted that other apparently factual dynastic material, reported in *Beowulf* and the Scandinavian legendary sources, represents genuine Scandinavian legend or history. The Old English and Old Norse name forms and narratives which tell of the Danish king Hrothgar and his nephew Hrothulf, and their royal hall of Heorot, all also named in *Widsith*, are clearly if controversially similar to the fourth-century history of the Goths and Huns as reported by the Latin historian Jordanes and others, and Erulian histories as reported by Procopius and in Paul the Deacon's *Historia Langobardorum*. The name forms, consistent and widespread in the narratives of these figures, correspond strikingly with the forms used specifically by Jordanes. These detailed similarities extend across a range of names and narrative elements not generally typical of Germanic heroic legend, and seem to go beyond coincidence. If they are not coincidental, they point to a large-scale transference of fourth-century Gothic, Hunnish, and Erulian history on to Danish dynastic legend. If so, this is likely to have been a learned undertaking, using in particular material derived directly from Jordanes.

There is little direct evidence for a centralized, unitary Danish monarchy before the ninth century. Certainly figures who bore the title "king" (Old English *cyning*; Norse *konungr*; represented by Latin *rex*) existed far earlier, but then the term may have meant little more than "clan chief": "king" is derived from "kin" (kindred, family). There is good evidence for adjacent early or archaic Germanic societies without unitary monarchies, but ruled by local chieftains: such societies include the Old Saxons before their conquest by Charlemagne, the Norwegians before the late ninth century, and the Icelanders before the thirteenth century. *Beowulf* itself reports (lines 14–16) that the Danes had been kingless for a long time before the establishment of the legendary dynasty of Hrothgar. If a centralized monarchy was an innovation in Denmark in perhaps the ninth century, it would welcome a legendary origin to justify its legitimacy. This could be provided by pseudohistory, documented later at great length by Saxo Grammaticus. The Franks had acquired just such a legendary origin by the eighth century: they derived themselves and their new Holy Roman Empire from Troy, just as the Romans had done. Equally, the twelfth-century Plantagenet kings of England were provided with just such a legendary pseudohistory by Geoffrey of Monmouth: the tales of King Arthur.

Early English kings were similarly interested in legend, probably likewise to give themselves legitimacy and value, and elaborate genealogies were constructed for them, deriving their ancestry not from Troy or Rome, but through Germanic legend from euhemerized pagan gods, usually Woden. Part of Hrothgar's genealogy also appears in, for instance, the West Saxon royal genealogy composed for King Alfred and preserved in the *Anglo-Saxon Chronicle* for the year 855. Some of these English royal genealogies may have been composed as early as the seventh century, and show much interest in Scandinavian figures. This may provide a possible context in which learned legendary pseudohistory might have been created, to give suitably heroic legendary ancestors to the kings of the new kingdoms of England.

It is possible, therefore, that the fourth-century histories of the Goths, Huns, and Erulians were used to create such a legendary pseudohistory for Denmark, whether mapped across on to existing native figures, or using no basis of native legend at all. Such a pseudohistory could hardly have been created in pre-Christian Scandinavia, since there could have been no access to the written texts of Jordanes or Paul the Deacon, nor the ability to read them. *Beowulf* and *Widsith* preserve some relevant details, such as the name of the hall Heorot, not found in Scandinavian sources, and Jordanes seems to have been known in the circle of scholars around the Englishman Alcuin in the late eighth century. Therefore such a pseudohistory could have been created in Christian Francia or, since it studiously avoids any Roman association, more probably in England. There it was recorded in the Old English poems *Beowulf* and *Widsith*. It might then have been transmitted to Scandinavia, perhaps through the Viking settlements in England, the Christian but Anglo-Scandinavian Danelaw.

Legends other than that of Hygelac's Frisian raid and the Danish dynasty are cited in *Beowulf*. A few of these are common Germanic or English accounts, several are specifically Scandinavian, and a few are peculiar to the poem.

Beowulf mentions Sigemund (German "Siegmund"; Norse "Sigmundr") and his nephew Fitela (Norse "Sinfjötli"), telling how among other great deeds Sigemund slew a dragon (lines 875–897). These figures are known throughout the Germanic world from the Völsung/Nibelungen cycle of legends as recorded in Norse and Middle High German, and which formed the basis for Richard Wagner's cycle of operas, *Der Ring des Nibelungen*. The poem mentions (lines 1198–1201) a legendary theft of the *Brosinga mene* (neckring of the Brosings), stolen by Hama (Middle High German "Heime;" Norse "Heimir") from the tyrant-king Eormenric, the historical Gothic king Ermanaric famed in all surviving Germanic legend. This story may be related to the ill-attested Norse myth of the theft of the *Brísingamen* (neckring of the Brísings), for which the gods Heimdallr and Loki contended in a swimming contest. Two passages deal with a tyrannical Danish king Heremod (lines 901–915, 1709–1722), who apparently does not form part of Hrothgar's dynasty; he is unknown elsewhere, but a minor god in Norse myth bears the same name, and parts of his narrative may be paralleled elsewhere.

Beowulf tells of Offa the Angle, known elsewhere from English and Scandinavian sources, and how his marriage brought an end to his wife's previous tyranny so that she then became an exemplary queen (lines 1931–1962). It tells of Ingeld (lines 2024–2069 and elsewhere), known from *Widsith* and Norse sources, who married Freawaru, daughter of the Danish king Hrothgar, to end a feud, which then broke out again in war leading to Ingeld's death. Alcuin knows of this in the late eighth century, writing to English monks and reproving them for listening to heroic legend: "Quid Hinieldus cum Christo?" (What has Ingeld got to do with Christ?). The poem tells of the fight at Finnesburh (lines 1068–1159), also known from a separate surviving Old English fragmentary poem and a mention in *Widsith*, in which a feud breaks out between the Frisian king Finn and his Danish brother-in-law, Hnæf, in which the woman at the center of the feud, Hildeburh, loses her brother and son and finally her husband. The stories of Offa, Ingeld, and Finn emphasize the figure of the woman of contention, central to the heroic feud, who is at once cause, inciter, or victim of the action.

Beowulf contains four substantial passages telling of wars which involve Swedish kings such as Onela (Norse "Áli") and Eadgils (probably Norse "Aðils"); these wars are also recorded in Scandinavian sources although they appear nowhere else in English. One of these passages also recounts the fratricide in Hygelac's family, when his eldest brother, Herebeald, was killed by another brother, Hæthcyn. Three of these four passages appear in association with accounts of Hygelac's Frisian raid.

A long passage (lines 506–581) tells of a swimming contest between the hero Beowulf in his youth and a competitor named Breca; this narrative is presented as hostile debate between Beowulf and a figure named Unferth. It is not recorded elsewhere, and might have been composed for the poem. Two passages are in elegiac mode, the Lay of the Last Survivor (lines 2247–2266) and the Lament of the Bereaved Father (lines 2444–2462), but these are discursively lyrical rather than narrative.

This background of legend is presented in a fractured mosaic of incomplete allusion. The legends are often indirectly recounted by characters within the poem. On the evidence of other surviving texts, some of these tales were already known in Anglo-Saxon England. These stories are never fully told in *Beowulf*, and its audience must supply essential narrative material from their own knowledge in order to understand them. So the legends of Finn, Offa, and Ingeld are told only partially and incompletely; only specific aspects of the material are presented, and the audience receives only glimpses of specific dramatic scenes within the narratives. Apart from Beowulf's own stories and the widely attested tales of Sigemund, only the Swedish wars and the story of Hygelac's Frisian raid are wholly or largely unknown from other surviving English sources. These are recounted in full, but are each fragmented into four dislocated blocks, and the complex accounts of the Swedish wars are told largely in reverse chronological order. Even here, essential narrative elements have been withheld until nearly the end of the poem, so that only then are the stories complete and able to be assembled into a coherent whole. The effect is certainly of intentional difficulty: the audience is required to exercise considerable powers of memory, intelligence, and judgment in order to put the narratives together. This is not merely a narrative jigsaw puzzle; each narrative shard refracts images and themes of its context in the poem, and so serves as inexplicit commentary on that context. In particular these legendary narratives, apart from the Sigemund and perhaps Hama narratives, are usually grimly realistic and lack heroic hyperbole. They often serve to show how heroism works out in practice: the unending grimness, grief, and futility of human feud. In this they give a realistic human background; the foreground is reserved for a larger narrative of a different kind.

STYLE OF THE POEM

BEOWULF shows unusual unity of compositional technique, in that the same structural principles are visible at the smallest and largest of scales. The nonlinear parallelism and variation of its sentence structure is mirrored at the largest compositional levels, the overarching structure of the poem, with nonlinear blocks of narrative set in apposition to each other. It shares parallelism and variation, as a feature of poetic style, with almost all other Old English poetry, but seems to take this technique further and in different directions from most other poems. At least in *Beowulf,* the device hardly ever seems to be used solely for metrical purposes. More than one concept is often paralleled at the same time; references are interwoven or embedded in counterpoint to each other. The technique provides a means of controlling focus and of presenting multiple aspects of central concepts, so that these are seen in many dimensions at once. Often it is used to exploit rare or archaic vocabulary, creating an effect of distance, and often to allow the exploration of remote, even metaphysical imagery, which not only distances the subject matter but can give it a remarkable perspective of meaning. It also always controls the tempo of the poetry, governing the movement of the syntax and the sense.

Similes are rarely used; where they occur, influence from Christian Latin poetry may sometimes be suspected, since most instances are extended on the model of the classical "epic simile" and involve reference to the Christian God (for example, lines 1605–1611). This seems to be intentional; the different means of expression indicate shifts in mode of perception and meaning.

Metaphor is used only by the native device of the kenning: this is a compound expression made up of two nouns, a base word and a possessive qualifier, and usually exploits tension of sense between its base word and its meaning. Thus *swanrad,* "riding-place of the swan" (line 200), is a kenning for the sea, on which the swan rides as if it were a road. The kenning provides a riddling vision of reality, where meaning is seen through paradox. Kennings are used widely throughout Old English poetry, but are for the most part fossilized, though *Beowulf* sometimes seems to be innovative in their formation and use. No Old English poem shows any sign of the use of the kenning to refer to myth or legend, as in Norse skaldic poetry: given the eagerness for such reference in *Beowulf,* this is likely to show the independence from Norse of the English tradition.

Beowulf seems frequently to use wordplay, often to ironic effect. Puns and word-play, actual or implicit, fulfil much the same function as kennings: they allow one thing to mean another. This is not unusual in Old English poetry; obvious examples can be found in *The Battle of Maldon.* After giving the name "Heorot" (hart, stag) to Hrothgar's hall, the poet plays on the word "horn" (horn, gable; lines 79 and 82). The music in the hall, *sweg* (line 89), is ironically equated with the *micel morgensweg,* "much morning-music" (line 129), the following morning: the mourning and lamentation after Grendel's first raid on the hall. The boar-helmets worn by Beowulf's men as they approach Heorot hold *ferhweard,* "life-warding" (line 305), where *ferh-* can mean "piglet" (cf. English "farrow") as well as "life."

Sentences are grouped into verse-paragraphs. These units, usually under twenty lines in length, are not normally marked by editors, but are defined rhythmically and rhetorically. They begin and end with pauses in the movement of the verse and of the sense, and are often held together by internal, nonmetrical patterns of alliteration and assonance. They are sometimes marked at their ends by some sort of gnomic statement which expresses the point reached by the movement of sense in the paragraph or group of paragraphs. They are effectively the units of performance, between which the performer can pause for breath and rhetorical emphasis. They are unusually well-defined in this poem, and impose a much longer-breathed performance than does most Old English poetry. They of course create a rhythmic effect of their own within larger units, the scenes or speeches which tell the stories of the poem.

The following example, the description of the funeral pyre at the center of the Finnesburh episode, shows a verse paragraph which gives a complete if brief scene. The translation is very literal, follows the word order of the original, and is meant merely to show which word has which sense. Metrical alliteration is shown by italicization (all vowels alliterate with each other); parallelism and variation within sentences are marked in boldface.

In the first sentence, the word *icge* is not understood. In the second sentence the dead warrior (the Danish king Hnæf) is called both (best of) Here-Scyldinga, "Host-Scyldings," showing his

Að wæs geæfned, ond *icge* gold	Oath was accomplished, and […] gold
a*h*æfen of *h*orde. **Here-Scyldinga**	heaved up from [the] hoard. Of Host-Scyldings
betst beadorinca wæs on *b*æl gearu.	best of battle-warriors was on [the] pyre ready.
Æt Þæm *a*de wæs e*Þ*gesyne	At the pyre was easily-seen

swatfah syrce, swyn ealgylden,
eofer irenheard, æÞeling manig
wundum awyrded; sume on wæle crungon.
Het ða Hildeburh æt Hnæfes ade
hire selfre sunu sweoloðe befæstan,
banfatu bærnan ond on bæl don
eame on eaxle. Ides gnornode,
geomrode giddum. Guðrinc astah.
Wand to wolcnum wælfyra mæst,
hlynode for hlawe; hafelan multon,
bengeato burston, ðonne blod ætspranc,
laðbite lices. Lig ealle forswealg,
gæsta gifrost, Þara ðe Þær guð fornam
bega folces. Wæs hira blæd scacen.

blood-stained shirt, swine all-gilded,
boar iron-hard, [a] prince many
with wounds sent to [his] fate; some in slaughter fell.
Bade then Hildeburh at Hnæf's pyre
her own son to flame entrust,
bone-vessels burn, and on the pyre put
at [his] uncle's shoulder. [The] lady grieved,
lamented in lays. [The] warrior went up.
Twisted to the clouds of slaughterfires [the] greatest,
roared before [the] barrow; heads melted,
wound-gates burst open, when blood sprang out,
hostile bite of body. Flame all swallowed up,
of spirits greediest, of those that there battle took,
of both of [the] people. Was their glory gone.

(lines 1107–1124)

warlike dynasty in descent from Scyld (whose name means "shield," to be echoed by the armor terminology in the next sentence), and *betst beadorinca*, more simply "best of battle-warriors," The bloody armor is called "bloodstained shirt" (or "corselet"), "all-gilded swine" (reflecting the color of the blood; gold is conventionally "red" in Old English) and "iron-hard boar," in both cases referring to a helmet bearing the image of a boar, with both the richness of gold and the strength of iron. The dead nobleman himself is equated by parallelism with the corselet and helmet upon the pyre. The fire is called both *sweoloð* (flame) and *bæl* (blazing pyre); the bodies are called *banfatu* (bone vessels), containers for the spirit within, as the armor had contained the body. Hildeburh's lamentation is stated simply in *gnornode* (grieved), and expanded into poetic expression in *geomrode giddum*, where *gidd* is "poem of lamentation"; the sound of her grief is to be echoed by the roaring of the pyre. The wounds on the bodies open in the fire—"heads melted, wound-gates burst open."—where the heads melt like the metal of the treasure, the wounds open like the gates of a blazing hall, falling open to let the red blood burst out like flame, like molten gold. This implies the common Old English poetic concepts of the body as a building, habitation of the soul, a treasury containing the hoarded spirit. The hall as a place of treasure, to be destroyed by fire, is an image already well established in the poem for the Danish hall, Heorot, itself (for example, lines 81–83). The wounds are both *bengeato* (wound gates) and *laðbite lices* (hostile bite of the body), implying an animate mouth. This imagery has already been established in the description of the coming of Grendel to Heorot, where the door of the hall is its "mouth" (line 724) and Grendel has come to devour. The apparently unrelated images here are therefore unified within a wider context in the poem. The fire is both simple *lig* (flame) and *gæsta gifrost* (most rapacious of spirits), which certainly carries implications of diabolical fire, the blazing mouth of hell. The upward movement which lifted treasure from the hoard also lifted the dead bodies on to the pyre, and then the fire itself twists upward into darkness, the smoke into the clouds. The whole passage is unified by references to fire, expecially with verbal repetitions of *ad* (anticipated by *að*, "oath") and *bæl*, both meaning "pyre"; these fire references become more and more metaphorical as they proceed. The *bl* patterning established in *bæl* (pyre) is picked up by *blod* (blood) and *blæd* (glory), so linking key concepts in the passage. The meaning of the whole scene is summarized in the last half line: "their glory was gone": the wealth of treasure and the bodies that had borne it are devoured in metaphysically described flame.

STRUCTURE OF THE POEM

THE larger units formed by verse paragraphs are usually speeches and scenes. Either may contain the other, sometimes repeatedly, like Russian dolls, though all speeches are contained within a larger scene. Each is made up of at least one verse paragraph, and they often contain many. Direct speech is usually introduced by formulaic phrases, such as "Beowulf spoke, son of Ecgtheow." There is no such rhetorical marker at the end of speeches, but in the manuscript there is a punctuation mark at their close. The speeches are long, formal monologues, sometimes very long; dialogue, where it occurs, consists of symmetrical monologues in apposition to each other, rather than conversation. Speeches often serve to slow the action, and to that extent control tempo; they also often contain subordinate narrative scenes, and are an important means of integrating legendary and other allusion into the central narratives of the poem. So characters within the main story of the poem, such as Unferth, Beowulf, and Hrothgar, as well as several unnamed minstrels, themselves tell subordinate stories. Speeches also are the almost invariable means of emotional expression, both for the individual characters and for the burden of meaning carried within the scene.

The scene presents a single completed action within a single defined context at a single time. It proceeds at an internally regular pace, and gives a more or less coherent visualization of the action. Visualization involves sensory description of the action and its setting, but details cohere in effect, rather than pictorially. Only those details are given which have an emotional or intellectual impact. They give fractured pictorial glimpses of narrative that tease the mind; their emotional and intellectual effect is always coherent. Internal pacing is often quasi-realistic, though material of greater emphasis is usually paced more slowly. Scenes have no standard rhetorical markers for beginning and end, other than an often abrupt change of tempo; they are defined by the narratives of which they are the essential building blocks.

The stories of the poem are presented in an essentially dramatic way; that is, through scenes and speeches. Directly told third-person narrative, unless recounted by characters themselves within larger scenes, is usually brief and introduces or links scenes. Very few scenes present the whole of a story. The two parts of the swimming-contest narrative (the symmetrically opposed speeches of Unferth and Beowulf) cumulatively give a full account of the story. Similarly, the four accounts of Hygelac's Frisian raid and of the Swedish wars each give different aspects and details of the entire narratives, so that cumulatively they provide a virtually complete report and do not require the audience to supply further information from other sources. The Sigemund, Heremod, Finnesburh,

Hama, Offa, and Ingeld narratives are simply incomplete and do not make complete sense by themselves: as discussed above, all these narratives are mentioned in other surviving texts, and the poem's audience presumably possessed other essential knowledge of them. Again, the effect is of fractured glimpses of the story material which tease the mind.

The subordinate narratives of Beowulf are always presented as sharply bounded, disjunctive blocks, not causally linked to their contexts but presented in comparison and contrast. The model is static and architectural: balanced masses which hold the structure together by the equivalence and opposition of their meaning and emotional weight, as an arch is held together by the balance of the blocks on either side of the keystone. These blocks tend to be presented in double narratives: opposed and contrasted pairs of stories. The two opposed accounts of the swimming contest establish the pattern early in the poem with great clarity; they are linked by many verbal echoes between them to emphasize their symmetry. Thereafter the subordinate narratives cluster around Beowulf's own stories. Sigemund and Heremod are paired together, as contrastingly successful and unsuccessful heroic figures, but Heremod recurs symmetrically much later, in Hrothgar's sermon, so establishing a pair across a wide span of the poem. The Hama story is paired with the first account of Hygelac's Frisian raid, again in a contrast of success and failure; the other three accounts of the Frisian raid are paired with three of the four accounts of the Swedish wars. The Finnesburh and Ingeld narratives are not immediately paired with other narratives, though they are linked to each other by narrative and positional symmetry, so establishing another pair across a wide span of the poem. The Offa narrative and one account of the Swedish wars (the Wiglaf narrative) are effectively unpaired.

Another organizational principle is that of framing (or embedding, often known as the "envelope pattern"), where symmetrical items occur on either side of a central passage and thereby frame it. The effect of framing is to emphasize the center, which is the pivot on which the entire structure turns. Thus the Sigemund-Heremod double narrative, and the Hama-Hygelac double narrative, are positioned on either side of the far larger Finnesburh narrative, which itself is complex, formed of several scenes that create several levels of framing around its central scene: that of the funeral pyre. Framing is also used on the largest scale to relate these narratives to the stories of Beowulf's fights against Grendel and Grendel's mother. So the narratives of the swimming contest precede the Grendel fight. Then that is followed by the group of five legendary narratives clustering around the Finnesburh story, which itself precedes the fight against Grendel's mother. The next cluster of subordinate narratives is formed by Hrothgar's sermon, the Offa and Ingeld narratives, which stand between the contests against Grendel's mother and against the dragon. These clusters of narrative material therefore stand at the narrative hinges between Beowulf's own three adventures. Narrative symmetry between, for instance, the two Heremod narratives, and between the Finnesburh and Ingeld narratives, ties them together across a wide span of the poem.

There is also some degree of forward-looking symmetry between subordinate narratives and the story of Beowulf himself. His account of the swimming contest, where he is seized by man-eating water-monsters and dragged down to the bottom of the sea, there to kill them with his sword, looks forward to the point where he dives into the monsters' mere and is seized by Grendel's mother and taken to her underwater dwelling. Similarly, the story of Sigemund's dragon-slaying may look forward to Beowulf's own. These narratives therefore to some extent prefigure the main story over very large spans of the poem.

Another organizational principle is that of interlace, where several narrative strands are taken forward simultaneously, weaving in and out of each other. The narratives of the Swedish wars and of Hygelac's raid are interlaced with Beowulf's dragon-fight in this way, to form a three-strand interlace, with three double entries of each strand. This can be seen as a sort of narrative counterpoint, and it culminates in the threefold death of kings: the deaths of the young king Hygelac, of the aged Swedish king Ongentheow, both set against and reflecting different aspects of Beowulf's own death.

Framing, prefiguring, and interlace are now widely recognized as structural principles throughout early and high medieval literature, though they often confuse modern readers, who are used to the simpler, linear structures of, for instance, the novel. They can be compared with the similar devices used in English art of the sev-enth and eighth centuries, often called insular or Hiberno-Saxon art.

There has been a long lasting if intermittent debate about the overall shape of the poem: whether it falls into two unequal halves or three roughly equal thirds. Some of the discussion appears not to be based on actual analysis of the poem. For example, Whitelock's suggestion of a three-part structure intended for performance over three sessions is probably unworkable in detail and practice: the natural breaks in the poem and summaries of the action do not fall at suitable points; any such three sessions would either have to be gabbled at great speed or exceedingly long. It is difficult to define any single large-scale structure of the poem based on performance requirements, and the poem might be meant to be flexible in this respect. To judge from maximum lengths of shorter Old English poems certainly intended for performance in a single session, for instance the so-called elegies, performance sessions might be more like the fitts in *Beowulf,* or possibly small groups of fitts.

Tolkien argued powerfully that *Beowulf* was divided into two unequal but equivalent parts, expressing a thematic structure of youth contrasted with age. So the first two-thirds of the poem deal with Beowulf the young hero, contrasting with the final third, Beowulf the old king. The thematic structure which Tolkien observed is certainly fundamental to the poem, but the contrast of youth and age runs through it from its prologue to its end. Thematic structuring around the concepts of heroism and kingship is also always present through the poem. All these are wholly integrated with each other, often through the use of thematically significant imagery, such as of treasure and weapons, or fire. Tolkien's view also disregards the emotional change within the poem carried by the narratives told after the Grendel fight. Hitherto all has been bright and glorious, with only brief hints of grief to come. Grendel indeed brought a shadow, but that merely serves to emphasize the heroic achievement of Beowulf who overcame him. But the Heremod and Hygelac narratives tell of kingship and heroic endeavor that end in failure; the Finnesburh narrative expresses powerfully the tragic consequences of both kingship and heroism. Although only one narrative day separates the fights against Grendel and against Grendel's mother, the tone of the poem has deepened and darkened, and its world has become wiser and far more sad. This is no longer the world of the bright young hero, able to cleanse it from shadow, for darkness is now inherent to heroism itself. Beowulf himself reflects on this deeper and darker understanding; his fight against Grendel's mother is far more terrible and involves a descent into a personal hell. The aged king Hrothgar's sermon at the end of that contest introduces a new aspect: Beowulf as potential king, who must guard himself spiritually in conflict against diabolical pride and greed. Only after this can Beowulf come to kingship and after fifty years encounter his dragon. In short, Tolkien's altogether convincing observation of thematic structuring around the contrast of youth and age fits wholly within a physical structure which reflects the three conflicts of the poem's main story.

There are no close parallels or known literary models for this huge and intricate structure, nor for several of the structural principles on which it is based. Within surviving early Germanic literature, only *Deor* uses disjunctive blocks of incomplete narrative within an overall thematic structure and story. It is very short and small-scale (forty-two lines in total), and has little or nothing of the delicacy and complexity of *Beowulf*, nor do its narratives seem to function as commentary on each other. *Deor* is simply a short set of exemplary narratives on the theme of transience, a common enough concern in Old English poetry. The subordinate narratives of *Beowulf* might be related to the classical "epic simile," a sharply distinguished descriptive passage introduced for comparison, but the subordinate narratives of *Beowulf* are story, not description, and are on an altogether larger scale, far more complex, and given far wider and more important functions. *Beowulf* is unique in this as in many other respects.

INTERPRETATION

SEVERAL interpretative approaches have been suggested above, but the poem remains elusive in overall understanding. At Beowulf's death, for instance, it is not clear whether the poem condemns him to damnation or not: the judgment of his soul is twice discussed in connection with a curse upon the dragon's treasure. The first of these uses vocabulary which is entirely ambivalent, and the second is textually corrupt. At the end of the poem, as twelve of Beowulf's men ride around his barrow lamenting him, they praise him in terms which are lofty but ambiguous. In particular the last word of the poem, *lofgeornost*, is difficult to interpret. It is a compound of *lof* (praise, glory) and *georn* (eager), and so must basically mean "most eager for glory." This can be interpreted entirely favorably, as "most eager for heroic achievement." But the compound is rare, and is only elsewhere found in late-tenth-century religious prose; there it is uniformly unfavorable and appears in phrases translating Latin *iactantia* (boastfulness). The word may well have had different connotations in heroic poetry from those used in the prose of late-tenth-century preachers, because of differences of genre, poetic diction, or date. But, at least for the scribes of the actual manuscript at the end of the tenth century, this word could have constituted condemnation.

It is reasonable to consider that the poem should require more than one simple interpretation. It seems to carry a variety of meanings and to exploit the tension between these. Grief for the passing of human glory is certainly one of these. But that glory is presented throughout the poem as all too often ill won. It is destructive, despite the greatheartedness that may cause a man to seek it, and the valor of its winning. The final foe whom the hero must slay is himself. The pain at the end of the poem is not merely lamentation for transience, but arises from a deeper questioning of the value of human achievement. This is tragedy, not cynicism: such things matter far too much for the bitter laughter which Chaucer allows himself, or at least his hero, at the end of *Troilus and Criseyde*.

For a modern reader, the depth of time portrayed in the poem between a Christian audience and its legendary, pagan past is redoubled by the remoteness of the poem itself, its language and its poetic mode. It looks back into world beyond world of antiquity. The legendary past was "other" even for the poem's first audience or the scribes of its manuscript: monster-slaying heroes no longer strode the world of literate English monks, just as Agamemnon or Odysseus no longer sailed the Aegean of Homer or Pericles. The conversion to Christianity formed a greater gulf between the English and their past than did the invasions or eruptions that might have ended Greek Mycenaean civilization. In comparison, cultural continuity is unbroken across the millennium between ourselves and the scribes who wrote the *Beowulf* manuscript. The pre-Christian, legendary past is not only different, but it is also important because it still has meaning. This significance may be as trivial as that of origin legends for a colonial people, the English, and the dynasties of their several kingdoms. But it is also important in ideology: the definition of primeval values and their redefinition and evaluation by that colonial people. They had now not only created a new identity of "Englishness," but had also accepted Christian systems of ethics and belief. Metaphysical Christian ethics of good and evil, justice and mercy, were superimposed upon older, social values of honor and shame, not without continuing tensions between them. The new ethical system did not wholly supersede pre-Christian values but was integrated with them within the new identity of the English. This fusion of value systems has largely endured to the present in the English-speaking world.

Beowulf did not provide the English with a set of self-justifying narratives, as the Sagas of the Icelanders provided for another colonial Germanic people in the High Middle Ages, and, arguably, the stories of the Wild West provided for the United States during the earlier parts of the twentieth century. *Beowulf* is too questioning, too elusive, too remote to be seen in these ways. It does not, for the most part, provide answers, not even to the apparently simple questions "Who are we?" "What are our values?" "What is our value?" Instead, it takes a vision of the far, legendary past and shatters it into innumerable prismatic fragments around the figure of its hero, each reflecting or refracting some aspect of his meaning and value. The light so reflected or refracted illuminates all desire for achievement, the lust for being which devours itself.

SELECTED BIBLIOGRAPHY

I. FACSIMILE EDITIONS. Kemp Malone, ed., *The Thorkelin Transcripts of Beowulf in Facsimile* (Copenhagen, 1951); Julius Zupitza, *Beowulf, reproduced in facsimile with transliteration and notes*, rev. N. Davis (Oxford, 1959); Kemp Malone, ed., *The Nowell Codex* (Copenhagen, 1963); Kevin Kiernan, ed., *Electronic "Beowulf"* (London, 1999), on CD-ROM, with edition.

II. TEXT. Grímur Jónsson Thorkelin, *De Danorum rebus gestis* (Havniæ, 1815), first printed edition; Friedrich Klaeber, *Beowulf and the Fight at Finnsburg*, 3d ed. (Boston, 1950), with full notes and commentary; Elliott Van Kirk Dobbie, *Beowulf and Judith* (New York, 1953); Else von Schaubert, *Heyne-Schückings Beowulf* (Munich, 1963), with useful textual notes; A. J. Wyatt, ed., *Beowulf with the Finnsburg Fragment*, rev. R. W. Chambers (Cambridge, 1968); C. L. Wrenn, *Beowulf*, rev. W. F. Bolton (London, 1973); Howell D. Chickering Jr., *Beowulf: A Dual-Language Edition* (New York, 1977), with parallel translation; M. Swanton, *Beowulf* (Manchester, 1978), with parallel translation; George Jack, *Beowulf: A Student Edition* (Oxford, 1994), repr. with corrections 1997, with parallel glossary and commentary; Michael Alexander, *Beowulf* (Harmondsworth, 1995), with parallel glossary.

III. TRANSLATIONS. In addition to Chickering and Swanton texts above, see John R. Clark Hall, *Beowulf and the Finnesburg Fragment*, with prefatory remarks by J. R. R. Tolkien, rev. C. L. Wrenn (London, 1950), a literal translation, useful as a crib; G. N. Garmonsway and Jacqueline Simpson, *Beowulf and Its Analogues* (London, 1968), includes translations of many of the Norse analogues; Michael Alexander, *Beowulf* (Harmondsworth, 1973); Seamus Heaney, *Beowulf* (London, 1999).

IV. BIBLIOGRAPHIES AND SURVEYS. Donald K. Fry, *Beowulf and the Fight at Finnsburh: A Bibliography* (Charlottesville, Va., 1969); Douglas D. Short, *Beowulf Scholarship: An Annotated Bibliography* (New York, 1980); R. J. Hasenfratz, *Beowulf Scholarship: An Annotated Bibliography, 1979–1990* (New York, 1993), maintained at http://spirit.lib.uconn.edu/Medieval/beowulf.html; Robert E. Bjork and John D. Niles, *A Beowulf Handbook* (Exeter and Lincoln, Neb., 1997); *Anglo-Saxon England* (Cambridge, 1972–) publishes an annual *Beowulf* bibliography.

V. OLD ENGLISH POETRY CITED IN TEXT. Raymond W. Chambers, ed., *Widsith* (London, 1912); Kemp Malone, ed., *Deor*, 4th ed. (London, 1966); Michael Swanton, ed., *The Dream of the Rood* (Manchester, 1970); Donald G. Scragg, ed., *The Battle of Maldon* (Manchester, 1981).

VI. SECONDARY LITERATURE. Humphrey Wanley, in George Hickes, *Linguarum Vett. Septentrionalium Thesaurus* (London, 1705); Friedrich Panzer, *Studien zur germanischen Sagengeschichte*, vol. 1., *Beowulf* (Munich, 1910); Elias Wessén, *De nordiska folkstammarna i Beowulf* (Stockholm, 1927); Adeline C. Bartlett, *The Larger Rhetorical Patterns in Anglo-Saxon Poetry* (New York, 1935); J. R. R. Tolkien, *Beowulf: The Monsters and the Critics* (London, 1936); Caroline Brady, *The Legends of Ermanaric* (Berkeley, Calif., 1943); Niels C. Lukman, *Skjoldunge und Skilfinge: Hunnen und Herulerkönige in ostnordischer Überlieferung* (Copenhagen, 1943); Dorothy Whitelock, *The Audience of Beowulf* (Oxford, 1951); Francis P. Magoun Jr., "The Oral-Formulaic Character of Anglo-Saxon Narrative Poetry," in *Speculum* (1953); Neil R. Ker, *Catalogue of Manuscripts Containing Anglo-Saxon* (Oxford, 1957); Arthur G. Brodeur, *The Art of Beowulf* (Berkeley, Calif., 1959); Alistair Campbell, "The Old English Epic Style," in *English and Medieval Studies Presented to J. R. R. Tolkien*, ed. N. Davis and C. L. Wrenn (London, 1962); Raymond W. Chambers, *Beowulf: An Introduction to the Study of the Poem*, rev. C. L. Wrenn (Cambridge, 1967); Margaret E. Goldsmith, *The Mode and Meaning of "Beowulf"* (London,

1970); Antti Amatus Aarne and Stith Thompson, *The Types of the Folktale*, rev. ed. (Helsinki, 1973); David N. Dumville, "Kingship, Genealogies and Regnal Lists," in *Early Medieval Kingship,* ed. P. H. Sawyer and I. N. Wood (Leeds, 1977); Ashley C. Amos, *Linguistic Means of Determining the Dates of Old English Literary Texts* (Cambridge, Mass., 1980); Colin Chase, ed., *The Dating of Beowulf* (Toronto, 1981); Michael Lapidge, "Beowulf, Aldhelm, the Liber Monstrorum and Wessex," in *Studi Medievali* 23 (1982); John Hines, *The Scandinavian Character of Anglian England in the Pre-Viking Period* (Oxford, 1984); Fred C. Robinson, *Beowulf and the Appositive Style* (Knoxville, Tenn., 1985); David N. Dumville, "Beowulf Come Lately: Some Notes on the Palaeography of the Nowell Codex," in *Archiv für das Studium der neueren Sprachen und Literaturen* 225 (1988); R. D. Fulk, *A History of Old English Meter* (Philadelphia, 1992); Sam Newton, *The Origins of Beowulf and the Pre-Viking Kingdom of East Anglia* (Cambridge, 1993); Lars Hemmingsen, "By Word of Mouth: The Origins of Early Danish History: Studies in European Learned and Popular Traditions of Dacians and Danes before A.D. 1200" (Ph.D. diss., Copenhagen, 1995); Andy Orchard, *Pride and Prodigies: Studies in the Monsters of the Beowulf-Manuscript* (Cambridge, 1995); Carl E. Anderson, "Formation and Resolution of Ideological Contrast in the Early History of Scandinavia" (Ph.D. diss., Cambridge, 2000).

ANDRÉ BRINK

(1935–   )

Robert Niemi

ANDRÉ PHILIPPUS BRINK WAS born on 29 May 1935, in Vrede, Orange Free State, South Africa. His father, Daniel, was a magistrate and his mother, Aletta (Wolmarans) Brink, was a teacher. Brink grew up in a world that was strictly segregated by race and class, a world where, as Brink describes, "There was simply no possibility of encountering a black person in any role other than a servant or a laborer, questions about 'humanity' never entered the picture." Like most of his white contemporaries, Brink was inculcated with the belief that apartheid "had been ordained by God and was the result of the curse on the children of Canaan and the confusion of Babel" (Baker, p. 50). But there were countervailing influences as well. Brink would sit in the back of his father's courtroom and listen "in awe" to the cases tried there. He later wrote that most of these cases "stemmed from a world so remote from my own that they never penetrated my consciousness. Such things happened to black people; they didn't really concern me. Except that a deeply rooted respect was born in me, not just for the law, which my father represented, but for justice, which he incarnated" (Baker, p. 50).

Brink's abiding sense of justice guided his gradual moral development toward an anti-apartheid stance. Certain key events of his youth pointed the way. One day a sickeningly bloodied black man came to the Brinks' house seeking justice for severe beatings at the hands of his master—and the police, to whom he had initially complained. Not long after Brink matriculated to Potchefstroom University ("a bastion of Calvinism") in 1951, a young black servant of neighbors was beaten "nearly to death" for running away. In stark contrast to such instances of white racist brutality, Brink was exposed to an inspiring image of black dignity when Z. K. Matthews, a leading black academic, came to Potchefstroom to deliver a lecture. Brink recalls that Professor Matthews was "received with great enthusiasm, and for a long time afterwards some of us continued to discuss the event. Not the address so much, although that in itself had been remarkable; but the fact that, for the first time in our protected lives, we had encountered a black man who was not a labourer or a servant" (Baker, p. 50). Another instructive experience occurred in 1955 when 60,000 black residents were forcibly evicted from Sophiatown, outside Johannesburg, to make room for white housing. In 1956 Father Trevor Huddleston published *Naught for Your Comfort*, an empassioned moral attack on the Sophiatown evictions. Still under the influence of his conservative upbringing, Brink disagreed with Huddleston at the time but later conceded that "Father Huddleston opened my eyes to something I hadn't realized before" (Baker, p. 51).

From an early age André Brink aspired to be a writer. When he was nine Brink published what he has since described as "my first atrocious little poem." He wrote his first novel at the age of twelve. Brink was equally precocious in romance. At the start of his college years he married Estelle Naude on 3 October 1951, when he was only 16 years old. The marriage produced a son, Anton, but soon ended in divorce. Brink earned his bachelor's degree from Potchefstroom University in 1955, a master's degree in Afrikaans in 1958, and another master's degree in English in 1959. It was during this period that Brink first began to publish his writing, which he later judged as "very unimpressive stuff. The Afrikaner tradition then was all naturalistic."

Brink did postgraduate work at the Sorbonne, University of Paris, from 1959 to 1961. Presumably destined to become a fairly conventional bourgeois academic, Brink was irrevocably changed by his Paris sojourn. To the young and relatively inexperienced Afrikaner, the city was "that great metropolis where every single thing I had taken for granted now had to be tested, explored, validated—or rejected." Brink recalled the simple but illuminating experience "of sitting down for a meal in a student restaurant and finding blacks at the same table [which] came as a shock. What had previously been so impossible that it had never crossed the threshold of the thinkable, was now happening as a matter of course. To discover that many of my new black colleagues were able to hold their own in conversations about literature, philosophy, politics, and a thousand other subjects, and the fact they often had read much more, and knew much more, than I did, left me in an almost perpetual daze" (Baker, p. 50).

Primed for moral and philosophical transformation, Brink was hit hard by news from his homeland. On 22 March 1960 white police massacred sixty-nine unarmed black anti-apartheid protesters in Sharpeville. Panicked by the ensuing widespread unrest, the government declared a state of emergency, arrested more than 18,000 people, jailed the black leadership, and banned the Pan-African Congress and African National Congress. Sharpeville was a major turning point in South Africa's modern history. The massacre and its brutally repressive aftermath effectively isolated South Africa from the international community and marked a new phase in the bitter struggle against apartheid that would last another thirty-four years.

A defining moment for his country, Sharpeville was a watershed for Brink personally. Sitting on a park bench in the Luxembourg Gardens reading the terrible news from home, Brink had a resounding epiphany about his country. He remembered thinking, "If this were really the apocalypse, if 'my people' were really sinking—then it was their own fault, the inevitable retribution for what they themselves had done and allowed to be done." He later told an interviewer that the atrocity forced him "to re-examine all the convictions and beliefs I had previously taken for granted." After completing his postgraduate studies, Brink went home, took a teaching position at Rhodes University in Grahamstown, and dedicated himself to fighting apartheid through his writing. "Returning to South Africa," Brink explained, "meant one thing: that writing had become an indispensable dimension of my life; and that I was prepared to assume full responsibility for every word I would write in the future" (Manguel, p. 409).

Brink married for a second time on 28 November 1965. The marriage, to Salomi Louw, produced a second son, Gustav, but also ended in divorce. His personal life in turmoil, Brink returned to Paris in 1968 to investigate the possibility of settling in France permanently. The French student rebellion against the conservative Charles de Gaulle regime in the spring of 1968 was another personal watershed for Brink. He recalled "The nature of the student revolt of that year forced me to reassess my situation as a writer" (Jones and Jorgenson, eds., vol. 62, pp. 45–46). Brink returned to South Africa in order, he said, "to accept full responsibility for whatever I wrote, believing that, in a closed society, the writer has a specific social and moral role to fill. This resulted in a more committed form of writing exploring the South African political situation and notably my revulsion of apartheid" (Jones and Jorgenson, eds., vol. 62, pp. 45–46). The fruits of that deepened commitment were realized five years later when Brink brought out *Kennis van die aand* (*Looking on Darkness*), a novel that deals candidly with explosive issues: interracial sex, police brutality, and state repression. The South African Supreme Court immediately banned the book, prompting Brink to translate his novel into English in order to reach a wider audience.

Brink married for a third time, to Alta Miller, a potter, on 17 July 1970. Together Brink and Miller had two children, Danie and Sonja, but the marriage also ended in divorce. In 1974 Brink was promoted to senior lecturer at Rhodes University and in 1976 he was promoted to associate professor. In 1980 Brink was promoted to full professor of Afrikaans and Dutch literature at Rhodes. That same year he was awarded the Martin Luther King Memorial Prize for his fifth novel, *A Dry White Season*. Brink married for a fourth time to Maresa de Beer, on 16 November 1990. The following year he was appointed professor of English at the University of Cape Town.

THE AMBASSADOR

TRANSFORMED by his first stay in Paris, Brink sought to articulate the city's seductive power with *Die Ambassador*, a 1963 novel in Afrikaans (translated into English by Brink himself and published in London in 1965 as *File on a Diplomat*). The title character is Paul ven Heerden, South Africa's ambassador to France, a career bureaucrat and middle-aged family man of Dutch Calvinist stock in the midst of an impeccably ordered life when he meets Nicolette Alford, a sexy, flighty twenty-three-year-old South African working in Paris as a stripper. While his wife and daughter are away on vacation in Italy, the Ambassador strikes up an acquaintance with Nicolette that soon turns into a fixation on his part. The Ambassador's perilous conduct is made even more dangerous by the obsessive jealousy of Stephen Keyter, the twenty-three-year-old third secretary at the embassy who has been jilted by Nicolette in favor of his boss. Aptly described by the critic George Stade as "ambitious, driven, resentful, self-pitying, a sex-starved pip-squeak, a petty Nietzchean" (Stade, p. 21), the malevolent Keyter exacts vengeance on his rival by reporting the matter to the home office in Pretoria. To add insult to injury, Keyter seduces the Ambassador's wife after her return to Paris. His life and career in ruins, Paul ven Heerden still cannot control his passion for Nicolette. Ennui, the thrill of illicit sex with a beautiful woman half his age, nostalgia for his own lost youth: all are factors that drive the Ambassador's mania. On a deeper level, though, ven Heerden is compelled by an emotionally unresolved affair twenty five years earlier with a woman named Gillian who treated him in the cavalier way that Nicolette treats Keyter. He reenacts his troubled affair with Gillian through Nicolette partly to salve the lingering hurt of the young man he was then, partly to open up his torpid emotional life. "Through her," he admits, "I return to the past and call up all the possibilities left unfulfilled; through her I explore all my relations with those around me." As for Nicolette, her attraction to the Ambassador has strong oedipal overtones; "He's like daddy," the father who deserted her in her childhood. Likewise, Stephen Keyter is driven by largely unconscious motivations that are oedipal in the extreme. He betrays the Ambassador so as to get back at his own father, whom he hated. And Keyter's unconscious motives in sleeping with the Ambassador's wife are too obviously Freudian to require any elaboration. Ironically, the Ambassador sees a younger version of himself in Keyter, but also the son he never had. In a sense, then, ven Heerden is betrayed by an earlier incarnation of himself whom he understands and pities but is powerless to influence. For the book's epigraph, André Brink chose "É́love is a form of metaphysical inquiry," a quotation from Lawrence Durrell that nicely expresses the notion that intimate relationships are the working out of intensely individual psychosexual, moral, and existential issues for each person involved.

To emphasize the highly subjective nature of these interpersonal experiences Brink divided *The Ambassador* into a number of distinct sections, each told from a different point of view. Keyter's first-person account is followed by an objective, third-person "Chronicle," then ven Heerdon's first-person account, then Nicolette's rather brief soliloquy, then "Mosaic," a third-person denouement. This sort of modernist narrative structure, so well suited to psychological complexity and depth, suggests that there is no totality to experience, no unified truth to know, only the fragments of life created by the limited vision of each individual. Furthermore, the novel's sutured quality enacts the cracking and shattering of Paul ven Heerdon's tidy world by subterranean forces of desire too long repressed. Formerly stolid Afrikaners, ven Heerdon and Keyter both find themselves swept away by the fierce romantic currents of cosmopolitan, sybaritic Paris, as did Brink himself.

LOOKING ON DARKNESS

IN a 1976 essay entitled "Literature and Offence," Brink characterized reading as a libidinal transaction between author and reader: "The text is a fully emancipated person, not a mindless little creature ready to fall back and open up. Her challenge is not the token resistance of a whore, but that of the integrated personality which yields neither to gentle persuasion nor to force but makes her own responsible decision about sharing only when the challenge from the other side is worthy of such commitment." Brink argues that his use of sexual imagery is not salacious; it offers "a comprehensive imagery which 'contains' my approach to literature as offence, but also . . . the sexual in itself represents an area of 'offensiveness' which seems to attract more persistent attention than many others" (*Writing in a State of Seige*, p. 136). That Brink realized the importance of sex as the key locus of personal identity, political power, and resistance to repressive state authority is evident from the topic he chose for his second novel, *Kennis van die aand* (1973). The book focuses on an interracial love affair, the ultimate taboo in apartheid South Africa. Brink knew that writing about such a subject was the literary equivalent of waving a red flag in front of a bull. Accordingly, for one of several epigraphs, Brink chose an exquisitely appropriate Antonin Artaud quotation: "Toute vraie liberté est noire et se confond immanquablement avec la liberté du sexe qui est noire elle aussi." (All true freedom is black and inevitably confounds itself with sexual freedom, which is black also.)

Brink borrowed the basic scenario for *Kennis van die aand* from Albert Camus's *L'Étranger* (*The Stranger*, 1942). Both books are presented as self-illuminating confessions by condemned murderers awaiting sentence. There are, however, fundamental differences between Camus's novel and Brink's. Camus's protagonist, Meursault, is indifferent, shallow, and apathetic by nature. He comes to realize the inauthenticity of his life only after he kills a man and is sentenced to death. Apprised of the absurdity of existence and his own predicament, Meursault decides to embrace his fate and live consciously, as if life mattered. Thus he becomes a stranger to modern society, which thrives on rote convention and ritual.

Brink's doomed protagonist is Joseph Malan, a thirty-two-year-old "Cape Coloured" actor and theater producer turned anti-apartheid activist who is convicted of strangling his lover, a white Englishwoman named Jessica Thomson. Unlike Meursault—a blunted soul who kills impulsively and without reason—Malan is an artist, intellectual, and revolutionary who very deliberately enters into a suicide pact with Jessica. The pressures that bring them to such a desperate pass are manifold and intense. While unrelenting state harassment cripples Malan's efforts to mount the kind of political theater that is his life's passion, his clandestine love affair with Jessica is increasingly dangerous to both of them; they are guilty of violating the "Immorality Act," an infamous apartheid law proscribing interracial sex. Matters come to a head when Richard Cole, a white rival for Jessica's affections, threatens to report their illegal liaison to the police. Unwilling to quit each other or go into exile and abandon the fight against apartheid, they choose to make a statement by sacrificing themselves. Vital to the symbolism of this final act is Malan's refusal to commit suicide after dispatching Jessica. Addressing himself to his jailers, Malan reasons, "If I kill myself, it's an admission of failure. Then you'll believe you've hunted me to death, that I couldn't bear it. But if I prove myself ready to endure what lies ahead, if I give myself into your hands, you can never ultimately possess me. For then it will have been my own choice, part of my liberty" (p. 378).

A sexually explicit novel that valorizes interracial intimacy while it condemns the government with extremely graphic descriptions of police beatings and torture, *Kennis van die aand* was immediately banned by the South African Supreme Court for allegedly being "pornographic, blasphemous, and Communistic." It was the first novel written in Afrikaans to suffer such a fate. In an interview with John F. Baker for *Publishers Weekly*, Brink admitted that the banning "was devastating to me. It meant I'd lost my readership" (p. 50). Worse still, the interdiction of *Kennis van die aand* brought Brink unwanted attention from the South African state security apparatus. As he recalled in his interview with Baker, "My phone was tapped, my mail was opened in very obvious ways—they *wanted* you to know they were doing it. Then of course there were the anonymous phone calls, at all hours of the day and night, threatening to kill you and your family. Once a firebomb was thrown at my house. There was an attempt to sabotage my car. I would be called in for interrogation [and] they would search my house, turning everything upside down. Once they even confiscated my typewriter, but I borrowed one from a friend, and it inspired me to work harder than ever" (p. 50).

Deprived of his native audience Brink had no choice but to translate *Kennis van die aand* into English for foreign consumption. In 1974 W. H. Allen published a British edition entitled *Looking on Darkness* and William Morrow brought out a U.S. edition under the same title a year later. Though he had done it before, the experience of translating his own work from Afrikaans to English was especially illuminating this time around. In a 1976 essay ("English and the Afrikaans Writer") Brink recalled the creative process as

one of the most revealing experiences of my life: not "translating" the work, but rethinking it in the framework of a new language; even more important, perhaps, re-feeling it. It even underwent a change of title, to *Looking on Darkness*, indicative of the process involved. It helped me to discover a lot about my own language—more than any translation I had attempted previously. It is remarkable, for example, what difference there exists between the "loads" of emotional content the two languages carry. Afrikaans, like French, appears to offer a much higher resistance to overstatement; it is much more at ease with superlatives and emotions. In English the threshold of overstatement is reached much more readily; "valid" emotionalism in

Afrikaans soon becomes unbearable in English. And this [is] but one, obvious, illustration of how one is forced to "re-feel" a novel in a new medium.

(Writing in a State of Siege, p. 131)

AN INSTANT IN THE WIND

WHILE he was translating *Kennis van die aand* into English Brink started researching *'n Oomblik in die wind* (*An Instant in the Wind,* 1975), a novel that also focuses on miscegenation, but in a different historical context. The inspiration for *An Instant* came from the true story of Eliza Fraser, an Englishwoman who survived the shipwreck of the *Stirling Castle*, a brig homeward bound from Sydney, Australia, to London, that sank off Great Sandy (now Fraser) Island in May, 1836. After being washed up on shore, Fraser endured ten weeks' captivity by the island's aborigines before being rescued by a runaway convict living with the aborigines after his escape. To suit his own agenda, Brink transposed Eliza Fraser's story to a radically different place and time: South Africa in 1749–1751. In Brink's novel Mrs. Fraser becomes Elisabeth Larsson, the wife of Erik Alexis Larsson, a Swedish naturalist leading a geographic expedition into the country's interior. At the outset of the novel Elisabeth (who is pregnant) is stranded alone in the wilderness after the expedition's guide commits suicide, most of the oxen are stolen, the six Hottentot bearers desert, and her husband disappears into the bush. Out of nowhere comes Adam Mantoor, an escaped black slave, and Elisabeth reluctantly joins him to trek back to Cape Town and civilization.

Initially Elisabeth's attitude toward Adam is haughty and mistrustful but softens after he saves her life by bringing her to a Hottentot village for treatment when she begins to miscarry. She loses the baby but eventually recovers her health. As they continue to struggle across the arid, rugged terrain, they lose the wagon, the remaining oxen, and just about everything else, including the cultural indoctrination that defined and separated them as white woman and black man, bourgeois colonial and vassal. Living an elemental life in the wild—in all its stunning beauty and danger—they gradually grow to love one another and enter into a passionate union. Outside the oppressive confines of patriarchal marriage, Elisabeth finds sexual fulfillment and deep human attachment for the first and perhaps only time in her life. The

tragedy, of course, is that their idyll cannot last. Both Adam and Elisabeth must reenter society— separately. Indeed, Brink switched to the subjunctive in the book's closing moments to suggest that Elisabeth will likely betray Adam and get on with her privileged life.

RUMORS OF RAIN

HAVING exhaustively limned the taboo subject of interracial romance, past and present, Brink adopted an entirely new angle of attack for his next novel, *Gerugte van Reen* (*Rumors of Rain*, 1984). Instead of dealing with the subversive politics of racially illicit love, Brink chose to focus on the economic underpinnings of apartheid by creating an in-depth character portrait of the archetypal ruling class Afrikaner. The emblematic figure Brink came up with is Martin Mynhardt, a paunchy, middle-aged mining executive and land speculator who drives a Mercedes 350-SE, has a wife and a mistress, but nonetheless avails himself of hotel prostitutes when he travels internationally. A son of farmers, Mynhardt is part of the new breed of deracinated Afrikaners, having relinquished generations-old ties to the veld for the big-city capitalism of Johannesburg and all its trappings. In the words of the critic Jean Marquand, Mynhardt is "an urbanized and secularized being: wealthy, sophisticated, sensual" (p. 93). A chauvinist in every sense of the term, Mynhardt is also a cynic, an opportunist, and a moral coward who believes that people "are essentially economic propositions" whom he chooses to buy or not buy, depending on the other person's demonstrated "efficacity as a salesman" of himself (*Rumors of Rain*, p. 203).

Though a weighty tome of some 175,000 words, *Rumors of Rain* is intensively synchronic and unified in terms of viewpoint and setting. To best explore Martin Mynhardt's consciousness, Brink has him narrate the novel in the first person and most of the action Mynhardt describes takes place on the family farm over a single weekend. The novel's thematic unity is suggested by Brink's choice of title, which literally refers to a prevailing drought but also serves as a fitting symbol for the country's desiccated but ominous political climate, which threatens to erupt into a sudden deluge of rebellion at any moment.

The plot is simple enough. Martin Mynhardt cancels a planned weekend with Bea, his mistress, to drive up to the family farm with his son,

Louis, to try and convince his (Martin's) mother to sell the farm so that he can reap enormous profits from a secret land deal struck with a government minister. Another reason for the retreat to the country is to try and reconcile with his son, Louis, who was sent to fight in Angola by his government and came back a bitterly disillusioned and radicalized young man. Mynhardt's mistress also disagrees with him over the merits of apartheid. To add to the stress, there has been recent black rioting at the Westonaria mines and Mynhardt's best friend, a lawyer named Bernard Frankel, is in the midst of being tried by the government for treason for taking part in the anti-apartheid struggle. (Some critics have suggested that Frankel is a fictive portrait of Brink's friend, the writer and activist Breyten Breytenbach, but Jean Marquand argued that Frankel is based on Bram Fischer, an activist sentenced to life in imprisonment in Pretoria in 1965 who later died behind bars.) All indications, public and private, point to the need to adopt a forward-looking political stance—one that foresees the inevitable end of white minority rule—but Mynhardt stubbornly refuses to lift his head out of the sand. He simply has too much psychological and financial capital invested in the present system to consider any other point of view.

The results of his intransigence are tragic. Having forsaken his friend Bernard—who is convicted and sentenced to life imprisonment—Mynhardt fails to achieve an understanding with his son. Over the same weekend Mynhardt manages to alienate his mother, and break with his own roots, by forcing her to sign away the ancestral homestead. As he drives back to Johannesburg with Louis on Monday, it finally (symbolically) begins to rain. News comes over the car radio of Bea's arrest in a police raid. More ominously, it is reported that Soweto and the other black townships have erupted in rioting "on an unprecedented scale." Martin Mynhardt experiences shock and dread but, true to life, he has no moral epiphany. On the contrary, he easily abandons Bea to her fate by telling himself that "they wouldn't have arrested her without good reason." That Mynhardt is as obtuse as ever is painfully evident in a soliloquy he delivers near the end of the novel: "I've tried so hard, I've acted with the best of intentions. I've tried to remain loyal to the simple fact of my being here and the need to survive. Isn't that enough?" (p. 435). The entire dramatic weight of the novel answers Mynhardt's disingenuous question with a resounding "no."

A DRY WHITE SEASON

FROM the image of the downpour that breaks the drought at the end of *Rumors of Rain*, Brink returned to a picture of desiccation as the overarching motif of his next novel, *'n Droë wit seisoen* (*A Dry White Season*, 1979). The title comes from a poem by the black South African writer and activist Mongane Wally Serote, which Brink reprinted as the book's epigraph. Its final lines echo *Rumors of Rain* by suggesting the natural inevitability of change: "Indeed, it is a dry white season / but seasons come to pass." As for its sources, in 1982 Brink told the interviewer Jim Davidson that the novel is based on two specific incidents: the case of a "detainee who had allegedly hung himself near King William's Town—Mohapi. The Mduli case in Durban also contributed to it, but it was mainly the Mohapi one which triggered it" (p. 27).

For purposes of verisimilitude and objectivity, Brink employed a Conradian framing device for his narrative. His unnamed narrator is a hack writer of Harlequin-like romance novels suffering through a "dry spell" of writer's block when he receives a sheaf of personal papers from an old university chum named Ben Du Toit. After Du Toit's sudden and rather suspicious demise, his friend undertakes the task of writing the dead man's story, which is, of course, the sum and substance of *A Dry White Season*.

Ben Du Toit is, to all appearances, a perfectly ordinary and respectable white Afrikaner. Middle-aged, married, with two children, the affable Du Toit is a former rugby star turned schoolteacher with a modest but comfortable house in the suburbs of Johannesburg. Yet there is something inside Ben, a rebellious streak, a passion for justice that only requires the right impetus to ignite it into a life changing fire. Gordon Ngubene, a black janitor at Ben's school, supplies that impetus. Police unjustly arrest Ngubene's young son, Jonathan, and subject him to a vicious flogging, "six cuts incised on his buttocks like six gashes of a knife" (p. 36). Gordon pleads with Ben, who has been a friend and a benefactor to his son, to protest to the authorities but Ben advises him to forget the incident. The caning, however, has lasting repercussions. Formerly a good student,

Jonathan becomes a bitter and rebellious boy with "murder in his heart." A year later, in June 1976, he takes part in the Soweto student protests that erupt into the bloody riots alluded to at the end of *Rumors of Rain*. Jonathan disappears during the chaos and Gordon again turns to Ben for help in learning the fate of his son. The response that Ben is finally able to elicit from the Special Branch (secret police) a month after the riots is disturbing in the extreme: it seems that Jonathan has just "died of natural causes." When Gordon tries to collect his son's body for burial, he is repeatedly put off. Finally the police have to admit that Jonathan had never been in detention but had been shot dead the day of the rioting and buried in an unmarked grave. All the official evasions and contradictory reports prompt Gordon to start his own investigation into the case, despite Ben's warnings to leave well enough alone. With remarkable persistence and courage, Gordon collects affidavits from witnesses and begins to piece evidence together—to the considerable discomfort of the Special Branch. To quash the investigation they raid Gordon's home, arrest him, confiscate his papers, subject him to countless beatings, and eventually murder him, but claim he committed suicide by hanging himself in his cell.

Shocked and enraged by Gordon's suspicious death, Ben launches his own investigation into the incident, despite an official inquest that affirms a verdict of suicide. Venturing into the black township to view the corpse, Ben is horrified to discover that Gordon's body shows signs everywhere of severe beating. As he gets closer to the awful truth, Ben is subjected to police surveillance and harassment, ostracized by friends and colleagues, receives death threats, is shot at, sent a bomb, dismissed from his job, and generally branded a traitor to his own people. Eventually his own wife and family turn against him. In an atmosphere of increasing violence, isolation, and paranoia—which makes part 3 of the novel especially gripping—Ben persists in his investigation into Gordon's murder. By this point he has no alternative. His quest for the truth has irrevocably exiled him from the ordinary life he had and turned him into a pariah. Knowing that he is probably slated for the same fate that befell Jonathan and Gordon, Ben contacts his writer friend and passes on his papers just two weeks before he is killed in a mysterious hit-and-run accident, undoubtedly orchestrated by the Special Branch.

The story of a man who finds his soul and conscience but forfeits his life in the bargain, *A Dry White Season* can be considered a kind of inverse mirror image to *Rumors of Rain*. With *Rumors* Brink posited all the necessary conditions for his protagonist's moral transformation, but denied him that transformation to make a point about the resiliency of the ruling ideology. In *A Dry White Season*, Brink's protagonist seizes the opportunity to redeem his own alienated humanity but must die because the apartheid system in which he is immersed cannot tolerate compassion or truth. Taken together, the two books form a devastating portrait of a racist police state that will brook no opposition from blacks or whites. Indeed, as the scholar Rosemary Jolly observed, *A Dry White Season* implicitly calls into question "the problematic nature of bearing witness in the context of white liberalism." Jolly astutely noted that "Ben realizes that to be privileged with certain kinds of information—to have knowledge—does not, in this case, enable either the course of justice or a change in circumstances" (p. 97). Though they examine the potential for white resistance from entirely opposite angles, both *Rumors of Rain* and *A Dry White Season* reach the same conclusion: that the moral and political climate under apartheid presents the ultimate double bind. One can turn a blind eye and die spiritually (or choose exile, which is also a kind of avoidance). The only other alternative is to oppose a monstrously evil totalitarian state and risk imprisonment, torture, and death. In a chilling development in which life imitated art, Stephen Biko, the jailed founder of South Africa's Black Consciousness Movement, died of massive head injuries after a severe beating by security police in August 1977. The uncanny similarities between Biko's case and *A Dry White Season* were too much for Brink. He suspended work on the book for over a year before he was able to resume writing, this time with a renewed intensity of purpose. As he told Jim Davidson, "I realized that it was also a matter of making sure the people knew about it, and were forced never to allow themselves to forget it" (p. 27).

A CHAIN OF VOICES

FOR his next novel, *Houd-den-bek* (literally, "Shut Your Trap," translated into English as *A Chain of Voices*, 1982), Brink returned to South Africa's slavery era to try and shed some light on the psychosexual genesis of the country's race pathology.

The remarkable verisimilitude of *An Instant in the Wind* led many readers to believe, falsely, that Brink had simply fictionalized the story of Adam and Elisabeth from archival material. To write *A Chain of Voices* Brink did revert to real history, in this case, the record of a failed slave insurrection. On 1–2 February 1825, at a remote Cold Bokkeveld farm north of Cape Town called *Houd-den-bek*, eleven black slaves mostly belonging to Nicolaas and Barend van der Merwe rebelled against their white masters, killing three, and wounding two others before being captured. After an eleven-day trial a month after the revolt, guilty verdicts were returned in eight of the eleven cases. Three of the prisoners were sentenced to death by hanging, three sentenced to life at hard labor, and the other two sentenced to fifteen years. Such are the "official" facts of the case, presented by Brink in opening ("Act of Accusation") and closing ("Verdict") sections couched in legal language. These two passages, which are evidently derived from the actual court proceedings, bookend five hundred pages of narrative that constitute the heart of the novel. Therein the *real* history of the uprising is told by some thirty participants in first-person accounts that move the action along in increments as they detail the events that led up to the tragedy. Hence, the title *A Chain of Voices*.

Most prominent among the voices are those of Nicolaas, the murdered master, and Galant, the slave who leads the revolt. De facto brothers in childhood, despite the respective colors of their skin, they are forced into the master-slave relationship mandated by Boer society as they come of age. Neither man is suited to his role. Barend, Nicolaas's older brother, describes Nicolaas as "moody and secretive, often eager to ingratiate himself, but always ready, the moment one's back was turned, to turn against one or split to Ma or Pa" (p. 114). A duplicitous coward and weakling with a shaky sense of his own masculinity, Nicolaas is hardly the man to master Galant, who proves his exemplary strength and courage by saving Nicolaas's life on more than one occasion. Haunted by the yawning disparity between his social authority and innate worth, Nicolaas turns into a sadistic brute. When his embittered wife, Cecilia, accuses him of not being "a real man" for failing to produce a male heir, Nicolaas displaces all of his doubt and self-loathing on Galant's infant son, killing the boy in a fit of "mad, blinding rage." Nor does he stop there. To ritually obliterate

Galant's superior manhood, Nicolaas impregnates Galant's "concubine," Pamela, with a white child. Ultimately driven over the edge of human endurance, Galant retaliates by leading the uprising, killing Nicolaas, and delivering his own symbolic coup de grace by having sex with Barend's unresisting wife, Hester, whom Nicolaas loved.

Critical opinion over the novel was somewhat mixed. Typical of the majority view is Julian Moynahan's flattering observation that *A Chain of Voices* "shows convincingly that the inevitable product of slaveholding is intolerable human abuse: physical abuse of men, physical and sexual abuse of women, neglect and mistreatment of children and, finally, insult and injury to the soul" (p. 1). On the other side of the ledger, Jane Kramer termed the novel "a potboiler of oppression" that insults blacks and whites with . . . feverish impartiality" (p. 9). Offended by what she took to be Brink's stereotypical characterizations of Galant, the archetypal "Brave Black Man," and Hester, the "Good White Woman," Kramer went on to pronounce Brink an unwitting victim of Afrikaner racial clichés. "The Afrikaners in power now in South Africa feed their paranoia on fantasies of a revolution whose necessary end is the black man fucking the white women in the hayloft while the farm burns. Brink feeds his faith in a better future with the same fantasy" (p. 12). While unnecessarily caustic and mean-spirited, Kramer's remarks do point to a problem that dogs much of Brink's early work: a tendency toward miscegenetic melodrama that predictably foregrounds graphic sex and violence: "apartheid gothic," as Jane Kramer put it.

THE WALL OF THE PLAGUE

As if to redress the dramatic excesses of some of his previous work, Brink followed *A Chain of Voices* with a quieter, more allegorical novel: *Die muur van die pes* (*The Wall of the Plague*, 1984). The title literally refers to a wall built in the mountains of the Vaucluse, Provence, to check the spread of the Plague of 1720. The figurative implications of Brink's central image—which he, of course, borrows from Camus's novel, *La Peste* (*The Plague*, 1947)—are complex and many layered. As Anthony Olcott noted, "Brink equates the plague not just with apartheid, but with all the incomprehensible ways in which men hate and destroy one another. . . . The plague begins as a symbol of politics but becomes by the end of Brink's novel almost life itself, the death and corruption which pervades and surrounds life, and in so doing, defines it" (p. 1). Useless against a flea and vermin-transmitted bacillus that no one understood at the time, the now crumbling wall has devolved into a symbol of delusion and futility. In a larger sense, it represents the perennial human wish for sanctuary that can never be attained.

Brink's protagonist, Andrea Malgas, a young South African woman of mixed race, has built her own wall against the plague of apartheid by migrating to Europe, as did Brink himself for a time. Malgas's lover, Paul Joubert, a fifty-year-old white South African novelist and filmmaker living in France, has proposed marriage. Though inclined to accept his proposal, Malgas opts for a few days away from him to think it over. Her hesitancy inheres in the fact that she can never return to South Africa if she weds Joubert; apartheid law forbids marriages between whites and "Cape Coloreds." Though she loathes her homeland for what it has done to her and her family, some sort of conflicted attachment makes the prospect of permanent exile daunting. Brink's epigraph to part 1 of the novel notes that "one died in five days" from the onset of infection by the plague. It is symbolically fitting, then, that Malgas' hiatus involves a five-day tour through Provence to scout shooting locations for *The Black Death*, a film Joubert is making about the plague. Accompanying her, at Joubert's insistence, is his friend, Mandla Mqayisa, a black South African radical on the run from Security Branch agents shadowing his every move. Initially Mandla has little use for Andrea, whom he considers a "try-for-White" race traitor and a snob. Appalled by his apparent arrogance, she is equally disdainful of him. However, as they travel through the bucolic countryside of Provence in autumn, Mandla and Andrea come to share the bitter stories of their lives under apartheid and begin to discover affinities that run deep. Mingled with these vividly realized recollections are haunting historical accounts of the plague and Andrea's unsettling memories of two previous tours of southern France, one with Paul, another with Brian, a former lover. All of these complex influences conspire to disarm Andrea's emotional defenses and render her hopelessly in love with her traveling companion. After they have the sort of earth-shattering sex that makes Brink's detractors wince, Andrea realizes she is essentially, ineluctably black, not white, and has much more in common with Mandla, personally and politically, than she has with Paul Joubert. As she puts it in her farewell letter to Paul, "With Mandla I discovered for the first time that I'd been trying to live a lie for too long" (p. 187). After Mandla disappears from the hotel where they are staying, Andrea learns that he has been killed in a mysterious hit-and-run accident not unlike the one that fells Ben Du Toit in *A Dry White Season*. Finally convinced that trying to run from the plague is pointless, because it is everywhere, Andrea decides to return to South Africa and live out the destiny into which she was born.

In a relatively short coda (part 2), Paul narrates his grief-stricken reaction to Mandla's death and Andrea's leaving him. More importantly, though, Brink has Paul recount a heated political argument he once had with Mandla that speaks to Brink's own, increasingly vexed predicament as a political writer. A good white liberal who espouses nonviolent change, Paul considers his dissident writing and filmmaking a genuine form of political activism. Mandla, a real revolutionary who has suffered torture at the hands of Special Branch thugs, emphatically disagrees: "You stand for everything that's good and right, but you don't have enough faith in it to do something which will make it possible. Nice words you can stuff up your arse, man. It's what you *do* that counts. The rest is bullshit" (p. 439).

STATES OF EMERGENCY

THAT Brink himself was reaching political conclusions similar to those voiced by Mandla Mqayisa is evident in his next novel, his first written only in English: *States of Emergency* (1988). The title refers to the national state of emergency declared in 1985 by South Africa's president P. W. Botha in the wake of steadily escalating protests, counterrevolutionary violence, and economic chaos. Another state of emergency was the crisis of imagination that writers like Brink found themselves facing as they watched their country going up in flames all around them. How was one to write and what was there to write about in the midst of an apocalypse that made literature a triviality?

Brink's answer was to jettison the naturalist idiom that had heretofore been his stock in trade. Adopting a cunning postmodern narrative approach—partly to attack the elitist assumptions of postmodernism—Brink created an author-narrator closely resembling himself. Attempting to compose a pure and simple love story set in contemporary South Africa, Brink's alter ego finds that, despite his best efforts, his narrative keeps getting contaminated by the ugly political realities of apartheid.

The fault does not lie in the attempted novel's source, which is a brilliant but unpublishable novella the narrator has received from Jane Ferguson, a young writer from Natal who subsequently commits suicide by setting herself on fire—hardly a testimony to the redemptive powers of romance ideology! Much taken with Ferguson's manuscript nonetheless, Brink's author-narrator suspends work on a historical novel he was writing, and steals liberally from Ferguson to concoct a story about a "fiftyish," married professor of literary theory named Philip Malan having an affair with Melissa Lotman, his twenty-three-year-old graduate teaching assistant. In what is really an anti-novel, Brink's narrator tells his love story in fits and starts, but mostly makes the reader privy to the creative process by constantly thinking aloud. As he goes along, he enunciates alternative scenarios and plot twists, advances (and retracts) ideas, voices qualms about particular choices and strategies, supplies speculative footnotes, and makes memoranda to himself. By displaying tactical ruminations that are normally kept out of sight, Brink shows how a writer's every imaginative decision, however minute, is ultimately a *political* decision because it has to plausibly represent the complex social world that the protagonists inhabit. In the end, the transfixing political crisis of a security state under general siege invades the imagination of the writer to such a degree that he cannot finish his love story. Sounding like a Samuel Beckett character, Brink's narrator concludes that he "can't go on like this. There can be no end to what has had no beginning" (p. 247).

Brink reinforced the self-deconstructive aspect of the novel by making lots of direct references to the larger political crisis that surrounds the insular, secret affair between Philip and Melissa: another means by which the romance is destabilized and diminished. On a purely structural level, these numerous forays into current events also contribute to the disruption of narrative continuity and help to interfere with the reader's willing suspension of disbelief in the love story. Furthermore, Brink worked his demolition project from the inside out by showing that, as their love

grows in intensity, Philip and Melissa can no longer keep that love covert and compartmentalized; it must, perforce, spill over into the world at large. Whether merely personal or political, real passions have a way of crossing borders and breaking through barriers, much like the plague somehow circumvented the wall in Provence that was supposed to keep it out.

As if all this were not enough, Brink introduced yet another dimension of meaning by mounting a political critique of structuralism (a once fashionable literary theory based in Saussurian linguistics that forms the foundation for much postmodernist critical theory). It is not for nothing that Philip Malan is a professor of literary theory who subscribes to the structuralist notion that the text is everything and is absolutely separate from the world. Tellingly, despite his belief in the hermetic "text *über alles*," Malan finds the "text" of his affair with Melissa increasingly unmanageable as a discreet event—Brink's way of having a "textocentric" critic hoist himself by his own petard. Indeed, Brink went as far as to equate the structuralist impulse with the spirit of apartheid. He sees, in both endeavors, a desire to "keep things apart, distinct, separate (man and woman; life and death; beginning and end; the inside and outside of a text; life and story), to define them in terms of their exclusivity rather than in terms of what they have in common" (p. 83).

CAPE OF STORMS: THE FIRST LIFE OF ADAMASTOR

HAVING supplanted realism with metafiction for *States of Emergency*, Brink ventured even further afield, stylistically, with *Die Eerste lewe van Adamastor* (1988; English language editions published in 1993 as *The First Life of Adamastor* in the United Kingdom and *Cape of Storms: The First Life of Adamastor* in the United States). Indeed, *Cape of Storms* is a total departure for Brink: a comic fable rooted in classical literature and myth. As he explained in the book's introduction, Adamastor ("*In Greek,* adamastos *signifies 'wild,' 'untamed'*") is a character mentioned in passing in the long genealogy of giants catalogued by François Rabelais in the first chapter of *Pantagruel* (1532). Adamastor appears again, more fully realized, in Portugal's national epic, Luis de Camoes' *The Lusiads* (1572), a poem about Vasco da Gama's voyage in 1500 to discover a trade route to India by sailing round the southern tip of Africa. In *The*

Lusiads Adamastor is a repulsive Titan who falls in love with the beautiful sea nymph, Thetis, wife of Peleus and mother of Achilles. Thetis rejects Adamastor because of his deformed appearance and enormous size. Thetis' mother, Doris, tricks Adamastor into believing that she has arranged a tryst for him with her daughter after he agrees to "cease his war against the armies of the Sea." As he attempts to make love to Thetis, Adamastor finds himself embracing a rock, and is transformed by Zeus "into a jagged outcrop of the Cape Pennisula." Eternally punished for his lust, Adamastor utters his own "somber prophecy," that shipwrecks and "all manner of catastrophes [await] the explorers of the Cape of Storms": Camoes' thinly veiled malediction on his countrymen for the plundering, murder, and exploitation committed by the colonialist adventurers who followed in da Gama's wake.

Brink began his own version of the story by entertaining the whimsical hypothesis that there really was an Adamastor. He further imagined that this "original creature, spirit, or whatever he may have been" has "survived through the centuries in a series of disparate successive avatars in order to continue looking over the Cape of Storms" (p. 6). Wondering how such a creature would "look back, from the perspective of the late twentieth century, on that original experience," Brink offered *Cape of Storms* as an answer to his own speculations.

In Brink's rendition, the first incarnation of Adamastor is T'kama, a giant and a young chieftain of the Khoikhoi, southern Africa's aboriginal tribe derisively dubbed "Hottentots" by the Europeans. T'kama falls in love, at first sight, with a white woman inadvertently left behind by a Portugese raiding party routed by T'kama's warriors at what is now Algora Bay, near Port Elizabeth. Naming her "Khois," the Khoi word for "woman," T'kama kidnaps her and makes her his bride, but cannot consummate the marriage. On their wedding night T'kama dons a plumed helmut, ritually smears his entire body with goat fat grease, plasters himself with blue, yellow, and white flowers, and ties an ostrich feather to his outsized male member, to be "the male that is most brightly plumed." Khois' reaction is to burst into a fit of uncontrollable laughter that humiliates T'kama and turns the wedding night into a farce. Funny as it is, the scene points up the vast differences that separate T'kama and Khois. Despite the best of intentions,

custom, skin color, language—and, most of all, T'kama's enormous and ever-growing penis—are formidable obstacles to marital relations. In a parallel scene later in the story, Khois attempts to please T'kama by killing and cooking a hare: a gesture that unwittingly strikes terror into the hearts of the Koikhoi because the animal is deadly taboo. Khamab, the tribal shaman, must summon all his magic powers to make ward off catastrophe. Driven to despair by her failure, Khois complains, "I can't do anything right. I understand nothing about you or your people or this goddamned country. There's nowhere I can go to. My own people abandoned me long ago. Everything is impossible" (p. 121). Khois' lament succinctly expresses the dilemma of the modern Afrikaner, trapped, without a fallback position, in a country and culture he or she can never understand.

The long anticipated mating happens only after T'kama loses his impossibly large phallus to a crocodile while rescuing Khois. Borrowing from the Isis-Osiris myth, Brink has Khamab fashion a more appropriately sized prosthetic penis out of clay, which he then changes into flesh. Husband and wife are finally able to have intercourse, and produce offspring but, staying faithful to Camoes' story of Adamastor, Brink offered no happy ending. One day the Portugese return and Khois opts to rejoin to her people. Heartbroken, T'kama tries and fails to buy her back from the sailors. Worse still, the Portugese (enacted the mythic role of Doris) trick T'kama to a lone rendezvous on the beach. Instead of producing Khois, as promised, they fall upon T'kama, lash him to a boulder, and beat him to death for having consorted with one of their women.

As is true of any parable, Brink's *Cape of Storms* is subject to many interpretations. Suffice to say that, whatever else it might be, *The First Life of Adamastor* is a witty and ironic commentary on the clash of cultures, a clash that produces unending dissonance and frustration until one of the parties relinquishes power or has it wrested from him or her. Even so, peace is short lived. That the story ends with the first of an eternally recurring cycle of betrayals does not seem to bode well for South Africa's destiny.

AN ACT OF TERROR

AFTER his side-trips into metafiction and parable, Brink returned to realism with *An Act of Terror* (1991), a massive tome at 834 pages, and his second novel written only in English. Brink's protagonist is Thomas Landman, a university student and photojournalist from a venerable Boer family that stretches back thirteen generations. By no means an activist, or even very politically oriented, Thomas takes photographs of black South Africans and the violent apartheid street scene primarily for aesthetic and sentimental reasons. When the university shuts down his first one-man show, the police come by to suggest that he choose less controversial subject matter, and the people he photographs begin to wind up dead, Thomas is forced to face the political implications of his artwork. Thomas forms friendships with blacks in the resistance movement and transforms himself into a committed activist. Eventually he and his girlfriend, Nina Jordan, the intense, guilt-ridden daughter of a notoriously cruel Afrikaner judge, are recruited into a terrorist organization. Ordered to take the struggle to assassinate the president, they detonate a bomb but their intended victim escapes harm. Unfortunately, six bystanders are killed in the explosion. In the frenetic manhunt that follows, police track down and shoot Nina. Thomas takes up with another woman and tries to get out of the country with the help of his comrades, but is betrayed by his own brother and the father of his new girlfriend. At the border he is forced to shoot his girlfriend to spare her from being captured by the security police. Wounded himself but delivered into exile, Thomas pauses to reflect on his actions and their consequences: "Had I known then what I do now, would I have chosen a different course?" (p. 614). He finds that he cannot deny or justify what he has done; he can only remember it—and by remembering it, grant it meaning. "Perhaps the whole reason for the chronicle I have been driven for so long to write . . . is this very need to record, to thwart forgetfulness; to grasp at that truth which is not so much the opposite of the lie as of forgetting. *A-letheia*" (p. 614). As a culminating act of truth telling and remembrance, Landman pens a "supplement" that chronicles the entire history of his family, from the first Dutch settlers in the 1600s, to the present day. Though Brink's supplement was meant to offer a radical revision of the heroic myth of the Boer settlers, most critics found the 200-page Landman family history a failure. It is too prolix, boring, and anticlimactic, especially on the heels of the gripping suspense narrative that comprises the lion's share of the novel.

Despite its rather obvious narrative flaws, *An Act of Terror* marked a sea change in Brink's political thought. With this book Brink declared his acceptance of the *necessity* for strategic acts of violence in certain, extreme circumstances, namely when the aggregate, unceasing violence of the state overwhelms and nullifies all moral qualms concerning violent resistance. As Rosemary Jolly put it, in *An Act of Terror* there is "a post-1985 shift in consciousness, one [that] is intolerant of any perceived, facile aestheticization or historization of violence, and radically suspicious of the assumptions of liberal pacifism" (p. 119). Ironically, in 1989, when Brink was still in the midst of writing *An Act of Terror*, South Africa's hard-line president, P. W. Botha, resigned due to ill health. Botha's successor, F. W. de Klerk, proved to be a moderate who put South Africa on a fast track toward ending apartheid by freeing political prisoners (among them Nelson Mandela), lifting the ban on the African National Congress, and repealing apartheid laws. Thus, the pace of current events overtook Brink and rendered his espousal of revolutionary violence somewhat dated when the novel was finally published in 1991.

ON THE CONTRARY

THE title of Brink's eleventh novel, *Inteendeel* (*On the Contrary*, 1993) comes from Henrik Ibsen's last words. The elaborate subtitle is Brink's own: *Being the Life of a Famous Rebel, Soldier, Traveler, Explorer, Reader, Builder, Scribe, Latinist, Lover and Liar*. The life to which Brink refers is that of Estienne Barbier, a Frenchman who came to the Cape in 1734 and was conscripted into the service of the Dutch East India Company as a soldier. A rebel by nature, Barbier led a revolt of disgruntled white Afrikaner farmers in the interior against the corrupt and brutal Dutch administration. Though he managed to evade arrest for awhile, Barbier was captured in 1737, tried for and convicted of treason, and executed. To underscore their displeasure with him, the Dutch cut off Barbier's head and right hand and nailed them to a stake. The rest of his body was quartered and the parts displayed throughout the settlement.

Starting with this basic story, Brink transformed it into an extremely complex fiction: part history, part fantasy, and part allegory about the nature of writing, lies, and truth telling. Brink had Barbier narrate his story in the first person, in a series of

302 letters he writes while awaiting execution. It is immediately clear, however, that Barbier's narrative is impossible. The novel's opening sentence reads: "I am dead: you cannot read: this will (therefore) not have been a letter." Confined in the "stinking Dark Hole of the Castle," Barbier has no light to see, no pen or paper, and the intended recipient of these messages is an escaped slave woman whose whereabouts are unknown, and who cannot read anyway. In short, Brink began his tale by putting it under erasure so as to emphasize the point that the victors write the history and the losers disappear, unless they are imaginatively revived and given a voice. Hence the book's title, which refers not only to Barbier's rebellion against Dutch colonial authority, but also to Brink's imagined narrative, which "speaks against [the] accepted history" that silenced Barbier.

Brink's Estienne Barbier is by no means a hero, or even a reliable narrator. In his revolt against the government, Barbier becomes complicit in the oppression and decimation of the Hottentots being perpetrated by Dutch and Afrikaner alike. He later comes to that realization: "The enemy that first threatened me, the enemy I'm still fighting, is in Cabo [Cape Town]: it's officialdom, corruption, power. The Hottentots are powerless" (p. 139). Barbier, serving as Brink's mouthpiece, makes a related point about the Afrikaners then and now. "I understood at last something of what I'd been living with those past months: this violence, this energy, this seeming exuberant cruelty, this need to subdue all adversaries real and imagined by brute force, this passion to destroy. All of it sprang not from exaggerated confidence, nor even from hate, but from terror: the fear of this vast land, of its spaces, of its unmerciful light, of what lay lurking in this light, of its dark people"(p. 139).

IMAGININGS OF SAND

FORTY-SIX years of apartheid officially came to an end on 27 April 1994, when Nelson Mandela was elected president in South Africa's first democratic election open to the black majority. The issue that had obsessed Brink, and had driven his writings for more than twenty years, suddenly evaporated. Brink's first post-apartheid novel, *Sandkastele* (translated by the author as *Imaginings of Sand*, 1996), set at the time of the elections, celebrates that change in an unexpected way. Therein, Brink concentrated on Afrikaner *women's* voices

and the distaff history they have to tell—which turns out to be more central, and more moving, than the dreary Afrikaner male history of enforcing race and class oppression.

Brink's first-person narrator, thirty-three-year-old Kristien Muller, returns to the Little Karoo, South Africa, from self-exile in England a few days before the big elections in April 1994. The ostensible purpose of her return home is to care for her grandmother, Ouma Kristina, who has been seriously injured after her house was firebombed. However, as the narrative unfolds, it becomes clear that Kristien's real mission is to inherit—and perpetuate—Ouma's rich knowledge of the family's female ancestors. In the words of the critic Michael Kerrigan, the rambling stories that Ouma tells Kristien comprise "the true history of the Afrikaners, its conventional chronology mocked by incestuous relations and deceits between generations, its certainties called into question by a hundred hidden compromises, its purity informed against by centuries of secret miscegenation" (p. 22). A former African National Congress supporter and activist, Kristien had been blunted by politics. Ouma offers a radically different discourse, a kind of timeless tribal dream. Closely attuned to nature's elements and the land, the spirit revivifies instead of deadening it.

Thus *Imaginings of Sand* joins *A Chain of Voices*, *Adamastor*, the supplement to *An Act of Terror, On the Contrary*, and other works by Brink in presenting alternate or revisionist mythologies of the Afrikaner experience that subvert the equally mythic official history. Clearly, Brink believes that healing the wounds of apartheid involves an honest and searching reconstruction of national memory, one that transcends the reductive dualities of oppressor and oppressed. Accordingly, Brink's last several novels manifest an abiding concern with finding new ways to tell new kinds of stories, which may, in fact, be very old stories that were simply repressed, silenced, or forgotten.

SELECTED BIBLIOGRAPHY

I. FICTION. *Die meul teen die hang* (1958); *Die gebondenes* (1958); *Eindelose wee* (Kaapstad, SA, 1960); *Lobola vir die lewe* [*Dowry for Living*] (Kaapstad, SA, 1962), novel; *Die Ambassador* (Cape Town & Pretoria, 1963), novel, translated into English by the author as *File on a Diplomat* (London, 1965), revised edition of translation published in the U.S. as *The Ambassador* (New York, 1985); *Kennis van die aand* (Cape Town, SA, 1973), novel, translated by the author as *Looking On Darkness* (London, 1974; New York, 1975); *'n Oomblik in die wind* (Johannesburg, SA, 1975), novel, translated by the author as *An Instant in the Wind* (London, 1976); *Gerugte van Reën* (Kaapstad, SA, 1978), novel, translated by the author as *Rumours of Rain* (London, 1978, reprinted as *Rumors of Rain*, New York, 1984); *'n Droë wit seisoen* (Emmarentia, SA, 1979), novel, translated by the author as *A Dry White Season* (London, 1979); *Houd-den-bek* [Shut Your Trap] (Emmarentia, SA, 1982), novel, translated by the author as *A Chain of Voices* (London, 1982); *Die muur van die pes* (Kaapstad, SA, 1984), novel, translated by the author as *The Wall of the Plague* (London, 1984); *Loopdoppies: Nog dopstories* (Cape Town, SA, 1984); *States of Emergency* (London, 1988); *Die Eerste lewe van Adamastor* (Kaapstad, SA, 1988), novel, translated by the author as *The First Life of Adamastor* (London, 1993) and published in the U.S. as *Cape of Storms: The First Life of Adamastor* (New York, 1993); *An Act of Terror* (London, 1991); *Inteendeel* (Kaapstad, SA, 1993), novel, translated by the author as *On the Contrary: Being the Life of a Famous Rebel, Soldier, Traveler, Explorer, Reader, Builder, Scribe, Latinist, Lover, and Liar* (Boston, 1993); *Sandkastele* (Kaapstad, SA, 1995), novel, translated by the author as *Imaginings of Sand* (London, 1996); *Duiwelskloof* (Kaapstad, SA, 1998), novel, translated by the author as *Devil's Valley* (London, 1998).

II. DRAMA. *Die band om ons harte* (1956); *Caesar; 'n drama* (Kaapstad, SA, 1961); *Bagasie. Triptiek vir die toneel* [Three one-act plays] (Kaapstad, SA, 1964); *Elders mooiweer en warm* [Elsewhere Fine & Warm][Three one-act plays] (Kaapstad, SA, 1965); *Die verhoor* (1970); *Die rebelle; bestoogstuk in nege episodes* (Kaapstad, SA, 1970); *Kinkels innie kabel* (1971); *Afrikaners is plesierig* [Afrikaners Make Merry] [Two one-act plays] (Kaapstad, SA, 1973); *Pavane* [A three-act play] (Kaapstad, SA, 1974); *Die hamer van die hekse* (Kaapstad, SA, 1976); *Die jogger: 'n drama in twee bedrywe* (1997).

III. LITERARY HISTORY AND CRITICISM. *Orde en chaos; 'n studie oor Germanicus en die tragedies van Shakespeare* (Kaapstad, SA, 1962), literary criticism; *Aspekte van die nuwe prosa* [Aspects of the New Fiction] (Pretoria, SA, 1967; revised edition, 1975), literary criticism; *Die Poesie van Breyten Breytenbach* (Pretoria, SA, 1971), literary criticism; *Aspekte van die nuwe drama* [Aspects of the New Drama] (Pretoria, SA, 1974), literary criticism; *Inleiding tot die Afrikaanse letterkunde, onder redaksie van E. Lindenburg* (Pretoria, SA, 1973); *Voorlopige rapport: Nos beskouings oor die Afrikaanse literatuur van Sewentig* (Kaapstad, SA, 1976); *Jan Rabie se 21* (Pretoria, SA, 1977); *Waarom literatuur?* [Why Literature?] *Inaugural Lecture Delivered at Rhodes University on 23 July 1980* (Grahmstown, SA, 1980; reprinted with other essays, as *Waarom literatuur?* (Kaapstad, SA, 1985); *Tweede voorlopige rapport: Nog beskouings oor die Afrikaanse literature van sewentig* (Kaapstad, SA, 1980); (with others) *Perspektief en profiel: 'n geskiedinis van die Afrikaanse letterkunde*

(Kaapstad, SA, 1982); *Oom Kootjie en die nuwe bedeling* (Emmarentia, SA, 1983), literary criticism; *Mapmakers: Writing in a State of Siege* (London, 1983), published in the United States as *Writing in a State of Siege* (New York, 1983), essays; *Literatuur in die strydperk* [Literature in the Battle Zone] (Kaapstad, SA, 1985), essays; *Vertelkunde: 'n inleiding tot die lees van verhalende tekste* (Kaapstad, SA, 1987); *Reinventing the Continent: Writing and Politics in South Africa, 1982–1995* (London, 1996), published in the United States as *Reinventions: Old Literature, New Climates* (New York, 1996); *Destabilising Shakespeare* (Grahamstown, SA, 1996), literary criticism; *The Novel: Language and Narrative from Cervantes to Calvino* (Cape Town, SA, 1998), literary criticism.

IV. TRAVEL. *Pot-pourri; sketse uit Parys* (Kaapstad, SA, 1962); *Semper diritto; Ilaliaanse reisjoernaal* (Johannsburg, SA, 1963); *Ole! Reisboek oor Spanje* (1965); *Midi; op reis deur Suid-Frankryk* (Kaapstad, 1969); *Parys Parys; retoer* (1969); *Fado: 'n reis deur Noord-Portugal* (1970).

V. OTHER NONFICTION WORKS. *A Portrait of Woman As a Young Girl* (Cape Town, SA, 1973), photography; *Brandy in South Africa* [translated from Afrikaans by Siefried Stander] (Cape Town, SA, 1973); *Dessert Wine in South Africa* (Cape Town, SA, 1974); *The Essence of the Grape: A South Africa Brandy Book* (Cape Town, SA, 1992); *SA, 27 April 1994: 'n skrywersdagboek* (Pretoria, SA, 1994); *27 April: een jaar later* (Pretoria, SA, 1995); *Mal-en ander stories; 'n omnibus van humor* (Kaapstad, SA, 1995); *A Land Apart: A Contemporary South African Reader*, edited by André Brink and J. M. Coetzee (New York, 1987).

VI. TRANSLATIONS. Ester Wier, *Die Eenspaaier* [The Loner] (Kaapstad, SA, 1967); J. M. Synge, *Die bobaas van die boendoe* [The Playboy of the Western World] (Kaapstad, SA, 1973); William Shakespeare, *Die Tragedie van Romeo en Juliet* (Kaapstad, SA, 1975); Jeanne Goosen, *Ons is nie almal* [Not All of Us] (Strand, SA, 1992); Antoine de Saint-Exupery, *Die klein Prinsie* [The Little Prince] (Kaapstad, SA, 1994).

VII. INTERVIEWS. Richard Eder, "An Interview with André Brink," in *New York Times Book Review* 85 (23 March 1980); Jim Davidson, "An Interview with André Brink: Writing in South Africa," in *Overland* 94/95 (May 1984); Alberto Manguel, "Writers at the Brink," in *Commonwealth* 111 (13 July 1984); Sue Kossew, "Writing in the 'New' South Africa: An Interview with André Brink," in *Commonwealth Essays and Studies* [Dijon, France] 18, no. 1 (autumn 1995); John F. Baker, "André Brink: In Tune with His Times," in *Publisher's Weekly* 243, no. 48 (15 November 1996); John Higgins, "What You Never Knew: An Interview with André Brink," in *Pretexts: Studies in Writing and Culture* 8, no. 1 (July 1999).

VIII. FILM. *A Dry White Season* (directed by Euzhan Palcy, Metro-Goldwyn-Mayer, 1989).

IX. BIOGRAPHICAL AND CRITICAL STUDIES. Frank Pike, "Veldanschauung," in *Times Literary Supplement* 3888 (17 September 1976); Robert L. Berner, "South Africa: 'An Instant in the Wind,'" in *World Literature Today* 51 (autumn 1977); Lewis Nkosi, "Afrikaner Arithmetic," in *Times Literary Supplement* 3994 (20 October 1978); Jim Hoagland, "Storm Over Soweta," in *Washington Post Book World* (5 November 1978); Jean Marquand, "Selected Books: 'Rumours of Rain,'" in *London Magazine* 19 (June 1979); Mel Watkins, "A Novelist's Impassioned Indictment," in *New York Times Book Review* 85 (23 March 1980); Anne Collins, "Three Tales From the Land of Black and White," in *Maclean's Magazine* 95 (10 May 1982); Julian Moynahan, "Slaves Who Said No," in *New York Times Book Review* (13 June 1982); Jane Kramer, "In the Garrison," in *New York Times Book Review* 39 (2 December 1982); Anthony Olcott, "The Long Reach of Apartheid," in *Book World—The Washington Post* (17 February 1985); George Stade, "A Pipsqueak's Obsession," in *New York Times Book Review* 91 (29 June 1986); A. J. Hassal, "The Making of a Colonial Myth: The Mrs. Fraser Story in Patrick White's *A Fringe of Leaves* and André Brink's *An Instant in the Wind*," in *Ariel* 13 (July 1987); Philip Horne, "Tunnel Visions," in *London Review of Books* (4 August 1988); Rosemary Jane Jolly, "Spectacles of Horror: Violence in the English Prose Works of André Brink, Breytenbach and J. M. Coetzee" (Ph.D. diss., University of Toronto, 1991); Randolph Vigne, "The Argument for Terrible Deeds," in *San Francisco Review of Books* 17 (January 1992); Paul Preuss, "Digging Their Own Graves," in *Book World—The Washington Post* 22 (15 March 1992); Lillian Hilja Andon-Milligan, "André Brink's South Africa: A Quality of Light," in *Critique* 34, no. 1 (fall 1992); Abdulrazak Gurnah, "Prospero's Nightmare," in *Times Literary Supplement* 4691 (26 February 1993); Mario Vargas Llosa, "Love Finds a Way," in *New York Times Book Review* (25 July 1993); Clarence Major, "An Improbable Love," in *Los Angeles Times Book Review* (29 August 1993); Mark Wormald, "Images of Africa," in *Times Literary Supplement* 4718 (3 September 1993); Peter S. Prescott, "The Cape of Not Much Hope," in *New York Times Book Review* (14 August 1994); Sue Kossew, "Pen and Power: A Post-Colonial Reading of the Novels of J. M. Coetzee and André Brink" (Ph.D. diss., University of New South Wales, 1994); Michael Kerrigan, "A Vision of Birds," in *Times Literary Supplement* 4845 (9 February 1996); Amanda Hopkinson, "Hidden from History," in *New Statesman and Society* (23 February 1996): 45, 46; Rosemary Jane Jolly, *Colonization, Violence, and Narration in White South African Writing: André Brink, Breyten Breytenbach, and J. M. Coetzee* (Athens, Ohio, 1996); Alison Michelle Kenzie, "The Magnificent Sense of Being Relevant': A Comparative Study of Milan Kundera and André Brink" (Ph.D. diss., University of Ontario, 1998); Sussi Poulsen, "'Cry Freedom' and 'A Dry White Season,'" in *South African Resistance Culture*, ed. Gorm Gunnarsed (Copenhagen, Denmark, 1998); Peter Horn, "I Am Dead: You Cannot Read André Brink's On the Contrary," in *Writing South Africa: Literature, Apartheid, and Democracy, 1970–1995*, ed. Rosemary Jolly (Cambridge, 1998); Daniel Jones and John D. Jorgenson, eds., *Contemporary Authors: New Revision Series*, vol. 62 (Detroit, Mich., 1998); Sue Kossew, "From Eliza to Elisabeth: André Brink's Version of the Eliza Fraser Story," in *Constructions of Colonialism: Perspectives on Eliza Fraser's Shipwreck*, ed. Ian McGiven et al. (London, 1998).

GEORGE MACKAY BROWN

(1921–1996)

Sandie Byrne

GEORGE MACKAY BROWN was born in Stromness, on the main island of Orkney, on 17 October 1921. That statement, of a kind that routinely opens entries in works of reference and is often more or less inconsequential to the student of the writing, is highly significant to the life and work of this author. He was first and last an Orcadian, devoted to the landscape, people, history, culture, and language of the Orkney islands, and he spent most of his life among them. In "Enchantment of Islands," he asserts that a poet

could not choose a better place to be born than a group of islands, like Orkney. . . .

A poet is wealthy indeed who has such a store of symbols to draw upon. (If I had been born in Birmingham, for example, I would know that any creativity in me would be impoverished from the start, perhaps fatally.)

(*Northern Lights: A Poet's Sources*, p. 3)

The Orkneys are a group of islands to the north of Scotland and divided from that country by a stretch of water known as the Pentland Firth. The convergence of tides from the Atlantic and the North Sea produces turbulent seas, and the islands are wind-scoured and storm-battered. Continuously inhabited for over five thousand years by successive peoples, the Orkneys bear traces of their early human history in stone and earthworks built by the first inhabitants and the mantle of tilth that has gradually been built up on the islands' rock core since the Picts and the invaders who displaced them, the Celts, began to plow and plant. The more recent inhabitants have a dual heritage, Scottish and Norse. Trading routes were established between Norway and the Orkneys in the early centuries of the first millennium, and while most Viking ships came to exchange or plunder goods and move on, some remained to become fishermen and farmers, so that the Orkneys became an earldom held in vassalage to the king of Norway. The great narrative of the islands, the *Orkneyinga Saga*, is a Norse saga, and Orkney names for both people and places carry traces of the Norse language: Hamnavoe, Hrossey, Braal, Eric, Thorfinn.

By the eleventh century, Earl Thorfinn of Orkney was overlord to nine Scottish earldoms and equal in power to the king of Scotland. The earldom was often in dispute, however, and it was in the interests of Norway to foster both rival claims, since Orkney under a single strong lord could well have demanded independence. The story of one such dispute, preserved in the *Orkneyinga Saga*, captured the imagination of George Mackay Brown. The disputants, Hakon and Magnus, agreed to meet on the island of Egilsay on Easter Monday of 1117. Magnus came as arranged, with only two ships and a few trusted advisors, but Hakon came with eight ships full of troops. That night, Magnus stayed in the church of Egilsay; the next morning he faced Hakon, who ordered his death. None of the warriors would kill Magnus on the holy festival, so Hakon gave the axe to his cook, Lifolf, who could hardly refuse. Lifolf was unwilling, and wept, but Magnus spoke kindly to him, and absolved him of guilt. Lifolf cleft Magnus' skull with the axe, and Hakon became earl of Orkney. Magnus was buried in Birsay, and his tomb became a site of miraculous cures and visions. Later, his remains were removed to Kirkwall and put into a pillar of the cathedral being built there, where they still remain, and he was canonized as a saint.

As the clan chiefs of Scotland grew more united, the Orkneys were drawn toward the nearest mainland, and in 1263, when King Hakon of Norway was defeated in battle at Largs (in southwest Scotland), Norway lost control of the islands. The Orkneys have been officially part of the kingdom of Scotland since 1472 (and thus part of the United Kingdom since the Act of Union of 1707).

In *For the Islands I Sing*, Brown wrote of the historical events behind his stories and poems.

Without the violent beauty of those happenings eight and a half centuries ago, my writing would have been quite different. . . . There are, fortunately for me, many legendary and historical sources in Orkney from later centuries that any native-born writer can seize on with delight—but still the great story of Magnus and Hakon is the cornerstone.

(p. 9)

In the same book, he describes a visit to the Cathedral of Saint Magnus in Kirkwall during a day out from a sanatorium in 1941 as an intense experience that was to quicken his imagination again and again in the following years:

in the south-east corner of the Cathedral, there has grown a cluster of plaques to Orkney's writers and scholars. I would be glad, I suppose, to have my name and years there, after my death.

(p. 81)

A footnote reads "The Island Council's Cathedral Committee have agreed to have this done."

George was the youngest of the six children of a mailman and tailor, John (Jack) Brown, an Orkneyman whose family had probably come from Scotland in the sixteenth century or later, and Mhairi-Sheena Mackay, daughter of a crofter-fisherman of Strathy, in Sutherland (on the north coast of Scotland). The Mackays were Gaelic-speaking; by the time Mhairi-Sheena went to school, she knew only two words of English ("yes" and "no"), but the language was compulsory at school. Once at work in one of the hotels catering for the new tourist industry of Stromness, she soon became "Mary Jane."

The family lived in an old house near the coast until 1934, when they moved to a new, ugly council house on the outskirts of Stromness. After the death of his father in 1940, and the gradual dispersal of the older children through work and marriage, GMB, as he was known to his friends and readers of his columns, lived there with his mother until he enrolled in an adult education college in Scotland. His early education at the state school in Stromness did not inspire GMB to scholastic or literary endeavor; in *For the Islands I Sing*, he was to write of it as "a great mill grinding out sterile knowledge; there was no room for delight or wonderment," and to say, "I still shudder when I recall how English was taught" (p. 28). The only subject that made "the blood sing" along his veins and nourished his imagination was history, "the

romantic spindrift of history, not the great surges of tribes and economics and ideas" (p. 31). He excelled only at essay writing, and found that literature crept up on him by stealth. Early poetic influences were William Wordsworth, Percy Bysshe Shelley, John Keats, Robert Burns, and William Butler Yeats, and, in prose, Joseph Conrad's "Heart of Darkness" (1902) and George Douglas Brown's *The House with the Green Shutters* (1901), which GMB described as the best Scottish novel of the twentieth century. Douglas Brown was an important influence on many Scottish writers. He was the first since John Galt to break with the sentimental "kailyard" tradition of J. M. Barrie and Ian MacLaren and the equally escapist adventure romances of Robert Louis Stevenson, and he deployed the structure of Greek tragedy and the minute detail of realism in order to depict small town Scottish life in its grim repressiveness. While GMB suggests that he stumbled on novels that meant something to him, he was not an avid or wide reader, and built up a resistance to set texts. The effect of the enforced three weekly chapters of Walter Scott was such that even half a century later (1985), he could not open the novels with pleasure (see *For the Islands I Sing*, p. 45).

A severe case of measles compounded by heavy smoking (which he had taken up at twelve) led to a weakness in the lungs, and GMB's skill and enthusiasm for football ebbed away. He began to find himself gasping for breath on the steep hills of Orkney and was diagnosed as having pulmonary tuberculosis. At the time (1941) there was no cure but the sanatorium regime of rest, wholesome food, and fresh air. He notes in *For the Islands I Sing* that in some ways he was grateful for the tubercle that "saved me from the world of 'getting and spending' that I had dreaded," for if there were to be "much of a future at all, it would be passed in a kind of limbo where little or nothing was expected of me" (p. 58). Rendered "unemployed and unemployable," he read, dreamed, and wrote. For two years, his mother kept him in food, cigarettes, and clothes, until the government granted a small weekly allowance to sufferers from tuberculosis, from which he gave his mother £1 and kept ten shillings, "and felt as rich and free as a lord." He began to write poetry and to contribute news items and book reviews to the *Orkney Herald*, as well as a weekly column under the name "Islandman." Later the *New Shetlander* (published on the group of islands further north east of the Orkneys) also began to take his work. In 1942 he wrote his first play, now lost, set in the Viking era, and he sent it to the Orkney novelist Eric Linklater, who returned it with constructive comments. As well as the sagas that were constant models and sources of inspiration, GMB was reading Linklater, the Orkney poet Edwin Muir, E. M. Forster, and Thomas Mann; later came Berthold Brecht and Gerard Manley Hopkins.

Stromness had been a "dry" town (in which alcohol could not be sold) since the end of the First World War, but in 1947 the town became "wet" again, and the main hotel opened two bars. GMB recollected that on going in to try a glass or two of beer, he was instantly "hooked." For him, alcohol was the key to a world in which he had no cares, no worries, and no shyness. After that, he was often drunk, and several times led home and dumped like a sack on his mother's doorstep (see *For the Islands I Sing*, pp. 66–67).

The opening of the pub had introduced a new element into his writing: the change that alcohol brings about on personality, in particular in enabling the northern personality to shed its stoical mask and give vent to pent-up emotions. GMB was a drinker for thirty years, dividing his allegiance, as he put it, between drink and writing. Ultimately, though he continued to use his insights into the workings of the mind under drink, he chose to give his allegiance to writing (see *For the Islands I Sing*, pp. 69–70).

A local bookseller, Ernest Marwick, published some of GMB's poems in his *Anthology of Orkney Verse* in 1949 and introduced him to the first of several important literary mentors, Robert Rendall. In 1946 GMB visited the island of Hoy and explored its sea valley, Rackwick, whose beauty struck him forcibly. This was to be the setting for many of his poems and stories, as well as the subject of some nonfiction writing, and it became a recurring symbol in many of his stories and poems. The poem cycle *Fishermen with Ploughs* (1972) is based on Rackwick life.

In the winter of 1950–1951 GMB joined an evening class "out of boredom" and was asked by the director of adult education to consider entering the new adult education college of Newbattle Abbey in Dalkeith, on mainland Scotland, to which the Orkney poet Edwin Muir had been appointed warden. The college was a republic of letters that fostered passionate debates and inspired its students to creative as well as academic enterprise. GMB was to say that the influence of Muir and the four close friends he had as a student helped to make him a writer. Newbattle gave him the stimulation, purpose, and direction he needed (see *For the Islands I Sing*, p. 93).

In 1953 tuberculosis reasserted itself, and GMB was confined to a sanatorium for more than a year, but this time treatment with powerful new drugs enabled him to be discharged in the summer of 1954 with the progress of the disease at least postponed by several years.

He returned to Newbattle Abbey for a final term but was expelled for returning drunk after a spree. The intervention of a Church of Scotland minister then studying at the college gained him a reprieve, and he was permitted to stay, on the understanding that for the rest of his time as a student at Newbattle he would abstain from pubs. After Newbattle, he spent four years at Edinburgh University, during which time he met one of the few women to have a profound influence on his life. He describes Stella Cartwright as a star and a muse who was the inspiration for many of his contemporary Scottish poets.

After the university, the "desert"—Orkney—"waited; unless, that is, I found a job and settled down. For such as me, there was only one avenue open: teaching. . . . I enrolled, dully, at the Moray House College of Education in October 1960. There were lectures and tutorials of crushing boredom." His first teaching practice was salutary. He knew, he wrote, with absolute certainty "that God hadn't called me to be a teacher" (see *For the Islands I Sing*, pp. 144–145).

GMB records his near-gratitude for the return of his old enemy, which saved him from becoming a teacher. A bad attack of bronchitis incapacitated him: an X-ray showed that the tubercle was active again. He was treated in the City Hospital and at a sanatorium near Aberdeen. In February 1962 patched up once more, he returned to Edinburgh, still officially a student, but he withdrew from the teaching course and went back to Orkney. Learning of the funds available for graduate research, he applied and was accepted to do a year's work on Gerard Manley Hopkins, during which time he lived in Stockbridge, near Edinburgh.

It was in an Edinburgh bed-sitter in 1958 that GMB had received a letter that was to mark one of the turning points in his life as a writer. Norah Smallwood, a director of the Hogarth Press, wrote to offer publication of his poems, which she had been shown by Edwin Muir. *Loaves and Fishes* was published in 1959. The Hogarth Press was to publish several of GMB's poetry and short story collections, and Norah Smallwood remained a friend until her death in 1984, though the Hogarth poetry editor, Cecil Day Lewis, rejected a selection of poems submitted in 1962, on the grounds that some of the imagery was barren. Though initially disappointed, GMB was spurred on by the rejection to better things and was to write that, in retrospect, he was glad that the collection had not been published (see *For the Islands I Sing*, p. 167).

Although his early poetry collections were received with indifference, the nonfictional *Orkney Tapestry* (1973) and fictional *A Time to Keep* (1969) and *Greenvoe* (1972) found both critical approval and popularity, enabling GMB to make a living from his writing. In 1965 he was awarded an Arts Council grant for poetry; in 1968 he was awarded the Society of Authors Travel Award, which he used to visit Ireland. The volume *A Time to Keep* won the 1969 Scottish Arts Council Prize, and its title story the Katherine Mansfield Merton short-story prize for 1971. GMB continued to publish at regular intervals through the 1970s and into the 1990s; his *The Golden Bird* (1987) was awarded the James Tait Black Memorial Prize in 1988, and *Beside the Ocean of Time* (1994) was shortlisted for the Booker Prize in 1994 and judged Scottish Book of the Year by the Saltire Society. He was given honorary degrees from the Open University, Dundee University, and Glasgow University; in 1974 was awarded the OBE.; and in 1977 was made a fellow of the Royal Society of Literature. During this time he rarely moved far from the Orkneys, where he died on 15 April 1996.

Brought up in the Presbyterian faith, Brown converted to Catholicism in the early 1960s, an experience about which he wrote in an essay for the Catholic newspaper *The Tablet*, and which influenced many of his short stories. Though committed, his faith was unorthodox.

WRITING

ALTHOUGH famously reclusive and not fond of giving interviews, GMB left a wealth of detail about the sources, design, and techniques of his craft, in his column, published diary, and articles. His foreword to *A Calendar of Love* (1967) begins: "Orkney is a small green world in itself. . . . Round that still

centre all these stories move" (p. 9). Novels, short stories, poetry, nonfiction, which are not clearly demarcated in GMB's writing, all preserve the rhythm of life on the islands in its rituals and cycles and occasional disruptions. His weekly essays in *The Orcadian*, "Letter from Hamnovoe" (later published as "Under Brinkie's Brae"), follow the wheel of the year. The immediate concerns of the here-and-now—the way the fish are running, whether the weather will hold for harvest, the market bus—are no more real than the days and people of the past: the pirate John Gow, Saint Magnus, Lammastide, the bombing of 1941, the Johnsmas fires. GMB's sense of Orkney time is contained in an essay for the winter solstice (21 December) of 1995, an imaginative evocation of the building of Maeshowe.

Today is the shortest day of the year—winter solstice—and it must have been a time of great worry for the first Orcadians, those who came after the retreat of the ice.

Ever since midsummer—a time they had greeted with dancing and fires—the sun had begun to dwindle . . .

True, every winter hitherto the sun, after the time of bright stars and snow, had begun to revive. . . . It would, as every year, keep tryst with the new grass and the lambs and the shoals of fish and the wild flowers . . .

And yet the thinking men of the tribe . . . reasoned that this cycle of the sun might not necessarily last for ever . . .

For the dead islander, there was no new beginning . . . So it might happen with the sun.

There might come a winter in which there would be no miracle of renewing. No, the winter fire of the sun would cool to a glowing cinder and then go out, finally and for ever. And the tribe would perish in that last ice . . .

And to show that they had the welfare of the life-giving sun at heart (as well as, incidentally, their own welfare) they consulted with the quarry-men and the hewers of stones and the mightiest mason among them sketched plans on a sheepskin with a charmed stick.

They built, over a generation, a stone hymn to the sun on the moor between two lochs.

Then they attempted what seemed impossible: the building of a great sun-temple six or seven fields away. . . . They made niches in the walls where dead chiefs and young dead princesses were laid.

There, along the corridor of Orkahowe, the sun entered at the solstice, and touched, with a golden finger, a tomb with the dead jewelled bones in it.

We must imagine, perhaps, a great cry of lamentation changing to a chorus of joy. The sun would not die. And even the dead would taste the chalice of immortality (who knows how?).

(*Northern Lights: A Poet's Sources*, pp. 71–72)

Although the Vikings provide some of the most famous and colorful chapters in Orkney's history, and its earliest literature, GMB is attracted to these earlier peoples whom, in *Portrait of Orkney*, he calls "the first breakers of the earth, the hewers of stones, the subtle ones who divined water and opened wells. It is their quiet voices that will end the story" (p. 91).

Several of the short stories describe the importance of storytelling to a community, and of the importance of the storyteller as repository of the history and folk memory of the people. When the stories are no longer told and the last storyteller dies, the past dies with them: "contemporary Orkney, cut off from the story of its past, is meaningless" (*An Orkney Tapestry*, p. 19). In the same book, GMB places himself in a line of descent from the Celtic bards and *olaves*, and the Norse saga-men and *skalds*, whose responsibility it was to

get back to the roots and sources of the community, from which it draws its continuing life, from which it cuts itself off at its peril. With the help of the old stories, the old scrolls, the gathered legends, and the individual earth-rooted imagination, I will try to discover a line or two of the ancient life-giving heraldry.

(p. 23)

This is not to suggest that the purpose of his work was to produce empirical history; the fiction is as much a source as the nonfiction, and even the latter "takes its stand with the poets" (p. 1). Art, myth, folklore, and history are interrelated and sometimes indistinguishable, and each has a related function. The art of storytelling and the making of poetry, like all art for GMB, must be a utilitarian craft. The function might be practical, religious, or mystical, but there must be a function. In "Lore," the blind fiddler Storm Kolson insists that "Art must be of *use*"; it must be "a coercive rhyme, to strand a whale on the rock, a scratch on stone to make the corn grow." He asks: "What are all these statues and violins and calf-bound editions for?" (*An Orkney Tapestry*, p. 130).

THE NOVELS

GMB's first novel, *Greenvoe*, in some ways resembles his collections of linked short stories. Each chapter of narrative fiction, representing the actions, large and small, of a cast of islanders during one of six days, is interspersed with poetry,

and ends with a segment of a drama that resembles an ancient fertility ritual. There is a plethora of narrative perspectives, styles, and moods, and an interaction between the conventional characterization of the inhabitants of Greenvoe and Hellya as three-dimensional individuals and their roles as types, or archetypes, in a formal ritual. Particularly interesting is the character of Elizabeth McKee, whose imagination puts her in the dock each day, facing a tribunal of accusers who scrutinize episodes from her past. In *For the Islands I Sing*, GMB remarks that though *Greenvoe* had proved the most popular of all his books, he did not care to read it except to "commune with my old friend Mrs McKee. She is a consolation. We have things we can say to one another" (pp. 176–177). The character, he insisted, had taken on an independent life:

[She] emerged and began, in her shy self-effacing way, to assert herself . . . as if she said, "I won't be confined within two dimensions, there are facets of me that must be shown, I refuse to be an inert paper cut-out." And so Mrs McKee, whom I grew to love more and more as the novel unfolded, led me gently into her past life; and, wisely, she led me among places I was familiar with: Edinburgh, and chiefly the district of Marchmont where both of us had lived at different times. Also she led me into places of the mind that I knew a little about, those places of guilt, prosecution, judgement, which, while they last, make life bitter and terrible. . . .

I think Elizabeth McKee and I have had more joy and understanding of each other than any other character I have imagined.

(pp. 174–175)

The novel returns to the theme of the preservation of an Orkney way of life under threat from human greed in the guise of progress, here represented by the "Operation Black Star," which is to despoil the island of Hellya. Ten years after the final evacuation, a small rowboat draws up off the coast of Hellya, and a group of men climb its cliff face by dusk. In the ruins of an ancient keep they enact a ritual. "Young Skarf" plays the Harvester, who is trampled by "the horse-shoe he had borne so faithfully and so long" and lowered into a grave by the Master Horsemen and Lord of the Harvest. Symbolically resurrected, he shares a communion of bread and whisky, and the Lord of the Harvest declares that they have "'brought light and blessing to the kingdom of winter . . . however long it endures, that kingdom, a night or a season or a thousand ages,'" and that the "word has been found." The novel ends, "The sun rose. The stones were warm. They broke the bread" (pp. 248–249).

GMB appears to be suggesting that while individual personalities have their day, and might even have an effect on the islands (by, for example, selling their houses to Operation Black Star), the larger pattern continues without deviation. Beneath the small acts of everyday life are imperishable rhythms and cycles.

By the 1990s GMB was a legendary figure whose accounts of the background to his fiction were considered worthy of space in the national newspapers. "Et in Orcadia Ego: On the Dreams of War and Peace which Inspired *Time in a Red Coat*" (*Independent*, 3 August 1991, p. 25) is a fascinating example of an author's self-exposition, and a useful guide to *Time in a Red Coat*, which is a complex, allegorical, symbolic work. Both the central characters and the quest plot of the novel are archetypes. The heroine is both an elemental creature associated with water in all its forms and "all woman, princess and peasant-lass and fish-wife, who have lived or who will live," and she is "afloat on the river of time" (p. 33), which is "the life of the whole tribe, the whole nation, the totality of the human race, and indeed of all creation" (p. 31). The girl's task is to pursue the dragon (war), not to kill it but to reconcile it with other symbolic creatures, horse (earth), dove (air), and fish (water), using a magical ancient musical instrument made of ivory. After her quest is complete, the girl marries an Orkney fisherman, ceases to move through time and space, and sheds her universal persona for an individual identity: "Maurya." Her story is not linear, however, but circular, following the cycle of water from rain to stream, to well, to river, to ocean, to clouds, and back again.

The novel contains an image of the ancient perception of the oneness of things, which, for GMB, modernity has lost.

For the river folk and the peasant, roses and nightingales and the moon were there, parts of the web of creation like themselves, and so the lives of flowers and birds and winter skies were grained into their flesh and blood; all created beings belonged to each other.

(p. 36)

Magnus, though based on historical events, is similarly allegorical and archetypal and exemplifies GMB's doctrine that all forms of art must gather into themselves a huge scattered diversity of experience and reduce them to patterns; so that, for example, in a poem all voyages, past, present, and future—become The Voyage, and all battles The Battle, and all feasts The Feast. This is to look at those events of time which resemble one another yet are never quite the same, in a symbolical way. The symbol becomes a jewel enduring and flaming throughout history. Therefore all our little journeys and fights and suppers that seem so futile once they are over, are drenched with the symbol, and retain a richness they never had while they were being experienced.

(p. 140)

Thus, for GMB, a story of local incident becomes The Story of timeless universality, and the storyteller, in his or her self "a person of no consequence," in the telling of the tale becomes magical:

While the ballad lasted these great ones of Orkney were his utterly, he could make them laugh or weep as he chose, or beg for more like dogs. His slow formal chant probed them to their innermost sanctuaries; showed them, beneath their withering faces, the enduring skull; but hinted also at an immortal pearl lost under the vanities and prodigalities of their days.

(pp. 153–154)

The story of the martydom of Magnus becomes part of a pattern that, in *For the Islands I Sing*, GMB calls

an image or an event stamped on the spirit of man at the very beginning of man's time on earth; that will go on repeating itself over and over in every life without exception until history at last yields a meaning. The life and death of Magnus must therefore be shown to be contemporary. . . . I did not have far to go to find a parallel: a concentration camp in central Europe in the spring of 1944.

(pp. 178–179)

The novel reiterates the point: though events are never the same, they

have enough similarity for one to say tentatively that there are constants in human nature, and constants in the human situation, and that men in similar circumstances will behave roughly in the same fashion.

(pp. 139–140)

The twentieth-century manifestation of the archetypal figure of sacrifice and goodness becomes Pastor Dietrich Bonhoeffer, and his killers are the Nazis. Magnus is more than a willing sacrifice in this novel, he is also a predestined sacrifice, a chosen one from his conception, and he has a vision of himself as part of a "pattern within-flux," reborn to be that chosen one again, in different eras. He sees himself

in the mask of a beast dragged to a primitive stone. A more desolate image followed, from some far reach of time: he saw a man walking the full length of a bare white ringing corridor to a small cube-shaped interior full of hard light; in that hideous clarity the man would die.

(p. 141)

Magnus, whether as Erlenddson (son of Earl Erlend) or Saint, had been an important figure to GMB for many years before the novel was published in 1973, and the development of the fictional Magnus can be seen in two editions of the periodical *New Shetlander*, to which GMB was a regular contributor: "Magnus Martyr: A Fragment" in *New Shetlander* 24 (July–September 1950): 44–45 and "Magnus Martyr: An Episode from a Novel," in New Shetlander 25 (October–December 1950): 22–25.

The Norse sagas do not employ the techniques of characterization and the delineation of motivation that, for readers of modern realist fiction, seem essential for the development of an engrossing story. Character is lightly sketched in, and central protagonists are archetypes rather than complex individuals and are endowed with the conventional heroic virtues: courage, loyalty, stoicism, warcraft. There are no long passages of introspection; there is little psychological drama; and the reader is expected to understand certain things without being told. GMB's novels have something of the quality of a saga, and like the sagas will often follow a journey and a battle that are both physical and symbolic.

Vinland (1992), his fourth novel, is the story of Ranald, who sails from Hamnavoe in the ship of his father, Sigmund Firemouth, but after an unjust beating jumps ship at Reykjavik and stows away on the *West Seeker*, captained by the far kinder Leif Ericson, a better seaman. Leif sails to Greenland and on west, past the boundaries of the known world, to a land where they are met by strange, hawk-nosed men with black hair, eyes like stones, and faces painted yellow and red and white. In spite of the northerly latitude, the land grows sweet grapes, which Leif believes would make good wine, so he names the new territory Vinland. The explorers return to Norway to gather supplies and more settlers, and Ranald meets Olaf, the king. He returns to Orkney, where he finds his mother dispossessed of the family home and living in poverty under an usurping pirate at Breckness, her father's farm. Ranald reclaims his inheritance, becomes a successful farmer and counselor of the Earl, visits Ireland, marries, is embroiled in the politics of the lordship of the Orkneys, and finally makes his last voyage, to Tir-Na-N-Og, the land of youth. Within Ranald's story are woven many others, in song, legend, and the tales of travelers and poets.

The title of the novel at first seems deceptive— Ranald and the sailors make only a brief stay in the half-mythical territory. Vinland comes to stand for something more than a new settlement, however; it is the object of a quest, the elusive object of desire, the yearning for something once glimpsed and half remembered. Ranald wants to return, not to amass riches or establish a trading route or found a new colony but to make peace with a native boy. While the Viking and native warriors circle each other suspiciously, the two boys, without ingrained mistrust, splash in the sea, climb trees, and move toward a friendship, which is aborted by the adults. All his life, Ranald speaks of commissioning a ship to sail back to Vinland, but when he is an old man, making his soul in a small hut beyond his farmstead, the voyage to Vinland becomes interchangeable with his last journey, to the Isles of the Blessed after Saint Brendan, or to Tir-Na-N-Og, or to death.

GMB's narrative style has the directness of the oral tradition and the clarity of folktale. *Beside the Ocean of Time* (1994) opens in characteristic style:

Of all the lazy useless boys who ever went to Norday school, the laziest and most useless was Thorfinn Ragnarson.

"I don't know what to do with you, you're useless," said Mr Simon the teacher. "I'll speak to your father.". . .

On Friday morning, for example, he had been telling the class about the

Norsemen in Constantinople 800 years ago— Thorfinn had sat there taking nothing in—he was watching a thrush on the wall outside, inattention personified—"a dreamer," said Mr Simon.

(p. 1)

In fact, the dreamer has attended to the lesson, at least the part that has caught his imagination, from which he has spun an engrossing dream that becomes a secondary narrative of the novel.

Thorfinn at that very moment was on a Swedish ship, the *Solan Goose*, anchored off a port in the Baltic. The skipper, Rolf Rolfson, was making plans to meet the prince of Rus, with a view to trading with his people and establishing good relations.

It should be said that Thorfinn was actually in the barn of Ingle, lying curled in the bow of his father's fishing yole, with the collie Stalwart sleeping in the stern. But in his imagination he was walking up a beach in the eastern Baltic, along with six other Swedish vikings, to meet a troop of envoys from the court of Rus.

(p. 4)

Thorfinn's dreams take him through the history of Orkney, from its ancient Celtic and Pictish past to the disruption of technology and war, and to the threat of the oil industry that is his present. Each dream episode visits an occasion in the islands' past that is either historically significant (the Viking crusade) or archetypal (the story of the selkie [seal-]woman), and each adventure features a young boy called Thorfinn. Thorfinn strives to be a poet, but his major success as a writer comes from the novel he writes as a prisoner of war in a German camp, popular historical romances, and "something different":

the impact on a primitive simple society, close to the elements, of a massive modern technology. He had experienced it at first hand, in his native island, when that pastoral place had been almost overnight changed into a fortress in the months before the Second World War. He embellished the record, of course, and simplified it too, in the writing.

(p. 214)

But this is not the book he wants to write; his writing has everything "but the innocent poetry of the first imagining." He no longer sees truly, with the "eye of childhood," and decides that it is time to go home and to make a novel out of the fragments that are left there: "folk memories, legends, the seal people, the trows that loved music and lived under the green hill."

If he were to return to Norday (he reasoned) it might not be too late to celebrate what was left of "the glory and the dream." He had known the island was a desert now; but the spirit of a place is not so easily quenched. If he were to work a few barren acres, sail to the lobsters . . . Then—it was just possible—out of those endless immemorial arduous rituals, the dance might break.

(pp. 215–216)

Thorfinn's quest fails; he cannot write the kind of poetic novel he wants to make, but the story does not end in failure or despair. He comes to see his quest to produce good poetry, rather than its attainment, as sufficient goal, and with a woman who, long ago in the past, was a kind of beacon of hope and brightness, he finds contentment in a simple crofting life.

"I won't go on much longer with this writing," he said. "Till the bread and fish are assured, here I'll sit every lamplit night, toiling at the unattainable poem. In the end the pages will be food for moth and rust."

"I'll dig my three acres and milk my goat," said Sophie. "I'll settle for that. We never find what we set our hearts on. We ought to be glad of that."

(p. 217)

Though not an autobiography, *Beside the Ocean of Time* tells a story roughly parallel in place and chronology to GMB's life. Thorfinn dreams his early dreams in the 1930s, sees the islands changed by the coming of electricity, radio, the telephone, and finally an enormous and destructive aerodrome, and after a time away, returns to live out his old age in his former home.

THE SHORT STORIES

THOUGH the setting for many of GMB's stories is the islands he loved and knew so well, and though they feature local characters, including living men and women, and local events, such as the Fair, they are rarely purely occasional or purely biographical or personal. In *For the Islands I Sing*, however, GMB notes that the death of his eldest brother, Hughie, did coincide with the composition of a short story, "Tam," one of the earliest to survive into his published collections. He remarks that the writing of such a piece "infuses a mingling of sweetness and power, difficult to convey. It is quite unlike any other kind of pleasure" (p. 109).

Many of the short stories preserve the directness and compression of the oral tradition; sketching in character by a representative piece of behavior or telling turn of speech, and location by a vivid image. "There was a ploughman in every field, and between every ploughman and his ox was a shining wavering furrow, and behind every wet clay furrow was a madhouse of wheeling gulls" ("Ikey," in *Winter Tales*, 1995, p. 125). Flora, fauna, and human inhabitants are connected to the

Orkney elements in stories that illustrate the calendar of the year like an illuminated book of hours, and animal imagery is often used to describe the landscape and its changing weather, as though the islands were a living bestiary.

> On the hillside, a mile further on, Ikey sat on a stone. A little company of early daffodils, in bud still, hung their heads nearby. A small cloud moved over, scattering drops of rain. The green heads twinkled. Then there was a wash of sun across the hill.
>
> A lark went up and up into the new patch of blue and was lost, but the sky went on ringing, it seemed even louder, over the hill of Greenvoe.
>
> In the field above, a ewe called anxiously for her lamb, wandering here and there among the rocks and little marshes. . . . Then Ikey was aware of a small flutter beside him. It was a lamb like a tiny masker, all black with a white mask for eyes and white forelegs and a white tail. Ikey thought it strange that the very young have no fear, but soon the world is full of shapes of dread. The harlequin lamb nuzzled Ikey's knee. Ikey lifted it and carried it to the ewe.
>
> The lark went on stammering out sweetness between two rain clouds . . .
>
> The big cloud that had covered the sun ten minutes before dropped its rain, a lingering prismatic shower . . .
>
> Ikey held his face up to the rain until his hair and his hands were streaming, and his hundred rags clung wetly about him. The sun came out again. Ikey glittered like a fish or a bird. The whole island was clean and sparkling.
>
> (pp. 127–128)

Certain critics have read GMB's stories as elegies for the old ways; the ways of a preindustrial life in harmony with the seasons and without the (GMB suggests dubious) benefit of such luxuries as piped water, electricity, radio, and the internal combustion engine (see, for example, Roberts, p. 181, and Bold, p. 112ff.). "The Paraffin Lamp," also in *Winter Tales*, certainly celebrates a crofter, Thomas, who stubbornly adheres to the old ways: horse plow; open fire; well water; tilley (paraffin) lamp. Aged and rheumatic, Thomas is considered by the other islanders to have been "failing slowly, of course, for years" (p. 3). When he goes down with influenza, the islanders think it will be the end of him, but "Thomas did come home. . . . He had fought off the illness—some of the dark power of the earth, hoarded slowly over many generations, was still in him" (pp. 3–4). In his absence the islanders have tried to make his life easier by installing the modern convenience of electric light.

> That evening, when the minister went along to see how the old man was after the journey, he found him reading *The Pilgrim's Progress* by the dim light of the paraffin lamp. He was very pleased to see the minister. He said that was a very handy thing, the electric light. He could see by it to fill his old lamp, and trim the wick, and light it with a wisp of straw from the fire.
>
> (p. 4)

While GMB is not a reactionary, and occasionally depicts life in an insular farming community as boring, his stories do seem to yearn for an older time of undivided sensibility; of oneness between humankind and the natural world, between belief and practice, between life and death. The stories about prehistoric inhabitants of Orkney depict their society as stable and harmonious, and their rituals and art as equally meaningful. The coming of the Vikings, the Reformation, the ties to Scotland, union with Great Britain, and industrialization split the unities of the islands, humanity from animal and land, politics from religion, art from action. *Hawkfall* (1974) traces this process through five stages of Orkney history linked by a family line that lives through them all.

"The Day of the Ox" depicts the process advancing in a sudden and cataclysmic step. A peaceful community on an Orkney coastline has become stagnant; no new songs have been composed for a generation. The poets have forgotten what their ancestors knew, the identity between signifier and signified enacted in the mysteries of ritual, song, and myth. Soon, strangers come to disrupt the dull routine: large, dynamic, greedy, golden strangers. They are Vikings who will take over and destroy the static society (see *Andrina*, pp. 125–129). When a community ceases to compose new songs and stories but only recycles old ones, GMB seems to suggest, it ceases to change, and without change comes decline.

The point is made again in "The Seven Poets," in which it is "a sign of death, they say, to repeat a masque" (*The Sun's Net*, 1976, p. 261) and in the novel *Time in a Red Coat*, in which the masquer demands, "How shall I announce a new thing?"; the country has been at peace for so long that "only the Song of Tranquillity is sung" (p. 4). The price of peace is boredom, and the price of contentment with a boring round is vulnerability to violent disruption.

Many of the stories weave real events or people into GMB's Orcadian tapestry. One such, in the same volume as "The Paraffin Lamp," is a deceptively simple, deft picture of William Bligh of the *Bounty*, here lieutenant of HMS *Resolution*, back from the South Seas expedition during which Captain Cook had been killed, anchored in Hamnavoe harbor to take aboard fresh water. The story depicts Bligh's first meeting with two men who were to accompany him on his expedition to Tahiti, a young Orkneyman, George Stewart, who became a midshipman on the *Bounty*, and a carpenter with an Orkney name, Peter Linklater, who became ship's carpenter. The characterization of Bligh is compact and compelling; far from the caricature of the films, we see a sober, conscientious, principled, undemonstrative, but kindly man. He is no saint; his remarks on the backwater in which he finds himself are pithy and uncomplimentary; but neither is he fool or sadist. The grace of the story lies in its spareness of line and sentiment. The events are the routines of a ship in harbor taking on water and looking for a few recruits; two of the officers dining in a local house, the senior of them taking reports and dictating letters. No overt reference is made to Bligh's future and the future of the two Orkneymen. The reader is not invited to sigh wistfully over the doomed young lives. There is neither sentimentality nor melodrama. Simply, we are given an insight into what might have been William Bligh's real character, and the circumstances of the presence on the *Bounty* of two men, one who returned with the *Bounty* to Tahiti and a native wife, and one who stayed with his captain in the launch cast adrift in the South Seas. Nonetheless, "Lieutenant Bligh and Two Midshipmen" is both moving and resonant.

GMB also introduced Christ into his stories, both as subject of human interpretation through the Gospels ("A Treading of Grapes," in *A Time to Keep*, 1969, pp. 63–76) and as a character ("The Road to Emmaus," in *Winter Tales*, pp. 227–238). There are epiphanic moments in which islanders encounter Christ-like figures, or midwinter nativities in which Christ's presence is palpably felt. The figure of the Orkney islander, fisherman and farmer, is central to GMB's writing, and Christ was both. The Gospels depict him as a friend of fisherman and, as he reminded them, a fisher of men's souls, and in one aspect he is a corn king who was ritually sacrificed for the fertility of the land and the survival of the people. In "The Way of Literature: An Apologia" (*The Tablet*, 12 June 1982), GMB reminds readers that he lived

in a group of islands that have been farmed for many centuries; all round me in summer are the whispering cornfields turning from green to gold. "Except a seed fall into the ground, and die . . ." Those words were a delight and a revelation, when first I understood them. And at piers and moorings in every village and island are the fishing boats, and the daily venturers into the perilous west, the horizon-eyed salt-tongued fishermen. ("The kingdom is like a net . . ." "I will make you fishers of men . . .") The elements of earth and sea, that we thought so dull and ordinary, held a bounteousness and a mystery not of this world.

(p. 585)

The enactments of the fertility ritual in *Time in a Red Coat* and *Greenvoe* are thus one with the death of Magnus and, for GMB, prefigurings of the "truth" of Christianity. For GMB, as for other Catholics, Christ's crucifixion is not just reenacted but occurs in the now of every Eucharist. Thus Catholicism remembers the pattern-and-flux of time and the eternal presence (and present) of the divine. GMB suggests, however, that the Reformation, by demonizing the old religions and denying them any truth, severed the people's sense of the continuousness of the cycles and the perfection of the divine plan.

POETRY

ONE of GMB's earliest published poems, "The Storm" (in *Selected Poems 1954–1992*, 1996, pp. 1–2), is an account of a tempest-tossed crossing to the tiny island of Eynhallow, between the Orkney islands of Mainland (Hrossey) and Rousay. The small skiff and its passenger could belong to any time: the Sound between the islands is as rough now as it was a thousand years ago. Only stanzas seven to ten establish this as an historical storm, by their sensory glimpses of the monastery on Eynhallow: its "Stained chancel lights, / Cluster of mellow bells"; "scent of holy water"; and final refuge in "Brother Colm's cell."

There may be traces of Gerard Manley Hopkins' *The Wreck of the Deutschland* (1876) and of his early poem "Heaven-Haven" in the theme of "The Storm." The raging elements are personified as possessed of "evil joy" and "Loud with demons," yet the storm is "Godsent," since it represents the tumult of the world the new postulant is leaving, which makes the peace of Eynhallow the more appealing. The language also echoes Hopkins in its movement, alliteration, and word-pairing:

> What blinding storm there was! How it
> Flashed with a leap and lance of nails,
> Lurching, O suddenly
> Over the lambing hills . . .
> And flung us, skiff and man (wave-crossed, God-lost)
> On a rasp of rock!

Five years later, in *Loaves and Fishes*, "The Old Women" has more in common with Robert Graves ("Woman of Greece"; "In Her Praise") both in subject and form, which includes regular rhyme. The poem introduces one figure of GMB's archetypal Woman, the crone.

> Go sad or sweet or riotous with beer
> Past the old women gossiping by the hour,
> They'll fix on you from every close and pier . . .

> But I have known a grey-eyed sober boy
> Sail to the lobsters in a storm, and drown.
> Over his body dripping on the stones
> Those same old hags would weave into their moans
> An undersong of terrible holy joy.
> (*Selected Poems 1954–1992*, p. 6)

Whereas Graves synthesizes the seasons, the life of man, and his worship of the Goddess in his one true story, GMB weaves his stories into a framework of place (the Orkneys) and faith (his unorthodox Catholicism).

By 1965, with publication of *The Year of the Whale*, GMB had found a voice of his own and an economical, vivid, imagistic form, exemplified in "The Hawk."

> On Sunday the hawk fell on Bigging
> And a chicken screamed . . .
> And on Monday he fell on the moor
> And the Field Club
> Raised a hundred silent prisms. . . .
> And on Thursday he fell on Cleat
> And peerie Tom's rabbit
> Swung in a single arc from shore to hill. . . .
> And on Saturday he fell on Bigging
> And Jock lowered his gun
> And nailed a small wing over the corn.
> (*Selected Poems 1954–1992*, p. 32)

The later poems continue to be shaped by voyages through time and space, and many of them read like entries in diaries, chronicles, or notebooks of observations (see "The Scarecrow in the Schoolmaster's Oats" and "A Child's Calendar," in *Selected Poems 1954–1992*, pp. 66, 67; "Magi," in *Voyages*, 1983, pp. 118–119). The poems are logbooks that combine the recording of the passing of time with the recording of a voyage, or the completion of an enterprise. Of the same type are the "Tryst on Egilsay," "Foresterhill," and "Brodgar Poems" sequences, which were published as short books and collected in the 1996 edition of GMB's *Selected Poems*. "Foresthill" imagines the monastic founding of a modern hospital (pp. 152–165). The "Brodgar Poems" follow the painstaking raising of a Neolithic circle stone by stone, until it comprises a calendrical fifty-two stations. In his introduction, GMB asserts that "A circle has no beginning or end. The symbol holds. People in A.D. 2000 are essentially the same as the stone-breakers and horizon-breakers of 3000 B.C." (*Selected Poems 1954–1992*, p. 166).

Just as his fictional biographies and histories do not depend upon recorded fact, GMB suggested that his poems embodied poetic truths that were truer than mere facts. Introducing *The Wreck of the Archangel*, he wrote that though several of the poems were about voyages to and from far-off places, the poet himself rarely traveled beyond his rocking chair: "Is poetry then a fraud? Or is it a quest for 'real things' beyond the sea-glitters and shadows on the cave wall? I hope, very much, the latter" (p. ix). Again, GMB attributes the source of his craft to the Orkneys and describes that craft as one of synthesis and unity. As he said in his *Selected Poems*: "The minglings of sea and earth—creel and plough—fish and cornstalk—shore people and shepherds—are the warp and weft that go to make the very stuff of poetry: 'the embroidered cloths' that Yeats wrote about" (p. xi). Many of the poems record the milestones of life in formal, ritualistic language, and many concern time and the stations of a life. In "The Jars," a man entering a house opens a jar that transforms in shape and contents. In succession it holds honey, salt, and corn. He etches an ear of corn beside a carving of a fish on the wall. The changing jar may be equivalent to the ritual hollow stones dedicated to the sun's passage in the story "Cup" (in *The Sea-King's Daughter* and *Eureka!* 1991, pp. 90–91), and the seven women who come to the man in the poem may represent the stages in the life of a woman—an archetypal woman who bears, succors, loves, and finally mourns the fishermen-crofters in GMB's Orkney.

> The mid-most woman smelt
> Of roses and sunlight. Her
> mouth had the wild honey
> taste
>
> The oldest one dropped
> tears on his face.
> (p. 26)

Most of GMB's characters are archetypes rather than individuals: "he," "a man," "the helmsman," "village women," "a tinker boy," "she." As in "The Jars," GMB's later poetry is characteristically free verse in short stanzas, and while he does not often employ rhyme or regular alliteration, some of his poems, such as "Orkney: The Whale Islands," suggest Old English or Welsh poetry.

> Sharp spindrift struck
> At prow's turning.
> Then the helmsman,
> "Either whales to starboard
> Or this storm
> Is thrusting us as Thule,
> Neighbour to bergs, beneath
> The boreal star."
> (*Selected Poems 1954–1992*, p. 3)

GMB develops many of the themes of his narrative fiction in his poems, as in his "Songs for St Magnus Day" (pp. 13–15), and a figure familiar from the fiction thrives in his last collection of poems, *Following a Lark* (1996). In the title poem, the boy-dreamer is perpetually late for school, his progress retarded and his attention diverted by the ascending lark, thoughts of fishing, a passing tinker boy, and the gift of a pan-drop (pp. 1–3). He reappears as the now-adult Ikey the tinker in "Daffodil Time." Poems such as "Homage to Burns" and "The Lords of Hell and the Word" celebrate another dreamer, the Scots poet Robert Burns, whom GMB describes as "the great poet of winter," but the theme of the collection is the praise of light: the literal light of the sun, and the "Light behind the light, that gives life and meaning to all the creatures of earth" (Introduction, p. vii). "Lux Perpetua" lists the "glimmers" by which we seek the eternal light:

> A star for a cradle
> Sun for plough and net
> A fire for old stories
> A candle for the dead
> (p. 34)

THE PLAYS

A Spell for Green Corn (1970), which was first broadcast as a radio play in 1967, includes "Some seventeenth-century records from the Island of Hellya, Orkney, concerning a witch trial" (pp. 67–91), which have the appearance of authentic documents. In *Greenvoe*, they are quoted by the historian "The Skarf" in support of the case for dismissing the charges against Sigrid Tomson. "Even in her own day she was reported to be of a rare modesty and innocence—'the lewdest alehouse whispers do not call her maidenhood in doubt,' to quote one contemporary letter" (*Greenvoe*, p. 141). Yet they were as fictional as the rest of the story, that is, the work of GMB. He makes his own history, and in the figure of The Skarf underlines the point that history is also myth and poetry and therefore concerned with the poetically true.

The opening of the play dramatizes another conflict between the old ways and the new: the reluctance of the shore people to give up their precarious living from the sea by breaking the earth and planting seed. Though Brother Cormac tells them that the sea is a miser and a murderer and the hill is mild and generous, they resist. His miracle in turning stones into fish to feed the starving people in some way commits them, however: "OLD-WILLAG: We belong to the hill now." There follows "The Ballad of John Barleycorn, The Ploughman, and the Furrow" (*A Spell for Green Corn*, pp. 13–15). This is the coming of the corn, the birth of the agrarian way of life.

Subsequent sections of the play dramatize the cycle of growing: midsummer, ripening; January, the corn dormant in the cold earth, and the people under the sway of the kirk, represented by the trial of Sigrid; Sigrid's death amid the bread and ale consumed at her burning; the twentieth century; fragmentary memories of fire and a cornstalk, a fish and a stone; a girl, Freya, perhaps Sigrid, who throws bread to the gulls and leaves strands of her hair for fiddle strings for a blind fiddler, possibly Storm Kolson, from the seventeenth century. The fiddler provides a sacramental meal of bread and whisky (or red wine) and in a long monologue sums up the ritual meaning of the play. The cyclical poem of humankind—Death, Bread, Breath, Birth—has been broken by Dearth. Sigrid's understanding and Storm's fiddle have found the word, Resurrection, to speak over the corn to make it grow and start the poem again, the same word as spoken in the last ritual of the Master Horsemen and Lord of the Harvest in *Greenvoe* (p. 248). Connected to Dearth is "progress," and the last line of the play is Luddite:

BLIND FIDDLER [*to his fiddle*]: There's one thing you and I must do yet, fiddle, we must break the machines.

(p. 66)

CONCLUSION

THAT many of GMB's publications defy categorization as fiction, nonfiction, poetry, or prose is indicative of his vision of his writing as a continuum, and in a temporal continuum with folklore, legends, sagas, religion, myth, and history. This undermining of genre distinction, with the nonlinear forms of his fiction, the patterns and archetypes, rhythms and cycles of his work, might suggest that GMB's world is without a center, without absolute values and significance. But his spirituality, specifically his Catholicism, and his belief in an Orkney heritage (however diverse) are fixed points. Many of his major characters are seeking, and some attain glimpses of, transcendent truths or inner meanings, and that truth is the oneness of things, the indivisibility of divine Creation. As storyteller GMB weaves a tapestry representing the web in which all creation is bound together. As Sunniva tells the little queen in "The Sea-King's Daughter," a story is

a treaty between us and all the creatures. That we belong to one another. That we're parts of a single web, most subtle and delicate. Who strikes the seal on the rock makes a gash in the world. Who puts an axe to a tree wounds stone and star and himself. . . . the queen and the girl that sings for a penny at the fair are sisters. And the deer is their sister, and the fish, and the hawk in the cloud. . . . if you have understood this you have understood all. It is time to go.

(*The Sea-King's Daughter* and *Eureka!* p. 45)

SELECTED BIBLIOGRAPHY

WHEREVER possible, quotations and references are from recent paperback editions.

I. NOVELS. *Magnus* (London, 1973); *Greenvoe* (London, 1972; repr. 1976); *Time in a Red Coat* (London, 1984); *Vinland* (London, 1992; repr. 1995); *Beside the Ocean of Time* (London, 1994; repr. 1995).

II. SHORT STORIES. *A Calendar of Love and Other Stories* (London, 1967); *A Time to Keep* (London, 1969); *Hawkfall and Other Stories* (London, 1974); *The Sun's Net* (London, 1976); *Witch and Other Stories* (London, 1977); *Pictures in the Cave* (London, 1977); *Andrina and Other Stories* (London, 1983); *The Masked Fisherman* (London, 1983); *Orkney Short Stories* (Orkney, 1983); *The Golden Bird: Two Orkney Stories* (London, 1987); *The Sea-King's Daughter and Eureka!* (Nairn, 1991); *Winter Tales* (London, 1995); *The Island of Woman and Other Stories* (London, 1998); *Northern Lights: A Poet's Sources* (London, 1999).

III. POETRY. *The Storm* (privately printed, 1954); *Loaves and Fishes* (London, 1959); *The Year of the Whale* (London, 1965); *Fishermen with Ploughs: A Poem Cycle* (London, 1971); *Winterfold* (London, 1976); *Voyages* (London, 1983); *The Wreck of the Archangel* (London, 1989); *Following a Lark* (London, 1996); *Selected Poems 1954–1992* (London, 1991; rev. 1996).

IV. PLAYS. *A Spell for Green Corn* (London, 1970); *Three Plays: The Loom of Light; The Well; The Voyage of Saint Brandon* (London, 1984).

V. NONFICTION. *An Orkney Tapestry* (London, 1969); *Letters from Hamnavoe* (Edinburgh, 1975); *Under Brinkie's Brae* (Edinburgh, 1979); *Portrait of Orkney* (London, 1981); *Rockpools and Daffodils: An Orcadian Diary 1979–1991* (Edinburgh, 1992).

VI. FOR CHILDREN. *Pictures in the Cave* (London, 1974); *The Two Fiddlers: Tales from Orkney* (London, 1974); *Six Lives of Frankle the Cat* (London, 1980).

VII. AUTOBIOGRAPHY. "The Broken Heraldry," in *Memoirs of a Modern Scotland*, ed. Karl Miller (London, 1970); "An Autobiographical Essay," in *As I Remember: Ten Scottish Authors Recall How Writing Began for Them*, ed. Maurice Lindsay (London, 1979); "The Way of Literature: An Apologia," in *The Tablet* (12 June 1982); *For the Islands I Sing* (London, 1997; repr. 1998); also see *An Orkney Tapestry, Portrait of Orkney*, and *Northern Lights*.

VIII. BIOGRAPHY AND CRITICAL STUDIES. Alan Bold, *George Mackay Brown* (Edinburgh, 1978); J. G. Roberts, "Tradition and Pattern in the Short Stories of George Mackay Brown," in *Literature of the North*, ed. David Hewitt and M. Spiller (Aberdeen, 1983); Alan MacGillivray, *George Mackay Brown's* Greenvoe, Scotnotes 6 (Aberdeen, 1989); Osamu Yamada, H. D. Spear, and D. S. Rob, *The Contribution to Literature of Orcadian Writer George Mackay Brown: An Introduction and a Bibliography* (Lampeter, Wales, 1991); Berthold Schoene, *The Making of Orcadia: Narrative Identity in the Prose Work of George Mackay Brown* (Frankfurt am Main, 1995); Joanna Ramsey, *In Memory of George Mackay Brown* (Glasgow, 1998); Hilda D. Spear, ed., *George Mackay Brown: A Survey of His Work and a Full Bibliography* (Lampeter, Wales, 2000).

J. M. COETZEE

(1940–   )

Laban Carrick Hill

DURING THE TWENTIETH century the violent and oppressive racism perpetrated by the white minority on the black majority was the dominant paradigm for framing any discussion or examination of South African literature. Every South African writer—black or white—on the international stage was defined first in terms of apartheid. This narrow—though justifiable—focus had a powerful influence on readers outside of South Africa in raising their awareness of the injustices within the country and clearly played a role in bringing an end to apartheid. South African writers' tragic and brutal themes of racism have proven to drive extraordinary narratives of human struggle and redemption, as well as nihilism. However, once the overt racism of apartheid had been overthrown, the authority of these works seemed to shift, like their political and social contexts, toward a more historical resonance rather than a vital, crucial truth that must be heard, here and now.

For the last three decades of the twentieth century, J(ohn) M(icheal) Coetzee's novels has been viewed primarily within this framework of racism and colonial oppression. Even though in his work his choice of literary devices such as allegory, unreliable narrators, and enigmatic symbolic settings appear to abstract his narratives from the immediate social and political reality of South Africa at the time, the novels have consistently been understood in the context of the overwhelming historical circumstance of apartheid. Within this interpretive parameter he has been both praised as one of the most important contemporary writers exploring the effects of Western imperialism on native culture and criticized for his avoidance of clear historical, political, social, and geographical referants. In *International Fiction Review* Derek Wright praised Coetzee for his "fictional extrapolation from South Africa's current historical crisis" (p. 113). On the other hand, Coetzee's contemporary, novelist and Nobel laureate

Nadine Gordimer, chided him in the *New York Review of Books* for his lack of explicitness. She wrote that Coetzee:

chose allegory for his first few novels. It seemed he did so out of a kind of opposing desire to hold himself clear of events and their daily, grubby, tragic consequences in which, like everyone else living in South Africa, he is up to the neck, and about which he had an inner compulsion to write. So here was allegory as stately fastidiousness; or a state of shock. He seemed able to deal with the horror he saw written on the sun only—if brilliantly—if this were to be projected into another time and plane.

(p. 3)

The critic Irving Howe went even further in the *New York Times Book Review* when he reviewed *Waiting for the Barbarians* (1980), commenting that "[o]ne possible loss is the bite and pain, the urgency that a specified historical place and time may provide" (p. 36). He felt the novel would have benefited from a more explicit connection to contemporary South Africa. In addition to these criticisms, Coetzee's novels that do not directly address race or colonialism have been given secondary status. Most critics have dismissed the novels *Foe* (1987) and *The Master of Petersburg* (1994) as works of lesser merit because of their lack of explicit relation to the racial conflicts in South Africa. The critic Maureen Nicholson in her *West Coast Review* essay " 'If I Make the Air around Him Thick with Words': J. M. Coetzee's *Foe*" found Coetzee's emphasis on textuality in the novel more than just problematic:

"Textuality" is here the central issue: how the story is told and what gets hidden or suppressed; whose voices are heard in the story and in history; the relationships between author and characters; and the demands of readers and booksellers whose "trade is in books, not in truth."

Given this explicit emphasis on textuality, *Foe* is a departure from what readers have come to expect of Coetzee. But his strength was and remains the literary representation of race and personal relations, *not* inter-textual relations. . . . His demands on his readers with *Foe* sadden me, requiring a patience with literary con-trivance that many will give grudgingly.

(pp. 52–53)

In all of these comments, as well as others, the defining hegemony is that of the social and politi-cal status of South Africa under a repressive white regime. Now that this reality exists only in an his-torical sense there is a danger that Coetzee's novels will be relegated to a similar status. To do this, however, is to overlook Coetzee's more complex and crucial thematic concerns about the relation-ship between authorship and authority that come into focus when all of his novels, including *Foe* and *The Master of Petersburg,* as well as his most recent post-apartheid novel *Disgrace,* are read as a cohe-sive, unified body of work. In *Dusklands* (1974), the two novellas "The Vietnam Project" and "The Nar-rative of Jacobus Coetzee" function as a kind of diptych in which the paranoid ramblings of a U.S. intelligence officer during the Vietnam War are counterpoised by a Boer settler's historical docu-ment recounting the exploitation of native Africans. Together these fictional narratives expose the inherent bias in authorial perspective that when taken to its extreme can be so ghastly that they reach far beyond mere censorship. In *In the Heart of the Country* (1977), written in diary form, Magda lives on a farm out in the veld, totally out-side human society, almost outside humanity. Her story reveals the consequences of isolation from a community of narrative realities to counterbalance her biased perspective. In *Waiting for the Barbarians* an unnamed magistrate is imprisoned and tor-tured for attempting to protect the peaceful nomadic people of his district. Through his experi-ence he discovers the "barbarian way" and is inex-orably changed. In *Life and Times of Michael K* (1984) Coetzee took his first step outside the role of imperialist/oppressor and focused on the oppres-sion of a single character. The novel follows the journey of Michael K, a disfigured, slow-witted young man taking his dying mother to a place she fondly remembers from her youth. The story is told from two perspectives, a stark, impersonal narrator and a young intern at a hospital. The theme coalesces around an attempt to tell the true story of Michael K which is finally unknowable. In *Foe* the narrative pretense is that the story of Robinson Crusoe as written by Daniel Defoe is inaccurate. *Foe* operates as a kind of corrective text in which the woman, who was also shipwrecked on the island and was deleted from Defoe's account, recounts her story, and thus recovers *her* reality. In *Age of Iron* (1990) the narrator is a retired classics professor dying of cancer in Cape Town. The novel takes the form of a letter to her daughter in America who has cut off all ties to South Africa and begun a new life in her adopted country. The book reads like an entreaty for understanding and sympathy from a cancerous world. In these pages the question that is asked is who deserves to be entrusted with the story. In *The Master of Petersburg* Coetzee strayed from his allegorical and overtly political landscape to study the imagined crisis of the nineteenth-century Russian novelist Fyodor Dostoyevsky returning from exile to find out the truth about his stepson's murder. The conflict aris-es when he encounters a number of competing narratives, none of which offer a clear answer. Consequently, he must decide which author—the police or the anarchists—tells the true story, or conclude that the truth lies elsewhere. With *Dis-grace* Coetzee returned to South Africa, but a post-apartheid South Africa, in which political correct-ness and liberal guilt offers the world a new kind of authorship that is as totalitarian as all others. Throughout all of his books Coetzee has shown a conviction that authorship is implicitly tied to cen-sorship, and thus moved himself beyond the argu-ment of solely viewing his work through the lens of South Africa.

CHILDHOOD

DESPITE the fact that Coetzee's novels transcend the time and place in which they were written to address more universal issues, the origins of this work are just as clearly anchored in the circum-stances of growing up in the complex and contra-dictory apartheid environment where success was entirely dependent on the mercurial whims of those in power. John Michael Coetzee was born 9 February 1940, to Vera and Jack Coetzee in Cape Town, South Africa. Ethnically Afrikaans, the Coetzees chose to raise their children as English. His mother, Vera Wehmeyer Coetzee, was the fourth of six children to Piet Wehmeyer, who was Afrikaans, and Marie du Biel, who was of German heritage. She grew up in the Uniondale district which was exclusively Afrikaans. Nevertheless, the parents gave all their children English first names and spoke exclusively English at home. Jack Coetzee's background was similar in that he was one of eight children and grew up in an Afrikaans household in Prince Albert that chose to speak English at home. Coetzee and his younger brother were brought up speaking English as their primary language and went to English schools.

As a child Coetzee did not get to know his father until he was six because Jack Coetzee served as a Lance Corporal in the army during World War II. When he returned from the war, Jack Coetzee secured a political patronage job of controller of Letting in Cape Town, but lost that job in 1948 when the United Party was voted out of power by the conservative Nationalists, the perpetrators of apartheid. For young Coetzee these years in the Cape Town suburb, Rosebank, were the happiest time of his life. In his memoir, *Boyhood: Scenes from Provincial Life* (1997), an episodic, third-person reportorial account of the middle years of his childhood, Coetzee described this place as "the house with the great oak tree in the front garden where he was happy" (p. 73). Nevertheless, it was also a time when he first began to understand the differences of class and color in South Africa. When Coetzee was seven, the family made an arrangement for an eight-year-old "Coloured" boy, Eddie, to work for them. "In return for washing dishes and sweeping and polishing, Eddie would live with them in Rosebank and be given his meals, while on the first of every month his mother would be sent a postal order for two pounds ten shillings" (pp. 73–74). The boys became friends, but when Eddie ran away, Coetzee realized how different their worlds really were, in spite of the fact that they lived together in the same house. "One thing he [Coetzee] knows for sure: Eddie will have no pity on him" (p. 77).

The shock of leaving Rosebank for Worcester where his father became a bookkeeper for Standard Canners was dramatic. The house they moved into was one of those housing development boxes out on the veld. "Every time the wind blows, a fine ochre clay-dust whirls in under the doors, seeps through the cracks in the window-frames, under the eaves, through the joints of the ceiling. After a day-long storm the dust lies piled inches against the front wall" (p. 2). The development was almost exclusively Afrikaans, but the Coetzees maintained their English lifestyle. Here on the veld Coetzee never quite found his place, where distinctions between ethnicity defined how

he was educated, who were his playmates, where he lived, and what kind of jobs his parents had. He realized that he was not English because his family was not Protestant and did not have an English last name, but he was also not Afrikaans because his family's lifestyle was distinctly English. This paradox made it difficult for him to find a group with whom to belong and was further exacerbated by his parents' lack of religious affiliation. South African society was intricately delineated by ethnicity, religion, education, and economic status. This fact made it impossible for a young Coetzee to remain completely unaffiliated. The consequences even proved difficult—as well as extremely absurd—at times:

The decision to "be" Roman Catholic is made on the spur of the moment. On the first morning at his new school, while the rest of the class is marched off to assembly in the school hall, he and three other new boys are kept behind. "What is your religion?" asks the teacher of each of them. He glances right and left. What is the right answer? What religions are there to choose from? Is it like Russians and Americans? His turn comes. "What is your religion?" asks the teacher. He is sweating, he does not know what to say. "Are you a Christian or a Roman Catholic or a Jew?" she demands impatiently. "Roman Catholic," he says.

(pp. 18–19)

Coetzee naïvely chose Roman Catholic because of the stories of Roman conquests he had read. He did not understand that Catholicism had nothing to do with ancient Rome until much later when his fellow Catholics began to pressure him to attend catechism classes.

Coetzee's father was a lawyer who had never practiced law. Nevertheless, after several years in Worcester, his father decided to open a law office back in Cape Town. The family moved to another housing development in the suburb of Plumstead. His mother took a job as a teacher while his father worked to build his law practice. In Plumstead life was difficult. Because he had gone to a rural school, none of the better Cape Town schools would accept him. Instead he had to settle for a third-rate Catholic school which he found interminably restrictive. During this time the fortunes of the family made a steep decline as well. Jack Coetzee began drinking heavily and piling up debts while stealing from his clients' accounts. Vera Coetzee's salary could not make ends meet, and the family had to be rescued by a relative. In

Boyhood Coetzee wrote of these times as unsettling. He described himself as someone who always felt like an outsider. His story was never the same as anyone else's. Thus, his story was never told. He felt censored by others and by the social conventions required in such a stratified society. He described his childhood as such:

Always, it seems there is something that goes wrong. Whatever he [Coetzee] wants, whatever he likes, has sooner or later to be turned into a secret. He begins to think of himself as one of the spiders that live in a hole in the ground with a trapdoor. Always the spider has to be scuttling back into its hole, closing the trapdoor behind it, shutting out the world, hiding.

(p. 28)

These secrets are the stories to which Coetzee was drawn. They were stories that could not be told either because to tell the story was dangerous or because the story was of no interest to others. Eddie's story was dangerous because "he had dropped the pretence of being content" (74). The consequences of Eddie's honesty were that he was beaten and sent away to reform school. Equally powerful was the story of Coetzee's great Aunt Annie's devotion to her father's autobiography. The manuscript was an account of the voices he heard from the heavens. She "devoted most of her life, first translating the manuscript [her father and Coetzee's great-grandfather's autobiography] from German into Afrikaans, then spending her savings to pay a printer in Stellenbosch to print hundreds of copies, and a binder to bind some of them, then touring the bookshops of Cape Town. When the bookshops could not be persuaded to sell the book, she trudged from door to door herself" (p. 118). Through these experiences, along with his own encounters with being branded an outsider, Coetzee was able to understand just how tenuous a person's story can be. His memoir *Boyhood* demonstrates this insubstantiality by its third-person narration, as if it were not his experience, but rather some character in a story. By not possessing his own story with the pronoun "I," Coetzee suggested that even the story of his life cannot escape the contingency of authorial authority.

After graduating from high school, Coetzee attended the University of Cape Town where he received a B.A. in 1960 and an M.A. in 1963. Feeling no real ties to his home, he moved to London where he worked for International Business Machines (IBM) as an applications programmer until 1964. After that, he spent the next two years as a systems programmer at International Computers. While living in England he spent most of his spare time writing poetry and studying literature. Like many young intellectuals he described this time as one when he wandered the streets of London and haunted the stacks in the British Museum seeking the meaning of life. In 1965 he enrolled in the Ph.D. program for English Literature at the University of Texas, Austin, and received his degree in 1969. From 1968 to 1971 he was an assistant professor at the State University of New York at Buffalo. At this time the effects of the Vietnam War and the assassination of the South African prime minister H. F. Verwoerd back home weighed heavily. Eventually, he saw a connection between the United States' imperialism in Vietnam and the Nationalist imperialism back in South Africa that caused him to genuinely question the narratives told by those in authority. When he returned to the University of Cape Town as a lecturer in 1972, he began working on the two novellas which would become the material of his first book *Dusklands*.

DUSKLANDS

FIRST published by Ravan Press in Johannesburg, *Dusklands* probes the link between the powerful and powerless in unexpected ways. The title *Dusklands* invokes the old line that "the sun never sets on the British Empire," but gives it a twist by suggesting that empires are at their day's end. The first novella, "The Vietnam Project," applies this metaphor to the U.S. involvement in Vietnam. The story's main character is named Eugene Dawn, a mythographer employed by the American military in a California research station. The project is named "New Life for Vietnam" and has been assigned to Dawn by the director of the project, a man named Coetzee. The dawn in this story is the realization by the reader how destructive the colonial mentality is on the victimizers. In his report Dawn explores the potential of radio broadcasting for psychological warfare against Vietnam. The crux of his argument is the mythologizing of the Vietnam War into the pattern of a benign father putting down rebellious children who are incapable of taking care of themselves. With proper discipline the people of Vietnam will welcome American imperialism. Bracketing this report is

Dawn's first-person narrative illustrating how his commitment to his interpretation ultimately pollutes his entire life. His relationships become framed by his notions of colonialism. In describing his wife he writes:

Now is also the time to mention the length of gristle that hangs from the end of my iron spine and effects my sad connection with Marilyn. Alas, Marilyn has never succeeded in freeing me from my rigors. Though like the diligent partners in the marriage manuals we attend to each other's whispers, moans, and groans, though I plough like the hero and Marilyn froth like the heroine, the truth is that the bliss of which the books speak has eluded us. The fault is not mine. I do my duty. Whereas I cannot escape the suspicion that my wife is disengaged. Before the arrival of my seed her pouch yawns and falls back, leaving my betrayed representative gripped at its base, flailing its head in vain inside an immense cavern, at the very moment when above all else it craves to be rocked through its tantrum in a soft, firm, infinitely trustworthy grip. The word which at such moments flashes its tail across the heavens of my never quite extinguished consciousness is *evacuation*: my seed drips like urine into the futile sewers of Marilyn's reproductive ducts.

(pp. 7–8)

The repulsiveness of this passage demonstrates how an individual is not just complicit with a violent regime's persecution of "the other" through repression, torture, and genocide, but is also contaminated to a degree that his or her actions follow the same script. Dawn is abstracted from real ecstatic experience by his ideology to such an extent that even a wife with a sex symbol's name, Marilyn, cannot engage him. Like a good father/imperialist, he diagnoses the problem as an inadequacy in his wife. She need only be reeducated by the appropriate manuals to perform with proper enthusiasm, just as his own Vietnam manual offers a corrective guide to the pacification of the natives:

1.3 *Control.* Our propaganda services have yet to apply the first article of the anthropology of Franz Boas: that if we wish to take over the direction of a society we must either guide it from within its cultural framework or else eradicate its culture and impose new structures.

(p. 20)

The implication of this text is that violent military conquests are only one kind of dominance. Language itself is equally coercive.

Without "The Vietnam Project" Coetzee's second novella "The Narrative of Jacobus Coetzee" would seem narrowly confined to the genre of South African literature covering black-white confrontation. "The Vietnam Project" widens the horizon of "The Narrative" to expand on the theme of language's coerciveness by offering a document that contains several descriptive narratives of a single event. Coetzee presented this novella as a historical document with a translator's preface, a written account by Jacobus Coetzee, an afterword containing a contemporary perspective, and the official 1760 deposition to the local authorities. At the center of the narrative is the real story (which is never explicitly told): Jacobus Coetzee goes on an elephant hunt, but is robbed and humiliated by members of the Namaqua tribe. This leads him to insanity and to his massacre of the tribe on his return journey. The central text of the narrative is bracketed by scholarly glosses, the translator's note and afterword, and original documents. It is among this collection of perspectives that the reader can discover, partially, the real story that exists only outside of the book.

This arrangement in the novella inherently suggests that truth will always lie outside of the text and that those who hold the truth can never speak. The layers of opacity that Coetzee has heaped onto the novella underscore how difficult it is for language to contain anything. First, the novella is a work of fiction by an author named J. M. Coetzee so everything within its pages can be immediately dismissed as not real. Second, the work itself is a narrative by a historical figure with the same name as the "real" author. The confluence of names suggests that the narrative cannot be considered any more real than its outer fictional frame. To amplify its contingency, this narrative is not even the authentic document, but rather a translation from the original language of Dutch into English. Consequently, a translator, who is a descendant of Jacobus Coetzee and perhaps J. M. Coetzee himself, has functioned as a mediation device to transform an already conditional narrative into an even more uncertain text. At this point the occlusion is so great that authentic events can only be peripherally approached. Coetzee further obscured the truth by adding an afterword, which is a translation from Afrikaans, by the father of the translator and descendant of Jacobus Coetzee. This afterword is a third-person narrative by S. J. Coetzee with exaggerated intrusions of the "authorial" consciousness, as in "I hope I have succeeded in evoking something of the reality of this extraordinary man" (p. 121). S. J. admits in this passage that "[t]o understand the life of this obscure farmer requires a positive act of the imagination" (p. 109), but that does not stop him from presenting his version as truth. The explicit irony in this part can only function as a kind of reminder to the reader of the totalitarian lineage of authorship. There is no question that "the reality of this extraordinary man" has been fully conveyed in ways that the author of the afterword never intended. As a coda to the entire novella, an appendix contains Jacobus Coetzee's official 1760 deposition. This document, however, is a transcription, no less mediated than the translations, even though it is purported to be the "official" account in contrast to the "unofficial" narrative.

The paradoxes that J. M. Coetzee mined in this novella suggest that there is a sort of incest between texts that record personal experience and those that gloss that experience, and between these texts and their readers. Coetzee, however, went even further to suggest that all texts are glosses because they are the product of an author who can function only as a mediator for that authentic experience. Consequently, what really happened—the genocide of the Namaqua tribe—can never be known unless the dead somehow rise from their graves to speak their story in conjunction with Jacobus Coetzee's.

The final irony in both "The Vietnam Project" and "The Narrative of Jacobus Coetzee" is the fact that J. M. Coetzee is the guiltiest of all conspirators because he as author functions as the imperialist of the entire production. So finally, no one—except perhaps the mute—can escape guilt. Consequently, authorship is an act of censorship more than, or at least equal to, revelation.

IN THE HEART OF THE COUNTRY

JUST as experimental in its narrative strategies as *Dusklands* was Coetzee's first novel *In the Heart of the Country*. Published outside of South Africa, this very short novel presents a narrative whose soundness is in question from the start. Essentially, it is a stream-of-consciousness journal of a spinster daughter, Magda, recording her nightmarish and murderous fantasies of killing her own father:

There was a time when I imagined that if I talked long enough it would be revealed to me what it means to be an angry spinster in the heart of nowhere. But though I sniff at each anecdote like a dog at its doo, I find none of that heady expansion into the as-if that marks the beginning of a true double life. Aching to form the words that will translate me into the land of myth and hero, here I am still my dowdy self in a dull summer heat that will not transcend itself.

(p. 4)

What it means is exactly what Magda cannot fathom. Her isolation goes beyond the barren veld and reaches deeply into her psychological being. When she speaks of the servants, she does so in clichéd, racist characterizations: "They want to be in the big house but they also want to stay home malingering, dozing on a bench in the shade" (p. 7). "They" are the other with whom she could never ally herself. Her only connection is with her father who is a widower. But when he has an affair with the young wife of the farm's black foreman Hendrik, she becomes unhinged from the only social or psychological anchor with which she has been tethered. In a sense, her father joins the other side of the master/slave dichotomy and becomes black. In her mind this leaves her as the only white master on the farm. She cannot tolerate the betrayal and so murders her father. "The axe sweeps up over my shoulder. All kinds of people have done this before me, wives, sons, lovers, heirs, rivals, I am not alone. Like a ball on a string it floats down at the end of my arm, sinks into the throat below me, and all is suddenly tumult" (p. 11). The consequence of this sudden and decisive action is to isolate her even further. The product of such separation is a deranged, afflicted narrative that cannot adhere into a traditional, cohesive fiction. Two hundred and sixty-six separately numbered sections constitute the text. What would be a continuous flow of paragraphs becomes a sputtering, nonlinear collection of overlapping and obsessive spewing of outrage, paranoia, and indignation, out of which the story emerges.

The resulting text coalesces around the notion that there is a link between racial conflict and mental deterioration. It suggests that racism is merely a symptom of a larger psychological disturbance, such as paranoid schizophrenia, and raises the question of whether humankind should treat the symptom or the disease. Critics have described Magda as representing the stagnant policies of apartheid. In this view Magda becomes symbolic of the white's situation in South Africa.

Not only is what they believe simply not true, but the consequences of their beliefs will lead to their destruction. Because of her delusion, Magda is eventually co-opted by Hendrik who rapes her and takes over the farm. It seems Coetzee was making a point that the same will happen for South African whites as a whole. Clearly, time has proven this reading of *In the Heart of the Country* to be true. This reading, however, leaves the larger psychosis untreated. In this way, Coetzee's ambition was greater than simply righting the wrongs of apartheid. The utter surrender to the pathology presented in the text underscores the more ambitious intent.

Nevertheless, this yielding raises other difficulties that nearly erode the power of the novel. Magda's affliction causes the text to appear more like a psychological clinical study than literary fiction. In light of *Dusklands'* confluence of multiple documents, Coetzee plainly intended for this to happen. He wanted the clinical aspects to struggle with the fictive. It is in this tortured, unresolved state that Coetzee meant to leave the reader.

WAITING FOR THE BARBARIANS

WHILE *In the Heart of the Country* presents a character who exhibits no understanding, and thus is completely isolated, Coetzee's next novel *Waiting for the Barbarians* presents a character with the opposite tendencies of Magda. The magistrate who is at the center of this story is a man with an infinite capacity for empathy. For decades he has run a tiny frontier settlement located in an indeterminate country on the edge of an unknown frozen tundra. Now, a war between the barbarians and the Empire whose servant he is threatens his peaceful and isolated existence. When a brutal colonel from the "Third Bureau" arrives to interrogate prisoners, however, the magistrate finds himself sympathizing with the victims. At first, he believes he can walk the fine line between support of the regime and overt rebellion against its brutality until the obvious mistreatment and slaughter of innocent prisoners causes him to take action. These prisoners are not barbarians but instead are a pacified tribe that lives beside the lake that separates barbarian territory with the Empire. One of the prisoners, an old man, is tortured to death while his daughter is made to watch. Afterward, the interrogators blind her and break her feet so

that she is unable to return to her lakeside village once the colonel and his men have left.

The magistrate finds her wandering the outpost and takes to washing her feet as an act of repentance for the cruelty of the regime he represents:

I seat her, fill the basin, roll the drawers above her knees. Now that the two feet are together in the water I can see that the left is turned further inward than the right, that when she stands she must stand on the outer edges of her feet. . . .
I begin to wash her. She raises her feet for me in turn. I knead and massage the lax toes through the soft milky soap. Soon my eyes close, my head droops. It is rapture, of a kind.

(p. 29)

This ritual inevitably escalates to a kind of sexual activity without consummation that clouds his righteousness as his actions become both repentance and colonial usurpation. The magistrate tries to explain his actions: "Until the marks on this girl's body are deciphered and understood I cannot let go of her" (p. 31). For him the scars are the signs of a language that he must decode in order to understand the reasons behind this war. In reading them he hopes to journey toward understanding barbarian otherness, but this never really occurs because he can no more penetrate the barbarian consciousness than he can copulate with the woman.

He becomes frustrated by his impotence. This dissatisfaction eventually leads him to return the woman to her people. The journey is long and difficult because her people have left the lakeside and moved further into the barbarian territory where it is safer. After months of traveling, he finally returns to the outpost to find it overrun by the colonel and his men. For his act of treason, he is tortured and imprisoned. The magistrate endures his punishment with a sense of satisfaction because he has realized that when "some men suffer unjustly . . . it is the fate of those who witness their suffering to suffer the shame of it" (p. 139). There's a righteousness in his suffering because he knows the real barbarians are the civilized people of the Empire.

In the magistrate's story Coetzee has created a parable about civilization. The title of the novel comes from a poem by Constantine Cavafy entitled "Expecting the Barbarians": "And now what shall become of us without any barbarians? / Those people were a kind of solution." It seems Coetzee suggested that civilization cannot exist without an enemy and that all communities are doomed to operate within a dualism: master/slave, empire/barbarian, father/child, man/woman. Once the magistrate is able to realize this, he can return to his duties at the outpost. Nevertheless, he is forever changed. He knows that in order to have justice another way must be found. At the end of the novel, he says:

I think: "I wanted to live outside history. I wanted to live outside the history that Empire imposes on its subjects, even with its lost subjects. I never wished it for the barbarians that they should have the history of Empire laid upon them. How can I believe that that is cause for shame?"

(p. 154)

This thought offers hope to the reader, but the final image in the book, a snowman, suggests otherwise:

It is not a bad snowman.
    This is not the scene I dreamed of. Like much else nowadays I leave it feeling stupid, like a man who lost his way long ago but presses on along a road that may lead nowhere.

(p. 156)

By considering a world beyond the Empire, the magistrate has ineluctably altered what had been a safe and cozy existence and traded it for the most frightening of possibilities—the unknown. But aren't the answers to all questions unknown until they are answered?

LIFE AND TIMES OF MICHAEL K

COETZEE'S next novel, *Life and Times of Michael K*, shifts focus from the narrative of the oppressor to that of the oppressed. A number of critics have linked *Michael K* to Kafka's *The Trial* because of the similarities in name, but Coetzee's work is very different from Kafka's novel in that the world *Michael K* depicts is not so fascist and all controlling. It is more accidental and just plain mean. The *K* in Coetzee's story seems more connected to Coetzee himself than Kafka's *K*. Coetzee's middle name is Michael, and the letter *K* is often interchangeable with the letter *C* in variant spellings. Though there is some correlation between these works, their similarities are clearly secondary to other themes with which Coetzee's novel is concerned.

The novel comprises two separate narratives, a third-person limited omniscient from the perspective of Michael K and a first-person point of view of a doctor. Both of these points of view focus on Michael K, a feeble-minded outcast with a harelip of no specific racial origin who searches with his mother for a home during a turbulent period of an unnamed country's civil war. On the way his mother dies and is cremated. Michael K's journey then shifts from finding the idyllic of his mother's childhood to discovering his own place in the world. Perhaps, not surprisingly, this place turns out to be an abandoned farm that appears at first to have been forgotten by all.

The first and third sections of the novel follow Michael K's journey from a third-person point of view. These two parts follow the evolution of Michael K's consciousness from a passive laborer caught in the middle of a civil war. These pages describe in hour-by-hour, day-by-day, week-by-week detail Michael's struggle to escape this violent society and exist on its margins. Through this portrait readers track how he comes to realize that the only way he can be free is to need nothing, absolutely nothing, from the world that begins at the end of his own body.

Michael experiences two distinct worlds in the book, the triple internment in camp, prison, and hospital and that of an isolated farm. These two environments are contrasted to underscore the difference between a fallen world and that of an Eden. In his internment Michael is forced to exist within the master/slave relationship. He tries, as best he can, not to, by refusing to eat or take any kind of sustenance from his oppressors. Outside of the internment he lives in a hole and grows pumpkins on the forgotten farm he has stumbled across. Here he finds a sort of Eden:

What a pity that to live in times like these a man must be ready to live like a beast. A man who wants to live cannot live in a house with lights in the windows. He must live in a hole and hide by day. A man must live so that he leaves no trace of his living. That is what it has come to.

(p. 99)

But to live without a trace is impossible. Consequently, his Eden is constantly violated, first by the grandson of the farm's owners who has run away from the military and then by soldiers in search of deserters and guerillas. These outsiders destroy his crop and make it impossible for him to survive. Near death, he is discovered and brought to a prison hospital where he is revived with food. Here, a young doctor struggles to force Michael to eat, who refuses. Michael has come to realize that the only way to achieve true freedom is to die. His body is his last oppressor. The doctor, however, does not understand this. Though he is against the war and against the mistreatment of what is implied to be blacks, he cannot understand why anyone would not want to accept his charity. For Michael charity is just another form of oppression. For him to receive the doctor's help he would have to accept a reality where the doctor and his kind have the power to choose to help or not—without Michael's participation. In this construct he is still a slave because it is never his choice. Consequently, his only choice is not to participate, and to do that, he must die. Once he escapes the hospital he wanders back to the shore, where he thinks:

Perhaps the truth is that it is enough to be out of the camps, out of all the camps at the same time. Perhaps that is enough of an achievement, for the time being. How many people are there left who are neither locked up nor standing guard at the gate? I have escaped the camps; perhaps, if I lie low, I will escape the charity too.
(p. 182)

In the final sentences of the book Michael imagines the ideal existence as he lays in the closet where his mother had lived on the shore in Cape Town:

[H]e, Michael K, would produce a teaspoon from his pocket, a teaspoon and a long roll of string. He would clear the rubble from the mouth of the shaft, he would bend the handle of the teaspoon in a loop and tie the string to it, he would lower it down the shaft deep into the earth, and when he brought it up there would be water in the bowl of the spoon; and in that way, he would say, one can live.
(p. 184)

Cynthia Ozick wrote in the *New York Times Book Review* that the novel "has rewritten the travail of Huck's insight, but from Nigger Jim's point of view, and set in a country more terrible—because it is a living bitter hard-hearted contemporary place, the parable-world of an unregenerate soon-after-now, with little pity and no comedy" (p. 1). Clearly, Coetzee went beyond Ozick's observation to create a narrative solution to oppression that offers freedom, but ironically only by way of self-annihilation.

FOE

WHEN Tony Morphet asked Coetzee in an interview in *TriQuarterly* about his shift away from explicit South African themes in his next novel *Foe*, he responded, "Foe is a retreat from the South African situation, but only from that situation in a narrow temporal perspective. It is not a retreat from the subject of colonialism or from questions of power. What you call 'the nature and process of fiction' may also be called the question of *who writes?* Who takes up the position of power, pen in hand?" (p. 462).

Foe explores more directly and explicitly unanswerable questions about language, writing, and authorship that Coetzee addressed through his examination of colonialism and master/slave relationships in his other novels. Who has the right to tell a story? Who has the right to speak for someone else? Who is denied the right to speak? Who needs someone else to speak for them? All of these questions coalesce around the issue of how language contributes to oppression. In this novel, Coetzee proposed that the story of Robinson Crusoe's shipwreck and subsequent life on the desert isle with Friday was not the "true" narrative. Instead, Foe, who was in financial distress at the time, compromised the "authentic" narrative in order create a popular work that would earn him considerable money. The narrator of *Foe* is Susan Barton, a woman who was shipwrecked on the same island as Cruso and Friday. In order to survive she has sold her story to a man named Foe (Defoe), but before he finishes he disappears to escape creditors. Destitute, she struggles to keep shelter and food for her and Friday for whom she has taken responsibility. Friday is mute, having had his tongue cut out on a slave ship, and cannot tell his story of capture, shipwreck, and rescue. Mindful of this, Barton embarks on her own narrative of the experience of landing on the island and discovering Cruso and Friday already there.

This chronicle stands as a kind of corrective text to Foe's classic adventure story. In Barton's account the reader discovers crucial differences. Foe alters the truth first by deleting Barton's participation in the experience and then by presenting the characters of Cruso and Friday as idealistic and enterprising rather than indigent and depressed as Barton experienced it. Barton makes herself the center of her account. The novel begins with her arrival on the island. Readers then learn the background behind her shipwreck and the circumstances of her travels. She is in search of her kidnapped daughter. Now, after two years in a Portuguese colony she is sailing for Lisbon when she is set adrift in a lifeboat by the mutinied crew. She is washed up on the shore of the island where Cruso and Friday had previously landed. Through her story the reader learns that Cruso is more like a Boer colonialist, a rather literal-minded, complacent Afrikaner who sees himself as a survivor rather than a utopia builder. In a passage describing Cruso's colonial mentality, she writes, "Growing old on his island kingdom with no one to say him nay had so narrowed his horizon—when the horizon all around us was so vast and so majestic!—that he had come to be persuaded he knew all there was to know about the world" (p. 13). Later in the book she writes:

Let it not by any means come to pass that Cruso is saved, I reflected to myself; for the world expects stories from its adventurers, better stories than tallies of how many stones they moved in fifteen years, and from where, and to where; Cruso rescued will be a deep disappointment to the world; the idea of a Cruso on his island is a better thing than the true Cruso tight-lipped and sullen in an alien England.

(pp. 34–35)

Throughout the book Barton reminds the reader that there are economic as well as sociopolitical motives for telling this story and that for her the promise of financial security is much more important than authenticity. This is why she sacrifices her story by selling it to Foe and letting him write it without any acknowledgement of her participation. Nevertheless, she finds she must tell her story anyway once Foe disappears. Barton, fortunately, is not a Foe, who adds and deletes facts in order to heighten reality for the sake of literary interest. Her story is told with as little artifice as possible. Through her narrative the reader realizes that she is clearly aware that her words are a gross simplification of the circumstances. In fact, her story as a whole becomes a meditation on authorship in four parts. It begins with her introductory monologue to Mr. Foe. The next section contains accounts of her life in London, then shifts into a series of letters to Foe, and ends with some notes on her walk to Bristol with Friday to send him by

boat back to Africa. At the end when she sits at Foe's bedside, he compares himself as the author of the book to being a whore. Barton responds:

"Do not say that," I protested. "It is not whoring to entertain other people's stories and return them to the world better dressed. If there were not authors to perform such an office, the world would be all the poorer. Am I to damn you as a whore for welcoming me and embracing me and receiving my story? You gave me a home when I had none. I think of you as a mistress, or even, if I dare speak the word, as a wife."

(pp. 151–152)

With these words of comfort Barton acknowledges that the purpose of any narrative is murky at best. In a sense an accommodation must be reached between what really happened and what can be told.

WHITE WRITING

FOLLOWING Coetzee's most polemical novel is a book-length work of criticism, *White Writing: On the Culture of Letters in South Africa*. In this collection of seven essays, published in 1988, Coetzee attempted to provide a critical framework to the history of white South African writing from 1652, when Europeans settled at the Cape of Good Hope, to 1948, when apartheid was institutionalized. In *World Literature Today* Barbara Eckstein described the collection: "Focusing on writers of English and of Afrikaans, Coetzee traces the writers' relationship to the African land as landscape and as landownership (the farm)" (p. 718). In this work he explored the many paradoxes inherent in a African pastoral aesthetic created by Europeans. White writing of this period, he suggested, has as its goal the creation of a mythology to underpin colonial occupation of a resistant land. To support this premise, he looked at white South African writing from defenders of racism and a conservative, agrarian order, and from critics of the reigning dispensation. Enriched by cross-cultural comparison between South African responses to issues of the day and European and American responses, Coetzee's analysis attempts to define the literary history from which all white South African writing evolves. In his introduction, he defined this genre of writing as existing in a transitional topography. "White writing is white only insofar as it is generated by the concerns of people no longer European, not yet African" (p. 11).

AGE OF IRON

WHILE *Waiting for the Barbarians* explores the psyche of a functionary of the Empire who has second thoughts, Coetzee's novel *Age of Iron* traces the journey of an elderly white woman who finds herself dying of cancer in a land afflicted with its own mortal illness. Both novels are first-person narration by the main character, but *Age of Iron* holds an additional texture because Mrs. Elizabeth Curren's narrative takes the form of a letter, written over several months, to her daughter in America. Unlike Coetzee's other novels, *Age of Iron*'s setting is explicitly the contemporary South Africa of the black township and the suburbs of Cape Town. This shift away from the allegorical represents a major change for Coetzee and seems to parallel the changing political and social climate in South Africa with the release of Nelson Mandela.

A retired classics professor, Mrs. Curren is a woman who has spent most of her life insulated from the harsher realities of apartheid. Until her diagnosis with spinal cancer that spread from an earlier bout of breast cancer, her life had been spent studying a two-thousand-year-old European legacy—as non-African as possible for a South African—behind the safe walls of academia. The discovery of her relapse, however, causes a personal revelation. She realizes that she is no longer part of the living. Now she is a member of the "other." When her doctor explains his diagnosis, she observes, "But already, behind the comradely front, I could see he was withdrawing. *Sauve qui puet*. His allegiance to the living, not the dying" (p. 4).

This epistolary novel functions as a letter to the world by way of her daughter. The reader is essentially looking over her daughter's shoulder. Her daughter has left South Africa and has promised never to return because of apartheid's atrocities. As such, she stands in for the reader as the moral center of this novel. The narrative, itself, follows Mrs. Curren's journey through a world that turns out to be hell, much like Dante's *Inferno*. Her guide is a homeless man who enters her life accidentally. The critic Patrick McGrath cogently summarizes the novel in the *New York Times Book Review*: "Her maternal sympathies [are] aroused by her black housekeeper's son when she sees him brutalized by the police. Surrogate parenthood gradually opens her eyes to the vicious realities of the apartheid state; ironically, it is to her daughter . . . that she pours out her thoughts in writing. Her real children, she begins to see, are the black youths being murdered by the security forces under her nose. The personal and political are most elegantly conflated in this novel" (p. 9). The symbolic power of the type of cancer she has—breast and spinal—underscore the tragedy of her circumstances. Now that she finally understands what she has been insulating herself from, she is barren, incapable of nurturing her real children. The resulting despair that is at the core of this novel is exposed when the title's iron metaphor is explained. In a discussion of parental responsibility with her housekeeper Florence, Mrs. Curren comes to this realization:

"No," said Florence. "That is not true. I do not turn my back on my children. . . . These are good children, they are like iron, we are proud of them."
  Children of iron, I thought. Florence herself, too, not unlike iron. The age of iron. After which comes the age of bronze. How long, how long before the softer ages return in their cycle, the age of clay, the age of earth? A Spartan matron, iron-hearted, bearing warrior sons for the nation. "We are proud of them." We. Come home either with your shield or on your shield.

(p. 50)

Mrs. Curren thus stands as a witness to the coming of the age of iron. Her letter chronicles not just her own impending death, but the last vicious gasps of a dying regime. At another point in the novel she acts as a kind of seer: "[It is] time for fire, time for an end, time for what grows out of ash to grow" (p. 65). It is in this fire, she suggests, that the new generation is forged. Her role as an oracle represents a quiet, almost hopeful, vision of the future rising, phoenix-like, out of the past. As such her death becomes a metaphor for the doom of liberalism in South Africa and a vision of hope signified by Mrs. Curren's implied emphasis on rebirth and human continuity.

THE MASTER OF PETERSBURG

COETZEE'S seventh novel, *The Master of Petersburg*, takes an even more dramatic shift away from his previous work than the realism in *Age of Iron*. This novel's central character is the Russian novelist Fyodor Dostoyevsky. In Coetzee's story, the novelist goes to St. Petersburg upon the death of his stepson, Pavel. He is devastated by grief for the young man, and begins an inquiry into his death. Though there are clear issues of this kind of intertextuality in his earlier novel *Foe*, Coetzee broke from his previous concerns of exploring alternative stories to the dominant narrative and offered the author Dostoyevsky's version of a death that is clouded by competing accounts. In his investigation he discovers that Pavel was involved in a group of nihilists and was probably murdered by either their leader or by the police.

Many reviewers have voiced mixed feelings about *Master of Petersburg* because of the obvious manipulation of the facts of Dostoyevsky's life. In real life, he did have a stepson named Pavel, but he was a foppish idler, a constant source of annoyance and embarrassment to the writer. The younger man also outlived his stepfather, and as Dostoyevsky died, he would not allow Pavel near his deathbed. Others have shown no compunction toward Coetzee's fictive sleight of hand. "This is not, after all, a book about the real Dostoevsky [*sic*]; his name, and some facts are connected to it, form a mask behind which Coetzee enacts a drama of parenthood, politics and authorship," Harriet Gilbert argued in *New Statesman & Society* (p. 41). It is these themes of parenthood, politics and authorship that are quintessentially Coetzeean. Essentially, this novel raises classic questions that Coetzee brought up before regarding the nature of authoritarianism and how it subverts truth itself within such a system. By casting these concerns outside of the South African context, Coetzee seemed to be broadening his perspective by suggesting that censorship exists less regionally and more universally while at the same time positing a resolution that is quite unexpected.

In *The Master of Petersburg* a depressed Dostoyevsky returns from exile in Dresden to late-czarist Russia. On all fronts he is compromised and therefore alone. He is not a real father, because Pavel is the child of his late wife's previous marriage. As a former revolutionary, he is affiliated neither with the revolutionaries nor with the authorities. On one side, the nihilists consider him a compromised individual of the previous generation. "We were disappointed in you—you, with your background" (p. 115). Dostoyevsky, however, has little appetite for violence. He just wants to be reconciled with his stepson, or the ghost of his stepson. On the other side, the government also distrusts him because of his past crit-icism of the regime. In fact, he is so unwelcome in official St. Petersburg circles that he had to enter the country under a pseudonym.

Incapable of allying himself with either extreme, he sets out to find his own truth. The novel makes it clear that the nihilists and the authorities function under a similar rubric which Nechaev describes at one point:

History isn't thoughts, history isn't made in people's minds. History is made in the streets. And don't tell me I am talking *thoughts* right now. That is just another clever debating trick, the kind of thing they confuse students with. I'm not talking thoughts, and even if I am, it doesn't matter. I can think one thing at one minute and another thing at another and it won't matter a pin as long as I *act*. The people *act*.

(p. 200)

History, or the narrative of the past, is inconsequential except in how it effects what it happening at this moment. Consequently, stories are tools of power to be manipulated as needed. This is why the nihilists and the authorities have their own story regarding the death of Pavel. Each is the story they need to control the streets.

Dostoyevsky's refusal to participate in either narrative puts him at odds with both. He will not compose a pamphlet denouncing the police as Pavel's murderers, and he will not denounce the nihilists for the police. In both circumstances he would be using his words as a tool of power. Instead, he desires for words and writing to function as a means of identification with his stepson, and that identification is a means in turn to his own salvation. It is more of a feeling, rather than an answer, for which Dostoyevsky searches. "Nothing he says is true, nothing is false, nothing is to be trusted, nothing to be dismissed. There is nothing to hold to, nothing to do but fall" (p. 235). There is a sense of vertigo in the place the novel finally takes the reader. The irony is that the narrative resolution lies in the contingency of the imagination.

DISGRACE

COETZEE'S *Disgrace* (1999) returns to the landscape of contemporary South Africa. The protagonist, David Lurie, a fifty-two-year-old twice-divorced adjunct professor of communications at Cape Technical University, is a Byronic character who has seemed to outlive his era. In his career he has been marginalized by the change in the role of the institution at which he has spent his working life. He used to be a professor of literature at Cape Town University College, but once the school had been changed into a technical college, his scholarly training was no longer needed. As a result, his position was reduced to that of adjunct professor relegated to teaching composition courses. He finds this new subject matter deeply troubling:

Although he devotes hours of each day to his new discipline, he finds its premise, as enunciated in the Communications 101 handbook, preposterous: "Human society has created language in order that we may communicate our thoughts, feelings and intentions to each other." His own opinion, which he does not air, is that the origins of speech lie in song, and the origins of song in the need to fill out with sound the overlarge and rather empty human soul.

(pp. 3–4)

At the same time he has devoted his life to engaging in numerous seductions and liaisons without any sense of responsibility, much like the subject of his studies, the Romantic poet Lord Byron. Now, he has reached a point in his life where his "lifestyle" is no longer acceptable in society.

The novel begins when Lurie is at loose ends sexually after having to end a long-term relationship with a paid escort. He accidentally encounters her with her children in the marketplace, and neither can tolerate this additional knowledge. She quits the escort service and breaks her long-standing liaison with him. This is just the first instance in which the tidy narrative by which he has constructed his life is disrupted by unwanted details and information. The knowledge that the prostitute he has had a weekly appointment with for the past few years is also a mother threatens the anachronistic notion he has of himself as a romantic rake. He slides easily into a relationship with an attractive student from his class on the Romantic poets. The affair is obviously not what it appears to be. In fact, the way that Coetzee described their first encounter suggests more rape than romance even though Lurie would never characterize it that way:

He has given her no warning: she is too surprised to resist the intruder who thrusts himself upon her. When he takes her in his arms, her limbs crumple like a marionette's. Words heavy as clubs thud into the delicate whorl of her ear. "No, not now!" she says, struggling. "My cousin will be back!"

But nothing will stop him.

(pp. 24–25)

Lurie knows he is making a mistake, but his Byronic self cannot be stopped. In fact, he has surrendered himself to the fantasy. As a result, things quickly go awry. Her boyfriend threatens him, and she withdraws from class and then from school. Her father shows up at his office and threatens him. Then a formal complaint is lodged. He is called before a committee that includes the chair of his department, a woman who views him as some sort of prehistoric creature, which in a way he is. Being faithful to his Romantic sense of reality, he immediately pleads guilty, but refuses to explain his actions or express a sincere apology. He offers that this is just the way he is made. He understands that the wider community does not approve of his actions, but he will not apologize for who he is. His apparent recalcitrance angers the committee. In the end they decide to terminate him without benefits. Once the community denounces his behavior, he packs up and leaves, accepting his exile in a state of disgrace with a strange passivity that is in line with his submission to the Byronic Romantic ideal.

In the first one-third of the book the conflict converges around the fact that Lurie has spent his life as the interpreter, not only of literature, but also of his own life. Now that role has become the responsibility of others—the girl, the boyfriend, university colleagues, his ex-wife, the newspaper. The chairwoman of his department states this plainly: "The wider community is entitled to know" (p. 50). At this point the reader expects the issue of Lurie's transgression to be further explored. Instead, Coetzee raised the stakes by setting in contrast the remaining events of the novel because he was more concerned with exploring how the moral authority of South Africa near the end of the millennium has changed. As such, this first part of the novel is almost a set piece or fictional exposition, developed in order to create an ironic context for what is to come.

After giving up his teaching job, Lurie joins his daughter, Lucy, on a small farm she owns in the eastern Cape. He is not at all at ease with her choice to be a truck farmer and kennel keeper for neighboring dogs. He feels this is below her, but settles in and lends a hand, determined to work in his spare time on an opera he has been meaning to write about Lord Byron in Italy. This idyllic pastoral, however, is soon violated when three black strangers rob and gang-rape Lucy while locking Lurie in the bathroom and trying to set him on fire. Lurie is humiliated and wants justice, but Lucy, while obviously broken in spirit, asks him not to tell anyone what has happened to her. At first it seems that the novel is drawing a parallel between Lurie as a father and Isaacs, the father of his student Melanie, in order to suggest that Lurie is being punished for his sexual arrogance. This conclusion, however, is much too reductive for Coetzee. The aim in this novel is to examine the shifting values in post-apartheid South Africa and to suggest that as the liberal elite attempts to atone for the past, it perhaps falls into the same totalitarian construct as apartheid with its own moral rigidity. In this construct, liberals perhaps feel it is their duty now to suffer injustice. This position is symbolized by Lucy's acceptance of the resulting pregnancy from the rape in which she acknowledges that she will learn to love the child she is carrying. She is somehow suggesting that the child of reverse oppression will develop into some sort of hybrid, or mixed race, that will offer a resolution. The irony here is that one tyranny has been traded for another with the hope that tyranny can be eliminated. Whether or not they can cancel each other out, the novel is clearly positing the responsibility on future generations. In conjunction with this larger theme, Lurie discovers psychic peace by helping a neighbor euthanize and incinerate the sick and abandoned dogs in the community, suggesting that those who cannot adapt must be destroyed. Strangely, Coetzee's attempt at real closure was unusual for him, but indicates a much more hopeful position than his earlier work ever suggested.

With his last two novels, *The Master of Petersburg* and *Disgrace*, Coetzee acknowledged the change in the social and political landscape of apartheid and pointed to a future where tyranny can be reduced, if not wholly eliminated. This direction, however, is not easy. Much of his work examines how tyranny functions in almost every aspect of humanity. He decoded the oppressive construct of point of view that makes any story, any narrative, an act of totalitarianism because it excludes other perspectives. Then, in *Master of Petersburg*, he

posited an alternative construct in which the responsibility for the story's truth shifts from the author to the reader. This redistribution of responsibility challenges the reader to use his or her own imagination to determine the truth behind the conflicting perspectives, much like Dostoyevsky. A reader must feel his or her way toward truth, while never really discovering the definitive answer. Consequently, *Disgrace* follows *The Master of Petersburg* because it offers a map by which to move toward this Eden. What this Eden may be like is as yet uncertain.

SELECTED BIBLIOGRAPHY

I. Books. *Dusklands* (contains two novellas, "The Vietnam Project" and "The Narrative of Jacobus Coetzee") (Johannesburg, 1974; New York,1985); *In the Heart of the Country* (New York, 1977) (As *From the Heart of the Country* [New York, 1982]); *Waiting for the Barbarians* (Great Britain, 1980; New York, 1982); *Life and Times of Michael K* (New York, 1984); *Foe* (New York, 1987); *Age of Iron* (New York, 1990); *The Master of Petersburg* (New York, 1994); *Disgrace* (New York, 1999).

II. Nonfiction and Translations. *A Posthumous Confession*, trans. Marcellus Emants (Boston, 1976); *The Expedition to the Baobab Tree*, trans. Wilma Stockenstroem (Boston, 1983); *A Land Apart: A Contemporary South African Reader*, ed. André Brink and J. M. Coetzee (New York, 1987); *White Writing: On the Culture of Letters in South Africa* (New Haven, Conn., 1988); *Doubling the Point: Essays and Interviews*, ed. David Atwell (Cambridge, Mass., 1992); *Giving Offense: Essays on Censorship* (Chicago, 1996); *Boyhood: Scenes from Provincial Life* (New York, 1997); *What Is Realism?* (with Bill Reichblum) (Bennington, Vt., 1997); *Lives of Animals* (with Amy Gutmann) (Princeton, N.J., 1999).

III. Awards and Honors. CNA Literary Award, 1977, for *In the Heart of the Country*; CNA Literary Award, James Tait Black Memorial Prize, and Geoffrey Faber Award, all 1980, all for *Waiting for the Barbarians*; CNA Literary Award, Booker-McConnell Prize, and Prix Femina Etranger, all 1984, all for *Life and Times of Michael K*; D. Litt., University of Strathclyde, Glasgow, 1985; Jerusalem Prize for the Freedom of the Individual in Society, 1987; *Irish Times* International Fiction Prize, 1995, for *The Master of Petersburg*; Life Fellow, University of Cape Town; Booker McConnell Prize, 1999, for *Disgrace*.

IV. Critical and Biographical Studies. Ursula A. Barnett, "South Africa: *Dusklands*," in *Books Abroad* 50, no. 2 (1976); Paddy Kitchen, "Death in the Head," in *The Listener* 98, no. 2522 (1977); Blake Morrison "Veldschmerz," in *Times Literary Supplement*, no. 3932 (22 July 1977); Charles R. Larson, "Anglophone Writing from African and Asia," in *World Literature Today* 52, no. 2 (1978);

J. M. COETZEE

Barend J. Toerien, "South Africa: *From the Heart of the Country*," in *World Literature Today* 52, no. 3 (1978); Paul Ableman, "End of Empire," in *Spectator* 245, no. 7593 (1980); Peter LaSalle, "Insight into the South African Psyche in Fiction," in *Africa Today* 27, no. 3 (1980); Peter Lewis, "Types of Tyranny," in *Times Literary Supplement*, no. 4049 (7 November 1980); Shiela Roberts, "Character and Meaning in Four Contemporary South African Novels," in *World Literature Written in English* 19, no. 1 (1980); Nicholas Shrimpton, "Cold Feet in Moscow," in *New Statesman* 100, no. 2590 (1980); Anthony Burgess, "The Beast Within: *Waiting for the Barbarians*," in *New York Magazine* 15, no. 17 (1982); Irving Howe, "A Start Political Fable of South Africa," in *New York Times Book Review* (18 April 1982); Webster Schott, "At the Farthest Outpost of Civilization," in *Washington Post* (2 May 1982); Bruce Allen, "A Pungent Tale of Ordeal and Survival Set in South Africa," in *Christian Science Monitor* (12 December 1983); Christopher Lehmann-Haupt, "Review of *Life and Times of Michael K*," in *New York Times* (6 December 1983); Cynthia Ozick, "A Tale of Heroic Anonymity," in *New York Times Book Review* (11 December 1983); Mark Abley, "An Outcast in a Tormented Country," in *Maclean's Magazine* 97, no. 5 (1984); Nadine Gordimer, "The Idea of Gardening," in *New York Review of Books* 31, no. 1 (1984); Vivian Gornick, "When Silence Speaks Lauder than Words," in *Village Voice* 24, no. 12 (1984); James Lasdun, "Life Victims," in *Encounter* 62, no. 1 (1984); Lance Olsen, "The Presence of Absence: Coetzee's *Waiting for the Barbarians*," in *Ariel* 16, no. 2 (1985); Debra A. Castillo, "The Composition of the Self in Coetzee's *Waiting for the Barbarians*," in *Critique: Studies in Modern Fiction* 27, no. 2 (1986); Richard G. Martin, "Narrative, History, Ideology: A Study of *Waiting for the Barbarians* and *Burger's Daughter*," in *Ariel* 17, no. 3 (1986); Dick Penner, "Sight, Blindness and Double-thought in J. M. Coetzee's *Waiting for the Barbarians*," in *World Literature Written in English* 26, no. 1 (1986); Robert M. Post, "Oppression in the Fiction of J. M. Coetzee," in *Critique: Studies in Modern Fiction* 27, no. 2 (1986); Stephen Watson, "Colonialism and the Novels of J. M. Coetzee," in *Research in African Literature* 17, no. 3 (1986); Josephine Dodd, "Naming and Framing: Naturalization and Colonization in J. M. Coetzee's *In the Heart of the Country*," in *World Literature Written in English* 27, no. 2 (1987); Allan Gardiner, "J. M. Coetzee's *Dusklands*: Colonial Encounters of the Robinsonian Kind," in *World Literature Written in English* 27, no. 2 (1987); Tony Moffet, "Interview with J. M. Coetzee," in *TriQuarterly*, no. 69 (1987); Maureen Nicholson, "'If I Make the Air around Him Thick with Words': J. M. Coetzee's *Foe*," in *West Coast Review* 21, no. 4 (1987); Ashton Nichols, "Review of *Foe*," in *Southern Humanities Review* 21, no. 4 (fall 1987); George Packer, "Blind Alleys," in *Nation* 244, no. 12 (1987); Dick Penner, "J. M. Coetzee's *Foe*: The Muse, the Absurd, and the Colonial Dilemma," in *World Literature Written in English* 27, no. 2 (1987); Cherry Clayton, "Uprooting the Malignant Fictions," *Times Literary Supplement*, no. 4460 (23 September 1988); Barbara Eckstein, "Review of *White Writing: On the Culture of Letters in South Africa*," in *World Literature Today* 62, no. 4 (1988); Susan V. Gallagher, "Torture and the Novel: J. M. Coetzee's *Waiting for the Barbarians*," in *Contemporary Literature* 29, no. 2 (1988); Kelly Hewson, "Making the 'Revolutionary Gesture': Nadine Gordimer, J. M. Coetzee and Some Variations on the Writer's Responsibility," in *Ariel* 19, no. 4 (1988); Shaun Irlam, "Review of *White Writing: On the Culture of Letters in South Africa*," in *MLN* 103, no. 5 (1988); Luc Renders, "J. M. Coetzee's *Michael K*: Starving in a Land of Plenty," in *Literary Gastronomy*, ed. David Bevan (Amsterdam, 1988); Michael Scrogin, "Apocalypse and Beyond: The Novels of J. M. Coetzee," in *Christian Century* 105, no. 17 (1988); Dick Penner, *Countries of the Mind: The Fiction of J. M. Coetzee* (Westport, Conn., 1989); Robert M. Post, "The Noise of Freedom: J. M. Coetzee's *Foe*," in *Critique: Studies in Modern Fiction* 30, no. 3 (1989); Barbara Temple-Thurston, "Review of *White Writing: On the Culture of Letters in South Africa*," in *Rocky Mountain Review of Language and Literature* 43, nos. 1–2 (1989); Derek Wright, "Fiction as Foe: The Novels of J. M. Coetzee," in *International Fiction Review* 16, no. 2 (1989); Gabriele Annan, "Love and Death in South Africa," in *New York Review of Books* 37, no. 17 (1990); G. Scott Bishop, "J. M. Coetzee's *Foe*: A Culmination and a Solution to a Problem of White Identity," in *World Literature Today* 64, no. 1 (1990); Kevin Goddard and John Read, eds., *J. M. Coetzee: A Bibliography* (London, 1990); Rosemary Jane Jolly, "Territorial Metaphor in Coetzee's *Waiting for the Barbarians*," in *Ariel* 20, no. 2 (1990); John Rees Moore, "J. M. Coetzee and *Foe*," in *Sewanee Review* 98, no. 1 (1990); George Packer, "Manifest Destiny," in *Nation* 251, no. 21 (1990); Patrick Parrinder, "What His Father Gets Up To," in *London Review of Books* 12, no. 17 (1990); Peter Reading, "Monstrous Growths," in *Times Literary Supplement*, no. 4565 (1990); Lawrence Thornton, "Apartheid's Last Vicious Gasps," in *New York Times Book Review* (23 September 1990); Susan V. Gallagher, *A Story of South Africa: J. M. Coetzee's Fiction in Context* (Cambridge, Mass., 1991); Derek Cohen, "Review of 'White Writing: On the Culture of Letters in South Africa,'" in *Dalhousie Review* (fall 1992); David Attwell, *J. M. Coetzee: South Africa and the Politics of Writing* (Berkeley, Calif., 1993); Julian Gitzen, "The Voice of History in the Novels of J. M. Coetzee," in *Critique* 35, no. 1 (fall 1993); Mark D. Hawthorne, "A Storyteller without Words: J. M. Coetzee's *Life and Times of Michael K*," in *Commonwealth: Novel in English* 6, nos. 1–2 (1993); Michael Marais, "'Omnipotent Fantasies' of a Solitary Self: J. M. Coetzee's 'The Narrative of Jacobus Coetzee,'" in *Journal of Commonwealth Literature* 28, no. 2 (1993); Michael Valdez Moses, "The Mark of Empire: Writing, History, and Torture in Coetzee's *Waiting for the Barbarians*," in *Kenyon Review* 15, no. 1 (1993); Rita Barnard, "Dream Topographies: J. M. Coetzee and the South African Pastoral," in *South Atlantic Quarterly* 93, no. 1 (1994); Harriet Gilbert, "Heir Apparent," in *New*

Statesman & Society 7 (25 February 1994); Patrick McGrath, "To Be Conscious Is to Suffer," in *New York Times Book Review* (29 November 1994); Michael Valdez Moses, ed., *The Writings of J. M. Coetzee* (Durham, N.C., 1994); Caroline Rody, "The Mad Colonial Daughter's Revolt: J. M. Coetzee's *In the Heart of the Country*," in *South Atlantic Quarterly* 93, no. 1 (1994); James Wohlpart, "A (Sub)Version of the Language of Power: Narrative and Narrative Technique in J. M. Coetzee's *In the Heart of the Country*," in *Critique* 35, no. 4 (1994); Philip R. Wood, "Aporias of the Postcolonial Subject: Correspondence with J. M. Coetzee," in *South Atlantic Quarterly* 93, no. 1 (1994); T. Kai Norris Easton, "Text Hinterland: J. M. Coetzee and the South African Novel," in *Journal of South African Studies* 21, no. 4 (1995); Joseph Frank, "A Review of *The Master of Petersburg*," in *New Republic* 213, no. 16 (1995); Martha Bayles, "The Silencers," in *New York Times* (22 September 1996); Graham Huggan and Stephen Watson, eds., *Critical Perspectives on J. M. Coetzee*, introduction by Nadine Gordimer (New York, 1996); Rosemary Jane Jolly, *Colonization, Violence, and Narration in White African Writing: André Brink, Breyten Breytenbach, and J. M. Coetzee* (Athens, Ohio, 1996); Sue Kossew, *Pen and Power: A Post-Colonial Reading of J. M. Coetzee and André Brink* (Amsterdam, 1996); Michael Marais, "Places of Pigs: The Tension between Implication and Transcendence in J. M. Coetzee's *Age of Iron* and *The Master of Petersburg*," in *Journal of Commonwealth Literature* 31, no. 1 (1996); Jennifer Wenzel, "Keys to the Labryrinth: Writing, Torture, and Coetzee's Barbarian Girl," in *Tulsa Studies in Women's Literature* 15, no. 1 (1996); Dominic Head, *J. M. Coetzee* (New York, 1997); Michiko Kakutani, "Childhood Hurt and Fear as a Writer's Inspiration," in *New York Times* (7 October 1997); Sue Kossew, ed., *Critical Essays on J. M. Coetzee* (New York, 1998); Michael Gorra, "After the Fall," in *New York Times* (28 November 1999); Christopher Lehmann-Haupt, "Caught in the Shifting Values (and Plot)," in *New York Times* (11 November 1999); Jonathan Levi, "Eros Enters," in *Los Angeles Times* (12 December 1999); Rita Barnard, "J. M. Coetzee," in *Research in African Literatures* 31, no. 2 (2000); Ian Hackling, "Our Fellow Animals," in *New York Review of Books* 47, no. 11 (2000); James Hynes, "Sins of the Father," in *Washington Post* (16 January 2000); Carol Iannone, "The Horror," in *Commentary* 109, no. 3 (2000); Shula Marks, "Negotiating the Past: The Making of Memory in South Africa," in *The American Historical Review* 105, no. 3 (2000); Joseph McElroy, "Salvation in South Africa," in *Nation* 270, no. 9 (2000).

WILKIE COLLINS

(1824–1889)

Stephen Amidon

IN THE PREFACE to the second edition of his immensely successful novel *The Woman in White*, Wilkie Collins claimed that he had "always held the old-fashioned opinion that the primary object of a work of fiction should be to tell a story" (p. 4). At first glance, this appears to be an obvious and even banal assertion for a novelist to make. After all, storytelling and fiction writing are widely deemed to be synonymous enterprises. But Collins' seemingly benign remark is in fact a stirring defense of one of the most radical fictional agendas of his era, an approach to storytelling which drew down upon him a barrage of outraged criticism, but also won him a broad, diverse readership which at times threatened to eclipse that of his close colleague, Charles Dickens. By advocating the primacy of pure narrative over the ethical and social concerns which had customarily governed how a story could be told, Collins was able to create a wild, unbridled, crowd-pleasing genre of fiction known as the "sensation novel." Working in an era when the novel was usually deemed a tame, domestic, deeply moral enterprise, he ignored the accepted restraints of the day, employing unprecedented complications of plot and extremities of circumstance to scandalize the critics and create intense reactions in a public which was only too eager to consume his work. With Collins, story became a landmine planted beneath the reader rather than a comfortable chair into which he could sink. Employing the principle so often attributed to him—"Make 'em cry, make 'em laugh, make 'em wait"—Collins was able at his best to produce work in which storytelling became an immediate, visceral sensation, rather than an instructive medium for the reader's education or moral betterment.

This is not to say that his novels are glib or shallow in the manner of so much popular fiction. In fact, Collins' work—once dismissed as mere trickery—is now seen as providing valuable glimpses into the murkier realms of the Victorian psyche, as well as employing a number of innovative literary games and strategies. By stripping his fiction of his era's received moral truisms and pet psychologies, Collins could plum depths which his more circumspect colleagues resolutely avoided. Pure story became a means of reaching the deepest imagination of the contemporary Victorian reader, whose buttoned-downed life usually covered up anxieties and longings beyond the scope of "proper" fiction. Although twenty-first-century readers might find the gross coincidences and violent passions of his plots hard to swallow, careful reading shows that at their best they follow a nightmare logic which can still strike a chord with anyone who gives him- or herself over to the text's exaggerations and ambushes. In this way, Collins was ahead of his time, creating archetypes which resonate in ways moral or tutelary fiction seldom can.

It is revealing to note that Collins' stranglehold on the darker precincts of his reading public's imagination was only relaxed when, in the latter part of his career, he abandoned the pure story in favor of "issue novels" that dealt with such topics as divorce, prostitution, vivisection, and religious prejudice. By hitching his fiction to these topical bandwagons, he lost the dark, incalculable energy that characterized his great work of the 1860s. Gradually, his novels really did take on the "old-fashioned" quality he ingenuously laid claim to in 1860. But this was not before Collins had left behind at least four novels—*The Woman in White*, *No Name*, *Armadale*, and *The Moonstone*—in which the craft of pure storytelling was radically and innovatively exercised.

LIFE

WILLIAM Wilkie Collins was born in London on 8 January 1824 into a family whose stability, cultivation, and relative prosperity were to ease his way into a successful writing career. His father, William Collins, was an accomplished painter and a member of the Royal Academy; his mother, Harriet Collins (née Geddes), was from a family that would produce several well-known artists. Collins' childhood was spent among a remarkably rich group of painters and writers, including Samuel Coleridge, William Blake, John Constable, and William Wordsworth. His unusual Christian name even had artistic overtones—it was in honor of his father's close friend, the painter Sir David Wilkie. But this is not to say that the Collins household was a den of bohemianism. William Collins may have been an artist, but he was also an austere, strictly religious man whose sense of propriety Wilkie was to rebel against for his entire adult life, in both his writing and his personal arrangements.

Collins was educated at home before being sent to an exclusive London boy's school at the age of eleven. His education was interrupted when he was twelve by a two-year-long family trip to France and Italy, an experience which would give Collins' writing the sophisticated, worldly air that was to shock so many critics and electrify the British public. Upon return he was boarded at another private school, though he proved an indifferent student. Around his seventeenth birthday he left school and was apprenticed to Antrobus & Co., a London tea merchant, though his energies were focused more on his growing literary ambitions than the world of commerce. In 1846, after five years of desultory apprenticeship, he left the tea trade to study law, an endeavor which had more impact on his plots, with their sensational crimes and complicated judicial issues, than the legal world (although Collins qualified for admission to the bar in 1851, he never actually practiced law). In 1847 his beloved father died, inspiring Collins to write his first published book, *Memoirs of the Life of William Collins, Esq., R.A.* (1848). Among its admiring readers was a man who was to become even more important in Collins' life than his father—Charles Dickens. Collins also had a painting hung at the Royal Academy's summer exhibition around this time, though it was to be the only work of art he was ever to exhibit.

After unsuccessfully trying to sell a romance set in Polynesia, Collins published his first novel, *Antonina; or, The Fall of Rome*, in February 1850. The story of the fifth-century sacking of Rome by Visigoths has little to do with his subsequent work and scholars view it as nothing more than spirited juvenilia. However, it did cement his reputation as a writer to watch, and a year later he was intro-

duced to the undisputed master of the Victorian literary scene, Charles Dickens. They soon became firm friends, acting together in the famous amateur theatricals Dickens produced at his London home and traveling to Switzerland and Italy in 1853, the year after Collins published his second novel, *Basil: A Story of Modern Life*. The two men also shared a secret enjoyment of the Victorian demimonde, visiting East End slums, Soho brothels, and Parisian theaters together, much to the chagrin of Dickens' more respectable friends. Collins' third novel, *Hide and Seek*, was published in 1854. The response to his writing remained respectful but somewhat tepid. His reputation was growing but still not secured.

In 1856 Collins joined the staff of Dickens' influential magazine, *Household Words*, where he published numerous stories as well as the serialized version of his fourth novel, *The Dead Secret*. His artistic intimacy with Dickens deepened throughout 1857. The two men appeared together on stage in Collins' melodrama about Arctic exploration, *The Frozen Deep*, and co-authored an account of their travels in the north of England, *The Lazy Tour of Two Idle Apprentices* (1890). They also became close readers and critics of one another's works. Not only was Dickens' role as Collins' magazine editor influential, but the younger author's passion for well-plotted stories in turn affected the later work of Dickens. By 1860 their relationship had become familial, with the marriage of Collins' younger brother Charles to Dickens' daughter Kate.

The year 1859 saw two enormous milestones in Collins' life. The first was the beginning of his relationship with Caroline Graves, which was to last (with one notable interruption) for the remainder of Collins' life. Legend, no doubt stoked by Collins, has it the two met in dramatic circumstances on a dark Hampstead street as the recently widowed single mother was trying to escape the clutches of a mesmeric seducer. Whatever the origin of their relationship, it was to endure, even though they never married, a circumstance which provides clear evidence of the mutinous stance Collins took against the strictures of Victorian propriety. But even without legal sanction, Collins remained personally and financially devoted to Caroline and her daughter Harriet (Carrie). The other defining event of that year was the commencement of the serial publication of *The Woman in White* in Dickens' new magazine,

All the Year Round. The work immediately created a sensation. Lines formed outside shops on the days a new installment was due; a cottage industry of "White Woman" clothes, perfume, waltzes, and other ephemera sprouted. The sensation novel, the genre originated by the book, became the literary fashion of the decade. By the time a bound edition was released in 1860, Collins' reputation as a first-rank author was cemented. He was now the Victorian equivalent of a superstar, recognized everywhere, a circumstance aided by his short stature, flowing beard, mincing gait, and large head. Although his two subsequent novels—*No Name* (1862) and *Armadale* (1866)—did not quite achieve the feverish success of *The Woman in White*, they continued to be best-sellers in both serialized and bound forms. Their sensational depictions of domestic crime and sexual intrigue earned the author a reputation as a literary outlaw, constantly skirting the borders of propriety. It was during this time that Collins, suffering from a severe case of arthritic gout as well as the pressures of writing his novels "hot" for magazine serialization, began to use opium in its liquid form, laudanum. In fact, during the composition of *No Name* (1862), Collins was so debilitated that Dickens felt compelled to offer to finish the book for him. Though the offer was declined, it was clear evidence of the strong intimacy of these two outsized talents.

The year 1868 was among the most eventful in Collins' life. It saw the publication of his second acknowledged masterpiece, *The Moonstone*, considered by many to be the first true detective novel in English literature. It was also during this year that Collins' private life underwent considerable disruption. When, after the death of his cherished mother, he refused to formalize his relationship with Caroline through marriage, she left him to marry a younger man. The undaunted Collins not only blessed the union by attending the ceremony, but he also formed a relationship with Martha Rudd, a shepherd's daughter he'd met while traveling in Norfolk. Once again, the iconoclastic novelist did not marry his lover, even though they were to have three out-of-wedlock children. His personal life became even more complicated two years later when Caroline, clearly unhappy in her marriage, returned to Collins. She lived with him in London until his death, with Martha and her children established in a household nearby as the "Dawson" family.

Around this time, 1870, Collins' work had begun a gradual decline from the heady zenith of the previous decade. The death of Charles Dickens on 9 June was a considerable blow, ending a relationship that had been deeply beneficial to both writers. Although their friendship had cooled somewhat over the troubled marriage of Charles Collins to Kate Dickens, they remained remarkably close for two such hugely successful writers. Still only forty-six, Collins now appeared more elderly than middle-aged. His novels gradually lost their aura of mystery and danger as they tackled "issues" such as marriage laws, Catholicism, and vivisection, rather than the nightmarish, often ineffable terrors present in *Armadale* and *The Moonstone*. Despite the slow drying of his creative juices, Collins remained a popular favorite throughout the reading world, evidenced by the continued box-office success of his plays (usually adapted from his novels) as well as a triumphant reading tour of America in the winter of 1873–1874.

The last years of Collins' life saw him struggle against ill health, opium addiction, and changing public tastes. The one time *bon vivante* had become a prematurely aged recluse. His consumption of laudanum reached staggering proportions—he was once witnessed downing an entire wine glass of the drug, enough, according to a contemporary physician, to kill a roomful of non-users. His drama *Rank and Riches* (1882) was laughed off the stage; novels such as *The Fallen Leaves* (1879) and *"I Say No"* (1884) were given only somewhat less churlish treatment by critics. Undaunted, the boundlessly energetic author continued to work until the stroke that led to his death, even securing the help of Walter Besant to finish his twenty-first and last novel. He died on 23 September 1889, dividing his estate equally among the two families he had dearly loved but stubbornly refused to legitimize during his lifetime. Respectable Victorian society had its revenge on this literary outlaw, however, citing his unconventional private life and the alleged shallowness of his work as reasons to deny him a memorial in either St. Paul's Cathedral or Westminster Abbey.

THE SENSATION NOVEL

WILKIE Collins was the pioneer and chief practitioner of the sensation novel, a genre that thoroughly dominated English fiction in the 1860s. The sensation novel can be defined as a book whose primary goal is to create extraordinarily intense reactions in the reader by employing vivid, spectacular, and bizarre scenarios. It is storytelling boiled down to its purest, most dramatic essence. Like the modern thriller, it seeks to keep the reader both enthralled and continually off balance. Unlike most thriller writers, however, Collins saw his work as having a deeply serious dimension as well, exploring the most pressing sexual, social, and psychological concerns of the day. In the sensation novel, the line between good and evil is often blurred, while the benevolent and just hand of providence is replaced by an arbitrary fist of cruel accident and ironic coincidence. Because the author's intent is to create a sensation among his readership—to provide vicarious thrills and renegade emotions—moral authority is often disrupted by complex plotting, wicked irony, and outrageous set pieces. At first glance, it is a surprisingly anarchic and amoral form of fiction to emerge from the staid Victorian world, though the success of the books of Collins and his followers suggest they provided a powerful release valve for the pent-up libidinal energies of their readers.

The sensation novel has its roots in the Gothic and Romantic fiction of the late eighteenth and early nineteenth centuries, works that focused on supernatural scenarios and exotic locales to create melodramatic effects. Another source was the Newgate novels, epitomized by the early work of Dickens, which explored the criminal underworld of Victorian London as a means of protesting against social inequality. A more outlaw source of Collins' fiction was the penny-dreadful serials and sensational stage dramas that formed the core of working-class entertainment. But unlike any of these sources, the sensation novel situated its frenzied action squarely in the quiet homes of the British middle class. Suddenly, under Collins' skilled and feverish hand, the most extreme scenarios were transplanted from distant settings into the modern, workaday world. As Henry James, writing in the *Nation* in November 1865, said, Collins introduced into the universe of the British novel "those most mysterious of mysteries, the mysteries which are at our own doors" (pp. 593–595). Instead of the decrepit, ghost-ridden castle of the Gothic romance or the East End hovel of the Newgate novel (named for the infamous London prison), Collins looked no further than the hearths and drawing rooms so familiar to their

bourgeois readers for their tales of murder, adultery, bigamy, and revenge. He largely banished the supernatural and the uncanny from his story lines, replacing them with a realism inherited from the domestic sagas of the previous two decades. Ghosts and demented aristocrats gave way to secretly conniving gentlewomen, corrupt merchants, and private detectives. Whereas a novel like *Armadale*, filled with generational revenge and prophetic dreams, might have once taken place in a ruined Scottish castle filled with oracular apparitions, Collins was satisfied to situate the primary action in a London apartment, a sunny country home, and a garden cottage.

The sensation novel also differed from the various forms of melodrama which preceded it in its complicated, often subversive morality. Where a Newgate or Gothic novel might contain scenes of violence and transgression, the morality underpinning these tales was almost invariably black and white, reflecting the current middle-class orthodoxies. Following the formidable example of Sir Walter Scott, Victorian novelists, even at their most outlandish, worked in an idiom that was highly and invariably moral. Villains may have been temporarily ascendant but they were also inevitably punished; any fleeting pleasure adulterous wives may have derived from their affairs was soon erased by suffering and death. With Collins, however, this good versus evil dynamic was obscured in order to pump up the volume of his stories. Traditionally "good" people misbehaved and were not always punished for it, while "bad" people were often dealt with sympathetically. Qualities that made a character compelling, such as cunning and persistence, were as likely to be rewarded as were virtue and patience, which often detracted from their dramatic potential. Thus, *No Name*'s Magdalen Vanstone, who first appears as a flower of that most venerated of British institutions, the Victorian lady, descends into a pattern of deceitful scheming and virtual prostitution in order to retrieve her family fortune, conduct which receives precious little in the way of authorial censure. Meanwhile, in that same novel, the criminal swindler Captain Wragge is both lovable and triumphant, while *The Woman in White*'s Count Fosco, an altogether more lethal rogue, compels a degree of attraction and sympathy which must have severely wrong-footed the reader accustomed to having villains to hate and heroes to love.

Needless to say, Collins' radical transformation of the norms of fiction brought down considerable denunciation upon him, often of the most personal and violent nature. In an era when critics were as likely to see themselves as guardians of public morality as they were arbiters of public taste, an author as adventurous as Collins was sure to be a target of great hostility. In fact, no less a figure than the Archbishop of York, writing in the *London Times* on 2 November 1864, sermonized against the sensation novel, calling it "a mere welter of crime, misery and confusion" (p. 9). One of the main complaints against Collins in particular was that his novels appealed to elements of society hitherto left out of the fictional circle, especially the working classes. Indeed, his work clearly struck a chord with the reading public at large. From the publication of *The Woman in White* in 1860 to the end of that decade—and in some ways to the end of his career—Collins remained a writer whose popularity rivaled that of Dickens. Such was his notoriety that the term "Sensational Mania" became current, usually as a lightning rod for frowning editorials. Other popular novelists such as M. E. Braddon, Charles Reade, and even the Dickens of *The Mystery of Edwin Drood* were working under Collins' compelling influence. Clearly, with the sensation novel Collins and his followers were able to tap into a turbulent vein of anxiety covered over by a thick veneer of Victorian rectitude. For a once-stable society giving way to an increasingly tumultuous, urbanized and democratic culture, his radical vision held up a darkly compelling mirror.

EARLY WORKS

THE first decade of Wilkie Collins' writing life can be seen as an apprenticeship, producing work that even at its most interesting pales in comparison to what was to come. His first published book, *Memoirs of the Life of William Collins, Esq., R.A.*, is a tribute to a father who is pictured as an occasionally overbearing but fundamentally decent man. Thoroughly researched and surprisingly objective, its main achievement was to put Collins on the literary map. His first novel, *Antonina*, is also little more than verbose prologue to his mature work. Set in a decadent Rome under threat of barbarian conquest, the book is most notable for the young author's vivid imagination.

Collins' second novel, *Basil*, begins his real career, primarily, as the subtitle suggests, by bringing Collins into the world of the modern reader. It tells the story of a young aristocrat who secretly marries a working-class girl he meets on an omnibus, only to have his marriage wrecked by a caddish seducer. The book's energy and daring elicited considerable attention, most notably for a scene in which Basil listens through a flimsy wall as his wife commits adultery next door. His next novel, *Hide and Seek*, is most notable for introducing, through the character of its deaf protagonist, Madonna Grice, a theme that was to recur throughout Collins' work—the effects of disability on the human psyche. *The Dead Secret* (1857), the story of a servant girl who must pass off her illegitimate daughter as her mistress's, was the first novel Collins wrote for magazine serialization, a practice which was to spur him on to his remarkably generous output in coming years. The well-received short story collection *The Queen of Hearts* (1859) concluded his apprenticeship. During this period, Collins' lifelong relationship with the theater was also cultivated, first with his two-act murder mystery *The Lighthouse* (1855), which was produced by Dickens for the London stage in 1857, and then with *The Frozen Deep* (1857), a story of Arctic exploration in which Collins and Dickens were to co-star in 1866. Although these novels and dramas constituted a varied and well-received body of work, they were soon to be eclipsed by the book that was to catapult Collins to the forefront of the British literary scene.

THE WOMAN IN WHITE

ANY question as to the position Wilkie Collins affords his first great novel in his personal pantheon is answered by the inscription on his tombstone, which identifies the grave's occupant as "the author of *The Woman in White* and other works of fiction." It is without doubt his masterpiece, incorporating all the author's best qualities—intricacy of plot, intensity of emotion, and severity of social criticism. After nearly a century and a half, it remains an extraordinarily vibrant and original work. Its effect on the British literary scene when it was released was almost unprecedented, creating a sensation worthy of the genre it instituted. Even a reader as ill disposed to popular fiction as William Thackery confessed to reading it "from morning till sunset."

The story is told by a series of narrators brought together by a drawing master using the pseudonym "Walter Hartright." It opens with Hartright accepting a post as tutor to the half-sisters Marian Halcombe and Laura Fairlie at Limmeridge House, their stately home in northern England. Just before he leaves London, Hartright encounters a ghostly "woman in white" racing along a deserted nighttime street (an event based upon Collins' own meeting with Catherine Graves). The mystery woman asks for his help, hinting she is escaping from a titled gentleman. Hartright also learns, to his astonishment, that she has a mysterious connection to Limmeridge House. He impulsively helps her, only to learn moments later she has just escaped from a lunatic asylum.

Upon arriving at Limmeridge, Hartright falls in love with the beautiful Laura, then discovers she is engaged to Sir Percival Glyde. He also learns that the woman in white is one Anne Catherick, who was raised by Laura's now-dead mother and who bears an uncanny resemblance to Laura. It is revealed that Anne was locked in the asylum by Glyde himself to suppress a dark secret she possesses about his past. Realizing his love for Laura is impossible, Hartright leaves Limmeridge.

The marriage of Laura and Percival soon goes wrong. He proves an insensitive bully who is mired in debt. When Laura refuses to sign over her inheritance to him, he begins to plot against her, aided by his brilliant, grotesque Italian friend, Count Fosco. Their scheme involves switching Anne and Laura by locking up Laura as Anne in an asylum, where her protestations about her true identity will fall upon deaf ears, then murdering Anne, so Glyde will receive the inheritance from his dead wife. The resourceful Marian ferrets out the scheme and is able to rescue her sister from the asylum, though not before Laura has been disinherited.

Hartright learns of the sisters' fate and decides to help them regain their legacy. The trio first match wits with Glyde, discovering Anne's secret in the process—Glyde is in fact illegitimate. After a panicked Glyde dies trying to destroy the evidence, Hartright then takes on Fosco, learning that the Italian is in fact a spy. He blackmails Fosco into confessing his crime, thereby reestablishing Laura's identity. The master criminal flees to Paris, where he is murdered by the brotherhood he betrayed. The novel ends with Laura and Hartright marrying, and Marian joining them in the role of spinster aunt, rounding out an unconventional but undeniably strong trio.

What is perhaps most striking about *The Woman in White* is the ingenious technique Collins employs to tell his high-octane story. Using a method John Sutherland in his introduction to the 1996 Oxford World's Classics edition shrewdly terms "forensic," Collins called a series of witnesses, plaintiffs, and defendants to testify to the reader by writing firsthand accounts of the events. Although none of them know the whole story and indeed a few, such as the doctor who certifies Laura dead, provide only a paragraph or two, the cumulative effect is one of startling immediacy. The omniscient, avuncular narrator who can comfort and guide the reader has been replaced by an array of often-conflicting voices. In an era when cheap newspapers were just beginning to popularize sensational murder trials, Collins brilliantly approximated the turbulent, anything-can-happen feel of a courtroom to the medium of the novel.

Another innovative feature of the novel is the attitude Collins adopted toward the subject of crime. Not only did he posit the seemingly respectable gentleman Percival Glyde as a person capable of the most heinous felonies, but he also implied a value-neutral attitude toward the notions of detection and justice. Breaking with the time-honored truism that divine justice will prevail, Collins suggested that it is instead whichever person is most cunning and persistent—not the one who is good and just—who will win out in the struggle between victim and criminal. Virtue and providence alone will not do the trick. As Fosco, the "Napoleon of Crime," himself says, "The hiding of a crime, or the detection of a crime, what is it? A trial of skill between the police on one side, and the individual on the other" (p. 236). Walter and Marian may have right on their side, but it is only due to their extraordinary energy and, more important, their willingness to engage in acts of espionage, blackmail, and even complicity to murder that they are able to win the day. By removing the inevitability of virtue's victory, Collins was once again able to place the reader precariously on the edge of his seat, thereby increasing the power of his story.

In fact, this scandalous suggestion that extra-legal maneuvers might be necessary for good to prevail over evil is only part of the extreme vision that made *The Woman in White* such a sensation. Also inherent in the book is a radical critique of marriage as it was practiced in Victorian England, a theme that is perhaps not surprising coming from a man who was able to maintain two happy families without ever going to the altar. Instead of being the repository of all that is good and fair in English life, marriage is portrayed as a snare in which the unsuspecting woman just might find slavery and even murder. Although Laura Fairlie is in every way the dutiful young Victorian lady—marrying the titled gentleman who her father commands she must—her happiness and very life are threatened by this act of fealty. It is only when she rebelliously refuses to play the blindly obedient wife by not signing over her fortune to Glyde that she enters the labyrinthian path to salvation and happiness in the form of a true (if unconventional) marriage to the man she loves.

NO NAME

THE *Woman in White* was a tough act to follow, especially for a writer working under the extraordinary deadlines imposed by serial publication. With *No Name*, Collins created a novel that was both less and more than its predecessor—less sensational in its style and effects, but more radical in its attack on Victorian propriety. If the dark, masculine, self-sufficient Marian Halcombe of the former novel suggests a new kind of literary heroine as she does battle with the corrupt men around her, then Magdalen Vanstone, the complex and troubling protagonist of *No Name*, sees this new model woman come decidedly into her own.

The novel opens quietly, with an image of blissful domestic rectitude that was sure to warm the hearts of Collins' critics. Sisters Magdalen and Norah live with their beloved parents in the comfortable country manor of Combe-Raven, engaging in the balls, amateur dramatics, and harmless flirtations expected of women of their age and station. Even the news that their mother is unexpectedly pregnant is received with optimism and good cheer. But the Vanstone's tidy Victorian arcadia begins to crumble with the arrival of a letter from America, which causes Mr. and Mrs. Vanstone to travel hastily to London on secret business. And then disaster strikes—Vanstone is killed in a railway accident. His shocked wife goes into premature labor, which results in the death of both her and her child. Suddenly, Magdalen and Norah have been transformed from privileged daughters into orphans.

Worse is to come when the will is read. They learn the reason behind their parents' secret journey to London—to get married. Vanstone, it transpires, had foolishly married many years earlier while a soldier in Canada, an unwise alliance that both negates his will and renders his daughters illegitimate. As their lawyer darkly says, "Mr. Vanstone's daughters are Nobody's Children" (p. 138). The result is that the girls are made dependent on a distant uncle, Michael Vanstone, who, because of a long-standing feud with his brother, refuses to give them more than a pittance.

Norah accepts her fate with quiet resignation, though Magdalen decides to do whatever is necessary to win back her legacy. After a chance meeting with her distant relative and professional con man Captain Wragge, she decides to team up with him to achieve her goal. She first enters that most risqué of Victorian occupations, professional acting, in order to raise enough capital to swindle Michael Vanstone. But after he dies and his fortune passes onto his weak-willed son Noel, she decides to get back her inheritance by marrying the man who now owns it.

One things stands in her way, however—Vanstone's formidable Swiss housekeeper, Mrs. Lecount, who also has an eye on her master's inheritance. An elaborate battle of wits ensues between Wragge and Magdalen on one side and Lecount on the other. Magdalen eventually does manage to marry Noel, who obligingly dies of heart failure not long afterward. But once again Magdalen is frustrated in her quest for justice—at the last minute Lecount had convinced her master to leave his money to an uncle, Admiral Bartram, rather than Magdalen. Undeterred, Magdalen disguises herself as a maid in order to infiltrate Bartram's house to look for a secret codicil to the will that might give her her legacy. She is once again defeated, however, and winds up sick and alone in a derelict neighborhood in London. While on death's door she is rescued by a kind-hearted sailor, Captain Kirke. He reunites her with Norah, who, as fortune would have it, has married George Bartram, the Admiral's nephew and heir. After considerable toil and strife, the sisters have regained their inheritance.

Although *No Name* lacks the mystery and sheer invention of *The Woman in White*, it earns its place at the forefront of Collins' fiction through the innovative intensity of the "cat-and-mouse" structure the author was to make his own. Indeed, so skillful was Collins' use of this game-like configuration that he was to influence a wide range of later detective writers. At its best, Collins' work can be likened to a masterful game of chess, where opponents such as Wragge and Lecount are constantly reacting to one another's moves, raising the dramatic tension and momentum all the time.

Another striking aspect of *No Name* is the continued radical departure from Victorian norms inherent in the author's depiction of his heroine. Although Collins cannot be said to have had an explicitly feminist agenda, he was clearly interested in depicting resourceful, unconventional women who fought against an oppressive system. It is not hard to see why many contemporary critics were shocked and even disgusted by Magdalen, who, not yet out of her teens, was willing to engage in all manner of deviousness to achieve her goal—even going so far as to marry and have sexual relations with a man she deeply loathes. "Any conspiracy, any deception, is justified to my conscience by the vile law which has left us helpless," she states to Wragge, who, despite his long experience as a con man, is stunned by her behavior (p. 336). Although Collins was criticized for mere sensationalism in his creation of this "bad girl" heroine—allegedly using her schemes for nothing more than titillation—a more serious point is being made about the status of women and the injustices of marriage and inheritance law in Victorian England. For the Vanstone sisters to be utterly crushed because of a legal technicality and the distant acts of their parents, Collins suggested, is a scandal that only the most callow social conservative can defend. Although the author pays lip service to the passive, dutiful (and notably uninteresting) Norah and duly rewards her at novel's end, it is impossible to deny that his sympathies lie with the strong-willed Magdalen and even with Lecount, both of whom are dynamic and resourceful female characters shown to have been made dependent on the whims of a pathetically weak man, Noah Vanstone.

Collins' other subversive gesture in the book is his creation of Captain Wragge, the "moral agriculturalist" who seeks to reap his rewards from the folly and ignorance of his fellow men. As an undeniably lovable rogue, he is one of Collins' most Dickensian characters, but where the eminently proper Dickens would have most likely meted out some sort of punishment to Wragge at novel's end, Collins depicts him as triumphantly establishing himself in the role of respectable purveyor of curatives and medicines. In the often amoral hurly-burly of Victorian capitalism, the author playfully suggested, a rogue is just as likely to become a pillar of the community as he is a convict—provided he has sufficient cunning, application, and money.

ARMADALE

IN a typically defensive preface to his third great novel, Collins anticipated some of the negative reaction that was to greet the eight hundred pages to follow. "Readers in particular will, I have some reason to suppose, be here and there disturbed—perhaps even offended—by finding that *Armadale* oversteps, in more than one direction, the narrow limits within which they are disposed to restrict the development of modern fiction. . . . Estimated by the Clap-trap morality of the present day, this may be a very daring book" (p. 4). To claim that *Armadale* is a "daring" book that "oversteps" contemporary fictional norms is a rare understatement by this most hyperbolic of novelists. It is, in fact, the sine qua non of sensation fiction, a book of such frenetic complication and passion that it at times threatens to burst in the reader's hands.

The novel opens in a German spa in 1832, where a man named Allan Armadale lies dying of a "paralytic infection" (syphilis). On his death bed, he makes a harrowing confession. While a young man in Barbados, he inherited a large fortune from a distant relative at the expense of that man's estranged son. Not long afterward, the disguised son (also named Allan Armadale) arrived and duly stole his rival's wife and identity. In revenge, the first Armadale murdered the second, who left behind a widow and a son, also named Allan Armadale. At the spa, the dying storyteller composes a will in which his own son (yet another Allan Armadale!) is warned of ever having anything to do with the son of the murdered man: "I see My Crime, ripening again for the future in the self-same circumstance which first sowed the seed of it in the past; and descending, in inherited contamination of Evil, from me to my son" (p. 55).

The action resumes nineteen years later. The son of the murderer, ignorant of his ancestry, calls himself Ozias Midwinter. He is a melancholy wanderer whose travels take him to the small English fishing village where Allan Armadale (son of the murdered man) lives quietly. The two soon become inseparable friends. When the carefree and somewhat fatuous Allan unexpectedly becomes heir to the wealthy Thorpe-Ambrose estate, he offers Midwinter the position of steward so the two friends can remain close. Despite discovering his father's letter warning him off any connection with Allan, Midwinter decides to spurn destiny and embrace the first true friendship of his life. He accepts the job and moves into Thorpe-Ambrose.

Enter Lydia Gwilt, the former servant girl who helped Allan's murdered father forge the documents needed to gain control of his rival's fortune. Now a formidable beauty with vivid red hair and a dark past, she is looking to make her fortune by disguising her identity and marrying Allan. To do so, she becomes governess to Allan's shallow young lover, Eleanor Milroy. When the cunning Lydia is prevented from attaining her goal, however, she decides upon an even more desperate plot—to secretly marry Ozias under his legal name, then, armed with a marriage certificate identifying her as Mrs. Allan Armadale, orchestrate Allan's death and claim to be his widow. Her ability to carry this radical scheme out is made clear when we learn that she has already murdered her abusive first husband. After marrying Midwinter (who she has come to love), she lures Allan to a corrupt asylum, where she will have him "accidentally" poisoned. But at the last minute Midwinter joins his friend and it is he who winds up in the gas-filled room. Realizing she has lost, Lydia frees her husband and takes her own life, leaving Allan and Eleanor to marry and Midwinter to escape at last from his father's curse.

As the above summary suggests, *Armadale* is an immensely complicated and feverishly dramatic performance. Indeed, many critics have complained that with this book Collins finally travels a sensation too far, creating a world of such rank improbability and immorality (nearly every significant character in the story spies on another) that the whole enterprise collapses under its own weight. Certainly the excesses of the sensation novel are fully exposed in a plot that contains no fewer than five characters with the same name and a host of extreme coincidences, such as the scene in which Allan and Ozias just happen to stumble upon the wreckage of the ship where Ozias' father murdered Allan's—several decades and many thousands of miles away from the original incident. The book's supporters, however, would argue that such a prosaic reading ignores Collins' deeper authorial purpose, which is to create a mythic, nightmare world in which the wheels of fate can be more efficiently spun. Even the strangest coincidence, after all, can be imbued with meaning once the existence of an ordering power is acknowledged.

In fact, it is in *Armadale* that the concept of destiny fully enters the author's fictional universe, albeit in a manner often more expedient than coherent. The book's considerable action is founded upon a series of prophetic moments, most notably the murderous Allan Armadale's warning to his young son to stay away from his victim's son at all costs. Equally portentous is the youngest Allan Armadale's elaborately detailed, seventeen-part dream in which he first encounters the figure of the "Shadow of the Woman," who will eventually arrive in the lethal form of Lydia Gwilt. Although Collins was clearly suggesting the existence of a guiding force behind his story's events, it would be a mistake to see this as being the agent to which Victorian readers were accustomed—a providential hand that bestows a moral, rational structure on the story. Collins has in fact conjured a darker, more anarchic pilot to steer his action. Fate may *seem* to order the world of *Armadale*, but it proves to be a mercurial, random power, one that serves the author more as a storytelling device to heighten tension than a way of adding ethical coherence to his work. For instance, the sympathetic figure of Midwinter continually challenges destiny's decree that he avoid contact with Allan, yet he is never truly punished for this defiance. And it is difficult to see the purpose behind Allan's elaborate dream other than to provide a dramatic impetus for the plot to come. Once again, Collins subverted traditional fictional devices to further his own agenda of pure story.

As with his previous work, Collins may have provided a happy ending for the likes of Allan and Eleanor, but his sympathies clearly lay with the novel's darker folk, most notably Lydia Gwilt. If the book's intricate story pushed plotting to its outer limits, than the brazen figure of Lydia Gwilt does the same with characterization. A murderer and swindler who associates with a prostitute's madam and an abortionist, she nonetheless commands a good deal of sympathy from the reader as an ill-used wife in a society that will not come to her aid. Take away Victorian values and she is simply a woman who won't lie down under a crushing fate. (In his 1889 essay "Wilkie Collins," Algernon Swinburne cogently suggested that she would have been perfectly sympathetic to Collins' frowning critics had she possessed a French name rather than an English one.) Collins also cunningly shows her to have a heart of sorts when she briefly develops a true romantic attachment for Midwinter, a quality unthinkable to his more conventional colleagues when they came to fill in the portraits of their painted ladies. Once again—and never again so radically—Collins demonstrated that, in his female characters, self-reliance and self-preservation are just as formidable virtues as fealty and chastity.

Another strikingly original aspect of the novel is its wide-ranging questioning of the static nature of identity, the notion of "strong character" to which so many of Collins' readers must have subscribed. As Collins' foremost biographer Catherine Peters has pointed out, the question of identity stands at the center of every one of his novels. In *The Woman in White*, for instance, Laura's and Anne's personalities are so fragile that they are easily interchanged and even run the danger of being snuffed out altogether. In *No Name*, Magdalen and Norah, as the title suggests, forfeit their very identities—are rendered fundamentally identity-less—by an act utterly beyond their control. It is left to Magdalen, a skilled natural actress who ironically employs a variety of false guises, to win them back their selfhood. In *Armadale*, this existential dilemma is explored most fully, with a number of characters vying for the gentlemanly identity of Allan Armadale. Comically reinforcing the importance of this struggle, Collins branded the losers with such absurd anti-names as Ozias Midwinter and Fergus Ingleby. Beyond the undeniably rich dramatic possibilities offered by this obliteration of personal identity is a frightening reflection of the changes disturbing the Victorian world, in which urbanization and industrialization were challenging and obscuring age-old notions of stable character and unified personality. In a society where reinvention was suddenly possible and often necessary, figures like the role-playing Magdalen Vanstone and the deadly duplicitous Lydia Gwilt served as telling archetypes.

THE MOONSTONE

IN his introduction to the 1928 Oxford World's Classics edition of *The Moonstone*, T. S. Eliot famously referred to it as "the first, the longest and the best of modern English detective novels" (p. v). Since then, longer and perhaps better police procedurals have been written, and if it is now known that other novels of detection preceded Collins', there can still be no doubt he had a pioneering hand in instituting his second genre in less than a decade. *The Moonstone* employs a series of innovative characters and techniques that were eventually to become conventional in the detective novel—the disarmingly astute police inspector, the missing gem, the gallery of multiple suspects, the bushel of red herrings, and the stunning revelation of guilt. It was perhaps inevitable that this author would come to write a novel in which detection was the primary fictional catalyst, given his previous penchant for cat-and-mouse plots that were built upon a foundation of lurid crime.

The Moonstone opens with the story of the theft of the precious diamond that gives the novel its name. Rumored to carry a curse upon whoever dares to steal it, it is taken from a statue of an Indian moon god during a military operation by a callous British officer, John Herncastle. The action then moves forward fifty years, to the death of Herncastle. In order to avenge himself on his hated sister Julia, he has arranged in his will that Julia's beloved daughter, Rachel, will receive the Moonstone on her eighteenth birthday, thus bringing its curse upon their family. It is brought to Rachel by her cousin, the dashing young Franklin Blake, whose arrival coincides with that of three Indian "jugglers" who are in fact out to retrieve the sacred gem. Blake and Rachel are immediately attracted to one another, even though the young lady is also involved with Godfrey Ablewhite, a well-known philanthropist and inspirational speaker. Ablewhite and Blake contend for her heart, a contest Blake eventually wins.

But everything changes when the diamond is discovered missing the morning after Rachel's birthday. Suspicion immediately falls upon Rachel's servant girl, Rosanna Spearman. When the local police can make no headway, the celebrated detective Sergeant Cuff is summoned from London. Improbably lean and possessed of an eccentric passion for roses, he comes to suspect that Rachel, with the help of her servant, stole it herself to pay off private debts. His suspicion seems to be confirmed when Rosanna commits suicide in a tidal miasma known as The Shivering Sand, and Rachel inexplicably breaks up with

Blake. But since the girl's mother will not countenance bringing charges against her daughter, the investigation is stopped in its tracks.

The action switches to London, where the diamond continues to cause trouble. Ablewhite is attacked and searched by the three Indians, putting the light of suspicion on him. But Rachel asserts his innocence, proving her faith by accepting his marriage proposal, even though she still loves Franklin. Blake returns from overseas, where he had unsuccessfully traveled to forget Rachel. Finding he is still snubbed by her over the case of the missing Moonstone, he decides to find out who stole it. His investigations dig up a letter Rosanna wrote before her death, which in turn leads to evidence implicating himself in the theft. Utterly confused, Blake confronts Rachel, who sensationally says she saw him steal the diamond with her own eyes.

Blake is then unexpectedly summoned by Mr. Candy, a doctor with whom he quarreled about the efficacy of modern medicine on the night the diamond was stolen. It turns out the doctor secretly gave Blake a dose of opium to prove that it worked. Drugged, Blake sleepwalked into Rachel's room and stole the gem, whereupon it became missing. With the help of Candy's melancholy, opium-addicted colleague Ezra Jennings, Blake recreates the crime scene, right down to taking another dose of opium, hoping to find where he hid it. But it is to no avail. The stone remains missing.

The mystery is finally solved when the pawnbroker who has possession of the stone, witnessed by Blake's agents, turns it over to a mysterious sailor. Before Blake and Sergeant Cuff can arrest the man he is murdered by the three Indians, who disappear with the gem. The victim is Ablewhite, who took the diamond from the drugged Blake. He turns out to be a rogue who hid a mistress and considerable debt. Blake and Rachel are reunited, as is the Moonstone with the statue from which it was so egregiously stolen a half century earlier.

If *Armadale* was criticized for promoting pure sensation at the expense of narrative coherency, then *The Moonstone* can be said to rectify this imbalance—with a vengeance. Never before or after in Collins' work was a story's form so carefully and minutely crafted. This is primarily due to the fact that Collins here focused on the recovery of a single object, rather than the churning mechanics of an ill-defined destiny or the dark mysteries of human behavior. Using modern techniques of structural analysis and game theory, late-twentieth-century critics have been able to elucidate the novel's remarkably well-detailed plot, showing why it has served as a standard for so many of the page-turners that followed it.

While some nineteenth-century reviewers claimed that this perfection of plot tended to swallow the novel's characters just as irrevocably as the terrifying Shivering Sand consumed Rosanna Spearman, later readers have come to see a penetrating humanity at work in the novel. In no other major Victorian novelist can there be seen such a thoroughgoing sympathy for society's previously voiceless characters. The novel's chief narrator, for instance, is the wise, *Robinson Crusoe*–loving steward Gabriel Betteredge, whose very name suggests that he is at least on a par with those considered his "betters." There is also the compelling figure of the ugly former inmate Rosanna, whose love for Blake could have easily been parodied but is here treated with a pathos and respect far beyond anything Anthony Trollope or even Dickens might have mustered. Equally unforgettable is the outcast doctor Ezra Jennings, with his mixed parentage and parti-colored hair, who suffers his social exile and opium addiction with a striking dignity that puts his more mainstream colleagues to shame. Indeed, Jennings can be seen as a gloss on Collins himself, who was in such pain during the serial composition of the novel that he supposedly had to tell the secretary taking his dictation to ignore his cries of anguish and concentrate only on his prose. Even the three Indian temple guards sent to England to retrieve the sacred diamond are pictured with a degree of seriousness and self-sacrifice utterly at odds with the racist conceptions of Collins' public. What other Victorian novelist, after all, would imply that the appropriation of scared objects from conquered countries was simple theft, rather that the righteous spoils of war?

Accompanying this sympathy for characters who must live below stairs or out of bounds is Collins' usual impatience with the "respectable" members of Victorian society. Ablewhite, that champion of fallen women, is shown to be a hypocrite of the first order, whose murder is lamented by neither writer nor reader. And Drusilla Clack, the pamphlet-pushing Christian zealot who assists in the book's narration, is a gossip and a spy whose sanctimonies cannot conceal a mean-spiritedness and an almost erotic hunger for tales of transgression. It is hard to conceive of another contemporary novel in which the notion of respectability was so comprehensively and incisively challenged as it was in this allegedly shallow thriller.

LATER WORK

THE publication of *The Moonstone* marked the end of the four-novel cycle that was to be the high point of Wilkie Collins' career. It is widely accepted that, from 1870 until his death, Collins' work was clearly of a lesser order than it had been during the 1860s. His famously intricate plotting often careered into rank preposterousness; the sensational energy fizzled into sentimentality and melodrama. There remains some debate over the reasons for this decline. Certainly, the author's continued ill health and increasing dependence on opium must have contributed to the diminished quality of his output, cutting him off from the public whose taste and judgment were vital sounding boards for him. Additionally, literary tastes changed—the passion for the "quick fix" of sensation fiction was always destined to be a relatively short-lived phenomenon. And there was also the fact that his dear friend, mentor, and editor Charles Dickens was no longer part of his life.

The most oft-cited reason for Collins' decline, however, is the increasingly important role he allowed overtly social issues to play in his work. Admittedly, these concerns were not absent from his earlier writing—*The Woman in White* contains a plea for the reform of private mental asylums, while *No Name* strenuously protests English inheritance law. But in no way could these grievances be seen as the bedrock of his work. This changed so notably after 1870, however, that Swinburne in his 1889 "Wilkie Collins" essay dismissed much of the author's later work with a lacerating bit of doggerel:

What brought good Wilkie's genius nigh perdition?
Some demon whispered—"Wilkie! have a mission."
(p. 305)

This change of course can be seen in Collins' first work after *The Moonstone*, the play *Black and White* (1869), which dealt with the thorny issue of the slave trade in the British colony of Trinidad. English audiences, suffering from slavery fatigue after years of exposure to the wildly popular *Uncle Tom's Cabin*, stayed away in droves. In fact, even though Collins began to identify himself as much

as a playwright as he did a novelist during this latter phase of his career, his stage successes were usually dependent on adaptations of his already renowned novels. Collins' first ostensible issue novel, *Man and Wife* (1870), rather prosaically made the case for marriage law reforms. The novel also contains an idiosyncratic but topical attack on the cult of sports and physical education which was currently in vogue at English universities. This was followed by *Poor Miss Finch* (1872), which was summed up dismissively by D. E. Williams in the magazine *Athenaeum* as "a sensation novel for Sunday reading" (pp. 202). Although containing a story of mistaken identity typical of Collins, it proves more preposterous than sensational in its rendering of a blind woman who regains her sight just as the skin of the man she loves is turned blue by the administration of medicine. *The New Magdalen* (1873) treads a more conventional path, telling the story of a Mercy Merrick, a prostitute who is reformed by the love of a noble-minded clergyman. But the novel lacks the ironic edge and narrative buoyancy of Collins' previous work— gone are the days of a Lydia Gwilt. Instead of masking trenchant social attack in high drama, the novel is more a sustained pamphlet supporting the rights of reformed prostitutes.

The Law and the Lady (1875) continues the author's fictional war against social injustice, this time assailing a Scottish law that allows a courtroom finding of "Not Proven" against a defendant, a result which allows society to suggest the guilt it cannot establish. In it, the formidable Valeria Woodville attempts to remove just such a judicial stain from her husband's record by proving him wholly innocent of the murder of his first wife. Besides this ground-breaking example of a female detective, the book was also notable for its bizarre villain, the legless, monomaniacal Miserrimus Dexter. *The Two Destinies* (1876) deals somewhat pointlessly with a man and a woman, childhood friends, who develop telepathic abilities that cause their paths to cross at key moments in their lives. *The Fallen Leaves* sees Collins once again resurrecting the story of a reformed prostitute. With its mix of preachiness and sentimentality, it is widely considered his worst novel. Both *The Black Robe* (1881) and *Heart and Science* (1883) take on issues of considerable concern to his readership, the former an alleged Jesuit conspiracy to take over British society, the latter the horrors of animal vivisection for the purposes of medical research.

"*I Say No*" sees Collins returning to his stock character of a respectable young woman forced by circumstance to become an amateur detective. This time an orphaned girl discovers the truth behind her father's apparent murder, which was in fact a suicide caused by his rejection by a woman of questionable character. Despite its lurid title, *The Evil Genius: A Domestic Story* (1886) is a divorce drama in which a governess and wife do battle over the same man. Collins' penultimate novel, *The Legacy of Cain* (1888), is the story of two sisters, one of whom is the daughter of murderess, who are brought up together but turn out very differently. Collins died during the composition of his last novel, *Blind Love* (1890), which was published posthumously.

CONCLUSION

FROM the prestigious *Saturday Review*'s complaint that readers of the just-published *The Woman in White* could only esteem its author "as we hire out a Chinese conjuror—for the night," to *The Spectator*'s reference to *Poor Miss Finch* as "that repertory of wasted cleverness," to the posthumous campaign to keep the author out of Britain's artistic shrines, Wilkie Collins was to have a deeply distrustful relationship with the literary establishment. His audacity on social issues, combined with a reckless showmanship in matters of characterization and plot, made him anathema to critics and social commentators who saw it as their job to tame the talented and censure the adventurous. Also, the reaction to Collins epitomized the longstanding (and still prevalent) prejudice against serious writers who write page-turning stories. Indeed, so mistrustful was Collins of the ability of critics to understand his work that he adopted the controversial habit of beginning each novel with a preface in which he directly addressed the reader on the merits and intentions of the story to come. The most extreme example of this was *Armadale*, with its preemptive appeal to the reader to ignore "the Clap-trap morality of the present day" in assessing the novel. Needless to say, these solicitations often served as red flags to the critical bulls circling the literary arena, causing Collins to be gored with alarming regularity.

By the time of his death, Collins' reputation had reached a low point. The enfant terrible had become an aged vaudevillian, shuffling off the stage to catcalls and derisive laughter. His banishment from the hall of fame at Westminster Cathedral had as much to do with his being viewed a "literary trickster" as it did with his outlaw private life. His work was seen, at its best, as being in the vanguard of the discredited literary movement of sensation fiction and, at its worst, as being preposterous grandstanding. The following decades were equally unkind, with Collins being relegated to the second division of the mid-Victorian canon—and beyond.

The twentieth century saw the steady resuscitation of his reputation. T. S. Eliot's appreciation of *Armadale* in his "Wilkie Collins and Dickens" essay may seem somewhat grudging, but it certainly improved on what had come before by claiming that the book "has no merit beyond melodrama, and it has every merit that melodrama can have" (p. 468). Critics such as Dorothy L. Sayers and Walter de la Mare also began to treat Collins' work as serious fiction rather than mere entertainment. By the 1970s a full-scale reassessment of Collins' work was underway, transforming him from a facile conjuror into a writer whose brilliant literary pyrotechnics illuminated the darkest realms of his era. Late-twentieth-century commentators have also discovered in his work deep structural complexities and an often revolutionary interest in literary games. Indeed, with his detonations of rigid orthodoxies and his disdain for shallow respectability, with his probing of the nature of identity and his frequent descents into the caverns of the unconscious, and with his unprecedented sympathy for the voiceless, Wilkie Collins can now be appreciated as a writer ahead of his time.

SELECTED BIBLIOGRAPHY

I. NOVELS: FIRST EDITIONS. *Antonina; or, The Fall of Rome*, 3 vols. (London, 1850); *Basil: A Story of Modern Life*, 3 vols. (London, 1852); *Hide and Seek*, 3 vols. (London, 1854); *The Dead Secret*, 2 vols. (London, 1857); *The Woman in White*, 3 vols. (London, 1860); *No Name*, 3 vols. (London, 1862); *Armadale*, 2 vols. (London, 1866); *The Moonstone*, 3 vols. (London, 1868); *Man and Wife*, 3 vols. (London, 1870); *Poor Miss Finch*, 3 vols. (London, 1872); *The New Magdalen*, 2 vols. (London, 1873); *The Law and The Lady*, 3 vols. (London, 1875); *The Two Destinies*, 2 vols. (London, 1876); *The Fallen Leaves*, first series, 3 vols. (London, 1879); *Jezebel's Daughter*, 3 vols. (London, 1880); *The Black Robe*, 3 vols. (London, 1881); *Heart and Science: A Story of the Present Time*, 3 vols. (London, 1883); "*I Say No*," 3 vols. (London, 1884); *The Evil*

Genius: A Domestic Story, 3 vols. (London, 1886); *The Legacy of Cain,* 3 vols. (London, 1888); *Blind Love,* 3 vols., completed by Walter Besant (London, 1890).

II. NONFICTION AND SHORT FICTION: FIRST EDITIONS. *Memoirs of the Life of William Collins, Esq., R.A.,* 2 vols. (London, 1848); *Rambles beyond Railways; or, Notes in Cornwall Taken A-Foot* (London, 1851); *Mr. Wray's Cash Box; or, The Mask and the Mystery* (short stories) (London, 1852); *After Dark* (short stories), 2 vols. (London, 1856); *The Queen of Hearts* (short stories), 3 vols. (London, 1859); *My Miscellanies* (journalism), 2 vols. (London, 1863); *Miss or Mrs? And Other Stories in Outline* (London, 1873); *The Frozen Deep and Other Tales,* 2 vols. (London, 1874); *The Haunted Hotel, A Mystery of Modern Venice* (novella) (London, 1879); *A Rogue's Life: From His Birth to His Marriage* (novella) (London, 1879); *The Guilty River* (novella) (Bristol, 1886); *Little Novels* (short stories), 3 vols. (London, 1887); *The Lazy Tour of Two Idle Apprentices: No Thoroughfare; The Perils of Certain English Prisoners* (with Charles Dickens) (London, 1890).

III. COLLECTED EDITION. *The Works of Wilkie Collins,* 30 vols. (New York, 1970).

IV. SOME RECENT EDITIONS. *The Haunted Hotel: A Mystery of Modern Venice* (New York, 1982); *Blind Love* (with Walter Besant) (New York, 1986); *No Name,* ed. Virginia Blain (Oxford, 1986); *Armadale,* ed. Catherine Peters (Oxford, 1989); *Basil,* ed. Dorothy Goldman (Oxford, 1990); *Hide and Seek,* ed. Catherine Peters (Oxford, 1993); *Mad Monkton and Other Stories,* ed. Norman Page (Oxford, 1994); *Poor Miss Finch,* ed. Catherine Peters (Oxford, 1995); *The Woman in White,* ed. John Sutherland (Oxford, 1996); *The Dead Secret,* ed. Ira. B. Nadel (Oxford, 1997); *The Law and the Lady,* ed. David Skilton (London, 1998); *Man and Wife,* ed. Norman Page (Oxford, 1998); *The Moonstone,* ed. Sandra Kemp (London, 1998).

V. BIOGRAPHIES. Kenneth Robinson, *Wilkie Collins* (London, 1951, 1974); Robert P. Ashley, *Wilkie Collins* (London, 1952; New York, 1952); Nuel Pharr Davis, *The Life of Wilkie Collins* (Urbana, Ill., 1956); Dorothy L. Sayers, *Wilkie Collins: A Biographical and Critical Study* (unfinished), ed. E. R. Gregory (Toledo, Ohio, 1977); William M. Clarke, *The Secret Life of Wilkie Collins* (London, 1988); Catherine Peters, *The King of Inventors: A Life of Wilkie Collins* (Princeton, N.J., 1993); William Baker and William M. Clarke, eds., *The Letters of Wilkie Collins,* 2 vols. (New York, 1999).

VI. CRITICAL STUDIES. Archbishop of York, "The Archbishop of York on Works of Fiction," in *London Times* (12 November 1864); Henry James, "Miss Braddon," in *Nation* (4 November 1865); D. E. Williams, "Poor Miss Finch," in *Athenaeum* (17 February 1872); Walter C. Phillips, *Dickens, Reade, and Collins: Sensation Novelists* (New York, 1919; repr. New York, 1972); Algernon Charles Swinburne, "Wilkie Collins," in *The Complete Works of Algernon Charles Swinburne,* ed. Sir Edmund Gosse and Thomas James Wise, vol. 15 (London, 1925; repr. New York, 1968); T. S. Eliot, "Introduction," in *The Moonstone* (London, 1928); Walter de la Mare, "The Early Novels of Wilkie Collins," in *The Eighteen-Sixties,* ed. John Drinkwater (Cambridge, 1932); T. S. Eliot, "Wilkie Collins and Dickens," in *Selected Essays* (New York, 1964; London, 1986); William H. Marshall, *Wilkie Collins* (New York, 1970); Norman Page, ed., *Wilkie Collins: The Critical Heritage* (London, 1974); John Sutherland, *Victorian Novelists and Publishers* (Chicago, 1976); Kirk H. Beetz, *Wilkie Collins: An Annotated Bibliography, 1889–1976* (Metuchen, N.J., 1978); Ray Vernon Andrew, *Wilkie Collins: A Critical Survey of His Prose Fiction* (New York, 1979); Winifred Hughes, *The Maniac in the Cellar: Sensation Novels of the 1860s* (Princeton, N.J., 1980); Sue Lonoff, *Wilkie Collins and His Victorian Readers: A Study in the Rhetoric of Authorship* (New York, 1982); Philip O'Neill, *Wilkie Collins: Women, Property, and Propriety* (London, 1988); Jenny Bourne Taylor, *In the Secret Theatre of Home: Wilkie Collins, Sensation Narrative, and Nineteenth-Century Psychology* (London, 1988); Thomas Boyle, *Black Swine in the Sewers of Hampstead: Beneath the Surface of Victorian Sensationalism* (New York, 1989); Nicholas Rance, *Wilkie Collins and Other Sensation Novelists: Walking the Moral Hospital* (Rutherford, N.J., 1991); Tamar Heller, *Dead Secrets: Wilkie Collins and the Female Gothic* (New Haven, Conn., 1992); Peter Thoms, *The Windings of the Labyrinth: Quest and Structure in the Major Novels of Wilkie Collins* (Athens, Ohio, 1992); Nelson Smith and R. C. Terry, eds., *Wilkie Collins to the Forefront: Some Reassessments* (New York, 1995); Lillian Nayder, *Wilkie Collins* (New York, 1997); Andrew Gasson, *Wilkie Collins: An Illustrated Guide* (Oxford, 1998); Lyn Pykett, ed., *Wilkie Collins (New Casebooks)* (New York, 1998).

DONALD DAVIE

(1922–1995)

Neil Powell

"THE SCHOLAR'S PLEASURE is the poet's vice," wrote Donald Davie in an early poem, "The Poet-Scholar" (published in the journal *Essays in Criticism* 5, January 1955, p. 43); nevertheless, he conceded, "The poet-scholar cannot keep apart / The gift and the investment." Perhaps that was one of the pieces "published in periodicals which I have lost sight of," as Davie wrote disarmingly in the foreword to his 1972 *Collected Poems 1950–1970*, or perhaps it was so honest and so prescient a poem that it seemed worryingly to preempt his later work; whatever the reason, it remained uncollected during his lifetime. Davie was indeed a poet-scholar whose literary career fully embraced both the blessings and the conflicts of his dual allegiance. Such writers are rare: Matthew Arnold in the nineteenth century, and William Empson and Yvor Winters in the twentieth are among the very few who achieved a similar parity of reputation as poets and as critics; and it is to this distinguished company that Davie belongs.

Donald Alfred Davie was born on 17 July 1922 and spent his childhood in Barnsley, Yorkshire, where his father, George Davie, was a small shopkeeper and deacon of the local Baptist chapel; his mother, Alice (Sugden Davie), a schoolteacher, was passionately devoted to English poetry. Thus the "unflurried connections . . . between literary culture and Dissenting religious allegiance," which Davie identified in *These the Companions* (p. 13), and which resonate through his poems, his two anthologies of Augustan verse and his 1976 Clark Lectures, published as *A Gathered Church*, were made early on. From Barnsley Grammar Holgate School he won a scholarship to read English at St. Catharine's College, Cambridge, in 1940; but Cambridge proved to be a "predictable and inevitable disappointment" (*These the Companions*, p. 20), a place of frighteningly unfamiliar social *mores* for an intellectually ambitious, yet unconfident and somewhat priggish, lad from the North. In fact, he spent only a single wartime year there before joining the Royal Navy, which would take him, via Iceland, to Arctic Russia: "once I was in the Navy," he recalled, "my world, simply my experience of geography, exploded outwards very fast" (*These the Companions*, p. 34). He fell in love in, and with, Russia: he shed much of the inhibiting shyness that, nurtured in Barnsley, had been intensified by Cambridge; he enjoyed the social freedoms of a foreigner; and he discovered Russian poets, including Pasternak, whose work he was subsequently to translate. In short, he grew up.

Quite by chance, a motif in Davie's career—exasperation with an English intellectual establishment resolved by foreign travel—had been established. On his return home in 1944, he met Doreen John, whom he married the following year, and resumed his studies at Cambridge. He seemed to have slipped back easily into conventional academic life, yet his wartime experience validated his impatience with more insular contemporaries, which would resurface, sometimes explosively, throughout his career. After graduating in 1947, he remained in Cambridge as a research student and was awarded his Ph.D. in 1951; meanwhile, he had been appointed lecturer in English at Trinity College, Dublin, where he stayed until 1957. During these years, as we shall see later, his reputation both as poet and as critic grew rapidly; and by the time he returned once again to Cambridge in 1958, as a lecturer and (from 1959) fellow of Gonville and Caius College, he was a leading figure in the new literary generation that had come to be known as The Movement.

But Davie's characteristic restlessness—his need to work against the grain which would prove so stimulating and occasionally so frustrating in his writing—was already asserting itself once more. He spent the academic year 1957–1958 as a visiting professor at the University of California at Santa Barbara, where he met for the first time one of his literary mentors, Yvor Winters, and he returned to the United States to lecture at the University of Cincinnati in 1963. However, his most momentous move—momentous not only in itself but in its wholly unexpected repercussions—came the following year, when he joined the new University of Essex as professor of English and, from 1965, pro-vice-chancellor. It seemed to be a brilliant appointment, enabling him to devise courses in which English literature was combined, for instance, with politics or with Russian literature; for a time, he felt he was overcoming the insularity he had so disliked at Cambridge. Yet only four years later, in 1968, when students rioted at several English universities and at Essex in particular, Davie had once more come to find cultural and academic life in his native country intolerable. Gratefully, and fully aware of achieving a neat intellectual congruence, he succeeded Yvor Winters as professor of English at Stanford University. "Finally Davie emerged as the compromise candidate," he recalled. "Winters, I am told, replied, 'I have less objection to Davie than to any of the others'; which is the nearest you would ever get from him to laying on of hands" (Tredell, p. 275).

Davie stayed ten years at Stanford and another ten at Vanderbilt University before he and Doreen returned home to retirement in Devon in 1988. In some ways, this contentious and conservative pipe-smoking Yorkshireman was an unlikely expatriate; yet his openness to the diversity of American poetry and his appreciation of American hospitality earned him many friends. Furthermore, California and Tennessee were excellent vantage points from which to berate the English in print, although, as he well knew, his polemical style, with its conversational tone and firm moral emphasis, remained not only very English but specifically Cantabrigian, owing a good deal to the example of F. R. Leavis. When he died in Devon on 18 September 1995, he was justly described by his obituarist in the *Independent* as "the defining poet-critic of his generation" (20 September 1995, p. 16).

POETRY I: A NEUTRAL TONE

DONALD Davie describes himself in "Homage to William Cowper," which opens his *Collected Poems*, as "A pasticheur of late-Augustan styles" (p. 17; page references are to the 1990 edition unless otherwise noted); and, beyond that seemingly modest self-deprecation, one can clearly glimpse the veiled challenge of a manifesto. Davie

is claiming eighteenth-century qualities of clarity and rationality as well as kinship with a specifically Christian poet. Indeed, his first substantial collection, published in 1955, was called *Brides of Reason*, and in it he insists almost too earnestly on maintaining the virtues of civilized discursive prose: "A neutral tone is nowadays preferred," as he says in "Remembering the 'Thirties" (p. 35). In much of *Brides of Reason*, the tone is "neutral" in the sense of being fastidious, detached, and unashamedly academic; the results are highly intelligent but just a little chilly, and in pieces such as "Poem as Abstract" (p. 24) or "Method. For Ronald Gaskell" (p. 43) there is an alarming tendency for the subject to vanish altogether beneath the density of the argument. Davie's distinctive habit of arguing where another poet might describe extends even to poems firmly rooted in places. Of Plymouth, his wife's home town, he can only conclude, "What has and not what might have been / It serves to show" ("Among Artisans' Houses," p. 19). At a Belfast Orangemen's Parade he finds that he "stayed to worry" until he "remembered with a sudden scorn / Those 'passionate intensities' of Yeats" ("Belfast on a Sunday Afternoon," p. 27).

A notable exception to this somewhat buttoned-up stance occurs in "The Garden Party." Here Davie finds himself revisiting the North to attend a grand social function, envying the "moneyed ease" of the wealthy young and encountering the "phantom of my earliest love": "I shook absurdly as I shook her hand." He continues:

As dusk drew in on cultivated cries,
Faces hung pearls upon a cedar-bough;
And gin could blur the glitter of her eyes,
But it's too late to learn to tango now.

My father, of a more submissive school,
Remarks the rich themselves are always sad.
There is that sort of equalizing rule;
But theirs is all the youth we might have had.
(p. 29)

This poem is interesting for several reasons: it shows how fluent and direct Davie can become when he taps into his autobiographical past; it successfully combines local detail, moral reflection, and easy colloquialism ("too late to tango"); and, in the wryly clinching final line, it strongly resembles the work of his exact contemporary Philip Larkin.

That point is worth emphasizing because in 1956 both poets appeared in Robert Conquest's anthology *New Lines*, the book that firmly established the idea of The Movement as a literary force; apart from Conquest himself, the other contributors were Kingsley Amis, D. J. Enright, Thom Gunn, John Holloway, Elizabeth Jennings, and John Wain. "We ridiculed and deprecated 'The Movement' even as we kept it going," wrote Davie in 1959 (*Prospect*, summer 1959, p. 13), but by 1967 he regretted that "we did not acknowledge our common ground," which, he wrote in a postscript to the second edition of his *Purity of Diction in English Verse*, might have provided them with "a common manifesto" (pp. 197–198). The practical importance of The Movement in general and of *New Lines* in particular for Davie's poetic career was that when his second full-length collection, *A Winter Talent*, appeared in 1957, it was from a major publishing house rather than a small press, the work of a recognized writer.

Davie's increased confidence is evident immediately. Whereas *Brides of Reason* opened with "Among Artisans' Houses," that constrained tribute to his wife which in the end is scarcely even about his wife's home town, *A Winter Talent* opens with a wonderfully uninhibited love poem, "Time Passing, Beloved": "Time passing, and the memories of love / Coming back to me, carissima, no more mockingly / Than ever before" (p. 46). One can't imagine that relaxed lyrical flow, nor the touching endearment "carissima," fitting comfortably into *Brides of Reason*; nor, for that matter, this fine last stanza:

What will become of us? Time
Passing, beloved, and we in a sealed
Assurance unassailed
By memory. How can it end,
This siege of a shore that no misgivings have steeled,
No doubts defend?

(p. 46)

That no longer sounds at all like the habitually disillusioned Larkin; if there is a resemblance here, it is to that master of the sensuous lyric, Robert Graves. But a writer does not as a rule discard all his early allegiances in one go, and *A Winter Talent* finds Davie expanding rather than rejecting the formal and rational criteria of The Movement. For instance, in "The Fountain" he begins by seeming to write one sort of poem—conventionally descrip-

tive, with an unusually heavy shower of similes and metaphors—but finishes with something altogether different, a philosophical meditation on Berkeley's *The Principles of Human Knowledge*, fusing the two strands in a final couplet stretched over a stanza break, where the last line completes a rhyme from three lines earlier: "We ask of fountains only that they play, / Though that was not what Berkeley meant at all" (p. 68). That trick of finishing a poem off with a single line rhymed across the stanza break is one of Larkin's, and it doesn't seem fanciful to suspect Davie of a joke at his friend's expense in applying it to just the kind of poem Larkin wouldn't write; we should notice, too, how "The Fountain" ties in with prose essays written by Davie at around the same time—"Yeats, Berkeley, and Romanticism" (*Irish Writing* 31, summer 1955) and "Berkeley and 'Philosophic Words'" (*Studies: An Irish Quarterly Review* 44, winter 1955). Elsewhere in the collection, the four-poem sequence "A Gathered Church" allows him to explore his Baptist inheritance in language that will echo much later on in his career: "So here I take the husk of my research, / A form of words— the phrase, 'a gathered church' . . ." (p. 59).

However, his most decisive advantage over such contemporaries as Amis and Larkin is his willingness to travel, physically as well as intellectually, and to make full use of these experiences in his poetry. One group of poems finds him in Italy, if not quite at ease: he knows that painters praise Italian light, but worries that "Our eyes may not be fine enough" to appreciate its effects ("Going to Italy," p. 63); and although in "Via Portello" (p. 65) he gently and justly chides Amis for his English insularity, it can't be said that the poem comes to descriptive life. Davie, as he was ruefully to admit a little later, was still inclined to make *thinking* do the work of *seeing*, and his poems could consequently seem starved of visual life. The Dublin pieces are more relaxed—it was a city in which he enjoyed living—and the "existential weather" of "Samuel Beckett's Dublin" (p. 61) is sparsely yet evocatively caught. Davie's was, after all, the winter talent of his book's title—"Winter is come again, and none too soon / For meditation on its raft of sticks" ("A Winter Talent," p. 71)—and so it should come as no surprise to find that the other outstanding poem in the collection, "Heigh-ho on a Winter Afternoon," is an oblique celebration of that season's ruminative, melancholic pleasures:

There is a heigh-ho in these glowing coals
By which I sit wrapped in my overcoat
As if for a portrait by Whistler. And there is
A heigh-ho in the bird that noiselessly
Flew just now past my window, to alight
On winter's moulding, snow; and an alas,
A heigh-ho and a desultory chip,
Chip, chip on stone from somewhere down below.

(p. 74)

The tone is soft-voiced, confidential; it is only with the fleeting introduction of an unspecified "you" (presumably his wife) in the second stanza that we realize that this is also a very subtle love poem: "Yes I have 'mellowed,' as you said I would, / And that's a heigh-ho too for any man" (p. 74).

POETRY II: AGAINST THE GRAIN

THE three collections of poetry that followed *A Winter Talent* represent significant deviations from the conventional slim volume pattern followed by most of the *New Lines* poets. The first, *The Forests of Lithuania* (1959), is a version of *Pan Tadeusz*, an epic poem by the Lithuanian Adam Mickiewicz (1798–1855); Davie had of course become interested in Eastern European literature during his wartime service in the Baltic, but he did not read Polish and relied upon an earlier prose version to produce what he cheerfully conceded, in a "Note" in his 1972 *Collected Poems*, was neither an "imitation" nor a "paraphrase" but, strictly speaking "a travesty" (p. 300). Its hurtling quality—the short suspended lines are peppered with proper names, snatches of conversation and self-interruptions—looks forward to his own longer poems (such as "England") and interestingly suggests that he was already reading some of the new, very different American poets who were to influence him so strongly a decade later.

Next came a *New and Selected Poems* (1961), published by Wesleyan University Press in Middletown, Connecticut; there has never been a British edition. Among the new poems is one widely regarded as a significant turning point in Davie's career, "With the Grain," in which he grapples with the problem of abstraction and concreteness, and attempts a partial reconciliation between them; in the eyes of his English readers, the poem acquired an additional mystique through its relative inaccessibility, for it was not to appear again in book form until the *Collected Poems* of 1972, where

it was accompanied by a "vulnerable" note. "With the Grain" opens with a reflection on the ways in which concrete activities cross over into abstraction as they become metaphorical ideas. The indisputably solid business of carpentry, for example, supplies such abstract phrases as "an ingrained habit" (p. 84). It continues with a second section—recalling Davie's earlier, not always wholly successful poems about painting—in which he attempts to find an equivalence between the "merciful" Cornish light falling upon a painter's subject and "an equable light upon words":

The purest hue, let only the light be sufficient
    Turns colour. And I was told
If painters frequent St. Ives
    It is because the light
There, under the cliff, is merciful. I dream
    Of an equable light upon words
And as painters paint in St. Ives, the poets speaking.

(pp. 84–85)

The notion is attractive and eloquently expressed, but, as Davie admits, it is a "dream"; poets cannot in fact speak as painters paint. In the third and final section he returns to carpentry as metaphor: "And will the poet, carpenter of light, / Work with the grain henceforward?" (p. 85). Again, the paradoxical congruence of concreteness and abstraction is brilliantly effective, yet it is in the accompanying prose note that Davie confronts his underlying difficulty. "It is true," he writes, "that I am not a poet by nature, only by inclination; for my mind moves most easily and happily among abstractions"; a little later he goes on:

Most of the poems I have written are not natural poems, in one sense not truly poems, simply because the thought in them could have been expressed—at whatever cost in terseness and point—in a non-poetic way.... Nevertheless I have taken a decision to write no more poems of this kind, only poems which are, if not *naturally*, at all events *truly* poems throughout.

(*Collected Poems*, 1972, p. 301)

It is a crucial distinction: one in which Davie almost contrives to hint that the writing of poems *against* the grain might be a nobler vocation than that of the "natural" poet.

In 1961, the year that Davie's American readers were offered his very English *New and Selected Poems*, his English readers were, conversely, introduced to his poems about American history, *A*

Sequence for Francis Parkman. This is the most eccentric of all his publications, presented as a Listenbook with a seven-inch LP record of Davie reading (evidently into a portable tape-recorder and through a surface like a sandstorm); it contains six poems, each with a prose commentary, followed by "A Letter to Curtis Bradford." Bradford was a New Englander by birth, with whom Davie stayed in Grinnell, Iowa, during his first visit to the United States in 1957–1958. "I see Curtis," he would write much later, in *These the Companions,* "as representative; representing an American type which, though rarer than it used to be, can still be met with—the sort of American who, knowledgeable about the Old World, is sure that his New World has surpassed it—not just politically and industrially, but culturally too" (p. 155). He was, therefore, an important emblematic figure in Davie's continual quest to understand the nature of Americanness, at which, he admitted,

> I only guess,
> I guess at it out of my Englishness
> And envy you out of England. Man with man
> Is all our history; American,
> You met with spirits. Neither white nor red
> The melancholy, disinherited
> Spirit of mid-America, but this,
> The manifested copiousness, the bounties.
> (p. 99)

These lines are doubly prescient, foreshadowing both the bitterness with which Davie was to regard his native country and the characteristics ("copiousness," "bounties") which he would find most enticing about American life and literature.

His next more conventional collection of poems, *Events and Wisdoms* (1964), was, as one might expect, very much an Anglo-American affair. It includes, as one of two "Dedications," perhaps the most wholly English in subject and tone of all Davie's poems, "Barnsley Cricket Club." These are home thoughts from abroad, written by their "demoralized" author during a California heatwave. Unable to complete any task to his satisfaction, he remembers Shaw Lane Cricket Ground in Barnsley, his father's "love of craft," and the dictum "A thing worth doing is worth doing well"; yet "things which would be natural" may be half-finished and "an art's / More noble office is to leave half-done" (p. 102). The affectionate ending is also gently equivocal (and the key word is surely "Ought"):

> How soon the shadows fall, how soon and long!
> The score-board stretches to a grandson's feet.
> This layabout July in another climate
> Ought not to prove firm turf, well-tended, wrong.
> (p. 102)

Against this guarded nostalgia should be set a poem such as "In California," in which Davie accumulates seemingly outlandish details with a wide-eyed curiosity that is by turns elated and affronted—"Chemicals ripen the citrus; / There are rattlesnakes in the mountains"; "Beef in cellophane / Tall as giraffes"; "Claypit / Yellow burns on the distance" (p. 116)—and delightedly adopts colloquialisms that are very far from his own:

> At Ventucopa, elevation
> Two-eight-nine-six, the water hydrant frozen,
> Deserted or broken settlements,
> Gasoline stations closed and boarded.
> (p. 116)

Almost every usage in these four lines—"elevation," "Two-eight-nine-six," "hydrant," "settlements," "gasoline"—is a consciously American deviation from the standard British English of the time. Davie could hardly have signaled his shifting allegiance more clearly. The collection's final poem, "The Hardness of Light," finds him once again in Italy, glancing back to "Via Portello" of eight years earlier and resolutely moving on: "Touched by that wand of transit, / Californian, hopeful . . . / I grow older, harder" (p. 131). As a self-description, "older, harder" seems a very long way from "mellowed" at the end of *A Winter Talent.*

POETRY III: ESSEX AND AFTER

DAVIE'S most remarkable poems date from his most turbulent years, those he spent at the University of Essex in the mid-1960s, and they were indeed published, with an allusive nod to Thomas Hardy's *Wessex Poems* of 1898, as *Essex Poems* (1969). They are energized by the tension between his English past and his American future, a tension both geographical and intellectual which thus becomes, paradoxically, also a resolution of his concrete/abstract dichotomy. No less paradoxical was the fact that the starkly lit, bleak landscapes and seascapes of East Anglia, which he was so soon to leave, had at last taught him to see and to write about seeing: it is no coincidence that the handsome first edition of *Essex Poems* was the first of Davie's books to contain illustrations (fine, spare line drawings by Michael Foreman).

"The North Sea" (p. 136) perfectly exemplifies his Anglo-American tension. It begins—and its title surely proclaims that it means to continue—as an evocation of the "Protestant sea," "one long arm of the cold vexed sea of the North," near whose shore he has come to live; and it continues, reasonably enough, with a digression on other seas and their particular associations. Then comes an urgent self-interruption: "But somewhere in mid-America / All of this grows tiresome, / The needles waver and point wildly"; and when they settle on a direction, it is toward the Pacific, "the end of the world," a destination he both fears and finds irresistible; the almost adjacent "Out of East Anglia" (p. 138) is, incidentally, a footnote or companion piece.

But for the time being at least Davie was *in* East Anglia and discovering an entirely new way to write about it, sometimes loosely basing his poems on models by Pasternak; his translation of *The Poems of Doctor Zhivago* appeared in 1965. At Holland on Sea he notices how "The light wheels and comes in / over the seawall / and the bitten turf" ("Sunburst," p. 140); in Tunstall Forest he relishes the rainy quiet in "the dripping ride, / The firebreak avenue" ("Tunstall Forest," p. 143); near Ely he finds "faintly coffee-coloured / Gridiron marks on the snow" "heart-breaking" ("A Winter Landscape near Ely," p. 145); and in a ruined church at Orford he notices "earth in every pockmark of the stone," "fragrant thick convolvulus," and "lilac double-hued" ("Orford," p. 144). What makes these finely observed images all the more striking is the pared-down sparseness of the verse that contains them: "Excellence is sparse," he writes in "Ezra Pound in Pisa" (p. 142); and that dictum informs these poems.

This is equally true when the subject is entirely literary or personal (for Davie, these are often the same thing) rather than geographical. "July, 1964" begins by remembering three deaths—those of Theodore Roethke, an unnamed friend, and a neighbor's wife—while in the second stanza Davie moves on to reaffirm his own vocation: "Love and art I practise; / they seem to be worth no more / and no less than they were" (p. 137). But it is the third and final stanza that develops this point, before turning with merciless irony on those who assume that the poet-scholar's dedica-

tion to his work is somehow at the expense of his personal life:

> The practice of an art
> is to convert all terms
> into the terms of art.
> By the end of the third stanza
> death is a smell no longer;
> it is a problem of style.
> A man who ought to know me
> wrote in a review
> my emotional life was meagre.
> (p. 137)

This is characteristic of Davie's newly astringent tone and prosody: the taut, suspended three-stress lines give additional edge to an occasion that, ten years earlier, he would almost certainly have treated in rhymed iambic pentameters.

At the end of *Essex Poems* are three pieces—"Iowa," "Back of Affluence," and "Or, Solitude"—that are collectively entitled "From the New World." These take us back quite specifically to Curtis Bradford's landscape; the last of the three, which opens with "A farm boy lost in the snow," also casts a wistful backward glance, for "Or, Solitude" was originally the subtitle of another poem about snowbound isolation, Wordsworth's "Lucy Gray." It ends, in its first and final forms, in the *New Statesman* of 31 December 1965 and in the *Collected Poems* (for in its original edition of *Essex Poems* that key word "metaphysicality" became, less effectively, "transcendental nature"), with this candid and impassioned yet still sparse quatrain:

> The metaphysicality
> Of poetry, how I need it!
> And yet it was for years
> What I refused to credit.
> (p. 155)

One reason why the *Essex Poems* succeed so notably is that Davie keeps his bitterness just in control, although this is not always so in the supplementary group of "More Essex Poems" that he added to the *Collected Poems*. They are interesting and revealing, as intemperate writings often can be, and they are not to be confused with their finer predecessors. Titles such as "New Year Wishes for the English" (p. 160) and "To Certain English Poets" (p. 162) largely tell their own stories; but the reader might pause at the stark self-analysis called "Revulsion" (p. 159). This finds Davie (not for the last time) on a train, carefully leaving there a presumably pornographic book and reflecting that his "strongest feeling" has always been "revulsion / From the obscene" and this amounts to "My life-consuming passion"; that this passion has been essentially reactive rather than active is, he says, "the heaviest charge / That can be brought against / Me, or my times" (p. 160). The point is more complex than it at first looks. Davie courageously redefines his own rigorous moral stance, one very much at odds with fashionable views in the late 1960s, yet his tone admits that this "life-consuming passion" might almost be a kind of affliction; then he twice qualifies his argument, first by suggesting that the *passivity* of his position makes him culpable, and secondly by implying (in the poem's final words) that the times in which he lives, rather than the poet himself, are to blame. Some strikingly similar phrases appear at the start of his memoirs, written a decade or so later: "throughout my boyhood but also ever since, my strongest and most common emotion has been fear. . . . I have been a coward before life; always, against the run of the evidence, I have expected the worst" (*These the Companions*, p. 2). Although "revulsion" and "fear" may seem unpromising controlling impulses for a poet, in Davie's case they were powerful and effective ones.

POETRY IV: FROM THE NEW WORLD

IT would be tempting—and not wholly misleading—to suggest that after Davie went to California in 1968 he did nothing but write about England. If he was a restless writer he was also, still more deeply, a rooted one. His feelings about his native country were fueled by an indignant patriotism that now found itself in creative collision with new literary influences. Davie, who had long championed American poets as diverse as Ezra Pound and Yvor Winters, developed during the 1960s a strongly advocated enthusiasm for the work of the Black Mountain poets in general and Edward Dorn in particular; it is Dorn's voice above all that informs the long poem *England* (pp. 172–186), with its hectic, fragmented allusiveness and its excited jumble of registers, from the archly decorous ("And this is a poem not about you / but FOR you, for / your delectation, lady," p. 175) to the rancorously incoherent ("Scotswoman on the make / at 70 plus, where the make / now is, with the teen-age newsmen," p. 179). *England* is not an easy piece, nor is it meant to be. Writing

furiously against the grain, Davie chastises himself and his readers; and he will do so again. Another long poem, *Trevenen* (pp. 191–200), presents a rather different sort of challenge. Densely detailed historical material is shaped into crisp, wonderfully sustained rhyming couplets, but most readers will need to look up Captain Cook's Lieutenant James Trevenen (1760–1790) in the *Dictionary of National Biography* to make much sense of the poem. The effort will be rewarded, for this rich narrative combines two of Davie's enduring interests, exploration and the eighteenth century. The same verse form is used for the still more ambitious *Six Epistles to Eva Hesse* (pp. 209–246), addressed to Pound's German translator, at the heart of which is another rueful glance over the shoulder or across the Atlantic to "My native land! secure, humane, / Where no one works (I mean, for gain)":

> What price myth
> In such a world? What price the lives
> Lived there, where computation thrives
> To breed the social engineers
> Who have the nation by the ears?
> Tickets for *Lear* are not much prized
> Where all's been de-mythologized,
> Nor much of merriment survives
> In Windsor's bright unhappy wives
> Financing, out of foreign loans,
> Welfare and the Rolling Stones.
> (pp. 228–229)

However, the most extensive and in some ways the most surprising of these retrospective works came in 1974, with the publication, in the same handsome format as *Essex Poems*, of Davie's next book-length collection, *The Shires*. Here, adapting the geographical methods of Olson and Dorn to the far smaller map of his native country, he revisits in alphabetical order the English counties: in some, the main associations are literary rather than autobiographical, of course, yet the two can converge in unexpectedly touching ways. The first poem, "Bedfordshire," begins naturally enough with John Bunyan; then, noticing the "Dissenting nineteenth-century demureness" of a chapel, Davie reflects: "I have never known / What to do with this that I am heir to" (p. 247). An affectionate piece on Cheshire, by contrast, brings to mind Auden's fondness for northern industrial landscapes, prompting this coda:

And Mr. Auden, whom I never knew,
Is dead in Vienna. A post-industrial landscape
He celebrated often, and expounded
How it can bleakly solace. And that's true.

(p. 249)

Sussex, on the other hand, though "most poeticized / Of English counties," has become strangely alien to the Davies when they return as "transatlantic / Visitors"; the author of "Barnsley Cricket Club" admits, "We had to pinch ourselves / To know we knew the rules / Of cricket played on the green" (p. 268). We may suspect he is making much of this to bolster a doubtful concluding point, and so it proves: "There is / Another emigration: / Draining away of love," he writes (p. 269), yet the impetus behind *The Shires* is, unmistakably, an inexhaustible if exasperated love for England.

That is a point to be borne in mind when reading the gnarled, ambitious poem that gives its title to Davie's 1977 collection *In the Stopping Train*. The occasion glances toward Philip Larkin—catching a slow train from Hull to London enabled Larkin to observe those famous whitsun wedding parties—and the poem itself at once recalls the self-lacerating aspects of "Revulsion" or *England*:

I have got into the slow train
again. I made the mistake
knowing what I was doing,
knowing who had to be punished.

(p. 285)

This is "the man going mad inside me," the "he" of the poem, a deranged doppelgänger who provides a narrative perspective only slightly and unnervingly distinct from that of the authorial "I." This "he" articulates in an exaggerated form some of Davie's own less admirable qualities: his irritability with his fellow human beings, his ignorance of the natural world. "Jonquil is a sweet word," he thinks, but he finds himself quite unable to visualize the plant it identifies. This "he" is tormented by the problem that haunts so much of Davie's work, the paradoxical tendency for abstract thought to drive out the concrete reality it is supposed to elucidate: "He never needed to see, / not with his art to help him," he says (p. 286), thus recognizing the very need he once sought to deny. Meanwhile, proving the point, the poem's "I" is trapped with the teasing circularities of language: "A stopping train, I thought, / was a train that was going to stop" (p. 286); "pane" puns mercilessly with

"pain," while "the man going mad" is plainly going "off the rails." As he says later on, "The dance of words / is a circling prison" (p. 291); yet he knows that words are equally our only way out of the prison and that this stopping train has turned out to be, with inescapably punning intent, an intermittent and interrupted train of thought.

"In the Stopping Train" is best viewed as a kind of catharsis. Its vulnerable, irascible candor seems finally to liberate Davie from at least some of his demons. Had he, then, "mellowed" at last? Not entirely; nevertheless, a poem such as "Townend, 1976" (p. 305) celebrates with gentle nostalgia, and in iambic quatrains only a little loosened since the 1950s, a childhood place as a "drab old friend"; while "Morning" (p. 299), which is a variation on Christopher Smart's "A Morning Piece, Or an hymn for the hay-makers" (1750), records an unexpectedly generous pleasure in "nondescript, barged-through streets," a reality now only lightly and jauntily at odds with "that mob of ideas? Don't knock them. The sick pell-mell / Goes by the handsome Olympian name of Reason." From here on, too, there is a strand of poems addressed to fellow poets, no less rigorously though far less impatiently than in his earlier work. "To Thom Gunn in Los Altos, California" (p. 294) moves from a wonderfully baroque opening—"Conquistador! Live dangerously, my Byron, / In this metropolis / Of Finistère"—to embrace elements borrowed from Gunn's very different poetic world in Davie's own referential, discursive style. "Winter's Talents" (p. 334), for Peter Scupham and Robert Wells, is a somewhat ambiguous "salute" that urges them to "Rehearse, / Voices not mine, in England's / Interminable winter" (with, surely, a punning suggestion that their "talents" owe something to Winters' influence). "Summer Lightning" (p. 372), dedicated to Seamus Heaney, which seems to bring Davie very nearly back full circle, is a redefinition of poetry in heroic (or possibly anti heroic) couplets, a mode once again appropriate to the poet who called himself "a pasticheur of late-Augustan styles":

The gift of poetry is like the fire
Seen of a summer's night: flames that transpire
Like a foreboding over a river, over
A field, or again there, flickering, hover
To silhouette some plume on a far coppice
Become a sacred grove.

(pp. 372–373)

"Summer Lightning" pulls together, in a mostly amiable and self-deprecating style, several of Davie's recurrent ideas about poetry: its dependence on the unpredictable and unfakeable creative occasion; its punishing demands on its creator ("this art of mine has flayed / Me, and still does. I'm skinned!"); its necessary imperfections and its civic responsibilities. With a nod to Samuel Johnson, whom he admired and in some ways resembled, Davie offers a self-portrait in which a familiarly disputatious character is presented in a new and benign light:

> I am opinionated and embittered,
> Inconsiderate, gruff, low-spirited,
> Pleased and displeased at once, huffy and raw;
> And yet I fear God, fear the Crown, the Law,
> Am spry enough by nature, cordial,
> Content to have vexed nobody at all.
> So there you have me, Heaney . . . I suppose
> All of our lot have vices much like those.
>   (pp. 373–374)

No one who had followed Davie's poetic career to this point would have dared to dissent.

POETRY V: GOODBYE TO THE USA

THE final section of the 1990 *Collected Poems* is called "Goodbye to the USA," a title that might spread out to embrace the slim volumes on either side of it, *To Scorch or Freeze* (1988) and the posthumous *Poems and Melodramas* (1996). In one way or another, these are Davie's homecoming. This is most plainly the case in "Sounds of a Devon Village" (pp. 451–453), a series of neatly observed pastoral sketches in which the natural sounds of the country jostle with the haymaker's radio ("country music" of another sort) and the tractor driver's "grinding gear-box," until at last the poem veers—as one might expect from this writer—into a charming, wry etymological digression on the word "sylvan." But this poem is an exception: Davie was not the kind of poet who could readily settle to the contemplation of local scenes, even after his retirement—although he admired writers, such as Hardy, who could.

In fact, Davie's homecoming was primarily spiritual—a return to the Christian faith he had doubted and abandoned earlier in his life. *To Scorch or Freeze* is a sequence of fragmented psalms—shards of scriptural text are embedded in their texture rather as snatches of Pasternak and Pound recur elsewhere in Davie—and many readers have found it a difficult or, indeed, impenetrable collection. "It baffles some people and offends others," Davie himself said of it, adding: "It is exploring what it means to be Godfearing, which is not a term very much used, though it's a usage in perfectly good odour—'he's a Godfearing man'" (Tredell, pp. 280–281). Godfearing men are perhaps not as common as they might be, and even they may have trouble with a style that is often a throwback to the impatient disrupted syntax of the early 1970s. But the finest poem in the book, "Brilliance," a delayed companion piece to the meditation on "excellence" in "Ezra Pound in Pisa" (pp. 142–143), recalls the spare clarity of *Essex Poems*:

> Brilliance, then, is noble;
> not in the subject but
> in what the subject attains to:
> a metaphysical, not
> in the first place human, property.
>   (p. 420)

Brilliance, Davie tells us, is God's "preferred / supernal way of moving," the perfection that distinguishes Him from His imperfect creations (and in turn from *their* imperfect creations), but this recognition is only reached after a subtly probing argument, complete with characteristically Poundian resonances; this is one of Davie's most engrossing "abstract" poems.

The ten-part meditation "Our Father" in *Poems and Melodramas* (pp. 18–22) forms a coda to *To Scorch or Freeze*; indeed, *Poems and Melodramas* is a book of codas. Some of the poems are rediscovered early works: one, "Tiger at the Movie-Show" (pp. 28–29), a reflection on postwar European culture ("The singing robe of Europe is shrugged on / By every would-be poet"), first appeared in the magazine *Prospect* in 1949 and may be Davie's earliest published poem. Another poem, "The Lost Bride (Arkhangelsk, 1943)" (p. 3), though written much later, recalls Granya, the "Dear vanished one" who made such a strong impression on him during his wartime service in Russia (for an account of this, see *These the Companions*, pp. 54–63). Three poems record his long friendship with Charles Tomlinson, which he had previously celebrated as an amiable rivalry between different sorts of "mastery" in "To a Brother in the Mystery" (*Collected Poems*, pp. 81–83); another remembers his late friend Philip Larkin. But there are no grand flourishes, no Yeatsian invocations of a mad old age (some might say, not unkindly, that there were times when the younger Davie was quite mad enough). In any case, poetry did not come often or easily to him in his last decade: he had thought that *To Scorch or Freeze* would be his last book, and very near the end of the *Collected Poems* comes a touching poem, dedicated to his wife, in those loping three-stress lines he had made his own, which starts from summer-induced writer's block. "Dry season. Block. So, rain . . ." it begins ("Though dry, not dry," pp. 441–422), but it turns into a gently ironic commendation of sloth—which at least spares "The inattentive world" from his shows of "Sardonic paradox"—before ending on a note both riddling and heartfelt:

How merciful is our God,
My love, that it should be
Not Love but only love
In this abstracted mode
I cannot stir the will
To ask that I be stirred to!
　　　　　　(p. 442)

CRITICISM I: ARTICULATE ENERGIES

DAVIE'S critical writing closely parallels his poetry in its unresolved tension between a patriotic view of literary culture, with particular concerns in eighteenth-century English history and in religious dissent, and a compulsive need to challenge this with exploratory, outward-looking interests that often seem to go very deliberately against the grain. Of his first critical book, *Purity of Diction in English Verse* (1952), he wrote in a postscript of 1966 that it had not been conceived primarily "as a teaching-manual, nor as foundation-stone of my own career in universities (though it has usefully performed both these functions), but principally so as to understand what I had been doing, or trying to do, in the poems I had been writing" (2d ed., p. 197). The same could be said about much of his critical writing.

Purity of Diction in English Verse—with its influential distinction between "language" and "diction," its advocacy of nonmetaphorical rationality, and its focus on eighteenth-century writers such as Cowper, Johnson, and Wesley—is the essential companion to Davie's own poetic apprenticeship;

it also anticipated, and indeed helped to shape, the prevailing literary climate of England in the mid-1950s. Like its immediate successor, Articulate Energy (1955), which analyzes different kinds of poetic syntax (subjective, dramatic, mathematical, musical), it is notable for its implicit insistence on the intellectually rigorous nature of poetry, in sharp contrast to the slacker neo-romanticism of the 1940s. But *Articulate Energy*, in embracing a far wider range of poetic procedures than its predecessor, also signals the beginning of Davie's long journey beyond eighteenth-century paradigms. In a remarkable chapter called "What is Modern Poetry?" he confronts a question that would continue to trouble him, in one form or another, throughout his writing life, both as a poet and as a critic (the apparently thunderstruck italics are his):

What is common to all modern poetry is the assertion or the assumption (most often the latter) that syntax in poetry is wholly different from syntax as understood by logicians and grammarians. When the poet retains syntactical forms acceptable to the grammarian, this is merely a convention which he choose to observe.

　　　　　　　　　　　　　　　　(p. 148)

If this is true—and in its context it is certainly persuasive—then it is, among other things, a barely veiled reproach to his colleagues in The Movement, who for the most part would never have dreamed that they were "merely" choosing to "observe" a "convention" when they wrote in the syntax of everyday speech; Davie, by contrast, was always eager to explore new directions of prosody. And, as if to emphasize the point, a little later in the same chapter he offers a comparative analysis of Wordsworth's "Stepping Westward" and Pound's "The Gypsy," praising the latter's "musical syntax" and "far finer economy"; that the logical, prose meaning of "The Gypsy" is unclear "doesn't matter," says Davie, for "syntax has become music" (p.156). Pound, after all, was hardly a poet likely to be invoked model by other members of The Movement.

His next critical book, *The Heyday of Sir Walter Scott* (1961), looks like an eccentric digression, and so in a sense it is: yet, as so often with Davie, it both reaches back into his personal past (Scott was a favorite author of his father's) and out toward new imaginative territories. Davie is interested in Scott as an exploratory writer of the wilderness, who is thus to be compared with such figures as

Mickiewicz and Parkman, both of whom inform substantial poems of Davie's—*The Forests of Lithuania* (1959) and *A Sequence for Francis Parkman* (1961). After this, it was time to turn his sustained attention to Pound, for the first but by no means the last time, in *Ezra Pound: Poet as Sculptor* (1964): even the title recalls the comparisons between poetry and painting or carpentry in the contemporaneous poem "With the Grain." Pound, it would be fair to say, was Davie's familiar demon, a poet who in many respects was utterly unlike him yet continually fascinating and instructive. Davie would return to Pound frequently in his essays and twice more at book length, in a contribution to the Modern Masters series (1975) and in a collected volume, *Studies in Ezra Pound* (1991). He was well aware that this protracted engagement frustrated certain readers: "Some reviewers," he told Nicolas Tredell, "find *Studies in Ezra Pound* maddening because at the end, Davie is still oscillating between angry exasperation with this poet and adulation and devotion to him. I'm sorry, but that's the way it's always been for me with Pound" (pp. 280–281).

In *Thomas Hardy and British Poetry* (1972), Davie turned his attention to another modern master, to explore the claim that "in British poetry of the last fifty years (as not in American) the most far-reaching influence, for good and ill, has not been Yeats, still less Eliot or Pound, not Lawrence, but *Hardy*" (p. 3). Hardy's status as a major poet became assured during the late twentieth century, but thirty years ago that was an unfashionable proposition, and Davie typically set about substantiating it with an eclectic choice of contemporary examples—not just poets such as Amis and Larkin, who are very obviously indebted to Hardy, but Roy Fisher and J. H. Prynne. *Thomas Hardy and British Poetry* contains many of Davie's most perceptive readings of English poems as well as some lethal asides (Robert Graves and Ted Hughes, inhabitants of "mythological Never-Never Lands" who write "mumbo-jumbo," are both felled with a single swipe on p. 102); in this book, one again notices how closely Davie's engagement with apparently incompatible opposites mirrors the progress of his own poetry.

When Davie returned to Cambridge to give the Clark Lectures for 1976, published as *A Gathered Church* (1978), he also returned to his Baptist upbringing and to his literary interests of two decades earlier. In 1958 he had edited an anthology of longer poems, *The Late Augustans*, which had eventually been followed, in 1974, by a companion volume, *Augustan Lyric*. He began his second lecture by reflecting on a poem he carefully called "Man frail, and God eternal" (although his audience would have been more familiar with it as the hymn that begins "O God, our help in ages past"), by Isaac Watts, who is strongly represented in *Augustan Lyric*. Not only was Davie drawing together preoccupations that may be called lifelong; he was preparing the ground both for his compilation of *The New Oxford Book of Christian Verse* (1981) and for his own use of biblical material in *To Scorch or Freeze*.

CRITICISM II: ADVOCACIES AND CONTROVERSIES

A casual glance at Davie's bibliography during the 1960s and 1970s might suggest a slowing down of critical activity: these were turbulent years professionally, and productive ones poetically, so that would have been entirely understandable. In fact, his critical output was enormous, though it was mostly in the form of reviews, articles, and essays; some of these remain uncollected, while others were included in *The Poet in the Imaginary Museum* (1977) and *Trying to Explain* (1979). As a frequent book reviewer for *The Guardian*, *The Listener*, the *New Statesman*, and the *Times Literary Supplement* he wrote on authors with whom he had no strong connection—among them Fulke Greville, Percy Bysshe Shelley, John Clare, Samuel Beckett, T. S. Eliot, Vladimir Nabokov, George Lukacs, Stephen Spender, William Empson, and Robert Lowell—as well as on authors, such as Pound and Pasternak, with whom he was more closely associated; he also contributed longer pieces to literary journals and from 1977 was a coeditor of *P. N. Review*.

Even more than his prose books, these items in periodicals enhanced Davie's reputation as an exceptionally thoughtful critic, a strenuous advocate, and a fiery controversialist. His most characteristic qualities—the impatient yet precise urgency, the button holing, conversational tone—were all the more effective at article length. One recurring theme, the relationship between poetry and the other arts, specifically informs some of his most important essays, such as "The Poet in the Imaginary Museum" (*The Listener*, 11 and 18 July 1957), "Two Analogies for Poetry" (*The Listener*, 5 April 1962), and "Poetry and the Other Modern

Arts" (*Michigan Quarterly Review* 7, summer 1968). The first of these takes as its starting point Malraux's notion that modernism in the arts coincided with technological developments (sound recording, color printing) that enabled the modern composer, painter, or sculptor to inhabit an imaginary museum largely unknown to his predecessors; whereas poets have had access to their own imaginary museum ever since the invention of printing. However, whereas the visual and musical arts have access to an *international* imaginary museum, the fact of language means that the international accessibility of poetry is limited and arguably, since the disappearance of Latin and Greek from the common curricula and the common heritage, declining. So the poet is left, says Davie in one of his favorite phrases, "betwixt-and-between" (*The Poet in the Imaginary Museum*, p. 52), chronologically an inhabitant of the modern artistic world yet alienated from it by the material of his art.

By the time he came to write "Poetry and the Other Modern Arts," however, Davie had managed to turn poetry's inescapable separateness from the other arts to its advantage. Poetry, he decides, "has built into it, in a way that is not true of the other arts, a principle of conservatism" (p. 158); precisely because its medium is the non-international one of language, it cannot be experimental in the same way as painting, sculpture, architecture, music, or dance. "The art of poetry imprisons, whereas all other arts liberate" (p. 162), he quite cheerfully remarks; it is the positive version of "the dance of words" that more menacingly becomes "a circling prison" in "In the Stopping Train." At the end of the essay the cause of his cheerfulness becomes apparent: "for the most part I am pleased and grateful that my art is the conservative art; that there cannot be abstract poetry; that there cannot be action-poetry as there is action-painting" (p. 164). Furthermore, since the writer, uniquely among artists, uses the same material—language—for creation and for criticism, his commitment to "a principle of conservatism" is also a commitment to a principle of scholarship: he cannot be other than a poet-scholar.

Perhaps the most remarkable example of Davie's persuasive advocacy is provided by his prescient and sustained efforts to commend Edward Dorn to British readers. There are passing references to Dorn in Davie's reviews of the early 1960s, but he begins in earnest, characteristically, by contrasting the American poet's sense of civic responsibility with his English counterpart's lack of it and focusing on Dorn's "Mourning Letter, March 29, 1963," in a piece called "A Poetry of Protest" (*New Statesman*, 11 February 1966); yet this is merely a prelude to an astonishing chapter on "The Black Mountain Poets: Charles Olson and Edward Dorn," which he contributed to a critical anthology called *The Survival of Poetry*, edited by Martin Dodsworth in 1970. Here, as well as audaciously comparing Dorn's "Idaho Out" with Winters' "The Journey," he concludes with a spectacular claim for Dorn's then latest work, the "comic and profound, narrative and piercingly lyrical" *Gunslinger*, of which "the form and idiom . . . transcend completely the programmes of Black Mountain, just as they transcend (dare one say?) any programme so far promulgated or put into practice in Anglo-American poetry of the present century" (*The Survival of Poetry*, p. 234). Nor was that the end of the matter. Davie returned to the subject in "Edward Dorn and the Treasures of Comedy" (*Vort* 1, fall 1972) and in "Sharp Trajectories," published in the Vanderbilt campus magazine *Maxie's Journal* in 1978, which ringingly ends: "But who ever thought that poetry is a safe commodity? The stuff is dynamite!" (the last three pieces are reprinted in *Two Ways Out of Whitman*, pp. 161–175, 176–178, 179–181). The significant point is that Davie not only championed so disparate a poet as Dorn over two decades but that he also, as we have seen, continually sought ways to incorporate lessons from Dorn's work into his own poetry.

No less important were the public controversies in which Davie energetically involved himself. One notable and arguably infamous row centered on the unhappy circumstances of his departure from England in 1968; another, more strictly literary one was triggered by his review of *The Oxford Book of Twentieth-Century Verse*, edited by Philip Larkin, in *The Listener* of 29 March 1973. Larkin was, of course, an exact contemporary and an old friend, but Davie had long disagreed with what he saw as the insularity and unadventurousness of Larkin's literary taste. "Recoiling aghast from page after page of the anthology," he now concluded, "This volume is a calamity, and it's very painful that it falls to me to say so." There followed three months of excited debate in the *Listener's* letters pages, as well as a "Views" column (10 May 1973) in which Davie, in a sort of half-term report, set about demolishing the contrary opinions that had been expressed. The whole affair, apart from providing the amusing spectacle of literary people losing their tempers, was a rare example of a serious, extended debate about poetic values in a nonspecialist journal—something Davie had a remarkable knack for initiating.

Toward the end of his life, he began to reorganize much of his earlier critical writing into thematic collections, such as the already mentioned *Studies in Ezra Pound*, and since his death the series has been continued, with volumes edited by Doreen Davie and Clive Wilmer. *Slavic Excursions* (1990) and *Essays in Dissent: Church, Chapel and the Unitarian Conspiracy* (1995) assemble material on two of his most enduring concerns, Eastern European literature and English religious dissent. *Older Masters* (1992) and *With the Grain* (1998) contain essays on English poetry. The former valuably gathers together material written during more than forty years on poets who range chronologically from Chaucer to Browning, as well as related pieces such as "Berkeley and the Style of Dialogue" and the 1963 pamphlet *The Language of Science and the Language of Literature*. The latter is essentially an augmented version of *Thomas Hardy and British Poetry: Two Ways Out of Whitman: American Essays* (2000) collects pieces of varying length on American writers: the title's "two ways" are the routes via Pound and William Carlos Williams on the one hand or Winters on the other; and the book is also concerned with a recurring preoccupation, the English writer's experience of "Americanness."

One further volume, *Under Briggflatts* (1989), subtitled "A History of Poetry in Great Britain 1960–1988," does not quite fit into this category, since it purports to be an original critical book; but much of it, understandably enough, is closely based on Davie's reviews and articles about contemporary poetry. It takes its title from Basil Bunting's long poem of 1965: "British poetry," says Davie, "looks very different if we take *Briggflatts* to be . . . central to it" (*Under Briggflatts*, p. 40). Yet, unlike *Thomas Hardy and British Poetry*, this book is not sufficiently unified or well enough argued to support the claims made for its presiding genius, and it is certainly too selective and opinionated to be properly called a "history." Readers will do best to treat *Under Briggflatts* as a series of brief, incisive essays on aspects of twentieth-century British poetry, which is really what it is.

CONCLUSION: DISSENTIENT VOICE

"F. R. Leavis is one of the important English authors of the present century," wrote Davie in 1967. "He is one of our *authors*, not just one of our critics, though the critical essay is the only form of literature he has practised" (*The Poet in the Imaginary Museum*, p. 150). Of course, Davie was also, and at least equally, a poet; but his judgment of Leavis (as well as his sympathetic analysis of Leavis' prose style, which he finds "colloquial all through" yet difficult in a way "which gives the writing substance and savour") is one that might surely be applied to himself. And it is one of his unmistakable distinctions that he is among the rather few critics of his time and ours who can be read for enjoyment—as well as for instruction and exasperation—as a writer. In the foreword to *These the Companions*, he worried about this business of self-definition. What was he to call himself? Writer? Poet? Critic? Teacher? He had been, he said, all these things, "but it's impossible to single out any one of them and declare that one to be my profession, or my vocation." Then he added: "'Writer' is the one I like best, because it's the most capacious" (*These the Companions*, pp. xii–xiii). That should be good enough for us, too.

Nevertheless, one other word resonates too persistently around Davie's work to be altogether avoided, and that is "dissenter." Born into religious dissent, he almost made a religion out of dissent, finding himself so often out of sympathy with his country or his culture or his time. Yet it is exactly this working against the grain that makes him so consistently interesting. It is the dissentient voice of both his poetry and his criticism, continually challenging the lazy and the conventional (in his subjects, in his readers and in himself), that gives his work its extraordinary "substance and savour." He is not an easy writer. Despite the amiable lucidity of his prose and the accessible metrics of his earlier poetry, he is more devoted to the pressure of his language than to the comfort of his readers. "What I notice is words, and the sounded or unsounded cadences that words make when they are strung together; names, not the things they name," he writes, at the end of *These the Companions* (p. 175). That is a stern imperative, and to a lesser writer it might have proved an unbearably constricting one; but in Davie it informs an ambition, and an achievement, which made him the outstanding English poet-scholar of his generation.

DONALD DAVIE

SELECTED BIBLIOGRAPHY

I. POETRY. *Poems* (Fantasy Press Pamphlet) (Oxford, 1954); *Brides of Reason* (Oxford, 1955); *A Winter Talent and Other Poems* (London, 1957); *The Forests of Lithuania* (Hessle, Yorkshire, 1959); *A Sequence for Francis Parkman* (Hessle, Yorkshire, 1961); *New and Selected Poems* (Middletown, Conn., 1961); *Events and Wisdoms* (London, 1964; Middletown, Conn., 1965); *Essex Poems* (London, 1969); *Six Epistles to Eva Hesse* (London, 1970); *Collected Poems 1959–1970* (London and New York, 1972); *The Shires* (London, 1974; New York, 1975); *In the Stopping Train and Other Poems* (Manchester, 1977; New York, 1980); *Three for Water-Music, and The Shires* (Manchester, 1981); *Collected Poems 1970–1983* (Manchester and Notre Dame, Ind., 1983); *Selected Poems* (Manchester and New York, 1985); *To Scorch or Freeze* (Manchester and Chicago, 1988); *Collected Poems* (Manchester, 1990); *Poems and Melodramas* (Manchester, 1996). A new edition of the *Collected Poems*, edited by Neil Powell, is scheduled for publication in 2002.

II. CRITICISM. *Purity of Diction in English Verse* (London, 1952; New York, 1953); *Articulate Energy: An Inquiry into the Syntax of English Poetry* (London, 1955; New York, 1958); *The Heyday of Sir Walter Scott* (London and New York, 1961); *The Language of Science and the Language of Literature 1700–1740* (London and New York, 1963); *Ezra Pound: Poet as Sculptor* (London and New York, 1964); *Thomas Hardy and British Poetry* (New York, 1972; London, 1973); *Modern Masters: Pound* (London, 1975; New York, 1976); *The Poet in the Imaginary Museum: Essays of Two Decades*, edited by Barry Alpert (Manchester and New York, 1977); *A Gathered Church: The Literature of the English Dissenting Interest 1700–1930* (London and New York, 1978); *Trying to Explain: Essays* (Ann Arbor, Mich., 1979; Manchester, 1980); *Czeslaw Milosz and the Insufficiency of Lyric* (Cambridge and Knoxville, Tenn., 1986); *Under Briggflatts: A History of Poetry in Great Britain 1960–1988* (Manchester, 1989); *Slavic Excursions* (Manchester, 1990); *Studies in Ezra Pound* (Manchester, 1991); *Older Masters* (Manchester, 1992); *Essays in Dissent: Church, Chapel and the Unitarian Conspiracy* (Manchester, 1995); *With the Grain*, ed. Clive Wilmer (Manchester, 1998); *Two Ways Out of Whitman: American Essays*, ed. Doreen Davie (Manchester, 2000).

III. MEMOIR. *These the Companions: Recollections* (Cambridge, 1982).

IV. TRANSLATION. *The Poems of Doctor Zhivago*, by Boris Pasternak (Manchester and New York, 1965).

V. VOLUMES EDITED. *The Late Augustans* (London, 1958); *Selected Poems of Wordsworth* (London, 1962); *Modern Judgements: Pasternak* (with Angela Livingstone) (London, 1969); *Augustan Lyric* (London, 1974); *Collected Poems of Elizabeth Daryush* (Manchester, 1975); *Collected Poems of Yvor Winters* (Manchester, 1978; Chicago, 1980); *The New Oxford Book of Christian Verse* (Oxford, 1981; New York, 1982).

VI. INTERVIEWS. "A New Aestheticism? A. Alvarez Talks to Donald Davie," in *The Modern Poet*, ed. Ian Hamilton (London, 1968); Kevin Jackson, "Exorcising Coleridge," in *Independent* (10 September 1990); "Clive Wilmer in Conversation with Donald Davie," in *P. N. Review 88* 19 (November–December 1992); Nicolas Tredell, "Donald Davie," in *Conversations with Critics* (Manchester, 1994).

VII. CRITICAL STUDIES. Bernard Bergonzi, "The Poetry of Donald Davie," in *Critical Quarterly* 4 (winter 1962); John Press, *Rule and Energy* (London, 1963); William Cookson, ed., *Agenda: Donald Davie Issue* 14 (summer 1976); Michael Schmidt, *An Introduction to 50 Modern British Poets* (London, 1979); Neil Powell, *Carpenters of Light* (Manchester, 1979); Neil Powell, "Donald Davie, Dissentient Voice," in *British Poetry Since 1970*, ed. Peter Jones and Michael Schmidt (Manchester, 1980); George Dekker, ed., *Donald Davie and the Responsibilities of Literature* (Manchester, 1984); Vereen Bell and Laurence Lerner, eds., *On Modern Poetry: Essays Presented to Donald Davie* (Nashville, Tenn., 1988); Michael Schmidt, ed., *P. N. Review 88: Donald Davie at Seventy* 19 (November–December 1992).

RADCLYFFE HALL

(1880–1943)

Julie Hearn

To SAY THAT Radclyffe Hall is not usually included in the canon of modernism is something of an understatement. Rejected by the mainstream and patronized by early feminist scholars who dismissed her notorious novel, *The Well of Loneliness* (1928), as a misguided apologia for an outmoded discourse on lesbianism, Hall seemed destined to go down in literary history as a cross-dressing, angst-ridden melodramatist rather than a writer of any worth. It is only in the last fifteen years or so—with the benefit of sociohistorical hindsight and a more multifaceted approach within feminist criticism to transgendered subjectivities—that her work has been rescued from relative obscurity and placed alongside that of Gertrude Stein, H. D., Djuna Barnes, Dorothy Richardson, and Mina Loy on the map of interwar literature long colored by the masculinist aesthetics of Lawrence, Joyce, Eliot, Yeats, and others.

If Hall's right to a stake in this literary landscape is to be acknowledged, perhaps it needs to be recognized, as Margaret Lawrence did in 1936, that Hall's reputation has exemplified "the inability of the public, even the reading public, to hold more than one idea about one writer" (*The School of Femininity*, p. 323). Move beyond the "idea" of Hall as a one-book writer, set aside homophobic images perpetuated by the English media's prurient fascination with her sexuality, and one can begin to tease out the perennial value of her work.

Although Hall rejected modernism's avant-garde modes of expression in favor of the traditional narrative form, she employed this form with a skillful blend of subtlety and audacity to deconstruct conventional and deeply gendered paradigms of the human condition as incisively as any experimentalist. And while her style may, at times, strike the modern critic as quaintly overblown, it was one that endeared her to the very people whose attitudes she wished to challenge—conservative, middle-class readers for whom subversive themes were more palatable served up by an omniscient narrator, in chronological time sequences, with a garnish of Edwardian sentiment and purple prose. There is humor too in Hall's fiction; the sudden, glinting quality was aptly defined by reviewer Ida Wylie when she wrote that Hall "sets out with no apparent intention at all of being funny but . . . surprises the chuckles out of you with the nonchalant air of a conjurer producing rabbits from the pockets of an astonished schoolboy" (*Queen*, 29 April 1925).

Contrary to popular assumption, Hall's career did not begin when she leapt spectacularly out of the closet with *The Well* nor end when the book was banned for obscenity, in November 1928, and subsequently lampooned without mercy (see Beresford Egan's *The Sink of Solitude*, 1928; Henry von Rhau's *The Hell of Loneliness*, 1929; and P. R. Stephenson's *The Well of Sleevelessness*, 1929). She made her literary debut as a lyric poet, publishing five volumes of pastoral verse between 1906 and 1915. Influenced by Algernon Swinburne, Robert Bridges, and particularly Robert Browning, most of these poems turn, with seeming conventionality, on themes of love, loss, and an aching desire for spiritual and personal fulfillment. In a number, however, lesbian themes are broached, or at least encoded. For example, "A Pearl Necklace" (in *A Sheaf of Verses*, 1908) recalls Hall's frustrated attempt to seduce Violet Hunt with the erotically charged gift of a string of pearls:

> Go, cold white pearls, with the luring eyes
> The woman is waiting who longs to win
> But the rainbow light that within you lies,
> But the soft cool touch of your satin skin.
> You are undefiled and the price of sin
> Has passed you by . . .
>
> (lines 1–6)

The lesbian content of this and other poems completely passed by the critics. Reviews were complimentary, albeit patronizing, and a number of Hall's verses were set to music by known composers to be sung at tea dances and in provincial theaters.

Coming late to fiction at the age of 44, Hall nevertheless had a clutch of widely acclaimed novels—*The Forge* (1924), *The Unlit Lamp* (1924), *A Saturday Life* (1925), and *Adam's Breed* (1926)—to her credit before fallout from *The Well* eclipsed the lot. In 1926, *Adam's Breed*, a serious study of religious suffering and redemption, won both the prestigious Prix Femina and the James Tait Black Memorial Prize—an achievement matched only by E. M. Forster's *A Passage to India*. The time was now ripe, Hall informed her publisher, to put her pen at the service of some of the most persecuted and misunderstood people in the world, namely, "congenital sexual inverts" like herself. Her editor, as Diana Souhami notes in *The Trials of Radclyffe Hall* (1999), "must have sweated" (p. 167). It was, after all, not long since 1921, when law lords in England had refused to make lesbianism illegal on the grounds that not talking about it might make it go away. It was also an era of deep-seated unease about new freedoms for women (full suffrage was granted in 1928) coupled with what Alison Light, in *Forever England* (1991), has identified as a painful rupturing and recasting of imperialist notions of masculinity, in the wake of the Great War.

Such instability around the meanings and limits of gender identity meant that writers who valued both their reputations and a steady income were studiously avoiding, or encoding, any treatment of unconventional sexual orientation in their work. (Vita Sackville West's account of her affair with Violet Trefusis was kept locked away in a Gladstone bag, not to be published until after their deaths. Likewise, although Forster wrote *Maurice* in 1913, it too, at his insistence, was published posthumously nearly sixty years later.) The establishment tolerated female homosexuality served as erotic fantasy by such French aesthetes as Charles Baudelaire and Paul Verlaine, or as a flight of fancy, a la Virginia Woolf's *Orlando* (1928). Hall's polemical justification of sexual relations between women was quite different; hence, it was stamped on—hard. "I would sooner give a healthy boy or a healthy girl a phial of prussic acid than this novel," thundered James Douglas in the *Sunday Express* (19 August 1928). "There is not one word from beginning to end of this book," proclaimed Chief Bow Street Magistrate Sir Charles Biron before banning it, "which suggests that anyone with these horrible tendencies is in the least blameworthy." Although the British ban lasted until 1948, copies of *The Well* sold steadily in France and the United States. By June 1929, Hall had amassed £6,000 in royalties from the American edition alone. At her death in 1943, the novel—translated by then into fourteen languages and selling 100,000 copies a year worldwide—was firmly established, for better or worse, as "the Bible of lesbianism."

Between 1932 and 1936 Hall published two more novels, *The Master of the House* (1932) and *The Sixth Beatitude* (1936), and a collection of short stories, *Miss Ogilvy Finds Herself* (1934). None carried the weight or impact of *The Well*, and each slipped quietly into insignificance.

EARLY LIFE

MARGUERITE Radclyffe-Hall was born on 12 August 1880 at West Cliff, near Bournemouth, the second daughter of Mary Jane Sager, of Philadelphia, and Radclyffe Radclyffe-Hall, a rakish dilettante known to his associates as "Rat." Within a month of Marguerite's birth her one-year-old sister, Florence Maude, had died from convulsions and her parents' marriage was over. She was to see her father no more than a dozen times after that and, in later life, blamed her mother for driving him away. Shunted to a new home in London, and only patchily educated, the young Hall was, by all accounts, a deeply unhappy child. Her mother's moods were unpredictable. In moments of rage she would beat her daughter with a silver hairbrush and curse the child's resemblance to the absent "Rat." Hall, as Diana Souhami records, became "solitary" and "strange" (*The Trials*, p. 10), unable to trust an adult or make friends with other children.

Inevitably, perhaps, Hall's evocation of the lonely child's inner world forms a striking element of her fiction, providing a metaphor for the alienation she saw at the very root of human existence. Gloomy as this sounds, she rarely wallows so deeply in pathos that her plots flounder. On the contrary, it is her central characters' determination to rise above their lot in life which set the tone of her work. As Sally Cline notes in *Radclyffe Hall: A Woman Called John* (1997): "It is courage, not defeat, that becomes her trademark" (p. 21).

Gian Luca, the illegitimate protagonist of *Adam's Breed*, is so neglected as an infant that his first word is "dog" instead of "mamma." In a rare moment of compassion, however, his grandmother tells him, "You have yourself." "'I have got myself,' wrote Gian Luca. Climbing on to the bed, he pinned up his motto, then he climbed down again the better to see it" (p. 55). It is the beginning of a lifelong search for self-realization in which sensual materialism conflicts with spiritual idealism, and food becomes a rich metaphor for experiences that either nourish, or starve, the soul.

This struggle to define one's self in relation to hostile others is compounded in *The Unlit Lamp, A Saturday Life, The Well,* and the short story "Miss Ogilvy Finds Herself." In each, the young protagonists become aware that at some fundamental level they are not like other girls and must kick hard against gender conditioning in order to simply "be." Ironically, it is in *A Saturday Life*—classified, along with *The Forge*, as a social comedy—that Hall is most trenchant in questioning the social and moral values that define what is "normal" and therefore "allowable" in terms of sexual behavior. Young Sidonia, who loves to dance naked, causes a scandal when she strips off in the cloakroom of the Rose Valery School of Greek Dance for an impromptu demonstration in front of the other children. Even Miss Valery, who considers herself progressive and Sidonia brilliant, is shocked. For

> It was one thing to worship the Greek in marble, always a modest medium; it was quite another to see it dancing minus clothes on linoleum in a Fulham cloakroom. Ah, that was it, the cloakroom was to blame, with its ugly and sordid personality, its dangling corpses of shabby coats. . . . Out in an oleander grove the child would have looked quite perfect.
>
> (p. 24)

As this passage reveals, Hall was adroit at critiquing anything or anyone, claiming universal truths about "normal" appearance and behavior. The well-meaning Miss Valery has clearly been seduced by a romantic *idea* of both art and eroticism and is as guilty as anyone of stereotyping and pigeonholing Sidonia. The oleander grove image may strike the reader as liberal-minded and lovely, but the de-personalization of Sidonia as "the child" within it unsettles the glib conviction that in a different time and place, away from the "ugly and sordid" cloakroom (which may or may not stand as a metaphor for postwar England), non-conformist femininity would flourish. By the end of the novel, despite her attraction to an older woman, Sidonia conforms to marriage and moth-

erhood; her fate is clearly preconditioned by the subtle yet stringent demands of class and society.

When Hall was ten, her mother married Alberto Antonio Visetti, her singing teacher and a founding professor of The Royal College of Music in London. Hall, as an adult, referred to him as her "disgusting" old stepfather. Early biographers have drawn a discreet veil over suggestions that she was sexually abused by Visetti. Una Troubridge, with whom Hall lived for twenty-eight years, referred to a sexual incident "with the egregious Visetti" in the first draft of her *The Life and Death of Radclyffe Hall* (1961), but omitted it for publication "lest we have psycho-analytic know alls saying [she] would have been a wife and mother but for that experience" (UVT, "Letters to John" from 1943, c. 1947, quoted in *Radclyffe Hall: A Woman Called John*, p. 31). Michael Baker, whose *Our Three Selves: A Life of Radclyffe Hall* was published in 1985, thinks Visetti was probably "not as black" as Hall later painted him, just "too wrapped up in his own concerns to give much thought to an unhappy, unloved child" (p. 16). Contemporary critics, however, have made connections between the psychopathology of child sexual abuse and the recurring motifs of lost innocence and damaged psyches that recur in Hall's fiction.

In the light of these connections, Hall's novella "The Lover of Things" (in *Miss Ogilvy Finds Herself*) can be read as far more than the tale of a man whose love of beautiful objects lands him in prison for theft. Claudia Stillman Franks, whose book *Beyond "The Well of Loneliness": The Fiction of Radclyffe Hall* (1982) provided a framework for closer literary analysis of Hall's work, sees "The Lover of Things" as "a parable of eternal war between flesh and spirit; a paradox of freedom and entrapment" (p. 137). Her analysis includes a suggestion that, for Dobbs, the ivory statuette he covets and eventually steals represents positive *anima*—that is, feminine psychological tendencies within his own psyche that he has repressed. Yet, there is also something disturbingly sexual about descriptions of Henry Dobbs's obsession with small, fragile treasures. He marries, we are told, "without emotion . . . for the good of his health" (p. 78) and is repulsed by the workings of the adult female body ("all the muck of bearing a child and other things . . . she was no longer nice . . . it made him heave," p. 97). Seeing perfection in the delicacy of Dresden nymphs "his fingers must itch to contact themselves with it, to stroke, to handle" (p. 69), and it is the taking of a small, "chaste" female figure—"that little white fragile thing, so . . . undefiled" (p. 92) for which he is punished. Such a deconstructive reading may seem at odds with Hall's largely sympathetic characterization of Dobbs. Placed, however, within the same belief system that shaped *The Well*'s overriding message (that sexual orientation is biologically determined, and ordained therefore by God Himself), "The Lover of Things" becomes an extraordinary comment on pedophilia, exploring the way essentialist, quasi-scientific theories on sexuality can be employed to excuse all manner of deviations from the "norm."

FINDING A VOICE

AT the age of twenty-one, Radclyffe Hall inherited a considerable fortune from her paternal grandfather, enabling her to leave home and, more importantly, to live as she pleased. For if, as Virginia Woolf famously said, a woman of this era needed a room of her own and five hundred pounds a year in order to write, Marguerite Radclyffe-Hall (soon to adopt the Christian name John, and the pen name Radclyffe Hall) was in literary clover. In 1907 she met Mabel Veronica Batten (Ladye) an amateur lieder singer of considerable repute, who introduced her to the work of George Sand, Sappho, and Vernon Lee (the nom de plume of French-born Violet Paget) and encouraged her to take her own writing more seriously.

Ladye also introduced Hall to the faith, music, art, and literature of Catholicism, leading to Hall's conversion in 1912. In one of the many paradoxes that shape both her life and her work, Hall later became deeply interested in spiritualism, attending seances to "communicate" with Ladye after her death, while continuing to appear at confession with her new partner, Una, Lady Troubridge. Neither Hall nor Una appear to have troubled themselves about the fact that their Church condemned spiritualism. And while religious thought colors much of Hall's fiction, it does so in a multiplicity of guises, from the Christian doctrine that informs *Adam's Breed* and, even more intensely, *The Master of The House*, through the Eastern theory of reincarnation used to explain Sidonia's passionate enthusiasms in *A Saturday Life* to a decidedly pagan celebration of nature's rhythms and female sexuality in *The Sixth Beatitude*.

Such a "pick and mix" attitude toward spirituality reflects Hall's propensity throughout her life and her work to both embrace and contest the dictates of patriarchy at whim. Her own appearance was deeply paradoxical. Although she accepted the sexologists' definition of herself as a "congenital invert"—a man trapped in a woman's body— and depicted her major heroines as unmistakably boyish, she did not cut her own waist-length hair until past the age of forty, and she wore tailored skirts, not trousers, in public so that no one would accuse her of "pretending" to be male. She flirted with feminism and took an interest in the activities of the suffragettes; yet, as Michael Baker notes, she "instinctively sided with the Establishment and held to the hierarchical view of society to which her class subscribed" (*Our Three Selves*, p. 49). Her somewhat patronizing take on organized feminism is reflected in *The Unlit Lamp* in a cryptic vignette of Lady Loo—a bloomer-wearing, bicycle-riding, post-menopausal woman who has taken up the cause of equal rights with the same "disregard of consequences" that once characterized her reckless fox hunting: "It is doubtful whether Lady Loo had any definite ideas regarding what it was that she hoped to attain for her sex; it certainly cannot have been equality, for in spite of her bloomers, Sir Robert, poor man, was never allowed to smoke a cigar in the drawing-room to the day of his death" (p. 117).

Introduced into Natalie Barney's modernist circle in Paris, Hall was both inspired and ruffled by the intellectual and sexual confidence she found there—an ambivalence she was to explore through *The Well*'s depiction of Valerie Seymour's literary salon as both a safe haven and pathetic refuge for inverts with no other place to call home.

Determined, to the point of arrogance, to champion "just causes" in her writing, Hall was aware, nonetheless, of the need to tread carefully to begin with through a minefield of literary censorship and conservative taste. She greatly admired May Sinclair, a popular writer who used "new psychology" (as the literature of psychoanalysis was then called) to address women's struggles against sexual or social repression (see *The Three Sisters*, 1914; *Mary Olivier: A Life*, 1919; and *The Life and Death of Harriet Frean*, 1920). Inspired by Sinclair, and perhaps influenced by unforgiving memories of her own mother, Hall decided to focus her own embryonic yet already discerning powers of psychological delineation on a subject of great and controversial interest in interwar England: spinsterhood.

THE UNLIT LAMP

As critic Maroula Joannou reminds us, the test of any text's progressiveness always takes place, at least to some extent, outside it, "within political discourse, and in generic, semantic and readerly interchange" ("*Ladies, Please Don't Smash These Windows,*" p. 100). Thus, in evaluating any text on literary spinsterhood in the 1920s, much depends on an understanding of the sociohistorical conditions under which Hall—along with Winifred Holtby (*The Crowded Street,* 1924), Sylvia Townsend Warner (*Lolly Willowes,* 1926), Katherine Mansfield ("The Daughters of the Late Colonel" and "Miss Brill," in *The Garden Party and Other Stories,* 1922), and Sheila Kaye Smith (*Joanna Godden,* 1921)—wrote and was read.

The situation of the "redundant" single female, although hardly new, took on fresh significance in the 1920s when the number of "superfluous" women living in England in the wake of the 1914–1918 War stood at an estimated two million. Moreover, The Matrimonial Causes Act of 1923, in allowing women to bring divorce suits for adultery, was adding thousands of ex-wives to the tally of women living independent and potentially "unnatural" lives. It was all too much for the establishment. In a reactive dissemination of a sexual ideology hostile to women's independence, "spinster" became a highly pejorative term, synonymous with shifting and conflicting states of frigidity, thwarted passion, dullness, and deviance. D. H. Lawrence's novella *The Fox* (1923) touches heavily upon this fear of women's autonomy in its depiction of a young man, Henry, made murderous in his determination to wrest the love of his life away from the woman friend with whom she has set up a farm. Henry's association with the feral makes his pursuit of Jill Banford seem both natural and understandable. The relationship between Jill and Ellen March, however, is presented as a most *un*natural state from which Ellen is longing to be rescued. ("She felt so strangely safe and peaceful in his presence. If only she could sleep in his shelter, and not with Jill. It was agony to have to go with Jill and sleep with her. She wanted the boy to save her," p. 96.)

That many spinsters had worked throughout the war and were now self-supporting was elided as social theorists and journalists of the day spoke of the dismal fate awaiting untold numbers of dependent single women: "Much of the home-life of our country is built up on a substratum of obscure martyrdoms . . . until the family is broken up by death. And then the luxurious, hospitable family home belches forth dismayed spinsters into an unsympathetic world, to wander about as aimlessly, and seek cover as nervously, as do the wood-lice when the flower-pot is lifted" (*Time and Tide,* 11 March 1921). Although this was undoubtedly the lot of some, it was by no means a balanced reflection of spinsterhood as lived by countless women—including Radclyffe Hall and her wide circle of friends. Yet, in the way of all propaganda, the image of the dowdy, dissatisfied spinster seeped into the national consciousness, reinforcing ideologies that tied women to the home and denying the existence of choice.

It was into this framework that Hall inserted *The Unlit Lamp,* a novel that goes beyond the popular stereotype of the sad old maid to show how circumstance, conditioning, and the stifling restrictions of family life thwart every move a young woman makes toward independence and self-realization. Although initially focused on the love-hate relationship that binds Joan Ogden to her mother, the growing attraction between Joan and her tutor, Elizabeth Rodney, provides a competing theme that struggles for attention as avidly as mother and mentor struggle for possession of Joan.

Hall was not ready to champion same-sex love openly and assertively. The relationship between Joan and Elizabeth is contextualized as romantic friendship rather than explicitly sexual. Nevertheless, Hall is incisive, even in this, her first novel, at speaking through and against the ostensibly straightforward surface discourse of her text; to create what renee c. hoogland, in *Lesbian Configurations* (1997) describes as "a variety of symbolic markers—sustained patterns of imagery, metaphors, personal names and other tropes— that are at once recognisable as expressions of 'the love that dare not speak its name' to those who know how to read them" (p. 7).

Ironically, it is Richard Benson, the suitor Joan rejects, who appeals most directly to the reader's understanding and approval of Joan's sexuality. He sees her always as "fine" and "splendid" and "beautiful because symbolic of some future state— a forerunner" (p. 209). Told by his mother that "a woman is only complete when she finds a good husband," he replies: "they can't all find husbands—and some of them don't want to" (p. 120).

Although Joan never does leave her mother for Elizabeth, Hall makes it clear that cultural, economic, and psychological forces beyond Joan's control are mostly to blame. As a young woman, Joan is determined to cut loose, to study medicine at Cambridge, and then to live with Elizabeth in a home from which "instead of seeing the undignified street you catch a glimpse of the trees in the square" (p. 142). The deaths of her father and her sister; the misuse of her trust fund, and the manipulative demands of her mother all conspire to weaken her resolve. Even the Church's phallocentric ontology is implicated in what may, or may not, have been an intentional reference to the way Christian dogma, dovetailed with quasi-scientific theories on sexuality, required unmarried daughters like Joan to stay close to hearth and home. Mrs. Ogden, we are told, has found "a new emotional excitement" through High Church ritual and the "ascetic, celibate and delicate" "Father" Cuthbert. As a result: "Her bedside table was strewn with little purple and white booklets: 'Steps towards Eternal Life,' 'Guide to Holy Mass,' 'The Real Catholic Church.' They found their way downstairs at times, and got themselves mixed up with Joan's medical literature" (p. 180). Whatever Hall intended here, there can be no doubt about her perspective elsewhere in this novel on the institution of marriage. The relationship between Mary Ogden and her husband, James, an ex-India colonel, is unremittingly awful:

> She had been little better than this man's slave for over twenty years, the victim of his lusts, his whims, his tempers and his delicate heart, the peg on which to hang his disappointments, the doormat for him to kick out of the way in his rages. She had lost youth and hope and love in his ungrateful service; at times she almost hated him.
>
> (p. 134)

Although extreme, such bitingly satirical depictions of conventional coupling serve an important function, in that both spinsterhood and the relationship between Joan and Elizabeth seem almost idyllic in comparison. James is a caricature, a red-faced brute of a man who functions as little more than a narrative device. Mary is not quite so one-dimensional. Indeed, her viewpoint, although restricted, allows readers some understanding of the psychological pressures that shape her cloying, clinging ways. Hall's working title for this novel was *Octopi*—an apt descriptor for a theme that reaches beyond the mother-daughter dyad to highlight the tragedy of numerous lives wasted due to an inability to cut through the "tentacles" that bind them to society, family, and custom.

Ten publishers rejected *The Unlit Lamp*, considering it too gloomy for a first novel. In response, Hall rattled off *The Forge*, a social comedy more suited to the tenor of the times. Although written to order, and undeniably formulaic, *The Forge* demonstrates Hall's preoccupation with sexual identity, which seeps, irreverently, through the lightness of her prose. A married couple, Hilary and Susan, split up to find their individual worth as creative artists. Susan embarks on an ambivalent relationship with the painter Venetia Ford—a "strange, erratic brilliant genius" (p. 123), based on the artist Romaine Brooks with whom Hall shared a "mannish" identity and a stimulating, although sometimes edgy, alliance. In *The Forge*, Venetia/Romaine is pivotal in making Susan realize that she will never be a great artist because she cannot be "whole-hearted" in her approach. For "artist," an astute reader might well read "lesbian." The following passage, in which Venetia criticizes Susan's flower painting, is loaded with sexual innuendo:

> "Those blue delphiniums," Venetia continued, "they're carefully grouped, the composition's charming; that's because you're clever Susan, you used your brain for that part. But the flowers themselves never grew in the soil, never lived in the sunshine, never felt the rain. They're just pretty forms with the colour of delphiniums, but without a vestige of spirit."
>
> Susan's eyes filled with tears, her lip trembled.
>
> "It's too terrible to be only able to paint corpses, I might as well be an undertaker at once. The queer thing is that I don't understand it, it never used to be like this."
>
> "It's not only the intrusion of everyday things that is ruining art in you Susan, it's something far more vital than that; I think your allegiance is divided."
>
> "My allegiance is divided? Oh, no, indeed not. How do you think I divide it?"
>
> "Ah, that only you yourself can know," said Venetia, very quietly.
>
> (pp. 284–285)

Susan's need for social approval is too great. She renounces her "art" for the world of "everyday things" and is reunited with Hilary. The world is full of chains, Hilary tells her—with love (for which read heterosexual, married love) both the heaviest and yet the easiest of all to carry (p. 318).

The Forge was snapped up by Cassells and published in January 1924, to be followed, eight months later, by *The Unlit Lamp*. Both sold well. Today, a number of critics regard *The Unlit Lamp* as Hall's finest novel. Zoe Fairbairns, in her introduction to the 1981 Virago reprint, thinks it curious that when Hall decided to describe and vindicate lesbianism to a hostile public she did not consider that *The Unlit Lamp* had already done so. According to Fairbairns, *The Well*, for all its "power, courage and passion," suffers from being the vehicle for Hall's cause: "She wrote *The Unlit Lamp* because she was moved, as a novelist, by a glimpse of a human predicament; and because in it she was not deliberately setting out to make a statement, that statement is powerfully made" (p. 7).

THE WELL

SAME-SEX relationships, during Radclyffe Hall's lifetime, underwent a dramatic re-classification, with distinctions clearly drawn between "acceptable" levels of female friendship and perversion. Sexologists Richard von Krafft-Ebing (*Psychopathia Sexualis*, 1882) and Havelock Ellis (*Studies in the Psychology of Sex: Sexual Inversion*, 1897) both pathologized female homosexuality as inborn congenital inversion, a "taint" as unavoidable as it was undesirable. By the mid-1920s this theory was being challenged by Freud's assertion that childhood trauma and arrested development triggered inappropriate sexual behavior. Freud's views, in holding out the possibility of a "cure" were popular with practicing analysts but not to a woman like Radclyffe Hall, who had no wish to be "cured," only to be accepted. The earlier theories, in both making female sexuality morbid and setting it in binary opposition to the heterosexual "norm" hardly seem preferable. Yet Hall, having set out to champion same-sex love to a barely post-Victorian society was in something of a no-win situation. As Lillian Faderman recognized in *Surpassing the Love of Men: Romantic Friendship and Love between Women from the Renaissance to the Present* (1981), if a woman argued that she *chose* a same-sex relationship she risked being accused of immorality, and if she accepted the psychoanalytic theory that childhood trauma was the cause of her inversion she had no excuse not to seek a cure. "But if she maintained that she was born with her 'condition,' although some might consider her a freak, she could insist, as Hall actually did, that God created her that way; that she had a purpose in God's scheme of things" (p. 318).

Since the implied preferred reader of *The Well* is heterosexual, it would seem that Hall deliberately foregrounded Krafft-Ebing and Ellis's beliefs in her portrayal of Stephen Gordon, the novel's protagonist, to win support and understanding for her cause. Ellis even wrote a short preface for the book, in which he commended Hall's "faithful and uncompromising" depiction of a congenital invert. However, as we shall see, the sexologists' definition of inversion is not as implacably upheld in *The Well* as might be expected. Indeed, it is constantly challenged by the creation of characters and subplots that offer an excellent standpoint from which to begin deconstructing sexological theory.

Diana Souhami, whose biography recognizes its subject as a strong-willed, unyielding character with the wealth and the temperament to act as she pleased, suggests that what appears in *The Well* to be an undermining of essentialist theory owes more to Hall's tendency to throw precisely what she wanted into her plots than to any deliberate attempt to subvert the stranglehold of her own homophobic discourse. So far as the sexologists' claims were concerned, states Souhami:

> Hall took the bits that suited her, mixed them with Catholicism, spiritualism and her own ideas on endocrinology and came up with a theory of lesbian identity about as empirically reliable as the paternity of Jesus Christ or Mabel Batten's whereabouts on sphere three. . . . She drew no conceptual distinction between belief and knowledge.
> . . . Her theories stemmed from her need to control her world, her untutored mind, her attraction to the folklore theories of her time and her religious implacability. She claimed scientific objectivity, but it was the world according to Radclyffe Hall.
> (*The Trials*, p. 155)

Perhaps, since we can never pinpoint authorial motivation with total certainty, it is enough to acknowledge *The Well* as a rich and multi-layered text that, like Hall herself, defies simple definition. Such an approach should also pave the way for an objective consideration of the diverse range of criticism leveled at *The Well* over the past seventy years—criticism that is itself the reflector of a complex mass of cultural, sociohistorical, class, and gendered perspectives.

Stephen Gordon, the novel's heroine, is "ejected" from her mother's womb as "a narrow-hipped, wide-shouldered little tadpole of a baby" (p. 9), marked from birth by the physical characteristics of a creature rather than a person. Her father, who longed for a son, gives her a boy's name and, to begin with, indulges her preference for "masculine" pursuits. His enlightened response to the realization that his daughter is an invert is sympathetically drawn; yet he dies without sharing either his knowledge or his sympathy with Stephen. Hall takes great pains to portray Sir Philip and his wife, Anna, as respected members of the landed gentry with no hint of neurosis or other forms of degeneracy in the family's genetic history. In doing so she both flies in the face of the sexologists' claim that inversion is a hereditary taint and posits sociocultural conditioning as an alternative explanation. As Gabriele Griffin suggests in her study *Heavenly Love? Lesbian Images in Twentieth-Century Women's Writing* (1993), the establishment—"a series of 'Sirs' just like Sir Philip"—might arguably have singled out *The Well* for prosecution because it "normalised" inversion by situating it within a family untainted by hereditary defects, implicit in this portrayal, says Griffin, is the assertion that "if inversion can occur in the Gordon family it can occur in *any* family" (p. 21).

In her late teens, Stephen rejects a marriage proposal from her friend, Martin Hallam, and falls in love with a neighbor's wife who ultimately betrays her to protect her own interests and reputation. It is only at this point, condemned by her mother as "a sin against creation . . . a sin against the father who bred you" (p. 203) that Stephen painfully acknowledges her difference. In her dead father's study, she reads and identifies with Krafft-Ebing's portrayal of the invert in *Psychopathia Sexualis*. "God's cruel" she laments. "He let us get flawed in the making" (p. 207). It is interesting to note, as Griffin does, that this gradual overturning of Stephen's originally secure identity *inverts* the usual narrative of social integration. Griffin sees this as part of the novel's underwriting of patriarchal society: "Framed by the exchange between an initially ignorant, then suffering daughter and an all-knowing merciful father-figure (Sir Stephen/God) who fails to reveal his knowledge/mercy, the novel constitutes a *Bildungsroman* in reverse" (*Heavenly Love*, p. 23).

Banished from Morton, the home she loves, Stephen lives temporarily in London and makes a name for herself as a writer. She returns to Morton to bury her horse but the "spirit" of Morton, once "all beauty and peace" (p. 144) evades her. Morton functions throughout the novel as a powerful symbol—an Edenic place of origin to which Stephen can never return. Hall stresses the importance of the house in the book's opening paragraphs, where it is personified as having "dignity and pride without ostentation, self-assurance without arrogance, repose without inertia" like "certain lovely women who, now old, belong to a bygone generation—women who in youth were passionate but seemly; difficult to win but when won all-fulfilling. They are passing away, but their homesteads remain" (p. 7). This is interesting on two counts. First, it hints, ironically, at an ideal of genteel womanhood to which Sir Philip's only successor—so at odds with her own femininity—will be unable to subscribe. Second, it intimates that such a paradoxical ideal has had its day (*They are passing away*) even though the constricting ideologies that "house" it remain firmly in place. Later, with Sir Philip dead and the country on the verge of World War I, we are given quite a different perspective on the Gordons' country seat. On Stephen's final visit to the stables she is filled with "a desolation too deep for tears . . . the desolation of things that pass, of things that pass away in our lifetime" (p. 225). There is mildew over a warped oak board bearing the stud-book title "Marcus." The currycomb is being eaten by rust, the brushes have lost their bristles, and "A jam pot of hoof-polish, now hard as stone, clung tenaciously to a short stick of firewood which time had petrified into the polish." Everything is out of place. A container made to hold jam has something inedible in it and even that is now useless. A stick meant for the fireplace is stuck and will never be lit. And yet, these disparate objects combined to be useful once and would have remained so with a little care and attention. Might not the same be said, within the context of this novel, about a female body "containing" a male psyche?

Hall's tone in relation to Morton—a blend of nostalgia and fatalism—neatly encapsulates the schism to be found in much interwar thinking about England: on the one hand, a rejection of Shelleyan optimism, and on the other, what John Lucas has called "a prolonged soft focus recall" of a time before the war (*The Radical Twenties*, p. 13). So far, so Lawrencian. Then, into this schism, Hall slips her own little piece of dynamite: a woman unwilling to uphold the Old Order; a woman who creates books—highly successful ones—instead of sons; a woman who, even at her most martyred and miserable, remains steadfastly true to a nature that defies the Patriarchy.

During World War I, Stephen goes to the front, as a member of a women's ambulance corps, and meets Mary Llewellyn—a younger woman whose appearance, character, and behavior evade simple definition within the hegemonic categories of sexological theory. After the war, Stephen and Mary set up home together in Paris, but their happiness is eroded by social opprobrium from the world at large and by Stephen's morbid conviction that Mary is not suited to life among "God's miserable army" of inverts. The timely reappearance of Martin Hallam sets the scene for an emotionally charged denouement, in which Stephen "gives" Mary to Martin and ends up alone.

One of the main criticisms leveled at *The Well* is that it upholds patriarchal values—promising nothing but anguish to same-sex lovers and supporting the view that any woman who is not a freak will always prefer a real man. Sonja Ruehl, arguing against this viewpoint in *Feminist Criticism and Social Change* (1985), draws on the work of French philosopher Michel Foucault to depict *The Well* as a novel that, although steeped in doom and gloom, shifts the balance of power from those who define homosexuality to those who are defined. In Foucauldian terms, Hall's pointing up of the social consequences of a lesbian identity imposed by medical-psychological discourse paves the way for others to demand the right to define that category in accordance with their own agendas. As Ruehl explains: "Through it [*The Well*] she takes a militant stance on behalf of all inverts *because she speaks as one herself*. She starts the process of the reverse discourse by opening up a space for other lesbians to speak for themselves, and later, through the contemporary gay and women's movements, to challenge the definition of the category from within" (p. 170).

Judith Halberstam, in her book *Female Masculinity* (1998), stresses the need to keep the catch-all label "lesbian" at bay in relation to both Hall and her work because it both stabilizes contemporary definitions of a term Hall did not use and can result in "an inadequate sense of the historical specificity of certain modes of self-understanding" (p. 106). In vigorously resisting readings that depict *The Well's* protagonist as either a failed lesbian or a pathetic male mimic, Halberstam places Stephen Gordon within a specific historical tradition of female masculinity within which complex ideas about clothing and masquerade were all a part of trying to "find a fit" at a time when a sex change would have been impossible. Halberstam also challenges the widely accepted notion that Hall purposefully depicted Stephen Gordon as a "mannish" lesbian to disassociate the novel from the asexual tradition of romantic friendship. Such a reading, she points out, is no longer credible given that we now have evidence of "rich female sexual cultures in the eighteenth and nineteenth centuries that revolved around gender deviance and nonheterosexual sex (such as tribadism)" (p. 98).

Hall's choice of third person limited omniscient narration makes focusing on anyone but Stephen tricky, but not impossible. Valerie Seymour (modeled on Natalie Barney) is allowed to voice some of Hall's own uncertainties over inversion theory and to point out that Stephen's "absurdly self-sacrificing" stance, although contrived to win sympathy from a potentially hostile readership, is not the only way her love affair might have ended. "For God's sake, keep the girl," she tells Stephen, "'and get what happiness you can out of life.' 'No, I can't do that,' said Stephen dully. Valerie got up: 'Being what you are I suppose you can't—you were made for a martyr'" (p. 443).

Contemporary critic Loralee MacPike has reconstructed the character of Mary Llewellyn to reveal her as a "new lesbian" whose standpoint is not only different from Stephen's but also so stunningly modernist in its construction that "it has required the current outburst of gender theorising to see it" (*Unmanning Modernism: Gendered Rereadings*, 1997, p. 81). It is Mary, argues MacPike, who turns inversion theory on its head by actively pursuing Stephen while failing to conform to the visual iconography of inversion theory. Although Mary's defection to Martin has been read as "proof" of her innate heterosexuality, it is *Stephen*, MacPike reminds us, who requires such a sacrifice, not Mary. *Stephen*, because of her conditioning, sees the heterosexual model of her parents' marriage as an ideal and is driven, therefore, to replicate the pattern in the only way available to her: by becoming as father to child and giving Mary away to marriage and reproduction. Mary leaves because Stephen makes it impossible for her to stay, and her marriage to Martin by no means precludes either her desire or ability to contract another emotionally intimate relationship with a woman. In Mary, concludes MacPike, lies the real danger sexology was keen to construct out of existence: "the possibility that one really couldn't tell an invert from a heterosexual woman. For then all women might be inverts. And the world would crumble. This is the threat of the modernist impulse in fiction: it splits open the world" (p. 85).

The British establishment, as noted earlier, was not prepared to risk so much as a tremor in its own part of the world on account of this book; and although such writers as Woolf, Forster, and Eliot rallied to *The Well*'s defense, they did so more in the name of literary freedom than out of admiration for either Hall or her work. Virginia Woolf, who considered *The Well* dull, was secretly relieved not to be called as a defense witness during the obscenity trial. She deplored the ban, however, and, in *A Room of One's Own* (1928), condemns (albeit obliquely) the sexual politics that, to her mind, influenced the outcome of the trial. In America, the New York Society for the Suppression of Vice took *The Well* to court in April 1929. Defense lawyer Morris Ernst called the book sincere, fearless, and beautiful, full of integrity and moral fervor. He referred to Theophile Gautier's *Mademoiselle de Maupin*, which had been recently cleared of an obscenity charge despite being far and away more salacious in tone and content than anything Radclyffe Hall had ever written. A letter of protest against *The Well*'s suppression was signed by Sherwood Anderson, F. Scott Fitzgerald, Ernest Hemingway, Upton Sinclair, Theodore Dreiser, and many other literary figures. The American judges concluded that *The Well* was not in violation of the law. It was a significant triumph but one that failed to appease Radclyffe Hall.

BEYOND THE WELL

REELING from the fate of *The Well*, it is perhaps unsurprising that Hall sought, through her next book, to recapture some of the respect and literary accolades accorded her prize-winning *Adam's Breed*. She failed rather dismally because, as critics past and present agree, *The Master of the House* is her weakest novel. Set in early twentieth-century Provence, it tells the story of Christophe Benedit, a carpenter's son whose spiritual quest and final martyrdom mirror those of Christ. So immersed did Hall become in her theme that, according to Una Troubridge, she developed the red stains and shoot-ing pains of stigmata on her palms and had to write with her hands bandaged. Such over-identification with her hero failed, however, to inscribe her text with the psychological insight and critical imagination that were Hall's greatest talents and that had set *Adam's Breed* apart as an artfully narrated quest novel. As Sally Cline says of *The Master of the House*: "Five hundred pages of unremitting virtue attached to a protagonist who never stumbles is simply too much to take" (*Radclyffe Hall: A Woman Called John*, p. 302). Claudia Stillman Franks calls the book "banal . . . little more than a bad example of speculative fiction" (*Beyond the Well*, p. 119) and deems it "nearly insufferable to the modern reader" (p. 116).

A quick glance at what was popular in 1932 shows that *The Master of the House*, as well as lacking emotional depth, was also badly out of step with the times. Aldous Huxley's *Brave New World* and Ernest Hemingway's *Death in the Afternoon*, both published the same year, reflect an ethos far removed from Hall's theme of unremitting religiosity. Damon Runyon's *Guys and Dolls* was running on Broadway. Noel Coward's play *Cavalcade* was playing to packed audiences in Britain and a little moppet called Shirley Temple was making her cinematic debut in *Red-haired Alibi*. Hall's latest offering, in comparison, was hard going.

Bitterly despondent and convinced that the literary world was set against her, Hall could not face starting a new novel. Instead, she reworked short stories written during her time with Ladye, added new ones, and published them in 1934 to good advance sales but mixed reviews. All five stories in *Miss Ogilvy Finds Herself* match the author's desultory mood following condemnation of *The Well* and the failure of *The Master of the House*. In each we find a protagonist whose search for love and self-fulfillment conflicts with either the dictates of their own psychological make-up or the laws of an antagonistic universe. This is familiar territory for Hall; yet there are new twists to the psychological landscape, all tightly contained in a format that, by its very nature, precluded the author's occasional tendency to ramble and lent her prose a fine cutting edge.

The title story bears comparison to *The Well* for its complementary yet in some ways more radical consideration of the invert as an outsider to conventional romantic narrative. The young Miss Ogilvy has much in common with Stephen Gordon in that she wears breeches "illicitly," loathes sisters and dolls, and later dreads the attentions of would-be suitors. She is, however, more stoical than Stephen, realizing early on that "she must blaze a lone trail through the difficulties of her nature" (p. 8). Her sisters, Sarah and Fanny, are both stereotypical spinsters of the saddest variety. A description of "their endless neurotic symptoms incubated in resentful virginity" (p. 9) seems a cruel and surprising snipe from the creator of Joan Ogden, yet works in unattractive opposition to their sister's feisty independence.

When World War I breaks out, Miss Ogilvy leaves Sarah and Fanny knitting "Jaeger trench-helmets" and "socks" (p. 10) and, like Stephen Gordon, finds her niche as an ambulance driver in France. On returning home she cannot settle and travels to an island off the coast of Devon. Here, she is shown the skull of a caveman and, that night, has a quasi-mystical vision in which she becomes a Bronze Age man aware of the impending extinction of his race. In an extraordinary section, describing this woman/man's struggle to speak (as primitive man his speech was "slow and lacking in words," p. 26), and he/she displays "wonder and terror" at the sight of forests "darkened fold upon fold" (p. 29), Hall comes remarkably close to evoking the pre-oedipal imaginary order of psychoanalytic theory. Jacques Lacan, who rethought Freud in the light of modern linguistic theories, defined the imaginary as preceding an individual's entry into the symbolic order of language and culture. And while his work has been censured by some feminists for its depiction of women as "lacking" in relation to the phallic signifier, others have welcomed his displacement of the idea of "natural" sexuality and rational discourse. In Lacanian terms, a return to an archaic, pre-verbal stage of the psyche is impossible, signifying the death of the self; yet "death of the self" would seem to be the only choice available and desirable to Miss Ogilvy, out of place as she is in both her female body and the twentieth century.

Indeed, the story ends with the discovery of her dead body outside the womblike cave she has "returned" to. The story's title, "Miss Ogilvy *finds herself*" suggests that the caveman she becomes is the "true self" she yearns to be. Yet Hall's description of this transformation of Miss Ogilvy-as-a-man is less than complimentary. The silence of the natural world, we are told, makes the man restless. He must menace the bears, in a display of superior strength, and make a lot of noise. Her/his sexual coupling with a young virgin is depicted in terms that pit her/his potency against the girl's vulnerability, yet allows, also, for ambiguity (the girl feels weighed down by "the terror of love." She "gasps" with fear, yet clings close to him "lest he should spare her." She repeats the word "no" four times, the implication being that she really means "yes," p. 33). If brute force and arrogance set in binary opposition to a kind of masochistic passivity represent Miss Ogilvy's, or, indeed, Radclyffe Hall's heterosexual ideal, this might well be considered a very sorry tale indeed. If, however, it is read as a comment on the monumental difficulties faced by women who seek to define and express a culturally mandated masculinity in relationships with partners who are themselves ambiguously tethered to a "feminine" identity, it is quite brilliant.

In June 1934 Hall and Una made one of their regular excursions to France where Una fell ill with gastroenteritis. The nurse hired to look after her, a thirty-year-old White Russian émigré called Evguenia Souline, became Hall's mistress, forming a love triangle that was to inspire Hall and infuriate Una on and off for the next nine years. More than five hundred letters written by Hall to Souline (as Hall preferred to call Evguenia) survive, providing valuable insight into the writer's passionate, often dictatorial nature; her class-ridden political conservatism; her views on inversion; and some of the events and relationships that inspired and shaped her fiction. Hall credited Souline with lifting her out of the doldrums and enabling her to write again. She began a new novel, *Emblem Hurlstone*, which she described as the "child" of their love affair. Metaphors linking creative writing to childbirth and maternity occur frequently in Hall's correspondence. *Emblem Hurlstone*, she informed Souline, needed special care, for "I can't see it go out with a button undone, with its left shoe off and its face & [sic] hands dirty!" (R. H. to E. S., 5 December 1934). In a letter dated Easter Sunday, 1935, she compared "sticky work"—that is, a novel that fails to "flow"—to "a long and difficult confinement." It is worth recalling, at this point, that in *The Well*, Stephen Gordon begins writing seriously only after accepting that as an invert she will never be a biological mother. Hall tells us next to nothing about Stephen's art apart from the fact that it is a commercial and financial success. This begs the question that for Stephen, as for Hall, the traditional forms of language, genre, and creativity remain in acute conflict with the invert's sexual identity and related perceptions. Thus the creative process becomes, for them, a complex and often painful act, during which the writer/mother is torn between the dualities of self-expression and compromise.

Emblem Hurlstone, which is about a man unable to deal with pain and a woman with many of Souline's mannerisms and characteristics, became a particularly "sticky" and truculent "child." Hall abandoned it unfinished and embarked immediately on *The Sixth Beatitude*. "I think it is the best thing I've ever written," she told Souline. "It is all, all YOU" (R. H. to E. S., 26 April 1935). Although *The Sixth Beatitude* notched up poor sales both in Britain and America, it remains a compelling study of diverse physical and emotional relationships and an interesting meditation on the supreme importance of perspective. Set on the Rye marshland—a part of England Hall knew and loved—it also contains some of the best descriptive passages Hall ever wrote. The central character, Hannah Bullen, has two illegitimate daughters. One was "the fruit of a sudden unruly impulse" in a disused shed (p. 12), and the other was conceived with a blonde-haired sailor on a "bewitched June evening," when the light had suddenly deepened and brightened "so that the Marsh looked unearthly green, and the river and dykes unearthly blue; so that the cuckoo's monotonous call had a curious power to disturb the senses" (p. 14). Although Hannah is clearly a "loose-living" woman by the standard of the times, Hall probes gently but firmly beyond moral conventions to establish her as a heroine worthy of respect. Toward the end of the novel, the children of Crofts Lane sing a Christmas carol in which the Virgin Mary wonders who will be kind to the infant Jesus. The third verse tells of a widow "in weeds of grief," a leper, a cripple, a thief, and finally Mary Magdalen in her "robes of sin" as the ones to rally round (p. 183). The point is succinctly made: society's outcasts (and the intertextual reference to Stephen Gordon and Miss Ogilvy is hard to miss) are the ones who, out of all humanity, frequently show the greatest nobility of spirit.

In her letters to Souline, Hall made frequent mention of the fact that she could no longer appreciate nature alone ("Beauty becomes sad if I am forced to see it without you" [R. H. to E. S., 8 September 1934]). She also referred to sex as "never quite enough" since "there is no perfection of union while we are still in the flesh" (R. H. to E. S., 27 March 1935). This desire of Hall's—both for the physical presence of her lover and for something beyond even that—finds expression in *The Sixth Beatitude* through Hannah Bullen's yearning to transcend both the poverty of her life in Crofts Lane and the limitations of fallen human nature. Hannah's sexual trysts with a married man "satisfy her body but not her mind. . . . When they were together her mind was unappeased and more solitary than when they were parted" (p. 146). The beauty of the changing seasons has the power to move her, but it is a "deathly sweet pain" (p. 69), tinged by an awareness of transience and the nagging demands of her daily life. Like most of Hall's protagonists, Hannah is doomed. Pregnant with her third illegitimate child, she goes out in a literal blaze of glory, having rescued a neighbor's children from a burning building. Her demise, however, has nothing to do with divine retribution. The reader is left in no doubt that it is Heaven, not Hell fire, that awaits this particular moral misfit.

In 1939 Hall's health began to fail. She continued working doggedly on a new novel, *The Shoemaker of Merano*, which she intended to dedicate to Evguenia Souline. Una was furious (the usual dedication in Hall's books, "To Our Three Selves," represented the original triangle of Hall, Una, and Ladye). Hall died of cancer on 7 October 1943, and her coffin was placed next to Ladye's in a vault at Highgate Cemetery. Una burned both the half-completed manuscript of *The Shoemaker of Merano* and all of Evguenia Souline's letters to Hall. She kept a fragment of the manuscript—about thirty pages—for the loveliness of the writing. They are enough, according to Diana Souhami, to reveal the book's compelling narrative tone and vivid characterization; enough to condemn the destruction of the rest as "a heinous act" (*The Trials of Radclyffe Hall*, p. 354).

CONCLUSION

IN 1885, when Radclyffe Hall was five years old, her grandmother commissioned a portrait of her in oils from society artist Katinka Amyat. The result, of which Hall was rather fond, showed a conventionally pretty little girl, with shoulder-length curls, clutching a bouquet of marguerites. Una Troubridge found the portrait unsettling and, after Hall's death, had the curls painted out to make the young Marguerite look more like a boy. Una died in Italy in 1963 and the portrait passed to her godson, Dr. Alessandro Rossi-Lemeni. He had the paint scraped away to reveal, once again, a curly-haired little girl. The contradictions evident in the two images, the conflictual play between what appears and what is, precisely echoes the multifaceted quality of Hall's writing. Scrape below the surface of her fiction, dense though it may sometimes appear, and there are flashes of stunning perception to be found. These more than justify the inclusion of Radclyffe Hall in any assessment of the shared tropes and ontologies that mark fine writing in general, and fine women's writing in particular, across the generations.

Influenced, as all writers are, by the historical moment she was born into and by the generic conventions to which she adhered, Hall's work, nonetheless, transgresses the boundaries of neat definition, employing metaphor, symbolism, and imagery to explore the human condition in all its destabilizing aspects. Loved or hated, *The Well of Loneliness* domesticated knowledge about same-sex love in an unprecedented way. It sidestepped rules of silence and invisibility to become a landmark in the history of both lesbian culture and literary censorship. Outdated as the book now seems to some critics, its very historical specificity is what marks it, for others, as a fascinating study of gender relations in a given sociohistorical context.

Viewed in its entirety, Hall's work reflects a vision that is timeless in its awareness of the internal and external forces that can conspire against individual happiness and fulfillment. Her compassion for the human condition, be it encapsulated in the tortured body of Christophe Benedit, the tormented soul of Stephen Gordon, or the restless spirit of Hannah Bullen, is both deep and wide-ranging. Her desire to affirm the possibility of joy is far more evident than a critique based solely on *The Well of Loneliness* might suggest.

Complex, contradictory, and passionately committed to her cause, Radclyffe Hall was a woman ahead of her time. Eschewing the linguistic fireworks of "high" modernism and the intellectual pretensions of the Bloomsbury Set, she went her own way, shocked the nation anyhow, then paid the price. A true outsider to the last—in relation to both society and the modernists—her place in the literary canon remains unjustifiably diminished. Her literary range, however, continues to speak for itself—in a voice that resonates with enduring authority, both in and beyond *The Well*.

SELECTED BIBLIOGRAPHY

I. POETRY. *'Twixt Earth and Stars* (London, 1906); *A Sheaf of Verses* (London, 1908); *Poems of the Past and Present* (London, 1910); *Songs of Three Counties and Other Poems* (London, 1913); *The Forgotten Island* (London, 1915).

II. NOVELS AND SHORT STORIES. *The Forge* (London, 1924; repr. March 1929); *The Unlit Lamp* (London, 1924; repr. 1983); *A Saturday Life* (London, 1925; repr. 1952); *Adam's Breed* (London, 1926); *The Well of Loneliness* (London, 1928; repr. 1973); *The Master of the House* (London, 1932; repr. 1952); *Miss Ogilvy Finds Herself* (London, 1934); *The Sixth Beatitude* (London, 1936; repr. 1959).

III. SECONDARY SOURCES. Una, Lady Troubridge, *The Life and Death of Radclyffe Hall* (London, 1961); Vera Brittain, *Radclyffe Hall: A Case of Obscenity* (London, 1968); Lovat Dickson, *Radclyffe Hall at the Well of Loneliness: A Sapphic Chronicle* (London and Toronto, 1975); Zoe Fairbairns, "Introduction" to *The Unlit Lamp* (London, 1981); Alison Hennegan, "Introduction" to *The Well of Loneliness* (London, 1982); Claudia Stillman Franks, *Beyond "The Well of Loneliness": The Fiction of Radclyffe Hall* (Avebury, 1982); Richard Ormrod, *Una Troubridge: The Friend of Radclyffe Hall* (London, 1984); Esther Newton, "The Mythic Mannish Lesbian: Radclyffe Hall and the New Woman," in *Signs: Journal of Women in Culture and Society* 9, no. 4 (1984); Michael Baker, *Our Three Selves: A Life of Radclyffe Hall* (London and New York, 1985); Sonja Ruehl, "Inverts and Experts: Radclyffe Hall and the Lesbian Identity," in *Feminist Criticism and Social Change: Sex, Class and Race in Literature*, ed. Judith Newton and Deborah Rosenfelt (New York, 1985); Angela Ingram, "'Unutterable Putrefaction' and 'Foul Stuff': Two 'Obscene' Novels of the 1920s," in *Women's Studies International Forum* 9, no. 4 (1986); Gillian Whitlock, "Everything Is Out of Place: Radclyffe Hall and the Lesbian Literary Tradition," in *Feminist Studies* 13, no. 3 (fall 1987); Rebecca O'Rourke, *Reflecting on the Well of Loneliness* (London and New York, 1989); Gabriele Griffin, "Becoming Visible," in *Heavenly Love? Lesbian Images in Twentieth-Century Women's Writing* (Manchester, 1993); Loralee MacPike, "Is Mary Llewellyn an Invert? The Modernist Supertext of The Well of Loneliness," in *Unmanning Modernism: Gendered Re-Readings*, ed. Elizabeth Jane Harrison and Shirley Peterson (Knoxville, 1997); Sally Cline, *Radclyffe Hall: A Woman Called John* (London, 1997); Joanne Glasgow, *Your John: The Love Letters of Radclyffe Hall* (New York and London, 1997); Judith Halberstam, "A Writer of Misfits: John Radclyffe Hall and the Discourse of Inversion," in *Female Masculinity* (Durham and London 1998); Diana Souhami, *The Trials Of Radclyffe Hall* (London, 1999).

IV. GENERAL READING. Margaret Lawrence, *The School of Femininity* (New York, 1936); Jane Rule, *Lesbian Images* (London, 1975); Lillian Faderman, *Surpassing the Love of Men: Romantic Friendship and Love Between Women from the Renaissance to the Present* (London and New York, 1981; repr. 1997); Catharine R. Stimpson, "Zero Degree Deviancy: The Lesbian Novel in English," in *Writing and Sexual Difference*, ed. Elizabeth Abel (Chicago, 1982); Sheila Jeffreys, *The Spinster and Her Enemies: Feminism and Sexuality 1880–1930* (London and Boston, 1985); Bonnie Zimmerman, "What Has Never Been: An Overview of Lesbian Feminist Criticism," in *Making a Difference: Feminist Literary Criticism*, ed. Gayle Greene and Coppelia Kahn (London, 1985); Alison Light, *Forev-er England: Femininity, Literature and Conservatism between the Wars* (London and New York, 1991); Maroula Joannou, *"Ladies, Please Don't Smash These Windows": Women's Writing, Feminist Consciousness and Social Change 1918–38* (Oxford and Providence, 1995); Bonnie Kime Scott, *Refiguring Modernism*, vol. 1 (Bloomington and Indianapolis, 1995); renée c. hoogland, *Lesbian Configurations* (Oxford, 1997); John Lucas, *The Radical Twenties: Aspects of Writing, Politics and Culture* (Nottingham, 1997).

T. E. HULME

(1883–1917)

Patrick McGuinness

BETWEEN 1909, WHEN he wrote his first polemical letter to *The New Age*, and his death on a battlefield in Belgium in 1917, Thomas Ernest Hulme published on a variety of issues central to the artistic and cultural movements of the early twentieth century in Europe. Poet and literary theorist, philosopher and avant-garde art critic, Hulme was also a political theorist, a soldier, and a relentless controversialist. He can be found at the intersection of many of the most significant currents of modernist art and culture: imagist poetry, literary theory, authoritarian politics, continental philosophy, and art criticism. His friends and acquaintances included such diverse figures as Ezra Pound, Henri Bergson, Rupert Brooke, Edward Marsh, Wyndham Lewis, Jacob Epstein, and Henri Gaudier-Brzeska. Among those who felt his influence scholars count T. S. Eliot, David Jones, Herbert Read, John Middleton Murry, and many more.

Hulme compressed a remarkable range of subjects into his short writing life; indeed, few areas remained untouched by his energetic, occasionally undisciplined, always provocative pen. He wrote poems described by T. S. Eliot as among the "most beautiful short poems in the English language" (p. 231); he wrote and lectured on poetry and poetic theory; he composed a "Sketch for a New Weltanschauung" ("Sketch for a New World View"); he championed the French philosopher Henri Bergson; he argued for classicism and what he called the "Religious Attitude" against romanticism and humanism; and he became one of the most daring theorists of the new art movements of the early twentieth century. He dabbled also in a specialized (though not unusual among contemporary intellectuals) and eccentric theology by claiming that the existence of God was mere "chatter" about "secondary notions," yet argued powerfully for a strong and vigorous conception of Original Sin: a religious attitude but without specific religion. Hulme remains, politically, difficult to locate: he translated and admired the work of the French radical syndicalist Georges Sorel and frequently referred to the great French anarchist Pierre-Joseph Proudhon, but was himself "a certain kind of Tory," that is to say, a man of the Right. Despite his prose style—commanding, assertive, muscular—and his dislike of what he called "romanticism in politics" (broadly speaking, the Left), Hulme believed in the absolute equality of all, and there is no trace in him, as there is in such contemporaries as Pound, Eliot, and Lewis, of anti-Semitism. Nor was he fascinated by authoritarian régimes or antidemocratic political figures.

Hulme was always hungry for knowledge and stimulation. He loved controversy and polemic, and although he wrote as a tough and opinionated personality, he did not expect people solemnly to agree with what he said. For him, dissent, provocation, and vigorous discussion were the oxygen of intellectual life. Something of this is evident in the preface to his earliest substantial work, "Cinders," written when he was in his mid-twenties:

A new philosophy is not like a new religion, a thing to be merely thankful for and accepted mutely by the faithful. It is more in the nature of food thrown to the lions; the pleasure lies in the fact that it can be devoured. It is food for the critics, and all readers of philosophy, I take it, are critics, and not faithful ones waiting for the new gospel. With this preface I offer my new kind of food to tickle the palate of the conoisseurs.
(*Collected Writings*, p. 7; hereafter *CW*)

Hulme kept abreast of European thought and philosophy, studied the work of Edmund Husserl, George Moore, and Bertrand Russell, pursued the aesthetic theories of Wilhelm Worringer, Alois Riegl, and Theodor Lipps, and promoted the painting and sculpture of Wyndham Lewis, Henri Gaudier-Brzeska, and Jacob Epstein. He wrote chronicles and reviews of modern French and German poetry, and although he unhesitatingly signed up to go to the western front in 1914, he could often be found reading German literature in his trench. He remained both a man of action and a man of letters. In one of his cantos, Ezra Pound remembers his friend Hulme returning wounded from the war and spending his time in the hospital reading German philosophy:

> And ole T.E.H. he went to it,
> With a lot of books from the library,
> London Library, and a shell buried 'em in a dug-out,
> And the Library expressed its annoyance.
>   And a bullet hit him in the elbow
> . . . gone through the fellow in front of him,
> And he read Kant and Hegel in the Hospital, in
>   Wimbledon,
> in the original,
> And the hospital staff didn't like it.
>
> (Canto XVI)

The first collection of Hulme's writings was put together by the poet, critic, and art historian Herbert Read and entitled *Speculations*. The book appeared in 1924. While Hulme was well known in avant-garde circles, it was the posthumous publication of *Speculations* that enabled him to take his place as one of the key figures in the artistic and literary history of these turbulent, creative, but also destructive years. For many years, *Speculations* was the authoritative volume of Hulme's work, although scholars recognize that there were serious problems with the editing and ordering of the writings. A recent *Collected Writings* was published in 1994, and though it is not quite complete (it does not contain all of Hulme's poems and fragments), it scrupulously dates and arranges the work thematically and chronologically. Nonetheless, *Speculations* was an event, saving Hulme from oblivion (he had been dead seven years), and receiving the following notice from T. S. Eliot in *The Criterion*:

When Hulme was killed in Flanders in 1917, he was known to a few people as a brilliant talker, a brilliant amateur of metaphysics, and the author of two or three of the most beautiful poems in the English language. In this volume he appears as the forerunner of a new attitude of mind, which should be the twentieth-century mind, if the twentieth century is to have a mind of its own.

(p. 231)

Despite the grandeur of Eliot's claims (Eliot was profoundly impressed by Hulme's ideas about classicism and the religious attitude), debates about Hulme's "influence" are confusing and per-

haps distracting. Critics have tended to feel the need to take sides, either by exaggerating his significance and making grandiose claims, or by belittling his originality and relegating him to the ranks of the "minor" modernists (in the latter category we might expect also to find Allen Upward, Richard Aldington, F. S. Flint, John Rodker, and others). However, this talk of "major' and "minor" modernists is counterproductive, and the perceived need to quote authors at canonical stock-exchange prices will not only misrepresent them but also impoverish one's sense of literary history. Because he died young, there is no substantial body of mature work by which to judge Hulme, and it would therefore be wrong to expect of him what we would expect from, say, Eliot or Pound or Joyce. But there is enough of interest and originality in his work, enough "food [for] the lions," to make him an important and enduring presence in scholars' configuration of modernists. Not all of Hulme's ideas are original (but whose are? the modernists were the great borrowers, the great anthologists), but he found new ways of applying them and new contexts in which they could bear fruit. Also, he was deft at combining the ideas of others in original and foresighted ways, while retaining his own unique style of thought and writing. Moreover, since he died in 1917, his career had ended before most of the great modernist works had appeared. There is no epoch-changing single work to compare with *The Waste Land* or *Ulysses* (both published four years after his death), and no vast lifetime-straddling project to set beside *The Cantos*. But why should there be? Unlike Pound and Joyce and Eliot, Hulme was only intermittently a poet and literary theorist: he composed a few poems, but moved on to literary theory, before moving on again to art and political theory. All of these he saw as subsections or facets of one overarching cultural-philosophical endeavour; indeed, Hulme refused to examine a single art or genre or discourse in isolation, but always had to map it onto others to understand its contexts and coordinates.

Twenty-first-century students or scholars will encounter Hulme in a variety of ways. They will perhaps have come to know him from anthologies of poetry for a few well-known "imagist" poems ("Above the Dock," "The Embankment," "Autumn"); or they may have read, in some anthology of key texts on literary theory, one of his famous essays such as "Romanticism and

Classicism," "Humanism and the Religious Attitude" (also entitled "A Notebook"), or "A Lecture on Modern Poetry." They may equally, however, have encountered Hulme in anthologies of art theory or in books on cubism and vorticism, in companions to philosophy or even, less obtrusively, as the translator of important texts by Bergson or Georges Sorel. But that is far from the entire extent of his reach: he can be found in the literary essays and memoirs of a number of key figures (the essays of Eliot and Pound, memoirs of Wyndham Lewis, Jacob Epstein, Herbert Read, and Michael Roberts). He will also feature with varying degrees of prominence in histories and critical accounts of twentieth-century poetry, criticism, and art. It is important to remind the student or scholar coming to Hulme for the first time that much of his most fascinating, important, and influential work did not appear in his lifetime. Six poems appeared during his life, as did a number of reviews and philosophical essays, but several of the key critical works—those for which he will be remembered and reread—did not: "Cinders," "Notes on Language and Style," "A Lecture on Modern Poetry," "Romanticism and Classicism" (among other texts) all appeared after his death.

LIFE AND WORK

A melancholy spirit, the mind like a great desert lifeless, and the sound of march music in the street, passes like a wave over the desert, unifies it, but then goes.
("Cinders," CW, p. 22)

THOMAS Ernest Hulme was born in Staffordshire on 16 September 1883, the son of a gentleman-farmer. He attended high school in Newcastle-under-Lyme in the northwest of England, from which he gained a scholarship to study mathematics at St. John's College, Cambridge University. Intellectually impressive, he was, in disciplinary terms, no model student: reports held in the archive of his college paint a picture of a rowdy, insolent, and rebellious character, willing to fight as much with fists as with words (later in his career, he suggested that "a little personal violence" (CW, p. 260) might have a place in intellectual debate). After several disciplinary problems, Hulme was "sent down" (expelled by the university) in 1904 for causing a riot in a theater. With typical Hulmian resourcefulness, he briefly

attended London University, before sailing to Canada in 1906, where he supported himself by working as a laborer.

His visit to Canada was a formative experience, and in one of his most famous works, "A Lecture on Modern Poetry," he recalled how he was spurred into writing poetry by the Canadian landscape:

the first time I ever felt the necessity or inevitableness of verse, was in the desire to reproduce the peculiar quality of feeling which is induced by the flat spaces and wide horizons of the virgin prairie of western Canada.
("A Lecture on Modern Poetry," CW, p. 53)

It was also around this time that Hulme began "Cinders," a series of meditations on philosophy, language, and knowledge. Even in his early twenties Hulme was thinking on a grand scale, and in one of the fragments discovered after his death he wrote, "Always I desire the great canvas for my lines and gestures" (Selected Writings, p. 13; hereafter SW). Characteristic of Hulme are an assertive, often bludgeoning style of writing, strutting confidence of tone, and an extraordinarily wide range of reference. All of these can be found in his early writings.

In mid-1907 Hulme returned briefly to England, before leaving for Brussels, where he taught English as a foreign language. He was adept at turning his experiences into material for writing, and it is likely that his work on language teaching and language acquisition helped him conceive his next substantial project, "Notes on Language and Style," which date from this period. Like "Cinders," these "Notes" take the form of fragmented jottings rather than seamlessly argued disquisitions. While "Notes" reflects broadly the same worldview as "Cinders," there is increased attention to the literary, as Hulme began to turn his restless mind to specifically poetic language. "Notes" is a kind of dramatized philosophy, in which Hulme intended to place a protagonist called Aphra. The figure of Aphra is described in a poem adapted from "Notes on Language and Style," in which Hulme evokes his dream of a precise language in "The Poet":

Over a large table, smooth, he leaned in ecstasies,
In a dream.
He had been to woods, and talked and walked with
    trees.
Had left the world

And brought back round globes and stone images,
Of gems, colours, hard and definite.
With these he played, in a dream,
On the smooth table.

(*SW*, p. 4)

It is around this point that Hulme entered the London literary world, and with it the circles of modernist writers and critics. In 1908 he joined a poetry discussion group called the "Poets' Club." This club was mostly a gathering of amateurs, founded and presided over by a banker, Henry Simpson. This genteel outfit was very different from the circles Hulme would soon move in, the noisy and controversial circles of Pound and Wyndham Lewis and others, and the evidence suggests that his presence at the Poet's Club shook things up, to say the least. "A Lecture On Modern Poetry," which has become one of Hulme's most anthologized works, was given to the Poets' Club in late 1908. Hulme began by dismissing the "bluff" and "hocus-pocus" of poetic discussions and proceeded to attack not only the respectable journals and their respectable views but also the club's president:

A reviewer in the *Saturday Review* last week spoke of poetry as the means by which the soul soared into higher regions. Well, that is the kind of statement that I utterly detest. I want to speak of verse in a plain way, as I would of pigs: that is the only honest way. The President [of the Poets' Club] told us last week that poetry was akin to religion. It is nothing of the sort.

(*CW*, p. 49)

Hulme was hardly aiming to endear himself to the Poets' Club, and indeed he perceived himself as something of an outsider in the London literary world. He despised what he saw as the social snobbery and upper-class attitudes of writers such as the Bloomsbury Group (whom he especially disliked), and had little respect for the gentlemanly amateurs of poetry and criticism. He certainly shared with Eliot and Pound a distaste for the lingering vagueness of the Pre-Raphaelites, and for the grand afflatus of Victorian poetry. Beneath the strutting provocation and the polemical tone, however, lay some serious theoretical issues as Hulme argued, in his imperious and aggressive way, for a modern poetry that was "tentative and half-shy" (*CW*, p. 54), written in free verse, and no longer concerned with great subjects and the so-called eternal verities. As Pound and the imagists were

later to do, Hulme staked out the claim for a poetic language (and a language of criticism) that was clean, precise, and robust.

The Poets' club produced two anthologies, *For Christmas MDCCCCVIII* and *The Book of the Poets' Club* in January and December 1909. Of the six poems Hulme published in his lifetime, "A City Sunset" and "Autumn" appeared in the first book, and "The Embankment" and "Conversion" in the second. In January 1912 *The New Age* published "The Complete Poetical Works of T. E. Hulme" ("Autumn," "Mana Aboda," "Conversion," "Above the Dock," and "Embankment"). These were published again in October in Ezra Pound's *Ripostes*. Pound himself wrote in his brief preface to the poems: "In publishing his *Complete Poetical Works* at thirty, Mr Hulme has set an enviable example to many of his contemporaries who have had less to say" (*Collected Shorter Poems*, p. 251). For those who are used to the hard-hitting bombast and aggressive vigor of his prose, Hulme's poems can come as something of a surprise. Indeed, some critics have suggested that Hulme's poetry, while constructed around the evocative image, was nonetheless imbued with a Georgian softness of focus, and an almost Romantic dreaminess.

The Poets' Club could not contain Hulme for very long. In early 1909, he left, and gathered another group of poets around him. These poets included F. S. Flint, Edward Storer, Florence Farr, and Francis Tancred. Ezra Pound, a recent arrival in London, was introduced to the group in April. It was this group that, according to F. S. Flint, forged the principles of imagism, and in such works as "Notes on Language and Style," "Cinders," and especially "A Lecture on Modern Poetry" Hulme was setting an imagist agenda or rather—in the absence of the imagist movement— a *proto*-imagist agenda. Pound called this group the "forgotten school of 1909" (*Collected Shorter Poems*, p. 251), though it is unclear who exactly had forgotten it, since more than enough writers, including some of Pound's own fellow imagists, remembered it very well in later years. Hulme himself called it the "Secession Club." "I refrain from publishing my own *Historical Memoir* of their forerunners," Pound wrote prefacing Hulme's poems, "because Mr Hulme has threatened to print the original propaganda" (ibid., p. 251). Even as early as 1912 the principles of imagism were being fought over. In May 1915 F. S. Flint wrote "History of Imagism" for *The Egoist*, giving

Hulme pride of place, with Pound coming later, and Edward Storer and Francis Tancred making up the background. According to Flint, recalling the group's meetings, "there was a lot of talk and practice among us, Storer leading it chiefly, of what we called the Image":

In all this Hulme was ringleader. He insisted too on absolutely accurate presentation and no verbiage; and he and F. W. Tancred . . . used to spend hours each day in search for the right phrase.

(pp. 70–71)

In January 1939 Pound tried to settle the question in "This Hulme Business," an article written for *The Townsman*, in which he claimed that Ford Madox Ford had been the motivating force behind imagism. Hulme himself seemed little exercised by questions of literary precedence, and soon moved on to new subjects and new passions.

It is clear, however, that Hulme was a central player in what *became* the imagist movement, but was not himself interested enough in literary movements to seek a place either in it or in the squabbling histories that emerged soon after. Within a few months of founding the "Secession Club," he had turned his attention to larger matters. From that time on, Hulme became increasingly interested in politics, philosophy, and aesthetics. He began translating and lecturing on the work of the French philosopher Henri Bergson.

Bergson was one of the most influential philosophers of the late nineteenth and early twentieth centuries, and his work had a profound impact not only on philosophy and aesthetics but also on literary and political theory. There were Bergsonian theories of poetry, art and music, religion and psychology, and Bergsonism penetrated almost every sphere of intellectual life. Hulme's translation of Bergson's *Introduction à la métaphysique* (*Introduction to Metaphysics*) appeared in 1912, and his own work between 1909 and 1911 is heavily influenced by Bergson. Indeed Hulme's second career as a translator and facilitator is also notable: he wrote some twenty articles on Bergson and lectured on his philosophy around England, becoming one of the clearest public exponents of an important movement in early-twentieth-century thought.

Hulme also began an association with one of the most prominent periodicals on the British literary scene: *The New Age* edited by A. R. Orage. *The New Age*, like Hulme himself, was ideologically eclectic, giving space to the political Right as well as the guild socialists and the Left. It was one of the most important periodicals of its time and has a significant place in any history of modernism, specifically in the cultural politics of early modernism. Hulme had begun writing for it in 1909, when he wrote a letter in response to F. S. Flint's mocking comments on the Poets' Club, whom he had disparagingly compared with the French symbolists. Flint (who very soon became Hulme's friend and collaborator) had claimed that the Poets' Club was staid and fusty, whereas French poetic groups led bohemian café-based lifestyles in an atmosphere of intellectual excitement. For Hulme, these were nothing but vacuous clichés, and he was swift and cutting in his response:

When, oh, when, shall we finish sentimentalising about French poets in cafés! . . . now comes Mr Flint, a belated romantic born out of due time, to carry on the mythical tradition of the poètes maudits. Nurtured on Mürger, he is obsessed by the illusion that poets must be addicted to Circean excess and discoloured linen. . . . It was natural for a Frenchman to frequent cafés. It would be dangerous as well as affected for us to recite verse in a saloon bar.

("Belated Romanticism," *CW*, p. 17)

Aside from the caustic wit of his letter, Hulme showed himself to be well aware of developments in French poetry, to the extent that he engages in a debate with Flint about the development of *vers libre* (free verse), which is soon to play a major part in modernist poetry. T. S. Eliot's essay "Reflections on *vers libre*" (in *To Criticize the Critic and Other Writings*) in fact quotes Hulme and uses one of his poems as an example of "the skilful avoidance of iambic pentameter" (p. 186). In this brief extract of his letter, Hulme's attitude to what he calls "romanticism" is evident. It is an amorphous and shifting category he spends his writing life attacking. For Hulme, soon to take up the struggle against literary excess, pretension, and self-regard, the "belated romanticism" of modern poetry, modern politics, and modern philosophy must be fended off. After the publications of this letter, Hulme became a regular contributor to *The New Age*. His ideas were reaching a wide public of like and unlike-minded intellectuals, and *The New Age* published essays and articles on subjects ranging from philosophy to art history to war. After his death, it was *The New Age* which published his last writings and poetic fragments under the title "Fragments (From the Notebooks of T. E. Hulme, who was killed in the war)."

In August 1911 Hulme reviewed an important book on modern poetry. It was one of the first histories of the symbolist movement in poetry and was by the poet and critic Tancrède de Visan. It was called *L'Attitude du lyrisme contemporain* (The Attitude of Contemporary Lyricism). The book was an important one for two main reasons: first, it was written by a poet who called himself a "Bergsonian" in both poetic and critical method; and second, it analyzed recent French poetry from the point of view of the image, free verse, and the symbolist heritage of modern French poets. For a sense of Hulme's context in his dealings with French poetry, one should note that F. S. Flint's Contemporary French Poets and Ezra Pound's Approach to Paris series were published in 1912 and 1913–1914 respectively. They represent more sustained and important engagements with French poetry, to be sure, than Hulme's, but Hulme was there before them. And once there, he moved on.

As his political consciousness developed, Hulme became increasingly attracted to the reactionary French group *Action Française*, and began to shift away from Bergson. The dominant figures of *Action Française* were the literary critic Pierre Lasserre and the politician Charles Maurras. The movement's principal articles were royalism, political ultraconservatism, and anti-romanticism; its secondary values took the form of anti-Semitism (the group was founded in the wake of the Dreyfus affair), nationalism, and a respect for the church and its institutions (though not necessarily belief in God). T. S. Eliot and Irving Babbitt were among Hulme's pro-*Action Française* contemporaries and exhibited a dalliance with the authoritarian Right. Artistically, politically, philosophically, it was becoming clear that there was no ready-made category for Hulme.

In July 1912 Hulme delivered a lecture at Clifford's Inn Hall on "The New Philosophy of Art as Illustrated in Poetry." It later became the much-anthologized "Romanticism and Classicism." In this lecture on poetry and poetic theory, politics and political theory, Hulme discussed Bergsonism, *Action Française*, conservatism, original sin, and anti-romanticism. It provided a foretaste of the way his later work ranged across genres, cultures, and centuries in its voracious need to extend its frames of reference. Until now, Hulme had only targeted specific issues or individual spheres of knowledge: poetry, art, politics, and philosophy. In "A Lecture," he began to see them all as intertwined, mutually dependent and fundamentally inseparable. The "sloppiness" and excess of Romantic verse is characterized not simply as an isolated literary phenomenon but as one symptom of a post-Rousseau (Hulme was relentlessly ill-disposed toward Jean-Jacques Rousseau, the French Romantic writer and social theorist) attitude of mind whose greater manifestations embrace political philosophy (democracy), history (a belief in progress and human perfectibility) and religion (the belief that man is innately good). By now, he was extending his notion of classicism and anti-romanticism into a more all-embracing antihumanism: it was not just the "spilt religion" of romanticism he attacked, but its roots in "Renascence" humanism.

But Hulme had not forgotten his studies, and in early 1912 he decided to try again at Cambridge, this time to study philosophy. How could Cambridge refuse him? He had a letter of recommendation from the most famous philosopher of his time, Bergson himself:

It is with great pleasure that I write to certify that I consider Mr T.E. Hulme to have a mind of great value. He brings to the study of philosophical questions rare qualities of subtlety, vigor and penetration. Unless I am mistaken , he is destined to produce interesting and important works in the domain of philosophy in general, and, more particularly perhaps, in that of the philosophy of art.

(SW, p. xv)

Bergson accurately predicted Hulme's future career, and especially his role in the radical art movements of Wyndham Lewis, Jacob Epstein, and David Bomberg, though he didn't know that Hulme's theories would soon position themselves much of the time against his own. Nor was he aware that the "vigor and penetration" (though minus the subtlety) would reach outside Hulme's studies and cause him to be expelled from Cambridge a second time. After writing "obscene" letters to the daughter of a Cambridge philosophy tutor, and with the angry father's solicitors in pursuit, Hulme left the country again. He escaped to Berlin, where he spent a few months in late 1912 and early 1913.

In Berlin Hulme met the poet and fellow soldier (and fellow war death) Rupert Brooke, whose company he found congenial, but with whom he was intellectually unimpressed. Hulme also became involved in the German poetry scene, visiting the cafés and cabarets of Berlin, and writing an essay entitled "German Chronicle" for *Poetry and Drama*. "German Chronicle" is one of the earliest pieces of informed criticism of expressionist and post-expressionist poetry in Germany, wholly unspoiled by anti-German sentiment, and showing that despite his own forceful opinions Hulme could be an open-minded critic with a gift for discovering the new. In Berlin, he also attended the Berlin Aesthetic Congress, where he heard lectures by the art theorist Wilhelm Worringer, who was to influence his essays and reviews on contemporary art. Germany in the year before World War I was an exciting but also a dangerous place, but Hulme, it seems, took the opportunity to learn and discover, and with his uncanny ability to find the literary and political action and his gift for turning adversity into advantage, returned to Britain informed and intellectually stimulated. He was ready for the next phase of his career: art criticism.

Largely self-taught (for want of a stable university education), Hulme devoured art theory with as much vigor as he had philosophy, politics, and literature. Worringer's 1908 book *Abstraktion und Einfühlung* (*Abstraction and Empathy*), provided a means of relating the art of the English avant-garde to the pre-Renaissance "geometrical" art of Egyptian and Byzantine civilizations. Though Hulme emphasized that "primitive" and "modern" art were *not* the same, he claimed that they were linked by temperamental similarities. These similarities consisted in what he called the "anti-vitalist" and "anti-humanist spirit" common to both periods. By this time in his career, his terms subtly but definitively shifted: the battle was no longer between romantic and classical but between Renaissance humanism and anti-humanism. It is a telling shift: romantic and classical, as well as being temperaments, might also connote chronology; "humanist" and "anti-humanist," however, denote absolute spiritual demarcations and because they do not imply chronological development, enabled Hulme to persist in his denial of "Progress." In the months to come, Hulme wrote about cubism, vorticism, and futurism, and his art writings have become valuable documents in the history and development of modernist art.

By the beginning of World War I in 1914, Hulme had been involved with a range of literary, politi-

cal, philosophical, and artistic movements. He had written on English and European poetry, translated and interpreted continental philosophy and political theory, founded and then discarded a school of poets, and engaged in a variety of controversies and arguments. He had written for the most important periodicals and journals; had five of his poems printed as an appendix to Ezra Pound's *Ripostes* (they can still be found in an appendix to Ezra Pound's *Collected Shorter Poems*); met, talked with, or argued against some of the most important figures of his day; and developed a substantial body of work in a variety of areas. For all his intellectual labors, Hulme was also rowdy, bullying, and macho. He was a womanizer and a fighter. He was known to carry with him a knuckle-duster, commissioned by him from Henri Gaudier-Brzeska, which was more than ornamental. There is also an account of Hulme returning from a sexual encounter on the London Underground, exhausted from discomfort but proud of his prowess. In *Blasting and Bombardeering* Wyndham Lewis recalled a fight with Hulme which culminated in Lewis being suspended upside down by his turn-ups from the railings of Great Ormond Street. In the memoirs and accounts of the period, he is remembered as a difficult, entertaining, and occasionally dangerous man.

In August 1914 Hulme enlisted as a private and was sent to the trenches. His experiences of war are recounted in "Diary from the Trenches," a series of letters to his family about life at the front, which was first published in 1955 in Samuel Hynes's *Further Speculations*, a book which collected writings by Hulme that had not appeared in *Speculations*. In the "Diary" Hulme recorded:

It's curious to think of the ground between the trenches, a bank which is practically never seen by anyone in the daylight, and it is only safe to move through it at dark. It's full of dead things, dead animals here & there, dead unburied animals, skeletons of horses destroyed by shell fire. It's curious to think of it later on in the war, when it will again be seen in the daylight.

(*CW*, p. 321)

Hulme's letters from the front make disconcerting reading. He is unsentimental, without illusions, without hope, yet utterly resolved to fight. "In reality there is nothing picturesque about [war]," he wrote, "It's the most miserable existence you can conceive of" (*CW*, p. 321). Hulme did not glorify or sentimentalize the war, and his war writings are disturbing because they show a man unwilling to subscribe to any of the comforting beliefs about patriotism and glory that were encouraged at the time, or to go over into the hardened cynicism that lay at the opposite end of the spectrum. His observations from the trenches occasionally display the gifts obvious in his poems: fragmented lyricism, intense observation, and striking images:

> The only thing that makes you feel nervous is when the shells go off & you stand out revealed quite clearly as in daylight. You have then the most wonderful feeling as if you were suddenly naked in the street and didn't like it. . . . It's really like a kind of nightmare, in which you are in the middle of an enormous saucer of mud with explosions & shots going off all round the edge, a sort of fringe of palm trees made of fireworks all round it.
>
> (CW, p. 319)

In April 1915 Hulme was wounded and sent back to England. It was probably on this trip home that Ezra Pound noted down, from Hulme's hospital bed, the poem "Trenches St. Eloi" ("abbreviated from the conversation of Mr. T.E.H."):

> Over the flat slopes of St Eloi
> A wide wall of sand bags.
> Night,
> In the silence desultory men
> Pottering over small fires, cleaning their mess-tins:
> To and fro, from the lines,
> Men walk as on Picadilly,
> Making paths in the dark,
> Through scattered dead horses,
> Over a dead Belgian's belly.
> The Germans have rockets. The English have no
>   rockets.
> Behind the lines, cannon, hidden, lying back miles.
> Behind the line, chaos:
> My mind is a corridor. The minds about me are
>   corridors.
> Nothing suggests itself. There is nothing to do
>   but keep on.
>
> (SW, p. 12)

Hulme was, and enjoyed being, an outsider: a middle-class northerner expelled from Cambridge, he was a right-winger who despised inequality and admired the radical politics of both the Left and the Right (though he himself assented to the latter). He was an admirer of German culture at a time when it was safer and wiser to detest it, and he sought out continental philosophy at a time when English philosophy turned inward. He was a cosmopolitan who remained at the same time aggressively English and who always learned about what he disagreed with. He supported a war he both found futile (because there would always be more wars and more wasted lives) and necessary (because the cost of defeat was unthinkable). Hulme detested the upper class and aristocratic snobbery of the English literary world and reserved his particular spite for the Bloomsbury Group, especially Bertrand Russell, the philosopher and pacifist Hulme saw as the symbol of privileged bohemianism. In an article called "Why We Are in Favour of This War," with the superbly barbed subtitle "The Case against Another Cucumber Sandwich," Hulme accused the eminent philosopher of having the cozy idealism of those who would never had to risk anything.

Less than two years before his death, Hulme began his final work. "A Notebook" ("Humanism and the Religious Attitude") was published in *The New Age* from December 1915 to February 1916. "A Notebook" is Hulme's most wide-ranging work. In it he drew on Bergson, Wilhem Dilthey, Friedrich Nietzsche, Husserl, and Moore, Original Sin, medieval and "Renascence" civilizations, poetry, modern and ancient art, war and contemporary politics. "A Notebook" is the summation of Hulme's thought, yet for years it was misunderstood because Herbert Read's *Speculations* for the most part presents Hulme's work backward. Read printed "A Notebook"—under the title "Humanism and the Religious Attitude," for which it is best known—at the beginning of *Speculations*, while "Cinders," Hulme's earliest piece, is published at the end. This has meant that critics have for years read Hulme out of order, and that misdating of his writings has led to claims of inconsistency and self-contradiction on Hulme's part. Since Hulme's writing career was so brief, and since his reception has been so bound up with his publishing history, it is important to be aware of the development of his thought. "A Notebook" allows scholars to chart the many changes it underwent and to trace the continuities that make his work, despite its spread of reference and attitude, a unified body of intellectual endeavor.

In March 1916 Hulme received his commission in the Royal Marines Artillery. An unexpected and solitary shell-burst, like those he described to his family in "Diary from the Trenches," killed him on

28 September 1917, at Nieuport St. Vaast, Belgium. An officer who encountered him while he was serving with his battery remembered: "What a man! He'd argue a dog's hind leg off" (in Roberts, p. 37). Michael Roberts, author of the first critical-biographical book on Hulme, *T. E. Hulme* (1938), has cause to believe that toward the end of his brief life Hulme was becoming more democratic and less of a bully:

[T]hose who met Hulme when he came home say that his outlook was greatly changed: "I remember Hulme remarking that the war had made him more tolerant, and that he was growing to be more and more democratic. I thought it wiser to ask no question on this remark as the knuckleduster was near at hand."

(p. 38)

POETRY, LANGUAGE, AND CULTURAL POLITICS

"CINDERS" and "Notes on Language and Style" contain the basis of Hulme's theories of poetry and poetic language, and are written in matchingly fragmented form. They are not simply intellectual ruminations; disjointed, dark, bleakly funny, they are a kind of poetic prose of spare and uncompromising beauty.

"The covers of a book are responsible for much error," wrote Hulme in "Cinders." "They set a limit round certain convenient groups of ideas, when there are really no limits" (*CW*, p. 11). From his earliest work, Hulme sought to expose the artificiality and expediency of systems, to emphasize their source and motivation in human need rather than in any stable "Truths" proposed by those he called "capital lettrists." In the same way, Hulme argued, a railway line built through a desert is necessary for getting from A to B across unpredictable and dangerous terrain. The dangers arise when the railway is believed to be a "given," rather than a "made" necessity, and when people forget, as Hulme wrote, that "the cosmos is only *organised* in parts; the rest is cinders." Systems are no more than facets of the human need to explain; they are in us rather than outside us. The "Cinders" are the great, systemless, incoherent world upon which humankind imposes its small sense-making categories. Hulme was an analogical thinker (and fascinated by analogies in poetry and language), and many of his analogies seek to express flimsy systematic order imposed upon fundamental chaos. These analogies turn up in many guises through-

out his writings: language (one of many sense-making systems) is a "chessboard," a "gossamer web . . . woven between real things"; words and phrases are "counters" moved according to artificial rules with abstract propositional cargoes; philosophy is a "Room" sheltered from the cinders, where "certain groups of ideas [are] as huts for men to live in"; ideas about "Good" are "like oases in the desert . . . cheerful houses in the storm." The process of thought and discovery, wrote Hulme, is of abandoning the systems humans have painstakingly erected and struggling with the chaos. As he put it beautifully: "All great men, all heroes, go to the outside, away from the Room, and wrestle with the cinders" (*CW*, p. 12). Or again, in these strangely comical and poetic lines:

Man is the chaos highly organised, but liable to revert to chaos at any moment. Happiness and ecstasy at present unstable. Walking in the street, seeing pretty girls (all chaos put into the drains: not seen) and wondering what they would look like ill. Men laughing at a bar— but wait till the fundamental chaos reveals itself.

(*CW*, p. 13)

For Hulme, the aim of all thought is "to reduce the complex and inevitably disconnected world of grit and cinders to a few ideal counters." Language is one aspect of the "manufactured chessboard laid on a cinder-heap." Hulme used analogies because for him there is no unity, and permanent comprehension is impossible; it thus becomes necessary not to look for absolutes, but to piece together items of knowledge analogically. To think in terms of analogies is to work horizontally: gathering parallels which mutually confirm each other's validity, moving step-by-step. To think in terms of absolutes (God, right, and wrong) is to think vertically: checking one's ideas against "higher" truths. The mind works by analogy, imposing laws, seeking likenesses and wishing for coherence; however, it must never forget that these laws and systems are projections of itself, its desires, and its need to make sense of the world. Hulme's work is caught between a sense of possibility and excitement at this lack of unity and this absence of absolutes, and a deep need to discover or impose the necessary unity and absolutes by which to live. As his work progressed, he moved more and more toward the latter position.

Images, analogies, metaphors, and similes are central to Hulme's literary preoccupations. These "shock" the mind out of the comforting pseudo-efficiency of language and, when employed in poetry, have the capacity to disrupt the mind's mechanical automatism. If this sounds to like imagism, then one should remember that for Hulme, "the Image" is part of a general interest in figurative language as a whole. Hulme was more interested in the mental processes and perceptual operations that the image provoked or disturbed than he was in the image per se, and in this respect his attitude was Bergsonian rather than "Imagiste." In one of his most famous poems, "Autumn" (published in 1909 in the first Poets' Club anthology), a number of Hulme's characteristics are at work:

> A touch of cold in the autumn night
> I walked abroad,
> And saw the ruddy moon lean over a hedge
> Like a red-faced farmer.
> I did not stop to speak, but nodded;
> And round about were the wistful stars
> With white faces like town children.
>
> (*SW*, p. 1)

This is no great complex edifice, but nor is it the kind of taut structure one might expect in an imagist poem such as Pound's "In A Station of the Metro" or a poem by Hilda Doolittle (H. D.). The poem is deliberately informal in address, anecdotal in substance, yet closing with a modest epiphany. In his "Lecture on Modern Poetry" Hulme argued for a "tentative and half-shy" poetry, written in free verse, and no longer beholden to the great formal structures, epic scale, and breadth of address of previous poetry. In a poem like this, the mixture of whimsy and intense observation seems to locate it somewhere between the Georgians and the imagists, as if the poem had one foot in either camp. A key feature of the poem, and one which distinguishes it from the work of the imagists themselves, is its use of simile. In the poem's seven lines, all of the figurative work is done by the word "like," leaving the reader with a sense of an imposed rather than a found relation, a similarity forced rather than fused. An imagist poem (or at least one by Pound or H. D.) would shun the simile altogether as evidence of verbalism and tired rhetoric. Hulme's "Autumn" is a poem based on images by a poet who asserts the primacy of the image in poetry; but it is not necessarily an imagist poem.

Hulme believed that poetic language was a compromise for a "language of intuition which would hand over sensations bodily," and there is in Hulme's writing on or about language a profound sensuality. In "Romanticism and Classicism," he wrote:

> In prose as in algebra concrete things are embodied in signs or counters which are moved about according to rules, without being visualised at all in the process. . . . One only changes the X's and Y's back into physical things at the end of the process. Poetry, in one aspect at any rate, may be considered as an effort to avoid this characteristic of prose. It is not a counter language, but a visual concrete one. It is a compromise for a language of intuition which would hand over sensations bodily. It always endeavours to arrest you, and to make you continuously see a physical thing, to prevent you gliding through an abstract process. It chooses fresh epithets and fresh metaphors, not so much because they are new and we are tired of the old, but because the old cease to convey a physical thing and become abstract counters. . . . Images in verse are not mere decoration, but the very essence of an intuitive language.
>
> (*CW*, pp. 69–70)

Poetry is language at its peak because it strains to create "fresh epithets and fresh metaphors" in a constant fight against vagueness and abstraction. According to Hulme, metaphors or similes, images or analogies, are first used in poetry, where they are alive and strange, then descend into prose, where they become figures of speech passed over unnoticed. For Hulme, prose is a "museum," a "graveyard," for once-fresh, once-living, expressions.

Scholars can appreciate how Hulme's ideas about language appealed to so many of the poets in whose circles he moved and argued. For Hulme, analogies have brief explosive lives before "dying" and becoming "counters." As he wrote in "A Lecture on Modern Poetry": "images are born in poetry. They are used in prose, and finally die a long and lingering death in journalists' English" (*CW*, p. 55). Hulme was concerned to develop and put into practice heightened forms of language awareness. He was no expert in linguistics, and it would be vain for scholars to seek the expertise that they would find in contemporary theorists such as Ferdinand de Saussure or the Russian formalists, but scholars may put him into context with those poets and critics, in the early part of the twentiethth century, who sought both to understand the mechanics of language and to revolutionize poetic usages. In "Notes on Language and Style," Hulme wrote:

Dome of Brompton in the mist . . . And the words moved until they became a dome, a solid, separate world, a dome in mist. . . . Aphra took the words, and they grew into a round smooth pillar.

(*CW*, p. 27)

On the one hand, Hulme's prose contains fantasies of solidity and precision; on the other, it contains fantasies of a language able to convey the transitory and the fugitive, a language of intuition. On the one hand, Hulme argued for precision and exactness, for a poetry that can convey the "solid," the "physical," the "visual"; on the other, he was fascinated with capturing the "blur," the fleeting and half-perceived. Hulme, like Pound (fascinated by the "sculpture of rhyme") used models borrowed from other arts to discuss poetry, and he shared with Pound a tendency to look to sculpture and the plastic arts when he wished to describe poetic effects. This is why so many of Hulme's analogies for writing are based around sculpture, modeling, planing, carving. For Hulme, language is a "Large clumsy instrument" that does "not naturally come with meaning" (*CW*, p. 29). In "Romanticism and Classicism" he expressed this struggle with language in the following manner:

[T]he fundamental process at the back of all the arts might be represented by the following metaphor. You know what I call architect's curves—flat pieces of wood with all different kinds of curvatures. . . . I shall here have to change my metaphor a little to get the process in mind. Suppose that instead of your curved pieces of wood you have a springy piece of steel . . . the state of tension or concentration of the mind, if he is doing anything really good in this struggle against the ingrained habit of the technique, may be represented by a man employing all his fingers to bend the steel out of its own curve and into the exact curve which you want. Something different to what it would assume naturally.

(*CW*, p. 69)

Beneath the heading "Example of the Plastic Imagination" in "Notes on Language and Style" he wrote:

The two tarts walking along Picadilly on tiptoe, going home, with hat on back of head. Worry until could find exact model analogy that will reproduce the extraordinary effect they produce. . . . Could be done by artist in a blur.

(*CW*, p. 28)

With his fascination with sculpture, painting, and carving, Hulme constantly measured linguistic effects against effects achievable in other arts. Often language is found wanting (it is an old attitude, and one that produces in the straining poet ever more sophisticated effects), as here, where painting is held to be better able to convey a certain visual experience than words. Hulme was an intense observer of the bustling transformations of the modern cityscape, and one might compare—for contrast rather than similarity—some of Hulme's observations of the modernist city with Eliot's in *The Waste Land*. While some of Hulme's poems have a Georgian, bucolic air, others are very much poems of the city and of daily life in the urban bustle, allied to the precision and immediacy of the best imagist poems:

The flounced edge of a skirt
recoiling like waves off a cliff.
(*SW*, p. 15)

Again the simile is cumbersomely wedged. But in another poem, one of the most suggestive of the posthumously published fragments, is this beautiful scale- and temporality-defying vision:

Old houses were scaffolding once
and workmen whistling.
(*SW*, p. 13)

This is much more like an imagist poem than most of Hulme's. It is a simultaneous presentation of different timescales and perceptions, present and past, the whole fused together into an original and suggestive *aperçu* on city life. As Hulme wrote: "Thought is the joining together of new analogies, and so inspiration is a matter of accidentally seen analogy or unlooked-for resemblance" ("Notes on Language and Style," *CW*, p. 30). In "A Lecture on Modern Poetry" Hulme wrote:

Say the poet is moved by a certain landscape, he selects from that certain images which put into juxtaposition in separate lines serve to suggest and to evoke the state he feels. To this piling-up and juxtaposition of distinct images in different lines, one can find a fanciful analogy in music. A great revolution in music when for the melody that is one-dimensional music was substituted harmony which moves in two. Two visual images unite to form what one may call a visual chord. They unite and suggest an image which is different to both.

(*CW*, p. 54)

Why all this emphasis on the image as component of poetry and language? Hulme was deeply influenced by Bergson's theory of "successive images" and especially by the idea of images "fusing" and creating a third image. Whereas Pound, Flint, and H. D. were influenced by Japanese haiku and Eastern poetry in their imagism, Hulme came to his ideas about images through Bergson. Here perhaps also lies a major difference between Hulme and the imagists who both learn from and move away from him. For Bergson, "successive images" prevented the mind from resting in a state of abstraction or fixity, and Hulme wrote that "analogies" were designed to prevent it "gliding through an abstract process." Juxtaposition of two images produces a third substance, a kind of energetic byproduct which Hulme described as akin to "fire struck between stones" (CW, p. 26).

"A Lecture on Modern Poetry" is full of references to death, decay, and putrefaction, as Hulme attempts to clear away the accumulated detritus of poetic tradition. The poet is in a different position from the actor or the dancer, who work in arts "of which no record can be kept, and which must be repeated for each generation":

The actor has not to feel the competition of the dead as the poet has. Personally I am in favour of the complete destruction of all verse more than twenty years old. . . . Meanwhile it is necessary to realise that as poetry is immortal it is differentiated from those arts which must be repeated . . . it is only those arts whose expression is repeated every generation that have an immutable technique.

(CW, p. 50)

Scholars cannot imagine Pound or Eliot, the great reverers of tradition, advocating the destruction of poetry more than twenty years old. But Hulme is unambiguous in his diagnosis of the modern "decay" of verse:

The latter stages in the decay of an art form are very interesting and worth study because they are particularly applicable to the state of poetry at the present day. They resemble the later stages in the decay of religion when the spirit has gone and there is a meaningless reverence for formality and ritual. The carcass is dead, and the flies are upon it. Imitative poetry springs up like weeds, and women whimper and whine of you and I, alas, and roses, roses, all the way.

(CW, p. 51)

Hulme continued by suggesting that modern poetry should learn from French vers libre: "the length of the line is long and short, oscillating with the images used by the poet; it follows the contours of his thought and is free rather than regular." Pretensions to permanence—whether of poetic expression or metaphysical systems—are no longer valid, because we "no longer believe in perfection, either in verse or in thought" (CW, pp. 52–53). The old certainties, Hulme argued, are gone, and with them must go the old pretensions to permanence and stability. The "modern spirit" retreats from pretensions to absolute truth, order, or immortality:

Instead of these minute perfections of phrases and words, the tendency will be rather towards the production of a general effect. . . . We are no longer concerned that stanzas shall be shaped and polished like gems, but rather that some vague mood shall be communicated. In all the arts, we seek for the maximum of individual and personal expression, rather than for the attainment of any absolute beauty.

(CW, p. 53)

"What is this new spirit, which finds itself unable to express itself in the old metre?" wonders Hulme, "before asking Are the things that a poet wishes to say now in any way different to the things that former poets say?":

I believe that they are. The old poetry dealt essentially with big things. . . . But the modern is the exact opposite of this. . . . it has become definitely and finally introspective and deals with expression and communication of momentary phrases in the poet's mind.

(CW, p. 53)

The new verse is, for instance, meant to be "read in the study" rather than solemnly "chanted" (note here a movement from the public to the private, the collective to the individual). In "A Lecture on Modern Poetry" Hulme claimed that "to put this modern conception of the poetic spirit, this tentative and half-shy manner of looking at things, into regular metre is like putting a child into armour." Hulme's *style*—his forceful, assertive, analogical way or arguing—is somewhat at odds with the substance of his argument: the "tentative and half-shy" modern spirit which he perceived at work in poetry.

"Romanticism and Classicism" is the article in which Hulme first began to address the political implications of his ideas. Hulme stage manages a fight between two persuasions, the Romantic and the classical. Briefly stated, the modern "classical" spirit employs fancy, while the outmoded (though still influential) Romantic still clings to "Imagination." To the Romantic, "man's nature is like a well"; to the classical, it is "like a bucket." Whereas Romantic verse "seems to crystallize . . . round metaphors of flight," the classical temperament "always remembers that [man] is mixed up with earth":

even in the most imaginative flights there is always a holding back, a reservation. . . . He may jump, but he always returns back; he never flies away into circumambient gas.

(*CW*, p. 62)

Though Hulme assembled specific targets to attack—Victor Hugo, Algernon Charles Swinburne, John Ruskin—"Romanticism" is also a catch-all term for things he disliked, such as Victoriana, Pre-Raphaelitism, dilettante criticism, and "emotions . . . grouped round the word infinite." To these standards, by which "poetry that isn't damp isn't poetry at all," he opposed the "dry hardness" of the classical.

(*CW*, p. 66)

In his nonpolitical writings (though in a larger sense, all of his writings are political, or at least heavily ideological) Hulme advocates control, order-imposition, stress, and violence. The artist struggles against the natural, the ingrained habits of the material (language, steel, wood, clay). So, now, it is against the natural and ingrained tendencies of a flawed human nature that politics should fight. It must do so by making rules and laws that act both as practical guides to living and as concrete reminders of more abstract limitations. There is, in this respect, a unity in Hulme's thinking: all he has done is extend his speculations outside the realm of poetic language and into the political. It is dangerous to speculate about how Hulme's politics would have looked had he survived the war, but one footnote to *Reflections on Violence* deserves to be quoted so that the reader is not tempted to identify Hulme with the extremist politics that developed after his death:

Some of these [attacks on democratic ideology] are merely dilettante, having little sense of reality, while others are really vicious, in that they play with the idea of inequality. No theory that is not fully moved by the conception of justice asserting the equality of all men,

and which cannot offer something to all men, deserves or is likely to have a future.

(*CW*, p. 251)

Hulme's discovery of Worringer's *Abstraction and Empathy* was decisive. Worringer attempted to analyse the "attitudes of mind" that lie behind "vital" and "geometrical" art and claimed that art was symptomatic of a race's or a period's sense of its place in the world. It was wrong to see ancient stylization as a sign of lack of skill gradually progressing, through the Renaissance, toward ever greater technical sophistication. Such account helped to confirm Hulme's sense that there was no such thing as by progress, if "Progress" means betterment or improvement. He did not believe in progress but in different conditions, what he called different "attitudes of mind." In "A Notebook" Hulme suggested that modern and pre-"Renascence" art share a certain "religious attitude" which can be gauged by "a feeling for certain absolute values that are independent of vital things":

Renascence art we may call a "vital" art in that it depends on pleasure in the reproduction of human and natural forms. Byzantine art is the exact contrary of this. There is nothing vital in it; the emotion you get from it is not a pleasure in the reproduction of natural or human life. The disgust with the trivial and accidental characteristics of living shapes, the searching after and austerity, a *perfection* and rigidity that human things can never have, leads here to the use of forms which can almost be called geometrical.

(*CW*, p. 426)

The attitude behind both the modern and the ancient arts is that:

Man is subordinate to certain absolute values: there is no delight in the human form, leading to its *natural* reproduction; it is always distorted to fit into the more abstract forms which convey an intense religious emotion.

(*CW*, p. 455)

By this time, the focus of Hulme's attacks moved from literary romanticism to what he called "Humanism." The root cause of this degeneration, Hulme believed, was the Renaissance, with its emphasis on progress, personality, and perfectibility. In "A Notebook" Hulme's thought is fully worked out, and the long essay appeared in installments while he was at war. It is an intense and sweeping essay full of generalizations, forceful assertions, and clever arguments. As a result, it can be somewhat confusing, since it synthesizes all of Hulme's major and minor interests: poetry, art, politics, algebra, philosophy, language, and culture. Briefly stated, these are its tenets: the "religious attitude," which does not imply religion itself, premises Original Sin, while "humanism" premises the perfectibility of man, placing the "divine" on the human plane. According to Hulme, romanticism in literature, relativism in ethics, idealism in philosophy, and modernism in religion are all "mixed or bastard phenomena"; placing perfection in *humanity* gives rise to "that bastard thing Personality, and all the bunkum that follows from it." For Hulme:

As man is essentially bad, he can only accomplish anything of value by discipline—ethical and political. Order is thus not merely negative, but creative and liberating. Institutions are necessary.

(*CW*, p. 444)

Humanity does not "progress," it merely shifts between possible attitudes of mind, misconstruing these changes as forward motion. He described the "religious attitude" as follows:

I am not . . . concerned so much with religion, as with the attitude, the "way of thinking," the categories, from which a religion springs, and which often survive it.

(*CW*, p. 455)

Humanism, as he depicted it, is unconsciously based on a belief in continuity and progress. But Hulme asserted that there are unbridgeable chasms between the three "regions of reality": the inorganic world (mathematical and physical science), the organic world ("dealt with by biology, psychology and history"), and the "world of ethical and religious values." The middle zone, the one in which humans move, is "covered with some confused muddy substance" (an echo here of "Cinders"), while the outer zones "have an *absolute* character," and thus "the perfection of geometrical figures." Humans are so submerged in the "muddy mixed zone" that they cannot see beyond it. Romanticism and humanism take a further dangerous step: they are so immersed that they see everything *through* the mud, and believe the other zones to be like—rather than radically other than—themselves. Philosophers such as Bergson and Nietzsche, Hulme argued, were useful inasmuch as they recognized the chasm between the organic and the inorganic, but no post-Renaissance thinker had recognized the chasm between the organic and the "ethical" or "religious." Humanism forgot that "man is in no sense perfect, but a wretched creature, who can yet apprehend perfection" (*CW*, p. 455). As Hulme wrote:

Romanticism . . . confuses both human and divine things, by not clearly separating them. The main thing with which it can be reproached is that it blurs the clear outlines of human relations—whether in political thought or in the literary treatment of sex, by introducing in them, *Perfection* that properly belongs to the non-human.

(*CW*, p. 427)

Classical and romantic, humanist and antihumanist, vital and geometrical: To what extent are these terms related, to what extent are they different? Critics disagree, and while the terms are related, the frames of reference from which they are drawn are substantially different. To the classical temperament, Hulme opposed the Romantic. But when he set the religious attitude against humanism, he reached further back, through the Renaissance, through medievalism, through ancient civilizations.

Ezra Pound, in a famous definition of writers and their place in literary history, distinguished between the "symptomatic" and the "donative" writers (*Selected Prose 1909–1965*, p. 25). The symptomatic figure is a symptom of a particular time and place, the ideas and intellectual currents that intersect upon him; the donative is one who actually gives something to his epoch, by adding to or changing it. It is a crude distinction, but one that conveniently encompasses the many debates that have surrounded the life and work of T. E. Hulme. For many years, scholars tended to place Hulme in the "symptomatic category," believing him at best to be a forerunner and at worst an isolated mixer and matcher of ideas and theories "in the air" at the time. In late-twentieth-century scholarship, however, he began to seem more of a donative writer, ahead of his time, voracious in his enthusiasms, and complex in his thinking. Such categories, however, need ultimately to be moved beyond; as Hulme wrote, "All theories as toys" ("Notes on Language and Style," *CW*, p. 45).

SELECTED BIBLIOGRAPHY

I. Separate Works. *Speculations,* ed. Herbert Read (London, 1924); *Notes on Language and Style,* ed. Herbert

T. E. HULME

Read, *Criterion* 3 (July 1925); *Notes on Language and Style,* ed. Herbert Read (Seattle, 1925); Michael Roberts, *T. E. Hulme* (London, 1938) (reprinted with an introduction by Anthony Quinton [Manchester, 1982] and contains poems and "Notes on Language and Style"); *Further Speculations,* ed. Samuel Hynes (Minneapolis, 1955); Alun R. Jones, *The Life and Opinions of T. E. Hulme* (Boston, 1960) (contains a number of Hulme's works and his "Poems and Fragments" printed as appendices); *The Collected Writings of T. E. Hulme,* ed. K. E. Csengeri (Oxford, 1994) (as well as containing all but a few of Hulme's writings, this edition also contains a full bibliography of Hulme's works); *T. E. Hulme: Selected Writings,* ed. with an introduction by Patrick McGuinness (Manchester, 1998).

II. BIBLIOGRAPHY. E. Csengeri, "T. E. Hulme: An Annotated Bibliography of Writings About Him," in *English Literature in Transition* 29, no. 4 (1986). (This bibliography goes up to 1984.)

III. CRITICAL STUDIES. F. S. Flint, "History of Imagism," in *The Egoist* 2 (1 May 1915); T. S. Eliot, "A Commentary," in *The Criterion* 2, no. 7 (April 1924); Laura Riding Jackson, *Contemporaries and Snobs* (London, 1928); Ezra Pound, *Collected Shorter Poems* (New York, 1949); Murray Krieger, "The Ambiguous Anti-Romanticism of T. E. Hulme," in *ELH* 20 (December 1954); Frank Kermode, *Romantic Image* (New York, 1957); Alun R. Jones, *The Life and Opinions of T. E. Hulme* (London, 1960); T. S. Eliot, *To Criticize the Critic and Other Writings* (New York, 1965); Christopher Middleton, "Documents on Imagism from the Papers of F .S. Flint," in *The Review* 15 (April 1965); Wallace Martin, *The New Age under Orage* (Manchester, 1967); Ezra Pound, *Selected Prose 1909–1965,* ed. William Cooleson (London, 1973); Ronald Primeau, "On the Discrimination of Hulme: Towards a Theory of the 'Anti-Romantic' Romanticism of Modern Poetry," in *Journal of Modern Literature* 3, no. 5 (July 1974); Richard Cork, *Vorticism and Abstract Art in The First Machine Age* (London, 1976); Miriam Hansen, "T. E. Hulme, Mercenary of Modernism," in *ELH* 47, no. 2 (summer 1980); C. H. Sisson, *English Poetry 1900–1950: An Assessment* (London, 1981); Michael Roberts, *T. E. Hulme* (London, 1938; reprinted with an introduction by Anthony Quinton [Manchester, 1982]); Michael Levenson, *A Genealogy of Modernism* (New York, 1984); Erik Svarny, *The Men of 1914* (Milton Keynes, Pa., 1988); Donald Davie, *Articulate Energy and Purity of Diction in English Verse* (Harmondsworth, 1992); Patricia Rae, *The Practical Muse: Pragmatist Poetics in Hulme, Pound and Stevens* (Lewisburg, Pa., London, and Cranbury, N.J., 1997).

HENRY KING

(1592–1669)

Diana E. Henderson

HENRY KING'S POETRY and sermons built on the mighty foundations of the Elizabethan Renaissance and the Anglican Church. Coming of age during the reign of King James I, he benefited from his intimacy with close family friend John Donne, who became a major influence on King's writing style in both sermons and poetry. He also esteemed and on occasion echoed the classicism of Ben Jonson's verse. During his student years he would have been witness to the first publication of Jonson's and Shakespeare's plays in Folio form, and dramatic language also added to the richness of King's writing; when he wrote an elegy for Sir Walter Raleigh, he used theatrical metaphors to laud the emblematic adventurer of Elizabethan England. Throughout King's long career, he continued to play with the poetry of Shakespeare and other great writers of his age. But even strong foundations may crumble in time, and Henry King lived to see the social institutions—if not the poetry—of the world in which he grew up dashed to pieces. Thirty years after his commemoration of Raleigh, he again wrote an elegy for a victim of beheading: this time, however, it was King Charles I. Bishop Henry King desperately tried to preserve the old hierarchies of King and Church through a period of radical change and, eventually, civil war. In this struggle, he was fighting against the tide of history, and in his writing we can see the changes it effected—including radical fluctuations in his poetic tone, at times bordering on hysteria. In each era, nevertheless, King achieved some lasting artistic success. King's life, his poetry, and his sermons thus provide not only fascinating material in their own right but also a vivid way for us better to understand a time of crisis and creativity that paved the way to modernity.

COMING OF AGE

HENRY King was born in 1592 at Worminghall, near Oxford, in his grandparents' home. He was the eldest son of John King, who was at that time Archdeacon of Nottingham and Chaplain to the Archbishop of York. The Kings came from medieval yeoman stock, and were among the many families that benefited from Tudor changes in religion and governmental structures. Henry's grandfather Philip inherited estates from an uncle Robert King, who became the first Bishop of Oxford at the time of the English Reformation (1530s). Henry's father John was an extremely eminent man of the cloth who attained a coat-of-arms before he died. Those who were to put on Henry's own tomb that he "descended from the ancient Kings of Devonshire," however, clearly exaggerated the importance of his pedigree. In this attempt to elevate the family through creative genealogy, Henry King was nevertheless in good company. Elizabeth I's chief minister William Cecil concocted a connection with the Norman twelve knights who supposedly "conquered" Wales as part of William the Conqueror's invasion, with minimal evidence for the wider claim—much less for the specific presence of a Cecil in the fray. Even Shakespeare managed to acquire a coat-of-arms for his father so that he could be, at least in retrospect, "a gentleman born." This craze for heraldry was one consequence of a sixteenth-century power shift from feudal aristocracy to a wider elite, who took on the trappings of ancient privilege whenever possible. These were the rising "new men" whose primary allegiances were to the Crown and the English Church. Henry King would try to uphold these loyalties under the Stuarts, an increasingly vexed enterprise.

After Henry's birth, his father was made one of Queen Elizabeth's Royal Chaplains and rector of St. Andrew's, Holborn. John King's rise continued unchecked under the first Stuart king, James I of England and VI of Scotland. James, who came to the throne in 1603, made John King his first Royal Chaplain, and the following year appointed him Dean of Christ Church, Oxford. Not surprisingly, this was the Oxford College that Henry was to attend, after study at Lord Williams' School, Thame, and Westminster (where he was an exact contemporary of another poet/minister in the making, George Herbert). In fact, all five of Bishop King's sons attended Christ Church. Throughout his schooling, Henry was accompanied by his beloved brother John—even though John was three years younger. They took their degrees at the same time (B.A., 1611, M.A., 1614). In 1624 they became Canons of Christ Church; in 1625 they received their Bachelor of Divinity and Doctor of Divinity degrees, even preaching as part of the degree-giving ceremonies on the same day.

The year Henry got his B.A., his father became Bishop of London. He was respected enough to be appointed to guard Frances Howard, the Countess of Somerset, when she stood accused of the murder of Sir Thomas Overbury. That poisoning, which led to the most sensational of Jacobean court scandals and trials, symbolized for many the growing corruption at Court and the Stuart tendency to give too much license to royal favorites. A generation later, under James's son Charles, discontent with these practices played a major role in allowing religious and political opponents of the Crown to marshal their forces and wage war against their sovereign. Back when John King was watching over the corrupt Countess in his London home, however, Anglican churchmen still commanded the respect of most parishioners and could help preserve a sense of community, bonding commoners and king. Bishop King also helped persuade a wavering John Donne that he was adequate to the job of holy ministry, ordaining him in 1615. As a surrogate father to Donne as well as actual father to Henry, Bishop King contributed much to the written legacy of Jacobean religion.

Henry's writing career in fact began prior to his ordination. His first published poem was, fittingly, an elegy—a genre in which he became a master. He contributed to an important volume of elegies honoring Prince Henry, the eldest son of King James, who died in 1612. The Prince had been a precocious patron and figure of hope for the future; consequently, his early death prompted a huge outpouring of grief, especially from poets and more activist Protestants. Dennis Kay, who has written extensively on the poetic collection honoring the prince, notes the new particularity and importance of the elegy form in the seventeenth century, as it took over some of the functions once served by the requiem mass. Henry King found the elegy an especially congenial and flexible form. King loved elegies and wrote them from first to last: from his tribute for Prince Henry, to his salute to his dear friend Lady Katherine Cholmondeley in the 1650s, a poem in which he vows to give up writing.

In King's love of elegies, he was indeed typical of his generation: the early seventeenth century saw an increase in these poems, often appearing in honorific collections. Although G. W. Pigman shows how this coincided with a loosening of strictures against grieving as immoral or unmanly, most elegies nevertheless remained formal exercises in composition deeply enmeshed with poetic self-advancement. King's presence in volumes commemorating Prince Henry and King Gustavus Adolphus of Sweden attests to his participation in such public assertions, but his poetic emphasis differs. Although his rhetoric of loss does become typically hyperbolic upon such occasions, Pigman remarks that King often seems more comfortable with the emotions and stages of mourning than do earlier poets and contemporaries such as Ben Jonson: King neither tries to hide his sadness nor chastise its display. It seems that the potential contradiction between grief and "manliness" or uprightness, inherited from both Stoic and Christian philosophical traditions, did not disturb Henry King. Consequently, his production of twenty-four elegies does not, as one might initially surmise, signal arrested development or an inability to move on in the face of death; on the contrary, the range and texture of these poems paradoxically attests to his having found a congenial form in which to meditate on the value of human life and his position as inheritor and survivor. Nor, conversely, does this formal "fit" diminish the historical man's evident sadness at the deaths of friends and loved ones.

Although we cannot date with certainty many of King's poems, he clearly began early and was dedicated to the craft. Some elegies were published in tribute volumes (to Prince Henry, to Gustavus Adolphus), and we know when other elegized persons died (though it may be false to assume that the poem necessarily was written close to the actual death date). Based on style and biography, eventual publication order, and other data, one can risk a few generalizations. Early in his life, King not only elegizes but also follows in the great lyric tradition of love poetry, writing many variations on the theme. While the imagined situations are familiar (attempted seduction, rejected affection, parting, and so on), they are handled elegantly, often displaying particular grace, an ingenious use of metaphor, or an unexpected shift in attitude. In "Tell me no more how fair she is," a creative variation on many a song of unrequited love, the lover finally burns in his own flames, becoming a sacrificial tribute to his beloved. The sonnet "The Double Rock" conjures a vivid image of the two lovers turning at last into stone. Because her hard heart has turned to stone, he too will "petrify" by "thinking on thy hardness." King uses the final couplet, often a place for generalized platitudes, to leave us with a perverse tribute: it will amaze the world to see "How both Revenge and Sympathy consent / To make the Rocks each others Monument" (Sylvester, p. 318).

"The Surrender" likewise begins at the end of an affair:

> We that did nothing wish that Heav'n could give;
> Beyond our selves, nor did desire to live
> Beyond that wish, all these now cancell must
> As if not writ in faith, but words and dust.
>
> (Sylvester, p. 319)

That grand, ambiguous "as if" moves the poem beyond mere lamentation for the lovers' shared past to meditate upon the very grounds of oath-taking and poetry, the "words" that become partners with "dust." The poem then turns away from the typical expectation that the lady has been false, instead blaming "the Starres" that work against them. The poem ends by imagining a mutual farewell in which they will move on to love others instead—evincing an odd maturity and acceptance about the world as it is. No Romeo and Juliet here: King shifts gear by first invoking the strong passions of the metaphysical lover (much indebted to the hyperbolic, tortured wit of John Donne) and then refocusing, turning outward from the lovers to acknowledge their bounded social place. Ultimately, the speaker survives by conceding to the societal or planetary forces that block their love. The poem seems biographically evocative, hinting at King's temperament in his professional as well as amorous choices: Henry had interests in the law and writing, but adapted his desires to fit his father's prescription that his son enter the Church and follow in his footsteps.

A similar turn, looking forward beyond a dejected lover's desperation, appears in "To his inconstant Friend." Here the premise is clichéd indeed, with the usual realization of his beloved's fickle womanhood; but then the speaker shifts his stance, declaring he won't turn into the typical rejected lover-poet. Instead of being a melancholy Petrarchan or justifying universal misogyny, he instead boasts, "Mark how wise Passion and I agree," and declares he will go love again, seeking a worthier object of affection. The Petrarchan image of the voyaging ship is re-deployed here, with self-consciousness and a new pragmatism: "Thus launch I off with triumph from thy shore" (Sylvester, pp. 324–325).

Several of Henry's early poems were set to music by John Wilson, first Professor of Music at Oxford, or Henry Lawes, Gentleman of the King's Music and of the Chapel Royal. From the first, connections with University, Church, and Crown inform King's artistic life and help shape his vision of social order. Bishop John King made his son a Prebendiary of St. Paul's in 1616, and Henry was probably ordained at that time. Thus, while Henry was twenty years younger than his father's friend Donne, he was a virtual contemporary in becoming a churchman, and would remain a close friend and associate of Donne until the latter's death. Soon after his ordination, Henry was also made archdeacon of Colchester and rector of Fulham. In 1617, at the age of twenty-four, he married Anne Berkeley, age sixteen, the daughter of Robert Berkeley of Canterbury, and an heiress. As a married man, he could no longer stay at Oxford. He gave his first public sermon at Paul's Cross in London on 5 November 1617, twelve years to the day after the Gunpowder Plot (to blow up Parliament and the King) had been discovered. Paul's Cross, by St. Paul's Cathedral, was the place up-and-coming university men often debuted, though some contemporaries implied that paternal connections had more to do with Henry's appearance than did any sparks of peculiar genius.

Henry and Anne lived in a Cathedral house in St. Paul's Churchyard, near the area where booksellers plied their trade. King loved his books, and his convenient access to the sellers' stalls must have helped him keep current. Over time, Henry created quite a library, even if much of it was to be lost during the Civil War. There are also signs that Henry would have liked to have been a lawyer; he was made an honorary member of Lincoln's Inn in 1619, sponsored by his uncle Philip (Henry would serve as his executor in 1636, as he did for

Donne in 1631). But his father had determined he would be a churchman, as Henry's sermon upon his father's death makes clear: John King "dedicated (in his desire) all his Sonnes to the Ministry of this Church, and [was] by no means willing to heare of any other course (though otherwise invited by gracious offers for some of them in particular)" (*Sermons*, p. 16). Henry's writings, nevertheless, continue to show his interest in the law, using legal imagery with unusual frequency.

Bishop John King provided a very large paternal footprint; if Henry felt he lived in his father's shadow, he seems ultimately to have been content there. Part of his satisfaction must have come from their congenial community, their shared vision of an orderly universe, and their belief in the naturalness of patriarchal succession. When John King died in March of 1621, his protege John Donne followed him as Dean of St. Paul's. That same year, King gave a sermon upon his father's death that was published immediately and went through three editions as *A Sermon Preached at Pauls Crosse, the 25. Of November. 1621*. In it, he yet again showed he was the faithful son, upholding his father's vision of hierarchy and Anglican order:

There is nothing so much sets out the Universe as *Order,* to see how subordinate causes depend of their Superiours, and this sublunary Globe of the Celestiall. Were not this method, what could hinder a second Chaos? For in the Worlds beginning all lay in one common wombe of darkenes. It was onely order and that Method God's *fiat* brought a long, which gave distinction and visibility to things. . . . Should all have been equall, what had man beene better then the beasts, save only his shape? . . . Since, then, it is established *per leges universitatis*, by the law of God and Nations, that the Lord must rule and the servant obey, it were preposterous, nay monstrous, that the *servant should bee greater then his Lord* . . . To serve is no base office, nor is slavery the badge of servants, but obedience: *Servants, obey your Masters.*

(*Sermons*, p. 70)

Despite plots and potentially unsettling astronomical discoveries, King's celestial and sublunary spheres remain firmly in their traditional places: at this point in his life the prospect of chaos and general upheaval was a rhetorical matter. Even when social upheavals took place later in his life, however, these words and ideas remained his foundation. In his relations both filial and affiliational, King epitomizes the ideal subject within Stuart ideology: he is a loyal follower of the King his father—both the biological and the royal one.

Henry King had in fact been instructed by King James to preach on this occasion, in defense of his father's Anglican Protestantism. As a rather backhanded form of compliment to the dead Bishop, it seems that Roman Catholics were claiming him for their own, reporting that he had a deathbed conversion. When this claim was printed in *The English Protestant's Plea*, King James felt a rebuttal was required, and the Bishop's own son was the one to do it. Apparently the slander had aimed at the whole family, for King wrote to refute "those calumnious tongues who gave out my Revolt, also as well as my Father's," and likewise to defend his brother John (*Sermons*, p. 82). The sermon fulfilled its mission: within four months, the third edition was printed, including a retraction by the libeler. Order and reputation were restored.

MATURITY AND LOSS

WITH the passing of his father, King seems only to have become closer to John Donne, his senior by twenty years. One can clearly discern the impact of Donne's poetry in King's "The Legacy." As Richard Sylvester has rightly remarked, King "shares something of Donne's fascination with the macabre horrors of the grave" (p. xxxi). First describing the physical decay to come after he dies, King then inserts a reference to figurative rather than literal cremation: using a typically flamboyant monosyllabic-against-polysyllabic rhyme to stress the point, he prays "may kind fate / . . . incinerate" the worst acts of his life. Thus, while having conjured in our imaginations a mouldering dead body that is difficult to forget, the poet forces us to move beyond the physical, transferring attention to the state of his soul. Unlike Donne, however, he tends to balance his vivid metaphysical wit with something more like Jonsonian classicism. For example, after meditating in detail upon rotting grave clothes, he steps back with a little aphorism: "He shall in story fill a glorious room / Whose ashes and whose sins sleep in one Tomb." The pithy balance of this couplet foreshadows Restoration wit, and will reappear in some of King's later sermons. Rather than remain immersed in the quirky or bizarre, as did some followers of Donne, King finds a way to include but not succumb to metaphysical extravagance. Equally notable, within this genre of metaphysical love poetry, is the reappearance of King's characteristic pragmatism. For "The Legacy" is addressed to his wife, and imagines her outliving him; rather than suggesting she find consolation by looking forward to their heavenly reunion, he instead argues that she should move on to a second husband:

> For (witness all things good) I would not have
> Thy Youth and Beauty married to my grave,
> 'Twould shew thou didst repent the style of wife
> Should'st thou relapse into a single life.
> (Sylvester, p. 322)

Only barbarians weep to death at their husbands' monuments, he elaborates, whereas she should repair her loss. How different from the norms of romantic young love! And how different was to be his and his wife's actual fate, as she died (having given birth to five children) at age twenty-three leaving him to grieve, not remarry—and write a magnificent, devastated poem that belies the ease of moving on as he advises in "The Legacy."

Perhaps it was his ability to see women as different from one another (some fickle, some faithful, rather than all standing for a single Platonic beloved) that begins to explain how Henry King, the conventional good son, could write one of the least conventional elegies of his age—one honoring a woman, and exclusively because of a private, domestic bond. That poem is known as "The Exequy," composed upon the death of Anne Berkeley King in January 1624 ("exequy" means the funeral ceremony or last rites; the first edition's actual title is "An Exequy To his Matchlesse never to be forgotten Friend"). During the last century, in great measure because of the advocacy of T. S. Eliot, this has become the most respected and anthologized of King's poems—and for good reason. Written in tetrameter couplets, it succeeds in adapting the elegy to honor a surprisingly unusual subject: a wife. Moreover, Ronald Berman observes, "Unlike the four other great elegies of our language, by Milton, Gray, Shelley, and Tennyson, this poem contains no elements of the pastoral, no sublimated wish for fame, no querying of the universal plan" (pp. 116–117). G. W. Pigman, describing new seventeenth-century attitudes to mourning which allowed the expression of grief rather than just encomia praising the dead, nevertheless find that in this poem, "King achieves an intimacy of address and a simple expression of

affection and sorrow that is unmatched in the period, although approached by passages in Milton" (p. 4; see also pp. 95–103).

Although many admirers place "The Exequy" in a class by itself, some have found points of resemblance with King's other elegies. Richard Sylvester, for example, notes that most of King's elegies are written in "freely moving and versatile couplets. King is a great poet of separation and parting; he writes of love affairs at the moment when they dissolve ('The Surrender,' 'The Retreat,' 'The Legacy') with a tough poise" (p. xxxi). One could argue that the same "tough poise" also appears in "The Exequy," where the very pulse of life in the speaker's veins is transformed into a soft drum accompanying him in his steady march toward death (and hence to eventual reunion with the dead beloved). But the poem is also heartbreaking in a way that distinguishes it from those earlier lyrics. There will be no second loves here. As Eliot himself remarked of these lines, which he found "greater than Marvell," they convey "that effect of terror which is several times attained by one of Bishop King's admirers, Edgar Poe" (*Selected Essays*, pp. 284/244). This is a poem in which "a human emotion is concentrated and fixed" (Chapbook, April 1921). Indeed, Eliot was so taken with it that Ezra Pound only with difficulty discouraged him from including his own "Exequy" in *The Waste Land*.

The tradition of writing elegies for other writers has had the effect of making most critics doubt the "authentic" quality of grief expressed—quite legitimately in many cases. But King's use of elegy works against overgeneralization. Similarly, many have seen "occasional verse" as a sign of artifice, especially in the few cases involving female subjects. Melissa Zeiger, for example, claims that "Only a few elegies for women are undertaken previously to [Thomas] Hardy's sequence—by Spenser, Donne, Milton, Henry King, Pope—and many of these are so clearly occasional as to preclude engagement with this ambitious genre" (pp. 43–44). King again seems an exception to the rule. In fact, "The Exequy" more closely resembles the mood and intensity of Jacobean tragedy than it does most other elegies: it stresses bodily decay and subjective loss, present darkness and the drumbeat of mortality, and the inadequacy of compensation for personal loss on this earth. Given King's frequent Shakespearean echoes, it is not far-fetched to hear Othello's lamentation for the dead Desdemona ("Methinks it should be now a huge eclipse / Of sun and moon, and that th'affrighted globe / Did yawn at alteration," 5.2.97–99) behind King's lines:

> And 'twixt me and my Soule's deare wish
> The Earth now interposed is,
> Which such a straunge Ecclipse doth make
> As ne're was read in Almanake.
> (Crum, p. 69)

Recognizing that this eclipse will outlast "the longest date," he can only look forward to the Last Judgment, the day

> Which shall the Earth to cinders doome,
> And a fierce Feaver must calcine
> The Body of this World, like Thine.
> (Crum, p. 70)

Unlike Othello, King is obviously not responsible for Anne's death in any direct sense: but it seems that no vocabulary, no vision except that of tragedy is sufficient for him to capture his grief in poetic form.

The future imaginings in the lines above signal a shift in the speaker's subjective experience of time as contrasted with the poem's beginning. At that point, time "creepes about" "lazily" and even goes "Backward and most praeposterous" for him—since he now can only dwell with his "dear friend" by thinking himself back into the past (Crum, p. 69). But if the poem thereby follows elegaic tradition (that is, by demonstrating a change in the speaker's attitude through the process of writing about the dead), the alteration hardly leads to simple displacement of grief or appreciation of the lost person. Unlike Milton's speaker at the end of his magnificent elegy *Lycidas*, King's first-person speaker cannot move on to "pastures new." King the sermonizer often emphasizes the consolation of the afterlife for Christians, but those who would find such a "solution" here must read his lines very flatly indeed. The conventional appeal to a supernatural frame to help him transcend his pain appears only in its most apocalyptic form, and even then it is the resurrection of the body that is emphasized:

> . . . Our Bodyes shall aspire
> To our Soules' blisse: Then wee shall rise,
> And view our selves with cleerer eyes
> In that calme Region, where no Night

Can hide us from each other's sight.
(Crum, p. 70)

Despite the allusion here to St. Paul's epistle (and hence to spiritual vision distinct from our mortal sight "through a glass darkly"), King's lines do not let us forget the body. His persistent attention to visual recovery serves less to sublimate desire than to lead us back to the poignant pain of his present loss and the distance between the two ex-lovers' bodies. Indeed, the next section of the poem turns back from heaven to her earthbound body, lent first to him and now to his rival earth whom he addresses directly and bitterly: "Meane time, thou hast Hir Earth: Much good / May my harme doe thee" (Crum, p. 70). He imagines the earth forced to account for her body "by weight," "Each Grane and Atome of this Dust" (Crum, p. 70). Again recalling Othello, King imagines his "Bride is lay'd" in a bed, black-curtained:

> Sleep on (my Love!) in thy cold bed
> Never to be disquieted.
> My last Good-night!
> (Crum, pp. 70–71)

But the poet cannot let go. Rather than relinquish her to God, he now anticipates their bodily "remarriage" as dust when he dies. Whereas before he looked beyond the apocalypse to imagine their mutual awakening, he now sounds more like Charlotte Brontë's Heathcliff in *Wuthering Heights*, digging to create a joint coffin with Catherine Earnshaw:

> Thou wilt not wake
> Till I Thy Fate shall overtake:
> Till age, or grief, or sicknes must
> Marry my Body to that Dust
> It so much loves; and fill the roome
> My heart keepes empty in Thy Tomb.
> Stay for mee there: I will not faile
> To meet Thee in that hollow Vale.
> (Crum, p. 71)

The final section of the poem, like its beginning, is addressed to his dead beloved: not to Time, Earth, God, or other living men, but to his wife. The wheel has come full circle, and in doing so, defies conventional consolation. The image of a journey informs this poem's literal progress toward the grave and its figurative movement beyond. This voyage, however, is not one of discovery or conquest but of recovery, and delayed recovery at that. If the journey itself is "life," it has been hollowed of meaning:

> At Night when I betake to rest,
> Next Morne I rise neerer my West
> Of Life, almost by eight Howres' sayle,
> Then when Sleep breath'd his drowsy gale.
> (Crum, p. 71)

Truly, it seems that the speaker continues to "Languish out, not Live the Day" (Crum, p. 69). Even the poet's pulse, the index of verse's rhythm and the biological sign of life itself, becomes instead the symbol of inexorable mortality, with the couple's reunion in death the sole and promised end.

> But hark! My Pulse, like a soft Drum
> Beates my Approach, Tells Thee I come;
> And slowe howe're my Marches bee,
> I shall at last sitt downe by Thee.
> The thought of this bids mee goe on,
> And wait my dissolution
> With Hope and Comfort.
> (Crum, p. 71)

If Othello was guilty of murder, this speaker is guilty only of the "crime" of his living "Divided, with but half a Heart"—but it is sufficient to make life empty. He will be remedied only with death, when "wee shall Meet and Never part" (Crum, p. 72). Thus with the heart and body remaining focal, his words still trying to cross the divide between life and death, the poem ends.

Anne left behind not only her husband but three living sons, two of whom (John and Henry) survived to adulthood. Their father went on soon after to receive his Divinity degrees, and survived the plague of 1625 (the worst of the century prior to the Great Plague of 1665). The marriage of the new King, James's surviving son Charles I, with Henrietta Maria of France was delayed as a result of the plague, finally taking place in February 1626. Henry King gave a sermon at Whitehall Palace the following month that according to Mary Hobbs, is "overlaid with an elegaic melancholy, which anticipates the harmonies of Sir Thomas Browne" (Sermons, p. 18). King's personal losses of father and wife were enlarged and made general by the recent plague and King James's death. Although Henry King does not seem to have written much poetry during this period, he did produce memorable sermons with artful imagery, as when he calls servants of Christ "Incarnate Starres" (Sermons, p. 145). His sermons also display increasing concern for certain widespread social injustices, especially the imprisonment of debtors.

In 1628 a collection of eleven of King's sermons was published, under the title An Exposition upon the Lord's Prayer. It was revised and reprinted in 1634 and went through a second printing that same year. Ten other sermons survive as well. Mary Hobbs, the premier student of King's sermons, emphasizes both the quality of their prose and their value as representative of the "true 'middle 'of the seventeenth-century Church of England (however that broad middle ground may have moved over the period)" (Sermons, p. 9). King's contemporary Thomas Fuller optimistically thought the sermons in An Exposition "remaining fresh in the minds of his Auditors will report him to all posterity" (ibid.); instead, they have for the most part been forgotten, overshadowed by the towering talents of Donne and Lancelot Andrewes, among others. King's strength as a preacher lay less in his distinctiveness than in his ability to synthesize elegantly and elaborately. He learned much from the achievement of the great Elizabethan synthesizer, Richard Hooker, whose Of the Laws of Ecclesiastical Polity gave intellectual weight to the expedience of the Anglican "middle way." King also worked closely with Donne, often preaching on the same texts from scripture and sharing his imagery. Not that this was necessarily a one-way relationship of borrowing, despite Donne's greater fame and legacy: given King's more extensive citation of sources, one might even surmise that the older man was at times relying on the younger friend's research! King's sermons exemplify the high Renaissance idea of syncretism, citing Greek and Latin classical poets as well as Biblical scripture, and taking delight in invoking familiar texts. As Hobbs observes, they display "grace of structure, sweetness of sound, elegaic intensity of mood, and occasional dry wit" (Sermons, p. 9).

On 31 March 1631, John Donne died. Near the end of his final sickness, he had a painting done of himself in his shroud, as if dead and awaiting the Second Coming of Christ. According to Izaak Walton's The Life of Dr. John Donne, he kept that picture by his bedside, "where it continued and became his hourly object till his death and was then given to his dearest friend and executor Dr.

Henry King, then chief residentiary of St. Paul's, who caused him to be thus carved in one entire piece of white marble, as it now stands in that church" (Hollander and Kermode, p. 1017). Henry King served as Donne's executor, and seems to have inherited some of the Dean's library. King wrote an elegy in honor of his friend that first appeared in the 1632 edition of Donne's sermon "Death's Duel," and then appeared among the elegies introducing the 1633 edition of *Poems by J. D.* Although many of Donne's poems had circulated in manuscript for thirty years, this was the first published edition of his poetic works. King most likely edited Donne's poems and certainly saw them through publication.

King's elegy, "To the Memorie of My Ever Desired Friend Dr. Donne," again illustrates how masterfully the poet includes his own distinctive twists within the elegy form. It beautifully contrasts elaborate and simple language, a technique perhaps learned from the stage's use of short lines in conversations; one thinks of the juxtaposition of large, magnificent speeches with understated, monosyllabic lines at key moments in Shakespeare (Prince Hal's "I do, I will" to Falstaff's effusions; Cordelia's "no cause, no cause" to Lear's apology). Thus, after much eloquent lament, wishing Donne had written his own epitaph and thus spared him this inferior labor, King begins a new poetic paragraph with a striking yet simple shift of tone that plays against elegy's formalities:

> Thou, like the dying Swann, didst lately sing
> Thy mournfull Dirge in audience of the King; . . .
> O! hadst thou in an Elegiack Knell
> Rung out unto the world thine owne Farwell,
> And in thy high victorious Numbers beat
> The solemne measure of thy griev'd Retreat;
> Thou mightst the Poet's service now have mist
> As well, as then Thou didst prevent the Priest,
> And never to the World beholden bee
> So much, as for an Epitaph for Thee.
>   I doe not like the Office.
>
> (Crum, pp. 76, 77)

But he must honor the greater poet and thus continues, though he finds it unfit that

> Thou, who didst lend our Age such summes of witt,
> Shouldst now re-borrow from her bankrupt Mine
> That Ore to bury Thee, which once was Thine.
>
> (Crum, p. 77)

The image carries forward an elaborate economic metaphor in which Donne was the husband of now-widowed "invention," the source of poetic excellence. Donne set such a high standard that nobody alive now can

> keep her at Thy rate,
> Though he the Indyes for her dowre Estate.
> Or else that awfull fire, which once did burne
> In thy cleare braine, now fall'n into thy Urne
> Lives there to fright rude Empericks from thence,
> Which might profane thee by their Ignorance.
>
> (Crum, p. 76)

Invoking the Indies first to conjure the idea of vast distance (since India used to be thought, quite literally, "the ends of the earth"), he shifts to the more contemporary focus of cultural distinction between [European] Christian knowledge and [Indian] "rude" "ignorance." But in this case—and despite writing at the moment of expanded English efforts to compete in East Indian colonialization—the cultural contrast then disappears, as if to acknowledge the universality of human inadequacy now that Donne has departed. Thus,

> Who ever writes of Thee, and in a Stile
> Unworthy such a Theame, does but revile
> Thy pretious Dust, and wake a Learned Spiritt
> Which may revenge his rapes upon thy meritt.
>
> (Crum, p. 76)

Ultimately, then, the speaker must not move beyond his subject, as many elegists try to do: he cannot put the dead to sleep and proceed to overgo the dead's poetic accomplishment with his own. Instead, along with others, "Committ wee then Thee to Thyself" and "thus to Thy owne Fame / Leave Thee Executor." He will be merely the guardian of the ashes.

> So Jewellers no Art, or Metall trust
> To forme the Diamond, but the Diamonds Dust.
>
> (Crum, p. 77)

Ashes to ashes, and dust to dust: like recycled Donne, rather than "outdoing Donne," he concludes.

King's elegy for Donne belies attempts, such as Richard Sylvester's, to categorize King among "social poets" and "secular metaphysicals" rather than "more strictly religious poets of the Donne tradition" (p. xxii). This difficulty in categorization is understandable (and to give Sylvester credit, he makes his uneasiness apparent), but invoking a modern division between secular and religious poetry is simply misleading: one can hardly imagine a more artful melding of religious and "societal" imagery than appears in King's elegies, shifting between types of dust and ash, aesthetic and religious profanation, and in many instances striving to convey a vision of the world that melds social order and consolation with religious order.

For those living in Stuart London, the interconnections among poets would have been more evident than any clear and consistent distinction between poetic schools. Ben Jonson teasingly averred he would have had Donne "hung" for the breaking of meter—that is, for writing in rough, irregular rhythms—but he shared with Dean Donne a respect for wit, artistry, and the cosmic and monarchic order. These were also fundamental tenets for Henry King. King honored Jonson as well as Donne with an elegy upon his death, in August of 1937. "To my dead friend Ben: Johnson" appeared with thirty-two other tributes in *Jonsonus Virbius* (1638). And as before, King does not attempt to supersede the early writer but to venerate him:

> What ends soever others quills invite,
> I can protest, it was no itch to write,
> Nor any vain ambition to be read,
> But meerly Love and Justice to the dead
> Which rais'd my fameless Muse;
> (Sylvester, pp. 329–330)

Of course, poets have to say such things—but King says them so consistently and emphatically that they carry the force of sincerity. For the discerning King, Jonson was the source of "The purest streams of language which can flow" (p. 330). He praises Jonson in terms that big Ben would have appreciated, most notably lauding his refinement of English. King also desires that his contemporaries learn from the master, asking those poets who study foreign tongues not to despise their own language "Untill by studying *Johnson* they have known / The height and strength and plenty of their own" (p. 330). Then they will realize that their own tongue is as good or better than the best of the continental languages. The achievement of the English Renaissance, its elevation of the vernacular to produce great poetry, can now be celebrated—even if, his

poem implies, not all his contemporaries yet acknowledge it. King does: and the clarity and artful simplicity of that couplet attest that he has learned Ben's lesson well.

Writing in praise of George Sandys' 1638 *Paraphrase upon the Divine Poems,* King shows further credentials as a literary critic as well as practitioner. He comments on various bad verse translations of the psalms and recognizes the need to update scripture to fit the times. He again concludes that English writers, beneficiaries of the generation that went before, are better stylists now: "And wheresoer the subjects best, the sense / Is better'd by the speakers eloquence." Here too, King interweaves issues religious and artistic—not to mention autobiographical. Sandys was, like King, the son of a bishop, and so the poet celebrates the

> . . . naturall joy I must impute
> To our Tribes honour, what by you is done
> Worthy the title of a *Prelates* son.
> (Sylvester, p. 335)

To be a good son, and especially to be the good son of a prelate, is for Henry King a worthy title indeed. Veneration for his elders—poetic, political, and personal—is a hallmark of his writing throughout his first forty years, and no doubt he wished such orderly succession to be part of his legacy. He cites the Sandys brothers (Edwin wrote a *View or Survey of the State of Religion in the Western Parts of the World*) as examples of the good "fruits" that derive from the marriage of priests, an obvious jab at the Roman Church's practice. He also regards the wide-ranging journeys of George and Edwin Sandys as signs of orderly progress in time, with new devotion accompanying new knowledge. His allusions to the scientific or geographical changes in these years, like his references to cosmic and artistic order, exude confidence and a sense of collective building, not self-doubt or anxiety. To be so assured at the time he was writing these lines, however, was no longer necessarily an indication of Renaissance wisdom and energy: viewed with historical hindsight, it begins to look like willful, conservative blindness. For not only new theories and information were rocking the foundations of thought in Stuart England; unwise governance was also moving the country to the brink of Civil War.

These were the years when Archbishop Laud rose to power, forcing the Church of England away from moderate Calvinism toward what his opponents somewhat misleadingly called Arminianism. Arminian theology rejected predestination in favor of a view in which God's sovereignty was compatible with free will, but what opponents of Laud found truly objectionable were his views on the importance of the episcopy and Church discipline. To extreme Protestants, Laud's Church looked virtually indistinguishable from Catholicism. He built rails in front of altars—to keep children and dogs away, but also reestablishing a strict separation between the minister and his flock. He purged those with strong Calvinist dispositions from the Church leadership. And he emphasized the kinds of ritual, display, and ceremony that Puritans found repugnant and idolatrous.

During the years of Laud's Archbishopric, Henry King's doctrinal positions shifted somewhat of necessity. He had never had much sympathy with extreme Puritanism: in his 1621 sermon, he attacked unlettered preachers "of both sexes" who "torment a Text," and wryly recommended "A little lesse preaching, and some more praying would do well" (*Sermons*, p. 17). He also believed in a great deal of ministerial authority and upheld practices that at first sound fairly close to those of Roman Catholicism: "We refuse not private confession made to God, nay, sometimes, a *private Confession* to our ghostly Father they Minister, who hath authoritie to pronounce an *Absolution*" (*Sermons*, p. 88). But then he elaborates:

Yet we will not loose or betray our Freedome so much as to do that Act by *Constraint* which ought to be as *free and voluntary* as David's resolution in this place: *I said, I will confesse.* We have no reason to stand to the courtesie of Rome for that Pardon which Christ hath freely given us. . . . We have no cause but to be very well assured that we may be saved without *Auricular Confession*; since in that sacred Booke which, we beleeve, containes all that may conduce to our salvation, we finde no tracke or mention of it.

(*Sermons*, p. 88)

Clearly, King's theology was more in line with mainstream Calvinist thinking than was Laud's. Henry King was not of the Archbishop's camp, nor did he receive advancement until Laud's own position had become sufficiently imperiled that he found it necessary to make wider alliances. From the time of Laud's elevation to Archibishop in 1633, King did not sit on the Church Court of High Commission, which was one of Laud's major power bases. Moreover, no sermons by King were printed during that decade.

On 27 March 1640, however, the fifteenth anniversary of King Charles's accession, King did give a sermon at Paul's Cross. By then, Laud had forced most Calvinist reformers into the opposition Parliamentary camp, and one surmises that the Archbishop needed every churchman who held Henry King's theological "middle position" on his side. What balanced King's disposition toward many aspects of Calvinism was his adamant monarchism. His March sermon, for example, anticipated Laud's notorious Canons (issued that May) "Concerning the regal power." Henry King argued for the Divine Right of Kings as the form of rule closest to God's pattern of natural order, and argued against Parliament's claim that the King was subject to them financially and judicially (*Sermons*, p. 21). While citing Old Testament scriptures and Revelations (texts popular with Puritans), King honored the character of King Charles extravagantly—and, as Mary Hobbs notes, did so "nine years before such an attitude became general among Royalists in the wake of the King's execution" (*Sermons*, p. 22). Even so, Laud's days were numbered, and by December of that year, he was imprisoned in the Tower of London. Before the decade was out, King Charles would follow him to the executioner's block.

THE CIVIL WAR YEARS

WHAT history has called the English Civil War, or even the English Revolution, Henry King would have viewed as a foul Rebellion, treacherous to the monarch and his land. The beheading of Charles shattered his faith in his countrymen. Yet years before the war, Anglican factionalism and financial arrogance had already exacted their toll upon the country. Ironically, Henry King's promotions within the Church coincided with the Church's own undoing: in 1639, while King Charles was engaged in his unwise "Bishops' War" against Scots Presbyterianism, Henry King was made Dean of Rochester Cathedral. And the year he was made Bishop of Chichester, 1642, marked the beginning of the actual fighting within England. The very day before he became a bishop, a Parliamentary bill deprived bishops of their place in the House of Lords. Moreover a few months later, during the autumn of 1642, Chichester fell to Parliamentary forces led by Colonel

William Waller after three days of bombardment. Henry King and his family fled first to Petworth, where he was rector; then to Shere, near Guildford; and by 1646, to his nephew's home in Blakesware, Hertfordshire. King was one of fourteen bishops harshly sequestered in March 1643, losing his palace, goods, book, and papers as well as his income. Thus he came to rely upon his friends and relations, even as he attempted to keep his finances afloat by making small loans and commissions. These were difficult years for the displaced bishop.

The move from Shere was in fact impelled not by the war but by family embarrassment: his son John seduced the youngest daughter of a family friend, the mathematician William Oughtred, Rector of Albany. Although at first upset, Henry King eventually decided to defend his son, for reasons that remain mysterious (unless we again consider his lifelong loyalty to the father-son bond). In any event, Oughtred drew up a Chancery petition in 1646, documenting the scandalous incident. Nor did Henry's forced journeying stop that year: later, he stayed with his sisters Anne and Dorothy, his brother Philip, and Dorothy's husband, Sir Richard Hubert at Lady Salter's, near Eton. Lady Salter was the niece of Bishop Brian Duppa, whom King would eulogize in a funeral sermon; this domestic enclave would have been an attempt to sustain a high Anglican, Royalist community in hostile times. For nearly twenty years, King lived in danger and impoverished, and the threats not only to his living but to his very structures of belief left very deep scars. His poetry and late sermons are both marked by the years of struggle, disillusionment, and anger.

The public execution of Charles I on 30 January 1649 was, for King, the last straw. He was living within six miles of Windsor when Charles's body was brought there in Feburary for burial. He refers to this event in the elegy "From my sad Retirement" dated 11 March 1649, published anonymously in 1659 on the eve of Charles II's assumption of the throne. What a startling contrast it is to read King's elegies for Charles I, brimming with rage and indignation, after reading the elegies and love poems of his youth! Never were the emotional costs of war made more apparent. "The Exequy" and the Civil War poems belong to entirely different worlds: one of intimate, large-minded contemplation, the other of polemical, political vitriol. The poetic line itself changes:

from light, artfully enjambed tetrameter to mournful and fitfully bombastic pentameter. While King's personal grief at Anne's death overflowed the measure of elegiac tradition, the elegies for his absolute monarch overflow *all* forms of measure-of number, length, even title—absolutely. The more than 240 lines of "A Deepe Groane, fetch'd at the Funerall of that incomparable and Glorious Monarch, Charles the First, King of Great Britaine, France, and Ireland,&c." (with the further elaboration: "On whose Sacred Person was acted that execrable, horrid & prodigious Murther, by a trayterous Crew and bloudy Combination at Westminster, January the 30.1648") were not enough. They were followed by the 520 lines of "An Elegy upon the most Incomparable King Charls the First"—King's longest poem, by some 200 lines. The loss of Anne led King to adapt the elegy in a distinctively uxorious, poignant way; the loss of his king left the poet railing against the loss of all order, all harmony, all value. His very core of subjectivity was imperiled.

The "Deepe Groane" (published soon after the event in 1649) begins by itself recognizing this greater, ultimate grief:

> When Griefe bleeds inward, not to sense, 'tis deep;
> W'have lost so much, that 'twere a sin to weep.
> The wretched Bankrupt counts not up his summes
> When his inevitable ruine comes.
> Our losse is finite when we can compute;
> But that strikes speechless, which is past recruit.
> (Crum, p. 110)

Like an earthquake or flood, this unnatural disaster engulfs and subsumes all other losses: "our Ruines are cast up, and sped / In that black Totall—Charles is Murthered" (Crum, p. 111). The act is fatal for people and church alike, as "Our Lives, Estates, Lawes, and Religion, All / Lye crush'd, and gasping at this dismall fall" (ibid.). Like the word "Murthered"—which the meter requires be pronounced as three syllables—the line break at "All" protracts and emphasizes loss. No longer can verse harmonize grief into a beautiful work of art. Now that the symbolic body of the Logos is gone, "all our words be but articulate groanes" (ibid.). Or rather, savage lamentation, as the speaker desperately redirects his attention toward the murderers' action, and thus repeatedly loses sight of his supposed monarchic subject. In the attempt to prove that King Charles's execution was "Above the scale of Crimes; Treason sub-lim'ed," the poem disintegrates into hyperpunctuated name-calling:

> Spirit-of-witch-craft! quintessential guilt!
> Hel's Pyramid! another Babell built!
> Monstrous in bulke! above our Fancies' span!
> A Behemoth! a Crime Leviathan!
>
> (Crum, p. 112)

Eventually (after a stream of rhetorical questions that follow these exclamations) the poet recovers to the point of imagining divine justice to come. Even here, though, the vision is presented as only hypothetical and includes a reminder of its bad timing for those trapped on earth at present: "Yet if just Providence reprieve the Fate, / The Judgement will be deeper, *though't be late*" (Crum, p. 114; emphasis added).

Only after producing this weak echo of a consoling universal order, more than halfway through the poem, can King turn to the elegiac task of memorializing Charles himself. As he recalls Charles's incomparable "Sweetnesse" in suffering, however, it is still the outrageous upheaval of hierarchy that dominates in King's imagination. His horror at a world turned upside down helps explain an otherwise strange association of this Christian king with a Turkish despot:

> Thus basely to be Dungeon'd, would enrage
> Great Bajazeth beyond an Iron Cage.
> That deep indignity might yet have layne
> Something the lighter from a Tamerlaine.
>
> (Crum, p. 114)

Whether this risky cross-cultural comparison works remains debatable. For one thing, it recalls another Renaissance play, Marlowe's *Tamburlaine*, which represented Bajazeth's humiliation but hardly portrayed him as heroic. (He "brains himself" against the iron bars of his cage, in what is certainly a vivid and horrific moment, but one more grotesque than magnificent.) More immediately, the allusion recalls the (not ungrounded) Parliamentary claim that Charles ruled despotically, a claim even included parenthetically within the poem itself: "(though blackmouth'd Miscreants engrave / No Epitaph, but Tyrant, on Thy Grave)" (Crum, p. 116). King's belief in the righteous traditional order is so complete that he assumes the Parliamentarians' assertion will appear patently preposterous. By

his logic, then, his evocation of Bajazeth will reflect back upon the tormenters baser than the heathen upstart Tamerlaine; and the comparison will focus our emotion on the horror of a king's degradation. "Enraged," "indignity," "insult," "Astonishment!": the words repeat and echo throughout the "Deepe Groane," deflecting attention from the king. What they really make us notice, however (at least reading from our distance of three centuries), is not the Parliamentarians' evil, but the poet's own horror and anger. When he again seeks consolation, it is imagined not as God's direct intervention but as the restoration of another Charles, who will "write Thy Chronicle in Red, / And dip His Pen in what Thy Foes have bled" (ibid.). This is a vivid although not beautiful conceit: the reconstituted royal line will write lines using the enemy's blood rather than the poet's (ineffectual) ink. However, it remains troubling and troubled, intellectually, coming as it does from a Christian claiming to take the higher moral ground. The current martyrdom will not serve, like Christ's, as a redemptive conclusion to a long history of suffering. And the poet's own thinking is stalled by the present time of violence.

Toward the end, the speaker imagines a future inscription on a monument to the dead King Charles, where "Such Characters as these shall there be read" (Crum, p. 116). They begin, "Here Charles the best of Monarch's butcher'd lies," and go on to praise the King for his sweetness and "Clemencie." But Bishop King seems to worry that such meekness might be confused with a "debase[ment]" of Majesty; he acknowledges that Charles's mercy was "Inviting Treason with a pardoning looke, / Instead of Gratitude" (Crum, p. 117). The ideal king is thus ill-suited to earthly rule over treacherous subjects. Again the betrayal and the poet's anger at the way men have in fact behaved overwhelms both King's poem and his confidence in the efficacy—as distinct from the propriety—of the patriarchal monarchism to which he remains devoted. After acknowledging that now "Heav'n conquered seem'd, and Hell to bear the sway," he abruptly concludes his English verses with an indented couplet, a sign of how tenuously it follows poetically or logically:

> A Prince so richly good, so blest a Reigne,
> The World ne're saw but once, nor can againe.
>
> (Crum, p. 117)

Which reign was as good? The proper answer must be either none, or else Christ's (symbolic) reign on earth; the latter reading would invoke the martyred King of Kings whom Charles repeatedly represents in Royalist remembrances. And yet, the couplet itself concludes on an apocalyptically negative note. Even should the king's son be restored to the throne, the treachery cannot be repaired nor his kingship match the past. The devastation wrought by this recognition leads to the poem's final movement back in time. Bishop King is unable to conclude with the English couplet above, despite—or perhaps because of—its bleak appropriateness as England's epitaph for mystical sovereignty. Instead the poet looks back: back to Latin, to Scotland, and to Charles's father King James, who was monarch in Henry King's happier youth. This long poem thus ends with a six-line Latin "parodia," a verse imitation, of the Scots humanist George Buchanan's "Genethliacon Jacobi sexti Regis Scotorum," which was written in the sixteenth century. Unable to keep his eye on present or future as fully redemptive, Henry King looks to the past.

Henry King's second and even longer attempt to elegize Charles calls for "that Trump of Death the Mandrake's Groan / Which kills the Hearers" as he recalls a story "which through time's vast Kalendar / Must stand without Example or Repair" (Crum, p. 117). Again the majority of the elegy directs its attention and anger (now more sardonic than raging) at the murderous sects, "Before whose fatal birth were no such things / As Doctrines to Depose and Murther Kings" (Crum, p. 123). Internal allusions suggest that King revised this elegy for publication close to the 1660 Restoration; if so, it would be his last verse publication and possibly his last poem.

Neither of King's two late elegies for women contains the exceptionally frank confrontation with grief characteristic of young Henry King's "Exequy." He sounds more hesitant now and full of doubt. He dares not complain of Lady Stanhope's death in a way that "Might doubt thy bliss, and shake our own belief" (Crum, p. 132); and when his "Best Friend L[ady]. K[atherine]. C[holmondeley]." dies, he strives to "bear th'Assaults of an uneven Fate." Indeed, like a gambler "Grow'n desp'rate through mischance," he resolves to "[fling] from me my now Loathed Pen / Resolve for your Sake nev'r to Write agen" (Crum, p. 134). In a telling transference, he compares his renuncia-tion to the action of "unoffic'd Servants" at their Princes' deaths, when they throw their staves into "their Masters' Graves" (Crum, p. 135). Whereas young Henry relied on father and king to support him through the loss of his domestic partner, now a female friend becomes the figure for his loss of king and symbolic father.

To read "The Exequy" and these poems composed during the interregnum makes vivid the war's subjective cost for this poet—beyond and alongside the very real loss of office, security, and even bodily safety that he endured. It helps us locate, too, where the fixation and trauma of his career lay: not in his turning again and again to the elegiac form to compose tributes in which he played second fiddle to the lost honoree, but rather in the loss of that position as loving son and faithful remembrancer. When a "doctrine" allowed the killing of the king, all King's own allegiances were challenged and disempowered. It was then that he lashed out venomously, in these putative elegies to Charles as in his vitriolic *ad hominem* attacks on the poet John Milton ("Iconoclastes") for his blindness—attacks that, read out of context, smack of a small-minded street-fighter:

Iconoclastes, so shamelessly rails That, as St. Paul said to Simon Magnus, so might I to him, *Thou art in the Gall of Bitterness*. And as the Apostle charged Elymas the sorcerer for *Mischief* and *perverting the Truth*; so it is very memorable This Wretch had the fate of Elymas, *Strook with Blindness* to his Death.

(*Sermons*, p. 271)

Despite such attacks, in some of King's holy writing in both sermon and verse forms, he sought—and on occasion found—a voice closer to his earlier Anglican "middle way." In 1651 he had his paraphrase of the psalms printed. He hated the traditional jingling of the sixteenth-century Sternhold and Hopkins translation, and wished to "deliver it from that dress which indeed made it ridiculous." To make the psalms readily available to the English laiety was consonant with radical Protestant ideology, and many versions of the psalms saw print during this decade of Commonwealth rule. King tried to find a stylistic middle ground as well, between the extreme simplicity of some Puritan versions, on the one hand, and over-wrought literary elaboration which sacrificed clarity for style, on the other. Though popular and fairly well received, his psalms did not succeed in their goal of displacing the much-loved barbarisms of Sternhold and Hopkins.

King's collected poems appeared in 1657, under the title *Poems, Elegies, Paradoxes, and Sonnets.* According to the title page, they were printed in London for Richard Marriot and H. Herringman, and sold in St. Dunstan's Churchyard, Fleetstreet, and at the New-Exchange. Although King did not claim to be responsible for their publication (nor would most Anglican churchmen of that era), the volume was well edited and included recent poems, implying he did have a hand in its reaching the public.

During the years when Parliament and then Cromwell ruled England, King continued in his attempts to uphold the old Church order, at great peril: he secretly ordained many priests using the Anglican Prayer Book service and even planned to go to the Hague, where Prince Charles held court, in order to consecrate new Bishops. This was an urgent task, as the war and the passage of years had greatly diminished the number of active Bishops: it was feared that a continuous Church hierarchy would be destroyed by attrition if something wasn't done immediately. As it turned out, a second Bishop well enough to accompany King across the English Channel could not be found-at least not before the restoration of the monarchy occurred. The Prince's return as Charles II was of course the end for which Henry King had most devoutly wished.

RESTORATION AND BEYOND

CHARLES II's return to England as monarch was only in legal terms the "Restoration" of a continuous monarchy uninterrupted by Charles I's beheading: the law now proclaimed that his son had become king at the very moment of his father's death, and all the confiscations of Royalist estates during the decade prior to 1660 were declared invalid. But the clock could not be turned back, nor changes in English thinking undone.

In 1661 King gave a sermon on Charles II's birthday, in which he discussed the importance of hereditary kingship. It was reprinted in 1713 (when Queen Anne's lack of an heir again made the succession problematic). A staunch defense of Jacobean absolutism, it was not particularly in keeping with Charles II's attempts to move on and repair the breaches in civil society caused by the Civil War. Henry King's sermon of 30 January 1664, given as a "Commemoration of King Charles the I, martyr'd on that day," shows that he held onto his old anger and venom against the King's murderers even in the new era. He recalled again the fall of Chichester in 1643, claiming the clergy were turned out in foul weather as Parliamentary troops of women paraded through the streets: for him, the world turned upside down.

Henry tried to carry on with his familial sense of order and loyalty as well. He made his brother Philip Archdeacon of Lewes. His second son Henry became a Gentleman of the Chamber to Charles II. Young Henry would receive his father's English books, whereas the Latin and other "serious" books went to John, the erstwhile seducer. Although he may not have been in great favor or accord with the frivolity of Charles II's Restoration court, Bishop King never gave up: he was still preaching a month before his death in 1669. He was buried in Chichester Cathedral, where, fittingly, one son would be buried with him.

During the nineteenth century, King's more generalized meditations about the passage of time, such as the short poem "Sic Vita," were his most popular and often anthologized. But between 1914 and 1925 three new editions of his poems were published, and they brought on a reassessment. Since the formalist praises of Eliot and Tuve, and the 1964 historical study by Berman, Henry King has faded for the most part from scholarly attention. Margaret Crum's edition of his poems and Mary Hobb's edition of his sermons have given us excellent texts to study, but much exploration remains to be done. For to read Henry King is to appreciate the achievements of the last generation of the English Renaissance; and to understand Bishop King is to learn much about the ways the Renaissance fell apart, and the costs of that loss. It is also to see the traces of modernity—which he himself would not necessarily have seen as such—in his tribute to his wife, his dedication to his family, and in his delight at the explorations and discoveries of his age. Sadly for him, he did not find a way to move forward with those turbulent times except in his prose style, which became sparer and more elegant with the years. In his heart and in his mind, Henry King remained a man of the English Renaissance, after the Renaissance was over.

NOTE: Portions of this essay were first published as part of a shorter article entitled, "King and No King: 'The Exequy' as an Antebellum Poem," in *The George Herbert Journal* 22, nos. 1, 2 (1998/1999): 57–75, simultaneously published as *The Wit to Know: Essays on English Renaissance Literature for Edward Tayler,* ed. Eugene D. Hill and William Kerrigan (Fairfield, Conn.: George Herbert Journal Special Studies & Monographs, 2000), pp. 57–75. I cite it here with the kind permission of the journal's general editor, Sid Gottlieb.

SELECTED BIBLIOGRAPHY

I. FIRST EDITIONS OF INDIVIDUAL WORKS. *Poems:* "An Elegy upon Prince Henryes Death," in *Iusta Oxoniensium* (Oxford, 1612); "An Elegy on Dr. Donne, Deane of Pauls," in *Death's Duell* (London, 1632); "An Elegy upon . . . Gustavus Adolphus," in *The Swedish Intelligencer, Third Part* (1633); "To my Dead Friend Ben: Johnson," in *Jonsonus Virbius* (London, 1638); "To my honourd friend Mr. George Sandys," in *A Paraphrase upon the Divine Poems* (London, 1638); "A Deepe Groane, fetch'd at the Funerall of . . . Charles the First" (London, 1649); "Tell me you Starrs that our affections move," in Walter Porter's *Madrigales and Ayres* (London, 1632); "Sic Vita," in *Poems by Francis Beaumont, Gent.* (London, 1640). *Sermons:* "A Sermon Preached at Pauls Crosse . . . 1621" (London, 1621); "Two Sermons Upon the Act Sunday . . ." (Oxford, 1625); "A Sermon of Deliverance Preached at the Spittle . . ." (London 1626); "Two Sermons Preached at White-hall in Lent . . ." (London 1627); "A Sermon Preached At St. Pauls March 27. 1640 . . ." (London, 1640); "A Sermon Preached at White-hall on the 29th of May . . ." (London, 1661); "A Sermon Preached at the Funeral of . . . Bryan [Duppa], Lord Bp. Of Winchester" (London, 1661); "A Sermon Preached at Lewis . . . Octob. 8, 1662" (London, 1663); "A Sermon Preached the 30th of January at White-Hall, 1664 . . ." (London, 1665).

II. FIRST EDITION OF COLLECTED WORKS. *Poems: Psalms of David* (London, 1651); *Poems, Elegies, Paradoxes, and Sonnets* (London, 1657). *Sermons: An Exposition Upon the Lord's Prayer* (London, 1628).

III. MODERN EDITIONS OF INDIVIDUAL WORKS, IN COLLECTIONS (referred to above). John Hollander and Frank Kermode, eds., *The Literature of Renaissance England* (New York, 1973); Richard Sylvester, ed., *English Seventeenth-Century Verse,* vol. 2 (New York, 1969).

IV. MODERN EDITIONS OF COLLECTED WORKS. Margaret Crum, ed., *The Poems of Henry King* (Oxford, 1965); Mary Hobbs, ed., *The Sermons of Henry King (1592–1669), Bishop of Chicester* (Rutherford, N.J., 1992); Eluned Brown, intro., *Poems, Elegies, Paradoxes, and Sonnets* [facsimile of 1657 edition] (Yorkshire, 1973). See also John Hannah, ed., *Poems and Psalms by Henry King D. D.* (London, 1843); John Sparrow, ed., *The Poems of Bishop Henry King* (London, 1925); and early-twentieth-century collections by Mason and Saintsbury.

V. BIBLIOGRAPHIES. Geoffrey Keynes, *A Bibliography of Henry King, D.D. Bishop of Chichester* (London, 1977); "The Bodleian Manuscripts of Henry King," in *The Bodleian Quarterly Record* 5 (Oxford, 1952–1953); William McCarron and Robert Shenk, *Lesser Metaphysical Poets: A Bibliography 1961–1980* (San Antonio, Tex., 1983).

VI. BIOGRAPHICAL AND CRITICAL STUDIES. Shyamal Bagchee, "Henry King's 'The Exequy': A Source for Hopkins' 'The Leaden Echo and the Golden Echo,'" in *Hopkins Quarterly* (1975); Ronald Berman, *Henry King and the Seventeenth Century* (London, 1964); R. Pollin Burton, "Poe, Henry King, and the Two Writers called Montgomery," in *Studies in American Fiction* (1980); Roger G. Clark, "Henry King and the Rise of Modern Prose Style," in *JEGP* (1975); T. S. Eliot, *The Varieties of Metaphysical Poetry,* ed. Ronald Schuchard (New York, 1993); Sidney Gottlieb, "Elegies upon the Author: Defining, Defending, and Surviving Donne," in *John Donne Journal* 2, no. 2 (1983); Mary Hobbs, *Henry King 1592–1669: Bishop, Poet and Refugee* (E. Sussex, n.d.); Dennis Kay, *Melodious Tears: The English Funeral Elegy from Spenser to Milton* (Oxford, 1990); Anthony Low, "A Metrical Device in 'The Exequy,'" in *Modern Language Review* (1968); Millar Maclure, *The Paul's Cross Sermons 1534–1642* (Toronto, 1958); G. W. Pigman, III, *Grief and English Renaissance Elegy* (Cambridge,1985); Rosamund Tuve, *Elizabethan and Metaphysical Imagery* (Chicago, 1947); Antoon Van Velzen, "Two Versions of the Funeral Elegy: Henry King's 'The Exequy 'and Thomas Carew's 'Elegie Upon Donne,'" in *Commitatus: A Journal of Medieval and Renaissance Studies* (1984); Melissa Zeiger, *Beyond Consolation: Death, Sexuality, and the Changing Shapes of Elegy* (Ithaca, N.Y., 1997). See also the editions of Crum and Hobbs, above.

DEREK MAHON

(1941–   )

Dillon Johnston

IF DEREK MAHON were actually a "British Writer," almost certainly he would be a very different writer than he is and perhaps not the highly esteemed and imitated poet he is today. Although no one can specify how his identity and experiences as a Northern Irish Protestant poet from Belfast shape his distinctive verse—nine books of poetry and four volumes of poetic translation from the French—almost certainly they separate him from his British peers. The British critic, and Mahon's future biographer, Hugh Haughton has said of Mahon's poems that they are "profoundly unlike those of his English counterparts. I can't think of any parallels among English poets for Mahon's metaphysical unease, his sense of damage and civilisational desolation, his sense of displacement and disenchanted mobility, or indeed for the poignant elegance of his lyric music" (*The Chosen Ground*, p. 90).

EARLY LIFE AND SCHOOLING

MAHON was born in Belfast, Northern Ireland, on 23 November 1941. His parents, raised in this "tough city of ships and linens" (*Collected Poems*, p. 261; hereafter *CP*), worked in the two principal industries—Protestant run—of what had been the only industrialized city of Ireland. Apprenticed as a pipefitter, his father rose to be an inspector of engines in the Harland & Wolff shipyard where Mahon's grandfather had been a foreman. His mother worked in the York Street Flax Spinning Company until she married and became a fastidious housekeeper and minder of her only child. Later, finding in a seventeenth-century Dutch painting an analogue to his own childhood setting, Mahon characterized himself as a "strange child with a taste for verse" which began, as with the very similar upbringing of John Ruskin, with close, highly focused observation: "the coal / Glittering in its shed, late-afternoon / Lambency informing the deal table, / The ceiling cradled in a radiant spoon" (*CP*, p. 105). As he said in an interview with Eamon Grennan for the Paris Review, "Since there wasn't any hurly-burly of siblings, I had time for the eye to dwell on things, for the brain to dream about things" (p. 155).

Religion and politics, the two sides of an Ulster sectarian identity, impinged on his childhood through unusual channels. From his regular childhood attendance at Anglican services, Mahon can recall neither the caloric nor thematic contents of sermons, but, as a young chorister at St. Peter's (Church of Ireland) on the Antrim Road, with two services on Sunday and choir practice on Wednesday night, "the hymnology invaded the mind," as he confessed to Eamon Grennan (p. 156). In political matters, what might have been the iron intransigence of Unionist politics within the male line of the family—father and uncles—was mollified by a working-class socialism opposed to the Tory element that supported the union with Great Britain. Growing up in an intersectarian neighborhood, religious aspects of sectarian differences remained mysterious to the young boy.

Belfast may be the most frequent identifiable setting in the early poems, "the kitchen houses / And echoing back streets of this desperate city" (*CP*, p. 13). With more frequency throughout the entire body of his work, the north coast of Antrim, especially Cushendun and Cushendall, where the family spent their summer vacations and where his own two children were baptized, becomes the landscape of the heart. As he said in his interview with Willie Kelly in 1981, "My home landscape, and here I mean North Antrim where I spent most of my childhood holidays, and not Belfast where I was born, figures largely in my poems." Finally he asserts, "The place that the poetry occupies is not a geographical location; it's a community of imagined readership" (*Cork Review*, p. 11).

The idea of a literary community, so important throughout Mahon's poetry, may have emerged as early as secondary school. Mahon attended one of the two most prestigious Protestant schools in Belfast, the Royal Belfast Academical Institution or Inst. Through childhood competition with his cousin Conacht, he had come to see himself as an inferior athlete, so at school he turned away from rugby and cricket to reading, writing, and other associated "fringe" activities. In his interview with Grennan, he recalls other nonathletes:

—oddities, weirdos—so I found a coterie, and there I was at home. Age fifteen, sixteen or seventeen, we would go precociously to something that was just coming into existence in a place like Belfast in the late 1950s . . . a coffee bar. And talk, and read Aldous Huxley.

(p. 158)

One especially enabling teacher of history and English at Inst. was John Boyle. He broadened the students' perspective on Ireland to include the teacher's native Dublin, Irish history, and writers such as William Butler Yeats, Louis MacNeice, W. H. Auden, Robert Graves, and, just before graduation, John Hewitt. Laboring under the influence of his personal favorite among living poets, Dylan Thomas, Mahon submitted an original poem for a school prize and, in what would be his junior year, won out over seniors and other contestants. In his final year at Inst, Mahon submitted a poem for the May Morton Prize, a national contest won in 1960 by John Montague's "Like Dolmens Round My Childhood," a poem often reprinted in Irish anthologies. Mahon claimed that this disabused him of the naive belief that he was the only poet writing in Ireland.

Although Mahon's revisions of his *Selected Poems* (1993) and then his *Collected Poems* (1999) reduce one's sense of his development, at his entrance to Trinity College, Dublin, in 1960, he was a precocious poet with, by various indications, a body of good poems. In an interview with Paul Keen in 1999, Michael Longley recalled the impossibility of competing with Mahon:

Mahon was already as a schoolboy writing extraordinary poetry. . . . It was painful for me as a fledgling poet to see how good he was. I think the first step I took to being a good poet, if that's what I am, was to say, this guy's so good I want to be in his company.

(*Books in Canada*, p. 10)

Mahon was two years behind Longley at Inst, where they moved in different circles, but at Trinity, they hung out in Longley's rooms ("Top of the Staircase, Number Sixteen in Botany Bay" in Longley's "River & Fountain"). Later they met in a basement flat in Merrion Square and formed the nucleus of a literary circle with Edna Broderick (Longley's future wife) and in his last year Eavan Boland, as well as Brendan Kennelly, Rudi Holzapfel, Eamon Grennan, and the aspiring poet Richard Eckersley, who became a celebrated book designer, as well as the Trinity graduates Timothy Brownlow and Rivers Carew, who edited *Dublin Magazine*. Among a faculty that seems to Mahon mediocre in retrospect, he found exceptional teachers in Alec Reid and Con Leventhal, as well as Owen Sheehy-Skeffington (Murphy, McDiarmid, and Durkan, p. 194). All three teachers admired Samuel Beckett, who would become a major influence on Mahon, and Reid founded *Icarus*, a journal for student writing that provided a meeting place for this circle of poets and, with *Dublin Magazine*, a showcase for their work, including many of Mahon's early poems.

These Trinity poets might be seen as an eddy within the currents of mature poets in Dublin, such as Austin Clarke and Patrick Kavanagh, often visible in the Palace Bar or McDaid's, respectively; Padraic Colum, Frank O'Connor, and poets from an earlier era; Thomas Kinsella and John Montague working with Liam Miller and the Dolmen Press. Nevertheless, as Terence Brown recognized in his introduction to Mahon's *Journalism*, "For the first time since Irish independence, Trinity-educated writers as an apparent group made more than an individual impact on the literary scene" (p. 15). Acknowledging this "Trinity school of young poets," as Brown called them, may be a helpful counterbalance to the wider recognition of the "Belfast Group," a weekly gathering of poets under the tutelage of the English scholar-poet Philip Hobsbaum who criticized each other's poems in a workshop setting. In a city that felt itself on the literary margins, the attention of this serious critic to Belfast poetry must have bolstered the confidence of Seamus Heaney and others who attended these sessions. Mahon, however, vociferously denied his participation in these workshops: "I was not a member of Philip Hobsbaum's . . . Belfast group. I was in a different city. I was a member of my own group in Dublin. . . . Philip's group didn't do anybody any good except perhaps Philip and Seamus, who carried it on after Hobsbaum left to go to Glasgow" (Murphy, McDiarmid, and Durkan, p. 193). Whatever Mahon's ability to judge the impact of the group on other writers, such as Paul Muldoon and Frank Ormsby, who attended these sessions later, clearly this was not an important experience for him.

Whether any influential literary friends were acquired in Paris—where Mahon went to study at the Sorbonne on a county fellowship in 1964, interrupting and extending his years at Trinity—one can discover only through his reviews, translations, and imitations of French writers. Gérard de Nerval, Charles Baudelaire, Arthur Rimbaud, and Paul Éluard have influenced his own verse; he has undertaken successful translations from the work of Jean-Baptiste Moliere, Jean Racine, Nerval, and Phillipe Jaccottet and reviewed books by or on Yves Bonnefoy, Alain Fournier, Albert Camus, Jean-Paul Sartre, Simone Weil, and other French writers. Mahon's attention to French poets, and European writers generally, added a level of sophistication to his literary studies and qualified him as a polyglot Irish poet, a credential acquired by most Catholic Irish poets with the early study of the Irish language.

Upon graduation from Trinity College, Mahon traveled to Canada where he spent a year teaching English to immigrants and manning the night phones for the Canadian Broadcasting Company (Scammel 5), before spending a year in Cambridge, Massachusetts, and elsewhere in the United States. He returned to teach in Belfast and Dublin before picking up a literary career in London that lasted from 1970 to 1985. In March of 1970, *Atlantis*, the literary magazine he co-founded and co-edited with Seamus Deane, made its appearance and continued as a quarterly until 1974. In the 1970s he spent a couple of years as a drama critic for the *Listener*, as features editor for *Vogue*, and for shorter periods as a poet-in-residence at East Anglia University, Emerson College in Boston, Wake Forest University (where he wrote "The Globe in North Carolina"), and finally New University of Ulster in Coleraine where he stayed for two years.

NIGHT-CROSSING *AND* LIVES

It would be difficult to imagine a more impressive poetic debut than *Night-Crossing* (1968; one might think of Auden's *Poems*, 1930, or Paul Muldoon's *New Weather*, 1973). Published in the poet's twenty-sixth year by one of the two major literary presses in Britain and Ireland, it was distinguished as a choice by the Poetry Book Society and uniformly praised by eleven reviewers in the *Times Literary Supplement*, *Poetry Review*, the *New Statesman*, *Poetry* (Chicago), and other prestigious journals. If the poems seemed remarkably polished, some had appeared six years earlier and undergone subsequent revision, and others were the product of a poet who had been writing serious poetry for eight years or so. Although some of the most characteristic aspects of Mahon's poetry emerged here, so did other qualities that would fade out of the poetry of his mid-career. For examples of the latter, the volume's opening poem, "Girls in Their Season," presents the *poète maudit* as a film-noir hero—Humphrey Bogart, or Albert Camus in trenchcoat—addressing the women of his past collectively. In a generally supportive essay recalling Mahon as a fellow student at Trinity, Eavan Boland regretted "that he preserved maleness as a sort of caste-system within the poem" (*Irish University Review*, 1994, p. 66). In another poem within the volume "The Poets Lie where they Fell," the title and poem seem to exclude the possibility of women poets. Neither poem survives intact in the *Selected and Collected* volumes of the 1990s (the latter poem is retitled in the *Collected Poems* "No Rest for the Wicked," so the collective *we* could refer to any group of slovenly males). The questioning of gender roles that Boland would ask of Mahon begins in the new poetry of the 1990s.

This volume does introduce characteristic interests and dispositions of the mature poet: his interest in phenomenology, in one's projection of humanity onto the insensate; a self-reflexiveness, especially about language and its relationship to the world; the epiphanic or transcendent moment, but actually only as a function of art, whether painting or poetry; encumbered reality from which humanity is freed by a liberating perspective; the human alone, an isolate or exile, who aspires to a collective relationship. Readers see some of these characteristics in the volume's second poem, "In Carrowdore Churchyard," addressed to Louis MacNeice. As a Belfast Protestant of the previous generation, MacNeice is Mahon's closest poetic forebear. The elder poet's stance as a "timeless vagrant" and a "tourist in his own country" is often shared by Mahon. The occasion for the poem is a visit to MacNeice's grave:

This plot is consecrated, for your sake,
To what lies in the future tense. You lie
Past tension now, and spring is coming round
Igniting flowers on the peninsula.

Your ashes will not fly, however the rough winds
        burst

                                    (*CP*, p. 17)

Although the diction is aimed at clear representation rather than the flamboyancy of later poetry, the puns here—*plot, tense, tension, spring*—call attention to language and its capacity for dual representation. Like so many of Mahon's poems, this poem about a dead poet, a master of "each fragile, solving ambiguity," also concerns the ways poetry mediates between the individual and life. By alluding to several of MacNeice's poems, he suggested how poetry shapes humankind's way of seeing. "The ironical, loving crush of roses against snow" refers to MacNeice's best-known poem "Snow" and the margins poetry recalls for joining rational incongruities. The form of the poem, four stanzas of six iambic pentameter lines, varies in each stanza the order of three rhymes and, thereby, suggests variation, even accident, within formal constraint. If poetry has a role, if in fact it "makes something happen," to contradict W. H. Auden, Mahon's allusion to Percy Shelley's "Ode to the West Wind" in the last line above excludes poetry from any political intervention. The poet brings "the all-clear to the empty holes of spring." Poetry announces the pacific moment and introduces an ironic gap across which we see the world more clearly in order to value our mortal lives, "the empty holes" being, perhaps among other meanings, the already dug graves that await humankind.

"Van Gogh among the Miners," which becomes "A Portrait of the Artist" in the *Selected and Collected*, represents the function of poetry as well as painting: "And the light on my forehead / Is the dying light of truth. / God gutters down to metaphor—" (*CP*, p. 23; in the *Selected and Collected, truth* becomes the more accurate and appropriate *faith*). The simile in an earlier stanza of the painter as a caged bird, a standard analogue to the poet, and the wrenched rhyme of the first and last line here, the only rhyme in the poem, remind readers that the painter stands in for the poet. In ekphrastic poems or references to painters' lives, Mahon employed the painter's medium of space, creating a mediated margin like the glass between snow and roses, and of light, whose sudden appearance can evoke the transcendent. Like the miner's lantern, the divine light the painter sees in his frequent subjects—chairs, faces, boots, sun-

flowers, fishing boats—actually emanates from his own head. The poem concludes by declaring that these radiant subjects are "each one a miner in disguise." Such an assertion would be too baldly declarative for the later poetry where, besides, insensate objects, the "mute phenomena," take on their own voices.

Perhaps the most accomplished poem in *Night-Crossing* is "Four Walks in the Country near Saint Brieuc," entitled later merely "Breton Walks." Boland recalled his suddenly reappearing from his sojourn in Paris in 1964 and brandishing new poems, "among them . . . the beautiful and persuasive 'Four Walks in the Country' which had come directly from his stay in Brittany" (p. 63). The four sections move fluently within their different forms and reveal other characteristics—extravagant diction, self-reflexivity about language, the alien status of the poet, his humorous self-deprecation, and different scales of time—not so clearly announced elsewhere in the volume. As in later poems, the extravagant, abstract diction, such as the "shadowy ingress of mankind" or the birds' "presuppositions of ill-will" calls attention to its own inadequacy. Doubtless, his actual status as "an enlightened alien," as Mahon said in "Man and Bird," and the necessity of his speaking a second language elicited some of these concerns. In the first "walk," language cannot accommodate the timescale of creation; in the second, no language can mediate between man and beast, yet, in the third walk, knowledge of one's precarious perch in the food chain lies deeper than language; and finally in "Exit Molloy," Beckett's character says, "I am not important and I have to die. / Strictly speaking I am already dead, / But still I can hear the birds sing on over my head" (*CP*, p. 22). Consigned to death, according to his own language, he turns to other senses, smell and silent listening, in this case to a language "over his head." The self-disparaging wit of these lines is reinforced by the slant rhyme (in one case rhyming of *propre* with *gap* guides us to syllibify correctly this foreign language).

So accomplished is *Night-Crossing* that readers could fail to measure accurately how far *Lives* (1972) exceeds that first volume. By opening with dissonant dimeter lines—"Has bath and shave, / clean shirt etcetera, / full of potat- / oes, rested yet"—Mahon revealed his intention to play with form in the volume and his skill at moving from abrupt rhythms to lyric epigrams at the poem's close: "we cannot start / at this late date / with a pure heart, / or having seen / the pictures plain / be ever in-/nocent again" (p. 1). For its subject matter, the volume draws on folk saying, poems in Irish, painting, other writers (Beckett, J. P. Donleavy, Constantine Cavafy), and, most significantly, archaeology and anthropology. "Lives," "Deaths," "What Will Remain," and "Entropy" establish this long view of civilization, implicit in the animism of *Night-Crossing* and developed into retrospective poems of *The Snow Party* (1975) that reflect on the decline of civilization or even the disappearance of humanity. "Lives" revises the song of Amergin, the legendary first poet of Ireland who asserts his negative capability by merging with the material world. Mahon wrote, "First time out / I was a torc of gold / And wept tears of the sun" as the poet regresses through increasingly darker civilizations until the first poet has become the retrospective anthropologist, who "know[s] too much / To be anything any more" (pp. 15, 45). Mahon's post-Apocalyptic settings, more extensive in *The Snow Party*, appear in two poems dropped from the *Selected/Collected*, "Entropy" and "What Will Remain." The latter poem begins, "What will remain after / The twilight of metals, / The flowers of fire, // Will be the soft / Vegetables where our / Politics were conceived" (p. 26). Like the opening sites of Mahon's later, most celebrated poem "The Disused Shed in County Wexford," these poems invite readers to "places where a thought might grow." As Shelley recognized in the conclusion of "Mont Blanc," sites of nothingness or of minimal life challenge, and threaten, human imaginations to fill in this space, and so they might be seen as petri dishes of poetry, as well as of "politics" or "a thought."

Beyond altering the scale of life, these poems move to vast time scales that enforce the brevity of life. In this respect, one of Mahon's most successful poems is "An Image from Beckett." The poem elaborates a comment made by Pozzo to Lucky in *Waiting for Godot* that humans are "born astride the grave. Although this essay will return to the question of Mahon's radical revisions for the *Selected Poems* and the *Collected Poems*, critics see here the poet's intention in reducing the poem from the original eighteen stanzas in *Lives* to fifteen in the later volumes. Having based the poem on an allusion, he kept the poem focused on Beckett's "bleak reductio" by omitting allusions to Stendhal and Mann. (He also deleted the dedica-

tion to his wife and lines concerning "my one marriage / over as soon as it started" which might now seem to entail a reference to the poet's broken marriage.) He also dropped a suggestion that the landscape is Danish which seems coy in light of how closely it approximates Northern Ireland. In its pared down form, the poem becomes a post-modern response not only to Beckett's emphasis on life's brevity but also to the modernist stance of the poet as isolated hero. For example, in Yeats's "A Dialogue of Self and Soul," confronting the ditch as life's situation rather than death's, the poet's Self declares "I am content to live it all again / it it be life to pitch / Into the frog-spawn of a blind man's ditch" (*CP*, p. 236). Where Yeats's poem employs high rhetoric ("When such as I cast out remorse") in making an heroic commitment to life even on its worst terms, Mahon employed understated humor in having the deceased speaker "haunted / By that landscape, / The soft rush of its winds // The uprightness of its / Utilities and schoolchildren" (*CP*, p. 41) where *haunted* and *uprightness* earn our doubletake. Yeats declared the poet's heroic intention to accept rebirth; Beckett invited us to muse lightly on life's brevity; Mahon offered as his fifteen-stanza last will-and-testament his poem that sees the quotidian "through a glitter of wintry light."

Akin to the shift from Yeats's heroic stance to a postmodern understatement are Mahon's elaborate epithets and multisyllabic phrasings, derivatives of and comments upon Yeats's combination of ordinary words, Latinate terms, and abstract generalizations: "Measurement began our might"; "Plato thought nature but a spume that plays / Upon a ghostly paradigm of things" (p. 217); "The ignominy of boyhood; the distress" (p. 236); "The Babylonian starlight brought / A fabulous, formless darkness in" (p. 213); "the barbarous clangor of a gong" (p. 208). Whereas Yeats recognizes the elevation of his language, and even confessed to his own stiltedness in more than one poem, his language—whether abstract or demotic—nevertheless serves his systematic views, the historiographic and psychological generalizations derived from *A Vision*. Mahon, however, employed a similarly elaborate diction humorously and without any metaphysical intentions: "They will have buried / Our great-granchildren, and theirs, / Beside us by now / With a subliminal batsqueak / Of reflex lamentation" (p. 40). As if Mahon removed Yeats's stilts, his patches of rhetoric float in ironic suspension above his clearly rendered scene.

One effect of Mahon's elevated phrasing is to call attention to the phrase-maker as standing aside from his contemporaries, detached in his commentary. Several poems in the volume emphasize the poet's isolation by focusing on him as outlaw or scorned object of the poem. In "As It Should Be" a fugitive, perhaps an Irish Republican Army (IRA) pariah, is gunned "down in a blind yard / Between ten sleeping lorries / And an electricity generator":

> Let us hear no idle talk
> Of the moon in the Yellow River;
> The air blows softer since his departure.
> (CP, p. 49)

The middle line's double allusion—through Denis Johnston's *The Moon in the Yellow River* to Li Po's association of the lunatic and the poet—substitutes the poet for the stalked quarry, the disturber and, consequently, victim of homicidal order: "Since his tide-burial during school hours / Our children have known no bad dreams. / . . . / They will thank us for it when they grow up / To a world with method in it."

Mahon offers a comic view of poet as victim in "I Am Raftery," a parody of the best-known poem by the blind, late-eighteenth-century Gaelic poet. No longer impoverished and scorned as the wild vagrant, he has been tamed as poet in residence and bought out by the "bright imperious music" of full pockets. The wit and deftness of this poem masks Mahon's intense distaste for the "poetry business." In a 1991 interview for the *Irish Literary Supplement*, Mahon said, echoing Yeats, "I believe in the lonely impulse of delight. I hate the 'business'" (Murphy, McDiarmid, and Durkan, p. 198). In his interview with Eamon Grennan, Mahon said, "What interests me is forbidden poetry written by solitaires in the cold, written by solitaires in the open, which is where the human soul really is. That for me is where poetry really is" (*The Paris Review*, p. 178).

In "Rage for Order" an agent of history condescends to the poet and, as the critic Neil Corcoran has pointed out, contradicts Wallace Stevens, to whose poetry the poem's title alludes. According to Stevens, whether as a jar in Tennessee or a song by the sea, the aesthetic gives shape and tempo to nature, as art exercises its "blessed rage for order."

In contrast to Stevens' Key West, Mahon's poem sets the poet among "the scorched gable end / And the burnt-out / Buses" of Belfast. In this setting, poetry "is a dying art / An eddy of semantic scruple / In an unstructurable sea" (p. 22), rather than "the maker's rage to order words of the sea." In its 1972 version, Mahon's poem concludes:

> Now watch me
> As I make history,
> Watch me as I tear down
>
> To build up
> With a desperate love,
> Knowing it cannot be
> Long now till I have need of his
> Germinal ironies.
> (*Lives*, p. 23)

Again, contrast with Yeats's poetry may draw Mahon's conclusion into perspective. In Yeats's "Lapis Lazuli" (in *Collected Poems*, 1989) one of the functions of art is to rebuild after history has cycled through destruction: "All things fall and are built again / And those that build them again are gay" (p. 295). Mahon's 1972 ending, as seen even through the eyes of this maker of "history," seems to endorse Yeats's view of the poet employing his double vision to speed history through its renewal. In the revision for the *Selected* and *Collected* poems, however, the poet can supply only "Terminal ironies," presumably poetic language as a dirge for unrenewable civilization.

As he will do in the next several volumes, Mahon concludes *Lives* with a verse letter, "Beyond Howth Head," voicing the persona we identify with the poet's witty, urbane self. No overheard confession, the poem exploits the vastness of postal networks from Dublin to London in its opening salute:

> The wind that blows these words to you
> bangs nightly off the black-and-blue
> Atlantic, hammering in its haste
> dark doors of the declining west . . .
> (CP, p. 52)

The value of the individual voice is enlarged by the same temporal and spatial scope that threatens to diminish it. In its revised form in the *Collected/Selected* the poem contains twenty-two eight-line stanzas (one less than the original), like Pope's Horatian epistles or Auden's "New Year Letter," using rhyming couplets. Like Auden,

Mahon employed slant-rhyme occasionally to mute the epigrammatic quality of couplets but gained a greater succinctness than Auden by using iambic tetrameter rather than pentameter lines. The poem ranges through space and time, from American imperial ambitions to the Danish sacking of Clonmacnoise. As Peter Denman has said in his most helpful account of Mahon's revisions, the presence of so many allusions "provides a personal literary analogy to the poem's general theme— the sweep of larger currents, imaged by the wind and tide, through the fractured perception of the immediate" (*Irish University Review*, 1994, p. 32). The effect of this poem's revisions, which include the dropping of "Notes to *Beyond Howth Head*" and deleting many of the allusions that occasioned the notes, is to make the verse-letter much less topical, much less a reflection of its extended moment indicated by the dates "March–April, 1970," appended to the original and deleted from, because less necessary for, the revision.

The epistolary fiction of an intimate audience of one, however, remains undiminished. Responding to the same unease about audience, widespread among twentieth-century poets, that occasioned, for example, "The Torn Letter," Hardy's poem to an unknown reader, Mahon developed a coterie of poets and readers, his verse-letters' addressees but also dedicatees of his poems, painter and poet subjects of his poems who are surrogates for himself, and other poets he appropriated by translations or imitations. Even in its potentially isolating uniqueness, implicitly the poet's vision is understood and endorsed by this "fit audience, though few," according to this poetic fiction.

THE SNOW PARTY, THE HUNT BY NIGHT, *AND* SELECTED POEMS

ALTHOUGH these three volumes gather Mahon's major work of the 1970s and 1980s, they represent neither clear stages in the poet's development nor especially coherent sequences. In his 1981 interview with Willie Kelly, Mahon said, "I'm basically the kind of poet who doesn't develop, who doesn't change, who just writes in the same voice, with slight modification and accretions of new tones of voice and new material" (*Cork Review*, p. 10). A decade later in the *Irish Literary Supplement* interview, he said, "Some poets—Montague, Heaney, for example—write . . . books like *The*

Great Cloak or North . . . almost novels. I don't write books of poems; I write individual poems" (Murphy, McDiarmid, and Durkan, p. 196). Whatever the viability of these two beliefs over the long run, they support Mahon's radical revisions of individual poems in his *Selected Poems* and allow him to neglect previous orderings of poems. Although the 1990s will prove both assumptions wrong or outgrown, in the "middle stretch" from 1975 to 1991, they help him survive crises to which they also contribute.

During these years, Mahon avoided involvement with Ulster politics and maintained a successful literary career, mostly in London. In 1972 he married Doreen Douglas with whom he would father and raise two children, Rory and Katie. In 1976 he was awarded the prestigious Denis Devlin Memorial Award from the Arts Council of Ireland, and he would go on to join the features department for the British Broadcasting Corporation in 1979, serve as poetry and fiction editor for the *New Statesman* from 1981 to 1984, and review for the *Irish Times* for over a decade beginning in 1986. Yet, despite his absence from the North, Mahon was touched deeply by the sectarian violence that became overt outside Derry in 1969. After years of suppression by the Protestant majority, Catholic activists began a civil rights campaign that escalated into sectarian fighting between the Ulster Constabulary, British troops, and Protestant paramilitary, on the one hand, and the IRA and its splinter groups, conducting a separatist campaign in the name of Catholic Ireland, on the other. In 1981 Mahon spoke darkly of "a life crisis which I won't talk about now, except to say that it's over and that my confidence has returned" (Kelly, p. 11). Referring to a two-year stint as poet-in-residence in the New University of Ulster, he said, "I went back there recently only to rediscover the impossibility of living there. . . . I have felt guilt. My feelings are very complex . . . because of the peculiar position of the Northern Protestant" (p. 11). At the close of this period in 1991, concerning the Troubles in Northern Ireland, he confessed to feeling "'beaten-up' . . . I felt that I had been guilty of something that I wasn't aware of" (Grennan, p. 164). He went on to characterize himself, James Simmons, and Michael Longley in, as "a middle-class, grammar-school-educated, liberal, ironical Protestants" who thought of themselves as "somehow not implicated. . . . One of the damnable things about it was that you couldn't take sides. . . .

In *Crane Bag* they'd call it 'colonial aphasia.' Perhaps, in fact, that's what it is" (pp. 164–165).

A second more personal problem arose from his own precociousness as a poet who over the first phase of his career could write poems such as "Breton Walks," "An Image from Beckett," and "A Disused Shed in Co. Wexford," lyrics so well wrought that they approached perfection. In the face of such accomplishment, one could change subject matter but otherwise only hope either to repeat prior successes or to find freer, more "organic" forms. In his talk with Willie Kelly, he revealed the strain of creating a different sort of poem: "Very often I throw things away because I'm conscious that I've been trying too hard to write a new kind of poem, and I know it's false" (p. 10). A decade later, in his conversation with Eamon Grennan, he had come to understand that his current creative endgame arose during his early career from his association of his unique way of seeing with alcohol, a "false consciousness, no doubt, especially the morning-after lucidity, which I thought of as being a kind of revelation" (p. 171). In the absence of drink, Mahon anticipated "a general sort of silence punctuated by a sudden burst of noisiness" (p. 172), which in fact led to a new creativity in the 1990s.

As with *Lives, The Snow Party* opens with a poem in the poet's voice, reflecting on Belfast as the road not taken. As an extension of this concern in *Lives*, the title "Afterlives" is appropriate although this poem might have exchanged titles with "Going Home," a poem later in the volume about the ghostly lives of shift-workers in Hull. Opening in London with what may have been "a morning-after lucidity," the poem, dedicated to James Simmons, a Protestant poet who stayed at home, speculates on this alternative life:

> Perhaps if I'd stayed behind
> And lived it bomb by bomb
> I might have grown up at last
> And learnt what is meant by home.
> (*CP*, p. 59)

This autobiographical poem is uncharacteristic of a volume, however, which more often sees the Troubles from a refracted viewpoint. In "Last of the Fire Kings," for example, adapted from its source in J. G. Frazer, according to Neil Corcoran's *After Yeats & Joyce* (p. 147), the king who expects his own ritual murder and succession prefers to "Die by my own hand / Rather than perpetuate / The barbarous cycle" among "the fire-loving people" which is what he knows as "history" (*CP*, pp. 64–65).

From the remote viewpoint of the seventeenth-century Japanese poet Basho, "The Snow Party" provides a perspective on Northern Ireland which may have been suggested by the resonant title of Basho's travel book, *Narrow Road to the Deep North*. In contrast to the genteel Japanese celebration of the first snowfall, the seventeenth-century religious wars in Europe erupt in violence:

> Elsewhere they are burning
> Witches and heretics
> In the boiling squares,
>
> Thousands have died since dawn
> In the service
> Of barbarous kings;
> (*CP*, p. 63)

That Mahon relocates the snow party—a ritual of the northern provinces during which ice houses and snow figures are built for children—in a peaceful, fictive drawing room confirms that this place out of time from which we can view history must be constructed from human imagination.

Beyond these refracted views of and oblique commentaries on the Troubles, *Snow Party* is preoccupied with reflections on the detritus of a wrecked or terminated civilization, to which its poems sometimes give a voice. The opening of "Thammuz"—"What will be left / After the twilight of cities, / The flowers of fire" (p. 11)—could be the setting for several of these poems, which may account for why it was dropped from the *Selected/Collected*. "The Banished Gods," also dropped from the later texts, concludes by envisioning a world "of zero-growth economics and seasonal change / In a world without cars, computers / Or chemical skies" (p. 31). Converted from a prose poem in *Snow Party* to poetic lines, "The Apotheosis of Tins" gives voice to civilization's trash, freed by its disuse from "the historical nightmare" to exist reflectively in the "terminal democracy of hatbox and crab, / of wine and Windolene" (p. 69). In extending Mahon's phenomenological concerns from earlier volumes, these poems challenge one's anthropocentric worldview. In revising the normal view of humanity's centrality, they relate to his poems that diminish humankind by enlarging space or time.

Lest readers forget with what tact and wit Mahon assumed these alternative perspectives on humanity, they should review the poem "The Mute Phenomena" in *Selected/Collected*. Originally entitled "After Nerval," Mahon's poem radically alters the tone and antique diction of the nineteenth-century French original, which Mahon approximated in the more literal translation of his little volume *The Chimeras* (1982). Consider the opening stanza:

> Man, do you think yourself the one reflective
> Thing in this lively world? Your urgent guile
> Works blithely on its raw material,
> But you ignore the spiritual perspective.
>
> (p. 20)

It is wonderfully transformed from *The Chimeras* by the broader spectrum of diction and the radical extension of Pythagoras' idea that "everything feels!":

> Your great mistake is to disregard the satire
> Bandied among the mute phenomena.
> Be strong if you must, your brisk hegemony
> Means fuck-all to the somnolent sunflower
> Or the extinct volcano . . .
>
> (*CP*, p. 82)

The pithy but parched line in the translation—"Note in the wall, a fierce interrogation"—becomes:

> An ordinary common-or-garden brick wall, the kind
> For talking to or banging your head on,
> Resents your politics and bad draughtsmanship.
>
> (*CP*, p. 82)

Mahon's wit is always cushioned by modesty and self-deprecation, here extended from the comic self-representation in this penultimate line to all of humanity.

These various concerns of *Snow Party*—Western society seen through refraction, humankind's anthropocentric worldview, animism—converge in "The Disused Shed in Co. Wexford" (pp. 89–90) and for that reason alone, it might be the most memorable poem in the volume, if not in Mahon's entire canon. So frequent and widespread are discussions of this poem, that critics might add little here except to emphasize one point concerning the poem's conclusion. The last stanza's analogy between the "thousand mushrooms [who] crowd

to a keyhold" in the shed of that abandoned hotel and the "Lost people of Treblinka and Pompeii" may be read allegorically, so the mushrooms are merely a vehicle to convey victims of the holocaust or an ancient natural cataclysm, but such an allegorical reading is too limited. More appropriately, the poem concerns all marginal life, which the poem teaches readers to notice from the opening stanza: the soft fricatives of "a flutter / Of wild flowers in the lift-shaft"; "a slow clock of condensation" where readers hear the three tocks of the water drops before they translate the abstract term *condensation*; the spondaic "a door bangs" trailing off into the unstressed syllables of "with diminished confidence"; the attenuated alliteration of "rippling rainbarrels"; and so on until readers can hear the variation of rhyme within the ten-line stanzas. As Mahon said in an earlier versions of his verse-letter "The Sea in Winter" (1979), he aspired to "Effect mutations of dead things / Into a form that nearly sings" (*Poems 1962–1978*, p. 113). The "Disused Shed . . ." does gives voice to marginal life: "You with your light meter and relaxed itinerary, / Let not our naive labours have been in vain!" (*CP*, p. 90). Edna Longley, one of Mahon's very best readers, calls attention to the pun on "light meter": "The pun summons poetry, not photojournalism, to order 'darkness' and 'pain'" (1986, p. 181). Yet, the poem suggests a contrast between photojournalism's "flash-bulb firing-squad" exposure of liminal suffering—the profile burned on the wall by Vesuvius; the newsreel exposure of the death camps, startling but momentary before being filed in the news' morgue—and poetry's slow, attentive lineation of survival and suffering. Longley's implication that the mushrooms, "groaning / For their deliverance," undergo a kind of birth through the midwifery of the poet, is bolstered by the last line where the root sense of *naive* (from *nāscī*, to give birth) confirms the "naive labours" as birth throes.

In the seven years between *The Snow Party* and the next major volume *The Hunt by Night* (1982), Mahon published two sequences, *Light Music* (1977) and *Courtyards in Delft* (1981), and a selection *Poems 1962–1978* (1979) which first revealed his predilection for revision. That volume concludes with "The Sea in Winter," a verse-letter of twenty-two ottava rima stanzas which is later rendered to twelve stanzas in *Selected/Collected*. One of the omitted stanzas concerns Botticelli's drawings for the *Divine Comedy*, which offer

Diagrams of that paradise
Each has his vision of. I trace
The future in a colour-scheme,
Colours we scarecely dare to dream.
(*Poems 1962–1978*, p. 114)

Although the New Age claims in the final couplet may have earned the stanzas' removal, all ekphrastic writing makes the appropriating claim to speak for the silent painting. In this sense, the several ekphrastic poems in *The Hunt by Night* extend Mahon's intention to "speak on . . . behalf" of the "wordless" while they also comment on the limitations of art.

The title poem "The Hunt by Night" deduces from Uccello's fifteenth-century painting that art tames and ritualizes those savage events that initiated society whether they be the real midnight hunt that Uccello "tamed and framed"or Freud's patricidal foundation of society. Poetic form supports the changes of civilization through primitive, civilized, and decadent stages, as is evident in the final stanza:

So long pursued,
In what dark cave begun
And not yet done, were not the great
Adventure we suppose but some elaborate
Spectacle put on for fun
And not for food.

(*CP*, p. 151)

The rhyme scheme—ABCCBA—does not reveal rhyme until the fourth line and then moves on to attenuated rhyme and a pattern seen retrospectively. As with cultures, the conclusion or decadent stage imitates the beginning or primitive stage, but the latter sophisticated phase embodies self-consciously the entire pattern not apparent in the opening. Rhyme is reinforced by the metrical movement from dimeter lines to tetrameter couplets back to dimeter lines, ending in an anticlimactic phrase. This particular reinforcement of meaning by form marks an even greater commitment to form by an already formally sophisticated poet.

In "Courtyards in Delft," the Dutch interiors of de Hooch, which represent the repressive, sanitizing functions of the Calvinist societies of the Netherlands and Northern Ireland, also reveal this art's aestheticizing transformations: "Nothing is random, nothing goes to waste. / We miss the dirty dog, the fiery gin" (*CP*, p. 105). As "Girls on the Bridge" asserts, the "Grave daughters / Of

time" arrested on the bridge in Munch's painting will have to reenter life as "The road resumes" (*Hunt*, pp. 32–33). By its removal from process, painting represents all art's marginal situation and its tendency to separate the artist, as an observer, from society. Consequently, many of these poems are spoken to or by writers in exile or on the margin such as Ovid in Tomis, Bertolt Brecht in Svendborg, Knut Hamsun on a boxcar top, and Paul Durcan in Berlin. Frequently, the poet extended his overview by assuming a theoptic view, a perspective from a vast time or space by which human endeavors dwindle "to the dim stone where we are reared" (*CP*, p. 141) as he said in the remarkable love poem "The Globe in North Carolina."

SELECTED POEMS, THE HUDSON LETTER, *AND* THE YELLOW BOOK

THE great ache of the 1980s—Mahon's dwindling stream of poetic production, his grinding will to write, alternative pump-priming strategies, alcoholism, and depression—finds partial expression in autobiographical poems such as "Dawn at St Patrick's," "Noon at St Michael's," and "Craigvara House." Whether the publication of *Selected Poems* in 1991 was a symptom or a solution to this depression was debated among the critics. Perhaps most saw the omission of well-known poems and the revisions to individual poems as unfortunate meddling. In a *Poetry Review* interview with William Scammell at the time of publication, Mahon seemed defensive: "The last poem in the book was written in 1985, so reviewers will say I am all washed up. . . . Buy it . . . and complain about the finicky revisions and re-revisions. . . . Valéry said that a poem is never finished, only abandoned" (p. 6). This interview precedes a review of *Selected Poems* by Edna Longley in which the critic denounces the poet-reviser's intention: "Poems themselves belong to history—not only their author's personal history or literary history. The poet cannot revisit the *period* of composition, let alone the mood" (1991, p. 8). She extended this criticism to what she perceived as the failure of individual revisions: "Mahon's revisions read like literal translations. It proves his original inspiration—it proves the fact of inspiration—that they should fall so flat and cold" (pp. 8–9).

The uprightness and warmth Longley associated with the original poems may have arisen from the topicality of the poems, the excitement of recognizing shared brand names, current events, or literary references which are expunged from the revised poems. For many readers in the 1990s and after, the revised poems are more accessible because they are more general. For example, when the long epistolary poems "Beyond Howth Head" and "The Sea in Winter" were shorn of many topical references, they could be read more as meditations than as letters. In the final stanza of "Beyond Howth Head," for example, when references to Arnold's "Dover Beach," to his *cailín bán* (his fair lover from whom he is divorced at the time of revision), and to Norman Mailer's Vietnam era account *Armies of the Night* (itself an allusion to "Dover Beach") disappear from the revision, the poem draws away from the historical moment toward a more universal condition, a statement neither flat nor cold nor necessarily inferior. By deletions such as the reference to "Dover Beach," however, cords are snipped that held together poems within separate volumes, an unbinding that some readers and critics regret.

In the mid-1980s, Mahon lived some months in the attic room of John and Evelyn Montague, "turning over a new leaf" as he said in "The Attic." He then moved to Kinsale, serving as regular reviewer for the *Irish Times*, producing versions of Molière's *School for Husbands* and *School for Wives* (performed in 1984 and 1989 respectively), and translating a selection of Phillipe Jaccottet's poetry, for which he won the prestigious Scott Moncrieff Prize for Translation in 1989. No doubt Mahon would have traded this very notable but extra-poetic success for a spate of poems that would evince a creative thaw. That thaw may have begun early in 1991 when he came to the United States to teach at Villanova University and, in the following year when he moved to Washington Square in New York, at New York University. The several tumultuous years that followed in New York became the basis for *The Hudson Letter* (1995), a sequence of eighteen cantos of one to three pages, some actually letters but others translations or imitations (Ovid, Jules Laforgue, Sappho, Marcabru) or dramatic meditations on or from the situation of other writers (Elizabeth Bowen, W. H. Auden, Yeats's father J. B. Yeats, and an imaginary, turn-of-the-century Irish domestic servant).

The sequence opens with an epigraph from Camus' *American Journals* ("remember this desert of iron and cement is an island") reminding readers that this is a Mahon setting—"one place only, / . . . Unique in each particular," as he said elsewhere (p. 131)—that confronts the Atlantic, Europe, and the cosmos and that the poem shares it with other exiles who have sojourned here. The poem opens, "Winter; a short walk from the 10th St. Pier— / and what of the kick-start that should be here?" (p. 19), a question asked by some of the critics who had been waiting a decade for Mahon's revival. For example, Tim Kendall declared in *Poetry Review*, "His admirers have been waiting too; but they will find nothing to satisfy them in *The Hudson Letter*." He then spritzed one of the cantos with faint praise: "'Beauty and the Beast' (a witty paean to *King Kong*, and Fay Wray in particular), although still falling short of earlier work, at least does enough to remind the reader of former glories" (p. 52).

Because this poem declares its independence from the high lyrical standard of the earlier poems—through the loose hexameters, the mixture of pop cult and demotic diction, the breathless narrative—readers probably should enjoy this poem according to another scale:

> a black speck outlined against the morning sky
> clutching Fay, said Noël Coward, "like a suppository."
> It's all inconsistent, of course, and disproportionate,
> he's too small there and too big on the street, *I know*,
> but it makes no difference, it's a magnificent show.
> (*CP*, p. 212)

The opening line of the poem "I go night-shopping like Frank O'Hara I go bopping" suggests that the stylistic model for Mahon's poem may have been O'Hara's loose line and catalogued round of errands in the Village on "The Day Lady Died" or of another of O'Hara's ad hoc Manhattan poems. Whereas O'Hara rarely used rhyme, Mahon's *fort-da* rhyme sets the light tone O'Hara achieves otherwise. Rather than accepting Mahon's line above—"it makes no difference, it's a magnificent show"—at face value, readers might assay the lightness of Mahon's ostensible subject, his fondness for *King Kong*, and recognize the degree of camp in his devotion to Fay Wray.

The poem's epigraph from *Peter Pan* tells readers that "none of the lost boys know any stories" (p. 211), suggesting the advancement of popular culture as a provider of narratives. Yet the myth-laden Mahon is no more one of the lost boys than he is one of the homosexuals in "Sneaker's," a poem (unfortunately dropped from *Collected Poems*) comprised of actual conversation in the bar of that name. In both cases, Mahon sympathized with those shut out from the larger society who have formed smaller marginalized groups, analogous to the artists and their audience celebrated as a community from the beginning of Mahon's poetry. Secluded within "A rented 'studio' apartment in New York / five blocks from the river, time to think and work" (p. 186), the poet says in the first poem, by the second poem he recounts the intrusion of those "out there." The most desperate of the excluded—"Poor banished children of Eve (brain damage, delirium, / peripheral neuritis), with nowhere to call home"—are represented in the twelfth poem "Alien Nation." The poet's sympathy with this group is credible: "I know you and you me, you wretched buggers, / and I've no problem calling you my brothers / for I too have been homeless and in detox" (pp. 207–208). Ultimately, the poet would have readers recognize in his status as "an undesirable resident alien on this shore" his cosmic vagrancy: "Blown here like particles from an exploding sun, / we are all far from home" (*CP*, p. 208). Although some readers may find this shift of perspective from the personal to the theoptic too frequently and easily achieved by Mahon, the sequence should be judged, nevertheless, according to this larger sense of "inside" and "outside." The final poem begins, "Once upon a time it let me out and let me go—" but concludes, "When does the thaw begin? / We have been too long in the cold.—Take us in; take us in!" (p. 222).

Perhaps the weakest poems in the sequence are those in which Mahon discoursed on life and offered encouragement and advice to his daughter and son respectively. Although self-mocking references to Polonius are meant to reduce fatuousness, too evident in his earlier long poem "The Yaddo Letter," artistic allusion cannot altogether transform him from being the ordinary, advice-giving father. For that matter, skepticism about the transformative function of art pervades *The Hudson Letter* from the looser, more self-conscious diction and rhyme to explicit comments about the muse, the nightingale, or other reminders of the artistic process. The most anomalous poem in the sequence—untitled in *The Hudson Letter*, titled "Ovid on West 4th" in the *Collected Poems*—concerns one of Ovid's metamorphoses, in which the rapist king Tereus is served his son in a filocidal fricassee by the boy's mother and aunt. To correct-

ly express the king's rage in discovering the contents of his meal, Mahon calls attention to the intervention of art, already twice removed from its subject by the fact of translation:

> Howling, he swept aside the candlesticks
> and called the furies from the depths of Styx—
> no, howling he overturned the dinner table
> and called the furies from the hobs of Hell.
>
> (*CP*, p. 198)

Mahon's self-correction also demonstrates his propensity to revise. Certainly, the revision of the title raises questions about the relation of art to life, here the application of the complex psychological relationships in Ovid's tale to the life of the poet-translator who lives on West 4th Street (in the next poem in the sequence, the first words in the poet's own voice are addressed to his own son: "Uneaten, you call home," p. 200). Mahon concluded his translation by adding a disclaimer that Ovid's story is not about arrogance, sex, or vengeance, "but about art / and the encoded mysteries of the human heart" (p. 199).

Of course, in Ovid's tale another transformation or translation occurs to the greatly wronged but murderous women who become birds to escape the king, his ravished sister-in-law Philomela becoming the nightingale. The appearance of an entire stanza of John Keats's "Ode to a Nightingale" as the first epigraph to *The Hudson Letter*, as well as the entrances and exits of Keats's nightingale, and John Milton's, throughout the sequence, reminds the reader not only of art's transformative power but also of its capacity to solace the refugee, whether this be Mahon in Manhattan or Keats's Old Testament émigré Ruth who "sick for home . . . stood in tears amid the alien corn."

In *The Hudson Letter*'s penultimate canto, Mahon contemplated his return to Dublin where he would continue to be, like J. B. Yeats, "an exile and a stranger" but "with the young audibly sneering behind my back" (*CP*, pp. 219, 218). That move actually occurred in 1995, when he returned to his top-floor flat in Fitzwilliam Square, and that persona of an aged, somewhat cantankerous reactionary, to some extent a literary creation, emerged in *The Yellow Book*. The poet's repatriation was supported in part by an award from the U.S.-based Lannan Foundation, and the poet began and maintained the sort of disciplined regimen he had once proclaimed difficult for his poetry but conducive to good health. The evidence for the resurgence of poetic powers appears more clearly in his *Collected Poems* than in *The Yellow Book*.

In a year when Medbh McGuckian and Ciaran Carson published poetry—*Shelmalier* and *The Twelfth of Never*—that, respectively, enlarged or deconstructed the myth of 1798 in Ireland, Mahon's poetry was revisiting the Victorian fin de siècle and subscribing to the decadence made famous by the writings of Oscar Wilde, Ernest Dowson, and others who often appeared in Aubrey Beardsley's journal *The Yellow Book*. Declaring himself "a decadent who lived to tell the story," he conceded that "burning without warmth or illumination / . . . / I keep alight the cold candle of decadence" (*CP*, p. 240). One critic has complained about the "proliferation of quotations" which "imply an abdication of authority" (Tinley, 1998, p. 87). One might argue that the authority of the decadent writer derives from his situation at the terminus of Western literature, which he looks back on and echoes when appropriate. For example, his statement above about the "cold candle" reflects the summons of the apologist for decadence Walter Pater, "to burn with a hard gem-like flame," itself a statement that incorporated metaphors from Gerard Hopkins, John Ruskin, and William Wordsworth of the diamond as an image for art. Mahon asked, "so let me write / in praise of yellow" (*The Yellow Book*, p. 36), the 1890s color of decay, and of the twenty sections of *The Yellow Book*, one is entitled wittily, "Remembering the 90s" (although changed in *CP*, unfortunately, to the insipid "Hangover Square"), and others are entitled or dedicated to Oscar Wilde, "Axel's Castle," Austin Clarke's Dublin of the 1950s, Mahon's own collegiate decadence in the 1960s, Arthur Schopenhauer's hermitism, and the heyday of the Gate Theatre. Beyond that, the volume's prologue and section XIII are translations by Baudelaire, the master of urban decay, and a translation of Juvenal in section X comments on his decadent age and modern times. Beyond that, poems on drinking and smoking defend decadent practices. The earlier of these "*An Bonnán Buí*" lifts off from a famous poem in Irish in which Cathal Buí (Cathal the Yellow) MacGiolla Ghunna expresses his deep sympathy for a yellow bittern who has died of thirst. Although diverted from the eighteenth century, the poem raises serious issues in Mahon's own life about "the lyrical madness" and whether we can have "music without hunger" (p. 27) but then descends into side issues—"Do we give up fighting so the tourists come / or fight the harder so they stay at home?"—that seem daft. If this poem that might be called "Drink" is a mixed success, "Smoke" is a satirical lyric that seems more thoroughly successful:

The last addicts gather at the last strand
for a last smoke-out on the burning sand
with Ekberg, Warhol, Guevara, Bowen and Cocteau,
ashes to ashes at the rainbow's end—
we are under a cloud, our world gone with the wind.
(p. 45)

Like a decadent pop artist, Mahon gathers here celebrities and familiar phrases, as if in balloons nudging each other, in what might be call a mockalyptic scene.

It may be appropriate to decadent poetry that it trails off, ends anticlimactically, or reaches for, but lacks energy to grasp, some effect as is the case with sections VIII, X, VIII, and XX. In section XVIII, an elegy for his mother entitled "Death in Bangor" ("Bangor Requiem," in *Collected Poems*), the poem intends to trail off. As the funeral ends—"something of you, perhaps the incurable ache / of art, goes with me as I travel south" (p. 261)—the scene flattens out into images of a muffled sadness.

Even critics who prefer Mahon's earlier work recognize his need "to explore alternatives to the kind of work he had polished to perfection in *The Hunt by Night*" and "that change of direction suggested artistic risk" (Tinley, 1998, 87). This admirable courage "to explore alternatives" reaches very hopeful conclusions in a dozen new poems that conclude *Collected Poems*. Some of these are imitations, considerable achievements in that sort of semidependent poem, but the final five poems signal a new start in several ways. In these poems readers are reminded that the decadence of *The Yellow Book*, like all of Mahon's poems of refuse and retrospection, is basically radical, one turn away from a minimalist starting over. These sites of possible gestation in Mahon's poetry, of departure with some long-awaited return, have become signatures with the sharp etching of an ideogram: "Like a claw-print in concrete / After the bird has flown" (88). These five poems also return readers to the signs of rebirth, not to the lithographic bird claw or the disused, static wombs of lift-shaft, dog corner, or lost hubcap, but to the primeval magma from which life arose. "A Swim in Co. Wicklow," for example, teems with images of first life:

> Spindrift, crustacean patience
> and a gust of ozone,
> you come back once more
> to this dazzling shore,
> its warm uterine rinse,
> heart-racing heave and groan.
>
> (p. 280)

In this "hissing wash" and "seething broth," among "slick algae, spittle, froth" the beloved swims "smart as a rogue gene." The stanzaic form—six line tercets with variations on three rhymes—just contains the slithering variation of rhyme and slant rhyme and lines alive with assonantal echoes. "The Dream Play" and "St Patrick's Day" also celebrate the world's flux, "a mist of glistening gism" and "frost off a ditch, ice in the sun" (pp. 282, 288).

"Shapes and Shadows" perceives in the abstract canvases of William Scott the "thick / but vague" suggestions of first forms and new beginnings, "shades of the prehistoric, / ghosts of colour and form":

> as if to announce the death
> of preconception and myth
> and start again on the fresh
> first morning of the world
> with snow, ash, whitewash,
> limestone, mother-of-pearl, . . .
>
> (p. 279)

From this process of radical new beginnings, the poet who has been called "one of contemporary poetry's great solitaries" finds new ways of imagining a material world in which we can honor the life of things and find ourselves at home, "the shadow of a presence, / a long-sought community."

SELECTED BIBLIOGRAPHY

I. COLLECTED WORKS (POETRY). *Poems 1962–1978* (London, 1979); *Selected Poems* (Oldcastle, Ire., 1990; Harmondsworth, Eng., and New York, 1991); *Selected Poems*, rev. ed. (New York, 1993; Oldcastle, Ire., 1993); *Journalism: Selected Prose 1970–1995* (Dublin, 1996); *Collected Poems* (Oldcastle, Ire., 1999).

II. INDIVIDUAL WORKS (POETRY AND PROSE). *Twelve Poems* (Belfast, 1965); *Design for a Grecian Urn* (Cambridge, Mass., 1966); *Night-Crossing* (London, 1968); *Beyond Howth Head* (Dublin, 1970); *Ecclesiastes* (Manchester, Mass., 1970); *Lives* (London, 1972); *The Man Who Built His City in Snow* (London, 1972); *The Snow Party* (London, 1975); *Light Music* (Belfast, 1977); *In Their Element: A Selection of Poems* (with Seamus Heaney) (Belfast, 1977); *The Sea in Winter* (Dublin, 1979; Old Deerfield, Mass., 1979); *Courtyards in Delft* (Dublin, 1981); *The Hunt by Night* (London, 1982; Winston-Salem, N.C., 1982); *A Kensington Notebook* (London, 1984); *Antarctica* (Dublin, 1985); *The Yaddo Letter* (Oldcastle, Ire., 1992); *The Hudson Letter* (Oldcastle, Ire., 1995; Winston-Salem, N.C., 1996); *The Yellow Book* (Oldcastle, Ire., 1997; Winston-Salem, N.C., 1998).

III. SCREENPLAYS / TELEVISION ADAPTATIONS. *Shadows on Our Skin*, prod. Kenneth Trodd, dir. Jean O'Brien (based on the novel by Jennifer Johnston, BBC 1, 1980); *How Many Miles to Babylon?* prod. Ennis Lloyd, dir. Moira Armstrong (based on the novel by Jennifer Johnston, BBC 2, 1982); *Summer Lightning*, prod. Paul Joyce (based on the novel *First Love* by Ivan Turgenev, RTE, Dublin, and Channel 4, 1982/1984); *The Cry*, prod. Andrée Molyneause, dir. Chris Menaul (based on the short story by John Montague, BBC 1, 1984); *Death of the Heart*, dir. Peter Hammond (based on the novel by Elizabeth Bowen, Shades of Darkness Series, 1985); *Summer Lightning* (RTE/Channel 4, 1985); *Demon Lover*, dir. Peter Hammond (based on the novel by Elizabeth Bowen, Shades of Darkness Series, 1986).

IV. TRANSLATIONS. *The Chimeras*, trans. of *Les Chimères*, by Gèrard de Nerval (Dublin, 1982); *High Time*, trans. of *A School for Husbands*, by Molière (Oldcastle, Ire., 1985); *The School for Wives*, by Molière (Oldcastle, Ire., 1986); *Selected Poems*, by Phillipe Jaccottet (London, 1987; Harmonsworth, Eng., 1988); *The Bacchae*, by Euripides (Oldcastle, Ire., 1991); *Phaedra*, by Racine (Oldcastle, Ire., 1996).

V. ANTHOLOGIES EDITED. *The Sphere Book of Modern Irish Poetry*, ed. Derek Mahon (London, 1972); *The Penguin Book of Contemporary Irish Poetry*, eds. Peter Fallon and Derek Mahon (London, 1990).

VI. INTERVIEWS. Willie Kelly, "Each Poem for Me is a New Beginning," in *Cork Review* 2 (June 1981); Terence Brown, "An Interview with Derek Mahon," in *Poetry Ireland* 14 (autumn 1985); William Scammell, "Derek Mahon Interviewed," in *Poetry Review* 81 (summer 1991); Paul Keen, "Playing Football in No-man's Land: Paul Keen Speaks with Michael Longley," in *Books in Canada* (March 1999); James J. Murphy, Lucy McDiarmid, and Michael J. Durkan, "Q. & A. with Derek Mahon," in *Writing Irish: Selected Interviews with Irish Writers from the Irish Literary Supplement*, ed. James P. Myers Jr. (Syracuse, N.Y., 1999); Eamon Grennan, "The Art of Poetry LXXXII: Derek Mahon," in *Paris Review* 154 (spring 2000).

VII. CRITICAL STUDIES. Michael Longley, "Strife and the Ulster Poet," in *Hibernia* (November 1969); Thomas D.

Redshaw, "Ri, As in Regional: Three Ulster Poets," in *Éire-Ireland* 9, no. 2 (summer 1974); Michael Allen, "Options: The Poetry of Michael Longley," in *Éire-Ireland* 8 (1975); Terence Brown, "Four New Voices: Poets of the Present," in *Northern Voices* (Dublin, 1975); Seamus Deane, "Irish Poetry and Irish Nationalism," in *Two Decades of Irish Writing* (Cheadle, U.K., 1975); D. E. S. Maxwell, "Contemporary Poetry in the North of Ireland," in *Two Decades of Irish Writing* (Cheadle, U.K., 1975); Douglas Dunn, "Let the God not Abandon Us: On the Poetry of Derek Mahon," in *Stone Ferry Review* 2 (winter 1978); Brian Donnelly, "The Poetry of Derek Mahon," in *English Studies* 60, no. 1 (1979); Adrian Frazier, "Irish Poetry after Yeats," in *Literary Review* (special issue on contemporary Irish poetry) 22, no. 2 (winter 1979); Timothy Kearney, "The Poetry of the North: A Post-Modern Perspective," in *Crane Bag* 3, no. 2 (1979); Dennis O'Driscoll, "Remembering the Past," in *Crane Bag* 3, no. 1 (1979); Brian Donnelly, "From Ninevah to the Harbour Bar," in *Ploughshares* 6, no. 1 (1980); Dillon Johnston, "Unaccommodated Mahon: An Ulster Poet," in *The Hollins Critic* 17, no. 5 (1980); Terence Brown, "An Ulster Renaissance? Poets from the North of Ireland 1965-1980," in *Concerning Poetry* (special issue on Irish poetry) 14, no. 2 (1981); John Byrne, "Derek Mahon: A Commitment to Change," in *Crane Bag* 6, no. 1 (1982); Serge Fauchereau, "Contemporary Irish Poetry: Confronting the Irish Situation," in *Critique* 38 (1982); D. E. S. Maxwell, "Semantic Scruples: A Rhetoric for Politics in the North," in *Literature and the Changing Ireland*, ed. Peter Connolly (Gerrards Cross, Buckinghamshire, 1982; Totowa, N.J., 1982); Stan Smith, "Margins of Tolerance: Responses to Post-War Decline," in *Inviolable Voice: History and Twentieth Century Poetry* (Dublin, 1982); Adrian Frazier, "Proper Portion: Derek Mahon's The Hunt by Night," in *Éire-Ireland* 18, no. 4 (1983); Eamon Grennan, "'To the Point of Speech': The Poetry of Derek Mahon," in *Contemporary Irish Writing*, ed. James D. Brophy and Raymond J. Porter (Boston, 1983); "Derek Mahon," in *Contemporary Literary Criticism* 27 (1984); Paul Durcan, "The World of Derek Mahon," in *Magill* (December 1984); Maurice Riordan, "An Urbane Perspective: The Poetry of Derek Mahon," in *The Irish Writer and the City*, Irish Literary Studies 18, ed. Maurice Harmon (Gerrands Cross, Buckinghamshire, Eng., 1984; Totowa, N.J., 1984); Seamus Deane, "Derek Mahon: Freedom from History," in *Celtic Revivals* (London, 1985); Seamus Heaney, "The Peter Laver Memorial Lecture 'Place and Displacement': Recent Poetry from Northern Ireland," in *Wordsworth Circle* 16, no. 2 (spring 1985); Mark Patrick Hederman, "Poetry and the Fifth Province," in *Crane Bag* 9, no. 1 (1985); Seamus Deane, "Contemporary Literature, 1940–1980," in *A Short History of Irish Literature* (London, 1986); Robert F. Garratt, "The Tradition of Discontinuity: A Glance at Recent Ulster Poetry," in *Modern Irish Poetry: Tradition and Continuity from Yeats to Heaney* (Berkeley, Calif., 1986); Edna Longley, "The Singing Line: Form in Derek Mahon's Poetry," in *Poetry in the Wars* (Newcastle-upon-Tyne, 1986); Ben Howard, "The Pressed Melodeon," in *Kenyon Review* 9, no. 1 (winter 1987); John Kerrigan, "Knowing the Dead," in *Essays in Criticism* 37, no. 1 (January 1987); Anthony Bradley, "Literature and Culture in the North of Ireland," in *Cultural Contexts and Literary Idioms in Contemporary Irish Literature*, ed. Michael Kenneally (Gerrards Cross, Buckinghamshire, 1988); Joris Duytenschaever, "History in the Poetry of Derek Mahon," in *History and Violence in Anglo-Irish Literature*, ed. Joris Duytenschaever and Geert Lernout (Amsterdam, 1988); John Wilson Foster, "Post-War Ulster Poetry: A Chapter in Anglo-Irish Literary Relations," in *Cultural Contexts and Literary Idioms in Contemporary Irish Literature*, ed. Michael Kenneally (Gerrards Cross, Buckinghamshire, Eng. 1988); Edna Longley, "MacNeice and After," in *Poetry Review* 78, no. 2 (summer 1988); Edna Longley, "'When Did You Last See Your Father?': Perceptions of the Past in Northern Irish Writing 1965–1985," in *Cultural Contexts and Literary Idioms in Contemporary Irish Literature*, ed. Michael Kenneally (Gerrards Cross, Buckinghamshire, Eng., 1988); Anthony Bradley, "The Irishness of Irish Poetry after Yeats," in *New Irish Writing*, ed. James D. Brophy and Eamon Grennan (Boston, 1989); John Engle, "The Vital Bond of Distance: Irish Poetry on the Road," in *New Irish Writing*, ed. James D. Brophy and Eamon Grennan (Boston, 1989); Seamus Heaney, "The Pre-Natal Mountain: Vision and Irony in Recent Irish Poetry," in *The Place of Writing* (Atlanta, Ga., 1989); Dillon Johnston, "Next to Nothing: Uses of the Otherworld in Modern Irish Literature," in *New Irish Writing*, eds. James D. Brophy and Eamon Grennan (Boston, 1989); Brendan Kennelly, "Derek Mahon's Humane Perspective," in *Tradition and Influence in Anglo-Irish Poetry*, ed. Terence Brown and Nicholas Grene (Basingstoke, Eng., 1989; Totowa, N.J., 1989); Edna Longley, "Poetic Forms and Social Malformations," in *Tradition and Influence in Anglo-Irish Poetry*, ed. Terence Brown and Nicholas Grene (Basingstoke, Eng., 1989); Barbara Carlisle, "Derek Mahon," in *Contemporary Authors* 128 (1990); William A. Wilson, "A Theopotic Eye: Derek Mahon's The Hunt by Night," in *Éire-Ireland* 25, no. 4 (winter 1990); Philip Hobsbaum, "Mahon, Derek," in *Contemporary Poets*, 5th ed., ed. Tracey Chavalier (London and Chicago, 1991); Edna Longley, "Where a Thought Might Grow," in *Poetry Review* 81, no. 2 (summer 1991); Peter McDonald, "History and Poetry: Derek Mahon and Tom Paulin," in *The Poet's Place: Ulster Literature and Society*, ed. Gerald Dawe and John Wilson Foster (Belfast, 1991); Bill Tinley, "International Perspectives in the Poetry of Derek Mahon," *Irish University Review* 21, no. 1 (spring/summer 1991); Elmer Andrews, "The Poetry of Derek Mahon: 'places where a thought might grow,'" in *Contemporary Irish Poetry*, ed. Elmer Andrews (Basingstoke, Eng., 1992); Terence Brown, "Home and Away: Derek Mahon's France," in *Ireland and France, a Bountiful Friendship*, ed. Barabara Hayley and Christopher Murray (Gerrards Cross, Eng., 1992); Hugh Haughton, "'Even now there are places where a thought might grow': Place and Displacement in the Poetry of Derek Mahon," in *The Chosen Ground: Essays on the Contemporary Poetry of Northern Ireland*, ed. Neil Corcoran (Bridgend, Wales, 1992; Chester Springs, Pa., 1992); Seamus Heaney, "Place and Displacement: Reflections on Some Recent Poetry from Northern Ireland," in *Contemporary Irish Poetry*, ed. Elmer Andrews (Basingstoke, Eng., 1992); Richard Kearney, "Myth and Modernity in Irish Poetry," in *Contemporary Irish Poetry*, ed. Elmer Andrews (Basingstoke, Eng., 1992); John Kerrigan, "Ulster Ovids," in *The Chosen Ground: Essays on the Contemporary Poetry of Northern Ireland*, ed. Neil Corcoran (Bridgend, 1992; Chester Springs, Pa., 1992); Edna Longley, "The Aesthetic and the Territorial," in *Contemporary Irish Poetry*, ed. Elmer Andrews (Basingstoke, Eng., 1992); Jody Allen-Rudolph, "Derek Mahon: Bibliography," in *Irish University Review* 24, no. 1 (1994); Eavan Boland, "Compact and Compromise: Derek Mahon as a Young Poet," in *Irish University Review* 24, no. 1 (1994); Terence Brown, "Derek Mahon: The Poet and Painting," in *Irish University Review* 24, no. 1 (1994); Catriona Clutterbuck, "Elpenor's Crumbling Oar: Disconnection and Art in the Poetry of Derek Mahon," in *Irish University Review* 24, no. 1 (1994); Peter Denman, "Know the One? Insolent Ontology and Mahon's Revisions," in *Irish University Review* 24, no. 1 (1994); Tim Kendall, "'Leavetakings and Homecomings': Derek Mahon's Belfast," in *Éire-Ireland* 29, no. 4 (1994); Edna Longley, *The Living Stream: Literature & Revisionism in Ireland* (Newcastle-upon-Tyne, 1994); Michael Longley, "The Empty Holes of Spring: Some Reminiscences of Trinity & Two Poems Addressed to Derek Mahon," in *Irish University Review* 24, no. 1 (1994); Christopher Murray, "'For the Fun of the Thing': Derek Mahon's Dramatic Adaptations," in *Irish University Review* 24, no. 1 (1994); John Redmond, "Wilful Inconsistency: Derek Mahon's Verse-Letters," in *Irish University Review* 24, no. 1 (1994); Kathleen Shields, "Derek Mahon's Poetry of Belonging," in *Irish University Review* 24, no. 1 (1994); Bill Tinley, "'Harmonies and Disharmonies': Derek Mahon's Francophile Poetics," in *Irish University Review* 24, no. 1 (1994); Terence Brown, "An Introduction," in *Journalism: Selected Prose 1970–1995* (Oldcastle, Ire., 1996); Tim Kendall, "Beauty and the Beast," in *Poetry Review* 86, no. 1 (spring 1996); Neil Corcoran, *After Yeats & Joyce: Reading Modern Irish Literature* (Oxford and New York, 1997); Dillon Johnston, "MacNeice & Mahon," in *Irish Poetry after Joyce*, rev. ed. (Syracuse, N.Y., 1997); Peter McDonald, "Louis MacNeice's Posterity," in *Princeton University Library Chronicle* 59, no. 3 (1998); Bill Tinley, "Jaundice," *Metre* 4 (spring/summer 1998); David G. Williams, "'The Writing Life': Derek Mahon's Journalism," in *Journal of Modern Literature* 21, no. 2 (1998); Neil Corcoran, *Poets of Modern Ireland* (Cardiff, U.K., 1999); Brian John, "Derek Mahon's Letters from America," in *New Hibernia Review* 3, no. 3 (1999).

NORMAN MACCAIG

(1910–1996)

Philip Hobsbaum

NORMAN MACCAIG IS one of the supreme lyric poets of the twentieth century. That is his strength, and also his limitation. He ranks with Robert Graves, Theodore Roethke, and Amy Clampitt in the twentieth century and, in a historical context, with Robert Herrick, Richard Lovelace, and Henry Vaughan. What he can do may be seen in one celebrated poem, his most anthologized: "Summer Farm" (in *Riding Lights,* 1955). Those readers who appreciate this will quietly but delightedly celebrate MacCaig. Those who do not like it had better go elsewhere.

> Straws like tame lightnings lie about the grass
> And hang zigzag on hedges. Green as glass
> The water in the horse-trough shines.
> Nine ducks go wobbling by in two straight lines.
> A hen stares at nothing with one eye,
> Then picks it up. Out of an empty sky
> A swallow falls and, flickering through
> The barn, dives up again into the dizzy blue.
> I lie, not thinking, in the cool soft grass,
> Afraid of where a thought might take me—as
> This grasshopper with plated face
> Unfolds his legs and finds himself in space.
> Self under self, a pile of selves I stand
> Threaded on time, and with metaphysic hand
> Lift the farm like a lid and see
> Farm within farm, and in the centre, me.
>
> (p. 17)

This poem is the essence of MacCaig's art, and of that art the essence is "A hen stares at nothing with one eye, / Then picks it up." One applauds the observation, in both senses. The poet sees, and the way in which he records what he sees enhances the seeing. MacCaig got tired of being called a metaphysical, but that is certainly an apposite term. As the critic James Smith wrote, "It is no association of things on account of a similarity due to an accident . . . but of things that, though hostile, in reality cry out for association with each other" (*Scrutiny,* December 1933, p. 235). The hen sees "nothing," then picks "it" up, thus showing

that there is more here than initially met the human eye. What is true of this metaphysical conceit is true of the poem as a whole, and also true of MacCaig's work at large. A good deal of his verse embodies the reconciliation of paradoxical entities. The "tame lightnings" can be accepted as such since they exist in the poem as metaphors for straws—the comparison being heightened by the word "zigzag" which is apposite to both straw and meteorological phenomenon.

The poem, like others by MacCaig, tends to become simplified in one's memory. When the text is confronted, however, one may find it little constrained by overt formality. The meter is remembered as being couched in straight quatrains, but these are arranged in pairs and not as alternations. Moreover, the third line of each stanza is truncated from the usual pentameter: "The water in the horse-trough shines." It may be taken over the line-division: "A swallow falls and, flickering through / The barn . . ." This shortened third line allows for a degree of sprung rhythm: "flickering through / The barn, dives up again into the dizzy blue." In spite of the apparently formal stanza, a line can be condensed to four stresses or, as here, elongated to six. Elongation makes for a greater extent of mimesis. The swallow's flight upward is, so to speak, enacted in the verse.

This lyric has an extent of self-consciousness that is not necessarily an appurtenance of the form. Its final stanza bears an exceptional amount of consideration.

> Self under self, a pile of selves I stand
> Threaded on time, and with metaphysic hand
> Lift the farm like a lid and see
> Farm within farm, and in the centre, me.

This summation of the poem reflects back upon previous images. None exists for its own sake. Each is part of a plan which, if mysterious at first, is revealed in the mode of telling.

The poet has already compared himself with a grasshopper that cannot unfold his extremities without projecting himself further than intended. He has empathized with creature after creature, and finds himself part and parcel of each one: "a pile of selves." In a gesture of self-reflexion he gazes down through this "pile of selves," and that gesture is ratified, again, by the springing of rhythm and the displacement of syntax. The alliteration of "Lift the farm like a lid" lends emphasis to the movement. The prolongation of the word "see" through its strategic placement at the end of a line, where the long vowel is allowed to trill on, leads to the weight given to the conclusion through the repeated "farm" and the revelation that, behind the imagery, is the eye. Beyond what is seen is the seer, and what is seen is an inalienable self at last.

EARLY LIFE AND WORK

IT was not easy for Norman MacCaig to find the self discovered in "Summer Farm." More than almost any other lyric poet, his was a prolonged gestation. One can attribute this to the confused identity of a Scot in the early twentieth century. Questions of education also factor in.

Norman MacCaig was born on 14 November 1910 in Edinburgh, Scotland, where he lived practically all his life, most of it at the same address—7 Leamington Terrace, in a district called Bruntsfield. He was married for fifty years to the same woman, Isabel, who had worked as a lexicographer. His origins, however, were more complex than this would suggest. His father, Robert MacCaig, came from Dumfriesshire and his mother, Joan (McLeod) MacCaig, from the Isle of Scalpay. She was a Gaelic speaker. One could hear this influence in MacCaig's voice: a characteristic prolongation of vowel sounds owing little to the urban setting with which he chose to surround himself.

His education was resolutely metropolitan. He received an excellent grounding at Edinburgh's famous Royal High School, and went on to Edinburgh University where he studied Latin and Greek and was awarded a first-class honors degree. That was a period when to gain a first in such a subject meant an uncommon mastery of fact and an assiduous application to study. He went on to become a primary school teacher, a profession which he followed for more than thirty years, lamenting toward the end that he had never

been placed on the panel of candidates from which head teachers were commonly selected.

This circumstance was due to the fact that he was a noncombatant in the Second World War. In fact, he went to jail for his beliefs, spending ninety-three days in Wormwood Scrubs Prison. He saw out the rest of the war as a nurseryman in Edinburgh, digging gardens. This suggests a romantic idealism that perhaps is a clue to the numinous quality of his verse. His youthful holidays in Scalpay, the place of his mother's birth, gave him a source of inscape that proved to be an unfailing fount of imagery. He was basically a poet of the West Highlands of Scotland. He said himself that, as a teenager and "a ferocious cyclist," he pedaled up a side road to a place called Achmelvich, north of Lochinver, and fell in love with this place; its two small crofts, its hills and its loch. His close friend until the older poet's death, Hugh MacDiarmid, pointed out the incidence of place names in the titles of MacCaig's poems: "Harris, East End," "Neglected Graveyard, Luskentyre," "Summer Waterfall, Glendale," "By Achmelrich Bridge," "Loch Roe" (*Akros,* March 1968, p. 22). For most of his life MacCaig spent each summer in this region, walking and fishing.

Yet the young poet found it difficult to develop. To see the place he had marked out as his Eden, he needed to find a technique. Here, his education was of less help than might have been expected. There was little to connect him with a living tradition of poetry in English, yet there seemed no other route to take. He eschewed the synthetic Scots evolved by his friend MacDiarmid and, equally, the Gaelic written by his distinguished contemporary, Sorley Maclean.

In metropolitan London, the 1930s was a chaotic time. The reigning school of poetry had been dominated by two Americans, T. S. Eliot and Ezra Pound. They had access to the mode of qualitative progression, an associative technique practiced by Walt Whitman. This was denied, at least in its entirety, to younger British poets of the era. Much of what even so major a poet as Wystan Auden practiced was flawed by American mannerisms that sat uneasily with his own early influences, Thomas Hardy, Wilfred Owen, and Edward Thomas. Auden and his associates, such as Louis MacNeice and Charles Madge, attempted forms of social realism that were alien to the more Romantic poets growing up before the Second World War.

Many of these were young Scots: not only Norman MacCaig but also J. F. Hendry, Tom Scott, G. S. Fraser, and W. S. Graham. Their revulsion from the School of Auden was voiced eloquently by J. F. Hendry, the editor of the anthology *The New Apocalypse* (1940), in which several of them initially appeared. He wrote in the book's introduction: "Freedom from matter is eternally impossible, and leads to the reaction of mechanistic-materialism, as found to-day in the English poets, Allott, Auden and others, via Bukharin and Deborin. . . . Logic, machine-made logic, has resulted from our fear of ourselves, fear of our uncontrolled energy, being translated into fear of the outside world" (p. 12).

What does he counsel otherwise, this prophet of a new process in poetry? It seems that he turned to the nineteenth-century French symbolist Arthur Rimbaud as representing the first flare up of that spirit of invention and search for novelty that distinguishes the modern movement. Certainly critics find in Rimbaud what may well pass for new forms, necessary for a discovery of the unknown: "Apocalyptic writing is therefore concerned with the study of living, the collapse of social forms and the emergence of new and more organic ones" (*The New Apocalypse*, p. 9).

That is quite tenable as theory. It is when critics look at the actual writing of Rimbaud that problems may be seen in matching theory with practice:

J'ai embrass é l'aube d'été.
Rien ne bougeait encore au front des palais. L'eau était morte. Les camps d'ombres ne quittaient pas la route du bois. J'ai marché, réveillant les haleines vives et tièdes, et les pierreries regardèrent, et les ailes se levèrent sans bruit.
La première entreprise fut, dans le sentier déjà empli de frais et blàmes éclats, une fleur qui me dit son nom.
Je ris au wasserfall blond qui s'échevela à travers les sapins: à la cime argentée je reconnus la déesse . . .
　　("Aube," in *Les Illuminations*, 1872–1875, p. 70)

I have held in my arms the summer dawn.
Nothing stirred yet in front of the palaces. The waters were still.
The shadows had not yet left their encampments in the woods.
I walked, waking the brisk warm winds; and precious stones gazed
at me, and wings rose around me noiselessly.
My first adventure was in a footpath already covered with splinters

of fresh pale light, where a flower told me her name.
I laughed at the waterfall which twisted its ragged way through the
pines: at the silver summit I espied the goddess . . .
　　　　　(Rootham, trans., p. 57)

Scholars agree that the unconscious is structured. The unconscious mind of Rimbaud is probably more structured than most. The imagery of his poetry has an eidetic quality, as though he was not merely describing but narrating. The effect is that apparently arbitrary collocations assume a degree of inevitability. This is brought about by a highly decisive mode of writing. The language is not transparent: there are internal rhymes and half rhymes, a marked extent of sonority, a verbal pattern existing as a system in parallel, it seems, with the experience conveyed.

There can be little doubt that Rimbaud was doing what the theorists of the New Apocalypse said they were doing. Yet Hendry, for instance, falls very far short of his exemplar in "The Four Seasons of War" (in *The Bombed Happiness*, 1942):

Snow banks the garden with its arabis.
Far out upon its seas white seagulls loop
The magic of white mimicry in trellised
Circles of incandescence and creation
Sung through hives of blue in the honeyed air.
Throughout man's temples sound the seasons' bells,
And ghosts of silence, loud in bomb reverberation,
Assassins of summer in these breathless chancels,
Swirl to his assault. Yet still the long and haunting
　waves swoop
Upon listening ears the peace of shining and inviolate
　shores . . .

　　　　　　　　(p. 25)

Hendry's poem reads like a ruinous adaptation of the French symbolist. In order to write like Rimbaud, it is not enough to feel like Rimbaud. One must take on, with his emotional outlook, a measure of his technique. The poems of the New Apocalypse—one could not, imagine Rimbaud with a label so overweening—do not use language with any degree of skill. There is no meaningful relationship between rhythm and syntax, indeed, between word and word. The result is verse of considerable obscurity. For example, consider Tom Scott's "poem" (in *The White Horseman*, 1941):

The brown-lapped cedars of years
Toll the bell of the times, the grave
And carrion drains to its wires,

The yearn of the blood lists to the wells
Of wounds and sad nerves walk abroad like fingers;
The gull wheels hard against the shrike's larder
And harvests a sowing of guns and mortars, the
    moon . . .

(p. 112)

For another example, take G. S. Fraser's "rhetoric in winter" (in *The White Horseman*):

Rich, with your leaves and streams and swans,
And every bronze eternal tree.
Valley shut in between the metal roads!
Where the cypress is sad, the poor shall have no
    picnics.
Where the grass is soft, the lovers shall not lie . . .

(p. 75)

And another example from W. S. Graham's "Over the apparatus of the Spring is drawn" (in *Cage without Grievance*, 1942):

Over the apparatus of the Spring is drawn
A constructed festival of pulleys from sky.
A dormouse swindled from numbers into wisdom
Trades truth with bluebells. The result unknown
Fades in the sandy beetle-song that martyrs hear
Who longingly for violetcells prospect the meads. . . .

(p. 7)

It is not that these extracts, characteristic of the verse of this school, are lacking in rhythm. It is rather that the rhythm is functionless. It has no necessary relation to what is being said. Critics would note, also, the overstated diction. The orchestra is relying too much on the percussion and the heavy brass. There is a lack of variegation and subtlety.

It is no coincidence, either, that the poets here quoted are all Scottish. There were English poets, certainly, connected with this school, but the affinity seems based on indefinability as regard to character. It was no easy matter growing up as a Scot in the early twentieth century. As Edwin Muir had said—provoking a controversy in doing so—"The Scottish consciousness is divided . . . Scotsmen feel in one language and think in another" (*Scott and Scotland*, p. 8). The technical name for this is "the Caledonian antisyzygy" (p. 36). This term was originally couched by a Scottish professor, Gregory Smith, and there is little doubt that Scottish education has a good deal to do with it. The Scots may have been well instructed in the

conventional sense, but at no time in the humanities were they brought face to face with the modern world. If the young poets were not to follow Hugh MacDiarmid into a Scottish amalgam, redeemed only by the genius of that solitary figure, where were they to go? The Calvinism that was dispersed through every level of Scottish life made for inhibition and low self-esteem. One can see why the unlocking of the unconscious associated with Rimbaud proved attractive.

That is why Norman MacCaig, who was eventually to emerge as such an exemplar of verse writing and meaningful imagery, was in his youth a key member of the New Apocalypse school. Four poems of his are included in the anthology of the same name and nine in *The White Horseman*. As can be seen in the ensuing extract from an untitled poem in *The New Apocalypse*, he shared in the nerveless rhythms and melodramatic diction of his fellows, though it seems he had a residual respect for metrical form, whether or not he was able to use it as a means of framing a genuinely mimetic rhythm:

The closer fist clamped my ell-head in
a butt of seaweeds and dawn rapidly
scalped my woolly night and left it
bleeding dismally on the window. Down
and upon hands, never in, a spot
of crumbly brow whispered like a butterfly

and out of the wings oozed a tongue of
mud protruding in spirals beneath me
so that I rose turning slowly, the young
man of sea . . .

(p. 64)

None of his poems from the first two Apocalyptic anthologies appeared in either of MacCaig's first two volumes of verse. He seemed to be gaining a degree of control over his diction, but unfortunately that was in the direction of mannerism. In *Far Cry* (1943)—where, as with the anthology pieces, there are no titles—a number of poems begin with a strongly voiced negative: "No rain falls, no weeping or rattling rain" (p. 5); "No time to talk, no eyes in the phosphorescent light" (p. 24). These are first lines, and the mannerism becomes even more evident in *The Inward Eye* (1946): "No more of honour in this sun-purged air" (p. 11); "No Chinese bird sings in its mounded wood" (p. 56); "No Christmas grief will hold your crying hand" (p. 58). And there are similar negatives, less prominently displayed, in the body of the verse: "No tree-root now" (p. 7); "No knife bleeds moonlight" (p. 32); "No priestly arm heaves heaven" (p. 32); "No shining armour is needed" (p. 42); "No angel curlew" (p. 58). Another mannerism, noticeable though not necessarily placed in the initial line of any given poem, is a reiterated "Out of." Thus, in *Far Cry*, there is "Out of the cry, the candle" (p. 11), and, in *The Inward Eye,* there are "Out of the harp of air" (p. 11); "Out of what sleep" (p. 19); "Out of a tombstone music" (p. 34); "Out of the shade of scarlet" (p. 38); "Out of the stone noose, out of the builded snare" (p. 41). There is also the insistent repetition of certain stock words such as "cry," "sky," "eye," "shadow," "light," "wind," "rain," "glass," "words," "angels." This gives the impression of a verse driven, but not in any meaningful direction. It is a clutching after identity, but not in any deep-seated form, so that one feels a McCaig poem could be constructed out of such mannerisms as though it were habiliment and not genuine personality.

The spelling of the name—McCaig—is important here. That was the styling used by the author of the poems in the Apocalypse anthologies and of the two early books—which he later did his best to suppress. None of the poems contained in them figure in his *Collected Poems* (1985). It is as though *Far Cry* and *The Inward Eye,* together with their author, McCaig, existed only in some limbo.

RIDING LIGHTS

THE gap between these earlier productions and the first acknowledged book is startling. It is marked by the spelling of the name familiar to readers—MacCaig—but this is a sign only of a far deeper movement in personality. What had happened to turn the misty poetaster of the Apocalypse into the superbly accomplished artist of *Riding Lights*?

Undoubtedly the trauma of an English prison had its effect, as did the subsequent years spent as a laborer in Edinburgh. One crucial event, however, was MacCaig's marriage to Isabel in 1940. The critic John Press, in an early consideration of *Riding Lights,* pointed out the incidence of love poems and characterized them as "metaphysical inquiries into the essence of love, and into the painful intricacies of a unique relationship between two people" (*Rule and Energy,* p. 176). Certainly the influence of the seventeenth-century poet John Donne is manifest in such a poem as "In Deserts":

Seeking a minute which is not a lair
From which your sleeping self suddenly will spring
On me and tear
With gentle violence this time-wanderer,
I turn to tree, stone, hill—that everything
Outside myself—as though you never were,
As much as hill, stone, tree, exactly there.

And in myself your alterations make
Images everywhere I cannot pass.
No dreams but wake
Into themselves, their own reality,
Where I and the world, through love's mad looking-
glass,
Are at once the cave where you sleep time away
And hunting-ground and daily and nightly prey.
(p. 22)

One can hear "Air and Angels," "The Dream," and "The Good Morrow" behind this lyric, and, for all its poise, the influences appear to be doing much of the work. There are other love poems, however, including "Not yet Afterwards," "Décor," "For a Greeting," and "You Went Away," where the influence is more absorbed.

In any case, such lyrics appear to be a means toward equipoise, not the equipoise itself. That comes in what might be called the nature poems of this collection—"Summer Farm" among them—except that the external world is refracted through a peculiar sensibility. The poems of *Riding Lights,* unlike those of its immediate predecessors and a good many of its contemporaries, are formalistic well below the surface of metric. They answer, more than most, to the ideals of the Russian Formalists, who, themselves a phenomenon of the 1920s, so influenced the later course of criticism in the twentieth century.

Take "Country House," for example (p. 47). It is written in loosely pentametric quatrains, with an unobtrusive but highly skillful use of pararhyme in alternating patterns: "fumbles" / "invisible" and "hollow" / "hill," for example. This pararhyme solidifies as the poem proceeds, ending with "slates" / "nights" and "rose" / "stars." This, however, is an effect upon the surface. The pararhyme aids the expression; it is not itself the key.

Rather, the poem seems to turn on what, taken by itself, is a fairly innocuous line toward its center: "He taps on the door; there's a letter come for you." But this is no postman following his route, or neighbor come across to visit. In context, the line is decidedly sinister. It is ruin that assails the country house, and the poem is couched in a series of personifications of that entity, especially stressing its manual aspects:

> Ruin creeps round the house, his wet hand fumbles . . .
> He sets the dogs barking, and goes by
> Swinging an axe . . .
>   he'll push hot grasses in
>
> Between the stones . . .
>
> Something that leaves on the disordered slates
> A thumbprint of green lichen . . .

And, in context, "He taps on the door; there's a letter come for you."

This is a brilliant way of characterizing the inevitable decay that assails a neglected or abandoned house. Critics may classify MacCaig as a minor poet, but linguistically he stands at the crossroads between Rimbaud and Shakespeare: "Ruin hath taught me thus to ruminate, / That time will come and take my love away" (Shakespeare's Sonnet 64). This is no less true in MacCaig, where the love is borne for hills, lochs, marshes, or, in this case, an old house. The figure of his love poems proper never assumes physical shape. The reader remains uninformed of her features, her semblance, her character. The poet's more specific attention is given to what might be termed inanimate objects—except that, in MacCaig's writing, they are informed, far more than his human figures, with sensible warm motion.

In this regard, one would point out for special attention such poems as "Wet Snow" ("to see / A tree stand there hugged by its own ghost," p. 9); "The Rosyfingered" ("Even the grass, grown soulful, hangs its head / Over the prim winks of its daisies," p. 9); "Same Day" ("A wind picks up the argument it had lost," p. 28); "Double Life" ("This wind from Fife has cruel fingers, scooping / The heat from streets with salty finger-tips / Crusted with frost," p. 30); "Hidden Law" ("The nightlong imprecation of the tide / Rides on my waking nerves," p. 35); "Wreck" ("Twice every day it took aboard / a cargo of the tide; its crew / Flitted with fins," p. 43). This is a definite way of seeing. It has something of the eidetic imagery scholars associate with Rimbaud, but deflected somewhat—filtered through an original reading of the original undiluted by translators. Possibly it has been redefined by a frequentation of Wallace Stevens. MacCaig is one of the few British poets who made sensible use of the great American metaphysician—who must, however, have produced a vibrant impression when first introduced to Britain in quantity through the agency of *The Faber Book of Modern Verse* (1936). At any rate, the influence, if influence there be, has been absorbed and used to considerable effect.

MacCaig has pieced together a world based on the area of the West Highlands that he had taken as his Eden. As Crombie Saunders wrote, "He had created his own environment. Since then it has been enriched, varied, refined; but in essence the world is that of *Riding Lights*" (*Akros,* March 1968, p. 27). Subsequent volumes added to the oeuvre; they did not significantly develop it. Riding lights, after all, are lamps posted upon a ship to show that it is at anchor.

This is not to say that MacCaig may be considered a poet of only one significant book. What he added to *Riding Lights* were many poems as fine as the best of the poems to be found in that collection. However, he did not effectively extend his technique, and, though he sought new subjects, he treated them in much the same way. They are entities brought under the sway of his highly individual universe.

THE SINAI SORT

The Sinai Sort (1957) is much the same mixture as, though perhaps more forcefully stated than, its immediate predecessor. Possibly some of the pieces date from a transition period, before the poet found his feet. That would not, however, be true of the poem that gives the book its title. It is, given MacCaig's usual approach, ambitious. A preference is expressed for the humility of ordinary speech, that of the "Golden Calf," which in turn gives the poem its title. Such speech is distinguished from that of "the Sinai sort," the "magniloquence of thunder," or the language of God. The poem, however, is rhetorical rather than moving. It has itself something of the "magniloquence" that it adversely criticizes: "the incorruptible lava of the word" (p. 10). If this is an example of MacCaig thinking, it cannot be said to come off. He is better at demonstrating his thought in action, deploying the speech of the Golden Calf in more modest poems, several of which can be found in the remainder of the book.

Consider the following: "Clachtoll" ("that stone ledge / That founders with each tide and then / Gasps itself dripping up again," p. 16); "Roses and

Thorns" ("I touch / The little ragged word, and my torn skin / Carries your signature," p. 18); "Celtic Twilight" ("This incandescent hush of water is / Neither one sentence nor parenthesis," p. 22); "November Night, Edinburgh" ("A high roof sails, at the mast-head / Fluttering a grey and ragged star," p. 26); "After Eden" ("Never mind the dark / That creeps through Eden. There's that savage flare / Will show us how to dream a desert there," p. 29).

This last gives readers an idea of how the vision of MacCaig works. Sometimes blamed for an absence of commitment—he was in no sense a political poet—he defended himself in an interview by saying that during dark times there was all the more value when writing of delights and pleasures "as steady perception of ordinary happiness" (*Guardian,* 24 January 1996, p. 24). Whatever the circumstances, he could dream a desert around them. The circumstances entailed living a quiet life as a primary schoolmaster in Edinburgh and calling to mind on solitary evenings, sometimes within the interval of smoking a cigarette, the image of a rock or a loch that itself conjured up a poem (*Times,* 21 November 1995, p. 18). Even when he attempted what might seem to be a more ambitious topic, his imagination circumscribed the imagined Eden. That, however, is also to say that he could accord to what subject matter he chose as a focus compounded of his favored images—almost always, remember, in that hard-won and singularly achieved style.

A COMMON GRACE

A Common Grace (1960) might well be considered a more cohesive book than its predecessor. The influence of Wallace Stevens is noticeable in such a poem as "Country Bedroom": "It must have been the moon, because it was. / Because it was, it must have been a shadow / Uglily collapsing on the floor" (p. 41). Another instance is "Blue Chair in a Sunny Day": "Nothing of blue or of the summer's colour / Nor of the moment in whose door it sits / Nor of that scratch in air that states a rose" (p. 19). The influence, pervasive as it is, seldom lies quite so near the surface, and indeed this poem failed to make its way into *Collected Poems* (1985).

Rather, the characteristic vision is somewhat understated, gathering about the word "grace" that is featured in several of the lyrics. One of the best of them, "Nude in a Fountain," has, referring to the subject of a statue, "that long helmet-plume of water waving, / In which the four elements hoisted from the ground, / Become this grace, the form of their enslaving" (p. 10). Another poem of high quality is "Feeding Ducks," and this has "my everlasting hand / Dropped on the hypocrite duck her grace of bread" (p. 31). "Two Ways of It," a poem about the dichotomy between legends and life, has "a god's grace that kills to keep its love" and also "[I] am no slave, but freeman of your grace" (pp. 32–33). While the excellent "Spate in Winter Midnight," referring to the rains of a storm, has "Black hills are slashed white with this falling grace" (p. 37).

The meaning of all this is surely that "grace" may be found everywhere if only humankind has the openness to experience it. This is MacCaig's version, it would appear, of "inscape." Certainly, with that marvelous technique, he could take the most ordinary events and settings and invest them with his own peculiar magic. "Edinburgh Courtyard in July" is almost an anthology piece, but MacCaig treated his subject as though it was one of his precious hills or lochs in Sutherland. The poem ends:

> And water from a broken drain
> Splashes a glassy hand out in the air
>   That breaks in an unbraiding rain
> And falls still fraying to become a stain
> That spreads by footsteps, ghosting everywhere.
> (p. 13)

In that one stanza a fractured drainpipe becomes an importunate limb, a stream "unbraiding" its locks, and the "unbraiding" becomes a "fraying," and the "fraying" becomes a "stain" which, the last of these transitions, becomes a ghost. The MacCaig magic is everywhere in this book. Or perhaps one should say, a long way after Robert Browning, a common grace silvers everything.

A ROUND OF APPLAUSE

A Round of Applause (1962) is a similar but perhaps stronger book. It contains several of MacCaig's anthology pieces: among them, "The Shore Road," "Moorings," and "July Evening." Consider this extract from "July Evening," which exemplifies the poet's verbal precision:

> A bird's voice chinks and tinkles

Alone in the gaunt reedbed—
Tiny silversmith
Working late in the evening . . .
                    (p. 54)

Perhaps the best known poem in this collection is "Byre":

The thatched roof rings like heaven where mice
Squeak small hosannahs all night long,
Scratching its golden pavements, skirting
The gutter's crystal river-song.
Wild kittens in the world below
Glare with one flaming eye through cracks,
Spurt in the straw, are tawny brooches
Splayed on the chests of drunken sacks.
The dimness becomes darkness as
Vast presences come mincing in,
Swagbellied Aphrodites, swinging
A silver slaver from each chin.
And all is milky, secret, female.
Angels are hushed and plain straws shine.
And kittens miaow in circles, stalking
With tail and hindleg one straight line.
                    (p. 39)

This, with its assured technique and quality of vision, is perhaps the pick of the bunch. The difference, however, is in quality, not kind. Perhaps the plot is stronger than in many of MacCaig's poems. The clue is given in the celestial terminology: "heaven," "hosannahs," "golden pavement." That byre is a light-hearted allegory of the universe, with the mice squeaking in the roof as substitutes for angels in heaven. Below, the "earth" is populated by the kittens, with their sensual connotations: glaring eyes, tawny brooches, drunken sacks. At nightfall the cows, proper denizens of the byre, enter, bringing with them connotations of Mother Eve: "milky, secret, female." This is a process of ordering the little universe. The mice cease squeaking and the kittens learn to behave themselves. Their minuscule savagery is replaced by miaowing [meowing] "in circles" and stalking in "one straight line." It is fanciful, certainly, and itself organized in the form of quatrains. Perhaps they are rather more formal on the surface as a means of containing the fantasy beneath the narrative surface: mice as angels, for example, and cows as mothers of humankind.

This form of meditative lyric, couched in an admixture of sophisticated rhyme and pararhyme, was by now well established. That MacCaig was duly conscious of what he was doing is attested by a somewhat neglected poem, very much self-reflexive, "Failed Mystic":

A stone remarked what he'd no answer to
And trees showered secrets he could only share
In remote reaches of himself—a country
He seldom travelled to. When winds were fair

He coasted with them, smelling of the Spring:
When they blew contrary he downed his head
And bullocked on, an ugly opposition,
Swearing to find himself—and found instead

What a wind is . . .
                    (p. 12)

The mystic is "failed," perhaps, because he sees the external surfaces rather than the depths of his own being.

Yet it may be answered that what the poet sees is at least in part a construct of his own personality. The quirky MacCaig imagery, seeing the likeness in apparent incongruities, abounds: "tall waves will run / Fawning on rocks and barking in the sun"; "The bird last night, whiskered with moths, flew out / From more than yonder into more than there"; "A hot winch huffed and puffed and gnashed / Its iron fangs and swallowed rope"; "In a salt ring of moonlight / The dinghy nods at nothing" (p. 12). "Mutual Life" contains more of this quirky imagery:

What do you know, mind, of that speck in air,
The high insanitary raven that pecks his claws
A thousand feet up and volplanes on his back
And greets his ancient sweetheart with coarse caws?
                    (p. 42)

This is a world of congruent incongruities, brought together by the poet's metaphysical imagination.

MEASURES

MEASURES (1965) brings together further remarkable poems: "Bull" ("Head's box, body's barrel, / Pinched haunches—tail's tuft," p. 14); "Fetching Cows" ("they roll / Their great Greek eyes and breathe out milky gusts," p. 16); "Aspects" ("Whales that have learned to drown, / Ballooning up, meet navies circling down" p. 18); and "Icy Road":

A show to hide the show outside, the newsreel
Flickering past, projected on the darkness,
That any moment will

Come to a stop with us its stars: a still.
(p. 39)

All these poems have been anthologized.

However, the true anthology piece in this book, one with perhaps a stronger plot and deeper emotional material than the others, is "Neglected Graveyard, Luskentyre." There are plenty of poems on this theme, but what makes MacCaig an especially valuable poet is that he brought something of his own to the spectacle; his own brand of irony, his peculiar compassion. The poem begins:

I wade in the long grass,
Barking my shins on gravestones.
The grass overtops the dyke.
In and out of the bay hesitates the Atlantic.

A seagull stares at me hard
With a quarterdeck eye, leans forward
And shrugs into the air.
The dead rest from their journey from one wilderness
    to another . . .
(p. 17)

That image of the "quarterdeck eye" would be hard to beat. Yet, with all this quirkiness, the poem ends on a note of restrained elegy, deceptively simple, quite unforgettable:

The edge of the green sea
Crumples. Bees are in clover.
I part the grasses and there—
Angus Macleod, drowned. Mary his wife. Together.
(p. 17)

It is the confrontation of death amidst life burgeoning on that makes for poignancy. More, it is the economy of phrase; no overstatement, not an unnecessary word; a distinction in itself.

This is so rich a book that the author was able to discard poems that would help to make the reputations of lesser men, notably "Hill Being Organ," a high-spirited piece that has appeared in at least one school anthology. However, a change was in the air.

SURROUNDINGS

BY the publication of MacCaig's eighth book, *Surroundings* (1966), the formal technique, it seemed, had begun to deliquesce. It is not that this is a bad book. Some well-known anthology pieces appear here. Among them are "Interruption to a Journey" ("The hare we had run over / Bounced about the road / On the springing curve / Of its spine," p. 17); "Sounds of the Day" ("When the air creaked, it was / A lapwing seeing us off the premises / Of its private marsh," p. 19); "Responsibility" ("They left the horse standing for two days / with a shattered leg / Till the vet signed a paper," p. 22). The tendency to dwell on injury is manifest. This is a disintegrating world, more redolent of cruelty than was previously the case in MacCaig's works.

There is another anthology poem that, with his characteristic prodigality, MacCaig left outside the *Collected Poems*. It is called "King of Beasts":

The indifferent lion lolling
Through the jungle in the back of
His Rolls-Royce. When you see him
Keep off the Zebra crossing—dive
Down an alley, if you're a rabbit,
Or sing, if you're a lark,
Straight up in the air . . .
(p. 16)

What one notices is that this is in free verse, and in that respect it is typical of the volume. The tight quatrains of previous books were often more syncopated than at first glance they seemed and, in any case, were a framework for paradoxes, fancies, and ironies that took one far beyond the expectations of traditional form. There was a sense of celebration.

In *Surroundings*, however, the preponderant free-verse form makes for discursiveness. There always was a tendency for MacCaig to preach, but this was contained by the exigencies of metrical structure and the focus on particulars of scene. Without sacrificing focus, the looser forms allow for an extent of reasoning as comment upon events. At this stage, events are still substantially present. One of the best-loved pieces in the collection is "Assisi," and it bears witness to MacCaig's travels, including a sojourn in Italy, and to his increasing confidence at handling his readership. It begins as sharply and anecdotally as any of the earlier poems:

The dwarf with his hands on backwards
Sat, slumped like a half-filled sack
On tiny twisted legs from which
Sawdust might run. . . .
(p. 35)

Its moral, too, is clear enough: the fact that the goodness of God can produce grotesques such as this, whose life is a testament of suffering. The poem ends with the tourists flocking after a priest who is describing the frescoes of Giotto:

> It was they who had passed
> The ruined temple outside, whose eyes
> Wept pus, whose back was higher
> Than his head, whose lop-sided mouth
> Said Grazie in a voice as sweet
> As a child's when she speaks to her mother
> Or a bird's when it spoke
> To St Francis.
>
> (p. 35)

The legend of St. Francis is doing a lot of the work here. This is not quite the imagery of paradox that made the poems of *Riding Lights* so telling. "A voice as sweet" is a phrase lucid enough. It is carrying on the narrative sufficiently. It does not, however, go beyond that narrative. The metaphysical wit is somewhat dimmed; the compassion, to an extent, is taken for granted.

With all that, this is a fine poem that deserves a place in the anthologies second only to, perhaps, "Summer Farm" and "Byre." The door to moralizing, however, has been opened by a certain looseness of form, and that door widens through the practice of subsequent books. A distinction of utterance is always there. What may be questioned is the grip on circumstance.

RINGS ON A TREE

MACCAIG'S travels widened, and a sojourn in the United States left its imprint in the earlier pages of *Rings on a Tree* (1968). Outside his Sutherlandshire Eden, however, the observation is not that of a poet so much as a journalist:

> The moderator's spectacles twinkle in the light.
> His brain twinkles in five languages.
> Two speakers sit on each side of him, desperately
> At ease . . .
> ("Writers' Conference, Long Island University," p. 25)

> I sit on a hard seat and do not raise
> my carton of weak beer to the green
> Statue of Liberty whose back is turned
> on Manhattan . . .
> ("Circle Line," p. 30)

> This morning I watched from here
> a helicopter skirting like a damaged insect
> the Empire State Building, that
> jumbo size dentist's drill . . .
> ("Hotel Room, 12th Floor," p. 27)

This is a little more than reportage, with its sly humor and observation of effects. But the MacCaig of Achmelvich or Lochinver would not have let himself get away so lightly with an image such as "damaged insect." There are traces of that poet in the present book, fortunately, and he shows up the skilled reporter with one or two pieces such as "Fog at Dusk," whose tighter forms bring about a more sharply fanciful imagery:

> The fog webs fatten the spiders' till they sag
> As thick as cloths. I touch one—its cold rag
> Becomes a filthy glove . . .
> (p. 38)

However, at times the reportage rises near this level, especially when something more than the lonely contemplation of transatlantic (and therefore alien) phenomena is attempted. "Leaving the Metropolitan Museum" has justly found favor. It describes a skillful sculpture in skillfully sculpted free verse—verse that, unlike the verse of previous books, has cast off the restriction of capital letters at the beginning of its lines:

> I went out from the unsheltered world of art
> into the unsheltered world,
> and there, by the door,
> Picasso's Goat—
>
> a shape of iron entered into by herds,
> by every aspect of goatishness.
> (What are you to say to a man
> who can carve a smell,
> can make a goat-smell out of iron?)
> (p. 34)

It is symptomatic that the speaker is leaving the museum. The familiar shape of the goat at the exit is an intercessor between MacCaig and his chosen paradise, and restores to him a little of his Edenic art. Even so, there is here a degree of repetition—"can carve" / "can make"—and perhaps a lowering of pressure that readers don't find in *Riding Lights* or *A Round of Applause*.

NORMAN MACCAIG

A MAN IN MY POSITION

TOO many of the poems in *A Man in My Position* (1969) begin with an explicit statement of thought:

I think of you
in gold coins.
My thoughts of you, each one,
is a gold coin—
I am their mixer but
they belong to you . . .
("Numismatist," p. 7)

or this:

What a pity thoughts are only to be contained
inside a skull.

My thoughts of you
are a string ball inside a canister . . .
("Transformations," p. 25)

or this:

Stand in this stage and think of me as me—
The moon's a pedant of the present tense
And I'm recessions, my own short history.

I changed before you changed me, as you must
Be differences in this moment's mode:
Stars once were gases or exploding dust . . .
("Structures," p. 43)

Perhaps the last of these doesn't qualify, since its opening is focused by its ostensibly stricter form. But there is a thinking about thinking in such poems, rather than a manifestation of thought. Too often the verse approaches the looseness of D. H. Lawrence's *Pansies,* English versions of *Pensées,* minor disquisitions. It is as though the idea were enough, and never mind the expression: "To see you from three places at once / is one of my impossible ambitions" ("It's Hopeless," p. 10); "I can no more describe you / than I can put a thing for the first time / where it already is" ("Sure Proof," p. 12); "When I look at you, / I, who prove better than some / that there are ways of telling / what there are no ways of showing, / have no words to say to you" ("Inarticulates," p. 19). MacCaig never was, perhaps, at his best in love poems, and the ones here expose certain weaknesses of his mature style. Among them is a tendency toward the prosaic.

Also there appears to be a growing and not altogether helpful extent of self-consciousness. This is manifest in the title poem, where it seems Mac-

Caig felt that a public persona, or at least an alter ego, was speaking out of his mouth:

Hear my words carefully.
Some are spoken
Not by me, but
by a man in my position.

What right has he
to use my mouth? I hate him
when he touches you
the wrong way . . .
(p. 15)

The verse here is sufficiently competent to carry the message, but only just. The language cannot be described exactly as "thin," yet it does not pick up and, in effect, create the meaning as was the case with some of MacCaig's earlier poems.

The poem's weakness reflects the heightened standing that MacCaig had attained. By this time, the poet was a personage. From 1967 he was no longer the primary school teacher of the last thirty years but the first holder of the writing fellowship at Edinburgh University and, subsequently, Reader in Poetry at the new University of Stirling. He was much in demand as a performer in public recitals, and his handsome presence graced many conferences. One sign of this public status was the commissioning for television by the British Broadcasting Corporation of what was to prove MacCaig's most ambitious poem, "A Man in Assynt." This makes explicit what had been implied over a long period, that MacCaig's true love affair, as far as his writing was concerned, was with the mountains, rocks, lochs and encroaching sea of the West Highlands:

Up there, the scraping light
whittles the cloud edges till, like thin bone,
they're bright with their own opaque selves. Down
    here,
a skinny rosebush is an eccentric jug
of air. And I,
somewhere between them,
am a visiting eye,
an unrequited passion,
watching the tide glittering backward and making
its huge withdrawal from beaches
and kilted rocks . . .
(p. 55)

The distinction is there still, but it seems to take the author several strokes to get across each effect. Critics miss the cohesion and indeed the conciseness of earlier work, where the thought was less explicit but the imagery more unexpectedly oneiric.

LATER WORKS

ALTHOUGH instances of MacCaig's earlier power occur even in *A Man in My Position* (consider "Venus Fly-trap" and "Basking Shark"), generally, as the volumes continue to succeed one another, explicit disquisition rises with respect to a diminishing quantity of achieved lyrics. Most of Mac-Caig's later volumes are couched in relatively formal verse. In *The White Bird* (1973) the title poem sums up the main theme, which is the sorrow of the world and one's relative lack of concern about it—and one's concern about not feeling sufficient concern.

However, MacCaig writes to more effect when summoning his sense of the immediate surroundings and their incongruities in such a poem as "Sparrow." It begins:

> He's no artist.
> His taste in clothes is more
> dowdy than gaudy.
> And his nest—that blackbird, writing
> pretty scrolls on the air with the gold nib of his beak,
> would call it a slum . . .
>
> (p. 26)

"Country Dance," too, has an almost liminal notion of an old fiddler: "He bowed lefthanded and his right hand / was the wrong way round. Impossible. / But the jig bounced, the gracenotes / sparkled" (p. 52).

Self-consciousness, however, keeps breaking in. Even in this charming, dancing poem, the author feels it necessary to add "There's a lesson here, I thought, climbing / into the pulpit I keep in my mind" (p. 52). There are too many pulpits, at least in relation to the images and inscapes the reader is allowed. "Inward Bound" goes on at some length, considering that what it has to utter are fairly routine meditations on life and death: "No journey is ever ended / Greyfriars and the melancholy double-blanks / in Warriston Kirk Yard / are no answers to that" (p. 37). That is a sentiment that might as well have been expressed in prose. While not wholly characteristic of *The White Bird*, this kind of writing represents an element of it.

There seems to be an attempt at consolidation in *The World's Room* (1974). The "room" in question

may very well be in the poet's head. However, the landscapes are evoked: tinged with melancholy, possibly fading with the sense of time passing and passed. The anthologists have avoided this volume, yet there are some quiet elegaic poems here that would have been worth culling. "Blackbird in a Sunset Bush" ends with a memorable image: "charcoal philosopher / in his blazing study" (p. 33). The dialogue with Eden continues: "Landscape and I get on together well. / Though I'm the talkative one, still he can tell / His symptoms of being to me, the way a shell / Murmurs of oceans" (p. 49). Fauna are present: "Ringed Plover by a Water's Edge," "Greenshank," "Stag in a Neglected Hayfield," and in "Birthdays," there is the poignant vignette, "In the earliest light of a long day / three stags stepped out from the birch wood / at Achmelvich bridge" (p. 64). There are people, too. On a return to Scalpay the poet encounters Johann "sixty years of size and astonishment" (p. 13), "Woodsman," and "Old Crofter," but they seem aged and run down. Even the two semblances of children, "Two Year Old" and "Wooden Chair with Arms," are composed, of necessity, from a grandfatherly vision. Attempts to make sense of it all in a broader perspective melt into disquisition, armchair philosophy: "When are the hymns to be written / in praise of the unimaginable power of the Word / that first made the chaos that made / creation possible?" ("Between Two Nowheres," p. 43).

There are signs of carelessness in *Tree of Strings* (1977). For example, there is the odd misprint—corrected, it must be allowed, in the *Collected Poems* (1985). There is also the peculiar circumstance that what might have been thought the best poem in the book was not, in fact, included, but appears, as an afterthought, under the book's generic title in *Collected Poems*. The poem in question, "Connoisseur," is one of the best of Mac-Caig's later efforts. Even though that disregard for meter which characterized his sunset years makes for a measure of discursiveness, there is a pattern of repetition that supplies a necessary integument:

> The rain makes a drumming on the roof
> and a splish-splash on the road.
> Nothing makes one sound only.
>
> That cloud is a camel, a weasel, a whale.
> Hamlet was right. Nothing
> has only one appearance.
>
> I collect
> Your laughter, your talk, your weeping.

I collect your hundred of semblances.

I store you in the cabinet of my mind
I'm a connoisseur, in love with the value only
of priceless things.

Though my eyes blur, I look at these treasures.
Though my hands tremble, I touch them.
Though my heart grieves, I love them.

And a seed falls from a tree and
in its lowly cabinet sets about
creating forests.

(p. 287)

If there is a slackening of rhythm in the stanza beginning "I store you in the cabinet of my mind," it is certainly redeemed by such emphases as are invoked by the repeated "though . . . though . . . though" of the following stanza, the penultimate stanza.

Of the poems in the book as it was first published, "Variations of Ten Summer Minutes" especially deserves attention. Again, there is a degree of discursiveness; again, a pattern of repetition provides a rhythmic spine. The plot, too, is an advantage. The speaker has paused in a village, and observes a boy flipping stones out to sea, the schoolmaster looking out of his window, a man leaving a shop with a pocket shaped like a whisky bottle, a melodeon wheezing a dance rhythm on board a boat. The poem ends:

The ten minutes are up, except they aren't.
I leave the village, except I don't.
The jig fades to silence, except it doesn't.

(p. 22)

This is an ingenious—but also elegaic—way of creating that mysterious quality, timelessness.

Norman MacCaig seldom dedicated his books to anyone, but *Tree of Strings* was dedicated to A. K. Macleod, and its successor, *The Equal Skies* (1980), is dominated by a sequence of poems commemorating Macleod's death. By now, MacCaig was using his peculiar mode of repetition as a definite technique in his verse. It certainly helps in framing into utterance a powerful set of emotions. The best of the twelve "Poems for Angus" is perhaps "Highland Funeral." This incorporates an attack on the sanctimonious minister spreading what MacCaig termed "a pollution of bad beliefs." However, what surrounds the funeral is the pagan setting that was an emanation of the dead man, a pagan himself:

The sea was boring, as grief is,
but beautiful, as grief is not.
Through grief's dark ugliness I saw that beauty
because he would have.

And that darkened the ugliness . . .

(p. 11)

The emphasis lies in that repeated "as grief is" and gives the poem its individual atmosphere.

This grim book, in which "Poems for Angus" are by no means the only elegies, supplies perhaps the last of MacCaig's anthology pieces in the cheerful shape of the poem "Toad." With its acuity of observation—"Stop looking like a purse" (p. 45)—this could fit seamlessly into D. H. Lawrence's *Birds, Beasts and Flowers*:

You clamber towards me on your four corners—
one hand, one foot, one hand, one foot . . .

(p. 45)

As is the case with Lawrence, the mode of repetition, by supplying a degree of mimetic patterning, prevents the verse from lapsing into prose. Clearly the poet in his mourning welcomed the inscape provided by this alien but friendly visitor.

A World of Difference (1983) draws, almost for the first time in MacCaig's oeuvre, on his store of classical learning, but those poems are not the most interesting in the book. A good deal of it reads like notes for poems rather than achieved works of art. Among those notes, however, are traces of the unique MacCaig imagery: "a summer inside a summer / died, leaving a useless crop" (p. 11); "inaudibly / a yellow flower dies giving birth to a yellow flower" (p. 17); and

An old ewe brings me down to the earth
she stamps her forefoot on. I look at her implacable
whisky and soda eyes. She knows all a sheep
needs to know: she's a black-stockinged blue-
   stocking . . .

("Camera Man," p. 25)

In spite of the images of old age and dying, the characteristic wit survives, even if it cannot quite prevail.

By now, Norman MacCaig was a living classic, his successive birthdays occasions for public rejoicing. Since the death of Hugh MacDiarmid in 1978, no one could doubt that he was Scotland's foremost poet. He was awarded the Order of the British Empire in 1979 and the Queen's Gold

Medal for Poetry in 1986. His final collection, *Voice Over* (1988), is in some ways less valedictory than its two most immediate predecessors. There is more of an acceptance of age, infirmity, and the passing of friends. "On a croft by the Kirkaig" provides a last reference to Angus Macleod in a tone of hushed resignation: "I'm sad / but not sad only, / for I share his possessions / and therefore himself" (p. 18). There is still room for a deprecatory view of a neighbor: "His eyes are two teaspoons / that have been emptied / for the last time" (p. 25). The veils of age seem to have dropped from his view of children: "young seraphs licking their fingers / and adding to the jewel-heap / of Praise-the-Lord / Coca-Cola tins" (p. 26).

In fact, the best poem in the book is a witty and kindly sketch, "Small Boy." The boy is throwing pebble after pebble into the sea, and the old master, with something of his former skill, allegorizes this as practicing for the future:

> when there'll be so many things
> he'll want to throw away
> if only his fingers will unclench
> and let them go.
>
> (p. 9)

In 1990 Isabel MacCaig died, and effectively that finished the poet's career. He said, quite frankly, that the impulse to write had left him, and he did not think it would ever return. To a great extent she seems to have been the stabilizing influence that was the foundation of his work. It had not been an easy pilgrimage. In his earlier years MacCaig had felt himself undervalued, and, until near the end, he had to exist beside the mighty presence of Hugh MacDiarmid. Though normally urbane and a good companion, in his cups he could lapse into a black sarcasm. However, his sense of merit, eventually matched by the world's encomium, kept him afloat.

He may have been more sensitive to applause than he revealed. At any rate, he stood high in the regard of his fellow poets. Roderick Hart produced a poem in his honor, which included lines such as, "It is always a joy / to see him, feeling hard pressed, / nip behind one of his clear hard images" (*Scottish Literary Journal*, May 1984, p. 79). Ted Hughes wrote of him, "His influence on younger poets has been pervasive and positive. And it continues. Whenever I meet his poems, I'm struck by their undated freshness, everything

about them as alive, as new and essential, as ever" (in Hendry and Cambell, p. 6). Edwin Morgan, perhaps his successor as the foremost Scottish poet, wrote, "MacCaig had a considerable influence on younger poets in Scotland, both from the quality of his work and from the popularity of his public readings; anyone who heard him read would find it hard not to hear that voice in his printed poems" (*Guardian*, 24 January 1996, p. 24). From this one may gather that it is MacCaig rather than the more spectacular Hugh MacDiarmid or Sorley Maclean that spoke to a rising generation. He helped the young Scots to find their voice in English. In this regard critics think of Liz Lochhead, Kathleen Jamie, and Kate Clanchy, whose eye for the heuristic image seems to have been developed under the aegis of this master. It is all the stranger that so many of his followers seem to be women. MacCaig, with his mildly bibulous social life and his interest in hill walking and fishing, seemed so essentially a man's man.

His rank as a poet is unlikely to suffer from vagaries of fashion. From that point of view, he seems to be in a truly great tradition. Yet, in the end, one would not necessarily call him a great writer. The most lyrical of poets seem to have at the center some masterpiece, some statement that summates the best of their work. One thinks of "Corinna's going a Maying" by Robert Herrick or "The World" by Henry Vaughan. In the twentieth century, there are "The Equilibrists" by John Crowe Ransom or "Church Going" by Philip Larkin. From the plateau of their musings rises some irrefragable peak. And the greatest poets—Thomas Hardy, William Butler Yeats, Wallace Stevens, Robert Frost—appear to be able to produce masterpiece after masterpiece in a manner that speaks of talent supernormal, if not superhuman.

Norman MacCaig, however, in common with Walter de la Mare, Robert Graves, and Theodore Roethke, seems destined to be read in selection, though a selection of his best poems would leave readers in no doubt of his genius. His two best books are probably *Riding Lights* and *A Round of Applause*. From the former one could pick out "Summer Farm," "Country House," and "Edinburgh Spring." From the latter, "Failed Mystic," "Byre," and "July Evening." One would have to add, for any decent selection, "Edinburgh Courtyard in July" from *A Common Grace* and "Neglected Graveyard, Luskentyre" from *Measures*; and, to judge from its incidence in anthologies and the amount of discussion it has provoked, many would add "Assisi" from *Surroundings*. Even these nine poems, however, would give only a sense of the sheer copiousness of the man, his invention, his cornucopia of ingenious imagery.

However, though conscious of his worth, the poet himself would eschew any hint of pretentiousness. He had, after all, his personal store of irony. He might have quoted from "The Shore Road": "He sounded his small history to make complete / The interval of leaf and rutting waves" (in *A Round of Applause*, p. 9). Or, from "Loch Sionascaig," "Hard to remember how the water went / Shaking the light" (p. 43). But Norman MacCaig remembered. He remembered for us all.

SELECTED BIBLIOGRAPHY

I. COLLECTED WORKS. *Selected Poems* (London, 1971); *Old Maps and New: Selected Poems* (London, 1978); *Collected Poems* (London, 1985); *Collected Poems* (London, 1990); *Selected Poems*, ed. Douglas Dunn (London, 1997).

II. SEPARATE WORKS OF POETRY. *Far Cry* (London, 1943); *The Inward Eye* (London, 1946); *Riding Lights* (London, 1955); *The Sinai Sort* (London, 1957); *A Common Grace* (London, 1960); *A Round of Applause* (London, 1962); *Measures* (London, 1965); *Surroundings* (London, 1966); *Rings on a Tree* (London, 1968); *A Man in My Position* (London, 1969); *The White Bird* (London, 1973); *The World's Room* (London, 1974); *Tree of Strings* (London, 1977); *The Equal Skies* (London, 1980); *A World of Difference* (London, 1983); *Voice Over* (London, 1988).

III. VOLUMES EDITED. *Honor'd Shade: An Anthology of New Scottish Poetry to Mark the Bicentenary of the Birth of Robert Burns* (Edinburgh, 1959); *Contemporary Scottish Verse 1959–1969* (with Alexander Scott) (London, 1970).

IV. CRITICAL STUDIES. James Smith, "On Metaphysical Poetry," in *Scrutiny* 2, no. 3 (December 1933); G. S. Fraser, "Norman MacCaig: Four Poems Examined," in *Akros* 3, no. 7 (March 1968); Hugh MacDiarmid, "Introduction to the Poetry of Norman MacCaig," in *Akros* 3, no. 7 (March 1968); Crombie Saunders, "A Case of Old MacCaig," in *Akros* 3, no. 7 (March 1968); Norman MacCaig, "My Way of It," in *As I Remember: Ten Scottish Authors Recall How Writing Began for Them*, ed. Maurice Lindsay (London, 1979); Roderick Hart, "Norman MacCaig," in *Scottish Literary Journal* 11, no. 1 (May 1984); Joy Hendry and Raymond J. Ross, eds., *Norman MacCaig: Critical Essays* (Edinburgh, 1990); Edwin Morgan, "The Poetry of Norman Maccaig," in *Crossing the Border: Essays on Scottish Literature* (Manchester, 1990); Kenneth Brown, *Poetry of Norman MacCaig* (Glasgow, 1993); Joy Hendry and Alan Campbell, eds., *Norman MacCaig: A Celebration* (Edinburgh, 1995); Magnus Linklater, "Still Dreaming of Achmelvich," in *Times* (London) (21 November 1995); Marjory McNeill, *Norman MacCaig: A Study of His Life and Work* (Edinburgh, 1996); Edwin Morgan, "Belief in an Ordinary Happiness" (Obituary), in *Guardian* (24 January 1996); "Obituary of Norman MacCaig," in *Times* (London) (24 January 1996); Anne Taylor, *Norman MacCaig* (Manchester, 2000).

V. FURTHER READING: SCOTLAND. Gregory Smith, *Scottish Literature: Character and Influence* (London, 1919); Hugh MacDiarmid, *Contemporary Scottish Studies* (London, 1926); Edwin Muir, *Scott and Scotland: The Predicament of the Scottish Writer* (London, 1936; repr. 1982); John Speirs, *The Scots Literary Tradition* (London, 1940); Hugh MacDiarmid, *Lucky Poet: A Self-Study in Literature and Political Ideas* (London, 1943); Robin Fulton, *Contemporary Scottish Poetry: Individuals and Contexts* (Loanhead, 1974).

VI. FURTHER READING: NEW APOCALYPSE. Helen Rootham, trans., *Prose Poems from "Les Illuminations" of Arthur Rimbaud* (London, 1932); Dylan Thomas, *18 Poems* (London, 1934); David Gascoyne, *A Short Survey of Surrealism* (London, 1935); David Gascoyne, *Man's Life Is This Meat* (London, 1936); J. F. Hendry, ed., *The New Apocalypse* (London, 1940); J. F. Hendry and Henry Treece, eds., *The White Horseman* (London, 1941); W. S. Graham, *Cage without Grievance* (Glasgow, 1942); J. F. Hendry, *The Bombed Happiness* (London, 1942); G. S. Fraser, *Home Town Elegy* (London, 1944); Henry Treece, *How I See Apocalypse* (London, 1946); Derek Stanford, *The Freedom of Poetry: Studies in Contemporary Verse* (London, 1947); John Press, *Rule and Energy: Trends in British Poetry Since the Second World War* (London and New York, 1963); Arthur Rimbaud, *Illuminations*, ed. Nick Osmond (London, 1976); Edward B. Germain, ed., *Surrealist Poetry in English* (London and Harmondsworth, 1978).

EDWIN MUIR

(1887–1959)

Peter Scupham

IN HIS FOREWORD to *The Estate of Poetry*, Muir's Norton Lectures of 1955–1956, Archibald MacLeish opened with this sentence: "Fame, in any generation, is a better guide to the generation than its poets—which is why the reputation of the author of this book is not commensurate with his accomplishment." Muir's life began in a remote, timeless agrarian society, and he lived through wars and social upheavals, ending while central Europe was frozen under Soviet hegemony; yet little of this tumult of event and change found its way into his poems. The whole tenor of Muir's work runs counter to fashionable orthodoxies now, as it did to fashionable orthodoxies half a century ago. The task he set himself when he started writing poetry in his mid-thirties was one of interpretation, but that interpretation was not of event, that passing show of history. His imagination was elsewhere, possessed by what he always thought of as man's "Fable" rather than his "Story," terms that need some explanation. Muir understood these terms as the twinned halves of mankind's existence.

In *An Autobiography* (1954), Muir wrote, "Our minds are possessed by three mysteries: where we came from, where we are going, and, since we are not alone, but members of a countless family, how should we live with one another" (p. 9). The mysteries are questions that Muir could only consider in the light of metaphysics and, after a tortuous journey, Christian metaphysics. The poetry and the autobiography, Muir's finest achievements, are not at heart concerned with the daily fabric of our lives; this belongs to the Story, and often resists interpretation; it may obscure rather than reveal our true nature. The Fable, which is Muir's constant theme, is concerned with simplification and sign, the ambiguous presentations given us in dream and waking vision. The Fable is alive in us when we recognize and celebrate the ritual stages in Everyman's passage through this world—in its most basic terms our progress from memories of Eden through the bitter world of the Fall, our travel lit by occasional redemptive visions and the hope of a restored unity. Of course the Story and the Fable are not exclusive; they live in a symbiosis, a necessary and mutually informing relationship.

THE STORY

EDWIN Muir was born on 15 May 1887 in the Orkneys, a cluster of islands off the Scottish mainland. His father, James Muir, was a farmer. In 1889 the family moved as tenants to a farm, the Bu, on the island of Wyre. The five or so childhood years that Muir spent there were crucial; their substance is central to Muir's imaginative life. In 1896 the family was forced to move to Garth, a farm on Orkney itself. The new farm, on difficult land, proved impossible to work profitably, and in 1901 the family left the Orkneys to make a new start in Glasgow.

The following years were a time of estrangement and personal tragedy. Muir started work at fourteen as a clerk and an office boy, taking successive jobs with a law firm, an engineering office, a publisher, a beer-bottling factory, his only respite was some months spent polishing cars and odd-jobbing on an Ayrshire estate. He summarized those early years in *An Autobiography* as "stupidly wretched, such a meaningless waste of inherited virtue, that I cannot write of them even now without grief and anger." Troubles thickened. Muir's father died in 1902, and in the same year his brother Willie died a lingering death from tuberculosis. After a fall from a tram car, in which he was knocked unconscious, Muir's brother Johnnie developed a brain tumor and died slowly, and in great pain, in 1906. His mother followed in 1907; as Muir laconically put it in *An Autobiography*: "The family now looked as if it had been swept by a gale" (p. 104). The last of Muir's hopeless jobs in the labyrinths of industrial Scotland was as clerk in a bone factory in Fairport, a post he held for the two years before the outbreak of the First World

War, a place where fresh bones arrived and were turned into charcoal.

In 1919 Muir married Willa Anderson, a college lecturer. "My marriage was the most fortunate event in my life" (*An Autobiography*, p. 154), is Muir's simple, defining statement of that event. The marriage was built to last and conducted in love, deep mutual respect, and shared work in translation from the German, most especially their introduction of Kafka to so many English-speaking readers; Willa wrote her own account of their life together, *Belonging*. After early intellectual and social experiments with the Clarion Scouts and Guild Socialism, Muir moved to London and became an assistant to A. R. Orage, working for Orage's periodical *The New Age,* which at the time was introducing its readers to the work of Freud and Jung. This in turn led Muir to undergo analysis. Willa was also earning, and Muir's criticism and reviews were accepted by *The Athenaeum* and *The Scotsman*; something was being established.

From 1921 onward, the Muirs lived for some years a nomadic life as a twentieth-century version of the Vagantes, the wandering scholars of the Middle Ages. A friend, Janko Lavrin, suggested that they should go to Prague. The Muirs grew increasingly at home in Europe, working for intellectual freedoms that crossed frontiers and with minds attuned to progressive and broadly socialist ideals—Willa taught for A. S. Neill, who was putting his ideas on child-centered education into practice in interwar Germany. Muir only started writing poetry at thirty-five; *First Poems* was published in 1925. By the time the Second World War began, he had published widely, his books including the biography *John Knox* (1929), three novels, *The Marionette* (1927), *The Three Brothers* (1931), and *Poor Tom* (1932), and, in 1935, *Scottish Journey*. In 1940 Muir published a memoir of his childhood and youth, giving it the title *The Story and the Fable,* and ending the account in 1922; the final version, charting the Muirs' progress from the twenties into the postwar world, was published as *An Autobiography*. During World War II Muir worked for the British Council, and in 1945 he went back to Prague as director of the British Council Institute. After the Communist takeover, Muir suffered a breakdown, and his postwar poetry is haunted by the Orwellian and apocalyptic visions that accompanied the Cold War period. He took a post equivalent to his Prague directorship in Rome and became warden of Newbattle Abbey

College in Dalkeith, Scotland, in 1950. Newbattle awarded no degrees but offered a period of cultural education to young men and women on meager grants. Faced with perpetual opposition, Muir's tenure ended unhappily. In 1955 he was Charles Eliot Norton Professor at Harvard, publishing his lectures under the title *The Estate of Poetry* in 1962. In 1956 came the final book of poems, *One Foot in Eden,* in which he certified and confirmed the precarious Christian vision he had always been working toward since his early loss of faith. He did not live to complete a commissioned work on ballad poetry, a subject always dear to him. Muir died in 1959. His greatest legacies are his autobiography, justly regarded as a work of great insight and literary distinction, and his poems. It is these to which the greatest attention must be paid.

THE STORY AND THE FABLE: AN AUTOBIOGRAPHY

WYRE

IN those years on the Bu, for that brief span when James Muir was surviving adequately as a farmer, his son was living in a world that was not circumscribed by the daily round of work. In those impressionable early years he felt the majestic otherness and power of the creatures that surrounded him, and the foundations of that habit he never lost of living simultaneously in both physical and spiritual dimensions were laid. Fed with balladry and tales of witches, phantom ships, the *Book of Black Arts,* mermaids—a whole gallery of supernatural beings, the young child was habituated to the fabulous and its intermingling with the routines of daily life. The grass itself was full of insects that were presences more than creatures: "I could never bear to touch any of these creatures, though I watched them so closely that I seemed to be taking part in their life, which was like little fragments of night darting about in the sun; they often came into my dreams later, wakening me in terror" (*An Autobiography,* p. 21). The boy's vision of the farm horses, their image endlessly recurrent in Muir's work, were seen by his adult self as built into the universal fabric of the world, their rolling eyes "like the revolution of rock-crystal suns," "the waterfall sweep of their manes," "their iron-shod hoofs striking fire from the flagstones" (p. 22). The total effect was to fill the child with a "stationary terror and delight from which I could get no relief" (p. 22). Muir always saw Wyre as suspended in time, his childhood's sense of timelessness transmuted into an image of eternity, the stationary terrors and delights the colors of a prism broken from a purity of endless light. The brilliance of Muir's apprehension of the secure and good was balanced by an equally vivid apprehension of the underside of life. The farm, that "carnival of life and death," was a place of crudity and pain, where a pig, its throat cut "flew on, quite strange to me, as if seeking something, with an evil, purposive look, as if it were a partner in crime, an associate of the pig-killer" (p. 37). When the pig was gutted, cleaned and hung, the child stared at it as if at an "infamous mystery"—and played football with its bladder. The farm is recreated in retrospect with an enormous physicality, the complex and practiced vocabulary of the mature writer put at the service of the child he once was, whose experiences were the more intense for his dumbness in the face of them.

An Autobiography is never content to rest with the Story, however rich and diverse its physicality. Puzzling over the meaning of his Wyre experiences, Muir considers the history of man's relationship with the animal creation, the long period when that relationship was not merely one of use but when creatures were "protagonists in the first sylvan war, half-human and half-feathered, from which rose the hearth, the community, and the arts" (p. 47). Muir, the farmer's son, sees man and beast traditionally united in a bond of necessity and guilt, a bond in which the sense of the sacred, the ritual mystery of killing played its part. For Muir, our dream life is not a mere working out or transposition of our daily problems into other imagery, but a deep link with our tribal past, a gateway into spiritual experience. Yeats would have said that dreams link us with the anima mundi, spiritus mundi, the world-soul; that "shape with lion body and the head of a man" is a "vast image out of *Spiritus Mundi*" in his poem "The Second Coming." Jung called that floating bank of interconnected images the Collective Unconscious. In 1919, on a Glasgow tramcar, Muir was given a waking vision, a revelation of desolation. Gazing at his neighbors, he found he could not see them as human beings; they had become animals "and I realised that in all Glasgow, in all Scotland, in all the world, there was nothing but millions of such creatures living an animal life and moving towards an animal death as towards a great slaughter-house" (p. 52). Muir's own belief

in immortality was only in part due to the intolerable nature of such a vision; it seemed to him to be the hard-won result of attending to his times of self-forgetting, his dreams, his contemplations, that "floating, half-discarnate state which precedes and follows sleep" (p. 54). What he meant by immortality was the everlastingness not of that thing he so distrusted, the "personality" of the individual, but of the soul. But the child whose early reading habits were to devour everything he could lay his hands on, and who found his sustenance in the *Bible, The Pilgrim's Progress, Christian World, Christian Herald, The People's Friend,* and *Sunday Stories,* had many sources to draw on when he found millenarian or apocalyptic images in the astonishing dreams he had when under analysis later, and which he related to the years in Wyre.

"For many years after leaving Wyre I never dreamed about it once; it was as if that part of my life was forgotten. My first dream came twenty-five years later, when I was being psycho-analysed in London," Muir wrote (*An Autobiography*, p. 63). One such dream was of a shipboard journey. He arrives at a transposed Wyre, where in a little shrine he touches the hanging image of an old woman, turning it into a living girl. Another took its origin from his first sight of a heron; in the dream, the heron is slowly transposed into a heraldic beast, forever fighting and defeating "an ancient, dirty, earth-coloured animal" (p. 65)—a dream later again made part of Muir's poem, *The Combat.* A third dream recounts Muir's version of Isaiah's prophecy of the day when lion and lamb will lie down together in amity. Led by a spiritual guide, and accompanied by a transfigured murderer, he is taken to a field where, on the little hills of his childhood, creatures are sitting or standing, "and each was separate and alone, and each slowly lifted its head upward as if in prayer" (p. 55). No place on this earth can ever be wholly a great, good place, but Muir found enough sustenance in Wyre to credit it with being exactly that, and because he chose it to be sacred, so, for him, it became.

To disentangle the factual components of a lost society from the accretions that imagination and the various forms of nostalgia confer upon it is not easy. George Marshall has attempted the task in his book *In a Distant Isle: The Orkney Background of Edwin Muir* (1987), entering a caveat against the belief Muir promulgates that he was living in a culture that was seamless, holding an unbroken converse with the legends of supernature and past balladry. Though it was important to Muir that his experiences on the Bu in Wyre formed part of an unbroken wholeness, Marshall sees Muir's childhood as taking place in a transitional world where farming on Wyre was at the mercy of "disturbing economic change and social conflict on the estate" (p. 86). James Muir was a tenant farmer for a landlord, Frederick Traill Burroughs, who needed more money than his tenants could provide. This was a world, too, where "the memories of legend and myth were being destroyed by the enmity of rationalist ministers" (p. 73). Marshall points out that James Muir, who told tales of the "fairicks," or fairies, and who claimed to hobnob with witches, also looked forward to the steamer bringing the weekly paper, that Victorian dispenser of superstition and dispenser of rational light. In many ways, Marshall suggests, Muir is clearly concerned to create a picture for his own childhood that might have been more true for the childhood of his father, and in Muir's lifelong attack on Calvin and Knox, whose theology of predestination doomed some to heaven, some to hell, irrespective of their actions, Marshall sees Muir as tilting at the ministers of a belief already much softened in practice in the Orkneys from its original ferocity. What is sure is that Muir never wavered in his belief that those five years on Wyre had given him the experience of living simultaneously in a harmony of seen and unseen worlds.

GLASGOW

The corresponding vision to that of Wyre which informs Muir's life and work is his youth in Glasgow and Fairport, but before the family left for Scotland, after their unsuccessful move to Garth, on the Orkney mainland, the fourteen-year-old Muir accepted a "conversion" at the hands of a revivalist preacher in Kirkwall. Though the conversion did not last, and was later followed by a second "dubious conversion" in Glasgow, Muir felt that "the change itself was so undeniable that it astonished me. I was not trying to be changed; I was changed quite beyond my expectation; but the change did not last long" (p. 88). Muir's alienation from Christianity, conditioned by the severities he perceived in its northern forms, lasted for many year, but the experiences show, perhaps, a latent readiness to interpret life in metaphysical terms that could only find its fruition by long and indirect ways. Glasgow, though, presented Muir with images of an intolerable contrast to those he carried with him there. His first clerkship took him each day through the slums: "These journeys filled me with a sense of degradation: the crumbling houses, the twisted faces, the obscene words casually heard in passing, the ancient, haunting sense of pollution and decay, the arrogant women, the mean men, the terrible children, daunted me, and at last filled me with an immense, blind dejection" (p. 91). Muir remembered remorseless, cruel fistfights, which he associated with the remorseless quality of Calvinism itself. One in particular became part of a dream in which a big man and a little man fought until the big one "lay down in the ring, tears oozing from his eyes, his limbs outspread, and let the little man do whatever he liked with him" (p. 108). This episode was also integrated into the poem "The Combat." At twenty-one Muir threw his emotional energies into socialism, deepening the fable of his life by seeing in the working faces around him "shoots of the glory which they would possess when all men were free and equal" (p. 113). Muir eventually rejected this vision as false if restricted to the building of a utopia on this earth only, but it started to predicate a solution to that third mystery in Muir's trilogy of questions: how should we live with one another? The conversion to socialism had the force of a religious conversion; a May Day demonstration gave him the sense that "all distinction had fallen away like a burden carried in some other place" (p. 114)—Muir had found there a strength to continue. With his customary hunger for guides to the truth, he found in Nietzsche "a last dying foothold on my dream of the future" and took refuge in "the fantasy of the Superman" (pp. 126, 127), a dream of being beyond the dictates of good and evil. Though false, the infatuation with Nietzsche helped him to survive when he might have foundered. Muir's subsequent time at the bone factory in Fairport, under the "clinging, sweet stench, suggesting dissolution and hospitals and slaughter-houses, the odour of drains and the rancid stink of bad, roasting meat" (p. 131) could only intensify the sense of degradation, the need to survive; yet that, too, has to be incorporated into the fable. Heine, another infatuation, could only intensify the wretchedness by his "sweet poison" and Muir's earliest poems, "lonely, ironic, slightly corpse-like" (p. 146), not republished, were accepted by Orage for *The New Age*. Between them, Wyre, Glasgow, and Fairport provide Eden and the Fall.

The early experiences in Glasgow helped to make Muir's relationship with Scotland a complex one. He had a troubled relationship with the theologies and rational habits of his own nation and in *Scottish Journey* (1935) goes some way to explaining why we must think of him as primarily a European and a citizen of those countries of the mind that lie beyond national frontiers. His ferocious diagnosis of Scotland, with its "derelict industries, its vast slums, its depopulated glens, its sweated peasantry, and its army of unemployed" (p. 250) is compelling. He offers no easy return to an agrarian society, claiming that the employed eighteenth-century peasant was worse off than the unemployed Clydesider of his own day, but he cannot make Scotland his home. In another telling passage he emphasizes his alienation from England's governing elite, his inability to cope with a public school tribe he found imbued with "this mechanical perfection of response, this unquestioning assurance that the game of life can be played in only one way" (p. 207).

Muir was never exactly at home in this world. He was an autodidact, a man whose uncertain and fairly workaday education had ended when he was fourteen and who had to fashion a meaning for his life from what fragments lay around him. The search for that meaning took him to Europe.

EUROPE
A great friendship and a happy marriage were of huge value to Muir's maturing thought; the friend was John Holms, whose intelligence led to the honing of Muir's own mind and whose patience gave Muir the confidence to grow. "Our minds were completely open to each other," Muir wrote (*An Autobiography*, p. 181). And if Wyre and Glasgow form the anchoring experiences of the fable, Europe and the long association with, in particular, Prague form another layer of experience crucial to the appreciation of Muir's poetry. Though Muir oddly gives as his and Willa's reason for leaving London in 1921 an acquaintanceship with so many people they couldn't get down to work, it seems natural that this questing young self-made man should home toward Europe, intimately associated with the great mappers of the internal world, Jung and Freud, always more intellectually aware than the coteries of London or the rational academics of Scotland. In Prague, Muir says, "everything seemed to be asking me to notice it"

(p. 189). There were new revelations to be found in what Muir sensed to be the proximity of theater, music, and political and social questioning to the lives of people of all classes. Those immediate postwar years were the serious beginning of Muir's cultural and intellectual life, and it was in Dresden in 1922 that he realized he must "live over again the years which I had lived wrongly" and, looking back at the years behind him, felt that "I was not seeing my own life merely, but all human life. . . . In turning my head and looking *against* the direction in which time was hurrying me I won a new kind of experience, for now that I no longer marched in step with time I could see life timelessly, and with that in terms of the imagination" (p. 192). He began to write poetry, and yet, as his cultural horizons expanded, a "terrible impersonality" grew and strengthened: the docketing and diminishing of human life at the service of industrial Glasgow, the rise of Fascism culminating in genocide in Germany, the dehumanizing of life under the Soviet imperium. Though the terrors brought about by Fascism and Communism were not dealt with directly in Muir's poetry, he had begun translating Kafka in 1929, and Kafkaesque images—the maze, the labyrinth, the gate, the castle, the outcast or refugee—give a deep and disturbing ambivalence to his mature work. Such things grew slowly; Muir often gave the impression that the unsealing of his eyes to the terrors slowly taking shape about him was a long, half-aware process; the flux of history was never a primary concern for one whose imagination was habituated to work on cycles and recurrences.

A crux came in February 1939 when Muir found himself unexpectedly saying the Lord's Prayer and realizing with the force of certainty that the prayer was "always universal and always inexhaustible" (*An Autobiography*, p. 246). He knew, irrevocably, that he was a Christian. After the war, Muir's sense of the labyrinth was immeasurably deepened by his presence in Prague for the two and a half years that culminated in the Communist revolution. His sense of the possibilities of a Christianity that could banish the ghosts of Calvin and Knox deepened with his experience of Rome and Italy: "I discovered in Italy that Christ had walked on the earth, and also that things truly made preserve themselves through time in the first freshness of their nature" (p. 280). *An Autobiography* and the *Collected Poems* are interwoven and complementary.

CRITICISM

MUIR'S life was not that of an academic. He was untenured, nomadic, making with Willa a life as a "translation factory," and burdened in the latter part of his life with administration, as alluded to in his W. P. Ker Memorial Lecture "The Politics of King Lear": "I have come to books when I could, in the intervals of a life spent on other things, many of them not of my choosing; books have not been my occupation" (*Essays on Literature and Society*, p. 33). Perhaps because of this Muir's critical writings and lectures are always generous in spirit, always marked by a desire to widen the audience for the good, as he saw it. Their style is lucid and unfashionably companionable. Two books in particular still challenge the reader with their insights and discussions of the interlocking relationships between literature, society, politics, and religious experience: *Essays on Literature and Society* (1949) and *The Estate of Poetry* (1962). These books were published at a time when the Fascist threat had only recently been defeated; when the Communist threat was at its height. Muir might now see consumer-materialism and the fissiparous nature of contemporary society as the more insidious enemies. The tenor of Muir's criticism is always to celebrate writing that expresses, or searches for, that unity in a society which he valued so highly, a unity at its finest when the relationship between that society and a metaphysical order that informs its being is acknowledged. The democratic bedrock of his mind distrusts hierarchy, but welcomes vision. This is reflected in *Essays on Literature and Society*. In his essay on Robert Henryson, the Scots poet of the medieval period, he finds the expression of a world when "all life, whether of the animals or of men, is a story and part of a greater story"; he can see in Henryson, as in the balladry of medieval Scotland, "a standard of proportion which has been lost," despite the trouble and lawlessness of those times (p. 11). In "The Politics of King Lear," Muir sets Lear's tragedy in the conflict between that older world of proportion and harmony that Lear inarticulately apprehends he is a part of, a world bound by "a sort of piety and human fitness" (p. 49) and the animal individuality of Goneril, Regan, and Edmund. We are reminded, in Muir's account of the animality with which Goneril and Regan are invested, of Muir's own desolation on that Glasgow tram car. The politics bare of morality that the opposition to Lear embodies did not seem a mere historical or literary phenomenon to Muir, who had experienced the crucifixion of Europe by fascist and communist regimes. The essay is constantly alive and alert to Muir's special concerns: our origin, our end, and our relationships with each other on this earth. Clearly, for Muir, the king understands the nature of the Fable; his vicious daughters only understand, existentially, the use they can make for their own ends of the Story. In his generous essay on Burns, Muir stresses the artistry of Burns as well as his prodigious and simplified popularity, but takes some issue with Eliot for his enclosure of poetry into a compound visited by the discriminating few, stressing that beyond Eliot's elite is a "fringe surrounding it which is not small, a working liaison between the discriminating few and the undiscriminating mass" (p. 63). Muir never loses sight of his belief in extending the democratic franchise; his essay on Walter Scott is full of dubieties, acknowledging the range, the power, but realizing that Scott's primary aim was "to achieve a distinguished position in society and to live a life of traditional grandeur" (p. 74). In his empathic essay on Friedrich Hölderlin, Muir might almost be writing the adverse criticism his own poetry has sometimes attracted when he talks of Hölderlin's "baffling depth, a certain radiant monotony," but he closes with a sentence properly appropriate to his own art as well: "He approached the mystery of time and eternity through the imagination" (pp. 88, 103). The brief essay on Kafka shines with an affection and respect for *The Castle* and *The Trial*, which contain, for Muir, "the most enchanting discoveries, the most startling riddles, the most profound insight into human life" (p. 123). Other essays in the book deal with Oswald Spengler, politics, and history. In his essay "The Decline of the Novel," he sees the twentieth-century novel reflecting its age in being trapped in time; uncertain of its ends, because "our existence, like our works, is an unfinished sentence" (p. 143). The Story, in life, in fiction, cannot satisfy if only seen as partaking in time, for it then becomes "a fleeting picture on an unstable substance" (p. 148). One's life can only be understood if seen as a having a permanent spiritual existence, freed from the shifting and random nature of time.

Muir's final essays, "The Poetic Imagination" and "A View of Poetry," are a sustained plea for the imagination as Muir defines it: "the faculty by which life is grasped in its individual forms, and human beings and all living things are shown as they live and move" (p. 220). He discusses the way in which the maker develops the capacity to partake in the life of the world by his absorption, and yet can simultaneously preserve his sense of detachment. He discusses the "inseeing" of Rainer Rilke, the capacity that John Keats, D. H. Lawrence, and Gerard Manley Hopkins had for vividly entering into the being of other life forms, but returns to his own central concern: how we use our imagination to express the historical continuity of human life and penetrate behind the Story to the Fable. Muir put it thus in a letter to Alec Aiitken in 1951: "I'm not much concerned with imaginative 'creation,' but rather with true and false imagination" (*Selected Letters of Edwin Muir*, p. 160).

The six lectures that Muir gave at Harvard in 1955 to 1956, published as *The Estate of Poetry*, are the distillation of a lifetime's experience and the considered credo of a man who had achieved distinction in the craft he spoke about. He began by defining what he meant by the "estate of poetry:" a communality including poet and audience, growing or shrinking according to cultural change, and, for Muir, becoming in his time the isolated poet confronting "the public." In the 1950s Muir wrote that "the rapid communication of information blunts the discriminating power of the mind, and may reduce it to a state of savage torpor" (p. 6). His reaction to the last half-century may be imagined. There is, of course, a sense in which the convictions Muir has come to disable him from both creation and appreciation outside the boundaries he has established. His belief that motor cars cannot enter poetry "except in the false rhetorical vein" (p. 8), because they have no inherent life of their own, and that consequently a car is "impervious to the imagination" is hardly useful and certainly not true, unless we accept Muir's world picture as incapable of enlargement. Again Muir returns to the ballad tradition as embodying a high tragic world in which the making of the ballads, and the oral tradition that gave them continuance, was in a sense a communal act of the imagination working on historical event and incorporating it into the Fable. For Muir, Wordsworth at his finest expressed the close bond between man, the earth he sprang from, and the spirit that informed him, just as William Butler Yeats was Muir's great contemporary who

achieved an audience and, having mastered his craft and assumed the authority, spoke of and to his countrymen in "love and fury." Both poets exemplified that reaching out into wider territories than those provided by small cultural elites that Muir cared about so passionately. Muir saw, though he was careful to enter some caveats and reservations, the growth of analytical criticism, intensifying the popular belief in the "difficulty" of reading poetry and consequently helping to corral poetry into a fenced-off compound—in his words, intensifying the divorce between poet and possible audience because "the method legalises the divorce as a settled and normal state" (p. 77). The lectures worry away at this gap between poet and audience; their positive if not necessarily optimistic tenor always asking the poet to focus on our common humanity and on our bond with both past time and the beyond-time experiences our imagination apprehends. The poet must, Muir felt, refuse to enter that enticing room where only the chosen few are waiting to applaud him.

FICTION: THE MARIONETTE

OF Muir's three novels, *The Marionette*, first published at the Hogarth Press by Leonard and Virginia Woolf in 1927, is the most compelling. Muir's two later novels, *Poor Tom*, with its Glaswegian autobiographical elements, a book Muir self-deprecatingly described in a letter to Mr. and Mrs. Thorburn in 1932 as " a very lugubrious one," and *The Three Brothers*, Muir's historical novel set in Renaissance Scotland, have not survived as triumphantly as his first, very much a poet's fiction.

The Marionette, an expressionistic novella rather than a novel, takes as its theme the maturing of Hans, the feeble-witted son of Martin, a reclusive Salzburg widower. Hans, fearing the terror, business, and inherent strangeness of the actual world about him, lives in flight from the people. The changeabilty of human faces seems to him "a violence of the flesh"; he takes refuge in dolls and a doll's house his father has given him. A visit to Herr Hoffmann's Marionette Theatre draws Hans into the world of marionettes, out of which he creates the image of a timeless, stationary universe parallel to the one he feels trapped in. The adolescent boy is drawn into the Faust legend he has seen enacted in the Marionette Theatre, and, given a suit in imitation of the one Faust wears and a

Gretchen puppet, he is drawn into a sterile enchantment with Gretchen in this world, while watching their double happiness in that illusory paradise he has created.. Martin attempts to draw his son gradually out into the natural world; the tale comes to a close with an orgy of sadistic violence, in which Hans drives nails into the Gretchen puppet till she is split into four. This act kills the enchanted garden of that other world, and Hans starts to build a mature life with his father after a visionary dream in which his father takes him to Gretchen's funeral and he weeps "with a desire to go on weeping till he should be free" (p. 150). Hans's tears bring life back to Gretchen, and the two of them walk together out into the life of green and growing things. The action is presided over by another controlling image, that of the twelve stations of the cross father and son must pass as they go downhill into Salzburg.

The bare bones of such a tale seem simplistic and banal. *The Marionette* is certainly neither. The narrative drive never slackens; the climax is sudden, horrifying, and right. The strangeness of a city to a newcomer—and this was written while Muir was responding to his own first impressions of Salzburg—is caught with an exact vivacity. In one ferocious scene where Hans, in his Faust suit and with puppet Gretchen beside him, is attacked and mobbed by a hostile crowd, critics have seen a pre-figuring of the Nazi terror about to be unloosed in Europe.

THE POEMS

Edwin Muir's *First Poems* was published in 1925, followed by *Variations on a Time Theme* (1934) and *Journeys and Places* (1937). The war years produced *The Narrow Place* (1943), followed by *The Voyage* (1946). Muir's finest collections, *The Labyrinth* (1949) and *One Foot in Eden* (1956), completed his poetic output. Though Muir had put this body of work together for his *Collected Poems*, his death left Willa Muir and J. C. Hall with the task of adding a final section of previously uncollected and unpublished work. *Collected Poems 1921–1958* was published by Faber and Faber in 1960; its definitive second edition, with a few textual revisions and a further poem added, was published in 1962. This is the most accessible text, containing the poems Edwin Muir wished his reputation to stand by and Willa Muir's additions. An annotated *Complete Poems* was finally

brought out in 1991. The bare titles of these books announce a poetry that is habitually stripped down to the essential concerns of the Fable, that positioning of man simultaneously in and out of time, in which the physical substance of the world becomes an endlessly suggestive, endlessly reforming mythic landscape. Though Muir sometimes speaks in the first person in his poems, he was uneasy with too close an identification of his speaker with his own personality. Since he was concerned with universals, much of his poetry is most appropriately expressed in the first person plural, the voice of that community that includes the reader. With Muir's own distrust of "explanation" in mind, the individual collections are discussed here sequentially: they were seen by the author as forming a journey, and though that journey is a complex one, often circular rather than linear, *Collected Poems* gathers strength and power as it progresses.

Muir only saved nine poems from his first book, *First Poems*, among them the two lyrical poems "Childhood" and "Horses," which have a memorable clarity of vision. Both were written in steady rhyming quatrains, a balladic form Muir often chose, and "Childhood" is a calm evocation of the boy Muir once was: "Long time he lay upon the sunny hill, / To his father's house below securely bound." Around him are the distinct contours of home, the "black islands," the "straight shadows" of the grass, and, shifting through those exact impressions, the mist, the "unseen straits," the "new shores" he can only guess at (*Collected Poems 1921–1958*, p. 19; subsequent page references are from this volume unless otherwise noted). It is a poem of home with a sense of departure built into it, a view seen through the wrong end of time's telescope. "Horses" is a dramatic contrast. Glimpsing a plow team, Muir is suddenly thrown back to the Bu, a child overpowered by his encounter with the otherness of the farm's heavy horses, their eyes filled with "a cruel apocalyptic light," their manes the "leaping ire of the wind" (p. 20). As the image with all its power dies away from him, Muir, caught in his longing, brings his poem to a passionate close:

Ah, now it fades! it fades! and I must pine
Again for that dread country crystalline,
Where the blank field and the still-standing tree
Were bright and fearful presences to me.

(p. 20)

The two poems are a point of embarkation for Muir's long journey: that kind of journey T. S. Eliot understood when he wrote, in "Little Gidding," how the conclusion of all our explorative journeys "Will be to arrive where we started / And know the place for the first time" (in *Collected Poems 1909–1962*, 1963, p. 222). From that first collection Muir also chose to save, as well as two or three descriptive pieces, his "Ballad of Hector in Hades." Hector recalls his headlong flight, Achilles on his heels, until the death blow comes and Achilles parades around Troy, "A corpse with streaming hair" (p. 26). This vigorous and clean-limbed poem is a transposition of an experience recounted in *An Autobiography* of a childhood flight from a bully: an early demonstration of Muir's technique of reworking experience into mythic form; it announces a concern with Greek myth, or rather a concern with the fall of Troy and the wanderings of Odysseus, which is an occasional motif in the poetry. It is perhaps curious that this child of the north made so little of Norse mythology, with all its ferocities of the dark; his legendary figures are primarily biblical or Greek. Three further ballads show Muir firmly under the spell of the border ballads of Scotland—and Coleridge's *The Rime of the Ancient Mariner*. There is an element of pastiche in the performance, but the energy of the imagery carries these ballads forward with an impetus and excitement often lacking in Muir; this is particularly so in "The Ballad of the Flood" with its Scottish vernacular phrases: the "crackling shell" of the Ark, the beasts who "sabbed and maned the leelang night," the "astonied ships" (pp. 32, 34, 35). Such usages are not often returned to.

"Variations on a Time Theme" is an ambitious poem in ten sections, and perhaps more ambitious than successful. The architectural shaping is unclear, and for all the interest inherent in Muir's theme, the sequence veers unsteadily, caught between rhyming couplets, blank verse, free verse, rhapsody, and lyric. Muir was never a great verse technician, and the forms he experiments with here are not handled with the kind of skill that gives the reader confidence in the poem's authority. The "Variations" are a reminder that Muir is often at his best when walking at his own pace or handling the balladic meters that had become second nature to him. He is not a natural lyricist; W. H. Auden would no doubt find him more of a Prospero than an Ariel—Prospero medi-

tates; Ariel sings because he must. The whole sequence is indebted to T. S. Eliot's *The Waste Land*: the opening lines are an Eliotean announcement, posed as an Eliotean question:

> After the fever this long convalescence,
> Chapped blood and growing pains, waiting for life,
> Turning away from hope, too dull for speculation.
>
> How did we come here to this broken wood?
>
> (p. 39)

The concerns here will never leave Muir, though they will find better and more varied expression. Time is the "sad stationary journey" down which humanity travels, the soul and the body in their brief uneasy pairing, seen as rider and horse. Expelled from Eden, human beings travel through Muir's own version of the waste, through "the comfortless smell of casual habitation" (p. 45), searching for release from Time's captivity. Part of Muir's technique in this sequence is to proceed by ambivalence of statement—a resounding ambivalence that seems to hold huge meaning but can also appear a nervous tic. We have "The peace that is won and lost," "Was it truth / That lured us here, or falsehood?" "one I know and do not know," "Buried alive and buried dead by Time," and many others (pp. 44, 39, 50, 48). This reliance on paradox as a means to approach spiritual meaning is hardly unique to Muir; it is part of his biblical inheritance, but it will be used rather more sparingly in the books to come.

With his collection *Journeys and Places* Muir started to build his poems into a unity and to find a voice appropriate to his subject matter. There is always something that seems a touch willed about the relations of the poems in a Muir collection to the title of that collection; the words "Journey" and "Place" occur in the titles in thirteen of the twenty-four poems gathered in the *Collected*. Ambivalences—"For small is great and great is small," The horizon's gates unlock and lock" (pp. 62, 59)—are still present, which are reminiscent of Eliot and such passages as the Fourth Tempter's address to Archbishop Thomas Becket in Eliot's *Murder in the Cathedral*: "You know and do not know, that action is suffering, / And suffering action" (in *Collected Plays*, 1962, p. 27). Such a true use of ambivalence closes the fine poem, "The Mythical Journey," as man "builds in faith and doubt his shaking house" (p. 63). The Greek world resurfaces with two poems taking the Trojan war as their theme, "Troy" being particularly effective in its creation of an old Trojan warrior who survives in Troy's ruins and still fights in imagination the long-victorious Greeks among scraps and refuse where

> The rat-hordes,
> Moving, were grey dust shifting in grey dust.
> Proud history has such sackends.
>
> (p. 71)

The free blank verse (never straying too long or too far from a ten-syllable, five-stress line) in which "The Mythical Journey" and "Troy" are written suits Muir exactly. It is a considering rhythm; it calls no special attention to itself and in Muir's hands is of an even texture, lacking bravura. It could be called a sober, serious mode; its detractors would call it pedestrian. In the balladic "The Town Betrayed"—betrayal and treachery interest Muir far more than frontal assault—Muir attempts the fusion of imagery drawn from different historical periods: the "harlot daughters" lean out of their windows like "painted prows," yet the ships in the harbor below are "crammed down with shells and guns" (p. 76). Such a fusion comes to its fruition in Muir's final book of poetry, *One Foot in Eden*. The poems of place do not attempt to turn into image the intimacy and uniqueness of any loved places on this earth; rather, they bear such titles as "The Private Place," "The Unattained Place," "The Original Place": places seen as staging posts on the spiritual journey. There is no final resting-place in these poems; there are only pauses beside signposts. However, "The Sufficient Place" captures a moment of equipoise between origins and ends "in this little house" with a grave processional beauty:

> If a man
> Should chance to find this place three times in time
> His eyes are changed and make a summer silence
> Amid the tumult, seeing the roads wind in
> To their still home, the house and the leaves and
> birds.
>
> (p. 87)

The Narrow Place starts to bear out some of the wisdom encapsulated in one of William Blake's Proverbs of Hell from *The Marriage of Heaven and Hell*: "Eternity is in love with the productions of time." Many of Muir's most memorable poems come when closely observed details of our human world are incorporated into Muir's larger vision. The opening poem for John Holms, "To J. F. H. (1897–1934)," is a brilliant illustration. He sees his friend "trussed to the motor cycle" and cannot tell "What world I walked in, since it held us two, / A dead and a living man," come back by "such a simple road from heaven" (pp. 91, 92). The vision is moving and convincing, as, in "The River," is the picture of the grandmother standing by her soldier grandson, who is about to set off to war:

> A bundle of clouts creased as with tribulations,
> Bristling with spikes and spits and bolts of steel,
> Bound in with belts, the rifle's snub-nosed horn
> Peering above his shoulder . . .
>
> (p. 93)

The presence of the war becomes overt, as does specific human activity in "The Wayside Station," when the farmer wakes and "feels the day like a familiar ache" before work starts (p. 92). "The Narrow Place" emphasizes the sense of constriction inherent in the period, constriction man has created, though Muir never closes the doors on the possibility of renewal, if only the renewal posited in the existence of "one little wild half-leafless tree" (p. 102). One of the finest poems in Muir's heraldic mode is "The Grove"; the "drugged thicket" or "smothering grove" that has to be passed through to achieve the good vision. The grove, with its "jungle cities," is ruled by the "well-bred sufficient animals / With clean rank pelts and proud and fetid breath, / Screaming their arrogant calls" (p. 109), in which it is perhaps not fanciful to see the image of Himmler's SS divisions of the Third Reich. To balance that, the collection contains one of Muir's most tender poems for Willa, "The Confirmation," with its lovely opening line: "Yes, yours, my love, is the right human face" (p. 118).

The Voyage is a somewhat unsatisfactory book, an eddy or swirl in the current before the two hugely impressive collections that bring Muir's poetic career to a triumphant conclusion. The end of a world war is rephrased in terms of the Trojan War in the lyrical "The Return of the Greeks," and much of the volume shows Muir eschewing his pentameters for love lyric and song. The task he sets himself in "In Love for Long," which is to "contrive a song / For the intangible" (p. 159), only results in a string of abstractions. Despite the obvious affection in the triple-stressed lines of

"For Ann Scott-Moncrieff," "Sorrow." and "A Birthday," the weightlessness of the verse makes the poems seem somewhat slight and casual, a mode not really suited to Muir's temperament. In some ways "Suburban Dream" is one of the most successful poems, strangely built out of daily suburban life, hovering over an almost timeless afternoon trance where women and children move like creatures in a dream until the trance is broken by the return of their menfolk in the evening. The poem is moving but feels as if it were written by someone else—Louis MacNeice perhaps—with its houses where "the air flows through the rooms / Fanning the curtain hems" and all is "a child's dream of a grown-up world" (p. 147). This book lives in a kind of waiting room, circling its themes lightly, curiously off-centered by its title poem, another ballad in the Coleridgean mode: "And blessing, we ourselves were blest" (p. 138).

The Labyrinth was published when Muir was in his early sixties; it is almost as if, with his particular concern for ancestral and inherited wisdom, he had been practicing in his earlier books to be an old man before his time. There was never a time when Muir's poetry had the sense of a new world opening before it; an old world opening behind it was always more his style. "Too Much," the first poem, announces the theme, the labyrinth being a version of the opening image in Dante's Inferno, the dark wood where all ways are lost: "Dark on the highway, groping in the light, / Threading my dazzling way within my night" (p. 163). The labyrinth lies all around Muir's narrator; the closed-off past itself becomes, in "The Return," "A sweet and terrible labyrinth of longing" (p. 167). Poem after poem in this assured and powerful collection carries an authority approaching that of Yeats in its security of tone, its assurance of the importance of what is being said. Occasionally the similarity is almost too close for comfort. Take the final lines of Yeats's "The Circus Animals' Desertion": "I must lie down where all the ladders start, / In the foul rag and bone-shop of the heart" (in *The Poems*, 1983, p. 348) Compare it to the end of the first section of Muir's "The Journey Back," as he returns "To my sole starting-point, my random self / That in these rags and tatters clothes the soul" (p. 171). Though most of the poems in *The Labyrinth* are written in the loose but stately blank verse that Muir is most at home in, the lyrical pieces have an assurance not always present in earlier work, particularly "The Child Dying," the

farewell of a dying child, its hand in its father's hand, and "The Combat." Many of Muir's earlier experiences went into the making of this strange account of the eternal conflict between two creatures, a "killing beast that cannot kill" and its eternal opponent, "A soft round beast as brown as clay" (pp. 180, 179). It is a poem whose suggestions widen out, ripples from a single stone thrown into a pond, a heartening poem. Two particularly impressive poems in Muir's meditative manner are "The Good Town" and "The Transfiguration." "The Good Town" takes us into the heart of postwar Europe, and into the center of the labyrinth, the Story and the Fable uniting; in the corrupted city, where you can tell the policemen and the spies "by their free and candid air" (p. 185), the citizens ponder how their slavery came about:

> We have seen
> Good men made evil wrangling with the evil,
> Straight minds made crooked fighting crooked
>   minds.
>
> (p. 186)

"The Transfiguration" leads us into Muir's final collection. The poem is lit with a visionary radiance. The animal creations join in "gentle congregations" or find their "leafy oratories," linked in praise; those who "hide within the labyrinth / Of their own loneliness and greatness" are freed (p. 199). Though the vision passes, it is a true token of the time when "he will come, Christ the uncrucified / Christ the discrucified, his death undone," and Judas will "take his long journey backward / From darkness into light" (p. 200). In this superb poem, Muir finds himself coming home.

In *One Foot in Eden*, Muir integrated for the first time the Christian myth and the Fable. Though Muir had always used biblical imagery, the full weight of his Italian experiences, by now deeply absorbed, certified his sense of the Incarnation, that living presence of the divine in the landscape, giving his final collection an astonishing freshness and sparkle. Muir seems to sum up the whole of quattrocento painting in "The Annunciation," whose grave beauty is a world away from his Presbyterian roots, as he senses the presence of "So great a wonder that it makes / each feather tremble on his wings" (p. 224). In "Adam's Dream," the Fall brings about a world where

The animals had withdrawn and from the caves

And woods stared out in fear or condemnation
Like outlaws or like judges.

(p. 211)

Still, the possibilities foreshadowed in "The Transfiguration" are never far away from this final collection. In the title-poem, the labyrinth gives way to the perpetual small redemption of the fallen world:

But famished field and blackened tree
Bear flowers in Eden never known.
Blossoms of grief and charity
Bloom in these darkened fields alone.

(p. 227)

In the fine poem "The Incarnate One," Muir sees Scotland as turning Christ, the Word Incarnate, back into Word again: "And God three angry letters in a book" (p. 228). Christ must continue on his unceasing journey for true recognition "Past the mirages and the murdering snow" (p. 229). The sense of a slow coming to terms with the fabric of Italy is beautifully captured in "The Difficult Land," where our longing for a relief from the labor of being human is alleviated by "faces of goodness, faithful masks of sorrow" and by the "dead / Who lodge in us so strangely" (p. 238). As summed up in *Dream and Thing*, Muir knows that we must bring "From the dull mass each separate splendour out. / There is no trust but in the miracle" (p. 242). The collection includes Muir's most celebrated poem, that anthology piece of the sixties, "The Horses," in which a nuclear holocaust is followed by the advent of the "strange horses." Muir envisages a new beginning in which the bond between man and creature is reestablished; the relationship at the heart of the community in Wyre comes around again:

Since then they have pulled our ploughs and borne
our loads,
But that free servitude still can pierce our hearts.
Our life is changed; their coming our beginning.

(p. 247)

POEMS NOT PREVIOUSLY COLLECTED

IN the miscellany of poems that Willa Muir and J. C. Hall added to the *Collected*, all of which they felt were written in Muir's last five years, there are one or two extraordinary pieces, of which easily the strangest is "The Song," a dream encounter with a giant creature, a horse, a centaur, giving out "A long breath drawn by pain, intolerable" (p. 259). This trapped creature, unable to break its bounds, is encapsulated in a poem whose strength and oddity bears comparison with Wilfred Owen's "Strange Meeting":

What wound in the world's side and we unknowing
Lay open and bleeding now? What present anguish
Drew that long dirge from the earth-haunting
marvel?
And why that earthly visit, unearthly pain?

(p. 259)

A poem showing how Muir might have built more of the fabric of the Story into the Fable is "There's Nothing Here," a kind of soliloquy given by his cousin Sutherland, lamenting the lack of physical substance in heaven: "Oh, for the plough stilts and the horse's reins, / And the furrows running free behind me" (p. 294). The last poem in the book, "I Have Been Taught," closes with what can be considered Muir's own final word:

And now the time grows shorter, I perceive
That Plato's is the truest poetry,
And that these shadows
Are cast by the true.

(p. 302)

CONCLUSION

MUIR brings into question all the most serious considerations that vex and perplex us as human beings. If we place no value on the idea of a world of spiritual meaning that informs this world we inhabit as we go about our daily business, if we have no sense of kinship with the dead, no faith that man's existence has more than an animal meaning in the place of things, we shall be blind to Muir's virtues. He offers no brilliant enticements; his poetry wears no finery. There are no concessions to wit or humor. In a letter to Joseph Chiari in 1946, Muir describes how he and Willa were whisked by night at breakneck speed through the wastes of Bohemia in an open car by a half-mad driver who occasionally brandished a revolver, Muir and the back seat getting gradually saturated by some honey he was carrying. It would make a good poem, but not a Muir poem. His patient probing can seem repetitive; his verse can seem pedestrian. In his Norton Lecture on Yeats, Muir disarmingly says: "There have been explanations of Yeats in plenty, and I have no wish to add to them, for I feel that to explain anyone is an attempt that should never be made" (*The Estate of Poetry*, p. 45). The poems and the autobiography ask for a re-tuning of the reader's wavelength, an open sensitivity to the mystery of things, for Muir is not concerned with entertainment, invention, or aesthetics but with the slow uncovering of what he tentatively feels to be universal truths.

Muir draws his images from primal sources: horse and plow, harvest and seedtime. The creation of novel metaphor is hardly his concern. Whether such imagery, drawn from a pre-industrial world, will gradually lose its power, whether our dream life will gradually eliminate it from our unconscious minds—these are troubles for Muir that his poems cannot charm away. Because Muir's incorporation of "timeless" imagery into his poems is so habitual, the occasions on which he incorporates more of twentieth-century daily life can seem contrived, as if that incorporation is a kind of duty rather than an inevitability. Muir seems unable to distinguish confidently between what he finds capable of being incorporated into the Fable and what for him is not; for him, the tractor must again be superseded by the horse, though surely everything that exists has to be susceptible to interpretation. That is his weakness, but his intense concentration on that search for the meaning that lies behind the flux of event is his strength, and the strength is such that in a busy and miscellaneous world, his poetry can offer a deep and sustaining wisdom.

It is appropriate to close with the final words of Willa Muir's memoir of their lives together, *Belonging*. Speaking of their love, she writes: "In reaching this personal harmony we made at least a start, we took a step or two along the road towards that greater world harmony which haunted us like a dream from the Fable. Edwin believed that it *was* a dream from the Fable which would ultimately come to pass, and he felt himself to be a spokesman for it in his poetry" (p. 316).

SELECTED BIBLIOGRAPHY

I. POETRY. *First Poems* (London and New York, 1925); *Chorus of the Newly Dead* (London, 1926); *Six Poems* (London, 1932); *Variations on a Time Theme* (London, 1934); *Journeys and Places* (London, 1937); *The Narrow Place* (London, 1943); *The Voyage* (London, 1946); *The Labyrinth* (London, 1949); *Collected Poems 1921–1951* (London, 1952; New York, 1953); *Prometheus* (London, 1954); *One Foot in Eden* (London and New York, 1956); *Collected Poems 1921–1958* (London, 1960); *Collected Poems* (London, 1963); *Selected Poems: With a Preface by T. S. Eliot* (London, 1965); *The Complete Poems of Edwin Muir,* annotated edition, ed. P. H. Butter (Aberdeen, 1991).

II. CRITICISM. *Transition: Essays on Contemporary Literature* (London and New York, 1926); *The Structure of the Novel* (London, 1928); *Essays on Literature and Society* (London, 1949; rev. ed., London, 1965); *The Estate of Poetry* (London and New York, 1962).

III. MEMOIRS. *The Story and the Fable* (London, 1940); revised as *An Autobiography* (London and New York, 1954); also, Willa Muir, *Belonging: A Memoir* (London, 1968).

IV. LETTERS. *Selected Letters of Edwin Muir,* ed. P. H. Butter (London, 1974).

V. OTHER PROSE. *We Moderns* (London, 1918; New York, 1920); *Latitudes* (London and New York, 1924); *John Knox: Portrait of a Calvinist* (London and New York, 1929); *Scottish Journey* (London, 1935); *Social Credit and the Labour Party: An Appeal* (London, 1935); *Scott and Scotland: The Predicament of the Scottish Writer* (London, 1936); *The Present Age: From 1914* (London, 1939); *Uncollected Scottish Criticism,* ed. Andrew Noble (London, 1982); *Selected Prose,* ed. George Mackay Brown (London, 1987).

VI. FICTION. *The Marionette* (London and New York, 1927); *The Three Brothers* (London and New York, 1931); *Poor Tom* (London, 1932).

VII. TRANSLATIONS WITH WILLA MUIR. *The Castle,* by Franz Kafka (London and New York, 1930); *The Trial,* by Franz Kafka (London and New York, 1937).

VIII. CRITICAL STUDIES. J. C. Hall, "Edwin Muir," in *Writers and Their Work* (London, 1956); P. H. Butter, *Edwin Muir: Man and Poet* (Edinburgh, 1966); Elgin W. Mellown, *A Bibliography of the Writings of Edwin Muir* (London, 1966); Daniel Hoffman, *Barbarous Knowledge: Myth in the Poetry of Yeats, Graves, and Muir* (New York, 1967); Peter C. Hoy and E. W. Mellown, *A Checklist of Writings about Edwin Muir* (London, 1971); E. Huberman, *The Poetry of Edwin Muir: The Field of Good and Ill* (New York, 1971); Allie Corbin Hixson, *Edwin Muir: A Critical Study* (New York, 1977); Elgin W. Mellown, *Edwin Muir* (Boston, 1979); Roger Knight, *Edwin Muir: An Introduction to His Work* (London, 1980); George Marshall, *In a Distant Isle: The Orkney Background of Edwin Muir* (Edinburgh, 1987); James Aitchhison, *The Golden Harvester: The Vision of Edwin Muir* (Aberdeen, 1998); Michael W. Russell, *In Waiting: Travels in the Shadow of Edwin Muir* (Glasgow, 1998); *Edwin Muir Centenary Assessments,* ed. C. J. M. MacLachlan and D. S. Robb (Aberdeen, 1990); Margery McCulloch, *Edwin Muir: Poet, Critic and Novelist* (Edinburgh, 1993).

NORMAN NICHOLSON

(1914–1987)

N. S. Thompson

"IF A MAN wants to see things 'strange, rich and rare,' he should cross not to the other side of the world, but to the other side of his own street. Familiarity breeds blindness rather than contempt, and nothing has more power to surprise us than the familiar looked at for the first time" ("Millom Delivered," p. 138). In these two sentences from a BBC Third Program broadcast in 1952, Norman Nicholson summed up most, but not all, of his position as a mid-twentieth-century poet, playwright, novelist, and topographer. Certainly, some poets have advocated seeing the universe in a grain of sand (William Blake, Emily Dickinson) or have been inspired by the localities of their birth (notably Nicholson's fellow Lakelander, William Wordsworth), but few poets in the twentieth century have successfully wedded these two elements, capturing both the essence of native place and the glimpse of something eternal there. Poets of the twentieth century generally followed its pattern of sweeping change, moving themselves from the region of their birth to a metropolis far removed, often in a different country. For many, James Joyce's prescription of "exile," for himself and his character Stephen Daedalus (*A Portrait of the Artist as a Young Man*, 1916), set the tone for the century. One only has to think of poets emerging at the time of Nicholson's birth—T. S. Eliot, Ezra Pound, and D. H. Lawrence, not to mention Robert Frost's sojourn in England. All of these, and many later writers, sought inspiration or a space to find themselves in a country or a background very different from their birthplace. Poets of the generation immediately preceding Nicholson's own were epitomized (if not led) by the restless energy of W. H. Auden, whose *Letters from Iceland* (with Louis MacNeice, 1937) and *Journey to a War* (with Christopher Isherwood, 1939), to say nothing of his poem "Spain" (1939), offered worldly, cosmopolitan vistas. (The sophisticated medleys of modernism, with its pan-cultural allusions and references, had already prepared the way) Auden's apocalyptic side was to spawn a short-lived school discerned in Nicholson's contemporaries, the so-called New Apocalypse poets (Henry Treece, G. S. Fraser, and J. F. Hendry). If these poets were reacting against the social and political agendas of the 1930s, it was seen to a greater degree in the poetry of imagination and personal liberation of Dylan Thomas and George Barker.

Norman Nicholson did not ally himself with any of these schools, perhaps in part because of his particular brand of Christianity. Brought into Methodism as a boy by his stepmother, he moved gradually, after a brief period of doubt in his teens, toward Anglicanism. He became a fully communicating member of the Church of England in 1940. In an era that saw many converts—including T. S. Eliot, C. S. Lewis, Evelyn Waugh, Robert Lowell, and W. H. Auden—Nicholson's religion was one of simple faith, expressed through his locality. He eschewed the intellectual and mythological expressions of belief favored by his fellow writers.

In making his native region so integral a part of his creative life, however, Nicholson was not wholly moved by elective affinity but rather clamped there firmly by the effects of tuberculosis contracted in his middle teens. And if he saw God as natura naturans, the creative spirit of nature, his appreciation of the natura naturata (created nature) of his birthplace was something that had to be worked at and achieved though the circumstances of personal difficulty. Thus, before looking at the various aspects of his work, which includes poetry, prose, and drama, it is essential to look at both his particular region and the circumstances of his life.

MILLOM

SITUATED on the west bank of the Duddon estuary in what is now Cumbria, Millom, Nicholson's birthplace, was a Victorian boom town, founded when super-rich hematite was discovered in the limestone coastal rock, with a large ironworks added to the mining activity behind specially built sea walls. On the coast, near the great landscapes of the Lake District, it was thus a singular locality in British topography: a typical industrial town, its rows of squat terraces interspersed with nonconformist chapels and railway sidings, but situated by the sea. Its prosperity was not long lived, however. At the turn of the century production peaked and, except for a brief respite during 1939–1945, its history during Nicholson's life was one of long, slow decline, exacerbated by the rigors of the Great Depression. Indeed, Nicholson saw not only the closure of the works in 1968 but also the flattening of the site some years later. Today the town survives on newer industries and, but for the mines and ironworks, looks much as it did as Nicholson remembers it in his work.

Norman Cornthwaite Nicholson was the first and only son of Joseph Nicholson and Edith Cornthwaite. He was born on 8 January 1914 above his father's tailoring and outfitter's shop at 14 St. George's Terrace, a three-story terrace house still standing and built originally as a family residence. Like many of the houses on that street, the front room facing the road had been converted into a shop, which Nicholson's father took over after a long apprenticeship to another local tailor and outfitter, who never forgave him for setting up in competition.

In his later years Nicholson wrote an engaging autobiography of his boyhood and youth, *Wednesday Early Closing* (1975). The title reflects the fact that most retail traders closed their business for a half-day during the week to compensate for remaining open on Saturday afternoons. The fact of his father's shop insulated the family from the worst effects of Millom's decline after its boom years as a mining and iron-producing town and, later, during the depression. In the main his customers were the middle and lower middle classes (Millom's white-collar workers) and farmers from the more southerly Lakeland region, not the industrial workers prone to layoffs and the "dole" (unemployment benefit) when demand slackened, then dried up. But the family was first hit by tragedy when Nicholson's mother died in the Spanish influenza epidemic immediately after the First World War. On his own admission, Nicholson was too young to be affected. He accepted his grandmother's statement that his mother had gone to join the angels and enjoyed the attention shown by his remaining family for the motherless

child. His paternal grandmother moved in and for several years he was brought up by her, his memory of the circumscribed world of back kitchen and narrow brick yard a warm if unspacious cocoon in which his life was sealed. In 1922 his father married Rosetta (Rose) Sobey, a younger woman who ran a piano shop on the same street.

If Nicholson inherited his father's pluck and determination, from his stepmother he was waltzed into a different kind of nurturing. Her parents, like Nicholson's Cornish grandparents, had come up from the southwest, attracted by employment in the new mining town. Like many Devonians, they were Methodists. Rosetta, a keen pianist, was in demand at many gatherings. Methodism, then, according to Nicholson, was a "social religion": "most Methodists went to chapel because they enjoyed it. The chapel was not only their place of worship—it was their place of entertainment, their ancestral home, their music hall, assembly room, meeting house, club and gossip-shop" (*Wednesday Early Closing*, p. 93). Until he was thirteen, he says that chapel was one of the happiest places in the town for him; indeed, his whole youth was bright: "No child has ever had a more comfortable feeling of belonging than I had in the Methodist schoolroom or, indeed, anywhere in Millom, for I was Joe Nicholson's lad in the streets, just as I was Rose Sobey's stepson at the chapel, recognized and greeted everywhere" (*Wednesday Early Closing*, p. 100). Chapel was a source of music, biblical narrative, and, indirectly, poetry, as the local musical festivals and competitions included verse recitation, at which Nicholson excelled.

At school Nicholson achieved greater recognition, quick, able and—as ever—loquacious. He won significant prizes at Millom Secondary School and looked set for a university education or, at least, like D. H. Lawrence, training as a teacher. He took his matriculation (school leaving certificate) in 1929 and went into the sixth form to study for the advanced certificate that led to higher education, the usual escape route for the able and bright out of the confines of the depressed mining town. He also became confirmed in the Anglican Church; folk mythology had it that that would ensure acceptance at a seat of higher learning.

After one year of an agreeable existence, reading and discovering literature, came the diagnosis of tuberculosis that put an end to these hopes. The local sanatorium had a poor reputation, so in 1930

Nicholson was sent to a private clinic at Linford, on the western edge of the New Forest in Hampshire. Although the setting was delightful, the doctors were clear that full recovery depended on Nicholson himself: apart from fresh air, warmth, and a good diet, there was then no treatment and, given that tubercles had reached his larynx, the precocious chatty boy who had won prizes for recitation was not only confined to bed for eighteen months, but also to speaking in a whisper (see "The Whisperer," in *Collected Poems*, p. 267). In all, he remained two years when, although not fully recovered, and still subject to hemorrhages, the strain of payment meant that he had to return home. What he can have felt like when he saw the "small, dark, drab, damp and mean" town again after the genteel company and congenial surroundings of the New Forest can only be imagined; Nicholson is silent on the matter. Nevertheless, he strived to recover, furthering his interest in the countryside discovered at Linford and continuing his literary reading.

At this point Nicholson's autobiography closes and leaves us wondering how this young man, disadvantaged by ill health and the consequent end to his formal education, came to be not only a poet but one published by Eliot at Faber and Faber.

In the absence of a biography, the only published source of information is the excellent literary study by Philip Gardner, *Norman Nicholson* (1973), the result of a Ph.D. thesis written during Nicholson's middle years. The only major study of the poet's work to date (although it excludes the original thesis's consideration of novels and prose), it benefits from the writer's close personal contact with the poet during his lifetime.

As Gardner notes (p. 25), three friendships sustained Nicholson throughout the decade the politically minded Auden claimed as "low" and "dishonest" ("September 1, 1939") but which people in northern industrial towns knew simply as "the Slump." All three friendships reflect the poet's growing interest in religion, as well as his interest in literature, and all three contributed to his intellectual development, when Eliot, Auden, and Sir James Frazer's *The Golden Bough* were required reading. Nicholson's classmate Bessie Satterthwaite went to read English at Manchester University in 1933 and maintained a close friendship, introducing him first to the Anglican vicar of Holy Trinity, the Reverend Samuel Taylor, an early encourager, but secondly in July 1937 to Brother George Every, a member of the Anglican order of the Society for the Sacred Mission. The occasion was a Student Christian Movement conference held at the important seminary of Kelhelm, which was used by T. S. Eliot for periodic religious retreats. Every, who lectured on modern poetry and was a poet himself, published by Eliot in the *Criterion*, became a seminal influence on the poet six years his junior, introducing him to important literary figures, including Eliot. Nicholson's first publications included several poems in *New English Weekly* and the *Listener* and the even more prestigious *Poetry* (Chicago) and *Southern Review* in the United States.

During this time Nicholson had begun to lecture for the Workers' Educational Association, first in Millom, then in Whitehaven. The lectures led to the publication of his first book of criticism, *Man and Literature* (S. C. M. Press, 1943). His first major book publication occurred the previous year with his editorship of the Pelican book *An Anthology of Religious Verse, Designed for the Times* (1942), a remarkable collection of contemporary religious verse ranging from Chesterton, Hardy, and Hopkins through Eliot and Auden to Every, Michael Roberts, and Nicholson.

The war gave rise to a boom time for poetry, and by the time of Nicholson's first two books, he had had work accepted in *Horizon, Penguin New Writing, Poetry* (London), and *Poetry Quarterly*. He was also reviewing regularly for the *New English Weekly* and later *Time and Tide*. In 1943 he published a dozen poems as one of three contributors, along with Keith Douglas and J. C. Hall, to a series of *Selected Poems* edited by Reginald Moore. When a full collection was rejected by Poetry (London) Editions, Eliot's secretary, Anne Ridler (whose work Nicholson had included in his Pelican anthology) suggested he try Faber and Faber and Eliot, who had earlier rejected a novel. Eliot found the collection strong enough for publication, and *Five Rivers* came out in July 1944 to favorable reviews. The book was reprinted twice and an American edition followed in 1945. A second volume, *Rock Face*, came out in 1948, followed by *The Pot Geranium* (1954), *A Local Habitation* (1972) and *Sea to the West* (1981), all published by Faber and Faber.

Once established as a man of letters at the war's end, still living in St. George's Terrace and still having to guard his health, Nicholson branched out into novels, plays, broadcasting, and topography, as well as his regular reviewing work, mainly for the *Church Times* and the *Times Literary Supplement*. In 1956 he was well enough to marry Yvonne Gardner, a local schoolteacher originally from London. Although there was a long gap between his third and fourth volumes, he was busy with other literary work. During the poetry boom of the 1960s, he became a popular performer at poetry readings, and he was the recipient of many grants and awards, including honorary degrees, the Queen's Gold Medal for Poetry (1977), and the OBE (1981). When he died in 1987, the *Times* obituary called him "the most gifted English Christian provincial poet of his century." He is buried with his wife, who died in 1982, in St. George's churchyard, Millom. His *Collected Poems*, edited by Neil Curry, came out in 1994.

POETRY

IN his autobiography, Nicholson wrote, "I did not want to be a solitary poet, talking to myself in an attic or beside a lake. I wanted an audience; I wanted to make people listen" (*Wednesday Early Closing*, p. 106). But what sort of poetry did that entail?

His first published (but uncollected) poem, "May Day, 1937" is a hymn to the "liberating earth" waking among an industrial setting recognizably Millom:

> Kangeroo derricks box the sky,
> Sunlight skittles the roofs away,
> Chimneys rear a spikey joke
> Quoited by the hempen smoke.
> (*The Serpent*, vol. 21, 1937, p. 141)

These opening lines are reminiscent of Auden, Spender, and MacNeice as the "Pylon Poets" of industry. Unlike them, Nicholson adds a joyous touch that leavens man's desecration and exploitation, noting the appearance of "snowdrop laughter," the "laughter. . . blossoming" when "The clownish spring will flower again." Although not a great poem, its celebration of vernal renewal shows the unique claim on the poet's imagination made by the strange juxtaposition of industry and nature on the Duddon estuary and in many ways sets the agenda for much of the landscape poetry to come.

Nicholson was striking a singular stance here. If Auden could write "Tramlines and slagheaps, pieces of machinery, / That was, and still is, my

ideal scenery" ("Letter to Lord Byron"), it was the setting for a poetry of social commitment, protest or satire. Landscape poetry itself was not familiar or popular before, or during, the war, even though Imagism had offered alternatives to cloying Georgian pastoralism. Perhaps the sestina Auden was later to call "Paysage Moralisé" (first published in the *Criterion* in 1933) gave a clue to the possibilities Nicholson was to develop. But where Auden has a generalized landscape of valleys, mountains, water, islands, and cities (the sestina rhyming words), Nicholson was able to attach human and eternal significance to his particular known industrial coastline. An early example is from "Now in the Time of This Mortal Life":

> Frost is tight upon the land
> Constricts it with a bony hand
> Yet with blade sharp as a nail
> The immanent crocus drills the soil,
> Man's nerves aver his spinal wish
> And feel the Word becoming Flesh.
> (*Collected Poems*, p. 66)

One obvious drawback to the development of landscape poetry in Nicholson's particular region was that Wordsworth had already mapped it poetically. Nicholson, however, was seeking far more than the Romantic poet's personal, though salvific, response to landscape, as the reference to the Incarnation here shows. Moreover, there had been significant changes since the early nineteenth century.

Thus, headed by the purely topographical title poem describing the five rivers that flow west from the dales to the Cumberland coast, *Five Rivers* contains a series of poems revising Wordsworth's Romantic vision in the light of subsequent industrial or urban development: "Egremont" (compare with "The Horn of Egremont Castle"), "The Duddon Estuary" ("The Duddon Sonnets"), and the pair "Askam Unvisited" and "Askam Visited" ("Yarrow Unvisited," "Yarrow Visited"). As might be expected, the collection contains themes relating to the war ("Corregidor," "Bombing Practice," "Stalingrad: 1942," "The Evacuees," "Cleator Moor," and "For St. James, 1943"), some based on the landscape. It also contains religious themes ranging from the quiet piety of "Carol," "Shepherd's Carol," and "Gethsemane" to the satiric sketch of "The Council of the Seven Deadly Sins," which depicts those sins as corrupt members of a local town council.

Although his first collection, it is by far Nicholson's richest in terms of variety and depth. It has an overly traditional caste for the times, with frequent rhyming couplets (often using slant rhyme), quatrains, tercets, and other stanza forms; there is also blank and free verse. The poems introduced many local words of Norse origin ("beck," "fell," "force," "pike," "tarn"). The three sequences that close the collection are an original fusion of Old Testament creation myths rendered modern by, paradoxically, using the medieval technique of substituting the poet's own landscape for the biblicalin order to establish a moral relationship between man and landscape.

"The Garden of the Innocent" presents an unsentimental catalogue of creatures red in tooth and claw who, as the poet says "have never been me." Having no will to sin, they are therefore innocent, but it is an amoral innocence, set apart from man's moral laws, which can teach man nothing. In "The Holy Mountain" the poet imaginatively reworks the narrative of the Fall. The first section establishes nature's essential interrelatedness in an Edenic Lakeland setting, before the creation of man is described from Noah's retrospective point of view on Mount Ararat, then, following Genesis 6:1–4, comes the creation of a race of truant men, noted for cruelty and violence, when rebel angels procreated with women. Section III returns to the Edenic garden. An apple containing all the elements "'transmuted to / My apple-ness'" literally falls, spreading disease and decay everywhere, but section IV ends in hope with the prophecy of redemption in a millennial kingdom, where the landscape gives back its fruits as the Incarnation: "Rain, rock, broken to wine and bread, / Are formed now into the Blessed Body." With this follows a description of the peaceable kingdom in a recognizably Lakeland setting, ending with the words of Isaiah 11:9—"For the earth shall be full of the knowledge of the Lord / As the waters cover the seas."

The final sequence, "The Bow in the Cloud," reworks the story of the Flood in seriocomic fashion, opening with an Ozymandias-like description of abandoned moonlit mineworkings and a chapel on a desolate sandy shore, waiting to be brought to life again. The next section moves to twenty-five stanzas in ballad meter recounting the comic events of the Lakeland farmer Old Tyson

("A statesman of the fell"), a Noah figure who, after he prays for rain, catches a stickleback, which grows into a "great fish" and swallows the tide in order to engulf the land. At the same time, it warns Old Tyson to prepare a vessel for the animals of farmyard and hedgerow, which he does. In section III, the tidal moon brings floods to the fells. Landing on Scawfell Pike, Old Tyson sees a rainbow and, in the last section (IV), addresses thanks to it for his salvation, "For the rainbow is the covenant of the Lord set that man may see it." He then ascribes first the theological virtues (faith, hope, charity), then the cardinal virtues (temperance, prudence, justice, fortitude) to the rainbow colors in their prismatic order (red, orange, yellow, green, blue, indigo, violet), with white "the colour of purity" containing them all.

This overt use of a mnemonic system linking the virtues to God's covenant is yet another medieval technique in a collection that recalls medieval lyrics ("Carol," "Shepherd's Carol"), the grotesquely comic description of the seven deadly sins in William Langland's *Piers Plowman* (Passus VII), and the reworking biblical narratives in local and contemporary ways (see Verse Plays, below).

Before looking at Nicholson's second collection, it is worth a pause to consider his synthesis of geological process and his transference of biblical landscapes to his native Cumbria, as it underpins his whole work. His effort to find the fresh and transcendent in the commonplace or everyday has a precedent in medieval works. The Mystery Cycles, for example, transposed biblical scenes to local settings, most notably the Shepherd's Plays in the Townley Cycle, a technique Nicholson adopts in his own Old Testament plays. One might note, too, that Western art has sanctioned such transpositions, from Masaccio to Rembrandt to the present day, thus reinforcing the relevance to different times and places of the original biblical message.

Nicholson creates a subtle but profound meaning from this precedent, which takes him toward modern ecology on the one hand, and, on the other, the fourfold levels of meaning of biblical exegesis. His reverence for created nature led him to an early awareness of the forces that create a particular landscape, from the geomorphology of its rocks to the patterns of settlement, agriculture, and industry that the geological base provides. He was able to see balances and imbalances that have now become familiar to us, and moralize the landscape according to man's use or misuse of it.

For the medieval mind, the world abounded in a further level of signification, with four levels of meaning available (although not always applied) to any individual sign. An early commentary on Dante's *Divine Comedy,* the *Epistle to Can Grande* (often attributed to Dante himself), is one of many texts that explain the system. Any particular sign possessed its literal, everyday meaning; a metaphorical meaning; a moral meaning in the Christian scheme; and an anagogical level, which only operated in the eternal spiritual world. "Rock," for example, is the mineral substance of the earth but can stand for "endurance." In Matthew 16:18 it is the rock on which the church was built or the church's temporal body. Finally, by anagogical extension, the rock is the church, which exists through eternity. For Nicholson, the landscape can be the literal physical one of the Lake District, or a "paysage moralisé" on a variety of levels, from the numinous page of the Book of Nature, where God writes his message, to a modern paradigm for the Holy Land. This train of thought leads to the creation of "The Seven Rocks," the final sequence of *The Pot Geranium,* his third collection.

Five Rivers was followed quickly by Nicholson's second collection *Rock Face.* It has been described as "transitional" and "oddly disappointing." Although not without successful poems, the collection lacks focus, and the main charge against it could be that there is nothing new in it—a particular danger if a poet limits himself to inspiration from a single environment. A quarter of the poems are simple lyrics, with "Song" as the title, and do not reflect the environment. Those that do, such as "The Land under the Ice" and "Silecroft Shore" concentrate on impersonal geological processes rather than creating the kind of fully moralized landscape found in "Across the Estuary," which conforms to the exegetical hierarchy of meanings previously outlined. As neatly summarized by Gardner, the dangerous estuary, which used to be crossed on foot at low tides, functions in three ways:

It is real, and thus involves the reader physically in the careful steps which must be taken to cross it carefully; it is the natural context in which man is tried and found wanting; and it is also symbolic of the moral choice itself, in that the firm sand of reason all too soon changes into the dangerous quicksand of uncertainty and mistake.

(1973, p. 65)

Two interesting departures are the use of dramatic monologue in two poems, "Caedmon" and "Naaman" (see 2 Kings 5), the latter poem continuing the Old Testament themes of "Belshazzar" and "The Raven" in *Five Rivers* (and reflecting the poet's venture into biblical drama, of course), and the entry of urban Millom itself into the poet's topography in "Millom Cricket Field" and "A Street in Cumberland."

It is in the third volume that this unassuming working-class town comes fully into view, sheltering under its backdrop hill of Black Combe, which almost seems to push it toward the sea. In his first two volumes, Nicholson established a magisterial landscape panorama of uplifting and ennobling geological remnants, with more than a touch of Wordsworthian sublimity achieved in the vast perspective of geological time and change. In *The Pot Geranium,* the poet fulfills the suggested manifesto of his own radio broadcast two years earlier of looking down his own street, of listening to local people, and of bringing "A human meaning to the scene" ("From Walney Island"), which perhaps his earlier landscape work had not.

Nicholson also first introduces here a favorite gambit of opening a poem with a direct quote of someone's speech, be it phrase or whole sentence, upon which the poem enlarges. "Millom Old Quarry" starts with an unnamed interlocutor stating "They dug ten streets from that there hole," the story being told in the ensuing dialogue with the poet; the same technique is exploited in "Five Minutes," where a man resting on a wall says he is "having five minutes" but the poet hears the next day that he died "having five minutes to the end of time." "Young Him" and "Rising Five" also explore ironies of time and mortality.

Furthermore, a new consciousness of the poet's shaping vision emerges in this collection, an awareness of how vision transforms what it sees, perceiving deeper significances in what is seen, or again reminding both poet and reader of life's transience. As ever, a good number of poems set these reflections against a landscape, such as "On the Lancashire Coast" or "The Boat House, Bank Ground, Coniston," but Nicholson's hometown is set center stage in the nocturne "Old Main Street, Holborn Hill, Millom." Under the "tiered, theatrical night skies" the street seems "built of canvas," a stage set indeed, but daylight brings a platonic chain of relationships between entity and idea, leading to love:

Beneath the shape, the wall, beneath the wall, the
    stone,
Beneath the stone, the idea of a stone,
Beneath the idea, the love.
                    (*Collected Poems*, p. 183)

Nicholson often builds this kind of linkage out of the natural landscape but cannot bring in the purely human element as here. In the title poem he shows how the imagination can transcend physical limits placed on the physical body. Confined to his bed in his attic room, presumably during a period of ill health ("Thighs and spine / Are clamped to the mattress"), the poet sees a box kite flying over the rooftops and feels his imprisonment acutely until he sees the pot geranium in his dormer window as it also "flies its bright balloon," a crimson that cannot be bettered in the tropics; in fact, it "Contains the pattern, the prod and the pulse of life, / Complete as the Nile or the Niger" (*Collected Poems*, p. 180). In a rhetorical flourish as sweeping as the last lines of Donne's "The Sunne Rising," he sees the warm rain blowing down the chimney as the Gulf Streamand the draft under his door as the Trade Wind, and he finds a whole world in that space:

My ways are circumscribed, confined as a limpet
To one small radius of rock; yet
I eat the equator, breathe the sky, and carry
The great white sun in the dirt of my fingernails.
                    (*Collected Poems*, p. 180)

This attempt at aggrandizement is fully explored in a series of poems on astronomical themes—"The Motions of the Earth," "Gathering Sticks on Sunday," "The Unseen Centre," "The Undiscovered Planet," "The Expanding Universe," and "The Outer Planet"—used to reveal the human significance of how little we know in our everyday lives and how much there is to discover, especially in God's love. The instrument of astronomical distance is used in a similar way to that of geological time, giving perspective on the small compass that is man. Nicholson feels time acutely in this collection, as in "On My Thirty-fifth Birthday," where he reflects under the urgency of time that everything should have a purpose,

including his "songs," and that human love should reflect love of God, for all time is subsumed and—presumably—will be judged under his eternal perspective.

The redemption of time in eternity through the Incarnation is the theme of a dramatic monologue, "A Turn for the Better," spoken by Joseph of the *Protoevangelium*, and the attempted prevention of the Incarnation is the subject of "Innocent's Day," spoken by Herod. With an irony worthy of Browning, Herod commends himself on the "good bargain" he has made with history in putting a stop to the further tribulations of his people by ridding them of the potential troublemaker for "the price of a two-year crop of children."

The collection ends with a sequence that again returns to Nicholson's favorite imagery, the rock. In "The Seven Rocks" he imposes a medieval allegorical meaning on the seven main types of rock composing the Lakeland series, namely the three theological and four cardinal virtues. The analogies are, for this writer, stretched too far, but the varied verse patterns and delight in Lakeland topography make it a fitting climax to a collection concerned with the themes of landscape, time, and change:

The crest of the rocks is cracked like a breaking wave,
The land declines again to its old rebirth:
Ashes to ashes, sand to sand.
                    (*Collected Poems*, p. 251)

Although he continued to publish individual poems at intervals in prominent journals and magazines, as well as a short pamphlet of religious lyrics, *No Star on the Way Back* (1967), Nicholson published no collection after *The Pot Geranium* until 1972 when *A Local Habitation* appeared. He was extremely active on the literary front, writing reviews, two further verse plays, and topographical works. He also did a lot of broadcasting. In 1956, he commented to a student magazine that he had "lost his first wind" as a poet and was "not yet . . . sure of his second" (Gardner, 1973, p. 95). Elsewhere, in a conversation with David Wright (*PN Review* vol. 46, 1985, p. 43), Nicholson says it was reading Robert Lowell's Life Studies (1959) that inspired him to write again.

To judge from the poems that eventually went to make *A Local Habitation*, it would seem that Nicholson's main problem was keeping up with the times. During the 1960s a new critical spirit arose among the young, who looked for different expressions of spirituality. Orthodox Christianity no longer enjoyed the support it did when Nicholson was a young man. Attitudes toward the new consumer culture were mixed. On the one hand, it had become so firmly entrenched it was satirized and protested against, but on the other hand, "pop" culture was an integral part of the "swinging sixties." In the literary world, London and its metropolitan values reigned supreme until regional presses were founded that contributed to the poetry boom. Liverpool poets' performances, the founding of magazines and presses in Manchester, and readings in Newcastle all became part of a mythology of popular poetry.

In many ways Nicholson must have benefited from the above as much as he would have been dismayed by the change in values from the early 1950s. He probably wondered if, wonderfully eccentric as he became, his poetry would become a dinosaur like that of John Betjemen, a topographical poet of a very different hue (but who also enjoyed a revival precisely because of what he was). Nicholson's nature poems obviously could be seen as a protest of sorts, or at least as resistance to growing urban and suburban sprawl; his landscape was northern and was welcomed by the new provincial publishing and reading scene; he could also be seen as a poet with a heart who was sympathetic to the working class, especially of a small mining and iron-working town.

Although Nicholson did not have to change his subject matter very much in the 1960s and 1970s, he did have to modify his style and, to some extent, the way he perceived certain things, including poetry. Gone were the allegorical meanings in the landscape, the overt devotional lyrics, and the semantic density of the 1940s and early 1950s; in came a conversational style, at times even chatty, even though he maintained loose formal structures in many poems.

Nevertheless, the topographical poems are charged with a new sense of edge and danger. "Windscale" was written in 1957 after a leak at the nuclear plant (now named Sellafield) on the Cumberland coast, which caused contamination of local milk and meat; it is an early protest poem against the nuclear age, where "toadstool towers infest the shore" (*Collected Poems*, p. 282). Other poems turn to local flora and fauna for inspiration, emphasizing the struggle of nature against the changing topography of the old town as it

tries to keep pace or repossess the scars left by industry ("The Elvers," "The Black Guillemot," "Bee Orchid at Hodbarrow"). Elsewhere he writes elegiacally of transformation in the local scene. "On the Closing of Millom Iron Works" is the poet's farewell to the industry on which the town was built. As part of a nationalized industry, the works was finally closed, after a long decline, in September 1968, and Nicholson notes humorously how much cleaner the town will be once freed of the continual showers of dust and soot the wind blows; but the layoff of men reminds him uncomfortably of 1928, when the fathers of these men stood idle with their backs to the wall; whichever way the wind blows, "it's a cold wind now." Most of the poems are personal and local, with Nicholson's family the main subject. Reticent until now about his earlier ill health, he also writes a long poem about his time as "The Whisperer" and one about the sudden death of a classmate crippled as a young man—"He a crock below the waist / And me a crock above it"—with whom he continued to exchange brief inquiries as to health on the odd occasions they met ("Nicholson, Suddenly").

Sea to the West (1981) was Nicholson's last collection, apart from a group of children's poems published three years later in a group anthology, *The Candy Floss Tree* (1984). It continues the themes of more immediate time and change in the local landscape, with special emphasis on the littoral scene, and concentrates far less on family and personal memories. In contrast to the previous volume, it is a more impersonal, even "colder" work. "The Shadow of Black Combe" introduces the theme of death, which pervades the collection as both a personal and a community concern, with the death of the town's main industry. The greatest change in the local landscape is recorded in "On the Dismantling of Millom Ironworks." Nicholson reflects on the final disappearance of the works, which, along with the slagbanks, were plowed into the ground. The landscape returns once more to that which Wordsworth knew:

The proud battery of chimneys, the hell-mouth roar
   of the furnace,
The midnight sunsets ladled across a cloudy sky—
Are archaeological data, and the great-great-great-
   grandchildren
Of my father's one-time workmates now scrounge
   this iron track
For tors and allies of ore bunkered in the cinders and
   hogweed.

And maybe the ghost of Wordsworth, seeing further
    than I can,
Will stare from Duddon Bridge, along miles of sand
    and mudflats
To a peninsula bare as it used to be, and, beyond, to a
    river
Flowing, untainted now, to a bleak, depopulated
    shore.

                  (*Collected Poems*, p. 360)

If the poet expresses concern for the survival of the town with its industry gone (and, to date, Millom still happily stands), he lauds the tenacity of nature to survive where it will, often against man's depradations, as in his eulogy for "The Bloody Cranesbill," and of "Weeds" in general, which will repopulate the scarred landscape like rosebay willow-herb's "new town" of "a thousand towers, / Every spiky belfry humming with a peal of bees" (*Collected Poems*, p. 341). This same tenacity is applauded in his family, and—modestly—in himself, especially in the face of death ("Comprehending It Not"). Elsewhere he expresses a humanist defiance of death, as in the "The New Cemetery," where he hopes he will "fling / [his] hooves at the boundary wall and bang them down again" as he once saw the old railway draught horses do when put to pasture on Saturday afternoons. A similar sentiment occurs at the end of "At the Musical Festival"; using the local phrase from prewar competition days—"to give it Wigan," meaning to have "a damned good try" (a "try" is a goal in rugby, for which Wigan was famous)—Nicholson makes the plea, "God grant me guts to die / Giving it Wigan" (*Collected Poems*, p. 368). Making the most poignant of these expressions is the title poem, "Sea to the West," in which Nicholson recalls the blinding glow of sunsets in his youth and, making the submerged connection between sunset and death, asks "Let my eyes at the last be blinded / Not by the dark / But by dazzle" (*Collected Poems*, p.339). These sentiments suit a man who, in his youth, with no known cure for tuberculosis, had to "give it Wigan" in order to survive, a poet who expressed the joy he felt in the landscape God had given to him, a joy for which he also had to try.

SHORT STORIES AND NOVELS

NICHOLSON began writing short stories at the same time as poetry. He succeeded in placing a couple in the popular journals of the day: "Pisgah" in *New English Weekly* (1938) and "The Price of Sixpence" in *Time and Tide* (1943). Two more appeared in *Modern Reading*; in all, he published a dozen stories up to 1952. In the main, they are what one would expect of the time, with local ironies, such as the A. E. Coppard–influenced "The Price of Sixpence." Two parables set in the future betray the influence of H. G. Wells. Nicholson's two novels, *The Fire of the Lord* (1944) and *The Green Shore* (1947), are coming-of-age novels that contain evocative descriptions of Millom's shoreline settings and lamplit rain-filled terrace streets. The lack of credible character, motivation, and dialogue make their lack of recognition entirely understandable.

Set during the war, *The Fire of the Lord* recounts the fate of Benjy Fell, an old and half-crazed prophetic character who returns to Odborough (recognizably Millom) after a long absence. His reappearance upsets Maggie Birker, a local baker, now regretting her recent marriage to Jim—a much younger man—after her older husband, who turns out to be Benjy, abandoned her many years before. Benjy's presence also upsets the local constable, who has to evict him from squatting in the abandoned farmhouse of his youth, now encroached by slagbanks of the local ironworks. When Jim falls for Maggie's assistant, Elsie, a young deaf girl who is intensely religious, he leaves the house and the ailing, evicted Benjy is taken in and cared for by Maggie on the understanding he will not reveal the past. Obsessed by the necessity for a "burnt offering" to assuage the continuing encroachment of the works on his native farm, the old man becomes an offering himself when, wandering on the slagbank at night with Jim, a load of hot slag is accidentally tipped on him. This sacrificial death frees Jim and Elsie to marry and frees Maggie to pursue the local constable she now has set her sights on.

The Green Shore depicts another strange religious character, a middle-aged recluse named Anthony Pengwilly (Pen), who lives in an abandoned lighthouse on the shore property of an iron works. He befriends Alice Dale, a local girl in her teens whose shyness is exacerbated by a weak leg. In a long flashback we learn of Pen's mining family origins and his religious conversion as a younger man, after which he has renounced the world and is kept on by the ironworks as a token watchman and gamekeeper. After a disastrous performance at a musical competition, Alice tells Pen she wants to live with him as his daughter. But her singing and the love of nature they share now awaken Pen, who is so drawn to her he has to test his resolve by asking Alice to strip for him. Although he is able to resist the temptation to look on her naked body, something is awakened in Alice, who later wants to strip for him again. Pen becomes angry and meetings cease. Finally, he says he will consider going away with her and is to announce his decision at the end of seven days. When Alice goes to find him, he has left for Scotland on a coaling vessel. Walking back along the shore, she meets the young man she was with when Pen and she first met and we assume, as Pen has now rejoined the world, that she has overcome her own difficulties and will settle down to a normal courtship and future life.

Thus both novels present the tension between a religious and a sexual life and attempt to resolve it for these particular characters. If the conclusions are unconvincing, especially those of *The Green Shore*, it is because they do not issue from satisfying character development. Indeed, the faith, scruples, and obsessions of all the characters are presented superficially, almost for the sake of the plot, as if they are mere literary pawns for Nicholson to work out his own very understandable tensions. Had he persevered and worked longer on these novels, they might have gained him the recognition he evidently wanted, but he would have had to portray character more convincingly, describe much more succinctly, and use the richness of local speech instead of an anodyne standard English. It would take the working-class novelists of the 1950s, such as Stan Barstow, John Braine, Alan Sillitoe, and Keith Waterhouse, to fulfill what Nicholson only sets out in embryo.

VERSE PLAYS

NICHOLSON wrote four verse plays (some mixed with prose), but only one of these was intended for the commercial theater; the other three are reworkings of Old Testament narratives for amateur production or local, unsophisticated audiences, or both.

The idea of the Christian verse play had come to the fore with the success of T. S. Eliot's *Murder in the Cathedral* (1935), for the Canterbury Festival, begun a few years earlier. The diocese of Chichester had founded a similar festival, for which

Eliot collaborated with its director of religious drama, E. Martin Browne (a seminal figure in the revival), with whom he wrote *The Rock* (1934). Other plays of the time were Christopher Fry's *The Boy with a Cart* (1937), Dorothy Sayers' *The Zeal of Thy House,* and Andrew Young's *Nicodemus* (all 1937). In 1939 Browne founded the Pilgrim Players to take religious plays to local community venues. What Nicholson and others envisaged for religious drama and wished to emphasize was the shared quality of a local audience of "ordinary lower-middle-class people in Church Halls and Methodist Sunday Schools" (Gardner, 1973, p. 111). It is therefore unfortunate that two of the plays premiered in unsuitable professional settings, resulting in unfavorable reviews.

The Old Man of the Mountains (1946) was commissioned in 1944 by E. Martin Browne for his Pilgrim Players group. Although it was later taken on tour, Browne included it first as part of a new season of religious verse drama put on at the Mercury Theatre in London in 1945, which included Anne Ridler's *The Shadow Factory* and Ronald Duncan's *This Way to the Tomb*. The play imaginatively recasts the two narratives of Elijah, his miracles for the Gentile widow and his contest with the Baal-worshipping king of Samaria (1 Kings 17–18), set against the prophet's prediction of drought. Living in the Lakeland dales, Elijah is now a statesman-farmer who truly fulfills the role of idiosyncratic prophet Nicholson tried to create in Benjy Fell (*The Fire of the Lord*). While not doubting the Lord, he is not convinced by his own powers that he is a true prophet and can bring the people back to the God of Israel. King Ahab becomes a grasping landowning squire and Obadiah his more reasonable overseer. Naturally, on this diminished scale, there is no antecedent murder of the Hebrew prophets, and the challenge on Mount Carmel is simply between Elijah and Ahab, not the Bible's four hundred priests of Baal. Where Nicholson's mastery in adaptation shows is in the clever interweaving of the two episodes, so that the miracles that help the widow (the flour and milk) are set against Ahab's depredations on the land, raising prices and oppressing the local population, represented by the widow, Ruth, her son Ben, and a neighbor. Indeed, Elijah's strength to challenge Ahab's idolatry comes after the successful healing of Ruth's son; as a direct consequence he is able to raise the sacrificial altars on Mount Carmel. After a suitable amount of dramatic tension, rain clouds are seen when God successfully lights Elijah's altar in a triumphal, if entirely predictable, ending. Set in three "Parts" with a small cast that includes a chorus of Raven (voice of God) and the Beck (nature), the diction modulates effortlessly between verse and prose, according to register, and the characters revel in a local and colloquial diction, which somehow escaped the characters in Nicholson's novels. The published text was reprinted almost immediately, and a second, revised version (responding to criticisms of Part III) came out in 1950. Gardner reports the play had "at least twenty four" different productions between 1945–1960 (1973, p. 125). The same cannot unfortunately be said for the other plays, which suffer from confused intentions; where they might have been successful for a local audience in a community setting, they have not enjoyed many such productions, although local groups have attempted them.

Nicholson's second play was commissioned by the Little Theatre Guild and premiered in the Newcastle People's Theatre in January 1949, with two further performances in the London area in the next two years. Gardner notes that *Prophesy to the Wind* has a plot of the poet's "own invention" (1973, p. 125); in fact, being asked for a play about the post-atomic age, he went (consciously or unconsciously) to a short story published as "The Colonists" in *Modern Reading* 8 (1943). In this short Wellsian parable Nicholson anticipates global disaster two years before the bomb was dropped on Hiroshima. A Viking-like people from the north are leaving settlements across a "new" landscape. One group, sailing into a small, lagoon-like harbor, finds "evidence of a former race" in "queer, tower-like buildings" that can be recognized as Millom's blast furnaces. The clever young Quentin sets about discovering more about this lost people and with the help of Father Xavier, the wise man of the tribe who discovers instruction books ("blocks of white pulp bound in leather"), he pieces together machine parts he finds and, overjoyed, says that with his discoveries he can now "do everything." But Xavier, who has read more of the "language of the lost race" and knows the misery and sorrow of the people of the machines, tries to dissuade the eager young man (p. 95). Quentin, of course, will not listen. Wielding a dagger, Xavier dispatches him down a disused mine shaft, feeling genuine sorrow because Quentin was a "man of true innocence." To this

narrative, Nicholson welds the basic idea of Mark Twain's *A Connecticut Yankee in King Arthur's Court* (1889), where a technician is sent through time to a nonindustrial people.

Prophesy to the Wind opens with a short prologue in which a nuclear explosion, with voices screaming "time is on fire," blows a technician named John into the smoking future. He "lands" among a pastoral community, a new Norse race led by Hallbjorn, a landowner and elder, who has a daughter Freya courted by the elder's kinsman, a pirate raider named Vikar. Hallbjorn's brother, a farmer named Ulf, is continually digging up pieces of meaningless metal from a landscape based directly on Millom and its environs. As in *A Connecticut Yankee* and "The Colonists," the strange young technician determines to bring technology to the people, resurrecting a dynamo he has found. Although Ulf attempts to persuade him to take up farming, John succeeds in turning a wheel with his machine. Having thus proved his word, he fulfills a bargain with Hallbjorn, who said John would be free to marry Freya but then refuses to agree to it. As John is about to try his fortune elsewhere, embarking on a voyage with Vikar, Hallbjorn hands him a dagger to give to the pirate, saying, "Vikar will understand." In the last scene Vikar reports that both John and the dagger lie at the bottom of a disused mine shaft. But we also learn that John has sown a different kind of seed, as Freya is about to bear his child, whom she defiantly predicts will take up his father's work.

Prophesy to the Wind is a short morality play in prologue and four scenes, as bleak perhaps as Orwell's *Animal Farm*. Although full of evocative verse, the characters are not finely drawn. Nicholson has added a love interest and jealousies to his earlier parable, but there is little characterization or depth, the characters serving merely to support the narrative. Hallbjorn's fear of a technological future is less informed than Father Xavier's; he has merely looked across the estuary and seen "the ruins; / Great bird-nests of brick where the hawk was hatched / That cracked the world in its claws" (p. 61). Although such verse poetically evokes the ruined world of the present and John's flights through the technological past are equally fine, elsewhere the language of the pastoral world is contrived, with a rather too heroic Victorian version of Old Norse sagas at the top, a silly "below stairs" banter from the servants at the bottom, and a mawkish drawing-room delicacy of "loves" and "darlings" from John and Freya in the middle, which stands oddly with a physical relationship pursued under problematic circumstances. The main difficulty with the play is that its subject is not so much a "post-atomic" as an anti-technological morality in the tradition of Twain, Wells, and Huxley, a morality later developed by the serious science fiction writers of the 1940s and 1950s. Against these writers, Nicholson's work could not hope to stand out.

For his last two plays Nicholson again turned to the Old Testament, but the infusion of new sensibility into the original is nowhere near as successful as in *The Old Man of the Mountains*. A Match for the Devil (1955), originally a commission by E. Martin Browne and the Religious Drama Society for the New Pilgrims group in 1952, was rejected on the grounds of subject and taste by the Society when already in rehearsal, but picked up by the London Club Theatre Group and taken to the Edinburgh Festival in August 1953. For its subject, Nicholson took the first three chapters of the Book of Hosea, to which he added the figure of the prophet Amos and the High Priest Amaziah, as well as several local characters of his own invention. Given Hosea's use of baking analogies ("adulterers / like an oven heated by the baker [7:4], Israel "a cake not turned" [7:8]), tradition has it he was a baker; such is the paucity of real-life reference in the book in which God's command to Hosea to marry "a wife of harlotry" (1:2) who is unfaithful, with whom he then separates and is later reconciled, is often viewed as an allegory of God's love for his wayward people, who were at that time following Canaanite practices such as worship of Baal, fertility rites, and even temple prostitution. Thus Nicholson has Hosea as a kind but dim-witted baker who falls dotingly in love with and marries Gomer, a temple prostitute whose young son, David, he has already befriended. Bored with being Hosea's ornament, Gomer returns to the temple and appears to be a "match for the devil." Humiliated, his business failing, after a time Hosea goes to the temple to offer forgiveness if Gomer will return, only to find himself upbraided by her for his presumption of superiority and moral high ground. The two are only reconciled when her son appears looking bedraggled and hopelessly in need of responsible parents, a piece of theater on the boy's part that proves he is also "a match for the devil," in the same way that Hosea's love and forgiveness are (p. 83).

The faults in the play's conception may be obvious, but the breezy local characters carry the play a long way to lulling an audience into a willing suspension of disbelief, and the message is obviously a good one, even if shown by a narrative that is too difficult to believe. However, setting in purely local terms a narrative that, even if not wholly allegorical, has depth of symbolic interpretation, was asking for theological, if not theatrical, trouble. If the Book of Hosea is about the sins of a nation, an audience—or theological committee— will hardly be persuaded by the representation of a young, and apparently willing, temple prostitute with a better head for business than her bumbling husband of a baker. No matter how much loving kindness Hosea shows her in the end, he is still a comic figure of a cuckold rather than a wronged prophet; indeed, he is no prophet at all, and the reconciliation has to be engineered by David's stratagem of needing them. If, as Gardner reports (1973, p. 142), local papers ran favorable reviews, reflecting an unsophisticated audience's enjoyment, and Nicholson hoped to be vindicated against the Religious Drama Society's rejection, the London press took him to task for the naive comedy and mock biblical language.

The play's original producer was supportive enough to offer the poet another opportunity for the kind of drama he wanted to write. Unfortunately *Birth by Drowning* (1960) suffers from much the same faults as the previous play, albeit for different reasons. It was first performed by theological students in the open-air Quarry Theatre for the Commemoration Festivities of the Community of the Resurrection, at Mirfield, Yorkshire. The basic narrative is the healing by Elisha of the leper Naaman, captain of the King of Aram's army (2 Kings 5), a moving tale showing the undoing of the pomp and majesty of competing kings by the prophet's humble cleansing of an enemy general, and the unnerving punishment he metes out to his servant Gehazi, who insists on taking the large reward Elisha had refused and is given Naaman's leprosy as a punishment. Instead of all this, Nicholson brings forward events from 2 Kings 6 and makes the issue of disputed borderland of a dales landscape (with much descriptive verse) a central issue that occupies the first two of the play's three acts, leaving only a short third act for the ostensibly key events of 2 Kings 5. Elisha is a gruff old Lakeland physician, and Gehazi, the son of a local farming couple, is his apprentice. What could, and perhaps should, have been a moving scene when the disbelieving general immerses himself (however symbolically on stage) in the Jordan is treated with levity, and the main moral seems to be the preservation of the dales from strife.

OTHER WORKS

NICHOLSON'S enforced leisure, the need for fresh air, and his love of the countryside, together with his talent for descriptive prose, made him the ideal topographer of his native region. In 1949 he wrote *Cumberland and Westmoreland* for Hale's popular County Books series, still a standard work despite the renaming of the area as Cumbria in 1974. His second work, *The Lakers* (1955), was about famous visitors to the Lakes, from the first tourists to the present. *Portrait of the Lakes* (1963) revised and updated the earlier *Cumberland and Westmoreland,* as did *Greater Lakeland* (1969). For the reader of Nicholson's poetry who wishes to know about the Lakes and the environs of his youth, the first volume has much on Millom's earlier social and cultural identity, as well as evocative photographs of the mines and ironworks. *Provincial Pleasures* (1959) is a record of the calendar year in Millom, embellished with much local history and anecdote, written in a sprightly style.

Although a prolific reviewer, Nicholson published only three main works of criticism, beginning with a book on modern literature based on lectures his gave for the Workers' Educational Association in the early 1940s, *Man and Literature* (1943). He followed this later with work on H. G. Wells (1950) and William Cowper (1951). At the time of writing his many published broadcasts, essays, and articles remain uncollected, but a selection is given in the following bibliography.

CONCLUSION

NICHOLSON was a unique poet for his time, combining inspiration from a local industrial landscape with wilder rural elements from the surrounding Lakeland to create a positive vision. There is no protest or despair over human exploitation of natural resources and no unredeemed view of nature as in a later poet like Ted Hughes. An overtly Christian poet on many occasions, his vision of God and humanity is not bleak, like that of R. S. Thomas, but manages to combine an engaging faith in both with stoicism and a certain majestic quality, seeing timeless values in a changing, but also eternal, landscape.

SELECTED BIBLIOGRAPHY

I. POETRY. *Five Rivers* (London, 1944; New York, 1945); *Rock Face* (London, 1948); *The Pot Geranium* (London, 1954); *Selected Poems* (London, 1966); *A Local Habitation* (London, 1972); *Sea to the West* (London, 1981); *Selected Poems 1940–1982* (London, 1982); *Collected Poems,* ed. Neil Curry (London, 1994).

II. SHORT STORIES AND NOVELS. "Pisgah," in *New English Weekly* 13 (15 September 1938); "Tree of Knowledge," in *Fords and Bridges* 3 (6 June 1938); "The Bishop Who Was Never Lonely," in *Modern Reading* 6 (1943); "The Colonists," in *Modern Reading* 8 (1943); "The Price of Sixpence," in *Time and Tide* 24 (29 May 1943); "The Boys," in *Modern Short Stories* 1 (1944); *The Fire of the Lord* (London, 1944; New York, 1946); "The Lead Mine," in *Oasis* (summer 1944); "The Wedding Present," in *John O'London's Weekly* 51 (8 September 1944); "Easter Eggs," in *Time and Tide* 26 (31 March 1945); *The Green Shore* (London, 1947); "Flowers by Request," in *Here and Now Miscellany* 4 (1948); "Halifax," in *Here and Now Miscellany* 5 (1949); "Our Dad and the Rabbits," in *The Pick of Today's Short Stories: Third Series* (London, 1952).

III. VERSE PLAYS. *The Old Man of the Mountains* (London, 1946; rev. 1950); *Prophesy to the Wind* (London, 1950); *A Match for the Devil* (London, 1955); *Birth by Drowning* (London, 1960).

IV. TOPOGRAPHY. *Cumberland and Westmoreland* (London, 1949); *The Lakers: The Adventures of the First Tourists* (London, 1955); *Provincial Pleasures* (London, 1959); *Portrait of the Lakes* (London, 1963); *Greater Lakeland* (London, 1969); *Norman Nicholson's Lakeland,* ed. Irvine Hunt (London, 1991).

V. OTHER WORKS. *Man and Literature* (London, 1943; rep. 1973, 1977); "The Poet Needs an Audience," in *Orpheus* 1 (London, 1948); "The Image in My Poetry," in *Orpheus* 2 (London, 1949); *H. G. Wells* (London, 1950; rep. 1973, 1976, 1977); *William Cowper* (London, 1951; rep. 1977, 1978); "Millom Delivered," in *The Listener* 47 (24 January 1952); "The Comic Prophet," in *The Listener* 50 (6 August 1953); "On Being a Provincial," in *The Listener* 52 (12 August 1954); "The Provincial Tradition," in *Times Literary Supplement* (15 August 1958); "The Second Chance," in *The Listener* 70 (5 September 1963; repr. in *Writers On Themselves,* London, 1964); "Norman Nicholson," in *The Poet Speaks: Interviews with Contemporary Poets,* ed. Peter Orr (London, 1966); *Wednesday Early Closing* (London, 1975); "Norman Nicholson in Conversation with David Wright," in *PN Review* 46 (1985).

VI. CRITICAL STUDIES. Kathleen E. Morgan, "Some Christian Themes in the Poetry of Norman Nicholson," in *A Review of English Literature* 5 (July 1964); Philip

Gardner, "The Provincial Poetry of Norman Nicholson," in *University of Toronto Quarterly* 36 (April 1967); Robin Skelton, "The Poems of Norman Nicholson," in *Stand* 10, no. 3 (1969); Philip Gardner, "No Man is an Island: Norman Nicholson's Novels," in *Ariel* 3 (January 1972); Philip Gardner, *Norman Nicholson* (New York, 1973); Bill Ruddick, "Adding to Wordsworth: Norman Nicholson's Sea to the West and the River Duddon Sonnets," in *Critical Quarterly* 24 (summer 1982); William Scammell, ed., *Between Comets: For Norman Nicholson at 70* (Durham, Eng., 1984); Matt Simpson, "Still Giving it Wigan: Norman Nicholson at Seventy," in *London Magazine* 24 (July 1984); Colin Speakman, "And Sow My Peck of Poems. . . ," in *The Countryman* 89 (winter 1984); Peter Swaab, "The Poetry of Norman Nicholson," in *Cambridge Review* 106 (June 1985).

PETER REDGROVE

(1932–   )

Philip Hobsbaum

I learned from him, that poetry, even that of the loftiest and, seemingly, that of the wildest odes, had a logic of its own, as severe as that of science; and more difficult, because more subtle, more complex, and dependent on more, and more fugitive causes. In the truly great poets, he would say, there is a reason assignable, not only for every word, but for the position of every word.

(Samuel Coleridge on his teacher, the Reverend James Bowyer, *Biographia Literaria,* 1817, chap. 1)

PETER REDGROVE WAS born on 2 January 1932 in Kingston-on-Thames, to a comfortably middle-class family. His father, Gordon, usually known as Jim, was a successful advertising copywriter, associated through much of his career with the Vernon's Agency. His elder son Peter—the younger died in early manhood—inherited his robust physique and resonant voice of considerable beauty. Peter Redgrove attended Taunton School in Somerset, where he distinguished himself as a student and won a minor scholarship in natural sciences to the Queens' College, Cambridge. There he was expected to take a good degree and proceed possibly to a career in medicine.

Events took another turn, however. During a period of national service in the army, Redgrove was diagnosed with incipient schizophrenia, and the insulin shock treatments which resulted evoked hallucinations in which, at that stage, he could find little sense or coherence. Once at Cambridge, Redgrove fell in with a number of young poets, including Ted Hughes, Philip Hobsbaum and Harry Guest, and started a literary magazine, *Delta,* which continued long after he had left the university; as it turned out, without a degree.

During this undergraduate period, Redgrove wrote a great deal, and, in search of a mentor, was influenced perhaps especially by the anthropological works of Robert Graves, who had come to the university in 1954 to deliver the Clark Lectures. A sequence of poems by Redgrove that is a key to his entire output has unfortunately never been published in full. It is called "Lazarus and the Sea." As one might expect from the title, this is a series of meditations concerned with death and resurrection, with the fructifying influence of the sea as womb very much in the foreground. The first poem in the sequence was published in Redgrove's own magazine, *Delta,* and runs as follows:

The tide of my death came whispering like this
Soiling my body with its antique voice.
I scented the antique moistures when they sharpened
The air of my room, made the rough wood of my bed,
    most dear,
Standing out like roots in my tall grave.
They slopped in my mouth and entered my plaited
    blood
Quietened my jolting breath with a soft argument
Of such measured insistence, untied the great knot of
    my heart.
They spread like whispered conversations
Through all the numbed rippling tissues radiated
Like a tree for thirty years from the still centre
Of my salt ovum. But this calm dissolution
Came after my agreement to the necessity of it;
Where before it was a storm over red fields
Pocked with the rain and the wheat furrowed
With wind, then it was the drifting of smoke
From a fire of the wood, damp with sweat,
Fallen in the storm.

I could say nothing of where I had been,
But I knew the soil in my limbs and the rainwater
In my mouth, knew the ground as a slow sea unstable
Like clouds and tolerating no organisation such as
    mine
In its throat of my grave. The knotted roots
Would have entered my nostrils and held me
By the armpits, woven a blanket for my cold body
Dead in the smell of wet earth, and raised me to the sky
For the sun in the slow dance of the seasons.
Many gods like me would be laid in the ground,
Dissolve and be formed again in this pure night
Among the blessing of birds and the sifting water.

But where was the boatman and his gliding punt?
The Judgment' and the flames? These happenings
Were much spoken of in my childhood and the
    legends.

And what judgment tore me to life, uprooted me
Back to my old problems and to the family,
Charged me with unfitness for this holy simplicity?

(*The Collector*, 1960, p. 9)

This poem was given considerable weight by Neil Roberts in the first published book-length study of Redgrove's work, *The Lover, The Dreamer and the World* (1994), and by several of Professor Roberts' students, notably the poet Cliff Ashcroft in a thesis for Sheffield University. Essentially, the poem is a reproach to Jesus for interfering with the natural process of things by raising Lazarus from the dead. The power of the poem resides in the energy with which the state of death is portrayed. The wooden bed is transformed through the image of roots in a grave—not low but "tall"—into a tree "raised to the sky." Like Stevens in his poem, "Of Heaven Considered as a Tomb," Redgrove discounts the conventional images of death, "the judgment and the flames," in favor of being reassumed into the earth. His Lazarus therefore regards being brought back to life as a charge of unfitness for "holy simplicity"—not so much the simplicity of death as that of inclusion in the natural order of the seasons.

The poem contains a characteristic rearrangement of syntax: "The tide of my death came whispering like this." "This" is the speaker's dramatic way of referring to his sudden state of inanition, the natural state from which the intervention of Jesus has saved him. A characteristic mimesis, whereby the verse is made to whisper as the tide comes in with quiet insistence and overcomes the body, also comes into play. There is an anatomical attention to detail: "my plaited blood," "the still centre / of my salt ovum." The state of death is made to seem at one with the state of nature, and the latter is made to seem beautiful: "The blessing of birds and the sifting water." Truly, this is an astonishing achievement for a twenty-year-old!

The five other poems in the sequence were never published in any of Redgrove's collections. Possibly he felt he had said enough in that first poem, which indeed has been anthologized and has attracted respectful attention. It might be felt, however, that the unpublished poems would have made the direction of thought more apparent. Number three, for example, shows the corpse taking its place among nature's count of enchanted objects.

A footstep in snow is not more impermanent

Than the haste and facility in dressing that the sea
    accomplishes.
The mermaid tresses are disposed, the sands patted
Into place, the necklace shells bestowed on the nape
    of the beach,
In less time than it takes the muscles of the wind
To turn. The grey lady or the sparkling blonde
The clear salt water that runs in her veins
Her cold lips lying on the shore, the beat
Of her heart against the ribbed and inverted chest
That brave men launch on her icy motherhood;
All these are at your disposal, and with these
A holy simplicity of small-voiced currents that would
    rinse
Your dead mouth and nostrils clean of any human
    conversations
Should you fail to please.

A patterning rhythm—"impermanent," "accomplishes"—serves in place of rhyme. The restrained pararhyme—"wind," "blonde"—keeps the reader at a distance. The poem hints at rhyme but only delivers at the end, in the final line, "please," that echoes the word "these" four lines up. One may regret that so perfectly voiced a lyric should have been denied circulation for half a century. Apart from redundancy—if one feels that the first poem in the sequence has already spoken for the others—it may be that the author thought this particular line of water imagery navigated him too close to Elliot's "Death by Water," that remarkable elegy poised in the whirl and plenitude of "The Waste Land." Or he may have felt that "The Quaker Graveyard at Nantucket," Robert Lowell's masterpiece—much discussed at Oxford and Cambridge during Redgrove's time as an undergraduate—had drawn too close.

Whatever the reasons, the public has been deprived of some exquisite lyrics, set to their own incantatory music, as the opening lines of numbers IV, V and VI attest:

Rolling habitat of such pale ghosts as cold Ophelia . . .
("Lazarus and the Sea," IV)

It enters the hushed blue room
In a multitude of silences, glittering with fallen
    tongues . . .
("Lazarus and the Sea," V)

Walking on the shore of that sea where I had
Lately been drowned, mixed and haunted by the
    waves, my doubts

And designs, hopes, sins; torn from that great sea
Where lately the sliding waves had turn and swelled
   me
Like smoke, to planet-size, flung my cloak of flesh
Over the wide world, I tried to call to Him
Where He sank into the mocking lips of that same
   cruel sea;
The setting water like a fading rose, with its grey dust,
And the salt water rippling in like a slowly closing
   fan . . .

               ("Lazarus and the Sea," VI)

Of these touchstones, the one to which the reader inevitably returns is number IV, "Rolling habitat of such pale ghosts as cold Ophelia." Ghosts pervade the work of Peter Redgrove.They certainly are noticeable in his first four books, which for reasons both bibliographical and biographical are best understood when taken en bloc.

INFLUENCES AND EARLY PUBLICATIONS

AFTER Cambridge, which he left in 1954, Redgrove settled in London with his first wife, the sculptor Barbara Sherlock. She bore him in quick succession two sons, William and Peter, each respectively taking their father's second and first forenames. Possibly through the influence of his own father, Redgrove found a job in copywriting at an advertising agency.

Among his early acquisitions were the complete *Oxford English Dictionary* in twelve volumes, the W. H. Auden and Norman Holmes Pearson anthology, *Poets of the English Language,* the *Nonesuch Shakespeare* in six volumes and the *Collected Works of C. G. Jung*—who had succeeded Graves as Redgrove's anthropological reading—in twenty volumes. These, together with the works of Arthur Rimbaud—which Redgrove read constantly and adapted freely into English verse—give some idea of his basic source material.

His fluency with words meant that the writing of advertising copy took no especial trouble, though he may have resented the consequent distraction from his poetry. At this point he regularly read his work at a creative writing group organized by Philip Hobsbaum, whose members included the already middle-aged Martin Bell, with whom Redgrove formed a close friendship that lasted till the end of the older poet's life; Edward Lucie-Smith, a writer of a very different kidney with whom he had a not-altogether-friendly rivalry; the radio producer George Mac-

Beth, who made him the center of many broadcasts; and the non-university-educated, anti-Establishment Australian, Peter Porter. This last member admired Redgrove as *il miglior fabbro,* saying of him in a memoir written for *The Poetry Review*: "From the very beginning I knew that I could never be so absolute myself in pursuing poetic reality, and that I would never be able to believe that in language and its sacred ritualisation as art man had a tool which could make him a god, a fundamental part of Redgrove's canon." That is a statement coming from a poet who, with some reason, many take to be of major stature.

The first four books give only a rough guide to the chronology of Redgrove's writings. Indeed, *The Collector* (1960) and *The Nature of Cold Weather* (1961) drew upon the same mass of manuscript. One poem that gave unmistakable warrant of quality was "Bedtime Story for my Son."

Where did the voice come from? I hunted through the
   rooms
For that small boy, that high, that head voice,
The clatter as his heels caught on the door,
A shadow just caught moving through the door
Something like a school-satchel. My wife
Didn't seem afraid, even when it called for food
She smiled and turned her book and said:
"I couldn't go and love the empty air."

We went to bed. Our dreams seemed full
Of boys in one or another guise, the paper-boy
Skidding along in grubby jeans, a music-lesson
She went out in the early afternoon to fetch a child
   from.
I pulled up from a pillow damp with heat
And saw her kissing hers, her legs were folded
Far away from mine. A pillow! It seemed
She couldn't love the empty air.

Perhaps, we thought, a child had come to grief
In some room in the old house we kept,
And listened if the noises came from some especial
   room,
And then we'd take the boards up and discover
A pile of dusty bones like charcoal twigs and give
The tiny-sounding ghost a proper resting-place
So that it need not wander in the empty air.

No blood-stained attic harboured the floating sounds,
We found they came in rooms that we'd warmed
   with our life.
We traced the voice and found where it mostly came
From just underneath both our skins, and not only
In the night-time either, but at the height of noon
And when we sat at meals alone. Plainly, this is how
   we found

That love pines loudly to go out to where
It need not spend itself on fancy and the empty air.
                              (*The Collector,* p. 38)

This poem, with its hint of a rhyme scheme and
its refrain, pays more regard to form than many of
the later poems. It most immediately springs from
the Redgroves' occupancy of a Victorian villa in
the tree-lined district of Chiswick, and the desire
of the young couple to have a child. Reviewing
the book in which the poem appeared, Philip
Larkin wrote in the *Guardian:* "the first house, the
first pregnancy, the first child, all recorded in a
style at once eager, extravagant, obsessively
detailed, and a little mad." The "ghost" of the
poem, reified in this eager manner, is a glimpse of
the future. Already in Redgrove's work there is
the sense of what is palpably present being part of
an extended context, in time as well as space.

This sense of ghosthood manifests itself in several other poems: "Old House," "The Dust," "Mists,"
"Corposant," "At the Edge of the Wood" —

A ghost of the old man popping over his hedge;
Shrieking and nodding from the gate...
                    (*The Nature of Cold Weather,* 1961, p. 46)

"The Ghostly Father"—

His bare feet had worn through. Thorns shivered on
   them,
They sank in the pasture and rattled flints
As he padded to the blot of a distant town...
                    (*The Nature of Cold Weather,* p. 18)

and "Ghosts." This last relates more closely than
the others to "Bedtime Story for my Son," but this
time it concerns barrenness, not pregnancy, and
the ghosts are images of the couple's sterile age
caught proleptically in the rough mirrors of
reflecting surfaces:

... and start up like ghosts ourselves
Flawed lank and drawn in the greenhouse glass:
She turns from that, and I sit down,
She tosses the dust with the toe of a shoe,
Sits in the pond's parapet and takes a swift look
At her shaking face in the clogged water,
Weeds in her hair...

—almost like the drowned Ophelia, which takes
us back to the Lazarus sequence again. One might
say that, in Redgrove, a figure is not a ghost

unless it is lifelike. This effect is created by the
verse. Characteristically, as here, Redgrove writes
a free verse whose metric he himself has theo-
rized. This particular poem, "Ghosts," begins:

The terrace is said to be haunted
By whom or what nobody knows; someone
Put away under the vines behind dusty glass
And rusty hinges staining the white-framed door
Like a nosebleed locked; or a death in the pond
In three feet of water, a courageous breath?
It's haunted anyway, so nobody mends it
And the paving lies loose for the ants to crawl
   through
Weaving and clutching like animated thorns...
                    (*The Nature of Cold Weather,* p. 1)

The declaration, in line one, has three heavy
stresses in as few as nine syllables. This is what
may be called a line that thrusts. The next five lines
are a set of responses to the initial statement, that
the terrace is haunted. Both in meaning and in
meter they accept the thrust. This rhythmic acqui-
escence is in part achieved by a preponderance of
light over heavy syllables, in part by the enjamb-
ment which takes meaning and rhythm over the
line boundaries—"someone / Put away ...,"
"dusty glass / And rusty hinges ...," "white-
framed door / Like a nosebleed ...," "a death in
the pond / In three feet of water..."

The seventh line embodies a further thrust:
"It's haunted anyway, so nobody mends it." This
thrust is created partly by the line's declarative
emphasis and partly because it has four heavy
stresses plus a heavy caesura in a total of twelve
syllables. Redgrove's mode of free verse plays
off thrusting lines against acquiescent lines
receiving the thrust. The rhythmic pattern is
something he has in common with Wallace
Stevens and William Carlos Williams, as distinct
from the cadenced verse of Walt Whitman and
D. H. Lawrence and the loose-jointed blank
verse of T. S. Eliot.

This is most readily described in the shorter
poems. But there are larger works, too, drawing
more evidently upon the writing of C. G. Jung,
who plays a role in the thought of Redgrove similar to that played by Ralph Waldo Emerson in
Whitman or George Santayana in Wallace
Stevens. Jung's concept of the Trickster is very
much to the fore in such poems as "The Nature
of Cold Weather," "The Sermon," "Mr. Waterman," and "At the White Monument." Jung

defines this concept in his *The Archetypes and the Collective Unconscious*:

Ability to change his shape seems to also to be one of his characteristics, as there are not a few reports of his appearance in animal form. Since he has on occasion described himself as a soul in hell, the motif of subjective suffering would seem not to be lacking either. His universality is co-extensive, so to speak, with that of shamanism, to which, as we know, the whole phenomenology of spiritualism belongs. There is something of the trickster in the character of the shaman and the medicine-man, for he, too, often plays malicious jokes on people, only to fall victim in his turn to the vengeance of those whom he has injured.

(p. 256)

"Trickster" seems rather an ad hoc denomination for all this, and it could be objected that Jung's *Psychological Types* are at once rather broad in definition and have a distinct family resemblance, one to another. A similar objection to the presentation of personality evinced by Redgrove was voiced by George Szirtes, writing in *Quarto 25*: "Redgrove's Postmen, Plumbers, Doctors and TV contestants [are] defined not by personality but by psychic function. As such they become part of a gallery of grotesques."

Redgrove's Tricksters certainly are not naturalistic personalities. However, Redgrove delights in creating the Ice Giant of "The Nature of Cold Weather," the aberrant minister of "The Sermon" and the ambulant pond of "Mr. Waterman," especially malevolent though this last may seem:

If he's not lounging, he toys with his shape, restlessly. Stripping off his waterproof, he is a charming dolls'-house of glass with doors and windows opening and shutting; a tree that thrusts up and fills the room; a terrifying shark-shape that darts about between the legs of the furniture, or lurks in the shadows of the room, gleaming in the light of the television-tube; a fountain that blooms without spilling a drop; or, and this image constantly recurs, a very small man with a very large head who gazes mournfully up at my wife (she takes no notice), and collapses suddenly into his tears with a sob and a gulp . . .

(*The Nature of Cold Weather*, p. 56)

The prose of "Mr. Waterman" is close to Redgrove's mode of free verse, and sometimes the modes seem almost interchangeable. Another of his Tricksters is the ruined veteran of "At the White Monument," who suddenly emerges into the parterres of a civic park to insist that the statuary at its center belongs to him. As printed in the collection of that name, published in 1963, the climax—when the Trickster has set fire to his house—runs thus:

He shuffled and skipped as the beam of heat hit his
    back,
And skipped out of the way of the puff and crackle
    underfoot,
As he told how wet slag sparked the power, and his
    hair puffed out in a flash,
Past a coxcomb of flames from the old kitchen range
Weltering and glittering in its lead, and since
He has never lost smoke in his nostrils . . .

(*At the White Monument*, 1963, p. 41)

There is a manuscript version of this, published in 1973 and dedicated to the actor Peter Woodthorpe who read it on the radio (1963), running thus:

A beam of heat beat on my back. A sudden swathe of smoke caught me round the neck. Crackle and creak under my feet. What's up? That wet slag short-circuited her electric fire and the fuse-boxes were exploding! One thing after another! Was I to be robbed even of the consolation of a vigil by her tomb, in the draughty corridor, camping in the hall? Sarah! I cried, Sarah! and beat my fists on the stone till the blood ran down—Sarah!

But I turned and flung myself through the flames out of the house. My hair puffed out in a flash. The smock I was wearing spread stiff with concrete, glowed white as I ran through a great coxcomb of flames jetting sideways out of the old kitchen-range where lead pipes splashed like water and it weltered and glittered in its lead. I have never been able to stop my nose streaming since, or to get the smoke out of my nostrils . . .

But it takes twice the bulk of writing to get across in prose what had already been achieved in verse. Although the prose is in the first person and the verse, quoted earlier, is in the third, it is the latter that achieves the greater degree of immediacy. This is in part owing to the clogging effect of those realistic details—the exclamation "What's up?" the electric fire, the wife's name—that seem to be thought necessary for the authenticity of the prose. But mainly it seems to be that the sympathy of the persona evoked in the metrical version is dispersed in the prose. The prose persona in this instance seems to be, as the verse persona is not, a grotesque. It is a question of voice, and voice is conveyed through rhythm. The rhythm of the verse is at once more flexible and more concise. Clearly, it is verse that is Redgrove's medium.

FICTIONAL WORKS

THIS comparison should be enough to satisfy critics such as George Szirtes. It also throws light, however, on Redgrove's comparative lack of success as a novelist. There are seven of these productions, two of them in collaboration with Redgrove's second wife, the inventive poet Penelope Shuttle. Shuttle, in fact, was early on celebrated as a novelist and her first work in that form, *All the Usual Hours of Sleeping,* was published in 1969, when she was only twenty-two. It is a triumph of formalism, and certainly influenced the way in which Redgrove was to go in fiction.

His collaborative venture with Shuttle, *The Terrors of Dr. Treviles* (1974), is something like a search for the Holy Grail. In Jung's *Psychological Types*, this is a non-Christian symbol of life—affirmation associated with womanhood—but loses its magical power as it becomes understood. Redgrove crucially disagrees with Jung in an unpublished section of his and Shuttle's *The Wise Wound* (1978), called in the manuscript "The Menstruous Traveller," for he declares that the Grail, as with other symbols, is life-giving in so far as people need it in order to achieve fresh energies. Thus far the substratum of *Dr. Treviles* is more interesting than the novel itself, in which the quest reveals little more than the meaning of the protagonist's name. It is not "travail," as Treviles thought, but "the house on the old cliff " as a fellow-doctor, Brid, discovers.

The novel is self-referential: to Redgrove's own poems, to his experiences with the London creative-writing group, and to his previous venture in fiction-writing group, and to his previous venture in fiction writing, *In the Country of the Skin* (1973). This, perhaps the most moving of his prose fictions, derives directly from the scenes of interchanging personalities in Shuttle's early novel. In Redgrove's words:

And Silas must do his magic, and be called Jonas; and Teresa does her magic because she loves Silas, but not Jonas, and she instructs Silas without knowing it; and Silas discovers Jonas with his magic; and Jonas does not love Teresa, and she knows it.

(p. 14)

The clue is that there are two men, Silas and Jonas, within the one skin. It is an experience that owes a good deal to the shock treatment for incipient schizophrenia Redgrove underwent when he was in the army.

Much of *In the Country of the Skin* is interchangeable with *The Hermaphrodite Album,* a book of poems written in collaboration with Shuttle and published in the same year, 1973. A passage from Chapter Three, Section 11, called "Soliloquy by the Well" is, for example, almost word for word identical with a poem in the poetry collection, called "Water-Lady:"

He asked her to go into the wood and tell him what she saw there.
She walked between the trees and the first thing she noticed was a pond.
She knelt down and stripped off the thin skin of reflections, rolled it
up and put it in her pocket to show she had been there.
The water's new skin reflected with more brilliance and better colour.
So she knelt down and took this new skin and put it in her pocket, throwing the other skin away. But the colours of the newest skin were without equal, so she took
this instead. In due time she emptied the pond in this manner . . .

(*In the Country of the Skin,* p. 82)

The terse paragraphs of this prose correspond to the free verse of the poem. The verse is preferable, because the reader is used to the demands made by the linguistically dense form of poetry, whereas the demands made by Redgrove's prose fiction are liable to be met with a degree of resistance.

One would not like to suggest by this that Redgrove's prose does not offer its attractions, and indeed, it can be read quite lazily as a series of special effects and still give pleasure. Consider a passage like this (and there are many similar) from another collaboration with Shuttle, *The Glass Cottage: A Nautical Romance* (1976):

If they did indeed one day lie at the bottom of the sea's branches, bedded in sea-flesh of ooze, skeletons full of windows through which the sea-life swum, the moist-air currents fashioning the great stem from which the white clouds budded and the clear rain fruited, all the water of the world would flow past the bones of the lovers, and this water-shrine of pleasure was good practice for that state of being. "One thousand black-coated clergymen are at this moment raising me to their lips and gargling me in preparation for their Sunday sermon," she said.

(pp. 80–81)

The plot is elusive, or obscure, or fragmentary, according to how one approaches the book. Its action concerns a murder aboard ship in the present, and, in retrospect, a hideaway in a glass cottage associated with the spirit of water.

Like the other novels, *The Glass Cottage* really exists as a series of impressions, some of which may be adapted from existing poems, others of which almost certainly gave rise to those yet to be composed. We read these novels, and the later ones—*The God of Glass* (1979), *The Sleep of the Great Hypnotist* (1979), *The Beekeepers* (1980), *The Facilitators* (1982)—episodically, for high points. For example, the visit to the occult shop in *The Beekeepers* gives a startling glimpse of the dialogues that percolated over the years between Redgrove and his friend, Martin Bell. It also provides a context for the former's poems such as "The Idea of Entropy at Maenporth Beach" and "The Dowser." So far as the patient reader is concerned, however, these poems require no context other than basic knowledge and general intelligence. To that extent, then, the novels and the two collections of stories—*The One Who Set Out to Study Fear* (1989) and *The Cyclopean Mistress* (1993)—delightful though they are in places, may be seen as adjuncts to the decisive work, which is in verse.

BEST KNOWN WORKS OF POETRY

REDGROVE left London for the United States in 1961 to teach at the University of Buffalo, in New York, and, thirteen years later, at Colgate University, in New York. He was basically domiciled in England, though. Between 1962 and 1965 he was Gregory Fellow in Poetry at Leeds University. This began a period of transition in his life. There is a gap of six years between *The Force* (1966) and *Dr. Faust's Sea-Spiral Spirit* (1972). It is partly bridged by a privately issued production, Peter Redgrove's *Work in Progress* (1969), which, in fact, contains several of the poems which were to go into *Dr. Faust* and to make Redgrove famous.

During that period, his marriage to Barbara failed, leaving the two sons and also a "reconciliation baby," Kate. From 1966 Redgrove had been a lecturer in liberal studies at Falmouth School of Art in Cornwall. Though he retired from this post

in 1983, Cornwall remained his place of residence. He met the psychologist John Layard, who reintroduced him to the work of Jung and introduced him to his own controversial approach to psychology. As Redgrove says in *Manhattan Review*, "Here was this famous Jungian man in Falmouth who was offering an analysis on condition I would use his methods in teaching and other work."

In 1969, Redgrove met Penelope Shuttle, who was to become his second wife and mother of his daughter, Zoë. The alteration in his work was galvanic. He always had seemed, for all his brilliance, an unstable personality. Perhaps he answered to Jung's characterization of the "introverted feeling type:"

it is continually seeking an image which has no existence in reality, but which it has seen in a kind of vision . . . It strives after inner intensity, for which the objects serve at most as a stimulus. . . . But the very fact that thoughts can generally be expressed more intelligibly than feelings demands a more than ordinary descriptive or artistic ability before the real wealth of this feeling cart be even approximately presented or communicated to the world.

(*Psychological Types*, pp. 387–88)

At last this writer, of "more than ordinary artistic ability," seemed to have found a commensurate means of expression.

Water had always been one of Redgrove's themes, often associated with fertility. One could cite poems such as "Lazarus and the Sea," "Mr. Waterman," "Mediterranean," "Caught in a Hurry," "The Instant," "Fantasia," "The Force," and "The Salt Stream. " This last, from the book of which "The Force" is the title-poem, may be taken as the foil for a contrast:

> Water running all the time, fascination
> Of sharp water that cuts the breath in gasps
> Glittering its stone: my own blood
> Beats in sympathy. Though warm
> My own eyes glitter like that stone,
> I bathe in the smart good wishes of the saline
> That smarts my cuts.
> (But who would be so foolish as
> The lone suicide on the early beach
> Plunging his shadow up the shore
> With razor dashed like a new groyne
> And sun on water like a roasting spit
> To risk, such a gash to the salt air?)

(*The Force*, 1966, p. 53)

231

Water is compared with blood, and there is some suggestion that it has healing powers. There is also the suggestion that too much of it can be dangerous, as with "the lone suicide on the early beach," and that "it" can refer either to water or to blood. The inference is that both are fine under control and in the appropriate place. The verse here is under control, too, and there are allusions to other poems—the "roasting spit" here may have something to do with the "spinning spit" of an earlier poem, "The Sermon." One could not call this cozy, but, when compared with the later poems, what might be termed insistence has risen to the power of obsession:

> I have always loved water, and praised it.
> I have often wished water would hold still.
> Changes and glints bemuse a man terribly:
> There is champagne and glimmer of mists;
> Torrents, the distaffs of themselves, exalted, confused;
> And snow splintering silently, skilfully, indifferently.
> I have often wished water would hold still.
> Now it does so, or ripples so, skilfully
> In cross and doublecross, surcross and countercross.
> A person lives in the darkness of it, watching gravely...
> ("Young Women with the Hair of Witches
> and No Modesty")

The difference between this and "The Salt Stream" is the difference between insistence and obsession. In earlier poems about water, Redgrove is describing phenomena. His work could legitimately be termed "nature poetry." In the later work, there is what might be called a metaphysical dimension. The "water" is there, not for its own sake, but for a purpose.

This later work—it may be called Redgrove's middle period—makes demands upon the reader. Of course the verbal skill endures, and the poems can be read for the alliterative skill of their rhythms and for the abundance of their imagery. An attempt at interpretation, though, shows a tough intellectual structure. The distance between Redgrove the poet and Jung the philosopher has diminished. Both are visionaries. The image as decoration has become the symbol integral to argument.

In "Young Women with the Hair of Witches," there is a movement of narrative that is not found in "The Salt Stream." In the later poem, the water either holds still at the speaker's request or moves so subtly as to defy definition: "a person lives in the darkness of it, watching gravely." The person

watching gravely is a priest. To become involved in the experience, as through the course of the poem the speaker does, is to become shaman, and to suffer thereby.

The young woman of the poem is a kind of embodiment of water, a naiad. The waves of her hair betray her origin. She is described in the speaker's terms as a world manifesting itself as water. The imagery is of a remarkable richness but, at the same time, betokens a good deal more than what would be associated with natural description. It is rather a reconstruction of visible form in metaphysical terms. What is being presented is a religion, subsumed in the variegation of a water nymph:

> I told her that her thoughts issued in hair like the consideration of water,
> And if she laughed, that they would rain like spasms of weeping,
> Or if she wept, then solemnly they held still,
> And in the rain, the perfumes of it, and the blowing of it,
> Confused, like hosts of people all shouting . . .
> (p. 10)

Jung, in his discussion of the Type Problem in Poetry, envisages a spiritual knight that embarks on the adventure of the lower and upper worlds. He crosses a river and his mistress appears before him in divine form—woman as mother and woman as desirable maid. Such an impression has immense power. It releases forces that, irresistible and compelling as they are, might well be termed "divine." Jung explains that "Loss of soul amounts to a tearing loose of one's nature; it is the disappearance and emancipation of a complex." (*Psychological Types*, p. 226).

Surely that is what is occurring in this poem. It is an emotion akin to the ecstasy of love, though represented here in disillusioned retrospection, with a sad verbal echo of the earlier excitement: "cross and doublecross:"

> But she loosened her hair in a sudden tangle of contradictions,
> In cross and doublecross, surcross and countercross,
> And I was a shadow in the twilight of her late displeasure.
> I asked water to stand still, now nothing else holds.
> (p. 10)

232

The speaker's wish has been recognized, but the naiad is displeased by this attempt at proximity. The only way in which water can hold still is for him to be so absorbed in it, his new religion so to speak, that there is no solidity, no dry land. His previous life has departed.

Redgrove was from his youth aligned with Jung, but the intervention of John Layard in the late 1960s as his guru and analyst brought Jung nearer and made him more urgent, even when Redgrove presumed to disagree with him. Also there is the intervention of Penelope Shuttle in the same period, with whom he seems to have experienced an intensity unknown to him in earlier relationships. This is embodied in his middle-period poetry. There can be no doubt that Shuttle, who is a good deal younger than Redgrove, was the prototype of the naiads, dryads, nereids, and other slim young women who populate the books after *Dr. Faust's Sea-Spiral Spirit,* which itself is pivotal.

In the truly astonishing prose work that Shuttle and Redgrove wrote together, *The Wise Wound* (1978), menstruation is seen as crucial to dreams, fertility, creativity, and the whole being of woman. That this no longer seems a startling proposition is to no small extent a credit to the success of the book. It embodies, however, some heavy interpretation. In the magnificently erotic *Song of Songs,* that most startling of inclusions in the Bible, Shuttle and Redgrove read "wine" as "the red blood of menstruation" and "navel" as vulva or "pudendum" (pp. 22–23).

Whether or not the reader goes along with this, it has given rise to some of Redgrove's most admired poetry. Perhaps the turning point of his whole career is the poem "The Idea of Entropy at Maenporth Beach." This is an explicit answer to "The Idea of Order at Key West," in which Wallace Stevens, against the sense of his own poem, subordinates the genius of the sea to a woman's voice (*Collected Poems,* 1954, pp. 128–130). In Redgrove's poem, the woman is counseled by that which Stevens seems to deprecate. The sea which in his poem represents the shadow: the black tide, the unconscious, all the subterranean force which one has to face if one is not to be defeated as a human being. In this poem, the woman does not merely face the black tide, she immerses herself in it:

A boggy wood as full of springs as trees.
Slowly she slipped into the muck.
It was a white dress, she said, and that is not right,

Not quite right; I'll have a smoother,
Slicker body, and my golden hair
Will sprinkle rich goodness everywhere.
So slowly she backed into the mud . . .
(p. 20)

It is a kind of baptism. The "Entropy" of the title, which usually signifies a degradation of resources, is here represented as reification. That which we normally shun—menstrual fluid, mud, the black tide—is here seen as a source of fertility. Redgrove himself said of Jung that he concealed his chief purpose, which was that his therapeutic method, termed active imagination, was in fact the creative process as it is known in art (*Manhattan Review,* p. 10). The upshot seem to be that Jung, as seen through Layard to whom the poem is dedicated, embraces all the world, not just the clean, self-consciously rational area of it that is in general acceptance. The woman's baptism is a working out of this recognition:

The mud spatters with rich seed and ranging pollens.
Black darts up the pleats, black pleats
Lance along the white ones, and she stops
Swaying, cut in half. Is it right, she sobs
As the fat, juicy, incredibly tart muck rises
Round her throat and dims the diamond there?
It is right, so she stretches her white neck back.
Some golden strands afloat pull after her . . .
(p. 20)

This may be a representation of the irrational, but it needs to be done in public speech or else the reader will understand nothing. A good deal of Redgrove's writing, especially in this middle period, is what T. S. Eliot called in his *Four Quartets* "a raid on the inarticulate" (p. 182). Redgrove is pushing language to further and further extremes without loosing hold of its possibilities as a medium. One notices the rapid oscillation between the voice of the narrator and the consciousness of the woman: "she stops / Swaying, cut in half. Is it right, she sobs." One notices the patterned use of alliteration, always a feature in Redgrove but here of an insistence so marked as to render it a structural trait of the verse: "spatters" / "seed"; "rich seed" / "ranging pollens"; "black" / "pleats"; "rises" / "round"; "dims" / "diamond."

Scarcely less marked is the assonance: "seed" / "pleats"; "white" / "right"; "stops" / "sobs"; "darts" / "fat" / "tart" / "muck." Then there is the repetition: "black . . . pleats," black pleats"; "is it right" / "it is right"; "white ones" / "white neck." The strength of the meaning inheres in the highly active verbs: "spatters," "darts," "lance," "stops," "cut," "sobs," "rises," "dims," "stretches." This gives the mud being, life, activity, and that is essential to the meaning of the poem. This patterning does not form a system on its own but reinforces the plot at every point. The vocabulary, to put it no more strongly, is appropriate to the subject matter and creates a rhythm equally appropriate. However, the rhythmic patterning is not obdurate. There is a transition in tone, to the fifth section, when she emerges again from the mud, black and laughing:

> The mud recoils, lies heavy, queasy, swart.
> But then this soft blubber stirs, and quickly she comes up
> Dressed like a mound of lickerish earth,
> Swiftly ascending in a streaming pat
> That grows tall, smooths brimming hips, and steps out
> On flowing pillars, darkly draped.
> And then the blackness breaks open with blue eyes
> Of this black Venus rising helmeted in night
> Who as she glides grins brilliantly, and drops
> Swatches superb as molasses on her path . . .
>
> (pp. 20–21)

This, to an extent, is a reversion to past aspects of Redgrove's style. In particular, "then the blackness breaks open with blue eyes" reminds us of a relatively early piece, "Without Eyes," and also of "The Artist to his Blind Love." The dramatically encroaching mud is now presented more as being "dressed," "darkly draped." The immersion has been accomplished.

Cliff Ashcroft, in his unpublished thesis, has said that most of Redgrove's women are dead. This is not true, but a surprising number of the earlier ones seem to be blind. In "The Idea of Entropy at Maenporth Beach," baptism is an eye-opener. That revelation escorts us to the concept of the black goddess, voiced in the prose work of that name. In *The Black Goddess and the Sixth Sense* Redgrove notes that "The phrase 'Solomon's Wisdom' meant his consort, the Queen of Sheba, or Black Goddess of the Perfumed Way, as the Hindus say that his love-partner Shakti is Shiva's 'Wisdom' or 'energy'" (1987, p. 69). Baptism seems to incarnate the women of the poem into a new order of being. Elements of white are reasserted, though elements of black remain. The

spectator looking on would seem to be the poet in his role as magician, not (as in the previous poem discussed) as shaman. What he seems to desire is not to overcome the woman but to become female and black himself:

> She laughs aloud and bares her teeth again, and cries:
> Now that I am all black, and running in my richness
> And knowing it a little, I have learnt
> It is quite wrong to be all white always . . .
>
> (p. 21)

The point is demonstrated as concretely as poetry will allow by an enormous access of energy in the verse. Towards the end of the poem, the full range of alliteration, assonance, repetition, and verbal activity is enlisted to narrate, rather than describe, and exciting new landscape rendering the darkness of the subconscious truly visible in the light of day, and indeed, tactile:

> Ah, watch, she runs into the sea. She walks
> In streaky white on dazzling sands that stretch
> Like the whole world's pursy mud quite purged.
> The black rooks coo like doves, new suns beam
> From every droplet of the shattering waves,
> From every crystal of the shattered rock.
> Drenched in the mud, pure white rejoiced,
> From this collision were new colours born,
> And in their slithering passage to the sea
> The shrugged-up riches of deep darkness sang.
> ("The Idea of Entropy at Maenporth Beach," p. 21)

The theme of water as religion runs through *Dr. Faust's Sea-Spiral Spirit,* in such poems as "Intimate Supper," "Love's Journeys" and especially, "Water-Witch, Wood-Witch, Wine-Witch," three in one—"And when she came out it was raining, the night itself / Wanted to touch her, a silver stillness / stood waiting, she was wet all through" (p. 11).

A massive collection of ninety poems entitled, *From Every Chink of the Ark,* followed in 1977. Water dominates the title-poem and also "The Navy's Here," "Snowmanshit," "It's No Pain," "Three Aquarium Portraits," "Pictures from a Japanese Printmaker," "Aesculapian Notes," "A Clean Bill," "Laundon, City of the Moon," "Pictures from an Ecclesiastical Furnisher's," "The Waterfall of Winter," "Somebody," "A Thaw," "Music for Octopi," " In the Vermilion Cathedral," "The Wells," and "Dance the Putrefact."

It is true that there are poems on Redgrove's other recurring themes such as ghosts and witches. The spirit of Jung is found implicitly in an especially fine poem, "Tapestry Moths," and very explicitly indeed in "From the Answers to Job." Yet all these themes are interconnected. The connections are equally unmistakable in *The Weddings at Nether Powers* (1979), in which a key poem is "The Famous Ghost of St. Ives." Its initial gesture, with a dramatic quality by now recognizably Redgrovian, impels the reader into an unexpected story-line:

A single big drop of water rolls along the back streets,
Along the slim back streets of haunted St. Ives;
John Jabez, former mayor out for a stroll in his town
Walks into the man-sized lens. He thought it was
A constituent rolling the shadows under a street
      lamp,
Walked up to it with hand out but it is a water-drop
Higher than his hat with in it reflected
The whole of St. Ives with harbour intact and himself
Hand-out in the back street his face pulled round.
He leans on the tough skin to get a better picture
And pop he is through being taken far a walk
Like a foetus in a bottle or a sailor in a glass berth,
Breathing safely through his whole skin, thumb-suck-
      ing . . .

                                                        (p. 79)

One can spot at once a kinship with "Mr. Waterman"—the politician drawn into the world of the water-bubble. This outlandish circumstance is retailed with arch gravity and an apparent attention to naturalistic detail, even though none of this could really have happened.

What, however, is the force of that "really?" Mr. Jabez sees a vision, men like ships sailing: some are strung with bunting, some with full cargo, some empty, and one full of happy ghosts that dissolved in a sea that was itself the hold of a ship, as though that ship was the world. It is a way of seeing that becomes convincing as the narrative proceeds, partly through the sheer vivacity of detail. But that world within the bubble breaks up, as a dream does, leaving the Mayor "unjointed with joy, my face streaming."

This poem has a design upon us, as "Mr. Waterman" doesn't. The latter is a *jeu d' esprit*, existing in terms of its own virtuosity. "The Famous Ghost of St. Ives," however, bids us be aware that the apparent world around us, that of votes and handshakes, is a mere skin upon a vaster reality. One is reminded of William Blake in *The Marriage of Heaven and Hell*: "How do you know but ev'ry

Bird that cuts the airy way, / Is an immense world of delight, clos'd by your senses five?" That is the meaning of Redgrove's "sixth sense," alluded to in *The Black Goddess*. To confine oneself to social actualities is to lose most of sentient life. Redgrove's ghosts are far more "real" than that which E.M. Forster termed "the world of telegrams and anger" in *Howards End*.

The Apple Broadcast (1981), continues the theme of water. It is highly characteristic in "The Moisture-Number," "The Numina at the Street Parties" ("A mirror nailed to a tree, reflecting the waterfall"), "Full Measures," "Return from the Islands," the title poem itself, and "Streets of the Spirits":

The reeds, the carpeting of the spirits
Through which their immense feet swish

On their way to walking over the lake
Down the sliding street of the river to the ghost-
      maned sea . . .

                                                        (p. 39)

Perhaps best of all is "From the Life of a Dowser," which is sometimes in the third person and sometimes in the first, but which always has the immediacy of a monologue. It is reminiscent of "The Sermon;" however, the underlying vein is more serious: "Pondering like some long transparent god / Waiting to be consumed and joined to more of him" (p. 47).

This obsession with water reaches its peak not so much in *The Working of Water* (1984), which in several ways is a continuation of the previous book, but in *The Man Named East* (1985). In *The Observer,* Peter Porter has called the latter work "a sort of learned journal of the spirit." Even when writing of the death of his mother, that most searching of all bereavements, Redgrove employs the metaphor of water—"and she bent / And washed her tired face away with dew and became a spirit" ("The Funeral," p. 31). However, there are all of a hundred images of water in this book of eighty-eight poems. Some of these are not so much moments of vision as literary masterpieces, and one could instance "The Quiet Woman of Chancery Lane" ("The blind girl points to the stars . . . / a special breath from space / Tells her they are out in their moist fullness," p. 10). Or "The Work of Water" ("Fill the church with water! / Let those old stones be our Works," p. 21), or "The College in the Reservoir":

Thus the whole town drinks the College of ghosts
Drowned in the reservoir and dissolved in shivering
   mirrors,
Torn mirrors of the web, whole mirror of the ocean
                                                    (p. 61)

Or the title-poem, "The Man Called East:" "The dew, the healing dew, that appears / Like the dream, without warning, hovering, on the blades" (p. 61).

REDGROVE'S THIRD PERIOD

BUT the poems, though never less than alert with lyrical beauty are beginning to lose their narrative distinctness. More and more, such books as *The Mudlark Poems & Grand Buveur* (1986), in the *Hall of the Saurians* (1987), *The First Earthquake* (1989), *Dressed as for a Tarot Pack* (1990), and *Under the Reservoir* (1992) demand to be read as sequences. Since they have a good deal to do, one with another, the sets of sequences require to be read as one sustained sequence. In this respect, Redgrove has entered his third period. It true that individual poems stand out, but these tend to be sequels to already published poems, as "From the Life of a Dowser—2," in *The Working of Water,* or "Joy Gordon," the celebration of a life, which takes off from the poem about the mother's funeral in *The Man Named East.*

There is also the re-emergence of former themes, such as a son's enmity with his father, adumbrated as far back as "Prelude and History" in the second book, *The Nature of Cold Weather.* It is now reified as an entire collection, *My Father's Trapdoors* (1994), together with its companion volume, *Abyssophone* (1995). A fourth period does, indeed, seem to be dawning, with exercises that cross over from science into the supernatural, justifying the sobriquet Redgrove has given himself, "Scientist of the Strange."

This development was prefigured in *The Laborators* (1993) and fructified in books such as *Assembling a Ghost* (1996), *What the Black Mirror Saw* (1997), and its companion work of the same date, *Orchard End.* Here are remarkable poems hovering between science fiction and theology, such as "Leather Goods," "Aromatherapy," "Water Cinema," "The Mortier Water-Organ Called Oscar." Also, there are pieces as yet uncollected, such as "Circus Wheel" (*Last Words: An Anthology,* 1999), "The Interior Mountaineer" (*Manhattan Review,*

Summer 2000) and "The Flying Ace" (*Times Literary Supplement,* 14 July 2000):

The Flying Ace, the Ace of Birds,
That perfect soul-bird, the owl, the werewoman,
The perfect soul-woman;

The mask zooms under the trees
And hangs itself up, watching
Through 270 degrees, making uterus-face . . .

This poem seems to be a reminiscence of the "Three Aquarium Portraits" (*From Every Chink of the Ark*), with the lobster that walks "like three headless armoured dancers" and the glass-shrimps "something between a fruitcake and a boot . . . being entirely of glass with a few guts / But shining like a neon sign at every joint" (pp. 99–102).

On the whole, however, plot-lines of individual poems coalesce in numinous imagery. Some pieces seem to be versions of one another, almost interchangeable. Redgrove is a maker of myths; his poetry allegorizes his intuitions. It helps that he is a keen observer of nature and has a metaphysical wit capable of perceiving unexpected correspondences. He has access to a language procreant with word play that gets his vision across. A poem such as "The Harmony" in *A Man Named East* advances nature's far-fetched parable of grub and moth:

The birds studded inside and out
With the bolted seeds of their flight,
Unable to bear it
Burst in full-blooming bushes
Like shell-burst of green
That trace flowering tendrils in mid-air.
                                              (p. 136)

Perhaps it was too much to hope that Redgrove could get his sequences together in some definitive form. The task would be tantamount to a *Paradise Lost,* a *Prelude,* and even these great poems may be held only to work in their fragments. Redgrove makes enormous demands on the reader if he is to be appreciated in full.

Certainly one can recommend individual poems with the kind of confidence one reserves for anthology pieces. The reader can only benefit from enjoying such attractive lyrics as, "Bedtime Story for my Son," "Ghosts," "The House in the Acorn," "Young Women with the Hair of Witches," "Tapestry Moths," "The Famous Ghost of St.

Ives," "From the Life of a Dowser," "The Quiet Woman of Chancery Lane"—to go no further on with the canon than 1985. These alone would give the idea of Redgrove as a considerable poet.

Or one could canvass the larger-scale pieces, such as "The Nature of Cold Weather," "Mr. Waterman," "At the White Monument," "The Sermon," "The Idea of Entropy at Maenporth Beach," "The Wells." Those give every evidence that Redgrove is a prince among verse narrators. But they only take us to 1977, and by that time Redgrove seems to be thinking in terms of sequences of associated poems rather than large-scale narrations. There are the novels, of course, with their attendant extravagances, and a good many items, some of which cannot be determined as prose or verse, that use fictional techniques.

Without in any way disparaging the later art of this inventive poet, the defining fiction seems to have been absorbed into a plasm. It becomes harder and harder to take the poems as separate individuals. More and more they seem to be part of an embracing entity which is nothing less than Redgrove's vision of life. That is why the dedicated reader needs to accept Redgrove en bloc, demanding though the task may be. These are no discrete pieces of writing but building blocks of a mighty temple of art. Each one is enhanced by proximity to the other.

Some poets need to fabricate their own instruments before they can play on them. In consequence, their early work may be met with misunderstanding or even rejection. What they achieve is so unfamiliar as to provoke in their potential audience a measure of resistance. Redgrove is one of these, and his affinities are with such writers as Ted Hughes and Geoffrey Hill.

Thus his achievement, though it may have been anticipated by the more acute critics, has not adequately been recognized. Jonathan Bate, however, wrote an essay entitled, "What Are Poets For?" in which he speaks movingly of the fissure between mind and being that has grown up with the advance of technology. In his book *The Song of the Earth,* Bate speaks of a loss of wonder and writes approvingly of the philosopher Martin Heidegger who saw the poet's vocation as "to speak the earth." He envisages a kind of ecopoetics, which will require the vision of that earth to be populated, to be enhanced by the imagination. He sees the poet as being in the wake of John Clare "supreme-ly committed to localisation of the spaces of his intimacy with the world."

Redgrove in conversation once said that John Clare had so strong a grasp of things because he knew how powerful were the forces that could take them away. It is Redgrove who is the ecopoet for whom, it seems, Jonathan Bate has been waiting. The verse of other writers may be *vorhandsein*—they impose a pattern on the world. The verse of Redgrove is so overwhelming because it is *zuhandsein,* or exploratory. It creates the world it looks upon—and hears, and smells—not by adding patterns to it but by stripping away the accretions of past stylization. He has a sixth sense; an enhancement of perception. Redgrove's ghosts, witches, spirits, water are there for all to experience, if we alert ourselves sufficiently. It is not an otherworld that he explores but a world that is potentially open to the explorer. The poetry of Peter Redgrove is one means we have at hand of pursuing that exploration.

SELECTED BIBLIOGRAPHY

I. COLLECTED WORKS. *Sons of my Skin 1954–1974,* edited, with an introduction by Marie Peel (London, 1975); *The Moon Disposes: Poems 1954–1987* (London, 1987); *Selected Poems* (London, 1999).

II. SEPARATE WORKS OF POETRY. *The Collector* (London, 1960), *The Nature of Cold Weather* (London, 1961); *At the White Monument* (London, 1963); *The Force* (London, 1966); *Work in Progress* (London, 1969); *Dr Faust's Sea-Spiral Spirit* (London and Boston, 1972); *The Hermaphrodite Album* (with Penelope Shuttle) (London, 1973); *From Every Chink of the Ark* (London, 1977); *The Weddings at Nether Powers* (London, 1979); *The Apple Broadcast* (London, 1981); *The Working of Water* (Langley Park, Durham, 1984); *The Man Named East* (London, 1985); *The Mudlark Poems & Grand Buveur* (London, 1986); *In the Hall of the Saurians* (London, 1987); *The First Earthquake* (London, 1989); *Dressed as for a Tarot Pack* (Exeter, 1990); *Under the Reservoir* (London, 1992); *The Laborators* (Exeter, 1993); *My Father's Trapdoors* (London, 1994); *Abyssophone* (Exeter, 1995); *Assembling a Ghost* (London, 1996); *What the Black Mirror Saw* (Exeter, 1997); *Orchard End* (Exeter, 1997).

III. NOVELS. *In the Country of the Skin* (London, 1973); *The Terrors of Dr. Treviles* (with Penelope Shuttle) (London, 1974); *The Glass Cottage* (with Penelope Shuttle) (London, 1976); *The God of Glass* (London, 1979); *The Sleep of the Great Hypnotist* (London, 1979); *The Beekeepers* (London, 1980); *The Facilitators* (London, 1982).

IV. COLLECTIONS OF STORIES. *The One Who Set Out to Study Fear* (London, 1989); *The Cyclopean Mistress: Selected Short Fiction 1960–1990* (Newcastle upon Tyne, 1993).

V. PLAYS. *In the Country of the Skin* (Rushden, 1973); *Miss Carstairs Dressed for Blooding* (London, 1976).

VI. NONFICTION. *The Wise Wound: Menstruation and Everywoman* (with Penelope Shuttle) (London, 1978; rev. ed. with foreword by Margaret Drabble, London 1986; also published as *The Wise Wound: Eve's Curse and Everywoman,* New York, 1978, and as *The Wise Wound: Myths Realities and the Meaning of Menstruation,* New York, 1988, 1990); *The Black Goddess and the Sixth Sense* (London, 1987, 1988; also published as *The Black Goddess and the Unseen Real: Our Unconscious Senses and Their Uncommon Sense,* New York, 1988); *Alchemy for Women: Personal Transformation through Dreams and the Female Cycle* (with Penelope Shuttle) (London, 1995).

VII. VOLUMES EDITED. *Universities Poetry 7* (London, 1965); *New Poems 1967: A P.E.N. Anthology of Contemporary Poetry* (with Harold Pinter and John Fuller) (London, 1968); *Lamb and Thundercloud* (Hebden Bridge, 1975); *New Poetry,* vol. 5, *An Arts Council Anthology* (with Jon Silkin) (London, 1979); *Cornwall in Verse* (London, 1982; Harmondsworth, 1983).

VIII. INTERVIEWS. Jed Rasula and Mike Erwin, "Interview with Peter Redgrove," in *Hudson Review* (autumn 1975); Philip Fried, "The Scientist of the Strange," in *Manhattan Review* 31 (summer 1983); "The Dialogue of Gender: Penelope Shuttle and Peter Redgrove," in *On Gender and Writing,* ed. Micheline Wandor (London, 1983); Cliff Ashcroft, "Lazarus and the Visionary Truth," in *Arrows: The Magazine of Sheffield University* (Sheffield, Eng., 1984); Neil Roberts, "The Science of the Subjective," in *Poetry Review* 77, no.3 (June 1987).

IX. CRITICAL STUDIES. Roger Garfitt, "The Group," in *British Poetry Since 1960,* ed. Michael Schmidt and Grevel Lindop (Oxford, 1972); Anne Stevenson, "The Voice of the Green Man," in *Times Literary Supplement* (18 November 1977); Geoffrey Pawling, "Alchemy of the Green Man," in *Delta* 58 (1978); Philip Hobsbaum, *Tradition and Experiment in English Poetry* (London, 1979), chap. 12 ("The Poetry of Barbarism"); Roger Garfitt, ed., *Poetry Review: Peter Redgrove Special Issue* 71, no. 2/3 (September 1981); Philip Hobsbaum, "After Barbarism: The Later Poetry of Peter Redgrove," in *Poetry Review* 71, no. 2/3 (September 1981); Peter Porter, "Peter Redgrove—a Brief Memoir," in *Poetry Review* 71, no. 2/3 (September 1981); Neil Roberts, "Diving Waterfly," in *Poetry Review* 71, no. 2/3 (September 1981); George Szirtes, "Not Mad or Bad," in *Quarto* 25 (January/February 1982); Terry Gifford and Neil Roberts, "Hughes and Two Contemporaries," in *The Achievement of Ted Hughes,* ed. Keith Sagar (Manchester, 1983); Neil Roberts, "Implicate Order," in *The Times Literary Supplement* (28 June 1985); Cliff Ashcroft, "A Study of the Poetry of Peter Redgrove," M. Phil. thesis, Sheffield University, 1989; Paul Bentley, "Language, Self and Reality in the Poetry of Ted Hughes and Peter Redgrove," Ph.D. thesis, Sheffield University, 1994; Neil Roberts, *The Lover, the Dreamer and the World* (Sheffield, 1994); Paul Bentley, "Singing the Real: The Later Poetry of Peter Redgrove," in *English* 44, no. 179 (summer 1995); Jordi Doce, "Translating into Verse: A Study of Peter Redgrove's Working Method," M. Phil. dissertation, Sheffield University, 1995; Neil Roberts, *Narrative and Voice in Postwar Poetry* (London, 1999), chap. 10 ("Peter Redgrove: Composition as Transaction").

X. ARCHIVE MATERIAL. The most substantial archive of Peter Redgrove's manuscripts, notebooks, and correspondence is in the library of the University of Sheffield. Other archive material is at the University of Texas, Austin; the Brotherton Library, Leeds University; the Lockwood Memorial Library, University of Buffalo; the University of Indiana; and Glasgow University Library (The Hobsbaum Bequest).

XI. FURTHER READING: POETRY. Elizabeth Sewell, *The Structure of Poetry* (London, 1951), chaps. 14 and 15 ("Rimbaud and the World of *Les Illuminations*"); Wallace Stevens, *Collected Poems* (New York and London, 1954, 1955); Arthur Rimbaud, *Selected Poems,* ed. Oliver Bernard (Harmondsworth, 1962); Penelope Shuttle, *All the Usual Hours of Sleeping* (London, 1969); Arthur Rimbaud, *Illuminations,* ed. Nick Osmond (London and Atlantic Highlands, N.J., 1976); Arthur Rimbaud, *A Season in Hell,* trans. Norman Cameron (London, 1994); Martin Bell, *Reverdy: Translations* (Reading, 1997); Penelope Shuttle, *Selected Poems 1980–1996* (Oxford and New York, 1998).

XII. FURTHER READING: PSYCHOLOGY AND RELATED SUBJECTS. J. G. Frazer, *The Golden Bough* (London 1922; abridged, 1963); John Layard, *The Lady and the Hare: Being a Study in the Healing Power of Dreams* (London, 1944); Robert Graves, *The White Goddess* (London, 1952); C. G. Jung, *The Collected Works,* esp. vol. 5, *Symbols of Transformation,* vol. 6, *Psychological Types,* vol. 9, *The Archetypes and the Collective Unconsciousness,* vol. 11, *Psychology and Religion,* vol. 12, *Psychology and Alchemy,* and vol. 14, *Mysterium Coniunctionis* (London, 1952); Erich Neumann, *The Great Mother; An Analysis of the Archetype* (London, 1955); C. G. Jung, *Memories, Dreams, Reflections,* trans. Richard and Clara Winston (London, 1963); G. Wilson Knight, *Neglected Powers* (London, 1971); Marie-Louise von Franz, Introduction to *The Analysis of Fairy Tales* (New York, 1972); Emma Jung, *Animus and Anima* (Zurich, 1974); Gerald Massey, *The Natural Genesis* (New York, 1974).

SAKI (HECTOR HUGH MUNRO)

(1870–1916)

Sandie Byrne

HECTOR HUGH MUNRO was born in Akyab, Burma, on 18 December 1870, the youngest child of Charles Augustus Munro, an inspector general in the Burma police, and Mary Frances Mercer. He had a brother, Charles, and a sister, Ethel. When Hector was two years old, his mother met with a tragic and yet bizarrely Saki-esque fate. Having returned to the safety of England during her fourth pregnancy, Mary Munro took a walk in a quiet country lane, where she was charged by a runaway cow. The shock caused her to miscarry, and she died. This was not the only bizarre death in the family history; eighty years earlier in India General Hector Munro was immortalized in Staffordshire pottery as a much-reproduced tableau entitled "The Death of Munrow" [*sic*], which depicted the general's head between the jaws of a large tiger.

Their father left the three Munro children in the care of his mother and two sisters, Charlotte, known as Tom, and Augusta, at Broadgate Villa, in Pilton, near Barnstaple, North Devon. The eccentric and domineering aunts imposed a regime of confinement, restraint, and arbitrary rules enforced by corporal punishment. The children were thought to have poor constitutions; like Conradin in "Sredni Vashtar," they were not expected to reach adulthood, and Hector, the most sickly of all, was not allowed to go to school until he was twelve. They lived a secluded life enlivened only by the one Christmas party they were permitted to attend each year, the annual visits of their Uncle Wellesley, and their father's four-year leave. Hector compensated for the narrowness of their daily lives with highly developed imaginative powers and led Charles and Ethel in every form of mischief that might escape detection or from which his cunning might extricate them. One great pleasure and sanctuary was reading; *Robinson Crusoe* (1719), Charles G. Leland's *Johnnykin and the Goblins* (1877), *Alice's Adventures in Wonderland* (originally published as *Alice's Adventures Underground*, 1865) and *Through the Looking Glass and What Alice Found There* (1871) were early favorites.

The year after his grandmother died, Hector was finally considered strong enough to follow his brother to Pencarwick School in Exmouth and, at fifteen, to attend Bedford Grammar School. He remained only two years, however, because as soon as he retired, Charles Augustus, now General, Munro came to rescue his children and carried them off to an extended tour of France, Germany, and Switzerland. They stayed for some time in Davos, Switzerland, where Hector met John Addington Symonds, who may have been a formative influence on his writing.

In 1893 Hector followed his father and brother into the Burma police. He spent thirteen months studying the local flora and fauna, collecting eggs, and raising a squirrel, a duckling, and a tiger cub, but he had seven bouts of fever, the last of which proved to be malaria, and was forced (from his letters, not unwillingly) to resign and return to England. After convalescing with his family, he settled in London in 1896 and began a writing career, though his employment as foreign and political correspondent for a number of journals took him away from the city for extended periods of time. His first story, "Dogged," appeared in *St. Paul's* Magazine in 1899, signed only with his initials. His first book, *The Rise of the Russian Empire* (1900), was modeled on Gibbon's *History of the Decline and Fall of the Roman Empire* (1776–1788) but with considerably more romance and even more irreverence toward its subject. His first publications as "Saki" were political satires in the style of Lewis Carroll for the *Westminster Gazette* (illustrated by Francis Carruthers Gould and collected as *The Westminster Alice* in 1902, "With apologies to Sir John Tenniel and to everybody else concerned"). The pseudonym is thought to be taken from the last stanzas of *The Rubáiyát of Omar Khayyám*, in which "Saki" is a cup-bearer.

Yon rising moon that looks for us again—
How oft hereafter will she wax and wane;
How oft hereafter rising look for us
Through this same Garden—and for one in vain!

And when like her, oh Sáki, you shall pass
Among the guests Star-scattered on the Grass
And in your joyous errand reach the spot
Where I made One—turn down an empty Glass!
(trans. Edward Fitzgerald, 1859)

In 1901 "Saki" dedicated two parodies of the *Rubáiyát* to an attack on prominent political figures of the time. The following year, another parodic collection illustrated by Carruthers Gould, *Not-So-Stories*, made ironic play with Kipling's *Just So Stories* (1902). Meanwhile, the characteristic short stories, signed "Saki," were appearing in the *Westminster Gazette*.

Back in England after the Balkans, Warsaw, and Russia, where he witnessed the assault on the Winter Palace in St. Petersburg, and Paris, Saki settled into the life of a gentleman about town, with rooms at 97 Mortimer Street. He frequented the fashionable drawing rooms, theaters, restaurants, and clubs; his own was the Tory (right-wing) Cocoa Tree. Though the publications from this period (1910–1914) made Saki's name famous and are littered with duchesses, baronesses, archdukes and gräfins, he lived a private rather than a public life and did not move in exalted social circles. By 1912, he was writing for the *Outlook*, *Morning Post*, *Daily Express*, and *Bystander*.

Though officially too old to join up, when war broke out in 1914 Munro enlisted as a trooper in the 2nd King Edward's Horse, from which he transferred to the 22nd Battalion Royal Fusiliers. After training, a period of teaching German to his fellow soldiers, and other delays, which fretted Munro considerably and during which he was promoted to corporal, he was sent to France in 1915. He continued to write—producing *The Toys of Peace* (1914), which he dedicated to the 22nd Royal Fusiliers, and a series of articles for the battalion's *Fortnightly Gazette*—and to enjoy the amenities of town when he could, but those who knew him well felt that he had changed. During a brief leave in June 1914, he had outlined "a project of going out to Siberia, when the war was over, with a friend" and starting a farm.

"I could never settle down again to the tameness of London life," he told me. . . . "It would have been a remark-

able life, wild animals beyond the dreams of avarice, at our very doors, and, before long, inside them."
(Munro, pp. 108–109)

In "A Memoir of H. H. Munro" his friend Rothay Reynolds suggested that the war had purged Saki of the habits of adult life and reestablished his true nature, so that he experienced "the love of the woodlands and the wild things in them, that he had felt as a child, returning. The dross had been burnt up in the flame of war," and he had turned away from the city back to the wild (p. xxiii).

He steadfastly refused a commission, but accepted promotion to lance-sergeant in September of 1916. A recurrence of malaria put him in the military hospital in October 1916, but on hearing that his men had been ordered to the Western Front, he discharged himself and joined them. He was killed during a rest break in a shell crater near Beaumont-Hamel on 14 November 1916. In a final Saki-esque touch, his last words were "Put that bloody cigarette out" before he was shot through the head, presumably by a sniper aiming for the glowing tip of another man's cigarette.

SHORT STORIES

INTRODUCING, or, as he put it, reintroducing, the writer he had enjoyed for many years to a wider reading public, Noël Coward affirmed Saki's undiminished appeal yet placed him squarely in the Edwardian context.

His stories and novels appear as delightful and, to use a much abused word, sophisticated, as they did when he first published them. They are dated only by the fact that they evoke an atmosphere and describe a society which vanished in the baleful summer of 1914. The Edwardian era, in spite of its political idiocies and a sinister sense of foreboding which, to intelligent observers, underlay the latter part of it, must have been, socially at least, very charming. It is this evanescent charm that Saki so effortlessly evoked.
(*The Complete Saki*, p. xiii)

Saki's work is elegant, economical, and above all witty. The dominant tone of the short stories is worldly, flippant irreverence delivered in astringent exchanges and neat epigrams. In "Reginald on the Academy," "'To have reached thirty,' said Reginald, 'is to have failed in life'" (*Reginald*, p. 23); in "The Match-Maker," "brevity is the soul of widowhood" (*The Chronicles of Clovis*, p. 25). At the center of many of his short stories is a young man, socially poised, articulate, fastidious, fashionable, witty, hedonistic, if not actually cruel, amused by the maladroitness or discomfiture of others, vain, and utterly self-centered. In the ambiguously titled "Reginald's Choir Treat," Reginald advocates the imitation of the lilies of the field "which simply sat and looked beautiful, and defied competition":

"But that is not an example for us to follow," gasped Amabel.

"Unfortunately, we can't afford to. You don't know what a world of trouble I take in trying to rival the lilies in their artistic simplicity."

"You really are indecently vain of your appearance. A good life is infinitely preferable to good looks."

"You agree with me that the two are incompatible. I always say beauty is only sin deep."

Reginald, pp. 42–43)

The heroes belong by birth to a privileged and wealthy class but consider themselves not quite privileged or wealthy enough. As Clovis remarks in "The Match-Maker," "All decent people live beyond their incomes nowadays, and those who aren't respectable live beyond other people's. A few gifted individuals do both" (*The Chronicles of Clovis*, p. 25). Though not necessarily or overtly homosexual, the heroes appear to have little interest in women for romantic or sexual purposes. To stay young and beautiful is their obsession ("Reginald in his wildest lapses into veracity never admits to being more than twenty-two," *Reginald*, p. 6), yet sensuality is mostly displaced onto dress (their own) and luxurious food and drink (champagne, caviar, marrons glacés, asparagus, oysters, plovers' eggs, paid for by other people). While spending a great deal of his time in other people's houses, at other people's social functions, and dining at other people's expense, the young men do not consider themselves free loaders but ornaments whose presence conveys social prestige (at best) or amusement (at worst). They delight in flouting convention and shocking the older or more stuffy of their acquaintance. There are dark hints at decadence, as in "The Innocence of Reginald":

"Youth," said the Other, "should suggest innocence."

"But never act on the suggestion."

(*Reginald*, p. 8)

Clovis's only religion appears to be hedonism. In "The Match-Maker," he compares people who eat a healthy diet to the flagellants of the Middle Ages, except that

"They did it to save their immortal souls, didn't they? You needn't tell me that a man who doesn't love oysters and asparagus and good wines has got a soul, or a stomach either. He's simply got the instinct for being unhappy highly developed."

Clovis relapsed for a few golden moments into tender intimacies with a succession of rapidly disappearing oysters.

"I think oysters are more beautiful than any religion," he resumed presently. "They not only forgive our unkindness to them; they justify it, they incite us to go on being perfectly horrid to them. Once they arrive at the supper-table they seem to enter thoroughly into the spirit of the thing. There's nothing in Christianity or Buddhism that quite matches the sympathetic unselfishness of an oyster."

(*The Chronicles of Clovis*, pp. 24–25)

The heroes are not precisely amoral, however, and have been known to help a friend in need. In "Reginald at the Theatre," the hero almost gives himself away as having a social conscience, or, rather, he shows his awareness that the duchess, in spite of her advocacy of moral rectitude, has none.

The Duchess thought that Reginald did not exceed the ethical standard which circumstances demanded.

"Of course," she resumed combatively, "it's the prevailing fashion to believe in perpetual change and mutability, and all that sort of thing, and to say we are all merely an improved form of primeval ape—of course you subscribe to that doctrine?"

"I think it decidedly premature; in most people I know the process is far from complete."

The duchess continues:

"[O]ne is conscious of spreading the benefits of civilization all over the world! Philanthropy—I suppose you will say *that* is a comfortable delusion; and yet even you must admit that whenever want or misery or starvation is known to exist, however distant or difficult of access, we instantly organise relief on the most generous scale, and distribute it, if need be, to the uttermost ends of the earth."

The Duchess paused, with a sense of ultimate triumph. She had made the same observation at a drawing-room meeting, and it had been extremely well received.

"I wonder," said Reginald, "if you have ever walked down the Embankment on a winter night?"

"Gracious, no, child! Why do you ask?"

"I didn't; I only wondered . . . "

(*Reginald*, pp. 27–30)

The Embankment is the side of the Thames in central London, a place where the down-and-outs of London sleep and organizations such as the Salvation Army run soup kitchens. While preaching about Britain's far-reaching foreign aid, the duchess makes no move to relieve the misery and poverty and hunger on her own door step.

A lack of open-handedness, either to the poor who depend on it or to the hero himself, is deplored and often ridiculed or punished, either by providence, the hero in the plot, or the deadly irony of the narrative voice, as in "Mrs Packletide's Tiger":

Louisa Mebbin adopted a protective elder-sister attitude towards money in general, irrespective of nationality of denomination. Her energetic intervention had saved many a rouble from dissipating itself in tips in some Moscow hotel, and francs and centimes clung to her instinctively under circumstances which would have driven them headlong from less sympathetic hands.

(*The Chronicles of Clovis*, p. 48)

The heartlessness of Reginald and Clovis (as well as of the general tenor of many of the stories) is of quite a different order from the sanctimoniousness and hypocrisy of the assorted duchesses, baronesses, and family members of the short stories, and its audaciousness provides much of the (black) humor. In "Esmé," a hyena devours a gypsy child.

Constance shuddered. "Do you think the poor little thing suffered much?" came another of her futile questions.

"The indications were all that way," I said; "on the other hand, of course, it may have been crying from sheer temper. Children sometimes do."

(*The Chronicles of Clovis*, p. 19)

The stories can even force a guilty laugh out of their readers when the black humor is directed against a serious and worthy cause. Saki's, or his narrator's, irreverence, or misogyny, extends to the woman's movement, or at least the Suffragettes. As the "Suffragetæ" in "The Gala Programme: An Unrecorded Episode in Roman His-

tory," they disrupt the chariot race of the imperial games, which is to precede a "grand combat of wild beasts," rather as the Suffragettes did a race in which a royal horse was running.

Hundreds of women were being lowered by their accomplices into the arena. A moment later they were running and dancing in frenzied troops across the track where the chariots were supposed to compete. No team of arena-trained horses would have faced such a frantic mob; the race was clearly an impossibility. Howls of disappointment and rage rose from the spectators, howls of triumph echoed back from the women in possession.

(*The Square Egg*, p. 141)

The Master of Ceremonies is hysterical with rage and mortification, but the "popular and gifted young Emperor Placidus Superbus" remains calm and unruffled, and arranges what appears to be Saki's answer to the demonstrations:

"Close the stable gates," commanded the Master of Ceremonies, "and open all the menagerie dens. It is the Imperial pleasure that the second portion of the programme be taken first."

It turned out that the Master of Ceremonies had in no wise exaggerated the probable brilliancy of this portion of the spectacle. The wild bulls were really wild, and the hyaena reputed to be mad thoroughly lived up to its reputation.

(pp. 141–142)

While Saki's Reginald, Clovis, and Bertie may have been the models for P. J. Wodehouse's young men of independent means and effete habits, they are not well-intentioned upper-class twits in the Bertie Wooster mold (first seen in *The Man with Two Left Feet*, 1917), though they are perhaps closer to the characters of Evelyn Waugh's satires, such as *A Handful of Dust* (1934) and *Scoop* (1938), and may be ancestors of the dandies of Ronald Firbanks' novels *Vainglory* (1915), *Inclinations* (1916), and *Valmouth: A Romantic Novel* (1919). The dandyism and affectation of Saki's heroes might be reminiscent of Baroness Orczy's eponymous *The Scarlet Pimpernel* (first published in 1905), but while Sir Percy throws off his airs and graces to rescue doomed aristocrats from the guillotine, Saki's heroes would be more likely to be gleefully working it—and equally as likely to be constructing witty epigrams as they mounted its steps.

While their heartlessness constitutes much of the comedy and their *bon mots,* however cruel, the style of the stories, the young men are also to be feared and pitied. Something, it is suggested, has gone awry with their development. An exchange between Emily Carewe and major Richard Dumbarton in the "playlet" "The Baker's Dozen" contains a line that might well get a laugh, but it also has a painful resonance.

EM.: There's always a chance that one of them might turn out depraved and vicious, and then you could disown him. I've heard of that being done.
    MAJ.: But, good gracious, you've got to educate him first. You can't expect a boy to be vicious till he's been to a good school.

(Reginald in Russia, pp. 109–110)

The schoolboys in Saki's writing are far more vicious than the animals, and they inhabit a world impenetrable to feminine or adult influence (see "The Strategist," in *Reginald in Russia,* pp. 85–93). Abandoning a young boy to this world is tantamount to exposing him in the jungle. He will become either predator or prey.

There is something feral about the Saki heroes. They go for the throat of their prey (if only the bridge opponent) and for the essentials of survival (good clothes, fine wine, baubles) with all the single-mindedness of a ferret in a rat hole. They leave town only to rusticate, joining country-house parties given by reliable hostesses for the sake of the food or the chance to live cheaply and catch up on sleep. They abhor the usual country pursuits of the gentry and upper middle class, such as hunting, shooting, and fishing, and are soon bored by long damp walks, village philanthropy, and parlor games. If they dislike and are out of place in the tamed, estate-managed, pastoral kind of landscape, however, they are attracted to the real, untamed wilderness. They may not ride, or hunt, or enjoy country walks, and their habitat may be the West End (of London) rather than the West Country, but they are associated with predators, danger, and the wild, which Saki's women characters invariably detest and fear.

The female protagonist of "The Music on the Hill," Sylvia Seltoun, is the archetypal middle-class Englishwoman who professes a love of the countryside but is "accustomed to nothing much more sylvan than 'leafy Kensington,'" a tree-lined suburb of London *(The Chronicles of Clovis,* p. 150).

She congratulates herself on bringing about a loveless marriage with a cold and indifferent man, and on persuading her husband to go down to his ancestral home, Yessney, but the country manor is not what she expects.

In its wild open savagery there seemed a stealthy linking of the joy of life with the terror of unseen things. Sylvia smiled complacently as she gazed with a School-of-Art appreciation at the landscape, and then of a sudden she almost shuddered.
    "It is very wild," she said to Mortimer who had joined her; "one could almost think that in such a place the worship of Pan had never quite died out."
    "The worship of Pan never has died out," said Mortimer.

(p. 151)

Exploring, Sylvia has a sense of a sinister presence at Yessney. Even the estate is not the picture-post-card farm with tidy, hen-pecked yard, picturesque duck pond, and sanitary Jersey cow that she expects, but a hostile, claustrophobic, brooding place. Animals slink away from her, and she is frightened by a large sow. Then "as she threaded her way past rickyards and cowsheds and long blank walls, she started suddenly at a strange sound—the echo of a boy's laughter, golden and equivocal" (p. 153). One day, following her husband, she comes across a clearing in which stands a small bronze figure of a young Pan at whose feet, as if in offering, have been placed a bunch of grapes. Since grapes are none too plentiful at Yessney, she snatches them angrily and returns homeward. As she turns, she sees a boy's face scowling at her from a tangle of undergrowth. He is brown and beautiful, but his eyes are "unutterably evil" (p. 154). She finds that her husband, who wears a "Jermyn Street" urbanity in the town, has another aspect in the country. He remarks dispassionately on the consequences of meddling with offerings to the wood gods and suggests that she should avoid the woods and orchards and give a wide berth to the horned animals on the farm. Nervous of the cattle and the ram, Sylvia skirts the farm meadows and the woods and climbs the hill above Yessney, but she is drawn onward by a stag apparently driven in her direction by a hunt, and by a low, fitful, reedy piping coming from a nearby copse.

The pipe music shrilled suddenly around her, seeming to come from the bushes at her very feet, and at the same moment the great beast slewed round and bore directly down upon her. In an instant her pity for the hunted animal was changed to wild terror at her own danger; the thick heather roots mocked her scrambling efforts at flight, and she looked frantically downward for a glimpse of oncoming hounds. . . . in a flash of numbing fear she remembered Mortimer's warning. . . . And then with a quick throb of joy she saw that she was not alone; a human figure stood a few paces aside, knee-deep in the whortle bushes.

"Drive it off!" she shrieked. But the figure made no answering movement.

The antlers drove straight at her breast, the acrid smell of the hunted animal was in her nostrils, but her eyes were filled with the horror of something she saw other than her oncoming death. And in her ears rang the echo of a boy's laughter, golden and equivocal.

(pp. 158–159)

The supernatural force of the wilderness is associated with the beauty of a lovely, wild boy who might well have been an object of worship for the heroes of the stories, with their cult of youth and beauty, their indifference to the fate of mortal man, and their capricious hedonism. The object of desire in Saki's stories is often adolescent and inhuman, or at least outside human society and, therefore, constraints of class, manners, and mores. In "Gabriel-Ernest," the narrative voice lingers over the feral beauty of the eponymous youth.

On a shelf of smooth stone overhanging a deep pool in the hollow of an oak coppice a boy of about sixteen lay asprawl, drying his wet brown limbs luxuriously in the sun. His wet hair, parted by a recent dive, lay close to his head, and his light-brown eyes, so light that there was an almost tigerish gleam in them, were turned towards Van Cheele with a certain lazy watchfulness . . .

The boy turned like a flash, plunged into the pool, and in a moment had flung his wet and glistening body half-way up the bank where Van Cheele was standing. In an otter the movement would not have been remarkable; in a boy Van Cheele found it sufficiently startling . . . Almost instinctively he half raised his hand to his throat. The boy laughed again, a laugh in which the snarl had nearly driven out the chuckle, and then, with another of his astonish lightning movements, plunged out of view into a yielding tangle of weeds and fern.

"What an extraordinary wild animal!" said Van Cheele . . . .

(*Reginald in Russia*, pp. 48–51)

Van Cheele is correct; Gabriel-Ernest is a werewolf.

"The Music on the Hill" has affinities with E. M. Forster's "The Story of a Panic" (1904), in which the presence of Pan creates misrule and tumult. The horned, goat-legged Pan appears in myth as the deity of Arcadia, a peaceful pastoral land, but he has come to stand for the spirit of the wild, especially in Saki's writing. Pan, or his animals, become agents of revenge on an archetypal Saki character, the managing woman. She is inevitably a crass and insensitive figure who appears to thwart and manipulate the male in her charge simply for the pleasure of exercising her power over him. As wife, she attempts to "make something" of her husband, or order his life; as mother she withholds funds and adulthood; as sister, she tells tales and tries to reform her brother's morals. Either way, she is the diametric opposite of the young Dionysian or Pan-like figure, a naiad of suburbia, who carries the hero away from a life of romance and adventure (whether wolves and Cossacks or duchess-baiting and choirboys) and commits him to a life sentence of dullness and routine. In "Tea," the twin objects of horror for Saki, managing women and suburban life, coalesce in his depiction of the claustrophobia that overwhelms its protagonist, James Cushat-Prinkly, as he contemplates the numbing routine of domestic life as perpetuated by women.

Thousands of women, at this solemn afternoon hour, were sitting behind dainty porcelain and silver fittings, with their voices tinkling pleasantly in a cascade of solicitous little questions. Cushat-Prinkly detested the whole system of afternoon tea. According to his theory of life a woman should lie on a divan or couch, talking with incomparable charm or looking unutterable thoughts, or merely silent as a thing to be looked on, and from behind a silken curtain a small Nubian page should silently bring in a tray with cups and dainties, to be accepted silently, as a matter of course, without drawn-out chatter about cream and sugar and hot water. If one's soul was really enslaved at one's mistress's feet how could one talk coherently about weakened tea?

(*The Toys of Peace*, p. 24)

James postpones proposing to the woman he is expected to marry and avoids encountering her over the tea tray by visiting a remote cousin, Rhoda Ellam. He finds Rhoda in a Bohemian setting, surrounded by the impedimenta of her unorthodox but creative work, taking a picnic meal. Beyond offering him caviar and the proper accoutrements, and telling James to find himself a cup, she makes no other allusions to food and does not tinkle. James proposes. After the honeymoon,

Cushat-Prinkly came into the drawing-room of his new house in Granchester Square. Rhoda was seated at a low table, behind a service of dainty porcelain and gleaming silver. There was a pleasant tinkling note in her voice as she handed him a cup.

"You like it weaker than that, don't you? Shall I put some more hot water to it? No?"

(p. 28)

One can almost hear the screams.

While woman is not overtly accused of bringing about the awful fate of "Judkin of the Parcels," an unending sameness of fetching and carrying unimportant packages (*Reginald in Russia*, pp. 42–46), a wife is lurking darkly in the wings, and Saki brings all his upper-middle-class contempt for the drudge of trade to the story, and all his lower-upper-middle-class horror of being sucked into its maw through economic necessity to the depiction of its victim.

A more extreme form of conjugal hell is depicted in "The Reticence of Lady Anne" (*Reginald in Russia*, pp. 7–12), in which the husband, Egbert, is so used to prolonged frigid silence as a demonstration of his wife's displeasure that he makes futile and self-abasing attempts at conciliation and appeasement all afternoon, unaware that she has been dead for two hours.

Reginald, Clovis, and other young men in the stories can get back at domesticating or bullying women through social embarrassment, economic redress (bridge debts are always useful), or petty blackmail, but the younger boys are more vulnerable, and the blackest of the female villains are their aunts and other older female relations and guardians. The tormentor of "The Lumber Room," the young hero's cousins' aunt, is "the *soi-disant* aunt" and "alleged aunt." That is, she usurps the power and prerogatives of an aunt, and by virtue of her malignity is worthy of the title.

It was her habit, whenever one of the children fell from grace, to improvise something of a festival nature from which the offender would be rigorously debarred; if all the children sinned collectively they were suddenly informed of a circus in a neighbouring town, a circus of unrivalled merit and uncounted elephants, to which, but for their depravity, they would have been taken that very day.

(*Beasts and Super-Beasts*, p. 275)

Nicholas, the child hero, is robust, and has his defenses against the domestic tyrant; his *soi-disant*

aunt is merely confined to a rain-water tank for thirty-five minutes; in other stories, however, the neglected, unloved boy exacts a more violent and extreme revenge on his tormentors and abusers. If children are to be labeled "depraved" for the high spirits of childhood, and their minor misdemeanors held up as sins and falls from grace, then the children will take care to be depraved, and to visit their sins upon their aunts. The anarchic force of nature that manifests as both the faun-like Gabriel-Ernest and the laughing boy with the flute is aligned with the oppressed children, and perhaps called into being by them. In "Sredni Vashtar," the unloved child is Conradin and the unlovely abuser is Mrs. de Ropp. The story's opening is masterful: unsentimental and deadpan, yet immediately arresting, and both chilling and moving.

Conradin was ten years old, and the doctor had pronounced his professional opinion that the boy would not live another five years. The doctor was silky and effete, and counted for little, but his opinion was endorsed by Mrs. De Ropp, who counted for nearly everything. . . . One of these days Conradin supposed he would succumb to the mastering pressure of wearisome necessary things—such as illnesses and coddling restrictions and drawn-out dulness. Without his imagination, which was rampant under the spur of loneliness, he would have succumbed long ago.

Mrs de Ropp would never, in her honestest moments, have confessed to herself that she disliked Conradin, though she might have been dimly aware that thwarting him "for his good" was a duty which she did not find particularly irksome. Conrad hated her with a desperate sincerity which he was perfectly able to mask. . . . from the realm of his imagination she was locked out— an unclean thing, which should find no entrance.

(*The Chronicles of Clovis*, pp. 93–94)

Conradin has two sources of solace in his cheerless, loveless life, a ragged hen and a polecat ferret, whose hidden presence in a toolshed is

a secret and fearful joy, to be kept scrupulously from the knowledge of the Woman, as he privately dubbed his cousin. And one day, out of Heaven knows what material, he spun the beast a wonderful name, and from that moment it grew into a god and a religion. . . . in the dim and musty silence of the tool-shed, he worshipped with mystic and elaborate ceremonial before the wooden hutch where dwelt Sredni Vashtar, the great ferret.

(pp. 95–96)

The Woman finds the hen and has it taken away, then begins to suspect the existence of another concealed animal. She ransacks Conradin's room until she finds the key and marches down to the shed.

And Conradin fervently breathed his prayer for the last time. But he knew as he prayed that he did not believe. He knew that the Woman would come out presently with that pursed smile he loathed so well on her face, and that in an hour or two the gardener would carry away his wonderful god, a god no longer, but a simple brown ferret in a hutch. And he knew that the Woman would triumph always as she triumphed now, and that he would grow ever more sickly under her pestering and domineering and superior wisdom . . . and the doctor would be proved right. And in the sting and misery of his defeat, he began to chant loudly and defiantly the hymn of his threatened idol—

Sredni Vashtar went forth,
His thoughts were red thoughts and his teeth were white.
His enemies called for peace but he brought them death,
Sredni Vashtar the Beautiful.

(pp. 99–100)

Conradin watches. Finally, "out through that doorway came a long, low, yellow-and-brown beast, with eyes a-blink at the waning daylight, and dark wet stains around the fur of jaws and throat." While the maids have hysterics and wonder who is to break the news to the frail child, Conrad calmly consumes buttered toast (pp.101–102). Mrs. de Ropp is said to be a portrait of Saki's Aunt Augusta, but Aunt Tom is satirized for a more forgivable failing in "The Sex That Doesn't Shop" (in *Reginald in Russia*, pp. 25–30). The perpetual petty warfare between the two is immortalized in "The Blood-feud of Toad-Water," which begins with Mrs. Crick's hen scratching among her neighbor Mrs. Saunders' seedling onions, endures for decades, and is described in mock-epic language as Old Testament in proportion (*Reginald in Russia*, pp. 31–37).

THE NOVELS

ALWAYS politically aware, perceiving the threat to Great Britain from the coming First World War, Saki made an about-face in the treatment of the decadent young heroes of his fiction. The qualities that made Reginald and Clovis admired wits, arbiters of fashion, and sought-after guests become the very qualities that are sapping the morale of the young and leaving the country vulnerable to attack by stronger, healthier nations.

Though the author's note to *The Unbearable Bassington* (1912) suggests the cheerful cynicism and amorality of Reginald ("This story has no moral. If it points out an evil at any rate it suggests no remedy"), it is neither cynical nor cheerful. The characters are all doomed, trapped in a series of hells from which there is no escape. The decadence of the young men of the short stories was a matter of style, but Comus Bassington's decadence is unhealthy, unpleasant, and corrupt. Where Clovis and Reginald amuse themselves with elaborate hoaxes that amuse them and fool or foil their antagonists, Comus plots from motives of sadism and cupidity, sometimes against those who are both innocent and defenseless, as when he derives great pleasure from caning a younger boy.

In spite of his vicious nature, Comus is the hero of the story, and Saki manages to get us on his side, to the extent of willing him to win the heiress and avoid exile from London, his natural setting. Indeed, Comus seems a distillation of London society as represented by the cast of minor characters, except that he does not pretend to be good. London in this novel is both the only place where one would not be bored to death and is utterly bleak: full of loveless marriages, false friendships, rapacious women, malicious-tongued old men, and avaricious young ones, all fueled by gossip. Comus' mother, Francesca Bassington, personifies the brittle materialism of her circle. "Francesca herself, if pressed in an unguarded moment to describe her soul, would probably have described her drawing-room" (p. 10), a beautiful setting for the possessions she has gleaned and schemed for over many years, and which have become everything to her. We follow Francesca's gaze as she makes an inventory of precious objects and find that, "above all her other treasures, dominating in her estimation every other object that the room contained, was the great Van der Meulen" whose associations, personal and aesthetic, are described in detail (p. 14).

For all its ornaments and Aubusson padding, society is, as Comus knows, "an animal world, and a fiercely competitive animal world at that" (p. 59). Nonetheless, when he exchanges that world for a real animal kingdom, we know that death will result. Comus will not be killed by the real animals; he does not fear and seems scarcely to notice them, but away from his natural habitat he will pine and die. He is another young Pan figure, and as such seems to be removed from the usual human attachments and obligations.

In appearance he exactly fitted his fanciful Pagan name. His large green-grey eyes seemed for ever asparkle with goblin mischief and the joy of revelry, and the curved lips might have been those of some wickedly-laughing faun; one almost expected to see embryo horns fretting the smoothness of his sleek dark hair.

(p. 30)

He seems exempt from the usual forces that shape character and is described as more like a force of nature than a person. When a schoolmaster remarks to a colleague that he could tame Comus, the latter replies:

"Heaven forbid that I should try" . . .
  "But why?" asked the reformer.
  "Because Nature hates any interference with her own arrangements, and if you start in to tame the obviously untameable you are taking a fearful responsibility on yourself."

(p. 33)

This is a dark aspect of Nature, or Pan, however. The narrative voice lingers over Comus' athleticism and beauty, but the physical prowess is used for show and brutality, and beauty is inhuman and cold. The boy seems the quintessence of youth, laughing and vivid; but it is a youth both doomed and damned.

The chin was firm, but one looked in vain for a redeeming touch of ill-temper in the handsome, half-mocking, half-petulant face. With a strain of sourness in him Comus might have been leavened into something creative and masterful; fate had fashioned him with a certain whimsical charm, and left him all unequipped for the greater purposes of life. Perhaps no one would have called him a lovable character, but in many respects he was adorable; in all respects he was certainly damned.

(pp. 30–31)

The distinction between lovable and adorable, which depends upon Comus' looks, vitality, and youthful arrogance, is significant. Comus may be doomed, but he is also damned as the consequence of human actions; he is damned because his mother does not love him enough. Francesca has hoped for a marriage between Comus and the heiress Elaine de Frey, whose money would save her from losing her real love, her house and its furnishings, and secure the perfect setting for the Van der Meulen. When Comus alienates Elaine's affection by constantly asking her for money, Francesca is furious, and when she suspects that he thinks she should sell the Van der Meulen to enable them to continue to live in their present style, she is horrified beyond words and allows her brother to find Comus a post in a conveniently remote corner of the empire. Utterly unfitted for the job, exhausted by the climate, debilitated by the unhealthy environment, away from his native soil, Comus becomes ill. As his Pan-like vivacity ebbs away, he reveals, and remembers, that he did once have a tie of human affection:

One person in the whole world had cared for him . . . But a wall of ice had mounted up between him and her, and across it there blew that cold breath that chills or kills affection.
  The words of a well-known old song, the wistful cry of a lost cause, rang with insistent mockery through his brain:
  "Better loved you canna be,
  Will ye ne'er come back again?"
  If it was love that was to bring him back he must be an exile for ever.

(pp. 299–300)

In spite of everything, Comus achieves pathos. We pity him, sympathize with his loneliness and misery, and look for a reprieve from his inevitable death in the insalubrious swamps. No reprieve comes, and the narrator turns relentless eyes on the agent of Comus' death. Francesca Bassington's punishment is her awakening conscience. She dwells on the image of Comus:

the warm, living, breathing thing that had been hers to love, and she had turned her eyes from that youthful comely figure to adore a few feet of painted canvas, a musty relic of a long departed craftsman. And now he was gone from her sight . . . and these things of canvas and pigment and wrought metal would stay with her. They were her soul. And what shall it profit a man if he save his soul and slay his heart in torment?

(pp. 311–312)

Francesca, not Comus, is the unbearable Bassington. Even then, Saki seems to feel that she has not suffered enough. The final ironic blow, delivered by her voluble brother just as she has read the telegram announcing Comus' death, is that her precious Van der Meulen is a fake.

In his literary biography of Saki, A. J. Langguth suggests that the ending of *The Unbearable Bassington* is weak, depending on a twist that might have been appropriate for a short story but that can irritate the reader of a novel (*Saki*, p. 208), but for some contemporary critics, the denouement was the book's strength. Among the quotations from reviews featured on the end pages of the 1924 reprint of the novel is the *Observer*'s declaration that it is one of "the wittiest books . . . of the decade" and that it has "a deepening humanity towards the end that comes to a climax of really disturbing pathos." Also included was an extract from a review in *Outlook*, a Tory magazine for which Saki was by then writing, which called it "a great book": "We do not remember any book which has left us more saddened and more obsessed by a sense of dreary intolerable pain." As Langguth points out, however, it is the detail, of setting and character, especially the supporting characters, who are vividly drawn with wonderful economy, rather than the pain and sadness, for which more recent readers remember the novel (see pp. 203–204).

If Comus is the degenerate youth of the drawing room, the degeneracy of the political sphere is represented by Courtenay Youghal. The young MP is neither corrupt nor wicked; he is even good-looking and intelligent. He is simply a consummate politician, constantly self-promoting, ambitious rather than committed, self-confident, amoral, heartless. Well-groomed without being vain, single-mindedly self-seeking without being actively unkind, Machiavellian without being entirely devoid of sincerity, Youghal is an elusive character and a puzzle to Elaine, whom he pursues in rivalry with Comus.

Making a cameo appearance in the novel is a Saki archetype, the man of dual personality—almost dual nationality—who is equally at home in a cosmopolitan city and a primeval forest. Tom Keriway appears almost out of nowhere, wrapped in both kinds of Saki glamour, that of the witty, accomplished sophisticate and that of the lone hunter, and he functions as a kind of tempter against whom Elaine should measure each of her suitors and find them wanting. He has lived in Vienna but also rambled through the Near and Middle East

as leisurely and thoroughly as tamer souls might explore Paris. He had wandered through Hungarian horse-fairs, hunted shy crafty beasts on lonely Balkan hillsides, dropped himself pebble-wise into the stagnant human pool of some Bulgarian monastery, threaded his way through the strange racial mosaic of Salonika, listened with amused politeness to the shallow ultra-modern opinions of a voluble editor or lawyer in some wayside Russian town, or learned wisdom from a chance tavern companion, one of the atoms of the busy ant-stream of men and merchandise that moves untiringly round the shores of the Black Sea. . . . He seldom talked of his travels, but it might be said that his travels talked of him; there was an air about him that a German diplomat once summed up in a phrase: "a man that wolves have sniffed at."

(*The Unbearable Bassington*, pp. 142–143)

He might be a relative of Richard Hannay (*The Thirty-Nine Steps*, 1915) or an ancestor of James Bond but for his crippled state and his status as indigenous part of rather than master of the wilderness. Modern life, in the form of disease and financial disaster, has hobbled him, and having stirred Elaine's imagination and her sensuality, he vanishes from the story, only to reappear, under a different guise, in *When William Came*.

The *Morning Post* reviewer called *When William Came* (1913) "Mr Munro's first novel with a purpose" and, perhaps unconsciously aligning Saki with his own Comus Bassington, as well as placing him as a comic writer, announced that the author's "jester's bauble has become a whip, and every stroke tells" (endpapers, *The Unbearable Bassington*, repr. 1924). The novel opens on a note of reproach: a vision of an England in which complacency and liberal thinking has diluted the qualities of the people who were once assured of their fitness to be rulers of half the world. English youth has become effete and apathetic; the abolition of national service has robbed the nation of its gymnasium and removed the proper outlet for aggression. Long-standing peace and unshakeable belief in the invincibility of the empire has led to the disbanding of the Royal Navy and a careless indifference to the growing power of Germany. The result is that the once-great Britain has become a colony of the Hapsburg Empire.

The young men whom Cecily Yeoville picks up to act as her successive official "boy-friends" are representative of the degeneracy of both the lower classes (they are ruthless users and social climbers) and the upper (they are used to fill empty lives by women such as Cecily). Though he has once been a strong, active, energetic man, long illness in a foreign country has left Cecily's husband, Murrey Yeoville, drained, tired, and gripped by crippling inertia. As a traveler in eastern Europe, Yeoville is another man at whom wolves have sniffed. Equally at home in Vienna and Budapest and in the forests of Siberia, Yeoville could be both urban sophisticate and devotee of Pan. As with all Saki heroes, he is comfortable in extremes; the one place where he is not at home is the middle-class, middle way: the suburbs and "Garden Cities" of middle England (see the scathing description of modern villas and their inhabitants in "The Quest," in *The Chronicles of Clovis*, pp.119–128). Yeoville is a fierce patriot whose opinion on the occupation of Britain by Germany, and of those who tolerate it, is clearly the approved response of the narrative voice.

Given his dual nature, Yeoville ought to be a Sir Percy Blakeney who rescues the ruling class of England from its German enemies, but he arrives too late, after the war is over, and his own physical and spiritual state is broken down. Nor is he alone in his inability to act. Faced with a *fait accompli*, debarred from military service, forbidden to bear arms, those who have not fled abroad seem ready to sink into acceptance or apathy. There is no want of patriotism. Intense love of the country is represented in the characters who, unable to fight for their nation, either retire to their country estates or create a pocket of England abroad. In *When William Came*, these are represented by women: the indomitable Eleanor; Dowager Lady Greymarten, said by Ethel Munro in "Biography of Saki" to be based on a living person admired by Saki (p. 90); and Mrs. Kerrick, a character in an interlude unconnected to the rest of the plot. Her name is used only once after the beginning of the chapter; otherwise, she is "the hostess," "this lady," "the mother," and, most significantly, "the Englishwoman." She is Saki's vision of Englishwomen, preserving a vestige of their country in which to rear the next generation to revere and be prepared to die for England. A French visitor presses her to explain why she chooses to live in a remote spot with hardly any amenities or society.

"In all this garden that you see," said the Englishwoman, "there is one tree that is sacred."

"A tree?" said the Frenchman.

"A tree that we could not grow in England."

The Frenchman followed the direction of her eyes and saw a tall, bare pole at the summit of the hillock . . . A

cord shivered and flapped, and something ran swiftly up into the air, and swung out in the breeze that blew across the hills—a blue flag with red and white crosses. . . .

"That is why we live out here," said the Englishwoman quietly.

(pp. 273–274)

Finally, it is the youth of Britain, represented by the Boy Scouts, who show the way, or at least carry out a symbolic act of defiance that might be a beginning. The young boy as homoerotic object represented in "Reginald's Choir Treat" and other stories is replaced, or supplemented, by the young boy as soldier and hope of the realm.

Representatives of the new regime are gathered in Hyde Park for a rally designed to cement relations between the new rulers and the newly ruled. After a great display of strength by the German military forces, the high point of the day is to be a march-past by the Scouts. If the occasion is a success, with even a third of the Scouts showing up, it will demonstrate that the younger generation has accepted the *fait accompli*, which will be a large step toward entente and appeasement. Any miscarriage will be a serious embarrassment for the new regime. A character remarks: "nothing has been left undone to rally the Scouts to the new order of things. Special privileges have been showered on them" (p. 309).

The Scouts are to march in at three o'clock. As the hour approaches, the crowd becomes restive but is controlled by the ubiquitous police and plainclothes detectives. Watching from the back is Murrey Yeoville, whose thoughts turn from despair to hope and pride, and shame.

And now a dull flush crept into his grey face; a look that was partly new-born hope and resurrected pride, partly remorse and shame, burned in his eyes. Shame, the choking, searing shame of self-reproach that cannot be reasoned away, was dominant in his heart. *He* had laid down his arms—there were others who had never hoisted the flag of surrender. He had given up the fight and joined the ranks of the hopelessly subservient; in thousands of English homes throughout the land there were young hearts that had not forgotten, had not compounded, would not yield.

The younger generation had barred the door.

(pp. 321–322)

The final scene is strongly visual. A powerfully evocative image sets up parallels between the three flags of the novel: the Union Flag (of the scene abroad) as emblem of patriotism and hope, the German flag as banner of empty pageantry and ignoble humiliation, and Murrey Yeoville's metaphorical "flag of surrender."

> And in the pleasant May sunshine the Eagle standard floated and flapped, the black and yellow pennons shifted restlessly, Emperor and Princes, Generals and guards, sat stiffly in their saddles, and waited.
> And waited . . .
>
> (p. 322)

THE PLAYS

SAKI'S experience of the Balkans, eastern Europe, and Russia, and his extensive knowledge of their history, provided matter for some of his short stories and two of his plays. *Karl-Ludwig's Window* and *The Death-Trap* (1924) are both short, one-act melodramas set in eastern Europe, and each revolves around one idea: a crucial piece of set (a haunted window) in *Karl-Ludwig's Window* (*The Square Egg*, pp. 179–190); a twist of fate (the ruse that is to be the last-minute reprieve from assassination turns out to be true) in *The Death-Trap* (*The Square Egg*, pp. 167–176). *The Watched Pot* (1924), which Saki wrote jointly with Charles Maude, is in three acts and has a large dramatis personae. It is a country-house marriage-race comedy revolving around the question of who will secure the hand of Trevor Bavvel and thus oust the tyrannical Hortensia Bavvel as châtelaine of Briony Manor, except that, as is revealed in the last scene, the alleged eligible bachelor has been married for two months. The play is interesting chiefly for the way in which the male *ingenue* is substituted for the female as passive object of desire, jealously guarded by parent, and pursued with stratagem and artifice by rival suitors. It recycles a number of lines from the short stories, as well as characters such as Hortensia Bavval, the domineering older woman; Agatha Clifford, the insensitive and encroaching houseguest; Mrs. Vulpy, the pretentious social climber; and René St. Gall, the young aesthete (*The Square Egg*, pp. 191–318).

In his introduction to the plays for the 1933 *The Novels and Plays of Saki*, J. C. Squires makes an explicit comparison between the dialogue of *The Watched Pot* and that of Oscar Wilde's drawing room comedies:

> half his jokes depend for their force upon their exaggeration of truth. René remarks: "This suit I've got on was

paid for last month, so you may judge how old it is." Here the truth is not important, except to tailors: with no more elaboration or afterthought "Saki" would summarize aspects of "world-problems" as they appeared to him, as in:

> Government by democracy means government of the mentally unfit by the mentally mediocre tempered by the saving grace of snobbery.

The form of this reminds one of Wilde. Wilde also might have written:

> For all I know to the contrary, he may by this time have joined the majority who are powerless to resent these intrusions.

although it took "Saki" to put it into the mouth of an almost agreeable lady talking about her sick husband. We think of Wilde's plays again when, speaking of harvest festivals and the growth of imports, Clare says:

> It shows such a nice spirit for a Somersetshire farmer to be duly thankful for the ripening of the Carlsbad plum

and in

> So many people who are described as rough diamonds turn out to be merely rough paste. . . .

"Saki" had all Wilde's cleverness at the substitution of a word in a stock saying or the inversion of a familiar proverb, and was an adept at contradicting our favourite cliches of word or thought, or strangely adapting them to unsuitable contexts. Yet though many of his sentences might be mistaken for Wilde's none of his pages could be attributed to another man.

> (pp. 345–346)

CONCLUSION

INTRODUCING the 1930 omnibus edition of Saki's stories, Christopher Morley sums up H. H. Munro's gifts.

> Delicate, airy, lucid, precise, with the inconspicuous agility of perfect style, he can pass into the uncanny, the tragic, into mocking fairy-tales grimmer than Grimm. His phrases are always urbane and usually final . . .

> Saki writes so lightly that you might hardly notice how beautifully also. . . . Let me repeat what I once put into the mouth of the "Old Mandarin" in a pseudo-Chinese translation:

> There is something specially Chinese
> In Saki's Tory humour,

He has the claw of the demon-cat
Beneath his brilliant robe.
Suavest comedian, silkiest satirist,
Smooth as a shave,
With a new razor-blade.

(pp. 6–7)

This style, at once suavely smooth and razor-sharp, is the quality for which Saki is justly celebrated, but perhaps his very facility with words, his brio, has made readers skate over the surface and miss other qualities. His short stories were popular on first publication and continue to attract new devotees with every reprinting, but his work is not as widely read, or as acclaimed, as it should be.

One of the most refreshing things about reading Saki's work is his complete lack of sentimentality about children, animals, or indeed anything. One of the most unpleasant things about reading it is his appalling anti-Semitism, expressed both in the narrative voice and that of the central protagonists, and echoing that of contemporaries such as Kipling. There are also a number of fairly narrow-minded stereotypes of Americans (pretentious and philistine), Germans (sentimental, crude, and greedy), and the working classes (ponderous, slow, and comic).

Saki was no more sentimental about his fellow artists than he was about animals and children. Wilde, born sixteen years before Saki and dying sixteen years before him, is the figure to whom Saki is most often compared. Wilde was a much more successful dramatist, and Saki admired him (a letter to his sister berates her for missing *A Woman of No Importance*), but he was not a better writer of short stories, dialogue, and epigrams. The aestheticism that was presented as a daring and radical position in Wilde's work has become a fashionable pose and self-conscious affectation in Saki's. While Saki's writing shows an interest in eastern Europe and the exoticism of Russia, and even China, it is not inflected with the Orientalism of Wilde's fiction and criticism, nor does it adopt the cadences and syntax of pseudo-Arabic. Though his visual imagery is sometimes reminiscent of Aubrey Beardsley's illustrations (see the previous extract from "Tea"), it is hard to imagine Saki writing the whimsical and sentimental "The Happy Prince" with a straight face or sustaining the semi-mystical, *Arabian Nights* quality of *A House of Pomegranates*. One feels that he might

have enjoyed the "The Canterville Ghost" but would have made the ghost's performances more theatrical and blood-curdling and given a different twist to the happy ending.

The other writer against whose work Saki's might be measured, a near contemporary of Wilde's, though he outlived him by more than fifty years, is George Bernard Shaw. Saki had toyed with *Man and Superman* (1908) in *Beasts and Super-Beasts*, and of one of a series of "Heart-to-Heart Talks" in the *Bystander* (in July 1912) was ostensibly a conversation between Shaw and the German ambassador, except that the ambassador doesn't get a word in, and the piece is a monologue on Shaw's fear that future generations will misattribute his work to another writer. Again, Shaw is a dramatist of more seriousness and weight but cannot match Saki's prose for pithiness, wit, or brevity. Either Shaw or Saki could be "one of the leading playwrights of your nation" for whom the imps of hell are engaged in preparing a huge press-cutting book in "The Infernal Parliament." The protagonist of the story, a visitor in hell pending a decision, is not impressed.

"Some dramatic authors wouldn't so very much mind spending eternity poring over a book of contemporary press-cuttings," he observed.
    The Fiend, laughing unpleasantly, lowered his voice.
    "The letter 'S' is missing."
    For the first time Bidderdale realized that he was in Hell.

(*The Square Egg*, p. 148)

He could be lampooning Shaw's self-publicizing and vanity or it could be a piece of self-mockery. With Saki, one never knows. His legion of fans, however, including Evelyn Waugh, Graham Greene, G. K. Chesterton, A. A. Milne, and Noël Coward, wherever they are, might well find eternity without reading matter on, still less by, Saki very tedious.

SELECTED BIBLIOGRAPHY

I. Short Stories. *Reginald* (London, 1904); *Reginald in Russia and Other Sketches* (London, 1910); *The Chronicles of Clovis* (London, 1911); *Beasts and Super-Beasts* (London, 1914); *The Toys of Peace and Other Papers* (London, 1919); *The Square Egg and Other Sketches* (London, 1924); "The East Wing," discovered in 1946, collected in *The Complete Short Stories of Saki* (1930; repr. 1953); "The Pond," "The Holy War," "The Almanack," "A Housing

Problem," "A Sacrifice to Necessity," "A Shot in the Dark," all collected in A. J. Langguth, *Saki: The Life of H. H. Munro* (1981).

II. NOVELS. *The Unbearable Bassington* (London, 1912); *When William Came: A Story of London Under the Hohenzollerns* (London, 1913).

III. NONFICTION. *The Rise of the Russian Empire* (London, 1899).

IV. POLITICAL SATIRE. *The Westminster Alice* (London, 1902); "The Political Jungle Book" and "The Not-So-Stories," in *The Westminster Gazette* (11 February 1902; 23 May 1902; 9 October 1902; 15 October 1902; 5 November 1902).

V. PLAYS. *The Death-Trap; Karl-Ludwig's Window; The Watched Pot* (first produced 1943), in *The Square Egg and Other Sketches* (London, 1924).

There have been many selections of Saki's stories and a number of omnibus editions. A useful recent collection that includes most of the stories, the novels, the plays, and the "Alice" satires is *The Complete Saki* (New York, 1976; London, 1982).

VI. BIOGRAPHY AND CRITICAL STUDIES. Rothay Reynolds, "A Memoir of H. H. Munro," in Saki, *The Toys of Peace* (London, 1919); E. M. Munro, "Biography of Saki," in *The Square Egg and Other Sketches* (London, 1924); Christopher Morley, intro. to *The Complete Short Stories of Saki* (London, 1930); Lord Charnwood, intro. to *When William Came*, in *The Novels and Plays of Saki* (London, 1933); J. A. Spender, intro. to *The Westminster Alice*, in *The Novels and Plays of Saki* (London, 1933); A. A. Milne, intro. to *The Chronicles of Clovis* (London, 1937); J. C. Squires, intro. to the plays, in *The Novels and Plays of Saki*; Evelyn Waugh, intro. to *The Unbearable Bassington* (London, 1947); J. W. Lambert, intro. to *The Bodley Head Saki* (London, 1963); George James Spears, *The Satire of Saki: A Study of the Satiric Art of Hector Munro* (New York, 1963); Charles H. Gillen, *H. H. Munro (Saki)* (New York, 1969); Noël Coward, intro. to *The Complete Saki* (New York, 1976; repr. London, 1982); A. J. Langguth, *Saki: A Life of Hector Hugh Munro: With Six Short Stories Never Before Collected* (New York, 1981).

ANNE STEVENSON

(1933–   )

Nicolas Tredell

IN A CAREER as a published poet that spans over fifty years, Anne Stevenson has employed a variety of poetic modes and explored a wide range of topics. She has worked in orthodox metrical forms, rhymed verse, blank verse, and free verse; she has produced lyrics, elegies, epigrams, satires, and verse letters; she has written of the physical realities and symbolic possibilities of different kinds of landscape, the experiences of bereavement, birth, marriage, motherhood and grandmotherhood, the continuities and differences between succeeding generations; and the nature of the poet and the making of poetry. To borrow a phrase from her poem "The Mudtower," Stevenson is a "migratory lady," not only in the geographical sense of a woman who has lived in, and written about, the United States, England, Scotland, and Wales, but also in her oscillations between a partly romantic, partly religious aspiration to transcendence, liberation, and isolation and an affirmation of the ordinary, a lucid acceptance of the bonds of the commonplace, and a sense of the importance of belonging.

Through all the changes of her life, however, Stevenson has shown a consistent concern for combining what she called, in her 1966 study of the poetry of Elizabeth Bishop, precision and resonance. Stevenson's best work demonstrates a disciplined use of language that captures moments of experience and perception while also reverberating more widely through time and space. She is not, for the most part, a spectacular writer; while she can vividly evoke extremes, most of her effects are quieter, more nuanced, at times apparently casual. For all her concern with woman's estate in some of her poems, she has shown strong resistance to being pigeonholed as a woman poet or a feminist poet and has conducted a complex debate with feminism in her poetry and prose writing. Despite her scholarly credentials and her experience in a variety of teaching posts, she has kept her distance from academic literary criticism and literary theory; but she is a lucid, informed, and perceptive critic of poetry, especially of Elizabeth Bishop; her 1966 study was complemented by another book, *Five Looks at Elizabeth Bishop* (1998); and she has produced a compelling and controversial biography of a poet towards whom she appears to feel a complicated mixture of admiration and antipathy: Sylvia Plath.

LIVING IN AMERICA, TRAVELLING BEHIND GLASS

ANNE Stevenson's migrations began early. She was born on 3 January 1933 to American parents in Cambridge, England, where her father, Charles Leslie Stevenson, a graduate of Yale, was pursuing studies at Jesus College with Ivor Armstrong Richards, George Edward Moore, and Ludwig Wittgenstein. He had originally come to Cambridge to study English but had switched to philosophy after reading Richards' *Principles of Literary Criticism* (1924; second edition, 1926). Later in 1933 the Stevenson family went back to the United States and Anne grew up in Cambridge, Massachusetts, and in New Haven, Connecticut. Her father was an excellent pianist and she grew up in a musical household listening to Bach, Beethoven, Mozart, and Schubert. But she also heard much poetry, mainly Victorian; her father liked to read aloud from the poems of Matthew Arnold, Robert Browning, and particularly of Sir Walter Scott— *The Lady of the Lake* and *The Lay of the Last Minstrel*; she also heard readings of earlier poets, for instance Donne and Shakespeare, and began to write poetry herself in her early teens, producing ballads and sonnets and coming under the influence of the work of William Butler Yeats and Robert Frost. She chose, however, to follow her musical interests when, in autumn 1950, she entered the University of Michigan as a music major, studying cello with Oliver Edel. But she changed to French and Italian, and studied hard while continuing to write poetry. At the age of eighteen, she discovered T. S. Eliot's "The Love Song of J. Alfred Prufrock" (1915) and *The Waste Land* (1922) but retained her allegiance to the poetry of the past; while at the university, she wrote a masque for dancing in Elizabethan forms. She also published poems in the university magazine, *Generation* and won three Hopwood Awards from the university for her poetry—a *Minor Hopwood* in 1952 and 1953, and a *Major Hopwood* in 1954. She graduated Phi Beta Kappa in 1954.

Stevenson married an Englishman, Robin Hitchcock, and lived for five years in England where her daughter, Caroline, was born in 1957. She went back to America in 1959, and spent some time in New York City, Corinth, Mississippi, and Atlanta, Georgia; she returned to The University of Michigan in 1960, where she studied with the poet and critic Donald Hall. Her first marriage broke up and she married again in 1961; her husband, Mark Elvin, was a scholar of Chinese history and she returned with him to Cambridge, England, in 1961. She obtained her master's degree in 1962. By her own account, it was also around this time, in her late twenties, that she first read Elizabeth Bishop's poems "The Map" and "Rooster." In 1965, Generation Press in Ann Arbor brought out her first collection of poetry, *Living in America*; she was thirty-two.

The thirty-two poems in *Living in America* are, for the most part, technically accomplished and range over topics that will recur in Stevenson's later work: life in the United States and in England; the experience of travelling to another country and another culture; and the lot of women as wives and mothers. The title poem finds little to praise in American life: the inhabitants of Harvard look down on living in America while Californians congratulate themselves upon it; but the overall drive of life in the United States is towards uniformity and conformity, as East and West, New England and California, rush towards each other, and those in between can only hope for salvation from nature—mountains and deserts. "This City" presents metropolitan life as a form of romantic addiction in which people are engaged in a frenetic quest for love as the only possibility of fresh life and growth; Stevenson later made the target of the poem more specific by retitling it "New York." The aversion to life in the United States and in the big city expressed in these poems marks a limit that will persist in Stevenson's work; there are forms of modernity that she cannot assimilate into

her poetry. But while England may offer an escape from modernity, it cannot ensure an escape from one's self: "The Traveller" is about coming to England, a "foreign place" where the speaker hopes to break the mold of her established sensory, cognitive, and emotional responses and to shed her ghosts; but at the end of the poem, waiting for tea in an old-fashioned English inn, she is chilled to see her specters "standing there in rows" (*Collected Poems*, p. 3). The past also haunts the poem "After a Death," later retitled "After Her Death;" this evokes the aftermath of bereavement in a way that anticipates the portrayal of Professor Arbeiter's grief following his wife's death in Stevenson's *Correspondences* (1974). But it is the present that weighs on the women in the poem of that title: "The Women" powerfully evokes the boredom and frustration of women who sit among dahlias all afternoon, waiting for their husbands to return.

Past, present, and future are all active in "To My Daughter in a Red Coat," a vivid portrayal of a small girl who, walking with her mother in the park on a late October afternoon, violates the past as she walks over the fallen leaves. It is an affectionate poem that also registers the ambivalence of parenthood as the young displace not only the old—"Those shrivelled women" who "stare / At us from their cold benches" (*Collected Poems*, p. 4)—but also their own parents, bringing intimations of mortality as well as promises of continuity. The haunting, musical line with its succession of sibilants, "Small winds stir the minor dead", comes to apply not only to nature, the breezes that lift the fallen leaves, but to the small girl's effect on those, including the woman who has borne her, who are already starting to die (*Collected Poems*, p. 4). This kind of ambivalence will be evoked more strongly in some of Stevenson's later poems. The idea that nature may echo human emotions but offer no comfort is more explicit in the most impressive poem in *Living in America*, "Sierra Nevada." In long sentences running on across lines, and interrupted by the occasional short phrase or simple sentence, the poem powerfully evokes a harsh, beautiful landscape of rocks and water that cares nothing for human beings but in which "the most difficult earth / supports the most delicate flowers" (*Collected Poems*, p. 17) and which intimates a return to a condition of primal desire prior to our social identities:

if we were to stay here for a long time, lie here

like wood on these waterless beaches,
we would forget our names. would remember that
     what we first wanted
had something to do with stones, the sun,
the thousand colours of water, brilliances, blues.

(p. 18)

Most of the poems in *Living in America* are included, with minor revisions, in Stevenson's *Collected Poems* (1996), but there are three whose omission is regrettable. "Indian Summer, Vermont," vividly conveys the persistence of summer through October and its final dissolution; in a surprising, provocative switch, the last stanza invites us to draw an analogy with the prolonged dissolution of an ancient civilization. "Mademoiselle" portrays a French teacher in Georgia who is a refugee from Nazi-occupied France and who retains, in an alien culture, her native ways and her lonely independence. "Two Kinds of Motion" compares the dome of the Capitol in Rome with the dome-like shape made by the water of the fountain in front of it: while the dome is a frozen structure within which movement can take place, the water of the fountain, in contrast, fashions a structure from movement, rising, falling and rising again. These two kinds of motion can be interpreted as a metaphor for two kinds of art, two kinds of poetry: *Living in America* contains examples of both kinds of poetry, but it is the second kind—the fashioning of structure from movement—that will increasingly become evident in the forms and themes of Stevenson's work. As X. J. Kennedy says in his introduction to *Living in America*, some of the poems in the collection—"The Traveller," for instance—employ exact rhyme schemes, but Stevenson more often does not use rhyme, and her line length is flexible.

In 1966, Stevenson moved to Glasgow with Mark Elvin, and they had two sons. Her second collection of poetry, *Reversals*, appeared in 1969, and includes slightly revised versions of a number of poems featured in *Living in America*. Of the new poems in the volume, "England" provides an interesting comparison and contrast to the title poem of her first volume: life in England does not provoke so wholesale a rejection as life in the United States does in "Living in America," but the tone of disdain and the dislike of modernity are still strongly evident: England is a "cramped corner country" (*Collected Poems*, p. 31) displaying proliferating urban ugliness; and at first it seems that only a rural England resembling the kind constructed in the early nineteenth-century paintings of John Constable can still release the poet's lyric impulse:

Ploughland where the wind throws the black soil
     loose
And horses pull clumsily as though through surf,
Or stand, hoofs clapped to the earth like bells,
Braced in their fields between churches and seagulls.

(p. 31)

Although the poem then acknowledges the possible bias of the observer—"Americans like England to live in her cameo"—it turns from the stereotype of rural England only to evoke its complementary cliché, a degraded modern England of sodium street lighting, "stunted houses," and "tiny sick shops." It is, one could suggest, the view of modern England that might be expected of a young poet brought up in twentieth-century America and exposed, as a child, to a great deal of English Victorian poetry. While there is some resemblance between "England" and C. Day Lewis' poem-sequence *The Magnetic Mountain* (1933), Stevenson seems to ignore the attempts of English poets in the 1930s, like Lewis, and in the 1950s, like Philip Larkin, to assimilate positively into their work a different kind of England, one of pylons and cooling towers as well as plowed fields and churches. It is only in her fine evocation of London in Autumn, where urban pollution produces a kind of corrupt beauty, that the poem breaks through into an engagement with modernity that is troubling but not wholly negative; it culminates in a sunset scene that is like an apocalyptic vision of William Blake revised for the later twentieth century:

September. Already autumnal.
Lost days drift under the plane trees.
Leaves tangle in the gutters.
In Greenwich, in Kew, in Hampstead
The paths are dry, the ponds dazed with reflections.

Come with me. Look. The city,
Nourished by its poisons, is beautiful in them.
A pearly contamination strokes the river
As cranes ride or dissolve in it,
And the sun dissolves in the hub of its own explo-
     sion.

(p. 32)

A closer engagement with modern England, and with its people, will develop in Stevenson's later poetry. In the poem "England," she is still—to employ the key metaphor of her next collection of poetry—traveling behind glass, the detached observer.

Other notable poems in *Reversals* include the title poem, a complex and compressed meditation on imagination, desire, and love. In its first stanza, "Reversals" evokes the way in which the human imagination can transform clouds so that they look like a range of geographical features—mountains, islands, inlets, archipelagos—and comprise an insubstantial but impressive world that offers "more than what is usually imaginary" but "less than what is sometimes accessible" (p. 20). The second stanza starts by suggesting that such shifting cloudscapes are metaphors for the imaginary objects of desire and aspiration that remain elusive and "change continually away from what they are" (*Collected Poems*, p. 20). It goes on to ask whether it might be possible for love to stabilize objects of desire and to satisfy aspiration, to transform the cloudscape into an arable landscape that, while it provides "less than what was sometimes imaginary," does deliver "more than what was usually accessible— / full furrows harvested, a completed sky" (*Collected Poems*, p. 20). The idea that reality may not fulfil the dreams of the romantic imagination but can provide its own more stable marvels is echoed in three poems that, in different ways, engage with the significance of children. "The Spirit is Too Blunt an Instrument" observes, in a loving and detailed way, the "intricate / exacting particulars" of a baby and reflects that only "the body's ignorant precision," rather than "desire or affection", could have produced them. In "Stabilities," the child is seen as giving solidity to desire and affection; as the gull is the ballast of its wing and the word is the stone of the mind, so is the child "love's flesh and bone" (*Collected Poems*, pp. 24–25). In "The Victory," the new mother's expected sense of triumph in bringing forth her small son gives way to an awareness of the power of the "Tiny antagonist," the "Scary knot of desires" whom she is compelled to love and who has ousted her from the victor's podium (*Collected Poems*, p. 25). The sense of the triumph of offspring over progenitor is echoed in "The Mother," who, ambivalently, loves her children but gives them her life to please them, a life that they must pass on but that "has never been used" (*Collected Poems*, p. 35). The contradictions of the mother in this short poem will be amplified and further explored in a number of the women who figure in *Correspondences*. Of the poems in *Reversals* that are omitted from Stevenson's *Selected Poems* and *Collected Poems*, the absence of "Fungi" is especially noticeable. "Fungi" is a powerful poem in which fungi are seen as evil excrescences that monstrously mimic the human lifecycle as they grow in a day from babies into masturbating adolescents and then into hairless and huge parasites that corrupt the rosebed. As well as its echo of William Blake's "The Sick Rose" in its closing lines, the poem calls to mind, in its overpowering imagery, the work of Sylvia Plath.

In 1974, Stevenson published *Travelling Behind Glass*, a selection of her poetry written over ten years, from 1963 to 1973. It includes six poems from *Living in America*, twenty-one poems from *Reversals*, and twelve previously uncollected poems. These are assured works that range over such topics as memory, marriage, affairs, the end of relationships, an adolescent girl's awkward relationship with her mother, and the desire for love. "Siskin" conveys, with vivid, precise economy, a moment (more exactly, two seconds) of experience in which the sight of a siskin—"*Small bird with green plumage, / yellow to green to white*"—evokes the memory of a dead father, "alive againÉ.hoping for siskins in Vermont" before—bird and father are gone (*Collected Poems*, p. 37). The central idea—one that will recur in Stevenson's elegy for her parents, "Green Mountain, Black Mountain"—is that parents may live again in those moments in which their children experience phenomena as the parents would have done when alive. In the long title poem of *Travelling Behind Glass*, a car journey becomes a metaphor for the contemplation of different possibilities of existence. As the speaker of the poem—a woman—passes through lush plains and urban overspill, she imagines the lives she might lead in those places, the possibilities of happiness that they may offer and the constraints that they may enforce. Visualizing "the woman myself" who multiplies and divides into her three children, she reflects:

How easy to accept,
be content
with her invitation . . .
They were so beautiful,
your children in the park,
rolling down that embankment
into a black knot of rhododendrons.

But how will you describe
the conspicuous hush of the suburbs
when the children have grown up and gone?
(*Collected Poems*, p. 49)

She finally reaches the wider prospect of an estuary, but she cannot shed her sense of detachment. "Travelling Behind Glass" explores, powerfully and lyrically, the tension between belonging and being apart, choosing a role in life at the cost of freedom or preserving the aloof liberty of an observer. Some aspects of "Travelling Behind Glass" are echoed in "Generations," a poem that Stevenson has herself identified as crucial in her development. In an important essay, "Writing as a Woman," collected in Stevenson's *Between the Iceberg and the Ship* (1998), Stevenson recalls how she was haunted by her own mother's image after her death from cancer in the early 1960s; she wanted both to bring her back to life so that she could speak to her, and to exorcise her. "Generations" evokes three generations of mothers, her grandmother, her mother, and herself, and three degrees of self-sacrifice, from the grandmother, with a "hurt smile under each eye," through the mother who, in silence, "suffers each child / To scratch out the aquatints in her mind," to the daughter, now herself a wife and mother, who "says 'Darling' with her teeth clenched" and cooks "fabulous lies" (*Collected Poems*, p. 38). This poem seemed to Stevenson like a breakthrough, and she feels that it was probably the seed of her next, and most substantial, work: *Correspondences*.

CORRESPONDENCES

Soon after writing "Generations," Stevenson and her husband left Glasgow to accept residency fellowships in the United States; Stevenson's was at the Radcliffe Institute for Independent Women, where she worked on *Correspondences*. As its subtitle suggests, *Correspondences* is a family history, told through a variety of documents, including newspaper obituaries, journals, and verse correspondence, that purport to be from the archive of the Chandler Family in the Chandler Memorial Library in Clearfield, Vermont. The history is a fictional one; it is not based directly on Stevenson's own family history, though there are some similarities, and she has invented all the supposed documents; but it persuades us of its plausibility and of its application, beyond the specific family in ques-

tion, to broader strands of the cultural and social development of the United States. Stevenson herself has said, in "Writing as a Woman," that *Correspondences* "was intended to be a study of puritan values in New England—of their strengths, their weaknesses, their corruption by ambition and greed" (*Between the Iceberg and the Ship*, p. 15).

Stevenson expertly and economically catches a range of tones of voice that bring each of the actors in the family history before us. The letters and other documents in the volume follow the Chandler family from the early nineteenth century to 1968, showing how a cold religious spirit becomes confused and combined with the language of materialistic commerce and how successive sons and daughters of the family, and their spouses, suffer, try to escape and fail, fall back into conformity, or die. The reader can discern both the differences between the men and women of succeeding generations and the correspondences, or patterns that repeat themselves with variations. Stevenson suggests that religion is deployed to reinforce patriarchal authority and the operations of commerce; that women are called upon to sacrifice their freedom of choice and action; and that the efforts of young adults to break away from their parents and create new lives for themselves are often thwarted. The tensions between an ideology of conformity and an ideology of individualism play through the volume. *Correspondences* has some of the fascination of a novel, or a family saga, and some of the interest of a social history; but it is, above all, a series of poems, and it is the economy, precision, rhythm, and variety of Stevenson's poetic language that gives the book its distinctive quality and its depth of implication.

Correspondences begins in 1968—the year of rebellion and near-revolution in the United States. The first document in the volume is the formal obituary, in the local newspaper, of Mrs. Neil F. Arbeiter, which praises "her selfless dedication to her country, to her church, to her family and friends" (p. 1). *Correspondences* will later reveal the more complex reality behind this image. An exchange of letters between her two daughters follows: Eden, still in Clearfield, Vermont, writes to Kay, in Hampstead, London, evoking the contents of her mother's desk, which include "correspondences, / piles of old stuff, mostly letters" (p. 2), and describing herself "reading and sorting, rereading . . . / dead evidences, a / yellowing litter of scraps scratched over with lives" (p. 3). We are then transported from the late twentieth century back to September 1829, by a letter from the Reverend Adam Chandler, recently arrived in Vermont from England, to his daughter, whose young husband has drowned in a shipwreck. It is cold with self-righteous condemnation of a rebellious daughter who had, from childhood, preferred "the precarious apartments of the world / to the safer premises of the spirit" (p. 11). This letter is immediately succeeded by one from Chandler's wife that reveals her increasing difficulties in coping with her home and family in the New World and in keeping up her own reading and self-education: her words towards the end of the letter—"My hand's gone numb. / The stove's gone out" (p. 14)—take on a more profound meaning when we find her obituary on the next page.

We move on to the next generation with a letter from Reuben, the Chandlers' prodigal son, who has run away from home and from Harvard, and who is experiencing an intense religious crisis, a kind of nineteenth-century dream vision that resembles Eliot's Waste Land: a "desert / where it spills out in miles and miles of / nothing at all" (p. 19). After this comes a letter from Reuben's sister, Elizabeth, the widow of the young minister whose drowning was received so unsympathetically by her father; she reproaches her brother for his engagement to a Southern girl and for reawakening, by his anticipation of marital bliss, the pain of her own loss. It is evident that Elizabeth's rebellion against her father has failed; that, following the death of her husband, she has submitted to his religious ideology and become conventional and pious; but her grief at her husband's death, revived by Reuben's letter, is nonetheless raw and real. The letter that follows is from Reuben Chandler's wife, Marianne, to her mother, disclosing her trials in marriage; her husband reproves her for her high spirits and demands his nuptial rights every night, insensitive to the suffering caused by her menstrual periods. Then, in one of the most remarkable sequences in *Correspondences*, we come upon the supposed remains of a journal/letter from Marianne to her husband, written in 1849 during a cholera epidemic while she was on her way by ship to New Orleans without her husband's permission—a journey during which their baby daughter died. The idea that only fragments of the journal have survived permits Stevenson to produce a kind of modernist montage, in which incomplete lines are juxtaposed to create eloquent

enjambments: each line runs on to the next in ways that produce startling, thought-provoking combinations, as in the conclusion of the poem:

> [. . .] Our dear little girl
> among the blessed, my beautiful
>   authorities let no one near.
>   darkies. I am full of
> one who was without fault and so
>   lies shrouded in my sister's
>   blame God and myself, dear
> why have you left me without support?
>   (*page torn*)
>   (p. 29)

Like his father, Reuben takes refuge from loss in self-righteous condemnation, wholly blaming his wife for the breakdown of his marriage and for his daughter's death. We then move on a decade, to read Reuben's letter to his sons studying in Europe; this shows that his youthful spiritual crisis is long behind him and that he has now reconciled Christian ethics and commercial success, advising his sons, on their return to the United States, to "follow with humble spirits and pure hearts / the peaceful ways of commerce and just economy" (p. 33). But the sons, in different ways, repeat their father's youthful rebellion. The elder son, Matthew, joins the Confederate Army in the American Civil War and identifies the soldiers of the North with his hated father; he dies of wounds in 1865. His younger brother, Jacob, goes West in 1867, and a prose extract from his journal as he journeys across Colorado records an encounter with a thirty-year-old woman who looks fifty, a wife and mother, living in a rough cabin, an image of endurance that recalls his grandmother. But Jacob's rebellion also fails in the end; he returns home to take over his father's clothing business, and, as the end of the nineteenth century approaches, it becomes clear that he has absorbed his father's fusion of Christian and commercial ideology, turning them into a set of maxims such as "Advertising . . . is a language of faith between buyer and seller" (p. 38). When he writes disapprovingly to his daughter, Maura, who is studying at Oberlin College, to reproach her for her frivolity of tone in her correspondence and her apparent neglect of her family, he tells her that her mother's "kisses were loans . . . upon interest these many long years" and that now "it is time to repay them, gracelessly, selflessly, with little acts of kindness and understanding" (p. 41).

On 1 January 1900, at the start of the twentieth century, Maura Chandler writes in her journal on the eve of her wedding. Her intention to work, write, learn, and elevate herself has been thwarted; her submissive life in marriage, loving her husband and bearing children, is about to begin. Her sense of being on the frontier between two selves is captured in the metaphor of the reflection of her face and her room in the window:

Cold. Midnight-morning.
Candlelight out in the cold.
Oval on the near side
and the far of the
mimicking window.
My face on the far side
and the near. My life.
This room that I know,
doubled also, hung
there in the snow.

So the unknown begins as
reflections of the known.
(p. 43)

Maura's husband, Ethan, echoes his father-in-law's penchant for fusing Christian and commercial imagery; in a loving letter to his wife, he styles himself "a Salesman of the Lord" (p. 47)—but he does demonstrate a genuine idealism that finds an outlet in the ethical, social, and trade union movements of the later nineteenth and early twentieth century. This letter, written in 1910, is immediately followed by a newspaper announcement of 2 June 1929—the year of the Crash—announcing his insolvency. In November of that year, he writes a letter to God in a New York hotel, recognizing his own distracted condition—"I am ill, I know, / from my own earnestness" (p. 49)—and implying the suffering of his wife, who is now "silent. / For long periods, completely silent" (p. 49).

The second part of *Correspondences* returns us to 1968. Kay feels reluctant to respond to her sister's call to return home, and she tries to explain why by invoking the figure of Persephone as a symbol of the artistically fecund woman—implicitly, Kay—who rejects the ordinary and chooses to bite into the pomegranate. This act condemns her to spend half her life in the underworld but enables her to raise "a few seeds to green / from her creative darkness." Kay compares this with the mother—by implication, her own mother—who "spat out the aching seeds" and "chose to live in the light" (p. 54). She concludes her letter by suggesting that her

mother should be left to rest now. We return to a letter of 1930 to Kay's mother from her own mother, Maura Chandler. Ruth Arbeiter is now married and living in Cambridge, England, and she also writes poetry—Maura mentions that, as the family poet, Ruth ought to know about a young man from Harvard called "Something like Lawrence Eliott"— that is, T. S. Eliot (p. 56). If one repressed aspect of Ruth is her poetic vocation, another is her love for an English novelist, Paul Maxwell, a love that exists less in the real world than in what Ruth calls, in a later letter—or, rather, a lyrical love poem, "that brighter isolate planet where we two live" (p. 63). It is not, however, a planet on which she will actually take up residence.

But a new generation of women in 1950s America starts to find the sacrifices that husband and family demand less tolerable. Kathy Chattle's letter of 1954 from a mental hospital to her mother, Ruth Arbeiter, rejects the "whole damn bore" of marriage, baby, and house but can see no alternative: "for me, what the hell else is there? / Mother, what more? What more?" (p. 70). In "Writing as a Woman," Stevenson remarks: "The hysteria at the end of this poem is one many of us felt in the 1950s and 1960s"; and "Sylvia Plath was spokeswoman for a whole generation of Kays" (*Between the Iceberg and the Ship*, p. 17). At this stage of Kay's existence, it seems that she is compelled to repeat the life of her mother, a life that has not lacked joy or value but that has entailed renunciation and frustration. Stevenson has said that she suspects that both Ruth, and Maura before her, "took the *happiest* course open to them," since Maura would not have become an outstanding writer and Ruth was better off with Professor Arbeiter than with Paul Maxwell. She also observes that neither woman "was willing to take risks, and their happiness was bordered with wistfulness, with a longing for knowledge beyond their experience" (*Between the Iceberg and the Ship*, p. 20). It should be said, however, that the writing attributed to these two women in *Correspondences* conveys a rather more intense unhappiness than that which is suggested by Stevenson's own term, "wistfulness."

The third, concluding section of *Correspondences* shows Professor Arbeiter's grief and sense of loss at his wife's death, and then introduces his son, who, like many of his contemporaries in the 1960s, and like his grandfather Jacob Chandler before him, is going West and challenging the values of acquisitiveness and duty enshrined in his family history and the history of America: "It's dangerous to live in a noose of 'I want' and 'I ought'" (p. 84). The last words of *Correspondences* are left to Kay in a letter to her father that also serves as an epilogue to the whole volume; at this point it becomes clear that "Kay" is the Kathy who, in the 1950s, saw no alternative to the asylum but conformity, but who has now reinvented herself as an independent woman and a writer, thus realizing, at last, the intellectual and creative aspirations of her own mother and of her earlier female forebears.

> That Kathy my name was, that Mrs. Frank Chattle
> died in New York of divorce.
> Kay Boyd, the woman, the writer, has survived.
>
> (p. 87)

She ends with a question that reflects not only on her own letters but on the whole text of *Correspondences*—of which, it is implied, she may be the author:

> Can these pages make amends for what was not said?
> Do justice to the living, to the dead?
>
> (p. 88)

While it may be impossible to answer those questions, it can be said that *Correspondences* was praised on its first appearance and has since become Stevenson's most admired work. She appears to concur with this judgment, as she has placed it at the end of her *Collected Poems*, as if it were a summation of all her poetry.

ENOUGH OF GREEN *AND* THE FICTION-MAKERS

STEVENSON followed up *Correspondences* with a work whose very title seemed to speak of renunciation: *Enough of Green* (1977). But in contrast to *Correspondences*, *Enough of Green* does not associate renunciation primarily with repression; it is, rather, the road to aesthetic, and perhaps spiritual, discovery. Stevenson wrote many of the poems in her fifth collection between 1973 and 1975, when she was Compton Fellow of Creative Writing at Dundee University and lived in a cottage on the Tay Estuary in Scotland, and the collection takes on the dour colors of that landscape or what she calls, in the poem "Fire and the Tide," that "mudscape" (*Collected Poems*, p. 53). The collection opens with a poem that, placed before the contents page, acquires the force of an epigraph, a preliminary statement that applies to the whole of the book. It addresses one of Stevenson's recurrent concerns: the nature of the poet and of poetry. "To Be a Poet" makes it clear that poetry is a demanding vocation: a poet must "always be alone," but must refuse the temptations of isolation—loneliness, restlessness, memory and remorse—and keep faith with silence. Such fidelity reaps its reward: an awareness of "the presence, the privilege" (*Enough of Green*, p. V). The notion of an austerity that results in clarity of vision plays through the collection: in the first poem after the contents page, the November sun on bare boughs enables us to "see what lay under / confusing eloquence of green" (*Collected Poems*, p. 52), while the final poem in the volume rejects green, yellow, and red, and arrives at black, of which "there is never enough" (*Collected Poems*, p. 52). In "North Sea off Carnoustie," the shore is marked by "an absence of trees, an abundance of lighthouses" and by "marram-scarred, sandbitten margins" that tell us this is "a serious ocean" and provide an image of transcendence: "The sea is as near as we come to another world" (*Collected Poems*, p. 53). But if one part of Stevenson is drawn to romantic isolation, another part of her is drawn to domesticity; it is characteristic that, in "North Sea of Carnoustie," the pull of "the planet ocean" is countered by a concluding image that affirms homecoming; to those returning from that planet, the lighthouses become "candles in the window of a safe earth" (*Collected Poems*, p. 53). An uneasy acceptance of domestic security—of "that four-walled chrysalis / and impediment, home"—is evident in "The Price:" "the ropes that bind us / are safe to hold" (*Collected Poems*, p. 72). In "With my Sons at Boarhills," the beach becomes both an extension of home and family and an intimation of their inevitable transience, as the mother watches her "own strange sons" and reflects on their estrangement from her: "my each child laboured from his own womb, / bringing forth, without me, men who must / call me mother, love or reassess me" (*Collected Poems*, p. 59).

Enough of Green was largely well received and strengthened the reputation that Stevenson had gained with *Correspondences*. Leaving Dundee, Stevenson became a Fellow of Lady Margaret Hall College, Oxford, from 1975 to 1977, and then a Writing Fellow at Bulmershe College, Reading, from 1977 to 1978. In 1978, she and the poet Michael Farley, whom she was to marry, founded

The Poetry Bookshop in Hay-on-Wye, on the border between England and Wales; it was a worthwhile venture though in the end it failed financially. It was at Hay that she wrote most of the poems gathered in her fourth collection, *Minute by Glass Minute* (1982). The centerpiece of the volume is the long poem "Green Mountain, Black Mountain," in which two landscapes—the Green Mountains of Vermont in the United States and the Black Mountains of Wales—become the setting for an elegy to her parents and the exploration of divisions and relations in a personal, historical and mythical sense: the relation between childhood and adulthood, between past and present, between the dead and the living, between Wales and America. By her own account, Stevenson conceived the poem in 1980, when she left Wales, where she now had her home, and spent some weeks in the Green Mountains of Vermont. The work takes a loosely musical form; Stevenson thought of it as a kind of cantata, a short choral work, and had in her mind while writing it musical notions like prelude, recitative, aria, and chorale.

The poem presents a problem for the critic, however, insofar as Stevenson herself has repudiated it, quietly omitting it from her *Selected Poems* and explicitly rejecting it, in the Preface, from her *Collected Poems* "as representing an affected, impressionistic style that I hope I have left behind me" (p. V). This is an unfair judgment. In "Green Mountain, Black Mountain," each landscape is finely evoked: the "White pine, sifter of sunlight" (*Minute by Glass Minute*, p. 21) in the New England woods; the "mud-lashed winter" (p. 22) of the Black Mountains. Both are landscapes that humans have shaped over centuries but which still remain resistant: the Green Mountains, personified, speak of the changes wrought by the early American settlers: "You brought to my furred hills / Axes, steeples" (p. 21); in the Black Mountains, steeped in myth and "word-mist," "the drenched sleep of Wales / troubles King Arthur in his cave" (p. 23). Within these long perspectives the poet recalls her own childhood; her mother, who lives on not in words but in her daughter's responses to moments of experience— a blackbird, a thrush singing, a broken branch regenerating itself in water; and her father—"your shoulders' loosened stoop to the piano, / or the length of you decanted on a chair" (p. 27). The poem concludes by bringing together nature, language and music in an astonishing affirmation:

Swifts twist on the syllables of the wind current.

Blackbirds are the cellos of the deep farms.

(p. 29)

Swifts feature dramatically in another poem in *Minute by Glass Minute*, as a symbol of romantic aspiration, evoked in rhythms that recall Gerard Manley Hopkins' "The Windhover:"

But a shift of wing, and they're earth-skimmers, daggers,
Skilful in guiding the throw of themselves away from themselves.

(p. 76)

The poem goes on to offer a parable in which, when the Great Raven created the birds, the swifts rejected rest and chose liberty—"We abhor rest . . . / Let us be free, be air!" (p.77). We find once more in Stevenson a tension between a partly romantic, partly religious aspiration to transcendence and what she sees as the demands of reality—what the swifts in her parable call "the filth of growth" (p. 74). Transcendence is desirable but unattainable: the poem concludes with the image of swifts as a "way to say the miracle will not occur, / And watch the miracle" (p. 77).

The poem "Buzzard and Alder" evokes a more attainable kind of transcendence, one that is seen in terms of the processes of change and transformation that take place in time. The glass, which in "Travelling Behind Glass" was a metaphor for separation from experience and commitment becomes, in this poem, a metaphor for the present moment, which the flow of life in time constantly transcends: buzzard and alder are seen living in a thin layer and "breaking through it minute by glass minute" (p. 75); it is only the dead, for whom time has stopped, who remain behind glass. In "If I Could Paint Essences," the desire to capture the essential, the "mudness of mud," the "cloudness of clouds" is thwarted by the way in which particular phenomena attract the eye and the mind and generate metaphor: "just as I arrive at true sightness of seeing, / unexpectedly I want to play on those bell-toned / cellos of delicate not-quite-flowering larches" (p. 74). The poem ends with an image of a reflection and a reality that is similar to the key image in Maura Chandler's verse letter on the eve of her wedding in *Correspondences*. While, in Maura's case, the image symbolizes the difference between present and future and between two identities, here it symbolizes the difference between existence and an ever-elusive essence: "the inescapable ache / of trying to catch, say, the catness of cat / as he crouches, stalking his shadow, / on the other side of the window" (p. 75). If essence is ungraspable, if the only transcendence is that of passing time, it is a transcendence that also takes away what time gives: the title of the last poem in the volume, "Transparencies," suggests the fragility of those "glass minutes," and the poem itself, taking the story on from "With my Sons at Boarhills," registers the gulf that now gapes between mother and grownup sons and evokes her desire to grasp their being as they move on through moments of time: "Oh, / it's your particular selves I need to hold / to the light as you cross the impossible lens of now / and now" (p. 92). Given Stevenson's sense that the only transcendence available to us is transience and that this brings loss with it, it is not surprising that one of the "Sonnets for Five Seasons" in *Minute by Glass Minute* praises the provisional stasis of September, a moment of rest in between extremes:

> . . . September is the wisest
> time—neither the unbearable burning word
> nor the form of it, cooped in its cold ghost.
>
> (p. 97)

In 1983, Stevenson produced "A Legacy on My Fiftieth Birthday," with due acknowledgment to the French fifteenth-century poet François Villon, author of *Petit Testament* or *Lais* (*Legacies*) and *Grand Testament*. Stevenson's verse will offers a partly light-hearted, partly serious autobiography of her growth as a poet, a roll-call of the authors who have influenced her, and her views on the current state of the poetic art. Like "Green Mountain, Black Mountain," "A Legacy" did not appear in her *Selected Poems* and was excluded from her *Collected Poems*, since it was, in Stevenson's own view, "an amusing pastiche" that had become, by the 1990s, "utterly dated" (*Collected Poems*, p. V); but it did survive to feature as the last poem in her sixth collection, *The Fiction-Makers* (1985), and aspects of it are echoed in other poems in this volume. "Making Poetry" explores the nature of poetry, defining it as "the shared comedy of the worst / blessed," while "Re-Reading Jane" prescribes Jane Austen as an antidote to feminist flatulence: "Dear votary of order, sense, clear art / and irresistible fun, please pitch our lives / out-

side self-pity we have wrapped them in / and show us how absurd we'd look to you" (*Collected Poems*, pp. 103–104).

Despite Stevenson's suspicion of literary and linguistic theory, evident in a dismissive reference to structuralism in "A Legacy," the title poem of *The Fiction-Makers* and some of the other poetry in the volume does display an awareness of the way in which reality is constructed in narrative that resembles some structuralist and post-structuralist theoretical perspectives. "The Fiction-Makers" is about writers and artists who, in the very moment of living and creating, are already turning themselves into fictions, into myths: Ezra Pound "thought he was making now, / but he was making then;" Auden and Isherwood, "stalking glad boys in Berlin," "thought they were suffering now / but they were suffering then" (p. 100). And life becoming fiction, turning into painting or prose or poetry, is a harbinger of death.

A number of poems in the volume are elegies for the dead, for instance to Elizabeth Bishop and the English poet Frances Horovitz; while "Forgotten of the Foot," omitted from the *Selected* and *Collected Poems*, is an elegy for a mining community that is dying as its mines are effaced: "They've swept up the workings / As if they were never meant to be part of memory" (p. 45). "Taking Down the Christmas Tree," also left out of the *Selected* and *Collected Poems*, presents the Christmas tree as "the victim, decked out for worship" that is "at last lost, sacrificed, / so the rite of birth can be death's from the beginning" (p. 19). Despite the evocation of Christmas, the traditional Western response to death and loss—Christianity—is only a trace, a remnant here, as it is in the poem that opens the volume. In an interview with Helena Nelson in the summer 2000 issue of *The Dark Horse*, Stevenson recalled the origin of this poem in relation to her quest for Christian faith. For a time in the early 1980s, she was keenly interested in religion and started to attend Church of England services, but she appears to have been disappointed. Later she wrote a long poem, virtually a novel, about her disappointment, but threw away all of it except for what she herself calls the "fragment" that appears in *The Fiction-Makers* under the heading "From an Unfinished Poem." In this poem, fiction is seen as taking root "in the idea of the cross" between the "horizontal" idea of event and the "vertical" idea of personality. The fragment ends by seeing the idea of sacrifice issuing in fictional rather than bodily resurrection: "In the event / the event is sacrificed / to a fiction of its having happened . . . " (*Collected Poems*, p. 99).

If mortality and loss haunt *The Fiction-Makers*, they are not the whole story. "An April Epithalamium" celebrates the rite of passage of marriage in a way that, characteristically for Stevenson, seeks to embrace both the romantic and the down-to-earth:

Marriage, you know, is not a life-long wedding,
A launching of moony pairs to pearly islands
Where love, like light, illuminates pure meaning.
For just when truth's in sight, it's time for dinner.
Or lust, thank God, corrupts pure love of language.
(p. 197)

The month of marriage in "An April Epithalamium" becomes the month of momentary rebirth in "Signs:" this poem concisely captures a moment in which the senses, dulled by age, recover their youthful keenness:

A child again, beginning again to wake up
After fifty years of change in the same circle.
By light unnerved in this eggshell air of April,
Sharp, clean, chill to the astonished nostril.
(p. 113)

While the response to *The Fiction-Makers* was mixed, it nonetheless further consolidated Stevenson's standing as a productive and competent poet. This standing was confirmed and reinforced by the publication, in 1987, of her *Selected Poems 1956–1986*. It was also in that year that she married Peter Lucas. Two years later, in 1989, another book by Stevenson was to appear that would plunge her into harsh controversy and compromise her literary reputation; it was not a collection of poems but a biography of fellow poet Sylvia Plath; ironically its title came to apply to Stevenson herself: *Bitter Fame*.

BITTER FAME *TO* GRANNY SCARECROW

IN a number of respects Anne Stevenson seemed well qualified to write a biography of Sylvia Plath. She and Plath were exact contemporaries, born in the same year; both were high-achieving students; both had experienced the contradictory pressures of 1950s and early 1960s America upon young women who wanted both to be poets and to be good wives and mothers; both had come to live in England and married Englishmen; both had borne children; both had suffered broken marriages; both had established themselves as poets on the English literary scene. But there were concerns among critics of the biography about the constraints under which Stevenson had worked; it had been Olwyn Hughes, Ted Hughes's fiercely protective elder sister, who had asked her to undertake the biography, and Stevenson herself, in an author's note at the start of the book, had stated that "Ms. Hughes's contributions to the text have made it almost a work of dual authorship. The biography also contained three substantial appendices consisting of memoirs of Plath by Lucas Myers, Dido Merwin, and Richard Murphy, nearly turning it into a work of quintuple authorship. While *Bitter Fame* was widely praised, its hostile critics, such as the writer A. Alvarez and Oxford professor John Carey, complained that most of the incidents in the book were interpreted in a way that was unfavorable to Plath and ignored other possible interpretations. Stevenson herself, however, firmly maintained that the biography was fair and accurate.

It was inevitable that the controversy over *Bitter Fame* would, at least for a time, overshadow Stevenson's own poetry and cloud critical judgments of its worth. Moreover, Stevenson seemed to provoke her critics by including a verse "Letter to Sylvia Plath" in her sixth volume of poetry, *The Other House* (1990). "The "Letter" is a complex, powerful poem, and its most frequently quoted lines indicate the discomfort that writing the biography produced in Stevenson:

Dear Sylvia, we must close our book.
Three springs you've perched like a black rook
between sweet weather and my mind.
At last I have to seem unkind
and exorcise my awkward awe.
My shoulder doesn't like your claw.
(p. 144)

The "Letter" provides a provocative critique of Plath that functions as a poetic complement to Stevenson's biography; its very form is part of that critique, with its mixture of metrical discipline—it is written in tetrameters—and an epistolary casualness unimaginable in Plath at the time of her death. But it served to reanimate a charge that had been made against Stevenson's biography: that it revealed Stevenson's envy of Plath.

A second aspect of *The Other House* that aroused negative criticism was its poems portraying Stevenson's grandchildren, "In the Nursery" and "Little Paul and the Sea," which were seen as sentimental. Clair Wills, in a *Times Literary Supplement* review (November 1990), compared them unfavorably with the visions of babies and children offered by Plath. Wills' review occasioned an entertaining correspondence in the *Times Literary Supplement* about the accuracy of Stevenson's poetic description of her baby grandson. In fairness, it needs to be stressed that these are poems about grandmotherhood, not motherhood, and they should be read in conjunction with earlier poems such as "Victory," which capture more strongly the ambivalence of maternity. Stevenson, perhaps defiantly, included both "In the Nursery" and "Little Paul and the Sea" in her *Collected Poems*.

In 1993, Stevenson brought out her ninth collection, *Four and a Half Dancing Men*. The title poem describes how a small boy tears an arm and a thigh from a troupe of five dancing men made for him by his mother out of paper and how the half-man pleases him most. The poem avoids the grandmotherly sentimentality of which Stevenson had been accused in her previous collection; and the four and a half dancing men become, in the poem, an image of the imperfect, fragile but ongoing dance of life itself. Ongoing life is also the theme of "From My Study," a poem whose long loose sentences run on over many lines, giving a sense of an inclusive tolerance as the speaker observes, with affection, amusement, and compassion, the life of a former mining community, a "Theme park / on the art of failure" whose diverse components nonetheless compose "the substance of something / people call their lives" (p. 163). If the title of "From My Study" continues to suggest a certain detachment, the poem demonstrates a more sympathetic and less stereotyped response to English life than is to be found in her earlier poem "England."

The second part of the collection, "Visits to the Cemetery of the Long Alive," offers, as its title suggests, a range of portraits of elderly people falling into bodily and mental decay. The poems present their physical and psychological distress clearly, sympathetically, and sadly, without the harshness evident in a poem such as Philip Larkin's "The Old Fools" but without any easy

consolations. But aging can bring its reconciliations: in the third part of *Four and a Half Dancing Men*, in the poem "When the Camel Is Dust it Goes Through the Needle's Eye," the poet recalls her own long-dead mother and feels that, as she herself grows older, she is coming closer to her. Other poems in the third section of the volume take up the themes of the fragility of life and of mortality: in the tightly written "Trinity at Low Tide," a transformed reflection on a beach that the sea has turned into a natural mirror is "cleansed of human overtones," turning one's face into "a travelling sun" and one's breast into "a field of sparkling shells and stones;" but there is a "third trick of light," a black shadow, "that copies you / and cancels you" (p. 174), a foreshadowing of death that echoes both the fearful shadow of Eliot's *The Waste Land* and the black ship of Larkin's "Next, Please." In "Painting It In," the effacement of features in the landscape on a misty morning, which the poem compares to a canvas on which the details have yet to be painted, lessens the sense of isolation one feels among the indifference of objects: "when things are unmade, being also feels less alone" (p. 187). The final poem in the volume, "After you left," concludes by registering the difficulty, the serendipity, of both happiness and achieved art: "About four square inches on the canvas— / that's a piece of luck" (p. 192).

Oxford University Press brought out Stevenson's *Collected Poems 1955–1995* in 1996. It was generally well received and provides an excellent selection of her work, although, as discussed earlier in this essay, the omission of some poems from her early collections and of "Green Mountain, Black Mountain" is open to question. After *Collected Poems*, Stevenson thought she had no more poetry left in her and turned to prose; *Between the Iceberg and the Ship*, in the University of Michigan Poets on Poetry series, gathers together a valuable and illuminating range of previously published essays by Stevenson on her own work, on women and poetry, and on the work of Plath, Seamus Heaney, Louis MacNeice, R. S. Thomas, and Dana Gioia. The volume concludes with a 1995 interview conducted by Richard Poole. *Five Looks at Elizabeth Bishop* comprises Stevenson's mature view of Bishop's poetry and provides an important complement to her 1966 study of Bishop.

These prose projects occupied Stevenson for two years, during which time she wrote no poetry. She had settled into what she herself described as an agreeable, grandmotherly way of life. Then, surprising herself, she wrote ten or twelve poems in North Wales, and these form the core of *Granny Scarecrow*, brought out by Bloodaxe Books of Newcastle upon Tyne in England after Oxford University Press had, controversially, closed its poetry list in 1999. By Stevenson's own account, the title poem was written at a sitting after walking past a scarecrow of the kind described in the poem—a scarecrow made from a dead grandmother's flowered print housedress nailed to a pole. At first, in a comically macabre sequence, the granddaughters, Marjorie and Emily, wave to "Granny Scarecrow" on their way to school, and she usually waves back:

> Two white Sunday gloves
> flapped good luck from the crossbar; her head's
>   plastic sack
>   would nod, as a rule.
>
> (p. 33)

But winter comes, and the scarecrow thins, decays, grows moldy; Marjorie and Emily, seeing this, tacitly agree to take another route that avoids it. The last stanza of the poem telescopes time, registering Marjorie's divorce and successful career and Emily's own accession to grandmotherhood; but "with the farm sold, none found a cross to fit their clothes when / Emily and Marjorie died" (p. 33). The poem, strikingly original in its key image, recasts familiar Stevenson themes: it becomes an elegy to the dead, an ironic image of how the dead, or their remnants, are recycled and finally effaced, and a cameo of the continuities and differences between generations. The poem is possibly also an amused comment on Stevenson's own status as a grandmother, which became a butt of mockery in some reviews of *The Other House*.

Eight poems at the start of *Granny Scarecrow*, written mainly in 1994, are linked with Stevenson's own childhood. "Going Back," for instance, evokes the "haunted erasures" and "more haunting survivals" (p. 13) of which the speaker is conscious when she returns, after forty years, to Ann Arbor, Michigan. The latter part of the volume contains an effective, thought-provoking elegy for Ted Hughes. The poet begins by mythologizing him but is interrupted by the apparent figure of Hughes himself who resists such mythologization or commemoration: "I'm . . . / an invention of my own imagination. / You'll find me in all my books. / So please, no more poems about me" (p. 66). Two especially impressive poems in the last section of the book are dramatic monologues, one by a ninety-year-old Jewish doctor dying of cancer, the other by an Italian ex-prisoner of war coming back in 1992 to the Italian chapel on the Orkney island of Lamb Holm. Such monologues, imagining and exploring the experiences of imaginary or real others, indicate a direction in which Stevenson wants to develop. Now aged sixty-seven, her poetic impulses have revived; she is working on a series of dramatic monologues by both the celebrated and the obscure of the twentieth century—such as Henry Ford and Primo Levi—who are trapped by their own expectations. The provisional title of the book is one that might equally well cover a number of Stevenson's earlier poems, not least those about women: *Prisoners*.

CONCLUSION

ANNE Stevenson is a survivor. She is strongly conscious of the way in which people can become prisoners of society and of themselves, but she also recognizes how they can endure in spite of this and can sometimes escape. She has experienced the desire for transcendence and for perfection but understands the dangers and self-deceptions that indulging this desire may involve. Her poetry is made out of her quarrel with those aspects of herself that Sylvia Plath lived out to the extreme of self-destruction. It is a quarrel evident not only in the themes but also in the very techniques and forms of her poetry: she is capable of producing formally polished poems, as in "The Traveller," and generating images of extremity, as in "Swifts"; but her poetry constantly tends toward the condition of the verse letter, that expansive epistolary form that is large enough to accommodate the detritus of human lives and disciplined enough to capture what "From My Study" calls "the marvellous / banality of seeing as it is / the on-going act" (*Collected Poems*, p. 158). Stevenson's poetry can sometimes act on the reader like Sylvia Plath's, grasping and clinging like a claw; but for the most part it is much more varied, touching us lightly, tapping us, beckoning us, taking us by the hand. Inevitably this variety means that Stevenson can sometimes slip into cliché and commonplace; but at her best she enables us to share the poetic discourse of a sensitive, intelligent, resilient, richly experienced human being as she responds to the complexities of life in the modern world.

SELECTED BIBLIOGRAPHY

I. SELECTED AND COLLECTED POEMS. *Selected Poems 1956–1986* (Oxford and New York, 1987); *The Collected Poems 1955–1995* (Oxford and New York, 1996; Newcastle upon Tyne, Eng., 2000).

II. POETRY. *Living in America* (Ann Arbor, Mich., 1965); *Reversals* (Middletown, Conn., 1969); *Travelling Behind Glass: Selected Poems 1963–1973* (London, 1974); *Correspondences: A Family History in Letters* (Middletown, Conn. and London, 1974); *Enough of Green* (Oxford and New York, 1977); *Minute by Glass Minute* (Oxford and New York, 1982); *The Fiction-Makers* (Oxford and New York, 1985); *The Other House* (Oxford and New York, 1990); *Four and a Half Dancing Men* (Oxford and New York, 1993); *Granny Scarecrow* (Newcastle upon Tyne, Eng., 2000).

III. PAMPHLETS. *A Morden Tower Reading 3* (Newcastle Upon Tyne, Eng., 1977); *Cliff Walk* (Richmond, Surrey, Eng., 1977); *Sonnets for Five Seasons* (Hereford, Eng., 1979); *Green Mountain, Black Mountain* (Boston, 1982); *New Poems* (Leamington Spa, Eng.,1982); *A Legacy* (Durham, Eng., 1983); *Making Poetry* (Oxford, Eng., 1983); *Black Grate Poems* (Oxford, Eng., 1984); *Winter Time* (Ashington, Northumberland, Eng., 1986).

IV. CRITICISM. *Elizabeth Bishop* (New York, 1966; London, 1967); *Five Looks at Elizabeth Bishop* (London, 1998).

V. SELECTED ESSAYS. *Between the Iceberg and the Ship: Selected Essays* (Ann Arbor, Michigan, 1998).

VI. UNCOLLECTED ESSAYS. "An Autobiographical Essay: The Music of the House: Scenes from Childhood," in *Poetry Review* 72, no. 3 (September 1982); "Poetry Now: A Contemporary Poet Expresses Some Views on the State of Her Art," in *Poetry Wales* 27, no. 1 (23–26 June 1991); "Anne Stevenson Reviews Anne Stevenson" (review of *The Collected Poems*), in *Rialto* 36 (Winter 1996–1997).

VII. BIOGRAPHY. *Bitter Fame: A Life of Sylvia Plath* (London and Boston, 1989).

VIII. UNCOLLECTED INTERVIEWS. "An Interview with Anne Stevenson," in *Common Ground: Poets in a Welsh Landscape*, ed. by Susan Butler (Bridgend, Mid Glamorgan, 1985); Michael O'Siadhail, "An Interview with Anne Stevenson," *Poetry Ireland Review* 26 (Summer 1989);James Roderick Burns, "Personal Artifact, Public Language: An Interview with Anne Stevenson," in *Other Poetry* 2, no. 15 (Spring 2000); Helena Nelson, "Anne Stevenson in Conversation," in *The Dark Horse* (Summer 2000).

IX. CRITICAL AND BIOGRAPHICAL STUDIES. J. E. Chamberlin, "Anne Stevenson (3 January 1933–   )," in *Poets of Great Britain and Ireland Since 1960: Part 2: M–Z*, ed. by Vincent B. Sherry, Jr., *Dictionary of Literary Biography*, vol. 40 (Detroit, 1985); Dewi Stephen Jones, "The Transitory Walker: Feelings for Continuities in the Poetry of Anne Stevenson," in *New Welsh Review* 2, part 2; Chris McCully, "Better Fame: The Poetry of Anne Stevenson," in *PN Review 91*, vol. 19, no. 5 (May-June 1993); Janet Malcolm, "Annals of Biography: The Silent Woman," parts I–3, in The New Yorker (23 and 30 August 1993); Janet Malcolm, *The Silent Woman: Sylvia Plath and Ted Hughes* (New York, 1993; with a new afterword, London, 1994); Harry Marten, "Finkel, Stallworthy, and Stevenson," in *Contemporary Literature*, 21, no. 1 (1980); Jay Parini, "The Poetry of Anne Stevenson," in *Lines Review*, no. 54 (September 1974); Jay Parini, "On Anne Stevenson," in *Ploughshares* 4, no. 3 (1978); Stan Smith, "Anne Stevenson," in *Contemporary Women Poets*, ed. by Pamela L. Shelton (Detroit, 1998); Richard Tillinghast, "Poems of Innocence and Experience," in *Michigan Quarterly Review* 37, no. 4 (Fall 1998); Clair Wills, "Plath Fare," review of *The Other House*, *Times Literary Supplement*, no. 4570 (2–8 November 1990). See also the letters from Carol Rumens, *Times Literary Supplement*, (23–29 November 1990), and from Michael Horovitz, *Times Literary Supplement*, (14–20 December 1990).

ALEC WAUGH

(1898–1981)

D. J. Taylor

ALEC WAUGH WAS a modest man. "I have no illusions about the quality of my work," he wrote in his first autobiography, *The Early Years of Alec Waugh* (1962, p. xiii). "I know myself to be a very minor writer." This is true, up to a point, and yet Waugh's substantial oeuvre—he wrote over fifty books in a career that edged into its seventh decade—is of more than passing interest to any student of the twentieth-century literary scene. Waugh's two best-known novels—*The Loom of Youth* (1917) and *Island in the Sun* (1956)—were separated by an interval of nearly forty years. He supported himself by his pen for the whole of his adult life. In the course of a cosmopolitan existence that took in two world wars and extensive foreign travel, he was the friend, if not the confidante, of a vast array of modern literary figures. His career, in fact, is a triumph of persistence—the resourceful literary man's ability to carve out a niche, or rather a series of niches, for himself in an ever-changing marketplace.

EARLY LIFE

ALEXANDER Raban Waugh was born in Hampstead, London, on 8 July 1898, the elder son of Arthur Waugh, the literary critic and publisher, and the elder brother of the novelist Evelyn Waugh. The Waughs were lowland Scots who had migrated south in the early part of the nineteenth century. Helped by his kinship with the influential critic Edmund Gosse, Arthur Waugh had become a successful literary journalist—his essay "Reticence in Literature" was a highlight of the first *Yellow Book*—before, in 1904, being offered the managing directorship of the publishing firm of Chapman and Hall. There were also Pre-Raphaelite links: two Waugh cousins had successively married the painter Holman Hunt. The Chapman and Hall connection was central to Waugh's early progress as a writer, providing him with employment for nearly a decade and giving

him an entrée into an influential circle of interwar literary figures. From the moment his first novel was accepted by Grant Richards in 1917, he was launched on what was effectively the family trade.

The dominant influences on Waugh's early life were, pre-eminently, his father and, running the former a very close second, his schooling. Arthur Waugh idolized his elder son, whose thrice-yearly return from boarding school was marked by a banner proclaiming, "Welcome to the heir of Underhill" (the name of the family house in Golders Green). Alec reciprocated this affection, spending long hours in his father's study listening to Arthur Waugh reciting poetry, writing to him on a daily basis when the two were apart, and, twenty years after his death, dedicating *The Early Years of Alec Waugh* to his father's memory "with a love that the years have deepened." At the same time, the experience of being at an English boarding school in the years immediately before the First World War left an indelible mark both on his mental outlook and his voluminous writings. Waugh was sent to Sherborne in Dorset at the age of thirteen. From the outset he embraced its routines and rituals with an almost religious enthusiasm. Team games, sporting "colours," the exercise of petty authority—all these Waugh relished with an intensity that an early-twenty-first-century observer may find faintly bewildering. "The life of a public schoolboy is essentially dramatic" he later wrote (*Early Years*, p. 29). Elements of this drama colored at least three of his novels and an early work of nonfiction, *Public School Life* (1922). Even friendly reviewers occasionally wondered at the depth of this fixation, while to a hostile critic such as Wyndham Lewis, whose *Doom of Youth* (1928) contains a bitter attack on Waugh, it provided a handy supply of free ammunition. "If I had to say what I thought of the strange case of Alec Waugh," Lewis wrote, somewhat cryptically, "I should say that the feminine maternal elements were excessively developed in him and of course being a man were thwarted.

They relieve themselves by means of these incessant literary compositions about small boys with sooty faces and bulging pockets" (*The Best Wine Last: An Autobiography through the Years 1932–1969*, 1978, pp. 11–12). Waugh, taking this as an imputation of homosexuality, brought an action for libel, though the case was settled out of court.

THE LOOM OF YOUTH

IN fact, Lewis had a point about the sooty-faced small boys. He also—as Waugh well knew—had a point about the homosexuality. As a mature man Alec Waugh was an energetic womanizer, but his early passions, not uncommon among boys of his generation placed in the hothouse atmosphere of a public school, were expended on members of his own sex. This, at any rate, is the background to *The Loom of Youth,* a novel which one contemporary critic characterized as likely to become "the *Uncle Tom's Cabin* of the public school system" (*Early Years,* p. 48). But there were other factors at work. Waugh spent the last Tuesday of July 1914 with his father watching a cricket match between the counties of Kent and Surrey at Blackheath in Southeast London. The outbreak of the First World War was only a few days away, and the match was interrupted by a stream of telegraph boys bringing call-up papers to the players. Waugh believed that "for me, as for many thousand others, boyhood ended on that grey July evening" (*Early Years,* p. 56). He returned to Sherborne eager to enjoy the advantages of premature seniority—most of the older boys were instantly called up for military service—but conscious that what he most wanted to do was to fight in France.

At this point the minimum age for enlistment was seventeen. Waugh left school a year later, having been detected in a homosexual escapade. This, and a great deal else, is faithfully reproduced in *The Loom of Youth.* Waugh's attitude to English public school life, as represented in his autobiographical writings, was relatively complex. Outwardly no one could have believed more in its hierarchies and observances. At the same time he had a rebellious streak and spent his last years at school operating a kind of guerrilla war against authority. Above all, perhaps, he believed that conventional attitudes toward public schools were hypocritical and ignored the inevitable consequences of keeping several hundred adolescent boys on the same premises for eight months of the

year. The particular myth he was concerned to expose found its deepest expression in Rudyard Kipling's story *The Brushwood Boy,* a stirring tale of schoolboy purity and fair-mindedness, which, Waugh knew, bore no relation to the realities of public school life.

The overriding complaint lodged by Waugh's alter ego "Gordon Carruthers" is that the public school system retarded the intellectual and emotional growth of exceptional boys by its insistence on making them conform. As Gordon reflects:

The average person comes through all right. He is selfish, easy-going, pleasure-loving, absolutely without a conscience, for the simply reason that he never thinks. But he is a jolly good companion; and the Freemasonry of the Public School is amazing. No man who has been through a public school can be an outside. . . . Very few Public School men ever do a mean thing to their friends. And for a system that produces such a spirit there is something to be said after all. But for the boy with a personality school is very dangerous.

(*The Loom of Youth,* p. 80)

Waugh's moral lapses having been detected, the Sherborne authorities treated him with a certain amount of tact. He was not expelled from the school, but told that it would be better if he left at the end of summer 1915. In any case he was anxious to join the war effort. September found him enrolled in the Inns of Court Officer Training Corps and embarking on a stretch of military training that led, in August 1917, to his departure to northern France as a second lieutenant in the Dorset Regiment. This period had important consequences. On the one hand, it allowed him to complete *The Loom of Youth,* which was finished by the spring of 1916. On the other, it involved a temporary posting at Berkhamstead, Hertfordshire, where he met and formed an attachment to Barbara Jacobs, the daughter of his father's friend W. W. Jacobs, at that time possibly the most successful writer of short stories in England.

After several rejections, *The Loom of Youth* was accepted by the small and precariously financed firm of Grant Richards. It was published in summer 1917, a few days before Waugh took ship for Flanders, to a chorus of acclaim and also a great deal of hostility. Looking back at the book over eighty years after its first appearance it is difficult to imagine what the fuss was about. As a lightly disguised account of Waugh's four years at Sherborne, its criticisms of a way of life and an institution which Waugh had largely relished were correspondingly mild. Similarly, the homosexual episode was so discreetly framed that a modern reader could pass by unaware that it had happened. At the time, though, this was incendiary stuff. Waugh later noted his good luck at having, by chance, produced a novel that reflected, however indirectly, a shift in public feeling. By this point the First World War, begun three years before on a tide of optimism, was bogged down in stalemate. A book that criticized the educational methods used to train its officer class was guaranteed an appreciative audience. It was also guaranteed a large number of detractors. In fact, the book created a sensation. It was denounced from pulpits and in school assemblies. Its admirers included H. G. Wells and Arnold Bennett. The latter wrote to Arthur Waugh: "I think it is a staggering performance. . . . I am not particularly interested in the public school altercation and I don't much care whether the institution . . . can successfully survive your son's presentation of it or not. What interests me is the very remarkable narrative gift of this man" (*Early Years*, p. 116). Waugh remembered reading this letter in his forward position on the western front, where the mail was brought up each evening by mule carrier.

As a junior officer attached to the Machine Gun Corps, Waugh fought in the Flanders offensive of autumn 1917, seeing service at the battles of Passchendaele and Ypres. In March 1918 his unit was caught north of Arras behind a counterattack. He was captured, and spent the remainder of the war in an officers' prisoner of war camp at Mainz. The seven months spent behind barbed wire were a formative experience: Waugh later referred to it as his "equivalent for a university" ("The University of Mainz," in *My Brother Evelyn and Other Profiles*, 1967, p. 74) Conditions in the camp were relatively civilized, and an alcove was reserved for "authors, architects and other students." Waugh's fellow students included the biographer Hugh Kingsmill and Gerald Hopkins, the translator of Fran≤ois Mauriac. It was here, too, that he discovered many of the classics of modern continental literature: Gustave Flaubert, Honoré de Balzac, Anton Chekhov, Ivan Turgenev, and Fyodor Dostoyevsky (*Early Years*, p. 131). *The Prisoners of Mainz* (1919) is a record of this period in his life.

Waugh was released shortly after the November 1918 armistice and returned to England. At twenty, and already engaged to be married to Barbara Jacobs, he was aware that the future he had mapped out for himself four years before would have to be substantially readjusted. University, where in normal circumstances someone of his background would have spent the next three years, held little appeal to a man who had seen military action and written a best-selling book. He was anxious both to marry Barbara and develop his career. Accordingly, Waugh fixed his marriage date for July 1919 and was inducted into Chapman and Hall in the post of "literary adviser," with a brief to introduce younger writers to the firm. Each of these moves, he soon came to realize, was a serious mistake. The marriage to Barbara Jacobs, two years younger than her very youthful husband, was never consummated. As Waugh delicately phrased it in his memoirs, "I had been nicknamed Tank at Sandhurst, yet I could not make my wife a woman." (*Early Years*, p. 156). It broke up in 1922. Meanwhile, Waugh found the atmosphere at Chapman and Hall, where he spent most of his time reading unpublishable manuscripts, unexpectedly dull. Worse, it prevented him from getting on with his own work. Eventually he opted for part-time employment, spending Mondays and Fridays in the firm's offices at Henrietta Street, Covent Garden, and the rest of the week at his desk.

EARLY WRITINGS

WAUGH'S early work, written in the period from 1920 to 1925, is undistinguished. There were good reasons for this. *The Loom of Youth*, as Waugh well knew, was a one-off book, an "issue" novel attacking a particular institution, whose particular focus, if not its setting, could not be repeated. Throughout the early 1920s, consequently, he was an author struggling to find a subject. He was also a young man of vigorous and wide-ranging enthusiasms. These included sports, social life, and sex. Though short in stature and prematurely bald (his brother's college friends nicknamed him "The Baldhead"), Waugh was a success with women. His autobiographical writings are strewn with accounts of his exploits in what he somewhat quaintly termed "gallantry" or "dalliance." Once his marriage to Barbara Jacobs was judged indisputably to have failed, he set about enthusiastically making up for lost time. None of this, inevitably, was conducive to the production of great works of literature. As a teenager, Waugh had fancied himself a poet, but after an early volume (*Resentment*, 1918) produced nothing else in this line. Two other novels, *The Lonely Unicorn* (1922; published in the United States as *Roland Whately* the same year), and *Card Castle* (1924), sank without trace, along with a collection of stories, *Pleasure* (1921). There were other, miscellaneous volumes: the prisoner of war book *Public School Life: Boys, Parents, Masters* (1922) and a youthful autobiography, *Myself When Young: Confessions* (1923), transparently influenced by George Moore. Sales and critical reception were modest. Waugh later acknowledged at this point in his career his friends would have been entitled to write him off as a one-book man.

However, these were far from being wasted years. As a London "bachelor," inhabiting a flat in Kensington and dividing his week between Henrietta Street and the Hertfordshire Inn where he went to write, and accepting any invitation that he received, Waugh was able to worm his way into most of the citadels of interwar British literary life. Through his father he came across many of the writers published by Chapman and Hall: Gilbert Cannan, W. L. George, E. Temple Thurston, and Desmond Coke. He was a friend of Sir John Squire, editor of the *London Mercury*, Oscar Wilde's man-about-town son Vyvyan Holland, and the novelist and reviewer Ralph Straus, and on nodding terms with contemporary celebrities such as Hugh Walpole. Through Harold Monro and his Poetry Bookshop he met T. S. Eliot and the Sitwells. Eighty years later many of the "Georgian" writers with whom Waugh was associated have faded into obscurity, but at the time these were influential connections.

In 1925 Waugh's fortunes took a turn for the better, with the appearance of his fourth novel, *Kept*. This was a considerable departure from what had gone before and marked the first appearance of something resembling thematic unity in Waugh's fiction: "a group of post-war characters, most of whom were kept in a different way, living on the past, on capital, on a title, on a reputation won during the war; with the figure of England herself in the background living on the triumphs of the eighteenth and nineteenth centuries" (*Early Years*, p. 207). Something of the novel's symbolism can be detected in its hero, to whom Waugh gave the less than plausible name of "Ransom Heritage." At the same time, *Kept* offered a moral dilemma, or rather a moral process, that became central to

much of Waugh's mature fiction: the tracking back of the steps whereby someone who has started out with more or less honorable intentions finds him- or herself in a situation where he or she is forced to act dishonorably. Here the subject is a war widow, supported by a man whom she believed would soon be free to marry her. Discovering that she is mistaken, the woman drifts into a romance with Heritage, an idle man-about-town who has lost whatever ambition he once possessed during the war, wants no stake in the future, and intends to spend the rest of his life pleasing himself.

With its unvarnished presentation of a group of people who had lost their bearings in the postwar world, *Kept* clearly reflected Waugh's own disillusionment with the England of the 1920s. Looking back on his early life from the vantage point of the 1960s, he was careful not to overplay this feeling of personal malaise, while acknowledging that his habitual round of pleasure-seeking was balanced by definite unease. Waugh had fought in Flanders with the hope of a better postwar world. This hope had not been realized. The old men, as he put it, were still in the saddle and England was far from being the "land fit for heroes" promised by wartime propaganda. At this time most of the opposition to postwar social agendas, and to the conduct of the war itself, came from the Left. Waugh, seeing himself as part of a generation of traditionally minded young men disillusioned by the experiences of their early manhood, took a rather different line:

We had found ourselves with a part of ourselves out of sympathy with the left-wing movement with whose interests we had thought ourselves allied. They had been so smug, so self-righteous, those non-combatants exchanging anecdotes about their C. O. [Conscientious Objector] gaol experiences in Dartmoor, and with a part of ourselves we had found ourselves in sympathy with the conservative elements to whom we had fancied ourselves implacably opposed; they were stubborn and reactionary, with closed minds, but they were honest men and they had fought in Flanders.

(*Early Years*, p. 213)

All this, as Waugh acknowledged, scarcely amounted to a loss of faith, but it did mean that as the 1920s wore in he became increasingly discontented, restless, bored with his career as a novel-writing, article-scribbling young man about literary London, and on the lookout for fresh horizons.

ALEC WAUGH

THE WANDERING YEARS

To the English writer of the interwar years, "fresh horizons" invariably meant foreign travel. The period from 1920 to 1939 was the great age of the young man's travel book, with writers such as Robert Byron, Peter Fleming, Graham Greene, and Waugh's younger brother Evelyn making distinctive contributions to the genre. Waugh's initial involvement came about almost by accident. Staying with the novelist G. B. Stern on the Italian Riviera, he had found himself discussing Somerset Maugham's short story "The Fall of Edward Barnard," in which a young American sails to the South Seas with the aim of earning enough money to support his fiancée, only to end up raising coconuts in Tahiti in the company of his native mistress. All this, the two agreed—if not with complete seriousness—sounded highly alluring. Why not quit the rat race and practice one's art at a more leisurely pace in Tahiti? Unfortunately, Stern's husband sent an account of this conversation to a newspaper gossip columnist. Shortly afterward readers of the *Daily Graphic* were informed that Mr. Alec Waugh was leaving for the South Seas. Waugh later used this episode as a humorous opening to lectures, alleging that he bought his round-the-world ticket from the French Messageries Maritime shipping line in "self-defence," but the apparent frivolity of the circumstances in which he threw up his London life marked a deeper sense of purpose.

The London flat was disposed of. Chapman and Hall granted him a year's leave of absence. Trying to fix on the main achievement of his seven-year stint in Henrietta Street from the vantage point of his early sixties, Waugh settled on what at the time was a fairly minor event. During the 1920s the firm issued an annual collection of short fiction called *Georgian Stories*. The task of editing the 1926 volume fell to Waugh. In it he included "The Balance" by his twenty-two-year-old brother, thereby launching Evelyn's career as a professional writer.

ALEC AND EVELYN

THIS is as good a place as any to consider the relationship between the brothers Waugh. *The Best Wine Last: An Autobiography through the Years 1932–1969*, Alec Waugh's final volume of autobiography, prints a fragment found amongst Evelyn Waugh's papers after his death in 1966 and intended for his own second volume of memoirs, the incomplete—in fact scarcely begun—sequel to *A Little Learning* (1964). Here Evelyn poked a good deal of fun at his elder brother while acknowledging a genuine debt. "His later years have been spent among the palms of the Mediterranean, the Pacific and the Caribbean," Evelyn wrote. "They have been illuminated, I believe, by love affairs with ladies of a great variety of ages, race and appearance. It may well be that in contrast the early 1920s seem to him drab" (p. 309–310). Nevertheless, his younger brother regarded him as a sophisticated figure:

To me he was someone who owned Havelock Ellis's *Studies in the Psychology of Sex*, in which I lubriciously browsed, as a host who introduced me to the best restaurants in London, on whom I sponged, bringing my friends to his flat and, when short of money, sleeping on his floor until the tube opened when I would at dawn sway home to Hampstead among the navvies setting out for their day's work. . . . I have seldom shared his tastes either in friends or in women. My heart sinks when a new acquaintance introduces himself as a friend of Alec's. But in the years of my poverty and obscurity I was constantly at his table.

(*Best Wine Last*, pp. 309–310)

The two brothers enjoyed a complex relationship in which envy, suspicion, admiration, and family loyalty each played a part. Evelyn's diary for 1920 notes the varying family reactions to a piece of juvenilia on which he was then engaged: "Alec apprehensive of a rival, Mother of my ruin through becoming a public figure too soon. Father rather likes it" (*The Diaries of Evelyn Waugh*, p. 108). On a fundamental level, Alec's nursery dominance and the favoritism shown to him by their father always rankled with Evelyn. The letters of his maturity are strewn with vaguely critical references to his elder brother. "What does 'anal retentive' mean?" he is once supposed to have inquired of a friend, this Freudian catchphrase having come his way. When told what it meant, he commented: "Then I have an anally retentive brother." On book jackets he frequently described himself as the younger brother of "Alec Waugh, the popular novelist," in feline disparagement of what he assumed to be Alec's potboiling trifles. Several of his novels, too, contain glancing little references that would only be intelligible to Alec's eye: casting Brideshead in *Brideshead Revisited* (1945) as a member of a ceremonious gentleman's dining club not unlike the "Sette of Odde Volumes," of which Alec was an enthusiastic ornament.

For his own part, Alec combined unswerving loyalty to his brother's reputation—he regarded him as the greatest English novelist of the age and gave evidence on his behalf in a celebrated 1950s court case in which Evelyn successfully sued the *Daily Express* for libel—with an occasional mild resentment of these slights. As his autobiographical writings show, he was not above getting a bit of his own back—casting doubts on his younger brother's pretensions as a wine buff, for example. In practical terms, Alec's influence on his younger brother's life was considerable. Quite apart from printing his first published story, he may also have introduced him to his first wife, Evelyn Gardner. In later life the two saw much less of each other—"I should doubt if we have met twenty times in the last twenty years" Alec wrote in 1962 (*Early Years,* p. 216) —although they corresponded about family matters. Something of their temperamental differences can be glimpsed in a minor disagreement over Alec's habit in later life of receiving the sacrament at an Anglican church in Tangier, where he was then living, despite his lack of religious belief. Alec could not understand his brother's pointing out—Evelyn was a devout Catholic—that this would give great offence to genuine believers.

Much of this, though, lay in the future. For the remainder of the 1920s Waugh lived a vagrant existence, travelling to what at that stage were far-flung locations—his destinations included the South Sea Islands, North America, and the Far East—and luxuriating in the orbit of a married American woman ("Ruth" in his autobiographical writings) with whom he was conducting a high-octane affair. The story of this relationship was told—heavily disguised and with the setting altered from Tahiti to the South of France—in his 1931 novel *So Lovers Dream* (published in the United States as *That American Woman*). Professionally, these years were a crucial stimulus to Waugh's career. He visited the West Indies, which provided a subject for a travel book, *The Coloured Countries* (1930). Retitled *The Hot Countries* for American publication, the book achieved a wide circulation in America as a selection of the Literary Guild. New York, where Waugh now began to spend long periods of time, was a congenial environment. *The Early Years of Alec Waugh* ends with him admiring the towers of Manhattan in the knowledge that "This was to be my city soon" (p. 308).

THE THIRTIES

FOR Waugh the 1930s were dominated by two events: the discovery of America, both as a setting for his work and a place in which he could market it, and his second marriage to Joan Chirnside. This does not mean that the wider currents of the decade of Hitler, Stalin, and Mussolini passed him by. In fact, Waugh's sense of political awareness, though not fashionable in the manner of, for example, W. H. Auden, Stephen Spender, and Christopher Isherwood, was no less acute. Like many of his more left-wing contemporaries he spent some weeks in Russia in the mid-1930s, unimpressed with what he saw, and contributed, neutrally, to Nancy Cunard's celebrated pamphlet *Authors Take Sides on Spain*. Still it would be wrong—absurdly wrong—to characterize Waugh as a writer with any kind of large-scale political vision. As a professional operator his eye was on America rather than on the events unfolding in continental Europe, and the concerns of his characters tended to be narrowly domestic. His own view of the decade, represented by later commentators as a single stretch of time in which the same dilemmas and anxieties dominated, was that it divided into four distinct periods: two years of depression, culminating, in Britain, with the election of a "National Government" at the end of 1931; a period of recovery and relative prosperity when Adolph Hitler's rise was something that was happening elsewhere; the onset of the Spanish Civil War, which began in March 1936, and an awareness of the powerful forces marshaled behind it; and a definite "prewar" period running up to the summer of 1939.

It would be difficult to claim that any deep consciousness of these historical shifts is present in Waugh's work. All the same, Waugh had read his Auden, he had younger, left-wing friends—in particular the novelist Arthur Calder-Marshall and his wife Ara—and his writings reflect some of this changing outlook. One of his better books from this period, *Thirteen Such Years* (1932), is a direct response to the panic of Britain's retreat from the gold standard and the consequent political crisis, ended by the election of a "National Government" headed by the Labor Party prime minister Ramsay Macdonald. A woven together miscellany of short stories and comment, the work was intended to show "the transition of English life from the excitement of the Armistice celebrations to the

General Election of 1931" (*A Year to Remember*, p. 184). It concludes with an imaginary, and intensely symbolic, character sketch of an expatriate Englishman living in the South of France—a man gassed in the First World War who had been forced to go abroad for medical reasons but now thinks it his "duty" to return to England. Inevitably, the London fogs are too much for his damaged lungs.

Waugh's second marriage made a considerable difference to him financially. His new wife, the daughter of an Australian business magnate named Andrew Chirnside, was a wealthy woman in her own right, still more so on her father's death, which brought her an inheritance of $1.5 million. By the standards of the 1930s this was a substantial sum. The Waughs set up house together in some style, at first in Kent, then at a property called Edrington on the Hampshire/Berkshire border. They had three children: Andrew, Veronica, and Peter. Though Waugh appreciated the change in his circumstances he was made uneasy by this new mode of life. He missed the excitement of London and what he considered to be its beneficial effect on his work. However, the product of his first spell as a country gentleman, a long "cradle-to-grave" novel, *The Balliols* (1934), was a best-seller on both sides of the Atlantic. Still, though, Waugh was dissatisfied, wondering what had happened to the old Alec Waugh who only a few years before had sped round the world writing his books on the hoof and making assignations in Tahiti. The cure for his restlessness was a series of visits to America. Encouraged by his American agent, the legendary Carol Hill, Waugh spent the rest of the decade breaking into the lucrative American magazine market. This was unusual for an Englishman. So, too, was his acceptance into the close-knit circle of writers and cartoonists employed by the *New Yorker,* a group that included John O'Hara, Dorothy Parker, Charles Addams, and James Thurber. The editors of *Redbook* and *Cosmopolitan,* both of which commissioned his short fiction at this time, valued him for his ability to make use of English and European settings in which sophisticated American readers could feel interested: Ascot, the Oxford and Cambridge Boat Race, the Eton and Harrow cricket match at Lord's. The brief, Waugh recalled, was, "Give us something our own writers can't" (*Best Wine Last,* p. 85). "It Happened in 1936" (1937), for example, involved a transatlantic flight that Waugh himself had taken on the Hindenburg airship. Waugh devised a plot in which an American couple quarrel on a trip to London. She catches the boat to New York, but by crossing on the Hindenburg the husband is able to arrive at the docks to greet and reconcile her.

Waugh's late 1930s magazine work—examples, including "It Happened in 1936," can be found in *Eight Short Stories* (1937)—is very much of its time. Other books from this period include *Jill Somerset* (1936), an attempt to reprise the formula established by *The Balliols,* and *Going Their Own Ways* (1938), an examination of contemporary attitudes to marriage seen through several different groups of characters, with which Waugh himself was unhappy. Part of the problem, perhaps, was his unwillingness to shake the habit of re-using old material that had not previously appeared in book form: the novel weaves together several stories that had already had an airing in magazines. Reaching his fortieth birthday in July 1938, Waugh was conscious that, both professionally and personally, he was at a low ebb. The time spent in America was putting a strain on his marriage. Joan disliked Americans. Presumably she distrusted even more her husband's constant affairs with American women. As a novelist, such creative powers as he possessed seemed to have dried up. Sitting in a public library in the West Indies late in 1938 he chanced upon an almanac which contained a discussion of the year's literature. The references to himself were unflattering. By his own account Waugh wondered whether this might not be a good time to give up the life of literature altogether, go back to England, and become a full-time village squire.

CAREER BREAK

REJUVENATION lay at hand—in the short term via another trip to New York, in the long term by way of the career break offered by the Second World War. Reflecting on his life at a dinner given by his English publishers to mark his seventy-fifth birthday, Waugh attributed his literary longevity to his date of birth. Only a man born between November 1894 and November 1899, he calculated, would be old enough to have fought in the First World War and young enough to have served in the Second—both experiences that Waugh considered vital to his professional development. The First World War gave him the chance to command men in battle and, as a novelist, allowed him a four-year start on his rivals. Then, twenty years later, at exactly the point where he felt his creative juices were drying up, its successor offered him a six-year "breather" and a number of postings he could make use of in his work.

After demobilization from his first stint of military service, Waugh had kept his name on the Army Reserve—a list of persons with military experience to whom the government could turn in times of national emergency. This meant that, unlike many of his contemporaries (for example, his brother Evelyn) he was called up in the very early days of the Second World War. His wife, fearing food shortages, took their children to Australia for the duration. However, as a forty-one-year-old second lieutenant, Waugh presented a problem to his superiors. Too old for front-line combat, he was a difficult man to place in the inchoate backroom hierarchies. While attempts were made to find him something to do, he reverted to the routines learned two decades before and used what little time he had available in the intervals of training to write a novel. The result, *No Truce with Time* (1941), was another example of Waugh's fascination—it went back to *Hot Countries* ten years before—with the West Indies. Featuring a young, bored planter's wife who gets entangled with a young visiting Englishman, the novel is in many ways a preliminary sketch for *Island in the Sun*.

Eventually, for the second time in his life, Waugh was sent to join the British Expeditionary Force (BEF) in France, as an intelligence officer attached to the General Staff. His chief duty was to write morale-boosting articles and short stories which it was supposed would ultimately appear in French newspapers and magazines. Within a few months, however, following the German onslaught on the Maginot Line, the BEF was in sharp retreat. Holed up in a seafront hotel, Waugh witnessed the bombing of Boulogne, which he considered far worse than anything he had seen twenty years before. He escaped across the English Channel. Among the many literary memorials to the London of the Blitz—they include the novels of Evelyn Waugh and Anthony Powell and Henry Green's account of life in the Auxiliary Fire Service—Waugh's contribution, given in *The Early Years of Alec Waugh,* is well worth reading. As ever, he was involved in a passionate love affair with a much younger woman. By now attached to an organization concerned with "petroleum warfare," he was also trying to relaunch his military career. Later he was posted to the Middle East, at first to Cairo, subsequently to Beirut and Syria, ending up in Baghdad where he worked once more in military intelligence. In all, he was away for nearly four years. The experience produced two books: the autobiographical *His Second War* (1944), written—unusually for a book of this kind—in the third person, and, much later, the novel *The Mule on the Minaret* (1965), which, although its hero is a university professor, makes direct use of many things Waugh had witnessed, including espionage techniques and the interrogation of witnesses.

POSTWAR LIFE

As one of the oldest soldiers to have served in the Second World War, Waugh was "demobbed" immediately after it ended. What by this stage in his life had become a kind of homing instinct took him to New York, where there was money waiting from the sale of a couple of magazine stories and the film rights to *No Truce with Time,* which under current British law could not be transferred to the United Kingdom. Indeed, Waugh's decision, made a few years later, to become a "resident alien" of the United States—spending ninety days in England and thereby evading its tax laws—was partly brought about by the punitive currency regulations of the postwar years, which effectively meant that he had to spend his American earnings in America.

Meanwhile, for all the rejuvenative effect of his mid-career break, he was conscious that relaunching himself in a literary marketplace from which he had been six years absent would take perseverance. Professionally, the next ten years were the worst of his life. Initially, Waugh intended to pick up where he had left off—writing short stories for American magazines such as *Redbook* and *Cosmopolitan,* which would subsidize the peripatetic but increasingly American-based lifestyle he enjoyed. After an eighteen-year marriage, he was divorced from Joan Chirnside in 1950 on grounds of "incompatibility," but they remained friends. There were also novels, but these were difficult times even for established writers: paper was short, and *Unclouded Summer,* finished not long after the war's end, was not published until the end of 1948. Its successor, *Guy Renton* (1953), an ambitious novel of London life, took a further five years. To add to these tribulations, Waugh knew that he was losing the knack of writing short stories. The early 1950s, consequently, marked a descent into less elevated marketplaces: a life of Thomas Lipton, the founder of the firm of tea-merchants-cum-grocers that bears his name (*The Lipton Story: A Centennial Biography,* 1950) and a history of Gilbeys, the British wine company. Waugh later wrote several other books of this sort.

Though the Lipton assignment was attended by a certain amount of razzmatazz, these were not exalted commissions. Now in his mid-fifties, Waugh was faced with the uncomfortable realization that most of his bridges were burnt. He had divorced his wife and transferred himself to America:

I had no wish to marry again. . . . I was a born bachelor. I wanted to be alone to write. I could never be a satisfactory husband. In the last analysis I came to Reno (a favorite spot for the filing of American divorce petitions) because I wanted to clear my decks, to stand on my own feet as an emigrant alien of the United States though still a loyal subject of the British Crown."
(*Best Wine Last,* p. 249)

Once there, he found his income sharply reduced. According to his memoirs, Waugh, feeling that he was losing his self-respect, came close to suicide at this point. He had hoarded a bottle of barbiturates and planned to do away with himself on an obscure tropical island to minimize the embarrassment to family and friends. In the end he avoided this fate. "Circle of Deception," the last short story he ever wrote, was bought by Twentieth Century Fox early in 1953. The money kept Waugh for nearly two years and gave him the time to lavish on what turned out to be the most significant project of his career.

ISLAND IN THE SUN

READ nearly half a century after its first appearance, *Island in the Sun* may seem not much more than an averagely good commercial novel of the immediately postwar period. At the time, though, it created an extraordinary fuss. In fact the novel was a publishing phenomenon: one of the first books whose best-seller status seemed to be assured before a single copy had left the warehouse. From Waugh's point of view the runaway success of *Island in the Sun* was a tale of high drama. Not only was it written at a low point in his career, but the latter stages of the book's composition—undertaken at the Mac-Dowell Colony in New Hampshire—coincided with the start of perhaps the most substantial relationship of his life, with the American novelist and children's writer Virginia Sorensen. Though the manuscript—nine hundred pages long and markedly more ambitious in scope than anything Waugh had previously written—failed to impress his British agent, it was seized upon enthusiastically by his American publishers. Holidaying in the South of France, Waugh found himself bombarded with telegrams, each announcing a further lucrative prepublication deal: magazine serializations, a Book of the Month Club purchase, and finally the acquisition of the film rights by Darryl F. Zanuck. Once published, the book was a substantial best-seller. In all, Waugh must have made half a million dollars from it: an extraordinary sum by the standards of the time, and one which gave him financial security for the rest of his life.

Island in the Sun assembles many of Waugh's favorite preoccupations: murder, adultery, closely observed social interaction, racial tension. Its West Indian setting mined a vein apparent in his work since his fictionalized history of piracy, *No Quarter* (published in the United States as *Tropic Seed,* 1932). Essentially, the novel consists of five interrelated elements. In the first, a woman who kills a man by mistake—he hits his head on a table edge when struck by her during the course of an argument—decides not to inform the police. The second strand involves a young American from the South who falls in love with the daughter of a West Indian planter, who discovers that she has "coloured" blood. A third takes in a man's suspicion of his wife's adultery. To these domestic melodramas, Waugh added two more general plot lines: the appointment of a controversial new governor and a reactionary planter who tries to discredit a young colored agitator by inciting a riot in which he himself is killed. Modest, as ever, about the novel's literary merits—which even his brother Evelyn grudgingly acknowledged—Waugh attributed its commercial success to its topicality: the interracial theme appealed to a postwar society that had begun to consider these issues, while the locales were becoming more familiar to an affluent new American audience to whom the West Indies was now a viable tourist destination.

AFTER the roller-coaster ride of *Island in the Sun,* in the opinion of his brother Evelyn, Alec Waugh "never drew a sober breath" ("Alec Waugh," *Dictionary of National Biography,* p. 419). In fact, apart from indulging his lifelong taste for travel, Waugh led a modest and inconspicuous existence, much of it spent working quietly in foreign hotels. The essay "Self Portrait: Nearing Sixty," reprinted in *My Brother Evelyn and Other Profiles,* gives a good idea of his routines at this time: solitary writing jaunts in the South of France, trips to America, the statutory visits to England. He remained close to his second ex-wife and took a benign interest in the upbringing of their children.

Waugh's late-period work, though less voluminous than his early output, is still extensive: more novels, autobiographical volumes, travel books, a history of Bangkok. The fiction, beginning with *Island in the Sun*'s successor, *Fuel for the Flame* (1960), set on an imaginary Southeast Asian archipelago and offering many of the same themes, is without great interest. The titles alone—*A Spy in the Family* (1970), *The Fatal Gift* (1973), and *Married to a Spy* (1976)—gesture at the area of international espionage in which he came ultimately to specialize. *A Spy in the Family,* which contains what were, for the time, quite daring scenes of lesbianism, was rejected on moral grounds by his English publishers.

Much more enduring, however, are his four autobiographical books. *The Early Years of Alec Waugh* ends in 1930, providing along the way interesting accounts of life in the trenches and the London publishing world of the 1920s. *My Brother Evelyn and Other Profiles* contains portraits of many of the (fairly) eminent Georgians with whom he was friendly, an obituary of Somerset Maugham, and a long account of the writing and reception of *Island in the Sun.* Perhaps predictably, the title essay is the least interesting in the book. *A Year to Remember: A Reminiscence of 1931* (1975) is exactly that: a blow-by-blow account of Waugh's literary, amatory, social, traveling, and sporting accomplishments over a twelve-month period, while *The Best Wine Last* carries the story of his life—patchily in the later sections—through to 1969.

It would be idle to claim that Waugh is one of the great autobiographers. He can be garrulous, complacent, and frankly dull, occasionally all at the same time. And yet in some ways these four books are his lasting memorial, not merely for their ability to recreate, in minute detail, a series of historical and literary periods but also for the authorial voice that rises above them. Half-modest, half-self-satisfied, they are by no means as anodyne as they sound, and the occasional hint of inner disturbance—the anxieties about the course of inter-war British life, the mild sniping at Evelyn—benefit from their comparative rarity.

Having been on the move for most of his adult life, Waugh finally came to rest in Tangier, where he purchased a house and lived quietly with Virginia Sorensen, whom he married after his second wife's death in 1969. In his later years, clad in suits of ever more eccentric cut, he was a frequent visitor to England, often to watch test matches at Lord's cricket ground (he was a member of the Marylebone Cricket Club, the English game's ruling body, for nearly half a century) or entertain friends at his London clubs. He and Sorensen eventually relocated to Florida, shortly before his death at the age of eighty-three on 3 September 1981. Of his vast literary output, only a handful of titles remain in print.

SELECTED BIBLIOGRAPHY

I. FICTION. *The Loom of Youth* (London, 1917; repr. London, 1954; page references in the text are from the reprint edition); *Pleasure* (stories) (London, 1921); *The Lonely Unicorn* (London, 1922; published as *Roland Whately,* New York, 1922); *Card Castle* (London, 1924); *Kept: A Story of Post-War London* (London, 1925); *Love in These Days* 1926; *The Last Chukka* (stories) (London, 1928); *Nor Many Waters* (London, 1928; published as *Portrait of a Celibate,* Garden City, N.Y., 1929); *Three Score and Ten* (London, 1929); *"Sir" She Said* (New York, 1930; published as *Love in Conflict,* London, 1977); *So Lovers Dream* (London, 1931; published as *That American Woman,* New York, 1932); *Leap Before You Look* (London, 1932); *No Quarter* (London, 1932; published as *Tropic Seed,* New York, 1932); *Playing with Fire* (London, 1933); *Wheels within Wheels: A Story of Crisis* (London, 1933); *The Balliols* (London, 1934); *Pages in Woman's Life* (stories) (London, 1934); *Jill Somerset* (London, 1936); *Eight Short Stories* (London, 1937); *Going Their Own Ways: A Story of Modern Marriage* (London, 1938); *No Truce with Time* (London, 1941); *Unclouded Summer: A Love Story* (London, 1948); *Guy Renton: A London Story* (London, 1953); *Island in the Sun* (London, 1956); *Fuel for the Flame* (London, 1960); *My Place in the Bazaar* (stories) (London, 1961); *The Mule on the Minaret* (London, 1965); *A Spy in the Family: An Erotic Comedy* (London, 1970); *The Fatal Gift* (London, 1973); *Brief Encounter* (based on the screenplay by J. Bowen) (London, 1975); *Married to a Spy* (London, 1976).

II. NONFICTION. *The Prisoners of Mainz* (London, 1919); *Public School Life: Boys, Parents, Masters* (London, 1922); *Myself When Young: Confessions* (London, 1923); *On Doing What One Likes* (London, 1926); *The Coloured Countries* (London, 1930; published as *Hot Countries,* New York, 1930); *"Most Women . . ."* (London, 1931); *Thirteen Such Years* (London, 1932); *His Second War* (London, 1944); *The Sunlit Caribbean* (London, 1948; published as *The Sugar Islands: A Caribbean Travelogue,* New York, 1949); *The Lipton Story: A Centennial Biography* (Garden City, N.Y., 1950); *Where the Clocks Strike Twice* (New York, 1951); *Merchants of Wine* (London, 1957); *The Sugar Islands* (London, 1958); *In Praise of Wine* (London, 1959); *The Early Years of Alec Waugh* (London, 1962); *A Family of Islands: A History of the West Indies 1492–1898* (London, 1964); *My Brother Evelyn and Other Profiles* (London, 1967); *Wines and Spirits of the World* (New York, 1968); *Bangkok: The Story of a City* (London, 1970); *A Year to Remember: A Reminiscence of 1931* (London, 1975); *The Best Wine Last: An Autobiography through the Years 1932–1969* (London, 1978).

III. POETRY. *Resentment* (1918, London).

IV. CRITICAL BIBLIOGRAPHY. There is no sustained critical treatment of Waugh's work. A short but informative memoir by his nephew, the novelist and journalist Auberon Waugh, can be found in the *Dictionary of National Biography* (Oxford, Eng., 1990).

GILBERT WHITE

(1720–1793)

Sam Pickering

GILBERT WHITE'S *THE Natural History and Antiquities of Selborne* was published in 1789. Shortly afterward, the warden of Merton College, Oxford, told White's nephew, "Your uncle has sent into the world a publication with nothing to call attention to it but an advertisement in the newspapers; but depend upon it the time will come when very few who buy books will be without it" (quoted in Blunden, p. 132). Compliments are raised upon manners, not facts. The warden, however, spoke true. Some hundred editions of the *Natural History* have appeared. For Samuel Taylor Coleridge it was "a sweet delightful book." After reading it, Charles Darwin wondered "why every gentleman did not become an ornithologist." In 1833 Lady Dover "arranged" an edition for "young persons." During the next hundred years, the *Natural History* became an inspirational instructive text for "boys and girls." Lady Dover's edition was reprinted several times, and in 1870 the Society for Promoting Christian Knowledge published an edition for children. In 1882 the book became part of Routledge's Young Person's Library, and in 1905 F. A. Bruton edited the book for the English Literature for Secondary Schools Series.

In 1929 the English poet and critic Edmund Blunden noted that "White was very largely responsible for the fact that at one time hardly any periodical publication was without its column on Natural History" (p. 150). Beginning in the nineteenth century, devotees made pilgrimages to Selborne. Critics linked White to Izaak Walton, another writer remembered for a single book—*The Compleat Angler* (1653). White and Walton became mythical Adams whistling the sweet magic of rural virtues. "Nature," the American man of letters James Russell Lowell declared in 1891, "had endowed these men [White and Walton] with the simple skill to make happiness out of the cheap material that is within the means of the poorest of us. The good fairy gave them to weave cloth of gold out of straw. They did not waste their time or strive to show their cleverness in discussing whether life were worth living, but found every precious moment of it so without seeking, or made it so without grimace, and with no thought that they were doing anything worth remark" (p. 108). As the industrial revolution dislocated life and thought in the nineteenth century, sentimentalists who celebrated the past at the expense of the present viewed White as saint of the simple and the wholesome.

In June 1882 the American naturalist John Burroughs spent a night and two rainy days in Selborne. Later he speculated about the reason for the popularity of the *Natural History*. "So many learned and elaborate treatises have sunk beneath the waves of which this cockle-shell of a book rides so safely and buoyantly!" Burroughs gushed. "What is the secret of its longevity? One can do little more than name its qualities without tracing them to their sources. It is simple and wholesome, like bread, or meat, or milk" (intro. to *Natural History*, p. vii). Hagiography reduces bone and flesh to rosy words. White led, however, a relatively calm and spotless life. He never married and spent his last forty-four years in Selborne. Animals, not people, produced the only muck staining his days. In March 1756, for example, he noted in his *Garden Kalendar*, a journal he kept detailing work in his gardens, that he "Borrowed six good Dung-carts of hot dung from Farmer Parsons."

WHITE AND SELBORNE

WHITE was born in Selborne parish, some fifty miles southwest of London, on 18 July 1720. A fellow of Magdalen College, Oxford, White's grandfather (also named Gilbert) accepted the living, or benefice, of Selborne in 1681 and set about restoring the vicarage. White wrote the *Natural History* in epistolary form. In the first letter he carefully described Selborne parish, creating a firm sense of place, something that increased the book's appeal to nineteenth- and twentieth-century readers, who often viewed themselves as rootless. Selborne lay out of the beaten way, "in the extreme eastern corner" of the county of Hampshire. Winchester was fifteen miles to the west, but roads in and out of Selborne were poor. Time had worn the roads deep into chalk and sandstone. The chief road into the village from Alton to the north was only eight feet wide in places. In other places it had sunk eighteen feet below ground level. In winter, rain and snow often made the roads impassable, so much so, White wrote in Letter 5 of the book's first half, "that they look more like water-courses than roads" (p. 26). What was inconvenience for eighteenth-century villagers became a boon for later pilgrims. Isolation so protected Selborne from development that to the literary-minded it smacked of Eden. In approaching the village, travelers entered a different world. Because the roads had been worn below ground level they exhibited "grotesque and wild appearances" after floods and frosts. Tangled roots turned through dirt, and "torrents" cascaded down banks. When water froze, icicles hung "in all the fanciful shapes of frost-work." "These rugged gloomy scenes affright the ladies when they peep down into them from the paths above, and make timid horsemen shudder while they ride along them," White wrote, "but they delight the naturalist with their various botany." In 1830 a correspondent of the *New Monthly Magazine and Literary Journal* called the village a "fairy spot of the imagination." "A scene of more enchanting rural loveliness eye never beheld," he exclaimed (pp. 566, 565). Publishers celebrated Selborne's beauty, prettying editions of the *Natural History* with engravings, photographs, wash drawings, and colored plates, in the process turning the parish into England's Arcadia. In 1882, for example, the edition of the *Natural History* which appeared in Routledge's Sixpenny Series contained 160 illustrations.

Chalk hills twisted through the parish. To the southwest of the village rose The Hanger. Towering three hundred feet above the village, The Hanger consisted of sheep-down and woody slopes. Many of the trees were beeches, White's favorite tree. Fewer than seven hundred people lived in the parish. An appendix attached to the *Natural History* described the state of the parish on 4 October 1783. The number of inhabitants was 676: 313 living alongside village streets, and 363 in the rest of the parish. The number of "tenements," or families, was 136. In his fifth letter White noted that although many people were poor, they were sober and industrious. "The inhabitants," he wrote, "enjoy a good share of health and longevity; and the parish swarms with children." Villagers lived in "good stone or brick cottages" which were glazed and had chambers "above stairs." "Mud buildings we have none" (p. 28). Besides husbandry, men worked in hop gardens and felled and barked timber. In spring and summer women weeded corn and in September picked hops.

Selborne's largest landowner possessed only seventy-five acres. At his death White owned forty acres scattered in plots around the parish. For literary pilgrims Selborne became the antithesis of Oliver Goldsmith's Auburn in the 1770 poem "The Deserted Village." In Selborne "health and plenty" cheered "the labouring swain." Association transformed White, who never held a church living and remained a curate all his life, into Goldsmith's village preacher, "passing rich with forty pounds a year," a man who did not wish "to change . . . his place."

White's father, John White, was born in 1688. Although he became a barrister and a Justice of the Peace, he does not seem to have practiced law. His wife, Anne Holt, a clergyman's daughter, inherited money, and John White whiled days away playing the harpsichord and gardening. After the birth of Gilbert, the couple left Selborne, moving to Compton, near Guildford. They returned, however, to Selborne when Gilbert was nine years old. In 1728 Reverend Gilbert White (the grandfather) died. On his death his widow and her two unmarried daughters moved into a nearby house. The house was called "Wakes," then later "The Wakes." Reverend White purchased it so his family would have a place to live after his death, the vicarage going to the new holder of the living. In 1729 or 1730 Reverend White's two daughters married on the same day. Shortly afterward John White and his family moved into The Wakes with his mother. Little is known how young Gilbert White spent days in the village. But if Wordsworth's Lockean assertion that the child is father of the man is accurate, then one can speculate that White roamed the various landscapes of Selborne. Certainly among naturalists, declarations that love of nature is learned during childhood are platitudinous. John Leonard Knapp (1767–1845), for example, testified that he modeled his *Journal of a Naturalist* (1829) on White's *Natural History*, a book, he wrote, which "early impressed on my mind an ardent love for all the ways and economy of nature" (in Johnson, ed., pp. 199–200).

When White was thirteen or fourteen, he began studying with the Reverend Thomas Warton in Basingstoke. Warton had been Professor of Poetry at Oxford. He had two sons, Joseph, two years younger than Gilbert, and Thomas, some eight years younger. Thomas was bright. He translated the epigrams of the first-century Roman poet Martial at ten and eventually became Professor of Poetry at Oxford and Poet Laureate. Joseph Warton, too, wrote poetry. Throughout his life, White himself wrote competent occasional verse. The three boys probably studied together and perhaps exerted some influence upon each other. Joseph Warton became Gilbert's lifelong friend. When the *Natural History* appeared, Gilbert sent him a complimentary copy. Joseph Warton's most famous poem was "The Enthusiast; or, The Lover of Nature" (1744). Sentimental primitivism pervaded the poem as Warton celebrated nature's superiority to art. In terms of White's life, the poem is interesting because it foreshadowed themes that later readers discovered in the *Natural History.*

Warton's narrator begins "The Enthusiast" by invoking dryads, asking them to lead him "to forests brown . . . unfrequented meads, and pathless wilds," far from "gardens deck'd with art's vain pomps." The narrator declares the song of the dove excelled the music of viol, lute, and trumpet. "Artful sounds" pleased less than the "choristers of air." Happy, the narrator declares, were the first of men, not yet confined to smoky cities. At the conclusion of the poem, the narrator longs to escape "Britannia's isle" and travel to a simpler, more natural world, asking "O who will bear me then to western climes." In 1753 Warton translated Virgil. In an introduction he thanked Virgil for giving "life and feeling, love and hatred, hope and fear, wonder and ambition to plants and trees, to the very earth itself." Later tributes to White smacked of similar phrases. White's quiet life seemed magical. Instead of wand transforming a kitchen maid into a princess and a pumpkin into a golden chariot observation made ordinary life vital. "For it is in this quietness," the nineteenth-century English naturalist Richard Jefferies wrote, "that the invisible becomes visible. The vacant field gradually grows full of living things. In the hedges unsuspected

birds come to the surface of the green leaf to take breath. Over the pond brilliantly colored insects float to and fro, and the fish that never seem to move from the dark depths do move and do come up in sight" (preface to *Natural History,* pp. x–xi).

Beginning in the nineteenth century and continuing to the present, readers of White escaped the fret of contemporary life by traveling to Selborne or by adventuring in backyards, their private Selbornes. Although White never hectored (boasted or swaggered) as did Henry David Thoreau, people read social implications into the *Natural History.* Selborne seemed ideally far from, as Warton put it in "The Enthusiast," "the distant din of the tumultuous world." Away from the fret of the world, a better life was possible. To appreciate White's book, Burroughs suggested, "a quiet, even tenor of life such as can be had only in the country" was necessary. Burroughs wanted people to reform lives and attitudes. To do so, they had to change the rhythms of their commercial days. For Burroughs the *Natural History* was a secular Good Book, capable of guiding the wise to virtue. "A way of life," he continued, "that goes slow, and lingers upon the impression of the moment, and returns to it again and again, that makes much of little things, and is closely observant of the face of the day and of the landscape, and into which the disturbing elements of the great hurly-burly outside world do not enter" (*Indoor Studies,* p. 163).

In December 1739 White entered Oriel College, Oxford. Because his mother died that year, he did not go into residence until five months later. White was neither wealthy nor poor. He could not afford to waste money on extravagant high jinks, but he enjoyed means enough to live well. He was not a recluse. He hunted, boated, and joined a music club. In 1744 White became a fellow of Oriel College. Fellowships were not the honors they have now become. Some went to successful students, but the awards were often a means of sustaining individuals until they obtained livings or came into inheritances. Never possessing excess means, White held the fellowship until his death, something that provoked resentment as people imagined White to be independently wealthy, a man who did not need the one hundred pounds a year the fellowship provided. In truth, aside from the fellowship, White probably had a yearly income of a hundred pounds, property bringing him some forty pounds, and two curacies sixty pounds.

WHITE'S JOURNALS

In the years immediately after going down from Oxford, White traveled in Britain, managed family affairs, and held curacies. In 1752 he served as Junior Proctor at Oxford. In 1749 he returned to The Wakes and began gardening on page as well as in field, taking time out, however, to be Proctor. In 1751 he began the *Garden Kalendar*. For forty-three years he kept notes on gardening and natural history, stopping only eleven days before his death. He kept the *Kalendar* from 1751 to 1767. In the journal he tracked planting and reaping, the weather, and the yields of crops. The *Kalendar* was not published during White's life. Keen gardeners and those devoted to White and Selborne will find it interesting. White was a good gardener, and he grew flowers and foods. He planted trees and shrubs and grew sweet corn and sea kale. Melons were a favorite, and he devoted much energy to hotbeds for melons and cucumbers.

To a great extent White's journals were the seedbed of the *Natural History*. To be a successful gardener, White studied plants. He owned, for example, the third edition of John Ray's *Synopsis methodica stirpium Britannicarum* (1724). Entries in the *Kalendar* were straightforward. The experience of reading the journal is not literary, but the accounts of gardening satisfy. In perusing the *Kalendar*, one strolls through season and years. "To dwell," the German philosopher Martin Heidegger said, "is to garden." Certainly gardening fixed White's roots in Selborne. For 3 April 1759, he wrote,

The Cantaleupe-bed not coming to a proper degree of Heat, I ordered it to be pulled to pieces, & worked-up with 10 loads of fresh dung just brought-in. The Labourers made-use of about 16 loads of the first bed again: so the new bed contains 26 loads. Laid some loam all over to keep-down the steam; & some turfs under the Hills. Put one barrow of loam to each Hill. Bed more than seven feet wide; & two feet & half thick behind.

(vol. 1, p. 75)

In the entry for 16 November 1763, White noted,

Serene, beautiful weather for several days, with the Mercury within half a degree of settled fair. Planted my Hyacinths in two rows along the border opposite the fruit-border: dug-in first some well-rotted dung. Put the blue & best pink-eyed intermixed in front. Planted my Tulips, *Narcissus,* and Jonquils in the border opposite

the bank. Dug & cleared the banks, & dining-room shrubbery this fine season.

(vol. 1, p. 133)

The entries furnish days with the concrete, a word easily applied to White's writing style. The reader of White, Burroughs maintained, came "face to face with something real; objects, ideas stand out on every page" (intro. to *Natural History*, p. xi). Enjoyment of the entries in White's journals may run deeper than style. "The love of dirt is among our earliest passions, as it is the latest," the nineteenth-century American man of letters Charles Dudley Warner wrote in *My Summer in a Garden* (1887):

Mud-pies gratify one of our first and best instincts. So long as we are dirty, we are pure. Fondness for the ground comes back to a man after he has run the round of pleasure and business, eaten dirt, and sown wild-oats, drifted about the world, and taken the wind of all its moods. The love of digging in the ground (or of looking on while he pays another to dig) is sure to come back to him as he is sure, at last, to go under the ground, and stay there. To own a bit of ground, to scratch it with a hoe, to plant seeds, and watch their renewal of life-this is the commonest delight of the race, the most satisfactory thing a man can do.

(p. 13)

Occasionally an entry in the *Kalendar* provided matter for the *Natural History*. White used the entry for 20 May 1761, a description of crickets, in Letter 46 of the *Natural History*. The entry begins as follows:

My Brother Tho: & I went down with a spade to examine into the nature of those animals that make that chearful shrill cry all the summer months in many parts of the south of England. We found them to be of the Cricket-kind, with wings & ornamented Cases over them, like the House kind. But tho' they have long legs behind with large brawny thighs, like Grasshoppers, for leaping; it is remarkable that when they were dug-out of their holes they shewed no manner of activity, but crawled along in a very shiftless manner, so as easily to be taken. We found it difficult not to squeeze them to death in breaking the Ground: & out of one so bruised I took a multitude of eggs, which were long, of a yellow Colour, & covered with a very tough skin.

(vol. 1, p. 104)

White kept other journals, a notebook for the year 1766, the *Flora Selbornesis* in which he wrote botanical observations. On 22 February, for example, White returned from London and

found the snow-drop, & winter aconite in bloom; & the Crocus blowing; the Hazel, *corylus sylvestris*, blowing, with vast numbers of their male catkins opening which gives the hedges a yellowish tinge: the primrose, *primula veris*, is also blowing. The thrush, *turdus simpliciter dictus*, the chaffinch, *fringilla*, & the skie-lark, *Alauda vulgaris*, sing: the titmouse, *parus major*, makes his spring note. Soft grey weather, & the ground in fine order.

(vol. 1, p. 188)

From 1768 until 1793 White kept the *Naturalist's Journal*, a printed diary, each volume of which contained a year's observations. Devised by Daines Barrington, a barrister and Fellow of the Royal Society, the diary was published by White's brother Benjamin. The original journal contained nine columns and spaces in which the diarist could record the date when trees leafed, flowers bloomed, and birds appeared. The first six columns of the journal provided places to record place, date, barometric pressure, temperature, rainfall, wind, and other doings of weather. Over the years, however, White's observations sprawled and ran beyond the allotted space, forcing him to continue notes from one page to the next or insert pages. Many entries were brief. On Monday, 4 June 1770, for example, the barometric pressure was 29½. The temperature was fifty-seven degrees Fahrenheit; the wind was from the southwest. During the day "Great rain" and "wind" occurred. Lastly, "Fleas (pulex irritans) abound on the steep sand-banks where the bank-martins build." Other entries were more detailed. A severe frost struck on Wednesday, 8 March 1786. Temperature ranged between ten and twenty-four degrees. "Black-birds, & thrushes die. A starving wigeon settled yesterday in the village, & was taken. Mention is made in the newspapers of several people that have perished in the snow. As Mr. Ventris came from Faringdon the drifted snow, being hard frozen, bore his weight up almost to the tops of the stiles. The net hung over the cherry trees is curiously coated over with ice." The journals swam into print in the wake of the *Natural History's* popularity, the first selections from the journals appearing in 1795 as *A Naturalist's Calendar, with Observations in Various Branches of Natural History*, edited by John Aikin.

INFLUENCES, PHILOSOPHY, AND THEOLOGY

IN 1763 White came into full possession of The Wakes. In April 1767 White visited his brothers Benjamin and Thomas in London. During the visit, he met Thomas Pennant. A Fellow of the Royal Society, Pennant was a prominent traveler and writer. His books sold well, and the year before meeting White, Pennant had completed *British Zoology*, an encyclopedia of mammals and birds. White began to correspond with Pennant. In 1768 when the second edition of the *British Zoology* appeared, Pennant included material furnished by White. In 1769 White met Daines Barrington, the creator of the *Naturalist's Journal*. The two men began a correspondence, and in 1770 Barrington suggested that White turn his observations into a book, thus planting the seed of the *Natural History*. The book was twenty years in the making, and when it was published in 1789, it consisted of forty-four letters to Pennant, the dates running from 1767 to 1780, and sixty-six letters to Barrington, dated from 1768 to 1787.

Time makes neither man nor book. But the spirit of an age influences writing. The critic in the *New Monthly Magazine and Literary Journal* attributed the success of the *Natural History* to White's mind. "The chief attraction of his book," the 1930 article explained, "lies in the moral beauty of his mind, in its serene and benevolent temper, in its deep, fervent feeling for nature, in its reverential communing with the mysteries of creation, and above all, in the perfect envelopment of its intellectual pleasures in that religion of the heart which sends up its incense to its Maker, even in the diurnal and hourly contemplation of his works" (vol. 29, p. 564). For the critic in the *New Monthly*, White was an optimistic man of feeling, and certainly in field and wood White appeared latitudinarian, taking a broad view of religious belief and conduct, seeing for himself rather than letting dogma or others determine what he saw. John Burroughs exclaimed, "What an equable, harmonious, and gracious spirit and temper pervade the book, and withal what an air of summer-day leisure and sequestration!" (*Indoor Studies*, p. 165). When White wrote, Darwin had not darkened life. Nature was not red in tooth and claw. Part of White's success, Richard Jefferies stated, "was owning to his coming to the field with his mind unoccupied. He was not full of evolution when he walked out, or variations, or devolution, or degeneration" (preface to *Natural History*, p. ix).

Evolution did not occupy White's thoughts, but the *Natural History* both reflected and was influenced by the intellectual doings of White's day. During the Renaissance, interest in the tangible natural world increased. "Man's first giant step for mankind," the American anthropologist Loren Eiseley wrote in *The Invisible Pyramid* (1998), contradicting Neil Armstrong's statement on the moon, "was not through space. Instead it lay through time" (p. 67). Francis Bacon institutionalized science, "inventing" the scientific method and the laboratory. Instead of limiting observation to the immediate or the iconographic, Baconians viewed knowledge as cumulative. In *The Advancement of Learning* (1605), Bacon urged, "We are not to imagine or suppose, but to discover what nature does or may be made to do" (in Eiseley, p. 67). Over time, Baconians believed, observations would cohere and knowledge would grow. Thus instead of using observation to buttress the present and a comparatively static theological world, Baconians focused on the future, a future in which changing knowledge would enable man to progress. Bacon's empirical followers founded the Royal Society, and optimism about where empiricism would lead blew through the scientific air. In the mid-seventeenth century Thomas Browne entitled one of his works *Pseudodoxia Epidemica; or, Enquiries into very many received tenents and commonly presumed truths.* Centuries, of course, have tempered such optimism. "The laboratories of Bacon's vision produced the atom bomb and toyed prospectively with deadly nerve gas" (Eiseley, pp. 68–69).

White was in part a Baconian. He recorded what he saw and resisted the temptation to impose meaning upon observation. "White valued his facts for what they were," Burroughs wrote, "not for any double meaning he could wring out of them, or any airy structure he could build upon them" (*Indoor Studies*, p. 166). No "bias" stood between him and what he saw. Although White paid lip service to the glory of God and in Letter 20 to Pennant marveled at "the wisdom of God in the creation," he did not force religious iconography upon the natural world. Not only was he the scientific heir of the Baconians, but he was also influenced by British latitudinarians, men such as Isaac Barrow, Samuel Clarke, John Scott, and John Tillotson. Latitudinarians relegated doctrine to the background of faith and attempted to turn Anglicanism into a moral system emphasizing charity and goodness. "Zeal for particular forms and ceremonies more than for Virtue and Religion," Clarke wrote in *Works* (1738), hindered "the growth of Christian Charity, and like the Worm at the Root of *Jonah's* Gourd" ate out "the vitals of true Religion" (vol. 1, p. 299). Latitudinarianism freed Christian living and vision from doctrine, allowing White and later naturalists simply to report findings and at most only genuflect before doctrine.

Tillotson wrote that the happiest disposition was to be of kind and giving spirit. Tillotson's prescription for the good life smacks of nineteenth-century descriptions that transformed White into a man of feeling. Latitudinarianism led to romanticism, in which truth became a matter of impulse and feeling rather than thought. In "The Tables Turned," Wordsworth urged readers to quit their books and clear their looks. "Let Nature be your teacher," he preached, declaring that "one impulse from a vernal wood" could teach man "more of man, / Of moral evil and of good, / than all the sages can." Pilgrims to Selborne in the nineteenth century were Romantics. For most, sight of The Wakes and its environs provoked emotionally charged prose in which feeling was synonymous with truth. Although latitudinarianism freed White from doctrine, White remained too much a Baconian to preach the truth of impulse. He reported what he saw, not what he felt. Knowing exactly what he saw was important for White. He owned, for example, Francis Willughby's *Ornithology* and Philip Miller's *Gardener's Dictionary*. White used guidebooks, however, only as guides. When in doubt about the doings of birds, for example, he trusted his observation, not someone else's books. White's journals are testimonials to the Baconian aspect of his character. Impulsive gardeners harvest weeds, not melons and cucumbers.

Knowing the names of things is important. If a naturalist does not know the name of the object he studies, more than likely he will view the object at a remove and write in metaphor, thus clouding observation. White benefited greatly from the classification of species pioneered by John Ray in the seventeenth century and continued and refined by Carolus Linnaeus. "The first step of science is to know one thing from another," Linnaeus said. "This knowledge consists in their specific distinctions; but in order that it may be fixed and permanent distinct names must be given to different things, and those names must be recorded and remembered" (in Johnson, ed., p. ix)

Also forming part of the intellectual and theological fibers out of which White wove the *Natural History* was "natural theology." Physico-theologians taught that the existence and attributes of God could be inferred from the study of nature. White read John Ray and William Derham, leading physicotheologians. Both writers were very popular. First published in 1714, Derham's *Physico-Theology* reached a thirteenth edition by 1768. The "Works of this visible world," John Ray wrote in *The Wisdom of God Manifested in the Works of the Creation* (1691), afforded "a demonstrative Proof of the unlimited extent of the Creators Skill, and fecundity of his Wisdom and Power." If, Ray asked, "a curious Edifice or Machine" necessarily implied the existence of an intelligent architect or engineer, did not the "Grandeur and Magnificence" of nature, which far transcended human art, "infer the existence and efficacy of an Omnipotent and All-wise Creator?" (pp. 1–2). Such statements promoted study of the natural world. They also, however, undermined revelation and doctrinal authority and led to deism. As the eighteenth century unfolded, the curious edifice grew in importance. In his *The Wisdom of God*, Ray wrote, "Let it not suffice to be book-learned, to read what others have written and take upon trust more falsehood than truth, but let us ourselves examine things as we have opportunity, and converse with Nature as well as books"; and also, "If man ought to reflect upon his Creator the glory of all his works, then ought he to take notice of them all and not to think anything unworthy of his cognizance" (in Johnson, ed., p. x).

As people increasingly began to converse with nature, the religious impulse drifted from the particular attributes of God. In the case of "The Tables Turned," impulses rose from a wood and led to truths that lay beyond words. Physicotheologians provided an intellectual rationalization for White's ramblings. Meanderings that once appeared indulgent and, worse, endangered the soul by leading one into woods of error, were now justified. When one wandered nature, in contrast, say, to the man-made city, one entered, if not God's world, at least a landscape the features of which testified to the presence of a deity. Over time nature's wondrous diversity drew attention away from God, and references to God and His attributes became platitudinous. Eventually God vanished. In *The Story of My Heart* (1883), Richard Jefferies concluded that no deity had anything to do with nature. "There is no god in nature, not in any matter anywhere, either in the clods on the earth or in the composition of the stars" (p. 63). Abandoning a deity completely in the nineteenth-century was difficult, and as compensation Jefferies embraced an Emersonian oversoul, calling it "Highest Soul." "I conclude," he wrote, "that there is an existence, a something higher than soul-higher, better, and more perfect than deity. Earnestly I pray to find this something better than a god. There is something superior, higher, more good. For this I search, labour, think, and pray. If after all there be nothing, and my soul has to go out like a flame, yet even then I have thought this while it lives" (pp. 66–67). In the nineteenth century the will to believe spun thoughts into knotty sentences. Part of White's appeal, his simplicity, was that he could observe and remain free from doubt. In later writers, nature, not God, healed the wounds of contemporary living. Even though Jefferies drifted from Christianity, he still used conventional religious words. "From my home in London," he wrote in *My Heart*, "I made a pilgrimage almost daily to an aspen by a brook. It was a mile and a quarter along the road, far enough for me to walk off the concentration of mind necessary for work. The idea of the pilgrimage was to get away from the endless and nameless circumstances of everyday existence, which by degrees build a wall about the mind so that it travels in a constantly narrowing circle" (p. 97).

THE NATURAL HISTORY OF SELBORNE

THE form of the *Natural History* contributed to its success. Letters lend themselves to the neighborly and the familial. For many readers White became a friend, and when such readers traveled to Selborne, they followed his paragraphs. "The swallows, his favorite object of notice among the 'winged people,'" a writer recounted on seeing The Wakes, "were at the moment careening in circles round the house and twittering among its eaves" (*New Monthly Magazine and Literary Journal*, vol. 29, p. 568). Instead of being hauled through pages by plot, readers of White's letters sauntered through season and year. Burroughs claimed that "as a stimulus and spur to the study of natural history" White's text had "more influence than any other work of the century" (*Indoor Studies*, p. 164). The book determined the course and form of much natural history writing. Newspapers and journals devoted sections to letters reporting on natural history. In 1907 *British Birds*, for example, began a correspondence column devoted to the reports of bird-watchers, amateur scientists like White.

White forever counted and measured: fossils, trees, rain, almost everything he observed. He watched a pair of white owls care for their offspring. "I have minuted these birds with my watch for an hour together," he wrote in Letter 15 to Barrington, "and have found that they return to their nest, the one or the other of them, about once in five minutes." He studied "domestic economy" and suggested that villagers burn rushes instead of candles. After describing the process of dipping rushes in grease, he noted the following in Letter 26 to Barrington:

In a pound of dry rushes, avoirdupois, which I caused to be weighed and numbered, we found upwards of one thousand six hundred individuals. Now, suppose each of these burns, one with another, only half an hour, then a poor man will purchase eight hundred hours of light, a time exceeding thirty-three entire days, for three shillings. According to this account each rush, before dipping, costs $\frac{1}{33}$ of a farthing, and $\frac{1}{11}$ afterwards. Thus a poor family will enjoy 5½ hours of comfortable light for a farthing. An experienced old housekeeper assures me that one pound and a half of rushes completely supplies his family the year round, since working people burn no candle in the long days, because they rise and go to bed by daylight.

(pp. 198–199)

In reports in magazines and newspapers, White's intellectual descendants followed both his sentences and his ruler. On 5 September 1937, for example, two correspondents of *British Birds* watched a shag, or cormorant, diving off the northeast coast of Skokholm Island. The bird, they noted, was in the lee of the island and was diving in several fathoms of water. Their letter reported:

In all it dived 54 times, and we measured the duration of each dive, and in 35 instances the length of time spent on the surface. The average duration of a dive was about 53 seconds and between each dive the bird spent 21 seconds on the surface (average). Three dives lasted 10 seconds or under, thirteen lasted over 1 minute. Of these by far the most remarkable was one of 170 seconds. The next longest were of 85 seconds and 70 seconds. It appears that the length of the time spent on the surface bears little relation to the length of the dive, for after the dive of 85 seconds the bird spent only 15 seconds on the surface, whereas after a dive of 48 seconds it spent 33 seconds on the surface. It should be remarked that the longest time spent on the surface (37 seconds) was after the exceptionally long dive already noted.

The lack of a narrative influences reading, and one might suspect that many people read the *Natural History* fitfully. Instead of binding themselves to literary regimens, readers imitated White and followed the vagaries of their own minds. White's book appeals more to middle-aged readers than to the young, readers who have lived long enough to shape the stories of their lives and for whom small pleasure is as enjoyable and as rewarding as great. The *Natural History* is a book that people start, put down, then pick up again later, this last probably as ambition wanes. It belongs, Burroughs stated, in the class of books that "like certain fruits . . . leave a lingering flavor in the mouth that is much better than the first taste promised" (*Indoor Studies*, p. 163)

Like familiar essays, letters can be distastefully self-centered. But White's concentration on the world beyond self enabled him to escape egotism. Never did he jot down an observation and, like Jack Horner, exclaim what a clever boy am I. Moreover he is playful, often in appealing, eccentric ways. On Michaelmas Day 1768, White related in Letter 28 to Pennant that he "managed to get a sight of the female moose belonging to the duke of Richmond." Unfortunately when White arrived at Goodwood, the duke's estate, to see the moose, it was dead, having died the morning before. White examined the moose, which had not been skinned and was suspended by ropes and a sling in a standing position in a greenhouse. Unfortunately, the moose "was in so putrid a state that the stench was hardly supportable." The odor did not deter White, and he set about measuring the animal. From ground to wither, the moose five feet four inches, exactly sixteen hands. He continues:

Its neck was remarkably short, no more than twelve inches; so that, by straddling with one foot forward and the other backward, it grazed on the plain ground, with the greatest difficulty, between its legs: the ears were vast and lopping, and as long as the neck; the head was about twenty inches long, and ass-like; and had such a redundancy of upper lip as I never saw before, with huge nostrils. This lip, travellers say, is esteemed a dainty dish in North America.

(p. 88)

White measured the moose carefully, not so thoroughly as he would have liked, though. He apologized for not measuring the tibia, saying that in his "haste to get out of the stench" he forgot to "measure that joint exactly." White's delight in describing the moose, even while enduring the stench, created the appearance of boyish, naive enthusiasm, thus making him seem otherworldly. "In the same garden," he continued, "was a young stag, or red deer, between whom and this moose it was hoped that there might have been a breed, but their inequality of height must have always been a bar to any commerce of the amorous kind. I should have been glad to have examined the teeth, tongue, lips, hoofs, &c. minutely; but the putrefaction precluded all farther curiosity" (pp. 88–89).

On another occasion White tested Virgil's notion that echoes are injurious to bees. Not only did bees thrive in locations in Selborne where echoes were "very strong," but, White concluded, bees seemed inured to sound. He had, he reported in Letter 38 to Barrington, held a large speaking-trumpet close to their hives and yelled "with such an exertion of voice as would have hailed a ship at the distance of a mile, and still these insects pursued their various employments undisturbed, and without shewing the least sensibility or resentment" (p. 223). Quirky curiosity has become a staple of nature writing. Thoreau cooked and sampled groundhog. In the late twentieth century in Vermont, Noel Perrin subjected butter and margarine to the cat test. He left sticks of butter and margarine exposed in his kitchen overnight to see which appealed to his cat.

After locating Selborne in his first letter, White created the texture of place. In his second letter, for example, he described trees growing in Selborne and its environs. He blended anecdote with fact, noting the size of trees and the price they fetched when harvested. Some trees were individuals. "In the centre of the village," he recounted, "and near the church, is a square piece of ground surrounded by houses" (Letter 2 to Pennant, pp. 20–21). The ground was called The Plestor. Until a storm in 1703, "a vast oak" had occupied the middle of The Plestor. Stone steps topped by seats surrounded the tree, and during summer it was a place of "much resort," the old sitting under the tree, engaging in "grave debate," and the young frolicking and dancing. Not only did this sort of detail create place, but it encouraged readers and pilgrims to mold the Selborne they visited into the pastoral image depicted in White's text. In 1830 a visitor to the village visited The Plestor. In the middle of the ground stood a sycamore, "almost

as dignified," the traveler wrote, "as its predecessor" (*New Monthly Magazine and Literary Journal*, vol. 29, pp. 569–570). White's careful texturing created a visual world. The great landscape painter John Constable said he had "always envied" the "mind that produced the 'Selborne'" (in Johnson, ed., pp. 3–4). Proving White influenced Constable is impossible. But both men labored to create place, and at first glance a painting like Constable's *The Cornfield* smacks of White's descriptions of Selborne. A dog follows sheep down a sunken lane, above which big trees lean and blow. Beside the lane a boy stretches on the ground, not to frolic, but to drink from a stream. At the end of the lane a field opens like a pond, and the eye flows outward to a distant church tower.

"Men that undertake only one district," White wrote, "are much more likely to advance natural knowledge than those that grasp at more than they can possibly be acquainted with: every kingdom, every province, should have its own *monographer*" (Letter 7 to Barrington, p. 138). This democratizing apology for study of the local held great appeal for readers, many of whom knew they would never be part of the throbbing great world. Later nature writers followed White's suggestion. While Thoreau, for example, is now identified with Walden Pond outside Concord, Massachusetts, Edwin Way Teale is associated with Trail Wood in Hampton, Connecticut. In the advertisement attached to *Selborne*, White dubbed his book "parochial history." Advice to study the immediate and the local in contrast to the distant and the abstract had even appeared in Book VIII of Milton's *Paradise Lost*, Raphael warned against a roving "Mind or Fancy." "To know," Raphael preached, "That which before us lies in daily life, / Is the prime Wisdom." All else, Raphael declared, "is fume, / Or emptiness, or fond impertinence."

The danger of the parochial is that it can become oppressively narrow and xenophobic. In 1930 in *I'll Take My Stand*, Southern Agrarians urged southerners and by extension all Americans to return to what they, Raphael-like, saw as simpler and more virtuous ways of living. The Agrarians criticized the spiritual and physical dislocations of industrialism, and they warned readers against eating the forbidden fruit of "progress." "It is the character of our urbanized, anti-provincial, progressive, and mobile American life that it is in a condition of eternal flux," John Crowe Ransom, one of the book's contributors, stated. "Affections, and long memories, attach to the ancient bowers of life in the provinces; but they will not attach to what is always changing" (p. 5). Resembling an Old Testament prophet preaching against seductive luxury and worldliness, Andrew Lytle, another contributor, wrote, "We have been slobbered upon by those who have chewed the mad root's poison, a poison which penetrates to the spirit and rots the soul. And the time is not far off when the citizens of this one-time Republic will be crying, 'What can I do to be saved?'" (p. 203). Lytle sounded like Goldsmith in brogans and overalls, the poet's bold peasantry transformed by time and place into yeoman farmers. The worm gnawing at the root of this pastoral flower, the fragrance of which lured readers to the bower and provincial life, was racism. Although Selborne appeared as "Sweet Auburn" before enclosure, the worm at the heart of the English pastoral and its parochial life was poverty. Nevertheless, throughout the nineteenth century writers celebrated village life. In *Tom Brown's School Days* (1857), the English reformer Thomas Hughes lamented the disappearance of sturdy villagers and described The Veast, a country fair. Class amusements had arisen, Hughes worried, dividing Briton from Briton. "O young England," he exclaimed, "why don't you know more of your own birthplaces?" "Over-civilization" and the accumulation of wealth, he worried, had shred the fabric of British society. For nineteenth-century readers Selborne became Auburn before the fall, a place devoutly to be sentimentalized. The harsh environments of Manchester as envisioned in Elizabeth Gaskell's *Mary Barton*, and of London in Dickens's *Our Mutual Friend*, seemed distant. Selborne became an icon of the gentle past, an emblem of what had been lost. Blowing about cottages in the village, a nineteenth-century traveler wrote, was a "pristine air of industry and comfort." In this other Eden, the walls of cottages were "neatly covered with vines and creepers in full bloom." Nearby thrived "trim little gardens." In the village were no traces of "that heart-sickening spectacle of squalid abject pauperism, which now, alas, too often haunts our fairest island scenes of cultivation and abundance" (*New Monthly Magazine and Literary Journal*, vol. 29, pp. 566–567).

A STUDY OF THE OVERLOOKED

WHITE stressed the use of things in his letters, sounding like a gardener familiar with trowel and spade, not a doctrinaire utilitarian. He defended his observations against the standing objections to botany, that it amused the fancy and exercised the memory without improving the mind or advancing real knowledge. Real botanists studied plants "philosophically." They investigated the powers of herbs and laws of vegetation. To plants society owed timber, bread, beer, honey, wine, oil, and linen. The study of grasses, White suggested in Letter 40 to Barrington, would "be of great consequence to a northerly, and grazing kingdom" (p. 227). In his fourth letter to Pennant, he discussed freestone. In every quarry, he noted, appeared thin strata of blue rag freestone. Able to resist rain and frost, blue rag was "excellent for pitching of stables, paths and courts, and for building of dry walls against banks; a valuable species of fencing, much in use in this village, and for mending of roads" (p. 25). White devoted much attention to the everyday, the small, and the neglected. In doing so, he added the harvest mouse and great noctule bat to the list of British fauna. He was among the first naturalists to note protective coloration, writing about the camouflage of the stone curlew. According to Letter 16 to Pennant, the dam, or mother bird, and her young skulked among stones in fields and were difficult to spot, "for their feathers are so exactly of the colour of our grey spotted flints, that the most exact observer, unless he catches the eye of the young bird, may be eluded" (p. 55). On several occasions White stressed the importance of small creatures, a concern mirrored today by acts protecting endangered species. In part such species are protected because humans fear that the disappearance of a species may irrevocably influence all remaining life, something White pointed out in Letter 35 to Barrington:

Earth-worms, though in appearance a small and despicable link in the chain of Nature, yet, if lost, would make a lamentable chasm. For, to say nothing of half the birds, and some quadrupeds which are almost entirely supported by them, worms seem to be the great promoters of vegetation, which would proceed but lamely without them, by boring, perforating, and loosening the soil, and rendering it pervious to rains and the fibres of plants, by drawing straws and stalks of leaves and twigs into it; and, most of all, by throwing up such infinite numbers of lumps of earth called wormcasts, which, being their excrement, is a fine manure for grain and grass.

(p. 213)

In pointing out the importance of the minute, in a sense White popularized the study of the overlooked, in the process contributing to the democratization not only of natural history but perhaps of literature itself. Constellations of influences, not single stars, produce books. Nevertheless, it is worth noting that many of the most memorable animals in twentieth-century children's books are downtrodden, even repulsive creatures, repulsive at least until the reader examines them closely, much as White looked at earthworms. The main characters of Kenneth Grahame's *The Wind in the Willows*, for example, are not prestigious "leaders" of the animal kingdom, but the neglected and ignored: a mole, a water rat, a badger, and a toad.

In Letters 1 and 17 to Barrington, White dubbed himself an "out-door naturalist," a person who humbly attempted "to promote a more minute inquiry into natural history: into the life and conversation of animals" (p. 123; p. 166). He urged people to examine nature themselves rather than relying on accepted knowledge or superstition. In Letter 28 to Barrington he said that "it is the hardest thing in the world to shake off superstitious prejudices: they are sucked in as it were with our mother's milk" (p. 201). Elsewhere he warned, "one cannot safely relate any thing from common report, especially in print, without expressing some degree of doubt and suspicion" (Letter 21 to Pennant, p. 68). When a French anatomist suggested that the internal structure of cuckoos prevented the birds from hatching their own eggs, White tested the idea by dissecting several other birds that nested, and noted his finding in Letter 30 to Barrington, that their "internal construction" resembled that of the cuckoo. White wanted to believe that swallows did not migrate but hibernated. He doubted that birds that flitted from hedge to hedge during summer could "traverse vast seas and continents in order to enjoy milder seasons amidst the regions of Africa" (Letter 12 to Pennant, p. 48). Some of his contemporaries speculated that swallows hibernated in mud at the bottoms of streams and ponds, "conglobulated into a ball," as Samuel Johnson put it. The hankering to believe in hibernation did not lead White astray, however. Although he searched through decades for signs of hibernation, he meticulously described his failure to find conclusive evidence.

A NATURAL COMMINGLING

"ALL nature," White wrote, "is so full that that district produces the greatest variety which is the most examined" (Letter 20 to Pennant, p. 65). More than half the species of birds ever seen in all Sweden had, he noted gleefully, appeared in Selborne, Sweden being home to 221 species and Selborne home to 120. Nature's multiplicity was ever intriguing. "How diversified are the modes of life not only of incongruous but even of congenerous animals," he wrote enthusiastically in Letter 48 to Barrington, "and yet their specific distinctions are not more various than their propensities. Thus, while the field-cricket delights in sunny dry banks, and the house-cricket rejoices amidst the glowing heat of the kitchen hearth or oven, the *gryllus gryllo talpa* (the mole-cricket), haunts moist meadows, and frequents the sides of ponds and banks of streams, performing all its functions in a swampy wet soil" (pp. 247–248). White's enthusiasm was contagious, perhaps even medicinal. In the nineteenth century returns to nature and experiences in the natural world became an often-prescribed remedy for the "day-mare Spleen." In "Tintern Abbey," Wordsworth wrote that memories of country life lightened "the burthen of the mystery," the "heavy and the weary weight / Of all this unintelligible world." In "Nature," Ralph Waldo Emerson testified that "crossing a bare common, in snow puddles, at twilight, under a clouded sky, without having in my thoughts any occurrence of special good fortune, I have enjoyed a perfect exhilaration." "I am glad to the brink of fear," he continued. "In the woods, too, a man casts off his years, as the snake his slough, and at what period soever of life is always a child. In the woods is perpetual youth. Within these plantations of God, a decorum and sanctity reign, a perennial festival is dressed, and the guest sees not how he should tire of them in a thousand years. In the woods, we return to reason and faith" (in *Selected Essays*, 1985, pp. 38–39).

In Letter 43 to Barrington, White referred to "the infinite variety of the feathered nation" (p. 235). For White and later naturalists, love of nature did not pale. The natural world remained forever intriguing. Vipers might poison, but, more intriguingly, they were objects of study, indeed creatures to be treasured and loved. To escape the shades of the prison-house that closed upon Wordsworth's growing boy in "Intimations of

Immortality," one meandered the natural world. In nature a person returned to "the glory and the dream" of childhood and, in some vague sense, entered an earthly pastoral landscape. Throughout the *Natural History* White detailed his ignorance and by implication invited readers to fashion answers to puzzles. In Letter 10 to Pennant, White said he had been interested in nature since childhood, lending credence to those who saw him as eternal boy. He noted that it had been his misfortune not to have had neighbors or companions who, by sharing his enthusiasm, quickened his industry and sharpened his attention.

In the book White is not a solitary, but he often seems alone or at least a man without close companions. Being alone became a literary saw of later Romantics who wrote about nature. Alone, as William Hazlitt put it, people escaped "the hackneyed common-places that we appear in the world." We "lose," Hazlitt said, "our importunate, tormenting, everlasting personal identity in the elements of nature, and become the creature of the moment, clear of all ties" (in *Hazlitt's Selected Essays*, 1949, p. 77). From another point of view the mechanics of nature writing are easier if one does not describe companions of trail and wood. Thus Annie Dillard did not mention family in *Pilgrim at Tinker Creek* (1974). Thoreau focused on life in his shanty at Walden and neglected to report his many trips into Concord. The presence of family often reduces the poetic seriousness of nature writing to low buffooning paragraphs. Although White's being alone is tinged with melancholy, particularly as readers see years pass and realize that White is growing deaf and slipping toward the grave, the *Natural History* never smacked of melodramatic loneliness. Never did White resemble the archetypical romantic solitary and roamer, Byron's Childe Harold, "the wandering outlaw of his own dark mind." Moreover, in contrast to much later roaming, White's discoveries do not lead to self-knowledge but knowledge beyond self, knowledge that comforts because it is of a world that outlives the individual.

As much as he admired the *Natural History*, in a preface to an 1887 edition Richard Jefferies regretted that White "did not leave a natural history of the people of his day" (p. xii). Although White lamented the absence of friends who shared his love of nature, people filled his world. Village boys brought him eggs, and farmers presented creatures to him: female vipers, an otter, mice, birds. Usually the animals were dead, the birds having been shot and the vipers sliced open in order to view the young inside. White called the end of the barn where farmers nailed hides and bodies "the countryman's museum." The killing of the animals is not to modern taste. Only rarely did White endow animals with human attributes, and he seems to have done so not out of a belief in the humanity of animals but simply as a way of describing behavior. In 1798 Thomas Young published *An Essay on Humanity to Animals,* in which he argued that the rights of animals, like those of man, could be "deduced from the Light of Nature." Since animals were "endued with a capability of perceiving pleasure and pain" and since "abundant provision" was made in this world "for the gratification of their several senses, we must conclude," Young declared, "that the Creator wills the happiness of these creatures, and consequently that humanity towards them is agreeable to him, and cruelty the contrary" (pp. 4–8). White was not cruel, but he did not subscribe to the rights of animals. Like White, most early ornithologists shot birds in order to study them. James Audubon did so, and Burroughs even shot birds off the nest. Applicable to the early ornithologist is the old statement that if an angel flew low enough, he would shoot it.

In Letter 6 to Pennant in the *Natural History,* White lamented the disappearance of the heathcock, vanished because of overhunting. He criticized "unreasonable sportsmen" who shot "twenty and sometimes thirty brace in a day" (pp. 29–30). He also recounted the disappearance of red deer, so preyed upon by poachers that the Duke of Cumberland had them removed. At the beginning of the eighteenth century, White reported in Letter 7 to Pennant, "all this country was wild about deer-stealing" (p. 31). By tempting people to poach, deer, he thought, did more injury to morals than to crops. Typically White did not preach after making the observation. The tendency to resist preachment contributed to his image as a comfortable man. In contrast, for example, in the *Cheap Repository Tracts,* published at the end of the century by evangelical Anglicans, the Clapham Sect, poaching led not simply to imprisonment or transportation but to the loss of soul and damnation.

Occasionally White described local superstitions, the idea, for instance, that twigs or branches removed from a grotesque pollard ash, known locally as a shrew ash, relieved pains caused by shrews running over farm animals' backs. Often he described local characters, a leper, for example, or an idiot boy. This last, he said in Letter 27 to Barrington, was practically a bee bird. "Honeybees, humble-bees, and wasps, were his prey wherever he found them: he had no apprehensions from their stings, but would seize them *nudis manibus* [with bare hands], and at once disarm them of their weapons, and suck their bodies for the sake of their honey-bags" (p. 200). The boy often put captive bees down his shirt. He raided hives, taking bees as they came out and then eating the honey inside. When he ran about, he made "a humming noise with his lips, resembling the buzzing of bees" (p. 201). White's bee bird was a precursor to Wordsworth's Boy of Winander who blew "mimic hootings to the silent owls." Unlike Wordsworth's boy, the bee boy did not carry the freight of poetic significance. He was just an inhabitant of Selborne, an unfortunate who became the stuff of a curious anecdote.

Most of the anecdotes in the *Natural History* concerned animals: Letter 17 to Pennant tells of a huge toad that was fancied by ladies "of peculiar taste" and fed maggots until it grew "to a monstrous size." The toad lived in a hole under steps leading to a garden. After supper the ladies placed it on a table and fed it. After a tame raven pecked one of its eyes out, the toad languished and died. One summer a tame bat took flies out of White's hand. According to Letter 11 to Pennant, "the adroitness it showed in shearing off the wings of the flies, which were always rejected, was worthy of observation, and pleased me much" (pp. 44–45).

The most famous creature in the *Natural History* is Timothy the tortoise, who originally inhabited the garden of White's aunt and later moved to The Wakes after her death. White wrote in Letter 13 to Barrington that on the first of November Timothy "began first to dig the ground" in order to build his "*hybernaculum,* which it had fixed on just beside a great turf of hepaticas. It scrapes out the ground with its fore-feet, and throws it up over its back with its hind; but the motion of its legs is ridiculously slow, little exceeding the hour-hand of a clock; and suitable to the composure of an animal said to be a whole month in performing one feat of copulation." He continues:

No part of its behaviour ever struck me more than the extreme timidity it always expresses with regard to rain; for though it has a shell that would secure it against the wheel of a loaded cart, yet does it discover as much solicitude about rain as a lady dressed in all her best attire, shuffling away on the first sprinklings, and running its head up in a corner. If attended to, it becomes an excellent weather-glass; for as sure as it walks elate, and as it were on tiptoe, feeding with great earnestness in a morning, so sure will it rain before night.

(pp. 153–154)

"I was much taken," White noted after observing his aunt feed the tortoise, "with its sagacity in discerning those that do it kind offices: for, as soon as the good old lady comes in sight who has waited on it for more than thirty years, it hobbles towards its benefactress with aukward alacrity; but remains inattentive to strangers. Thus not only 'the ox knoweth his owner, and the ass his master's crib,' but the most abject reptile and torpid of beings distinguishes the hand that feeds it, and is touched with the feelings of gratitude" (p. 154).

Anecdotes about animals are the stuff of many nature books from the last half of the twentieth century. James Herriot raised his books upon descriptions of the doings of animals. In Gerald Durrell's *The Drunken Forest, Menagerie Manor, A Zoo in My Luggage,* and *The Whispering Land,* among a shelf of others, animals are main characters. In *My Family and Other Animals,* the best of Durrell's books, young Durrell buys Achilles the tortoise from the Rose-Beetle Man. After devouring crates of strawberries and like Timothy providing days of entertainment, Achilles tumbles down an abandoned well and dies.

White's greatest enthusiasm was for birds, and he wrote more about birds than any other creatures. He kept careful records of the appearance of species in spring and their disappearance in fall. He measured and weighed birds. He examined the contents of craw and stomach. Above all, his studies brought delight to him and later to readers. He watched birds feed. The flycatcher, he wrote in Letter 10 to Pennant, "takes its stand on the top of some stake or post, from whence it springs forth on its prey, catching a fly in the air, and hardly ever touching the ground, but returning still to the same stand for many times together" (p. 41). According to Letter 11 to Pennant, young barn owls are indiscriminate eaters, feeding on "snails, rats, kittens, puppies, magpies, and any kind of carrion or offal" (p. 44). The fern-owl fed in flight. More than once, White reported, he saw the bird "put out its short leg while on the wing, and, by a bend of the head, deliver somewhat into its mouth." Taking and eating prey in flight explained the use of the bird's middle toe, "which is curiously furnished with a serrated claw" (Letter 37 to Pennant, p. 102). As an aside White wondered in Letter 12 to Pennant if canaries could be naturalized to Selborne, by putting their eggs into the nests of "some of their congeners" such as goldfinches (p. 47). Then, perhaps by winter, he thought, canaries might be able to shift for themselves. White also described the nests of birds. In the middle of May, providing that the weather was good, the house martin

begins to think in earnest of providing a mansion for its family. The crust or shell of this nest seems to be formed of such dirt or loam as comes most readily to hand, and is tempered and wrought together with little bits of broken straws to render it tough and tenacious. As this bird often builds against a perpendicular wall without any projecting ledge under, it requires its utmost efforts to get the first foundation firmly fixed, so that it may safely carry the superstructure. On this occasion the bird not only clings with its claws, but partly supports itself by strongly inclining its tail against the wall, making that a fulcrum; and thus steadied it works and plasters the materials into the face of the brick or stone.
(Letter 16 to Barrington, pp. 161–162)

Not only did White increase interest in close observation of birds, and other creatures, but he showed that such studies could bring almost endless pleasure.

White described both the sounds and flights of birds. "The grasshopper-lark," he wrote in April 1768 in Letter 16 to Pennant, "began his sibilous note in my fields last Saturday. Nothing can be more amusing than the whisper of this little bird, which seems to be close by though at an hundred yards distance; and, when close at your ear, is scarce any louder than when a great way off" (p. 56). After visiting a friend, White described in Letter 10 to Barrington the man's efforts to analyze the hooting of owls. He tried all the owls "that are his near neighbours with a pitch-pipe set at concert-pitch, and finds they all hoot in B flat" (p. 148). White's favorite birds were swallows, and they swirl through many letters. "Wonderful is the address" that the chimney swallow shows, he wrote, "all day long in ascending and descending with security through so narrow a pass. When hovering over the mouth of the funnel, the vibrations of her wings acting on the confined air occa-

sion a rumbling like thunder" (Letter 18 to Barrington, p. 172). A swallow, White reported, built its nest "on the wings and body of an owl that happened by accident to hang dead and dry from the rafter of a barn." After the nest was removed, the owner of the barn stuck a conch shell in its place. The following year a pair of swallows built a nest "in the conch," and the female laid eggs (p. 175). White studied the flight of birds, noting in Letter 42 to Barrington, for example, that owls moved buoyantly, "as if lighter than air." While titlarks rose and fell in large curves, white-throats jerked over the tops of hedges and bushes. Sand martins also jerked in flight, "with frequent vacillations like a butterfly" (p. 233). Doubtless, he speculated, the flights of swallows were influenced by the insects on which they fed. "Hence it would be worthy inquiry to examine what particular genus of insects affords the principal food of each respective species of swallow" (Letter 20 to Barrington, p. 181).

AN HONOR OF NATURE

IN his last letter to Barrington, written in 1787, White said that he had considered writing a natural history of the twelve months of the year. But, he explained, since two books on the subject had already appeared and "as the length of my correspondence has sufficiently put your patience to the test, I shall here take a respectful leave of you and natural history altogether" (Letter 66 to Barrington, p. 289). He took leave of his book but not of natural history. He continued writing in the *Naturalist's Journal* until the middle of June 1793. On 1 June 1793, he noted that Timothy the tortoise was so "voracious" that when he could not get other food, he ate grass. On 6 June, he "sowed two rows of large white kidney-beans" and noticed that "the old Bantam brought out only three chickens." On 13 June, "Provence roses blew against a wall. Dames violets [were] very fine," and after ten weeks stocks were still in bloom. The next day he "cut four cucumbers," for a total of twenty-two cut in three days (vol. 3, pp. 465–467). Twelve days later, on 26 June 1793, he died.

In the entry in the *Journal* for 8 July 1792, White wrote that "The Poet of Nature," James Thomson, "lets few rural incidents escape him. In his *Summer* he mentions the *whetting* of a *scythe* as a pleasing circumstance, not from the real sound, which is harsh, grating, & unmusical; but from the train of summer ideas which it raises in the imagination. No one who loves his garden & lawn but rejoices to hear the sound of the mower on an early, dewy morning" (vol. 3, p. 420). Similarly, *The Natural History of Selborne* raised trains of association in readers' minds. Not only did Selborne seem like Auburn before wealth accumulated and men decayed, but it also resembled a village similar to that described in Thomas Gray's "Elegy Written in a Country Churchyard." Because galloping commercialism left Selborne or "this neglected spot" untouched, compared, say, to Thoreau's Walden Pond, pilgrims viewed it almost as fairyland. Development of Concord and Walden, for example, undermined place, making it increasingly difficult for people to escape the moment and indulge the imagination. For the most part, trips to Walden evoke cynicism and bemusement, not the spirit of Thoreau. In 1939 E. B. White described "fronting only the essential facts of life" on Highway 126. At the end of his piece on Walden, White parodied Thoreau instead of celebrating him as pilgrims to Selborne celebrated White. After recording that he bought a baseball bat and a left-handed fielder's glove in Concord to bring back to his son, White addressed Thoreau, saying, "You never had to cope with a shortstop."

In 1830 the writer for the *New Monthly Magazine and Literary Journal* sought out White's grave, much as a visitor to the country churchyard might seek out the grave of Gray's poet in order to pay elegiac homage. Poetic truth became actual truth. The tablet that stood above White's grave had been shifted. Knowing that White's grave was the "fifth grave from the wall," the writer eventually noticed a "slight heave of turf" and a low headstone, reading "G.W. Ob. 1793." "Far from the madding crowd's ignoble strife," White, the writer believed, lived the good life and through the *Natural History* showed readers ways to better their lives (p. 569).

In the last year of his life, W. H. Auden wrote "Posthumous Letter to Gilbert White." In the poem Auden speculated that Thoreau might have found White to be the ideal friend he never met. The two writers shared much. Both appeared immune to the seduction of worldly power. Instead they found creatures amusing and interesting. Auden then said he wished he had known White. That being impossible, however, he concluded the poem by declaring that he had the right

to "reread" White, something almost every naturalist seems to have done since the early nineteenth century. The warden of Merton was prescient. White's book became remarkably popular, not simply making readers appreciate nature more but also awakening imagination and enriching life. *Natural History*, Virginia Woolf wrote in *The Captain's Death Bed and Other Essays* (1950), "left a door open, through which we hear distant sounds, a dog barking, cart wheels creaking, and see, when 'all the fading landscape sinks in night,' if not Venus herself, at least a phantom owl" (p. 19).

SELECTED BIBLIOGRAPHY

I. NATURAL HISTORY. More than one hundred editions of the *Natural History* have been published. Most are interesting not for what they reveal about White, but for what they reveal about attitudes toward White and the study of nature. The first edition and standard text is *The natural history and antiquities of Selborne, in the county of Southampton: with engravings, and an appendix* (London, 1789). In 1970 the Scolar Press at Menston published a reprint of the first edition.

A selection of particularly interesting editions of the *Natural History* includes John Aikin, ed., *The Works, in Natural History, of the late Gilbert White . . . To which are added, a calendar and observations, by W. Markwick* (London, 1802), and the British Library has a copy of this edition, annotated by Samuel Taylor Coleridge; John White, ed., *The Natural History . . . To Which are Added The Naturalist's Calendar* (London, 1813); *The Natural History . . . Selborne: A New Edition, with notes, by several eminent naturalists. And an enlargement of the naturalist's calendar* (London, 1832); Edward Jesse, *Gleanings in Natural History. Second Series. To which are added some extracts from the unpublished MSS. of . . . Mr. White* (London, 1834); Edward Jesse, ed., *The Natural History . . . Selborne with observations on various parts of nature, and the naturalist's calendar. With additions and supplementary notes by Sir William Jardine* (London, 1849); Thomas Browne, ed., *The Natural History . . . with extensive additions* (London, 1853); G. C. Davis, ed., *The Natural History . . . Selborne* (1869); *The Natural History . . . with notes by Frank Buckland, a chapter on antiquities by Lord Selborne and new letters* (London, 1875); E. T. Bennett, ed., *The Natural History . . . Thoroughly rev., with additional notes by James Edmund Harting* (London, 1875), which includes an appendix containing ten letters White wrote to R. Marsham; Thomas Bell, ed., *The Natural History . . . Selborne* (London, 1877), containing letters, poems, and material from White's account books within its two volumes; *White's Natural History* (London, 1882), which was part of Routledge's Sixpenny Series; *The Natural History of Selborne . . . with a preface by Richard Jefferies* (London,

1887); *The Natural History of Selborne . . . with the text and new letters of the Buckland ed.* (London, 1895), including an introduction by John Burroughs; *The Natural History . . . with notes by Richard Kearton, F. Z. S., and 123 illustrations from photographs* (London, 1902); *The Natural History . . . with illustrations in colour by George Edward Collins* (London, 1911); Wilfred Mark Webb, ed., *A Nature Calendar* (London, 1911), a limited edition published by the Selborne Society and printed on Italian handmade paper; Walter Sidney Scott, ed., *The Antiquities of Selborne . . . with wash drawings of Selborne made in the year 1776 by Samuel Hieronymous Grim* (London, 1950); *The Natural History . . . with drawings by John Nash* (London, 1951); Walter Sidney Scott, ed., *The Natural History . . . Selborne* (London, 1962), published for the Folio Society and containing drawings by John Piper.

Editions of the *Natural History* published for children include Lady Dover, ed., *The Natural History . . . arranged for young persons* (London, 1833); *The Natural History . . . for young persons* (London, 1870), published for the Society for Promoting Christian Knowledge; F. A Bruton, ed., *Selections from White's Natural History of Selborne* (London, 1909), published for the English Literature for Secondary Schools Series under the general editorship of J. H. Fowler; *The School Selborne: Being selections from the Natural History* (London, 1910); Marcus Woodward, ed., *White's Selborne for Boys and Girls* (Oxford, 1927).

II. JOURNALS AND LETTERS. Francesca Greenoak, ed., *The Journals of Gilbert White* (London, 1986–1989). The Greenoak edition is in three volumes covering the years 1751–1773, 1774–1783, and 1784–1793. This edition, edited under the general editorship of Richard Mabey, is the definitive edition (and from which all page references in this text are to), superceding Walter Johnson, ed., *Gilbert White's Journals* (London, 1931).

Excerpts from White's journals were attached to many early editions of the *Natural History*. In 1795 selections from the journals first appeared, these being excerpts from the *Garden Kalendar,* "printed for B. and J. White," in *A Naturalist's Calendar, with Observations in Various Branches of Natural History; Extracted from the Papers of the late Rev. Gilbert White,* edited by John Aikin (London, 1795). In 1975 the Scolar Press published a facsimile edition of the "Garden kalendar."

Appended to several nineteenth-century editions of the *Natural History* are letters written by White. Two collections are important, however: Rashleigh Holt White, ed., *The Life and Letters of Gilbert White* (London, 1901), and John Mulso, *The Letters to Gilbert White of Selborne from his intimate friend* (London, 1907).

Timothy the tortoise became White's most popular "character." In 1946 Sylvia Townsend Warner introduced *The Portrait of a Tortoise, Extracted from the Journals and Letters of Gilbert White* (London, 1946).

III. BIBLIOGRAPHIES. Gilbert White, *The Natural History . . . Selborne,* edited by Grant Allen (London, 1899–1900), published by John Lane at the Bodley Head and issued in parts, includes a bibliography compiled by Alfred Paterson; H. B. Watt, *A List of Bibliographies of the Writings of Gilbert White* (London, 1910); Edward Alfred Martin, *A Bibliography of Gilbert White, the Naturalist and Antiquarian of Selborne: With a Biography and a Descriptive Account of the Village of Selborne* (London, 1934), a revised and enlarged edition of an 1897 text.

IV. BIOGRAPHICAL AND CRITICAL STUDIES. The standard biography is Richard Mabey, *Gilbert White: A Biography of the Author of The Natural History of Selborne* (London, 1986); Mabey's book won the Whitbread Biography of the Year Award. Introductions to the various editions of the *Natural History* are also a good source of critical and biographical remarks, particulary Richard Jefferies, preface to *The Natural History of Selborne* (London, 1887) and John Burroughs, intro. to *Natural History at Selborne,* 2 vols. (New York, 1895).

See also *New Monthly Magazine and Literary Journal* 29, part II (1830); John Burroughs, *Indoor Studies* (Boston and Cambridge, 1889); James Russell Lowell, *Latest Literary Essays and Addresses* (Cambridge, 1891); Richard B. Sharpe, *White Friars Club. Pilgrimage to Selborne* (London, 1901); John C. Wright, *"Saint" Gilbert: The Story of Gilbert White and Selborne* (London, 1908); Marcus Woodward, *In Nature's Ways . . . Being an Introduction to White's "Natural History of Selborne"* (London, 1914); Walter Johnson, *Gilbert White: Pioneer, Poet, and Stylist* (London, 1928); Edmund Blunden, *Nature in English Literature* (London, 1929); Walter Scott, *White of Selborne* (London, 1950); Ronald Lockley, *Gilbert White* (London, 1954); E. D. H. Johnson, ed., *The Poetry of the Earth: A Collection of English Nature Writings from Gilbert White of Selborne to Richard Jefferies* (New York, 1966); Charles F. Mullett, *"Multum in Parvo*: Gilbert White of Selborne," in *Journal of the History of Biology* 2 (fall 1969); *Gilbert White of Selborne* (London, 1970), publication 688 of the British Museum's Natural History Department; Anthony Rye, *Gilbert White and His Selborne* (London, 1970); James Devlin, "Henry Thoreau and Gilbert White: Concord and Selborne," in *Xavier University Studies* 11, no. 2 (1972); William Keith, *The Rural Tradition: William Cobbett, Gilbert White, and Other Non-Fiction Prose Writers of the English Countryside* (Hassocks, 1975); Leopold Damrosch Jr., "Gilbert White of Selborne: Enlightenment Science and Conservative Ideal," in *Studies in Burke and His Time* 19, no. 1 (1978); Paula R. Backscheider, ed., *Probability, Time and Space in Eighteenth-Century Literature* (New York, 1979); S. E. G. Curtis, "A Comparision Between Gilbert White's Selborne and William Bartram's Travels," in *Proceedings of the 7th Congress of the International Comparative Literature Association* (Stuttgart, 1979); Marian Clover, "Gilbert White: Father of British Naturalists," in *British Heritage* 4 (1983); Paul Foster, ed., "The Gibralter Correspondence of Gilbert White," in *Notes and Queries,* n.s., 32, nos. 2, 3 (1985); Paul Foster, "William Sheffield: Four Letters to Gilbert White," in *Archives of Natural History* 12, no. 1 (1985); Arthur Sherbo, "The English Weather, the *Gentleman's Magazine,* and The Brothers White," in *Archives of Natural History* 12, no. 1 (1985); Paul Foster, "The Hon. Daines Barrington: Annotations on Two Journals Compiled by Gilbert White," in *Notes and Records of the Royal Society of London* 41 (1986); Lucy B. Maddox, "Gilbert White and the Politics of Natural History," in *Eighteenth-Century Life* 10, no. 2 (1986); Paul G. M. Foster, *Gilbert White and His Records: A Scientific Biography* (London, 1988); Elizabeth Heckendorn Cook, "Selborne's Cultural Landscapes: An Exhibition," in *Cultural Landscapes: Gilbert White and the Natural History of Selborne* (Stanford, 1989); June Chatfield, "The Natural History and Antiquities of Selborne Two Hundred Years On," in *Selborne Association Newsletter* 31 (1989); Paul Foster, "Approaches to the Study of Gilbert White," in *Archives of Natural History* 17, no. 3 (1990); David Fussell, "The Greening Eye: Gilbert White, the Picturesque and Natural History," in *Critical Survey* 2, no. 1 (1990); P. A. Morris, "Examination of a Preserved Hawfinch . . . Attributed to Gilbert White," in *Archives of Natural History* 17, no. 3 (1990); Robert D. Pepper, "Gilbert White's Tiny Mouse: A Sceptical Objection in 1789," in *Notes and Queries,* n.s., 37 (September 1990); Clarence Wolfshohl, "Gilbert White's Natural History and History," in *CLIO* 20, no. 3 (1991); Robert James Merrett, "Natural History and the Eighteenth-Century Novel," in *Eighteenth-Century Studies* 25, no. 2 (1991–1992); Shelia Rainey, "Dear Molly," in *Selborne Association Newsletter* 34 (1992); Barry Baldwin, "The Bird Man of Hampshire," in *Hellas* 5, no. 1 (1994); Paul S. Cornelius, "Benjamin White (1725–1794), His Older Brother Gilbert and Notes on the Hibernation of Swallows," in *Archives of Natural History* 21, no. 2 (1994); Stuart Peterfreund, "Clare, White and the Modalities of Meditation," in *Wordsworth Circle* 27 (summer 1996); John R. Campbell, "A Secret Iridescence," in *Georgia Review* 51 (summer 1997); Peter Neumeyer, "Charlotte vive," in *CEA Critic* 60, no. 1 (1997).

A. N. WILSON

(1950–   )

William H. Pritchard

THE THIRTY-TWO BOOKS A. N. Wilson has published since his first in 1977 are of remarkably different natures and constitute a significant achievement for a writer who turned fifty on 27 October 2000. His fiction, his biographies, his criticism of religion and culture embody an extraordinarily lively mind, engaged with the main currents of British life as it transpired in the last quarter of the twentieth century. His literary operations are conducted always in a spirit of exhilaration that readers find appealing; Wilson's is a mind willing to entertain varied, sometimes contradictory, ideas in order to see which of them entertain him. His restless curiosity entails the willingness to change his mind and makes for a volatile, attractive, unpredictable presence. As he once remarked about John Ruskin, the Victorian sage he much admires, "You never know quite which way he will jump." This enlivening habit is evident in Wilson's own novels, in his religious and philosophical critiques, and in the subjects of his biographies and shorter portraits. The more one reads and rereads him, the deeper one moves into something that can be called "a world"—observed, imagined, and rendered with full articulateness by an exceptional intelligence. T. S. Eliot once wrote about Shakespeare that any one of his plays could be understood only in the light of his work as a whole. With A. N. Wilson the challenge is to acknowledge the surprise and variety of his books as they appear, while keeping an eye on the larger pattern of meaning they display.

CHILDHOOD AND YOUTH

ANDREW Norman Wilson was born in Stone, Staffordshire, the youngest of three children of Norman and Jean Dorothy Crowder Wilson. His father was a pottery owner (for a time the managing director of Wedgewood) and a designer of pottery, examples of which can be seen in London's Victoria and Albert Museum. The young Wilson, whose literary inclinations were on early notice, was educated by Dominican nuns, then sent away at age seven to a preparatory school, Hillstone, in Great Malvern, Wales. The seven years he spent at what he once called "a crummy, hateful little place" surely provided rich material for his later fiction, especially Julian Ramsay's school days in the first volume of Wilson's five-volume chronicle *The Lampitt Papers*. In 1964 Wilson entered Rugby School, then won a scholarship to New College, Cambridge, where he read English under John Bayley, to whom, along with Bayley's wife, Iris Murdoch, he would dedicate his first novel. His special academic interests at Oxford were Old and Middle English as well as linguistics, although the books to come reveal an immensely well-read student of English poets, novelists, and essayists generally. Wilson's interest in the fine arts (at one point he thought of himself as a painter) is also evident in his fiction, which has many examples of expert perception about particular artists and works of art. At Oxford, in 1971, he won the Chancellor's Essay Prize and that same year married Katherine Duncan-Jones, a Fellow in English at Somerville College and ten years Wilson's senior. Two daughters came of the union.

After taking his Oxford degree, Wilson did freelance teaching there at New College, and in 1973 spent a year in training for the Anglican priesthood at Saint Stephen's House, a theological seminary near Oxford. The experience was not a successful one. Over the next few years he lectured at Saint Hugh's College and New College, Oxford, and also served a term as master at Merchant Taylor's School in Northwood, Middlesex, where he wrote his first novel, *The Sweets of Pimlico*. This was followed over the next six years by five further novels, the last of which, *Wise Virgin*, marked his first publication in America in 1983. The years also saw his debut as a biographer of Sir Walter Scott and John Milton. As if these projects weren't sufficient to keep him wholly occupied, in 1981 he became literary editor of the *Spectator*, a conservative London weekly with an excellent book review section. Wilson himself contributed numerous reviews to the magazine and to the *Times Literary Supplement* and *Sunday Telegraph*—a selection of his journalism from the 1980s, *Penfriends from Porlock*, appeared in 1988. In the manner of a writer whose major interests lay elsewhere, Wilson prefaced the selection by claiming to be "appalled" at how many books he had reviewed and how few of them had stayed in his memory. Elsewhere he remarks, with humorous exaggeration, that he forgets journalism as soon as he writes it, sometimes even before he writes it. He resigned from the *Spectator* in 1983, later becoming literary editor of the *Evening Standard*, to which he contributed a weekly column.

In the second half of the 1980s, Wilson's attention to religion, always a central aspect of his fiction, expressed itself in more controversial, sometimes polemical, fashion; the polemic reached its height in a 1991 pamphlet, *Against Religion*, in which he rejected and urged others to reject Christianity. Although no causal relation should be claimed between his rejection of religious belief and his personal life, Wilson's marriage broke up during this period, and in 1990 he married the art historian Ruth Guilding, with whom he took up residence in London. Meanwhile his rate of production continued unrelenting, with biographies of Tolstoy and C. S. Lewis. Studies of Jesus and Paul, conducted in a skeptical, informed manner, followed in the nineties, along with *God's Funeral*, a survey of religious and philosophical debate about God over the past two centuries. Wilson makes no claim to be a man of action, remarking once that he has led a quiet life and plans to lead an even quieter one. Where the action—the noise, as it were—has been and will continue to be is nowhere else than in his individual books.

EARLY NOVELS

IN a somewhat arbitrary way, since Wilson's production of novels has been steady and unceasing, we may consider first the six he published in the years 1977–1982. In their different ways, these books share an interest in and expertise about what Kingsley Amis, speaking of light verse, called "manners, social forms, amusements, fashion (from millinery to philosophy), topicality, even gossip." Stylistically varied, they share over-all a narrative perspicuity, usually humorously directed, in their presentation of the London/Oxbridge milieu where Wilson found his real and literary home. They display this milieu through a comic-satiric mode that Wilson quickly made his own but whose ancestry he was well aware of, having observed it in writers such as Ronald Firbank, Evelyn Waugh, Anthony Powell, Kingsley Amis, Iris Murdoch, and Anthony Burgess. Others names could be added, but these are enough to suggest that Wilson is temperamentally closer to such ironic comedians than, say, to Doris Lessing or John Fowles or C. P. Snow. Yet any umbrella rubric such as "satire" is too crude to do justice to the delicacies of perception, wit, and feeling his novels contain.

His first, *The Sweets of Pimlico* (1977), won the John Llewellyn Rhys Memorial Prize. A poised and accomplished piece of work of less than two hundred pages, it has a capably managed plot in which a number of related characters work out their destinies. A young schoolmistress named Evelyn Tradescant, having recently broken off with her fiancé, is lonely, vulnerable to experience, and passionate about natural history, particularly insects (her name evokes a seventeenth-century naturalist, John Tradescant). One afternoon in Kensington Gardens, Evelyn meets Theo Gormann, a mysterious, elderly man with an enigmatic past. Gormann is rich and takes pains to draw Evelyn into his set, one of whose members is a sexually ambiguous figure named John "Pimlico" Price, a sweets manufacturer (hence the title). The novel is about Evelyn's growing realization of her love for Theo, which reaches a disastrous conclusion when he is seriously wounded by a bomb set off in the National Gallery. Evelyn comes to an awareness of sexual complication, particularly of the homosexual network in which Theo and Price, as well as her brother Jeremy (a lover of Price's), are involved. (There is even a rather gratuitous, or at least not deeply thought-out, moment of lovemaking between Evelyn and her brother.) The novel is attractive for its strong presentation of the London of Kensington and Pimlico, and for some well-executed comic scenes involving Evelyn's parents, letters that go astray revealing sexual indiscretions, and the like. But when Theo is crippled by the explosion, Evelyn moves him to Brighton, where she looks after him until he dies, and the novel's tone deepens as she tries to make sense of what has happened between her and the old man:

like every important thing in life, it seemed inevitable. But *how* they came to know each other, and love each other; by what degrees their intimacy had deepened, or unfolded—she was unsure which metaphor was the more apt—she found it hard to remember. The strands were too complex and delicate to be seen as it were with the naked eye of memory.

(p. 170)

Human beings in their mystery are more difficult to see clearly than varieties of insects; the "naked eye of memory" is a difficult faculty to trust. Wilson returned to this theme in later works, but it is convincingly, even movingly, set forth in his first novel.

The Sweets of Pimlico was quickly followed by *Unguarded Hours* (1978) and *Kindly Light* (1979), which are continuous in that they follow the "progress" of their hero, a hapless young man named Norman Shotover. These novels show Wilson at his most freewheeling and extravagant, since their satiric technique is loud and opportunistic, presenting us with a carload of "religious" figures—sinister priests, gay and transvestite seminarians, a leftish dean anxious to bring the church up to date—along with countless other improbable figures and institutions. The novels have a clear precursor in Waugh's *Decline and Fall*, in which Paul Pennyfeather, an innocent, good-hearted young man, is buffeted by the winds of chance into schoolmastering, white slavery, and prison, all of which occupations turn out to be essentially identical. One of the funniest scenes in *Kindly Light* occurs when Norman chaotically steers a class of boys through a scene in *Macbeth*, and even as the students behave and speak outrageously, Norman feels "glad that he had turned out to be such a success as a teacher." (The scene in *Decline and Fall* where Paul Pennyfeather attempts to keep order with the boys at Llanabba Castle school comes to mind.) Like Waugh's hero, or anti-hero, Norman is sensible, thoughtful, wanting nothing more than to find an acceptable life's calling; circumstances, as directed by the novelist, hilariously conspire to make such a discovery absolutely impossible.

Wilson enlists us in the effort to keep things going wrong for his hero, as when Norman hears Lady Bayswater, the woman on whose account he was fired from the firm of Windle, Windle, and Bight, declare, "There's no point in going gentle with them. . . . You've got to kill them, and the

younger the better." Norman assumes the worst, only to have it explained by his putative sweetheart, Cressida, that "Mrs Swanston" (another lady in the room) "is having trouble with slugs": "I've tried pellets and everything," replies the lady in question. Norman's career as a priest (he has been "consecrated" in *Unguarded Hours* by a wandering bishop named Skegg) lands him in *Kindly Light*, in a "modern" Christian retreat as conducted by Father Sporran and his dancing nuns, who "wore only black fish-net stockings and the briefest of tunics." They sing the Beatles' "All You Need Is Love" while Father Sporran serves a Communion repast of Hovis (an ordinary English loaf of brown bread) and Beaujolais. Observing the nuns, Norman decides that they look terrible, that "It had been a big mistake to give up wearing the habit," since one now became aware of "wobbling thighs, hairy armpits, varicose veins bulging their way through nylon."

The satire is external, broad, sometimes crude; the human figures it is directed at are caricatures—grotesque simplifications of life. But as T. S. Eliot has reminded us, "creative" satire invites us less to take pleasure in people being exposed than to delight in the grotesque proportions they have been given by the satirist. Wilson's negative attitudes and his unflattering view of most human beings as they go about their misconceived tasks give us the license not to take people seriously; he refuses to grant them an inner life with which we must sympathize. These two "Norman Shotover" novels show Wilson at his most unbuttoned and amusing in making artistic capital out of human follies.

With *The Healing Art* (1980), which won three prizes, including the Somerset Maugham Award, Wilson attempted something quite other than the theatrical extravagances of the Shotover novels. In its fine opening hospital sequence, two women who have had breast cancer operations visit their surgeon for six-week checkups. The younger woman, on whom much of the novel will focus, is an Oxford lecturer named Pamela Cowper; the older woman, Dorothy Higgs, is a working-class wife. In a drastic mistake, their charts get mixed up, and the harried, arrogant, indeed brutal Dr. Tulloch finds the healthy-looking Pamela to be terminally ill, while Dorothy, who looks and is indeed very ill, is assured she's coming along fine. Dr. Tulloch insists that Pamela have chemotherapy, to prolong slightly the two months she has left; Pamela, whose notions about the healing art have a pronounced religious tinge, refuses the medical advice and goes to America instead to visit her sometime boyfriend, John Brocklehurst, an Oxford philosophy don visiting at Cornell. Through a combination of circumstances, Pamela ends up in an Ithaca hospital, where she is found to be perfectly healthy; Dorothy, meanwhile, disintegrates rapidly, is back in the hospital with broken bones, and never finds out her true condition. Wilson ambitiously creates a cast of characters surrounding each woman and at a crucial moment brings them back together, just before Dorothy is killed in a car crash.

Pamela's spiritual counselor, Father Stickley (nicknamed "Sourpuss"), expresses the novel's animating idea when, on a visit to the shrine at Walsingham before Pamela flies to America, he tells her, "We don't expect *doctors* to work miracles, but that is not to say that we don't expect miracles." Yet there is no conclusive development of this theme, rather an undetermined openness about how much should or can be said, with confidence, about "the healing art." Despite many interesting successes—including some excellent university-directed satire and a sharp portrayal of the medical profession as glimpsed through one of its least lovely specimens—the novel goes on too long and tries to put too much in play. Pamela returns from America with a young woman she meets in Ithaca, seemingly pregnant by the don Brocklehurst, and a sexual relation develops unconvincingly between the women. The novel's violent conclusion, a fireworks blowup at Brocklehurst's rooms in college resulting in two deaths, feels like a desperate grasping at effects. The two previous Waugh-like novels each ended in the grossest of improbabilities (Norman jumping off a tower, Norman teaching Greek—or perhaps *Macbeth*—to a group of chimpanzees) suitable to the farcical tone of the books. *The Healing Art*, which begins so gravely and invites us to imagine inner lives for at least some of its characters, ends in a manner unworthy of its earlier promise. In the novel's combination of bizarre human about-faces—often sexual ones—and violent events (car crash, explosion), Wilson is writing in an Iris Murdoch vein. As with some of Murdoch's books the result is problematic.

At this point in his career, having published four well-received novels, Wilson had received little adverse criticism. This was to come, however, when in 1981, his fifth novel, *Who Was Oswald Fish?* appeared. Longer than *The Healing Art*, its plot was even more complicated, indeed the most elaborate one found in any Wilson novel. The question of its title refers to a late-Victorian architect, one of whose artifacts—a disused church in Birmingham—is about to be demolished. The city council's representative whose job is to make this happen is an unhappily married father of two named Fred Jobling, who in the course of attending to business meets a brash and glamorous businesswoman-entrepreneur named Fanny Williams. He falls in love with her (this is reciprocated, though complicatedly), with immediate and dislocating ramifications to Fred's marriage and to Fanny's London menage. (She has a live-in bisexual African lover, Charles Bulloweewo, and two unbelievably evil children named Marmaduke and Pandora; and an aunt, who turns out to be the architect's, Oswald Fish's, daughter.) At one juncture Wilson provides a chart diagramming some of the generational complexities, but even the closest of readers is going to get lost in the maze of interconnection, coincidence, and fiendishly manipulated events constructed by the novelist. The book's language and style are brash, outrageous, full of sexual jokes and "improper" diction. It is highly entertaining stuff, but it did not amuse the novelist A. S. Byatt, who reviewed it in the *Times Literary Supplement* and after suggesting what a favorable review might praise in the novel ("its verbal wit, the flamboyance of its sexuality, the co-existence of farce and tragedy") went on to chastise Wilson for what she called "a gossipy, sneering contempt for his world, his characters and his readers." Byatt found that Wilson treated life and death "with a flip sneer" and ended her review by professing not to understand how he had become a novelist of considerable reputation.

There is no point in attempting to "refute" Byatt's charge—readers of the novel must decide for themselves how telling a charge it is. But her review is important as an early, negative response to the way Wilson's fiction is willing, even eager, some feel, to "do dirt on life" (the language is D. H. Lawrence's). Does a novelist who presents, often in a satirical manner, a number of imperfect, unlovely instances of human behavior need also—as Henry James said was necessary—to project "the possible other case, the case rich and edifying"? Or is the piling-up of human follies and vices, without the novelist's explicit condemnation of or detachment from them, a perfectly respectable, indeed entertaining, mode of fictional behavior? *Who Was Oswald Fish?* makes us consider this question more pressingly than any of Wilson's previous books.

Undeniably, *Wise Virgin*, the novel that followed *Oswald Fish*, not only was his most accomplished but also manifests a human sympathy often absent from the earlier books. *Wise Virgin* is no less comic than its predecessors, but the comedy enriches itself especially in its resolution, by taking seriously the inner lives of its two main characters. Giles Fox, a medieval scholar who has lost his eyesight some years back, now lives with his daughter Tibba in a sparely furnished London flat where his overriding occupation is to finish editing a thirteenth-century treatise on virginity (details of the treatise effectively provided by Wilson). Giles has also lost two wives, the first to death in childbirth, the second in an auto accident. He is the recipient of a declaration of love by his research assistant, Miss Louise Agar, who is plain, dumpy, and fattish but whom her employer begins to feel is beautiful. Giles's daughter, moored to a routine of taking care of her father and attending school, has made up a fantasy love life involving Virginia Woolf and an aging, dubious figure, Captain de Courcy, from whom Tibba takes speech lessons in an effort to correct her stutter. There is also a satisfying complement of the usual Wilson comedy, focused on Giles' sister and brother-in-law, a prep school master named Monty Gore ("Ruddy G.," as known by his pupils), and a brash, non-student athlete named Peverill, who eventually falls for Tibba, and vice versa.

What Wilson does in *Wise Virgin* is to invest his own sharp and often dismissive irony, his eye for the absurd and unattractive, in the figure of his embittered protagonist. Here is Giles, waking in the night with stomach discomfort and ruminating on the dinner he and Louise Agar have been given by a Cambridge supervisor of hers (Louise is a medieval scholar whose thesis was not accepted):

How had he managed to survive for forty-seven years in the world without having social life of the kind provided by that supper party? Hard chairs, a cramped little dining "area" in what was obviously a living-room, hardly any room to stretch legs or elbows round the table; cold, rough, red supermarket wine in tumblers tasting (his at any rate) faintly of onion and washing-up liquid; the cassoulet, cooked not quite long enough so that every bean had to be vigilantly chewed with the

knowledge (and here it was, the wakeful proof of it) that it would "keep him up in the night."

The cold inner eye Giles is accustomed to cast on everything, including himself, is finally mitigated in a wonderful and unlikely Christmas visit paid to his lonely digs (Tibba has broken away into her own life) by Louise and her marvelously vulgar mother. Together, and to his own surprise, they melt the stony-hearted scholar, and in a touching moment he asks Miss Agar to marry him. In other words, *Wise Virgin* is that unexpected thing, a Wilson novel with a "happy ending" that along the way forgoes none of the astringent, superbly executed comedy one expects from him. *Wise Virgin* has some of the depth attained at the end of *The Sweets of Pimlico* and intermittently present in *The Healing Art*; but its economical assuredness surpasses anything Wilson had yet produced.

THREE BIOGRAPHIES

TO demonstrate that there was more than one string to his writing bow, Wilson brought out three biographies within the space of five years: *The Laird of Abbotsford: A View of Sir Walter Scott* (1980); *The Life of John Milton* (1983); and *Hilaire Belloc* (1984). These writers were the subjects of previous biographies and Wilson in no way sets himself up as a discoverer of new facts that will "explain" for the first time the particular writer's secret. In fact, there is a deliberately offhand tone to Wilson's enterprise; he calls the Scott biography a "view" or an "essay," declaring at the outset, "This is a work of pure self-indulgence." He sets down his admiration for Scott's life and art in the opening sentence of the preface—"Scott was not only a great writer, he was also a great man"—and in the less than two hundred pages that follow he provides a passionate, proudly subjective account of why he believes this to be the case. Events of Scott's life are selectively but effectively employed, and they alternate with useful, always critical accounts of the novels Wilson sees as most interesting. There is an excellent chapter on Scott as poet; an especially vivid account of the fascinations of *Ivanhoe* (Wilson would later introduce and annotate a Penguin edition of the novel); and a concluding chapter on Scott's Journal as a "record of how he made himself conform to the heroic standards of his own fiction." Wilson writes about the deeply moving passage in which Scott confronts the corpse of his just-deceased wife: "Perhaps no passage in his fiction matches this—and there are many others like it." If Wilson's book on Scott had done no more than call attention to the Journal as a great and today not well-known book, it would have justified itself. In fact, the entire commentary is a feast of intelligent perception.

The Milton biography is more conventional, useful enough in tracing the career of the poet, especially in locating Milton in a London, an England that Wilson renders with telling specificity. Perhaps because of the vast literature on Milton's poems, Wilson seems chary of hazarding much by way of criticism, as if it had all been said before. One doesn't use the book to rethink the Miltonic performance in *Lycidas* or *Paradise Lost*; rather, it helps us become more aware of the conditions—personal, religious, physical (Wilson is good on Milton's blindness)—of that performance. It is also helpful in guiding the nonspecialist student economically and sensibly through the vast corpus of Milton's prose tracts. *The Life of John Milton* doesn't have the personal edge found in the book on Scott; still, it is a lively, wholly readable treatment of a literary and human career.

Finally there is the little-read biography of Belloc, sometimes condescended to or dismissed by those who find neither the subject nor Wilson's treatment of him deserving of attention. In fact, and if one reads it through, *Hilaire Belloc* is a mine of lore with respect to religious and political matters in the late nineteenth and early twentieth centuries. For most of us, this is uncharted territory. Wilson's fascination with his subject is such that it animates these dead issues and draws a compelling portrait of a man with some unappealing qualities—most notoriously Belloc's anti-Semitism—who produced a few quirky and attractive books (*The Path to Rome*, for example). Wilson also manages to shine a new light on a number of poems, especially the *Cautionary Tales for Children*, that have permanently lodged themselves in a minor section of the English poetry canon. As with the Scott book, one detects in Wilson's liking of Belloc more than a whiff of "Tory" sympathy and a yen to demolish certain liberal clichés. As with similar inclinations in Wilson's novels, their expression in the biography makes for mischievous energy.

LONDON NOVELS OF THE MID-1980S

THE three novels Wilson published in the years 1983 to 1986 are mainly continuous with his six previous ones. *Scandal* (1983) and *Love Unknown* (1986) are contemporary portraits, often acerbic, of middle-class men and women involved in erotic adventures that turn into disasters; *Gentlemen in England* (1985) is a historical novel, set in the late nineteenth century, full of artistic and religious figures from the time and the appurtenances of Victorian domestic, architectural, and cultural life. From the beginning of his career, London was a central presence in Wilson's fiction, and these novels show the city front and center, though varied with excursions to Paris, the Malverns, Bedfordshire, always carefully limned. In *Scandal* the froglike hero, Derek Blore, is an up-and-coming Member of Parliament, soon to be a cabinet member, with a taste for kinky sex. Blore goes once a month to a squalid room in North London, there to be "disciplined" by a dim-witted young woman named Bernadette, herself the unknowing agent of a blackmailing scheme to discredit the minister and his party. The Profumo scandal is in the background, and Wilson's novel may have influenced a popular television series of the 1990s about a scheming minister, Francis Urquhart (*House of Cards* was the first of the series' three lives).

Emerging from the tube at Westminster after his monthly experience with Bernadette, Derek Blore notes that

absolute darkness had descended on London. Parliament Square was dankly misty. The sky was a dirty orange haze giving way to a cloudy blackness. Where there was light—from the headlamps of cars, from street-lamps and shop windows—it seemed to be a fuzzy, half-hearted sort of light, almost conspiring with the dark to lose itself in blackness. The windows of the Abbey glowed dimly like old jewels . . . . Further west, up Victoria Street in the Roman Catholic cathedral, a stately Latin Mass had been sung, imploring the mercy of the Lamb of God, who takes away the sins of the world. But in the fuzzy enclosures of light, and under the cover of dark, the sins of the world went.

(p. 29)

The camera continues tracking to Trafalgar Square and to Soho, in a Dickensian *Bleak House*-like view of things from the small to the large. *Scandal* is a highly plotted, relentlessly driven novel in which the ludicrous hero is painfully exposed, while his elegant wife, Priscilla (the book is ironically subtitled "Priscilla's Kindness"), grandly triumphs. But the book has none of the moments of human tenderness and vulnerability that showed in *Wise Virgin*.

Its successor, *Gentlemen in England*, is perhaps Wilson's most ambitious novel, at least in terms of its range and scope, and in its density of local specification. The time is roughly 1880, the central characters a professor of geology, Horace Nettleship, his wife, Charlotte, their daughter, Maudie and their son, Lionel, who is at Oxford, succumbing to Catholic conversion. Charlotte falls in love with a young painter named Lupton, a follower of the Victorian painter Alma-Tadema, even as Lupton falls in love with Maudie. Hovering over the action are two fantastic aesthetes, Mr. Waldo Chattoway ("Marvo," as he's known by Maudie) and Charlotte's father, Augustus Egg, an old man who remembers when times were livelier, earlier in the century. Whereas in *Scandal* Wilson's style is relatively spare and sharply ironic, *Gentlemen in England* presents a more cluttered surface, as if the prose has to live up to the heavy furniture of the late-Victorian era. Here is the Nettleship house ("The Bower") in a place called Abbey Grove, London:

The sun had been doing its best, since dawn, to shed a little light . . . but it was on the point of recognising its match in the Nettleships and going behind a thick black cloud. Earlier, from a bright cyaneous firmament, it had smiled down on St. John's Wood, but it found difficulty, when it came to The Bower, in getting past the high hedges, the tall fir trees in the garden, and the laurels in the shrubbery before it got to the house. Still, the sun had done it, and made a manly show of falling upon the garish mullioned Gothic, some thirty years old, where the professor and his household chose to reside, an asymmetrical, unhappy-looking house which sprouted turrets and porches and balconies where you least expected them.

(p. 3)

Such a passage, in its vigor of elaboration and humorously-cocked eye at the arrangements of things, reminds us of Dickens: it is "descriptive" writing that spawns itself, one sentence giving birth to the next, even more aggressively extravagant, one. As with so much of Wilson's writing (and like Dickens') the novelist appears to be having a good time at what he's doing. *Gentlemen in England* is so crammed with writers, painters, schoolmasters, and their products—with George Eliot, *In Memoriam*, Browning's "Youth and Art," Meredith's *Modern Love*, and countless others— that, as with the fir trees in the garden at Abbey Grove, it is difficult to get beyond them into a compelling plot with a clear outcome.

The book is Wilson's great curiosity hoard, full of the impressive historical and literary furniture of his own agile, well-stocked mind. And it provides an excellent test to distinguish the fervent admirer of this novelist's work from another sort of reader, willing enough to admit the impressive fireworks and dazzling skill of the presentation but unconvinced that it results in high literary distinction. Clever yes, very (says this sort of reader), but perhaps too clever by half. But it would be more generous and more imaginative to call the novel a challenge richly met both in the design of the whole and in the quality of the writing, sentence by paragraph.

After treating, with some amused sympathy, the unknown consequences of human love in the England of 1880, Wilson focused, in *Love Unknown*, on the England of the 1980s. Unlike the density of specification in *Gentlemen in England*, the successor novel shows Wilson in his most available mode of address, breezily confiding to us about his characters, "I am sorry to say that it is left to me, their chronicler, to record the happy time on their behalf." He is referring to the fortunes of three young women who shared a London flat in the 1960s, then separated to lead individual marital and erotic lives until twenty years later when fate—love unknown—brings them together again. The novel shows Wilson at his most detached, manipulating his characters into situations of extreme embarrassment, as when Simon, the presumed loyal husband of Richeldis (one of the three women) is recognized by the other two—Monica and Belinda—during a visit to Fountainebleau. Simon, alas, is there, under the false pretense of a business trip, with a young blonde woman who turns out to be his secretary. The consequence of this discovery is that Monica, unmarried after all these years, not only confronts Simon on his ruse but also declares her love for him. The usual complications ensue in a deftly told narrative where one feels the novelist, like Stephen Dedalus's notion of the artist in *Portrait of the Artist as a Young Man*, as removed from the creation, "indifferent, paring his fingernails." Like the earlier *Healing Art*, *Love Unknown* reminds us of Iris Murdoch but is without Murdoch's "deep" mysteries. Perhaps it is the better for such an absence, although its crisply rendered sequence of chapter on chapter can be criticized as clock like, mechanical. Even less than in his other novels is Wilson taken in, sympathetically, by his creations; there's a prevailing airiness and lightness of narrative touch as the novel gives us events that pass through our mind and leave little behind except the sense of a well-conducted tour of modern romantic foibles.

FURTHER BIOGRAPHICAL AND CRITICAL WRITING

THE years 1988–1990, in which Wilson published the first two volumes of *The Lampitt Papers*, also saw—amazingly, even for such a prolific writer— three further books of prose, each of much interest: *Tolstoy* (1988), his longest biography and the first one of his to receive wide attention; *Penfriends from Porlock* (1988), a miscellaneous collection of essays, reviews, and other occasional journalism; and *C. S. Lewis* (1990), perhaps the most personal of his biographies. The odd and striking title of the essay collection derives from Coleridge's account of how, while engaged in writing the poem that turned out to be the unfinished "Kubla Khan," he was interrupted by a "person from Porlock" who had business with him. In his preface to the essays Wilson aptly quotes Stevie Smith's poem "Thoughts About the Person from Porlock," which begins

> Coleridge received the Person from Porlock
> And ever after called him a curse,
> Then why did he hurry to let him in?
> He could have hid in the house.
>
> (p. IX)

Wilson admits to letting in many persons from Porlock who have invited him to give lectures, writes reviews and essays, or comment on the deaths of literary personages—activities that have interrupted his writing of novels and biographies but that, in their short-term diversions from larger projects, have been extremely welcome. (Stevie Smith eventually declares, in her poem, "I long for the Person from Porlock.")

In his small selection from a much wider list of items, Wilson pays short, admiring tributes to writers he is fond of—Ivy Compton-Burnett, Philip Larkin, Barbara Pym, Iris Murdoch—and to lesser-known English figures like the Gothic scholar Montague Summers, the humorist Peter Simple, and the ecclesiastic Dean Inge. The focus is insular, the criticism a mixture of anecdote, description,

and judgment. Perhaps the most interesting pages in the book occur in "Two Talks on Satire," where Wilson distinguishes fictional satire from comedy, with implications for his own novels. Satire works by concentrating on human weakness and imperfection, he says, while comedy, particularly in the novel, "delights in human beings as they are and thrives on all our weaknesses and imperfections." Yet despite—or perhaps because—of the Christian adherence of so many English comic writers, dwelling on human imperfection can bring with it a positive, even celebratory, element. Thus Wilson says about *Scandal*, the novel of his he calls closest to having "a satirical purpose," that while the protagonist Derek Blore is perhaps the most unlikable of all his characters, he, Wilson, grew quite fond of him, even pitied him, over the course of writing the book. Overall, *Penfriends from Porlock* invites us to take its occasional efforts with less than high seriousness, even as it holds out a number of lively Wilsonian formulations. When Wilson left the *Spectator* in 1983 he wrote a valedictory essay where he claimed to have ceased reviewing because he had more important things to do. This essay, however, is absent from the collection—no doubt a considered exclusion.

In *A Bottle in the Smoke*, the second volume of *The Lampitt Papers*, the narrator has some reflections about biographers (in particular a clever and unscrupulous one named Raphael Hunter) and how they are promoted by their publishers: "To sell the book, there would be a 'new line' or what publishers sometimes call a 'new angle.' If no new 'material' was forthcoming (and it almost certainly would not be there to be discovered), that would not prevent Hunter hinting at sensational discoveries." Nothing could be further from Wilson's own practice as a biographer; for example, he makes no claim in his book on Tolstoy to have penetrated to the heart of the matter by taking a new angle on his subject. The only "angle" is provided by Wilson's careful and sympathetic guidance through the life and works of the writer, an extended account that does not explain, justify, or censure Tolstoy's behavior. Wilson writes truly about *War and Peace*, "The book is unforgettable and endlessly rereadable not because of the accuracy or thoroughness of its historical research, but because each character in turn is imagined with all the intensity of Tolstoy's being." Something analogous to this vigorous impartiality is present in Wilson's biography.

In 1989 he did a series of programs for the BBC on the lives of "Eminent Victorians" that were published that same year under the Lytton Stracheyan title. In the preface Wilson is concerned to distinguish his enterprise in writing about six Victorian eminences—Prince Albert, Charlotte Brontë, William Ewart Gladstone, John Henry Newman, Josephine Butler, and Julia Margaret Cameron—by reminding us that these men and women, like the four Victorians Strachey had debunked, really *were* eminent, to be regarded by a post-Stracheyan writer like himself with admiration rather than contemptuous superiority. Wilson's fondness, even nostalgia, for things Victorian crops up often in his fiction, notably in the architectural creations of Oswald Fish and the whole of *Gentlemen in England*. His *Eminent Victorians* is a handsomely produced (by the BBC) book of six essays and numerous excellent illustrations of representative figures from the era. In justifying his annexation of Strachey's title, he allows that his predecessor's book will still be read when his own is forgotten, but that when both are forgotten people will still be reading *Jane Eyre* and Newman's *Apologia*. Wilson's refusal to assume attitudes of condescension toward the book's subjects is continuous with the same practice in his previous biographies, though this does not preclude the usual leavening element of wit through which the subjects are shown to us. The essays are an admirable introduction for lay readers to distinguished figures they would like to know more about.

Wilson's fifth full-length biography, of C. S. Lewis, is perhaps his best or most distinctive inasmuch as he takes on a twentieth-century figure whose appeal to legions of readers, especially Christian ones, has been and continues to be immense. He himself has felt this appeal, and he asks why it is that in talking to people about Lewis he found their memories unfailingly interesting. His book proposes to explore this question by investigating Lewis' marvelous capacity for projecting "images of himself into prose." For Wilson, the most attractive of Lewis' many books is *English Literature in the Sixteenth Century*, in which we hear "a fluent, highly intelligent man talking about books in a manner which is always engaging"—a claim that applies to Wilson's own forays into reviewing and criticism. But Lewis' larger appeal, in his speculations and books about Christianity, is to readers who associate Lewis' voice "with some of their deepest and most profoundly felt religious

moments." On this score, as well as on the literary one, Wilson's sympathy is patent, even as—the year after his biography appeared—he would publish the pamphlet *Against Religion*. But the centrality of both literature and religion to Wilson's own life, in addition to his authority in speaking about the Oxford-Cambridge world where Lewis taught for many years, makes him something close to an ideal biographer for the writer who, he says at the conclusion of his preface, "deserves our honour." The honor is richly paid in this book, a *literary* biography in the best sense.

RELIGIOUS POLEMIC

DURING the years 1985–1991 Wilson became more explicit in declaring his own religious position. In 1985 he published a short inquiry, *How Can We Know?* declaring that writing the book had made him discover "that in spite of everything I did believe the Christian religion to be inescapably and irresistibly true." Yet in the essay's concluding paragraph the word "but" appears, significantly, four times. It was not long until "Yes" was followed by the "But" that ushered in "No." In 1986, still from within the fold, it appears, he contributed an interesting essay ("The Clergy") to a volume titled *The Church in Crisis*, a critical assessment of the current state of affairs in the Church of England. Here he described himself as "a practicing Anglican," then provided a potent, if disillusioned, evaluation of current procedures in ordination and of the often grim circumstances of a clergyman's life. The following year, introducing a volume of photographs, *Landscape in France*, he referred to "the abolition of Christianity" that was being carried out in France, "not by the atheist state but by the Christian Church itself," in its increasing secularity and willingness to modernize itself. In 1989, prefacing a selection of Cardinal Newman's work (*Poems, Prayers, Meditations*), he says that in rereading Newman he found the controversies that exercised the great writer now uninteresting, but found also that he could still respond to the "inner" Newman.

Although in retrospect we can see evidence of disillusionment in some of these utterances, nothing in them could be seen as predictive of the wholesale rejection and disparagement of Christianity that the 1991 pamphlet *Against Religion* contains. Its first pages declare that religion is the "tragedy of mankind," then consider briefly the historical fact of persecution among the sects and the delusive fervency of individuals convinced that they and only they know the truth. Wilson notes the strength of his own religious impulses but argues that since "I have discarded any formal religious affiliations," this is exactly what makes these impulses so dangerous: "If it were not half so good," he says about religion, "it would not be capable of being so bad." Insofar as religion can be said to be making a comeback, it is "bad news for the human race." This would seem to constitute a last word on the subject, but in fact his dissociation from Christianity seemed, if anything, to spur him into further inquiry about the subject, though now as a skeptical historian rather than a believer.

Or so the appearance of his full-length studies *Jesus* (1992) and *Paul* (1997) suggests. "It was not in fact until they came to doubt the divinity of Jesus that historians thought of writing his life at all," Wilson writes in the preface to *Jesus*, and by analogy it is likely that only after Wilson made his definitive break with Christianity did it become necessary and compelling for him to expend the extraordinary amount of reading and research, including the study of Greek, that went into these two books. In *Jesus* he expresses the hope that therein he has "not written fiction"; yet considering the multifold difficulties in discovering the "facts" about the historical Jesus, as well as the important differences, explored in detail, between the historical Jesus and the Jesus of faith, any hope for a nonfictional account is beset with difficulties. So it may be wise to think of both *Jesus* and *Paul* as necessarily containing fiction in their biographical and analytical accounts of events, questions, and problems in the lives of their subjects.

If *Jesus* attempts to be a "dispassionate" account of the differences between the historical figure in all its inconsistencies, and the religion this figure was made to be the central avatar of, then *Paul's* importance becomes crucial. In the latter book Wilson describes the Gospels as "Passion Narratives" rather than "stories about a great preacher and exorcist who had the misfortune to be executed by the Romans." *Paul* argues that in fact it was this man, rather than Jesus, who deserves the title of founder of Christianity. In both books Wilson's tone is—surprisingly, considering his penchant for satire and ironic deflation of shibboleths—even-handed, thoughtful, and fair-minded in the attempt not to simplify complex matters. He admits that he is not a scholarly authority in the field (even though he surely knows a great deal), and as might have been expected responses to the books from scholars were very mixed indeed. But they are unquestionably impressive attempts to extend Wilson's thinking about the religion that has always occupied him—thinking that would culminate, at the end of the millennium, in *God's Funeral*.

THE LAMPITT PAPERS

THE title is Wilson's designated one for the sequence of five novels he published between 1988 and 1996—a twelve-hundred-page chronicle of English life in the latter half of the twentieth century, as seen through a particular lens. The lens is that of Julian Ramsay, events of whose life from his days as a public schoolboy to those of a sexagenarian writer and actor (on stage, in television) make up the central story. But the *Lampitt Papers* title, which Wilson first used when the third volume in the sequence was published, puts the emphasis not on Julian but on the extraordinarily interesting—at least to Julian—family that preoccupies him throughout his life. As a youth growing up in a Norfolk vicarage with his Uncle Roy and Aunt Deirdre (his parents were killed in an air-raid during the Second World War), Julian has been the recipient of his uncle's fascination, expressed in ceaseless anecdotes about its members, with the Lampitt family. One of these members, Sargent ("Sargie") Lampitt, is a friend of Uncle Roy's; but the main focus is on a Lampitt no longer living, James Petworth Lampitt, an Edwardian man of letters who wrote a much-praised book on the Prince Consort and left behind, as writers do, various "papers." The fate of these, of who will write Petworth Lampitt's biography and what it will reveal about circumstances of his life and death, is of great concern, especially to other family members who wish to protect his privacy—as well as to his biographer, Raphael Hunter. Later Julian himself is asked to write a book about Petworth Lampitt but from the beginning of the sequence his relations with the ubiquitous Hunter are featured, often in their erotic aspects (Hunter is a consummate ladies' man who keeps succeeding with women Julian himself is interested in). The sequence overall is not presented in strictly chronological progression, and especially as it develops there are frequent, sometimes rapid, changes of temporal perspective (Julian young,

Julian old, Julian in-between). On the whole, however, the presentation is fairly conservative, even old-fashioned as compared to that of Wilson's contemporaries such as Salman Rushdie, Julian Barnes, or Martin Amis.

Yet in another sense Wilson's decision to write this sequence was a radical one, at least in the terms of his earlier fiction: that is, he employs for the first time a first-person narrator endowed with a reasonable, relatively straightforward attitude toward life that makes a bid for our common-sense sympathies. This is not to say that Julian is a morally and humanly superior person; over the course of the books he is seen as a vessel full of imperfections, of much less than heroic character in his affairs, erotic and otherwise. But he is not created mainly to be an object of satire either on Wilson's or on our parts: this, the chronicle implies, is what an ordinary life might look like when imaginatively inspected over decades. In *A Bottle in the Smoke* Julian has just published his first novel and is on his way to an extremely unimpressive "party," given by his publisher, when he has a visionary experience in Bloomsbury Square. In both substance and narrative style, the moment suggests what differentiates the Lampitt books from anything Wilson had done previously.

Julian tells us, as he stands beneath "leaves of plane and horse-chestnut" that "rustled menacingly over my head," that though difficult to put into words he experienced something vital about his existence:

I did not really want to be an actor; I did not want to be married; I no longer cared about this book, though I felt the beginnings of a deeper desire to write fully, and honestly, not with the brittle surface of my mind, and not humorously or cruelly. This was the beginning of a simple, positive desire to record experience in prose as a homage to life itself, born from the certainty that I myself, before I was forgotten, would pass into forgetting, and owed it to experience, trivial or important, sad or joyful, to set down something of what I had felt.

Julian's sudden access to what seems an ultimate truth about his life will be exposed as naive, certainly in terms of the larger pattern his career will exhibit—a much less dedicated and unwavering portrait of the artist than he here entertains. Yet the passion, even the sincerity, behind this rendered moment is real, and Wilson does not scoff at it, nor hold it up for amusement. What makes the passage even more interesting, when placed against his earlier novels, is that Julian's aspiration to write prose that is simply and solely an "homage to life itself" is exactly what Wilson has *not* done in his own art. In fact, the qualities Julian here eschews, such as writing "with the brittle surface of my mind . . . humorously or cruelly" are much closer to a central aspect of Wilson's comic and satiric procedures. There may be a joke suggested here about the yearning—sympathetically indulged but also judged to be impossible—to pay homage to nothing more or less than life itself.

Wilson has numerous forebears in the enterprise of writing a long fiction that emanates from the mind of a single protagonist committed to exploring a consciousness in relation to society and history. Proust is surely an important precursor, as is, closer to home, Anthony Powell's twelve-volume *A Dance to the Music of Time* (1951–1977). There is some overlap in the mainly middle-class world both Powell and Wilson survey. However, Powell's narrator Nicholas Jenkins (compare "Julian Ramsay"), although similar to Julian in some respects—he goes to private school, spends a summer in France with a family, and moves in the London literary world—is presented through a style both more elaborate and more nuanced than Wilson grants Julian. Without that stylistic arrayal, Julian Ramsay—on the surface no more interesting a man than Nick Jenkins—often has trouble capturing our readerly engagement. This becomes increasingly true as the sequence develops: *Incline Our Hearts* (1988) and *A Bottle in the Smoke* (1990) are both strong novels in the realistic tradition, especially good in treating Julian at school, Julian in Brittany (there is some fine evocative writing about France, a place dear to Wilson's heart), and the London scene where he works for a time as bartender in a pub. But the business of the Lampitt papers and the complicated family involvements that ensue are drawn out rather thin in later books, where it often feels as if new characters are being brought in, new relationships started up, just to keep the kettle boiling. When the reader completes the final volume (*A Watch in the Night*, 1996), he may well say what Samuel Johnson said about Milton's *Paradise Lost*: "None ever wished it longer than it is."

THE LAST DECADE

THE studies of Jesus and Paul, along with most of *The Lampitt Papers* might, for a less driven writer, be considered a sufficiently impressive number of books to produce over the decade 1990–1999; for Wilson, they are in fact only accompaniments to four further books. The slightest, though by no means the least entertaining, is a mordant, often hilarious portrait of the royal family in *The Rise and Fall of the House of Windsor* (1993). That same year saw a novel, *The Vicar of Sorrows*, one of his best performances in a thoroughly familiar Wilson novel mode. Near the end of the decade came *Dream Children* (1998), one more treatment, and a highly original one, of the pleasures and pains of eros. And with *God's Funeral* (1999) Wilson could be said to have closed the book—although that is a dangerous statement to hazard about such a changeable figure—on his long affair with religion, by surveying a number of figures who announced or dealt with the "death of God"; each of these figures is "honourably at war with theology."

Given his lifelong preoccupation with theology, it is perhaps surprising that, until *The Vicar of Sorrows*, none of Wilson's novelistic heroes was a clergyman. In *The Healing Art* the heroine's religious mentor is an Anglican priest, and there are various parody-clerics of all stripes in *Unguarded Hours* and *Kindly Light*. But Francis Kreer, the sorrowful vicar of Wilson's longest novel, is treated with a combination of sympathy, satire, and unsparing judgment that makes for one of the novelist's most complex portraits of a man in trouble. Francis' troubles, or sorrows, are manifold: he despises his wife of many years, who is herself afflicted with crippling fantasies and fears; he learns, after the death of his mother, that she had an extramarital affair and bequeathed half her fortune to her lover, rather than all of it to her only son. Francis's own religious faith is anything but solid, and his performance of parish duties grows increasingly slack. When he falls in love with a young woman attached to a group of hippies who have camped near the parish, his dissolution is assured. Wilson pursues him relentlessly, though not unfeelingly, into eventual disgrace and madness. The novel's effect as a whole is tragicomic, and it has a range and particularity of reference that may justly be called Trollopean—although darker, it is every bit as readable as one of the master's products. We may also be put in mind of George Eliot's poignant, yet gently satiric, portrait of a minister in her early novella *Amos Barton*. These are but two of Wilson's many antecedents to his freshly imagined novel.

The Vicar of Sorrow's affiliation with earlier novels of Wilson's in which the hero's self-destruction is the central matter of action and interest—*Scandal*, for example, or the two Norman Shotover novels—makes it a familiar though engrossing product. The same cannot be said of *Dream Children*, which bids for the title of Wilson's most original and surprising (even shocking) piece of fiction by refusing to play the expected game of unraveling the protagonist. Oliver Gold, the novel's hero, is a philosopher *wunderkind*, a sort of A. J. Ayer or Isaiah Berlin figure whose lineage is with great culture critics of the previous century, such as Ruskin or Mill. Oliver also commands huge success with the media and is in much demand (as Wilson has been, relatively speaking) but at a certain point in his career spends a summer holed up reading Hegel and decides that his own mind is comparatively second rate. Whereupon he throws up his college fellowship and moves into a London household occupied by four women: Janet Rose, who lives in an imagined past when she and her deceased husband hosted famous literary folk; Janet's daughter, Michal, divorced, with a ten-year-old daughter named Roberta ("Bobs"); and a young philosophy don named Catherine Cuffe, who was a pupil of Oliver's and is now Michal's lover. In their different ways, all the women fall in love with Oliver; thus when he announces plans to marry Camilla Bayes, a not particularly distinguished American (so the four women feel), consternation sets in.

Oliver's great secret, and the main theme of the novel, is that he is a lover of young girls, the "dream children" of the novel's title, and "Bobs"—the object of his attentions—reciprocates (the *Lolita* allusion is wholly patent). What Wilson achieves in *Dream Children*, through writing that is by turns sprightly high-comic and at other moments (when Oliver's mind is being explored) introspective and intelligently full of life, is a quite unpredictable yet wholly satisfying story that resists the usual cliché of comeuppance doled out to the lovers. In its brief compass—just over two hundred pages—it represents a triumph of economy and resource by managing to keep us off-balance and alert, page by page. It was daring of Wilson to take on a subject that, especially after Vladimir Nabokov, threatened to be merely sensational. In fact, the novel manages to stir up, even confuse, a reader's feelings and principles about this incendiary subject, even as it exploits that subject in resourceful novelistic moves. Coming as it does after the latter adventures of Julian Ramsay in the Lampitt chronicle, *Dream Children* reads like a Wilson invigorated and freed by a subject and a dramatis personae that truly takes him into the realm of aesthetic delight.

Wilson's final book of the century, *God's Funeral*, is a sweeping presentation of major and minor figures who had something of interest to say about the Christian religion in its latter days: David Hume, Immanuel Kant, Auguste Comte, John Stuart Mill, Thomas Carlyle, John Henry Newman, George Eliot, Matthew Arnold, Herbert Spencer, Algernon Swinburne, Charles Darwin, Benjamin Jowett, Samuel Butler, Karl Marx, John Ruskin, George Bernard Shaw, William James—these are only a few of the characters who populate the crowded pages. Wilson treats each of them to a performance, sometimes briefly, other times at greater length; his role is that of showman, creating his subjects through a combination of biographical, analytical, and anecdotal energy. It is an extremely subjective survey insofar as Wilson is quite ready, even eager, to share with us his opinions and judgments about the value of the individual contribution. (Ruskin and Swinburne, for example, come off very well; Arnold and Shaw not so.) The book has no overall argument, lives in the vivacity of individual treatment. Wilson admits to not being a philosopher, a scientist, or a specialist in religion; rather his identity is that of novelist-biographer-cultural historian, caught up in individual and collective responses of impressive human beings writing about what he calls "the God-thing." His argumentative, deliberately provocative style invites disagreement.

Like Wilson's biographies, *God's Funeral*, in its generous sampling from literary, philosophical, and scientific figures, is above all an invitation to reading. At one point he urges us not to read *about* Kant but to *read* Kant, and his whole book constitutes a similar plea on behalf of the sages surveyed. The effect is that we come away from the discussion of Ruskin determined to attempt *Fors Clavigera*, Wilson's candidate for the single greatest book of the nineteenth century; or to pick up Swinburne's poems or Newman's prose. His appeal is to the reader as an intelligent, amateur lay person eager to extend boundaries and complicate responses. With a view of Wilson's own complicated engagement with religion, it is instructive that, after declaring (in *Against Religion*) that religion, especially the Christian brand, was a very bad thing, he concludes *God's Funeral* by noting that some of the most significant events of the twentieth century, like the collapse of Soviet Communism and the spiritual war against racism in America, show "the palpable and visible strength of the Christian thing, the Christian idea." In his own individual way as a novelist and critic, A. N. Wilson has made a substantial contribution to keeping that idea alive.

SELECTED BIBLIOGRAPHY

I. Collected Essays and Reviews. *Penfriends from Porlock* (London and New York, 1988).

II. Novels. *The Sweets of Pimlico* (London, 1977); *Unguarded Hours* (London, 1978); *Kindly Light* (London, 1979); *The Healing Art* (London, 1980); *Who Was Oswald Fish?* (London, 1981); *Wise Virgin* (London, 1982; New York, 1983); *Scandal; or, Priscilla's Kindness* (London, 1983; New York, 1984); *Gentlemen in England: A Vision* (London, 1985; New York, 1986); *Love Unknown* (London, 1986; New York, 1987); *Incline Our Hearts* (London, 1988; New York, 1989); *A Bottle in the Smoke* (London and New York, 1990); *Daughters of Albion* (London, 1991; New York, 1992); *The Vicar of Sorrows* (London, 1993; New York, 1994); *Hearing Voices* (London, 1995; New York, 1996); *A Watch in the Night* (London and New York, 1996); *Dream Children* (London and New York, 1999).

III. Biographies. *The Laird of Abbotsford: A View of Sir Walter Scott* (Oxford, 1980); *The Life of John Milton* (Oxford and New York, 1983); *Hilaire Belloc* (London and New York, 1984); *Tolstoy: A Biography* (London and New York, 1988); *Eminent Victorians* (London, 1989; New York, 1990); *C. S. Lewis: A Biography* (London and New York, 1990); *Jesus: A Life* (London and New York, 1992); *Paul: The Mind of the Apostle* (London and New York, 1997).

IV. Philosophical and Religious Speculation. *How Can We Know? An Essay on the Christian Religion* (London and New York, 1985); *The Church in Crisis* (with Charles Moore and Gavin Stamp) (London, 1986); *Against Religion* (London, 1991); *God's Funeral* (London and New York, 1999).

V. Other Works. *Lilibet: An Account in Verse of the Early Years of the Queen Until the Time of Her Accession* (anonymous, London, 1984); *Stray* (London, 1987; New York, 1989); *The Tabitha Stories* (London, 1988; republished as *Tabitha*, New York, 1989); *Hazel the Guinea Pig* (London, 1989; Cambridge, Mass., 1992); *The Rise and Fall of the House of Windsor* (London and New York, 1993).

VI. Books Edited and Introduced. Sir Walter Scott, *Ivanhoe* (London, 1982); Bram Stoker, *Dracula* (Oxford and New York, 1983); *The Lion and the Honeycomb: The Religious Writings of Tolstoy* (London and San Francisco,

1987); *Landscape in France* (text by Wilson) (London, 1987; New York, 1988); John Henry Newman, *Prayers, Poems and Meditations* (London, 1989; New York, 1990); *The Faber Book of Church and Clergy* (London, 1992); *The Faber Book of London* (London, 1993).

VII. BIOGRAPHICAL STUDIES. Alan Hollinghurst, "A. N. Wilson," in *Dictionary of Literary Biography*, vol. 14, *British Novelists Since 1960* (Detroit, 1983); James Atlas, "The Busy, Busy Wasp," in *New York Times Magazine* (18 October 1992); Brian Murray, "A. N. Wilson," in *Dictionary of Literary Biography*, vol. 155, *Twentieth-Century British Literary Biographies* (Detroit, 1995); Russell Greer, "A. N. Wilson," in *Dictionary of Literary Biography*, vol. 194, *British Novelists Since 1960* (Detroit, 1998).

VIII. CRITICAL STUDIES. William Boyd, "Comedy of Errors," in *Times Literary Supplement* (6 June 1980); A. S. Byatt, "Flourishing Fleshly," in *Times Literary Supplement* (23 October 1981); Pat Rogers, "Medieval Minds," in *Times Literary Supplement* (5 November 1982); John Sutherland, "Dark Places," in *London Review of Books* (18 November–1 December 1982); Michael Wood, "The English at their Vices," in *New York Times Book Review* (17 February 1985); John Sutherland, "Minor Victorians," in *Times Literary Supplement* (6 September 1985); Christopher Ricks, "Chronicities," in *London Review of Books* (21 November 1985); Anatole Broyard, "In and Out of Love and Faith," in *New York Times Book Review* (9 March 1986); John Melmoth, "What We Are Here For," in *Times Literary Supplement* (29 August 1986); Michiko Katkutani, "Friends for Life," in *New York Times* (16 May 1987); David Nokes, "In the English Gulag," in *Times Literary Supplement* (2 September 1988); Victoria Glendenning, "Grotesques in a Class of their Own," in *Times* (London) (30 August 1990); Joel Connaroe, "The Lamb of God in England," in *New York Times Book Review* (26 January 1992); Victoria Glendenning, "Cassocks in a Twist," in *Times* (London) (9 September 1993); Michiko Katkutani, "A Man among Women as Deluded as Himself," in *New York Times* (4 August 1998); William H. Pritchard, "Mr. Wilson's Literary Life," in *Hudson Review* 52, no. 4 (winter 2000).

MASTER INDEX

The following index covers the entire British Writers series through Supplement VI. All references include volume numbers in boldface Roman numerals followed by page numbers within that volume. Subjects of articles are indicated by boldface type.

"Americans in My Mind, The" (Pritchett), **Supp. III:** 316

"Ametas and Thestylis Making Hay-Ropes" (Marvell), **II:** 211

Aminta (Tasso), **II:** 49

"Amir's Homily, The" (Kipling), **VI:** 201

Amis, Kingsley, **Supp. II:** 1–19; **Supp. IV:** 25, 26, 27, 29, 377; **Supp. V:** 206

Amis, Martin, **Supp. IV:** 25–44, 65, 75, 437, 445

"Among All Lovely Things My Love Had Been" (Wordsworth), **IV:** 21

"Among School Children" (Yeats), **VI:** 211, 217

Among the Believers: An Islamic Journey (Naipaul), **Supp. I:** 399, 400–401, 402

Amores (tr. Marlowe), **I:** 276, 290

Amoretti and Epithalamion (Spenser), **I:** 124, 128–131

Amorous Prince, The; or, The Curious Husband (Behn), **Supp. III:** 26

"Amos Barton" (Eliot), **V:** 190

Amours de Voyage (Clough), **V:** xxii, 155, 156, 158, 159, 161–163, 165, 166–168, 170

Amphytrion; or, The Two Sosias (Dryden), **II:** 296, 305

"Ample Garden, The" (Graves), **VII:** 269

Amrita (Jhabvala), **Supp. V:** 224–226

"Amsterdam" (Murphy), **Supp. V:** 326

Amusements Serious and Comical (Brown), **III:** 41

"Amy Foster" (Conrad), **VI:** 134, 148

An Duanaire: An Irish Anthology, Poems of the Dispossessed, 1600–1900 (Kinsella), **Supp. V:** 266

An Giall (Behan), **Supp. II:** 71–73

Anacreontiques (Johnson), **II:** 198

"Anactoria" (Swinburne), **V:** 319–320, 321

Anand, Mulk Raj, **Supp. IV:** 440

"Anarchist, An" (Conrad), **VI:** 148

Anatomy of Exchange-Alley, The (Defoe), **III:** 13

Anatomy of Frustration, The (Wells), **VI:** 228

Anatomy of Melancholy (Burton), **II:** 88, 106, 108; **IV:** 219

Anatomy of Oxford (eds. Day Lewis and Fenby), **Supp. III:** 118

Anatomy of Restlessness: Selected Writings, 1969–1989 (Chatwin), **Supp. IV:** 157, 160

"Ancestor" (Kinsella), **Supp. V:** 274

Ancient Allan, The (Haggard), **Supp. III:** 222

Ancient and English Versions of the Bible (Isaacs), **I:** 385

"Ancient Ballet, An" (Kinsella), **Supp. V:** 261

Ancient Lights (Ford), **VI:** 319, 320

"Ancient Mariner, The" (Coleridge), **III:** 330, 338; **IV:** viii, ix, 42, 44–48, 54, 55

"Ancient Sage, The" (Tennyson), **IV:** 329

"Ancient to Ancients, An" (Hardy), **VI:** 13

"And country life I praise" (Bridges), **VI:** 75

"And death shall have no dominion" (Thomas), **Supp. I:** 174

And Our Faces, My Heart, Brief as Photos (Berger), **Supp. IV:** 94, 95

And Then There Were None (Christie), *see Ten Little Niggers*

And What if the Pretender Should Come? (Defoe), **III:** 13

Anderson, Lindsay, **Supp. IV:** 78

Anderson, Sherwood, **VII:** 75

Anderton, Basil, **II:** 154, 157

"Andrea del Sarto" (Browning), **IV:** 357, 361, 366

Andrea of Hungary, and Giovanna of Naples (Landor), **IV:** 100

"Andrey Satchel and the Parson and Clerk" (Hardy), **VI:** 22

Androcles and the Lion (Shaw), **VI:** 116, 124, 129

"Andromeda" (Hopkins), **V:** 370, 376

Andromeda Liberata (Chapman), **I:** 235, 254

Anecdotes (Spence), **II:** 261

"Anecdotes, The" (Durrell), **Supp. I:** 124

Anecdotes of Johnson (Piozzi), **III:** 246

Anecdotes...of Mr. Pope...by the Rev. Joseph Spence (ed. Singer), **III:** 69, 78

Angel at the Gate, The (Harris), **Supp. V:** 137, 139

Angel Pavement (Priestley), **VII:** xviii, 211, 216–217

Angels and Insects (Byatt), **Supp. IV:** 139, 151, 153–154

Angels and Insects (film), **Supp. IV:** 153

"Angels at the Ritz" (Trevor), **Supp. IV:** 503

Angels at the Ritz (Trevor), **Supp. IV:** 504

Anglo-Italian Review (periodical) **VI:** 294

"Anglo-Saxon, The" (Golding), **Supp. I:** 78

Anglo-Saxon Attitudes (Wilson), **Supp. I:** 154, 155, 156, 159–160, 161, 162, 163

Angrian chronicles (Brontë), **V:** 110–111, 120–121, 122, 124–125, 126, 135

"Anima and Animus" (Jung), **Supp. IV:** 10–11

Anima Poetae: From the Unpublished Notebooks (Coleridge), **IV:** 56

Animadversions upon the Remonstrants Defense Against Smectymnuus (Milton), **II:** 175

Animal Farm (Orwell), **VII:** xx, 273, 278, 283–284; **Supp. I:** 28n, 29; **Supp. IV:** 31

Animal Lover's Book of Beastly Murder, The (Highsmith), **Supp. V:** 179

Animal's Arrival, The (Jennings), **Supp. V:** 208

Animated Nature (Goldsmith), *see History of the Earth...*

Ann Lee's (Bowen), **Supp. II:** 81

Ann Veronica: A Modern Love Story (Wells), **VI:** 227, 238

"Anna, Lady Braxby" (Hardy), **VI:** 22

Anna of the Five Towns (Bennett), **VI:** xiii, 248, 249, 252, 253, 266

Annals of Chile, The (Muldoon), **Supp. IV:** 428–432

Annan, Gabriele, **Supp. IV:** 302

Annan, Noel, **V:** 284, 290

Anne Brontë (Gérin), **V:** 153

"Anne Killigrew" (Dryden), **II:** 303

Anne of Geierstein (Scott), **IV:** 39

Anniversaries (Donne), **I:** 361–362, 364, 367

Annotations of Scottish Songs by Burns (Cook), **III:** 322

Annual Register (periodical), **III:** 194, 205

"Annunciation, The" (Jennings), **Supp. V:** 212

"Annunciation, The" (Muir), **Supp. VI:** 207

Annus Domini (Rossetti), **V:** 260

"Annus Mirabilis" (Larkin), **Supp. I:** 284

Annus Mirabilis: The Year of Wonder (Dryden), **II:** 292, 304

"Anorexic" (Boland), **Supp. V:** 49

"Another Grace for a Child" (Herrick), **II:** 114

Another Mexico (Greene), *see Lawless Roads, The*

Another Part of the Wood (Bainbridge), **Supp. VI:** 17–19

Another September (Kinsella), **Supp. V:** 260

"Another September" (Kinsella), **Supp. V:** 260

"Ansell" (Forster), **VI:** 398

Anstey, Christopher, **III:** 155

"Answer, The" (Wycherley), **II:** 322

"Answer to a Paper Called 'A Memorial of true Poor Inhabitants'" (Swift), **III:** 35

Answer to a Question That No Body Thinks of, An (Defoe), **III:** 13

"Answer to Davenant" (Hobbes), **II:** 256n

"Answers" (Jennings), **Supp. V:** 206

"Ant, The" (Lovelace), **II:** 231

Ant and the Nightingale or Father Hubburd's Tales, The (Middleton), **II:** 3

"Ant-Lion, The" (Pritchett), **Supp. III:** 105–106

Antal, Frederick, **Supp. IV:** 80

"Antheap, The" (Lessing), **Supp. I:** 242

"Anthem for Doomed Youth" (Owen), **VI:** 443, 447, 448, 452; **Supp. IV:** 58

"Anthem of Earth, An" (Thompson), **V:** 448

Anthology of War Poetry, An (ed. Nichols), **VI:** 419

Anthony Trollope: A Critical Study (Cockshut), **V:** 98, 103

Antic Hay (Huxley), **VII:** 198, 201–202

"Anti-Christ; or, The Reunion of Christendom" (Chesterton), **VI:** 340–341

"Hymn to Pan" (Keats), **IV:** 216, 217, 222

"Hymn to the Name and Honor of the Admirable Sainte Teresa, A" (Crashaw), **II:** 179, 182

Hymn to the Pillory, A (Defoe), **III:** 13

"Hymn to the Sun" (Hood), **IV:** 255

"Hymn to the Winds" (du Bellay), **V:** 345

"Hymn to Venus" (Shelley), **IV:** 209

"Hymne of the Nativity, A" (Crashaw), **II:** 180, 183

Hymns (Spenser), **I:** 131

Hymns Ancient and Modern (Betjeman), **VII:** 363–364

Hymnus in Cynthiam (Chapman), **I:** 240

Hyperion (Keats), **IV:** 95, 204, 211, 212, 213, **227–231**, 235; **VI:** 455

Hypnerstomachia (Colonna), **I:** 134

Hypochondriack, The (Boswell), **III:** 237, 240, 243, 248

"Hypogram and Inscription" (de Man), **Supp. IV:** 115

Hysterical Disorders of Warfare (Yealland), **Supp. IV:** 58

"*I* abide and abide and better abide" (Wyatt), **I:** 108, 109

I Am a Camera (Isherwood), **VII:** 311

"I am Raftery" (Mahon), **Supp. VI:** 170

I Can Remember Robert Louis Stevenson (ed. Masson), **V:** 393, 397

"I care not if I live" (Bridges), **VI:** 81

I, Claudius (Graves), **VII:** 259

I Crossed the Minch (MacNeice), **VII:** 403, 411

"I dined with a Jew" (Macaulay), **IV:** 283

"I find no peace and all my war is done" (Wyatt), **I:** 110

"I go night-shopping like Frank O'Hara I go bopping" (Mahon), **Supp. VI:** 175

"I Have Been Taught" (Muir), **Supp. VI:** 208

"I have longed to move away" (Thomas), **Supp. I:** 174

"I have loved and so doth she" (Wyatt), **I:** 102

"I heard an Angel singing" (Blake), **III:** 296

"I, in my intricate image" (Thomas), **Supp. I:** 174

I Knock at the Door (O'Casey), **VII:** 12

"I know a Bank Whereon the Wild Thyme Grows" (Shakespeare), **IV:** 222

"I lead a life unpleasant"(Wyatt), **I:** 104

I Like It Here (Amis), **Supp. II:** 8–10, 12

I Live under a Black Sun (Sitwell), **VII:** 127, 135, 139

"I Look into My Glass" (Hardy), **VI:** 16

I Lost My Memory, The Case As the Patient Saw It (Anon.), **Supp. IV:** 5

"I love all beauteous things" (Bridges), **VI:** 72

"I never shall love the snow again" (Bridges), **VI:** 77

I promessi sposi (Manzoni), **III:** 334

"I Remember" (Hood), **IV:** 255

"I Remember, I Remember" (Larkin), **Supp. I:** 275, 277

"*I Say No*" (Collins), **Supp. VI:** 93, 103

"I see the boys of summer" (Thomas), **Supp. I:** 173

"I Stood Tip-toe" (Keats), **IV:** 214, 216

"I strove with none" (Landor), **IV:** 98

"I took my heart in my hand" (Rossetti), **V:** 252

"I wake and feel the fell of dark" (Hopkins), **V:** 374*n*, 375

"I Wandered Lonely as a Cloud" (Wordsworth), **IV:** 22

I Want It Now (Amis), **Supp. II:** 15

"I will not let thee go" (Bridges), **VI:** 74, 77

I Will Pray with the Spirit (Bunyan), **II:** 253

"I will write" (Graves), **VII:** 269

"I would be a bird" (Bridges), **VI:** 81–82

Ian Hamilton's March (Churchill), **VI:** 351

"Ianthe" poems (Landor), **IV:** 88, 89, 92, 99

Ibrahim (Scudéry), **III:** 95

Ibsen, Henrik, **IV:** 118; **V:** xxiii–xxvi, 414; **VI:** viii–ix, 104, 110, 269; **Supp. III:** 4, 12; **Supp. IV:** 1, 286

Ibsen's Ghost; or, Toole Up to Date (Barrie), **Supp. III:** 4, 9

Ice Age, The (Drabble), **Supp. IV:** 230, 245–246, 247

Ice in the Bedroom (Wodehouse), **Supp. III:** 460

Icelandic journals (Morris), **V:** 299, 300–301, 307

"Icy Road" (MacCaig), **Supp. VI:** 188–189

Idea of Christian Society, The (Eliot), **VII:** 153

Idea of Comedy, The, and the Uses of the Comic Spirit (Meredith), *see Essay on Comedy and the Uses of the Comic Spirit*

"Idea of Entropy at Maenporth Beach, The" (Redgrove), **Supp. VI:** **233–234**, 237

"Idea of Perfection, The" (Murdoch), **Supp. I:** 217, 220

Idea of the Perfection of Painting, An (tr. Evelyn), **II:** 287

Ideal Husband, An (Wilde), **V:** 414–415, 419

Ideals in Ireland (ed. Lady Gregory), **VI:** 98

Ideas and Places (Connolly), **Supp. III:** 110

Ideas of Good and Evil (Yeats), **V:** 301, 306

Identical Twins (Churchill), **Supp. IV:** 181

"Identities" (Muldoon), **Supp. IV:** 414, 424

Idiocy of Idealism, The (Levy), **VI:** 303

"Idiot Boy, The" (Wordsworth), **IV:** 7, 11

"Idiots, The" (Conrad), **VI:** 148

Idleness of Business, The, A Satyr…(Wycherley), *see Folly of Industry, The*

Idler (periodical), **III:** 111–112, 121

Idyllia heroica decem (Landor), **IV:** 100

"Idylls of the King" (Hill), **Supp. V:** 191

Idylls of the King (Tennyson), **IV:** xxii, 328, 336–337, 338

"If by Dull Rhymes Our English Must be Chained . . ." (Keats), **IV:** 221

If I Were Four and Twenty: Swedenborg, Mediums and Desolate Places (Yeats), **VI:** 222

"If I were tickled by the rub of lover" (Thomas), **Supp. I:** 172

"If in the world there be more woes"(Wyatt), **I:** 104

"If, My Darling" (Larkin), **Supp. I:** 277, 285

"If my head hurt a hair's foot" (Thomas), **Supp. I:** 176–177

If the Old Could…(Lessing), **Supp. I:** 253, 254

"If This Were Faith" (Stevenson), **V:** 385

If You're Glad I'll Be Frank (Stoppard), **Supp. I:** 439, 445

"Ikey" (Brown), **Supp. VI:** 68

Ikons, The (Durrell), **Supp. I:** 121

"Il Conde" (Conrad), **VI:** 148

Il cortegiano (Castiglione), **I:** 265

Il pastor fido (Guarini), **II:** 49–50

Il pecorone (Fiorentino), **I:** 310

"Il Penseroso" (Milton), **II:** 158–159; **III:** 211*n*; **IV:** 14–15

Iliad, The (tr. Cowper), **III:** 220

Iliad, The (tr. Pope), **III:** 77

Ill Beginning Has a Good End, An, and a Bad Beginning May Have a Good End (Ford), **II:** 89, 100

"I'll come when thou art saddest" (Brontë), **V:** 127

I'll Leave It To You (Coward), **Supp. II:** 141

I'll Never Be Young Again (du Maurier), **Supp. III:** 139–140, 144

"Illiterations" (Brooke-Rose), **Supp. IV:** 97

"Illuminated Man, The" (Ballard), **Supp. V:** 24

Illusion and Reality (Caudwell), **Supp. III:** 120

"Illusions of Anti-Realism" (Brooke-Rose), **Supp. IV:** 116

Illustrated Excursions in Italy (Lear), **V:** 77, 79, 87

Illustrated London News (periodical), **VI:** 337

Illustrations of Latin Lyrical Metres (Clough), **V:** 170

Illustrations of the Family of Psittacidae, or Parrots (Lear), **V:** 76, 79, 87

I'm Dying Laughing (Stead), **Supp. IV:** 473, 476

"I'm happiest when most away" (Brontë), **V:** 116

"Image, The" (Day Lewis), **Supp. III:** 115–116

Japp, A. H., **IV:** 144*n*, 155
Jarrell, Randall, **VI:** 165, 194, 200; **Supp. IV:** 460
"Jars, The" (Brown), **Supp. VI:** 71–72
"Jasmine" (Naipaul), **Supp. I:** 383
"Jason and Medea" (Gower), **I:** 54, 56
"Je est un autre" (Durrell), **Supp. I:** 126
"Je ne parle pas Français" (Mansfield), **VII:** 174, 177
"Je t'adore" (Kinsella), **Supp. V:** 263
"Jealousy" (Brooke), **Supp. III:** 52
Jeames's Diary; or, Sudden Wealth (Thackeray), **V:** 38
Jean de Meung, **I:** 49
Jeeves (Ayckbourn and Webber), **Supp. V:** 3
"Jeeves and the Hard-Boiled Egg" (Wodehouse), **Supp. III:** 455, 458
Jeeves and the Tie That Binds (Wodehouse), *see Much Obliged*
"Jeeves Takes Charge" (Wodehouse), **Supp. III:** 456, 457–458
Jeffares, Alexander Norman, **VI:** xxxiii–xxxiv, 98, 221
Jefferson, D. W., **III:** 182, 183
Jeffrey, Francis, **III:** 276, 285; **IV:** 31, 39, 60, 72, 129, 269
Jeffrey, Sara, **IV:** 225
Jenkin, Fleeming, **V:** 386
Jenkyn, D., **Supp. IV:** 346
Jennings, Elizabeth, **Supp. IV:** 256; **Supp. V:** 205–221
"Jenny" (Rossetti), **V:** 240
Jerrold, Douglas, **V:** 19
Jerrold, W. C., **IV:** 252, 254, 267
"Jersey Villas" (James), **III:** 69
Jerusalem (Blake), **III:** 303, 304–305, 307; **V:** xvi, 330
Jerusalem Sinner Saved (Bunyan), *see Good News for the Vilest of Men*
Jerusalem the Golden (Drabble), **Supp. IV:** 230, 231, 238–239, 241, 243, 248, 251
Jesus (Wilson), **Supp. VI:** 306
Jess (Haggard), **Supp. III:** 213
Jesting Pilate (Huxley), **VII:** 201
Jew of Malta, The (Marlowe), **I:** 212, 280, **282–285,** 310
Jew Sÿss (Feuchtwanger), **VI:** 265
Jewel in the Crown, The (Scott), **Supp. I:** 266–267, 269–270
Jeweller of Amsterdam, The (Field, Fletcher, Massinger), **II:** 67
"Jews, The" (Vaughan), **II:** 189
Jhabvala, Ruth Prawer, **Supp. V:** 223–239
Jill (Larkin), **Supp. I:** 276, 286–287
Jill Somerset (Waugh), **Supp. VI:** 273
Jimmy Governor (Clune), **Supp. IV:** 350
Jitta's Atonement (Shaw), **VI:** 129
"Joachim du Bellay" (Pater), **V:** 344
Joan and Peter (Wells), **VI:** 240
Joan of Arc (Southey), **IV:** 59, 60, 63–64, 71
Joannis Miltonii Pro se defensio…(Milton), **II:** 176
Job (biblical book), **III:** 307
Jocasta (Gascoigne), **I:** 215–216
Jocelyn (Galsworthy), **VI:** 277

"Jochanan Hakkadosh" (Browning), **IV:** 365
Jocoseria (Browning), **IV:** 359, 374
"Johannes Agricola in Meditation" (Browning), **IV:** 360
Johannes Secundus, **II:** 108
John Bull's Other Island (Shaw), **VI:** 112, **113–115**
John Caldigate (Trollope), **V:** 102
"John Fletcher" (Swinburne), **V:** 332
John Gabriel Borkman (Ibsen), **VI:** 110
"John Galsworthy" (Lawrence), **VI:** 275–276, 290
John Galsworthy (Mottram), **VI:** 271, 275, 290
"John Galsworthy, An Appreciation" (Conrad), **VI:** 290
"John Gilpin" (Cowper), **III:** 212, 220
John Keats: A Reassessment (ed. Muir), **IV:** 219, 227, 236
John Keats: His Like and Writings (Bush), **IV:** 224, 236
John Knox (Muir), **Supp. VI:** 198
John M. Synge (Masefield), **VI:** 317
"John Norton" (Moore), **VI:** 98
"John of the Cross" (Jennings), **Supp. V:** 207
"John Ruskin" (Proust), **V:** 183
John Ruskin: The Portrait of a Prophet (Quennell), **V:** 185
John Sherman and Dhoya (Yeats), **VI:** 221
John Thomas and Lady Jane (Lawrence), **VII:** 111–112
John Woodvil (Lamb), **IV:** 78–79, 85
Johnnie Sahib (Scott), **Supp. I:** 259, 261
Johnny I Hardly Knew You (O'Brien), **Supp. V:** 338, 339
Johnson, Edgar, **IV:** 27, 40; **V:** 60, 72
Johnson, James, **III:** 320, 322
Johnson, Lionel, **VI:** 3, 210, 211
Johnson, Samuel, **III:** 54, 96, **107–123,** 127, 151, 275; **IV:** xiv, xv, 27, 31, 34, 88*n,* 101, 138, 268, 299; **V:** 9, 281, 287; **VI:** 363; and Boswell, **III:** 234, 235, 238, 239, 243–249; and Collins, **III:** 160, 163, 164, 171, 173; and Crabbe, **III:** 280–282; and Goldsmith, **III:** 177, 180, 181, 189; dictionary, **III:** 113–116; **V:** 281, 434; literary criticism, **I:** 326; **II:** 123, 173, 197, 200, 259, 263, 293, 301, 347; **III:** 11, 88, 94, 139, 257, 275; **IV:** 101; on Addison and Steele, **III:** 39, 42, 44, 49, 51; **Supp. IV:** 271
Johnson, W. E., **Supp. II:** 406
Johnson over Jordan (Priestley), **VII:** 226–227
Joking Apart (Ayckbourn), **Supp. V:** 3, 9, 13, 14
Jolly Beggars, The (Burns), **III:** 319–320
Jonah Who Will Be 25 in the Year 2000 (film), **Supp. IV:** 79
Jonathan Swift (Stephen), **V:** 289
Jonathan Wild (Fielding), **III:** 99, 103, 105, 150
Jones, David, **VI:** xvi, 436, **437–439**
Jones, Henry Arthur, **VI:** 367, 376
Jones, Henry Festing, **Supp. II:** 103–104, 112, 114, 117, 118

Jonestown (Harris), **Supp. V:** 144–145
Jonson, Ben, **I:** 228, 234–235, 270, **335–351; II:** 3, 4, 24, 25, 27, 28, 30, 45, 47, 48, 55, 65, 79, 87, 104, 108, 110, 111*n,* 115, 118, 141, 199, 221–223; **IV:** 35, 327; **V:** 46, 56; **Supp. IV:** 256
Jonsonus Virbius (King), **Supp. VI:** 157
Joseph Andrews (Fielding), **III:** 94, 95, 96, 99–100, 101, 105
Joseph Conrad (Baines), **VI:** 133–134
Joseph Conrad (Ford), **VI:** 321, 322
Joseph Conrad (Walpole), **VI:** 149
Joseph Conrad: A Personal Reminiscence (Ford), **VI:** 149
Joseph Conrad: The Modern Imagination (Cox), **VI:** 149
"Joseph Grimaldi" (Hood), **IV:** 267
"Joseph Yates' Temptation" (Gissing), **V:** 437
Journal (Mansfield), **VII:** 181, 182
Journal, 1825–32 (Scott), **IV:** 39
Journal and Letters of Fanny Burney, The (eds. Hemlow et al.), **Supp. III:** 63
Journal of Bridget Hitler, The (Bainbridge), **Supp. VI:** 22
Journal of a Dublin Lady, The (Swift), **III:** 35
Journal of a Landscape Painter in Corsica (Lear), **V:** 87
Journal of a Tour in Scotland in 1819 (Southey), **IV:** 71
Journal of a Tour in the Netherlands in the Autumn of 1815 (Southey), **IV:** 71
Journal of a Tour to the Hebrides, The (Boswell), **III:** 117, 234*n,* 235, 243, 245, 248, 249
Journal of a Voyage to Lisbon, The (Fielding), **III:** 104, 105
Journal of Beatrix Potter from 1881 to 1897, The (ed. Linder), **Supp. III:** **292–295**
"Journal of My Jaunt, Harvest 1762" (Boswell), **III:** 241–242
Journal of the Plague Year, A (Defoe), **III:** 5–6, 8, 13
Journal to Eliza, The (Sterne), **III:** 125, 126, 132, 135
Journal to Stella (Swift), **II:** 335; **III:** 32–33, 34
Journalism (Mahon), **Supp. VI:** 166
Journalism for Women: A Practical Guide (Bennett), **VI:** 264, 266
Journals and Papers of Gerard Manley Hopkins, The (ed. House and Storey), **V:** 362, 363, 371, 378–379, 381
Journals 1939–1983 (Spender), **Supp. II:** 481, 487, 490, 493
Journals of a Landscape Painter in Albania etc. (Lear), **V:** 77, 79–80, 87
Journals of a Landscape Painter in Southern Calabria…(Lear), **V:** 77, 79, 87
Journals of a Residence in Portugal, 1800–1801, and a Visit to France, 1838 (Southey), **IV:** 71
Journals of Arnold Bennett (Bennett), **VI:** 265, 267

"Miss Pulkinhorn" (Golding), **Supp. I:** 78–79, 80

"Miss Smith" (Trevor), **Supp. IV:** 502, 510

"Miss Tickletoby's Lectures on English History" (Thackeray), **V:** 38

"Missing, The" (Gunn), **Supp. IV:** 276

"Missing Dates" (Empson), **Supp. II:** 184, 190

Mistake, The (Vanbrugh), **II:** 325, 333, 336

Mistakes, The (Harris), **II:** 305

Mr. A's Amazing Mr. Pim Passes By (Milne), **Supp. V:** 299

"Mr. and Mrs. Dove" (Mansfield), **VII:** 180

"Mr. and Mrs. Frank Berry" (Thackeray), **V:** 23

"Mr. Apollinax" (Eliot), **VII:** 144

Mr. Beluncle (Pritchett), **Supp. III:** 311, 313, 314–315

Mr. Bennett and Mrs. Brown (Woolf), **VI:** 247, 267, 275, 290; **VII:** xiv, xv

"Mr. Bennett and Mrs. Brown" (Woolf), **Supp. II:** 341

"Mr. Bleaney" (Larkin), **Supp. I:** 281

"Mr. Bodkin" (Hood), **IV:** 267

Mr. Britling Sees It Through (Wells), **VI:** 227, 240

"Mr. Brown's Letters to a Young Man About Town" (Thackeray), **V:** 38

Mr. Bunyan's Last Sermon (Bunyan), **II:** 253

Mr. C[olli]n's Discourse of Free-Thinking (Swift), **III:** 35

"Mr. Crabbe—Mr. Campbell" (Hazlitt), **III:** 276

"Mr. Eliot's Sunday Morning Service" (Eliot), **VII:** 145

"Mr. Feasey" (Dahl), **Supp. IV:** 214

"Mr. Gilfil's Love Story" (Eliot), **V:** 190

"Mr. Gladstone Goes to Heaven" (Beerbohm), **Supp. II:** 51

"Mr. Graham" (Hood), **IV:** 267

"Mr. Harrison's Confessions" (Gaskell), **V:** 14, 15

Mr. H (Lamb), **IV:** 80–81, 85

Mr. John Milton's Character of the Long Parliament and Assembly of Divines...(Milton), **II:** 176

Mister Johnson (Cary), **VII:** 186, 187, 189, 190–191

"Mr. Know-All" (Maugham), **VI:** 370

Mr. Macaulay's Character of the Clergy in the Latter Part of the Seventeenth Century Considered (Babington), **IV:** 291

"Mr. McNamara" (Trevor), **Supp. IV:** 501

Mr. Meeson's Will (Haggard), **Supp. III:** 213

"Mr. Norris and I" (Isherwood), **VII:** 311–312

Mr. Norris Changes Trains (Isherwood), **VII:** xx, 311–312

Mr. Polly (Wells), *see History of Mr. Polly, The*

Mr. Pope's Welcome from Greece (Gay), **II:** 348

Mr. Prohack (Bennett), **VI:** 260, 267

"Mr. Reginald Peacock's Day" (Mansfield), **VII:** 174

"Mr. Robert Herricke His Farewell unto Poetrie" (Herrick), **II:** 112

"Mr. Robert Montgomery's Poems" (Macaulay), **IV:** 280

Mr Sampath (Naipaul), **Supp. I:** 400

Mr. Scarborough's Family (Trollope), **V:** 98, 102

"Mr. Sludge 'the Medium'" (Browning), **IV:** 358, 368

Mr. Smirke; or, The Divine in Mode (Marvell), **II:** 219

Mr. Stone and the Knights Companion (Naipaul), **Supp. I:** 383, 389

"Mr. Tennyson" (Trevor), **Supp. IV:** 502

Mr. Waller's Speech in the Painted Chamber (Waller), **II:** 238

"Mr. Waterman" (Redgrove), **Supp. VI:** 228–229, 231, 235, 237

Mr. Weston's Good Wine (Powys), **VII:** 21

Mr. Whatnot (Ayckbourn), **Supp. V:** 2, 13

"Mr. Whistler's Ten O'Clock" (Wilde), **V:** 407

"Mrs. Acland's Ghosts" (Trevor), **Supp. IV:** 503

"Mrs. Bathurst" (Kipling), **VI:** 193–194

Mrs. Browning: A Poet's Work and Its Setting (Hayter), **IV:** 322

Mrs. Craddock (Maugham), **VI:** 367

Mrs. Dalloway (Woolf), **VI:** 275, 279; **VII:** xv, 18, 21, 24, 28–29; **Supp. IV:** 234, 246

Mrs. Dot (Maugham), **VI:** 368

Mrs. Eckdorf in O'Neill's Hotel (Trevor), **Supp. IV:** 501, 508

Mrs. Fisher; or, The Future of Humour (Graves), **VII:** 259–260

"Mrs. Jaypher found a wafer" (Lear), **V:** 86

Mrs. Leicester's School (Lamb and Lamb), **IV:** 80, 85

Mrs. McGinty's Dead (Christie; U.S. title, *Blood Will Tell*), **Supp. II:** 135

"Mrs. Medwin" (James), **VI:** 69

"Mrs. Nelly's Complaint," **II:** 268

"Mrs. Packletide's Tiger" (Saki), **Supp. VI:** 242

Mrs. Perkins's Ball (Thackeray), **V:** 24, 38

"Mrs. Silly" (Trevor), **Supp. IV:** 502

"Mrs. Simpkins" (Smith), **Supp. II:** 470

"Mrs. Temperley" (James), **VI:** 69

Mrs. Warren's Profession (Shaw), **V:** 413; **VI:** 108, 109

Mistral, Frederic, **V:** 219

Mistras, The (Cowley), **II:** 194, 198, 202, 236

"Mistress of Vision, The" (Thompson), **V:** 447–448

"Mists" (Redgrove), **Supp. VI:** 228

Mist's Weekly Journal (newspaper), **III:** 4

Mitford, Mary Russell, **IV:** 311, 312

Mitford, Nancy, **VII:** 290

Mithridates (Lee), **II:** 305

Mixed Essays (Arnold), **V:** 213n, 216

"Mixed Marriage" (Muldoon), **Supp. IV:** 415

Mo, Timothy, **Supp. IV:** 390

Mob, The (Galsworthy), **VI:** 280, 288

Moby-Dick (Melville), **VI:** 363

Mock Doctor, The (Fielding), III 105

Mock Speech from the Throne (Marvell), **II:** 207

Mock-Mourners, The:...Elegy on King William (Defoe), **III:** 12

"Model Prisons" (Carlyle), **IV:** 247

Modern Comedy, A (Galsworthy), **VI:** 270, 275

Modern Fiction (Woolf), **VII:** xiv

Modern Husband, The (Fielding), **III:** 105

"Modern Love" (Meredith), **V:** 220, 234, 244

Modern Love, and Poems of the English Roadside...(Meredith), **V:** xxii, 220, 234

Modern Lover, A (Moore), **VI:** 86, 89, 98

Modern Movement: 100 Key Books from England, France, and America, 1880–1950, The (Connolly), **VI:** 371

Modern Painters (Ruskin), **V:** xx, 175–176, 180, 184, 282

Modern Painting (Moore), **VI:** 87

Modern Poetry: A Personal Essay (MacNeice), **VII:** 403, 404, 410

Modern Utopia, A (Wells), **VI:** 227, 234, 241, 244

"Modern Warning, The" (James), **VI:** 48, 69

Modernism and Romance (Scott-James), **VI:** 21

Modes of Modern Writing: Metaphor, Metonymy, and the Typology of Modern Literature, The (Lodge), **Supp. IV:** 365, 377

Modest Proposal, A (Swift), **III:** 21, 28, 29, 35; **Supp. IV:** 482

"Moestitiae Encomium" (Thompson), **V:** 450

Moffatt, James, **I:** 382–383

Mohocks, The (Gay), **III:** 60, 67

Mohr, Jean, **Supp. IV:** 79

"Moisture-Number, The" (Redgrove), **Supp. VI:** 235

Molière (Jean Baptiste Poquelin), **II:** 314, 318, 325, 336, 337, 350; **V:** 224

Moll Flanders (Defoe), **III:** 5, 6, 7, 8, 9, 13, 95

Molloy (Beckett), **Supp. I:** 51–52; **Supp. IV:** 106

Molly Sweeney (Friel), **Supp. V:** 127

Moly (Gunn), **Supp. IV:** 257, 266–268

"Moly" (Gunn), **Supp. IV:** 267

Molyneux, William, **III:** 27

"Moment of Cubism, The" (Berger), **Supp. IV:** 79

Moments of Being (Woolf), **VII:** 33

Moments of Grace (Jennings), **Supp. V:** 217–218

Moments of Vision, and Miscellaneous Verses (Hardy), **VI:** 20

Monastery, The (Scott), **IV:** xviii, 39

Monckton Milnes, Richard (Lord Houghton), **IV:** 211, 234, 235, 251, 252, 254, 302, 351; **V:** 312, 313, 334

"Monday; or, The Squabble" (Gay), **III:** 56